Web Enabled Commercial Applications Development Using...

HTML, JavaScript, DHTML and PHP

4th Revised Edition

Web Enabled Commercial Applications Development Using...

HTML, JavaScript, DHTML and PHP

4th Revised Edition

By

Ivan Bayross

BPB PUBLICATIONS

20 Ansari Road, Darya Ganj, New Delhi-110002

Reprint: 2023

Fourth Revised Edition 2010

FIRST EDITION 2005

ISBN 13: 978-81-8333-008-4

Distributors:

COMPUTER BOOK CENTRE
12, Shrungar Shopping Centre,
M.G.Road, BENGALURU–560001
Ph: 25587923/25584641

DECCAN AGENCIES
4-3-329, Bank Street,
HYDERABAD-500195
Ph: 24756967/24756400

MICRO MEDIA
Shop No. 5, Mahendra Chambers,
150 DN Rd. Next to Capital Cinema,
V.T. (CST) Station, MUMBAI-400001
Ph: 22078296/22078297

BPB BOOK CENTRE
376 Old Lajpat Rai Market,
DELHI-110006
Ph: 23861747

BPB PUBLICATIONS
20, Ansari Road, Darya Ganj
New Delhi-110002
Ph: 23254990/23254991

Published by Manish Jain for BPB Publications, 20 Ansari Road, Darya Ganj, New Delhi–2 and Printed by him at Reva Printers, New Delhi

Foreword

All programmers know that programming for the Internet is a great place to be. This employment window is constantly renewing itself and is ever evolving. Coding in it will retain its fascination for a long long time.

Application development using the Internet as the delivery platform is really fairly traditional Client / Server type programming with a few twists. The break from traditional Client / Server programming on the Internet is because both the Client side and Server side programming environments are quite different.

The Internet is a huge number of heterogeneous computers with heterogeneous operating systems and programming environments all working together in complete harmony hence this difference.

The traditional Client side-programming environment for the Internet is HTML, DHTML, and JavaScript. Traditional Server side-programming environments are several, but this book focuses on PHP scripting as the Server side programming of choice.

Using this rather strange mix for programming environments dynamic, interactive web sites can be created and deployed on the Internet. There are many books written that cover these environments, so what makes this book different?

It's written in such a way:

- That you will gradually build a static web site using HTML
- Move this skill upward by creating some degree of user interactivity using JavaScript
- Finally, shift to Server side data processing by creating PHP scripts.

By the end of your studies and working through the examples in the book a lot of the skills you require to create sound, dynamic, Interactive Web Sites will grow firmly in place. Growth beyond this is by surfing the web and trying to figure out how specific functionality was brought to a website.

There are also a very large number of web sites on the Internet that give away excellent PHP scripts for free. Download these scripts, open them in any ASCII editor (Notepad is a good one) and decipher how they work. Most of these freebies are very well documented using 'REM' statements in the code block or have complete 'Help' files in HTML or PDF (Acrobat Reader files) format. This will really make you fly.

Concepts are built using simple language. Examples have easily understood logic. Several key areas in dynamic, interactive, web site development have been addressed. Once this is grasped the skill gained must allow any commercial application developer to create a dynamic, interactive website quickly, confidently and successfully

The enclosed CD-ROM has the code examples used in the book and several useful goodies to help you create your first few web sites. I've also added several web site snippets, which would help give you a direction when you are creating you're a web site for the first time.

Additionally, the CD-ROM contains Apache, PHP and MySQL executables that will help you setup the framework on any computer.

Having said this I must add that the very best way to create a good, user interactive web site is by surfing the Internet constantly and checking out web site's that interest you. Try and figure how the web site was coded to provide the functionally that it actually has.

My approach, (where possible) right click on an interesting web page and 'View Source'. This will give you an unparalleled insight into the coding techniques used by others to create the web site.

This foreword will not be complete without my thanking the many people who encouraged me and put up with the many revisions and updations of the manuscript with patience and tolerance.

My sincere **THANKS** go to:

- My publisher Mr. Manish Jain. He has brought enormous changes in my life. This is a debt of gratitude I will never be able to pay in full.
- Ms. Meher Bala and Ms. Kavita Mavani who carefully checked and rechecked the manuscript until all the errors of English Grammar and formatting were corrected (as humanly possible). Thank you for being so meticulous.
- The many programmers who read this material, without you all I would not be an author. I welcome both your brickbats and bouquets. You can contact me via BpB, New Delhi, else you could check out my web site appropriately named www.ivanbayross.com.
- Finally, my wife Cynthia who has always encouraged me whenever I thought that I'd never get a manuscript ready for publishing. You have always helped to keep my feet firmly on the ground, in you I am truly blessed.

Ivan N. Bayross

TABLE OF CONTENTS

SECTION – I: HTML

1. INTERNET BASICS 1

BASIC CONCEPTS *1*
COMMUNICATING ON THE INTERNET *2*
INTERNET DOMAINS *4*
INTERNET SERVER IDENTITIES *4*
Registering A Virtual Domain With InterNIC *4*
Domain Name Extension *5*
ESTABLISHING CONNECTIVITY ON THE INTERNET *5*
CLIENT IP ADDRESS *6*
How Client IP Addresses Are Assigned *6*
How ISP's Achieve The Task Of Assigning IP Addresses *6*
Getting A Temporary IP Address *6*
HOW IP ADDRESSING CAME INTO EXISTENCE? *7*
A BRIEF OVERVIEW OF TCP/IP AND ITS SERVICES *8*
Internet Protocol *9*
TRANSMISSION CONTROL PROTOCOL *10*
World Wide Web *10*
FTP 10
FTP As An Application 10
FTP As A Service 10
FTP As a Protocol 11
TELNET *11*
SELF REVIEW QUESTIONS 11

2. INTRODUCTION TO HTML **12**

INFORMATION FILES CREATION 12
WEB SERVER 12
WEB CLIENT / BROWSER 13
Understanding How A Browser Communicates With A Web Server 13
Establish Connection 13
Client Issues A Request And Server Sends A Response 14
Server Terminates The Connection 15
HYPER TEXT MARKUP LANGUAGE (HTML) 15
HTML Tags *15*
Paired Tags *15*
Singular Tags *15*
COMMONLY USED HTML COMMANDS 19
The Structure Of An HTML program *19*
Document Head 19
Document Body 19

Titles And Footers *20*
Title 20
Footer 21
Text Formatting *21*
Paragraph breaks 21
Line Breaks 21
Emphasizing Material In A Web Page *24*
Heading Styles 24
Drawing Lines 24
Text Styles *25*
Bold 25
Italics 25
Underline 25
Other Text Effects *27*
Centering (Text, Images etc.) 27
Spacing (Indenting Text) 28
SELF REVIEW QUESTIONS 31
HANDS ON EXERCISES 31

3. LISTS 33

TYPES OF LISTS 33
Unordered List (Bullets) *33*
Ordered Lists (Numbering) *33*
Definition Lists *34*
SELF REVIEW QUESTIONS 37
HANDS ON EXERCISE 37

4. ADDING GRAPHICS TO HTML DOCUMENTS 38

USING THE BORDER ATTRIBUTE 38
USING THE WIDTH AND HEIGHT ATTRIBUTE 39
USING THE ALIGN ATTRIBUTE 40
USING THE ALT ATTRIBUTE 41
SELF REVIEW QUESTIONS 45
HANDS ON EXERCISE 45

5. Tables 47

INTRODUCTION 47
The Caption Tag *48*
USING THE WIDTH AND BORDER ATTRIBUTE 48
USING THE CELLPADDING ATTRIBUTE 49
USING THE CELLSPACING ATTRIBUTE 50
USING THE BACKGROUND-COLOR PROPERTY 51
USING THE COLSPAN AND ROWSPAN ATTRIBUTES 52
SELF REVIEW QUESTIONS 56
HANDS ON EXERCISES 57

6. LINKING DOCUMENTS **58**

LINKS 58

External Document References *58*

Internal document references *59*

Hyper Linking To A HTML File (Starting At The Beginning Of The Document) *60*

Linking To A Particular Location In A Separate Document *61*

IMAGES AS HYPERLINKS 62

Image Maps *63*

SELF REVIEW QUESTIONS 71

HANDS ON EXERCISES 72

7. FRAMES **74**

INTRODUCTION TO FRAMES 74

The <FRAMESET> Tag *74*

The <FRAME> Tag *74*

Targeting Named Frames *75*

SELF REVIEW QUESTIONS 84

HANDS ON EXERCISES 84

A - PROJECTS IN HTML **86**

PROJECT SPECIFICATIONS FOR THE FIRST PROJECT IN HTML 86

PROJECT SPECIFICATIONS FOR THE SECOND PROJECT IN HTML 94

PROJECT SPECIFICATIONS FOR THE THIRD PROJECT IN HTML 100

PROJECT SPECIFICATIONS FOR THE FOURTH PROJECT IN HTML 105

ANSWERS TO SELF REVIEW QUESTIONS **117**

SOLUTIONS TO HANDS ON EXERCISES **119**

SECTION - II: JAVASCRIPT

8. INTRODUCTION TO JAVASCRIPT **124**

JAVASCRIPT IN WEB PAGES 124

Database Connectivity *125*

Client side JavaScript *125*

Capturing User Input *125*

JAVASCRIPT 126

The Advantages Of JavaScript *126*

WRITING JAVASCRIPT INTO HTML 128

BASIC PROGRAMMING TECHNIQUES 128

Data Types And Literal *129*

Number 129

Boolean 129

String 129

Null 130

Type Casting *130*

Creating Variables *130*

Incorporating Variables In A Script *130*

The JavaScript Array *131*

Dense Arrays 131
The Elements Of An Array 132
The JavaScript Array and its length Property *133*
OPERATORS AND EXPRESSIONS IN JAVASCRIPT 133
Arithmetic Operators *133*
Logical Operators *134*
Comparison Operators *134*
String Operators *135*
Assignment Operators *135*
The Conditional Expression Ternary Operator *135*
Special Operators *135*
The delete Operator 135
The new Operator 135
The void Operator 136
JAVASCRIPT PROGRAMMING CONSTRUCTS 136
CONDITIONAL CHECKING 137
The if - then - else Statement *137*
Immediate if (Conditional expression) *137*
SUPER CONTROLLED - ENDLESS LOOPS 138
For Loop *138*
While Loop *138*
FUNCTIONS IN JAVASCRIPT 139
Built-in Functions *139*
USER DEFINED FUNCTIONS 140
Declaring Functions *140*
Place Of Declaration *140*
Passing Parameters *140*
Variable Scope *142*
Return Values *142*
Recursive Functions *142*
PLACING TEXT IN A BROWSER 143
DIALOG BOXES 143
The Alert Dialog Box *144*
The Prompt Dialog Box *145*
The Confirm Dialog Box *146*
SELF REVIEW QUESTIONS 148
HANDS ON EXERCISES 149

9. THE JAVASCRIPT DOCUMENT OBJECT MODEL 150

INTRODUCTION 150
Instance *150*
Hierarchy *151*
THE JAVASCRIPT ASSISTED STYLE SHEETS DOM [JSSS DOM] 151
UNDERSTANDING OBJECTS IN HTML 152
Properties Of HTML Objects *152*
Methods Of HTML Objects *153*
BROWSER OBJECTS 153
THE WEB PAGE HTML OBJECT HIERARCHY 155
Access To Elements Of A Web Page *155*

How A Web Page Element Is Manipulated *156*
HANDLING (WEB PAGE) EVENTS USING JAVASCRIPT 156
Named JavaScript Event Handlers *157*
SELF REVIEW QUESTIONS 158
HANDS ON EXERCISES 159

10. FORMS USED BY A WEB SITE 160

THE FORM OBJECT 160
The Form Object's Methods *165*
Properties Of Form Elements 166
Methods of Form Elements 167
The Text Element *168*
The Password Element *168*
The Button Element *169*
The Submit (Button) Element *170*
The Reset (Button) Element *171*
The Checkbox Element *173*
The Radio Element *175*
The TextArea Element *176*
The Select And Option Elements *177*
Multi Choice Select Lists 178
OTHER BUILT-IN OBJECTS IN JAVACRIPT 181
The String Object *181*
The Math Object *181*
The Date Object *182*
USER DEFINED OBJECTS 184
Creating A User Defined Object *184*
Instances 184
Objects Within Objects *185*
SELF REVIEW QUESTIONS 189
HANDS ON EXERCISES 190

11. COOKIES 191

WHAT ARE COOKIES 191
SETTING A COOKIE 191
SELF REVIEW QUESTIONS 194

B - PROJECTS IN JAVASCRIPT 195

Project Specifications For The First Project In JavaScript – Guest Book *195*
Project Specifications For The Second Project In JavaScript – Pen Pals *197*
Project Specifications For The Third Project In JavaScript – Registration Form *201*

ANSWERS TO SELF REVIEW QUESTIONS 207

SOLUTIONS TO HANDS ON EXERCISES 208

SECTION - III: DYNAMIC HYPER TEXT MARKUP LANGUAGE

12. DYNAMIC HTML **213**

CASCADING STYLE SHEETS 213

Font Attributes *214*

Use Of Font Attributes 214

Color And Background Attributes *214*

Use Of Color And Background Attributes 215

Text Attributes *215*

Use of Text Attributes 216

Border Attributes *217*

Use Of Border Attributes 217

Margin Related Attributes *217*

Use Of Margin Attributes 218

List Attributes *218*

Use Of List Attributes 218

CLASS 219

Use Of Class 219

USING THE <SPAN>...</SPAN> TAG 220

Use Of SPAN Tags 220

EXTERNAL STYLE SHEETS 221

Use Of External Style Sheet 221

USING THE <DIV>...</DIV> TAG 222

Use Of DIVs 223

Use Of The DIV Tag And Visibility Property 223

SELF REVIEW QUESTIONS 225

HANDS ON EXERCISES 225

Answers To Self Review Questions **226**

Solutions To Hands On Exercises **227**

SECTION - IV: SETTING UP THE PHP FRAMEWORK

13. Introducing PHP **228**

PHP - A Server Side Scripting Language *228*

What Is A PHP File? *229*

Why PHP? *229*

INSTALLING THE FRAMEWORK 229

Internet Information Server *230*

Installing IIS 231

Testing IIS 238

Apache *239*

Downloading Apache2 239

The Apache2 Installation Process On Windows XP 240

Configuring APACHE Web Server 242

Binding An IP To A Domain Name Using The HOSTS File: 243

Creating Virtual Domains Under Apache 243

14. SETTING UP AND CONFIGURING PHP TO WORK UNDER APACHE AND IIS....248

DOWNLOADING PHP 248
Downloading PHP For Windows 249
THE PHP INSTALLATION PROCESS....250
PHP / Apache Installation On Windows XP 250
PHP Installation On Linux....253
Erasing An Older Version 253
Installing PHP From Its Source File....255
The Configure Command 257
The Make Command....258
The Make Install Command 259
Binding The PHP Installation With Apache2 259

15. TESTING THE PHP / WEB SERVER SETUP....262

TESTING THE PHP / IIS SETUP 262
Stopping And Starting IIS Via The XP Services Interface 262
Stopping And Starting IIS Via The Command Prompt 262
Testing The PHP Installation 263
TESTING THE PHP / APACHE SETUP 264
Testing PHP / Apache On Windows 264
Testing PHP / Apache On Linux 266

SECTION - V : PHP LANGUAGE BASICS

16. PHP & HTML 268

GETTING STARTED....275
Writing PHP....275
Naming Files....275
Comments....275
The Semicolon....276
Delivering Text As Output....276
White Space 276
Running the PHP Script - myfirst.php....277

17. THE BASICS OF PHP....278

DATA TYPES....278
VARIABLES 278
Numbers 280
Strings 280
Joining Strings....283
Variable Scope 283
Variable Variables 286
PHP Superglobals....287
CONSTANTS 289
HERE DOCUMENTS....291
OPERATORS....292
Unary Operators 292
Negation Operators 293

Increment / Decrement Operators 293
Cast Operators 295
Binary Operators *296*
Numeric Operators 296
Assignment Operators 298
Concatenation Operator 299
Comparison Operators 299
Logical Operators 300
Bitwise Operators 301
Ternary Operator *303*
Operator Precedence *303*
References *304*
ARRAYS 307
CONDITIONAL STATEMENTS 309
The if Statement *309*
Executing Multiple Statements 310
The elseif Clause 312
The switch Statement *315*
ITERATIONS 319
Looping *319*
The for loop 319
The while loop 322
Controlling An Array Using A WHILE Loop 324
The do...while Statement 326
The foreach loop 327
Infinite loops *330*
Special Loop Keywords *331*
Loops Within Loops *332*
Mixed-Mode Processing *336*
HANDS ON EXERCISES 337

18. FUNCTIONS 339

USER-DEFINED FUNCTIONS 339
Functions With Arguments *341*
Functions With Multiple Arguments *341*
Functions Accepting And Returning Values By Reference *343*
Functions Accepting And Returning Values By Value *346*
Accessing Global Variables Within A Function *346*
Globalizing Functions *347*
Functions In Files *348*
Recursion *349*
Anonymous Functions *352*
BUILT-IN FUNCTIONS 352
print() *353*
include() *353*
header() *354*
phpinfo() *354*
PHP SERVER VARIABLES 356
Functions For Variables *360*

Controlling Script Execution 363
Array Functions 365
WORKING WITH DATE AND TIME 371
The Date() Function 372
The time() Function 373
Converting From A String 374
Converting From Components 377
PERFORMING MATHEMATICAL OPERATIONS 378
Rounding Up A Number 378
Randomization 380
Other Mathematical Conversion Functions 382
Mathematical Constants 384
WORKING WITH STRING FUNCTIONS 385
Extracting Part Of A String 385
Finding A String Within A String 386
Returning The First Occurrence Of A String 389
Replacing Parts Of A String 390
Converting To And From ASCII 391
Measuring Strings 392
Trimming Whitespace 395
Wrapping Lines In Text Messages 396
Changing String Case 397
Secure Data Hash 399
Printing Number Formats 402
String Padding 403
Complex String Printing 404
Pausing Script Execution 406
HANDS ON EXERCISE 409
19. WORKING WITH FORMS 410
Introducing HTML Form Tags And Elements 410
The Main <FORM> Tag 410
FORM ELEMENTS 412
Text Box 412
Text Area 412
Password 413
Radio Button 413
Checkbox 414
The Combo Box Or Drop Down List Box 414
Hidden Field 415
Image 415
SUBMIT And RESET Buttons 416
ADDING ELEMENTS TO A FORM 417
Adding A TextBox 418
Adding A Text Area 419
Adding A Password Field 421
Adding Radio Buttons 422
Adding A Select Box 424
Adding Check Boxes 427

Adding A SUBMIT And CANCEL BUTTON *429*
Adding A Hidden Field *432*
Converting clientMaster.html To clientMaster.php *435*
Running clientMaster.php At The Web Server *440*
Preventing Forms Being Automatically Submitted To A Web Server *443*
Automatically Selecting The Contents Of Text Boxes *444*
UPLOADING FILES TO THE WEB SERVER USING PHP 445
The move_uploaded_file( ) Function *447*
HANDS ON EXERCISE 449

20. REGULAR EXPRESSIONS 450

Regular Expression Engine *450*
Common Uses Of Regular Expressions *450*
Types Of Regular Expressions *451*
Regular Expression Functions *452*
Symbols Used In Regular Expressions *453*
Using ^ and $ 453
Using *, + and ? 453
Using Bounds {} 453
Using Quantifiers 454
Using | The OR Operator 454
Using . The Period 454
Using [ ] Bracket Expressions 454
Using Regular Expression Functions *454*
HANDS ON EXERCISES 476

21. DEBUGGING AND ERRORS 478

GOOD PROGRAMMING PRACTICES 478
Visual Examination Of Code Spec *478*
Coding Style *478*
To Improve Code Spec Readability *479*
Commenting Code Spec *479*
Meaningful Variable Names *480*
Functions *480*
PHP Code Block Indicators *480*
ERROR HANDLING IN PHP 481
Displaying Errors *481*
Type Of Errors 482
Syntax or Parse Errors 483
Fatal Errors 485
Warnings 486
Notices 487
Logical Errors 488
Environmental Errors 491
Runtime Errors 491
Core Errors 492
Compile Errors 492
User Defined Errors 492

Error Levels In PHP 493
Setting Error Reporting Levels Via PHP.INI 493
Setting Error Reporting Levels Via error_reporting() 494
Logging Errors *498*
What Is A Log? 498
Using error_log() 498
Using php.ini File To Set Error Log File Path 500
Logging errors to a file 501
Logging Errors Via Syslog 503
Using trigger_error() 505
Ignoring Errors *507*
Acting On Errors / Exceptions *508*
Try Block 508
Catch Block 509
Throw Statement 509

22. A STANDARD CHALLENGE AND RESPONSE SYSTEM 513

THE LOGIN FORM: 513
ERROR HANDLING IN THE CHALLENGE AND RESPONSE SUB SYSTEM: 516
THE REGISTRATION SUB-SYSTEM: 519
CLIENT SIDE JAVASCRIPT BASED ERROR HANDING 522
WEB SERVER SIDE PHP BASED ERROR HANDLING 524

SOLUTIONS TO HANDS ON EXERCISES 525

APPENDIX - A 419

IITML Color Codes *419*
Resource On World Wide Web *419*
Resources On HTML Editors *420*
Resources On HTML Document Development *420*

APPENDIX - B 421

Resources For JavaScript *421*

APPENDIX C 421

HTTP *421*

APPENDIX - D 423

Resources For PHP *423*

SECTION - I: HTML

1. INTERNET BASICS

BASIC CONCEPTS

The Internet began in 1969, as an experimental four-computer network called ARPAnet, which was designed by the U.S. Defense Department so that research scientists could communicate. In approximately two years, ARPAnet grew to about two-dozen sites and by 1981, consisted of more than two hundred sites. In 1990, ARPAnet was officially disbanded and the network, which now consisted of hundreds of sites, came to be known as the Internet.

After a while, commercial organizations began to recognize the use of such a network which converted the whole world into a **Global Village** and allowed almost instant access to business or commerce data and a host of other services such as E-Mail and E-Commerce. The rapid growth of the Internet was due to networking giants like British Telecom, Hyundai, AT&T and others setting up fast and reliable networks that encircled the globe. The networking giants were very clear about their role. This was to setup and maintain, monitor and expand existing networks. Hence another layer was formed above this layer called ISP's (**I**nternet **S**ervice **P**roviders). The networking giants gave access to the Internet via **Gateways**. Using ISP gateways it is perfectly possible to route business or commerce data from one point of the globe to another by using a heterogeneous mix of networks owned by different networking giants who have worked out an agreement between themselves on the costs of usage.

ISP's in turn offer clients' access to the Internet via their gateways as paid for service. An ISP's gateway generally consists of a server with a permanent connection to the Internet. The Server's connection to the Internet is called its Internet **Pipeline**. Special hardware is used as the pipeline to connect an ISP's server to the Internet. ISP pipeline bandwidths of 2GB to 10GB are quite common. Multiple pipelines can be purchased by an ISP from a networking giant and used.

Clients that log into the Internet via an ISP commonly use only 33.6 Kilobyte of the ISP's bandwidth. Occasionally a client whose data traffic is very high will use special connectivity methods (ISDN) to an ISP's server and use between 64Kbps to 128Kbps of the ISP's bandwidth. If a client has huge data traffic then a client could directly negotiate with a networking giant to have its own private **Gateway** to the Internet and then make use of the huge bandwidth for its data transfers. These types of clients are not ISP's and as a general rule do not allow other clients access to their gateway. Even in such case physical access to the Internet is a server. The diagram 1.1 illustrates what was said earlier:

The Internet consists of two types of computers **Servers** and **Clients**
- ❑ Computers which offer information to be read are called **Servers**
- ❑ Computers that read the information offered are called **Clients**

Servers run special software (*Web Server software*) that allows them to
- ❑ Respond to Client requests for information.
- ❑ Accept data from Clients

Some of the most popular software which Servers run to allow them to respond to Client requests for information is, *Internet Information Server* (**IIS**), *Apache Web Server, Microsoft Personal Web Server.*

Clients run special software (*Browser software*) that allows them to

- Locate the appropriate Server
- Query the Server for the information to be read

Some of the most popular browser software that Clients run, to allow them to query Internet Servers for information are *Netscape Communicator, Internet Explorer.*

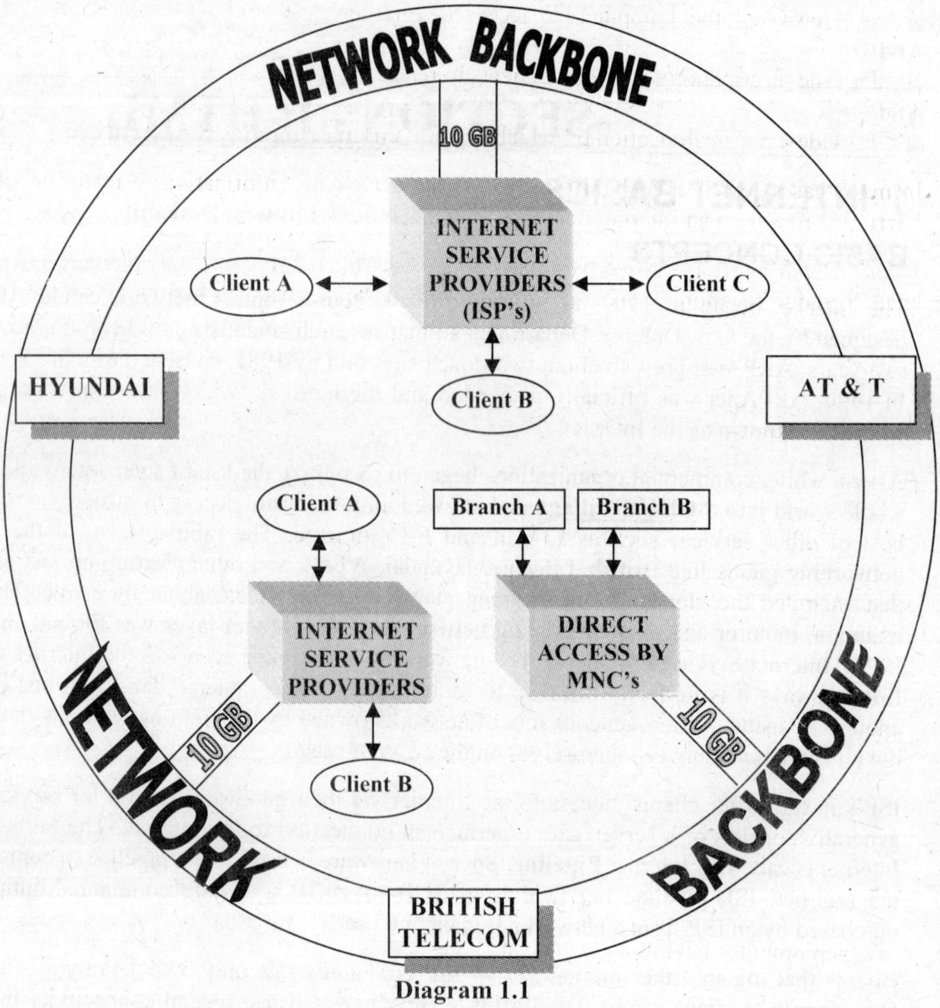

Diagram 1.1

COMMUNICATING ON THE INTERNET

TCP/IP is the only protocol used to send data all around the Internet. TCP/IP is really two individual sections, (TCP) a set of communication protocols and (IP) a unique address. Every machine connected to the Internet must have an address by which it can be located on the Internet. This is called the ***IP address*** of the machine. For the Internet to function smoothly, no two machines can have the same *IP address*. Hence each machine connected to the Internet must have a unique *IP address*, which identifies that machine.

The Internet is a worldwide network of networks. As the Internet grew over the years it became increasingly important to have a governing body, which allocated unique IP addresses to organizations linked to the Internet. An international body called InterNIC, located in the USA, is responsible for registering and assigning unique *IP addresses* to organizations wishing to manage networks, which will be part of the Internet. A unique *IP address* therefore points to an *actual computer* connected via a gateway to the Internet. This computer is known as a **Domain** i.e. a place where information is available. This is a Physical Domain on the Internet.

Conceptually, a Server, which has a permanent IP address (i.e. *a Physical Domain*), can provide

- ❑ A gateway to other computers to access the Internet

And/Or

- ❑ Provide information for Internet clients to read

And/Or

- ❑ Provide a physical location on which *several* **Virtual Domains** can be **Hosted**

In many cases, when a **Web Site** provides Internet clients information to read, the site is mounted as a **Virtual Domain** on an Internet Server, which is its (*host*) **Physical Domain**.

Virtual Domains are identified by a name (e.g. www.microsoft.com). Just like a *Physical Domain* needs to have a unique IP address, so also *Virtual Domain Names* need to be unique on the Internet. All *Virtual Domain Names* must be registered with InterNIC. One Internet Server may host several virtual domains.

Virtual domains can be conceptualized as sub directories on an Internet server's hard disk drive. The information that Internet clients wish to read would be **Files** within the sub directory.

When an Internet client connects to an Internet server some software running on the Internet server must respond to the Internet client's request for information. The software that runs on an Internet server and responds to an Internet client's request for information is called **Web Server** software.

An Internet Web server responds to an Internet client's request for information by going to a specific sub directory on its hard disk and forwarding a *pre-determined* file to the Internet client for the first time. After that the Web server will forward files to the client depending upon specific requests from the client.

Traditionally, this sub directory on the Internet server is '*wwwroot*' and the file automatically picked up and passed to the Internet client the first time is traditionally called '*index.html*'.

Note

However, web server software can be configured to go to any *user defined* sub directory and forward any *user defined* file to the Internet client.

Multiple Virtual Domains hosted on a Single Physical Domain:

A single computer having a permanent IP address and connected to the Internet can host *multiple virtual domains* on its hard disk drive. There are several Internet servers (i.e. physical domains) which do nothing but **Host** multiple virtual domains.

Companies who wish to have an Internet presence without registering a physical domain with InterNIC and then creating a virtual domain on the physical domain simply rent hard disk space on these ***Host*** servers. Most often host servers rent space on their hard disk drives in 25MB blocks.

Host servers offer several additional services such as multiple e-mail boxes, web site creation, web site creation tools and so on. This service makes the prospect of renting hard disk space and creating a virtual domain on someone else's physical domain very attractive due to competitive pricing. The price of hosting a virtual domain on someone else's Internet server is really a very tiny fraction of the setup costs of a physical domain on the Internet.

This has given rise to a situation where the number of virtual domains outnumbers the physical domains on the Internet.

Internet clients will now not only need to connect to the correct physical domain but also to the correct virtual domain hosted on the physical domain. Hence, the Web server software run on the physical domain must perform ***Virtual Domain Name*** resolution as well (*i.e. must be able to connect Internet client to the correct sub-directory on the hard disk drive and forward the correct starting file from this specific sub directory*).

Conceptually, a sub-directory is created on the Internet '*Host*' server. The company, which has purchased hard disk space on the Internet host server, creates its web site within this sub directory. This sub directory will hold the default startup file (e.g. *Index.html*) which the web server will send back to the client when the client connects to the physical domain and points to a specific virtual domain hosted on the physical domain.

When an Internet client requests for a connection to a virtual domain on the Internet, the request is routed to the proper Internet Server using TCP/IP. The Web Server running on this Internet Server then handles the request, resolves (*maps*) the *Virtual Domain Name* sent along with the request to an appropriate sub directory on the Internet Server where the web site (i.e. *virtual domain*) is hosted.

INTERNET DOMAINS

Each computer that has a permanent IP address, runs Server software and offers information to clients, is considered to be a **Physical Domain** i.e. a place *(domain)* where information is available.

The Physical Domain

All Internet Servers are connected to the Internet via an **Internet Gateway**. An Internet gateway is usually provided by one of the global networking giants that have setup these gateways. These networking giants are the companies who have spent enormous sums of money to set up the physical networks that circle the globe.

These physical networks are called the **Internet Backbone**. The Internet backbone is a heterogeneous mix of networking technologies, which have been successfully implemented and currently fully operational. The networking giants are companies like British Telecom, Hyundai, AT&T etc.

INTERNET SERVER IDENTITIES

InterNIC, a quasi government body in the U.S.A registers and issues Internet Servers their unique IP addresses.

InterNIC also authorizes organizations in other countries to issue IP addresses. In India, NCST (National Center of Software Technology) a quasi government body is authorized to issue permanent IP addresses. This really means that the Internet Server must be located within India.

Registering A Virtual Domain With InterNIC

Log onto an InterNIC Server. Fill up a registration form online. Pay the two-year registration fee to InterNIC. This registers a virtual domain with InterNIC.

Detailed Registration will ask for information like Personal Details, Billing Contact Information, Technical Contact Information, and Administrative Contact Information and so on.

When a company registers a virtual domain name with InterNIC, InterNIC requires a unique IP address to be specified. The unique IP address specified, is generally the IP address of the Internet server, which will host the **Virtual Domain**.

nterNIC's address is http://www.internic.net/regist.html

- InterNIC will scan its registered database to ensure that the domain name is unique
- If the name is unique, InterNIC will inform the registering company or individual that its registration has been accepted.
- Once the Domain name is registered the registering company has 30 days within which payment has to be made to InterNIC for the registration. Once registered, the Domain registration is valid for 2 years. After a two year period the registration must be renewed or the registration lapses.
- If the name is not unique, the registration is rejected and InterNIC will inform the company the registration has been rejected due to the Domain name being duplicate.

Note

InterNIC allows a company registering a Domain name to scan through its domain name database using a simple but elegant user interface. Hence, prior actual registration a company or individual can find out whether the domain name being registered is unique or not.

As the number of Domain registrations grew by leaps and bounds InterNIC began segregating Domains according to the services provided by the Domain being registered. This was done by adding an *extension* to the Domain name. The extension to the domain name indicated the kind of service being provided by that domain.

A Domain name extension structure is as follows:

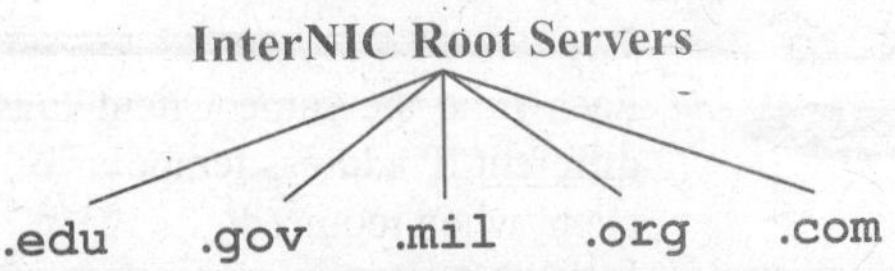

Diagram 1.2

Note

InterNIC has spread its *Root Servers* geographically across the United States to be able to handle the large number of physical Domain Name Servers being registered and virtual domain names being hosted on these servers.

Domain Name Extension

.edu	Servers that provide Educational services.
.gov	Servers that provide information about the government of a country
.mil	Servers that provide Military information
.org	Servers that provide information about the Organizations in the world.
.com	Servers providing commercial services on the Internet

Table 1.1

ESTABLISHING CONNECTIVITY ON THE INTERNET

The protocol used to setup communications between a Client and Server on the Internet is TCP/IP. TCP/IP, expands to read Transmission Control Protocol / Internet Protocol. TCP/IP is a connection independent protocol.

This means that TCP/IP works completely independent of the physical media used to create the network. The network can be a heterogeneous mix of any of the following networking technologies Ethernet, VSat, Fiber Optics, Infrared, VHF/UHF radio frequencies and so on, TCP/IP will work across all quite transparently. TCP/IP breaks up data into datagrams and guarantees that the data is correctly received at its destination

CLIENT IP ADDRESS

How Client IP Addresses Are Assigned

Computers that only read information offered, (i.e. Internet clients) need not necessarily have a permanent IP address. However, when logged into the Internet, a client requires a unique IP address. This IP address enables the Internet server called, to reply accurately.

The Internet Service Provider's (ISP's) Server via which the client connects to the Internet, temporarily assigns a unique IP address to the client.

In India, for a very long time, the only ISP was **V**idesh **S**amachar **N**igam **L**imited. (i.e. VSNL). Whenever a client logs into the Internet via a VSNL Server, the VSNL Server temporarily (*and dynamically*) assigns a unique IP address to the computer that successfully logs in.

How ISP's Achieve The Task Of Assigning IP Addresses

ISP's purchase a block of unique IP addresses from internationally recognized networking bodies. Thus whenever a client logs into the Internet via an ISP's Server, one of these unique IP addresses is temporarily assigned to the computer, which logs in.

Note

Each time the same Client logs into an ISP's Server, the Client will be assigned a unique but different IP address temporarily. This is the technique of **Dynamically assigning** an IP address to a client when required.

The maximum number of computers that can log into an ISP Server and access the Internet is therefore limited to the block of unique IP addresses purchased by that ISP from the international networking body.

Getting A Temporary IP Address

Assuming that the Client computer is a Windows machine, its TCP/IP stack is configured to Get an IP address dynamically from the ISP's DHNS **Server**.

The Client computer logs into the ISP's Server using a dial-up line and a modem. After a successful login is accomplished, the ISP's Server automatically passes one IP address from the block of IP addresses purchased, to the computer logged in.

Once a computer is logged on the Internet and has a unique IP address, any other computer on the Internet that is aware of this IP address can setup communications with it. *i.e. all the Clients become visible to all the other computers on the Internet, via their unique IP address through the ISP's Server.*

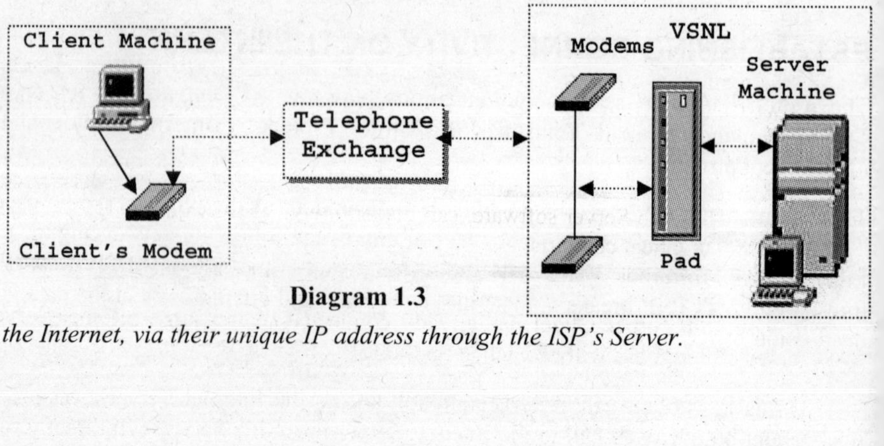

Diagram 1.3

HOW IP ADDRESSING CAME INTO EXISTENCE?

When the Internet was in its infancy, the US military, colleges and academics largely used it to exchange data. One master Server (called **Root**) held the entire set of computer IP addresses.

These IP addresses were held as pure text in a file called **Hosts** held in a sub-directory on the **Root** Server.

Note

On an M.S. Windows computer, to locate the **Hosts** text file search in: **C:\Windows**.
(*Replace 'C' with an appropriate drive letter*)

The contents of the **Hosts** file are as follows:

```
IP address       Domain Name
202.100.17.33    Microsoft
```

i.e. a unique IP address of the Internet Server, followed by a single **Tab** character, followed by a domain name.

Resolving Domain Names

When any Client wishes to communicate with any Internet Server using browser software, the Client sends out a broadcast using the Server's *Domain name* as the identifier.

The ISP's Internet Server intercepts this request first.

Should the **Domain Name** be unknown to the ISP's Internet Server.

The ISP's Internet Server will route this broadcast to an InterNIC Root Server.

In the InterNIC Root Server's *Hosts* file the Domain Name will be mapped to an IP address.

This IP address will be returned to the ISP's Server

The ISP's server will now pass this IP address back to the Client's browser

The Client's browser will now broadcast a request to connect directly to the Internet Server using its IP address.

As soon as this call is heard by the Internet Server it will respond and a link will be setup between the Client and the Internet Server.

Web Server software running on the Internet Server takes care of connecting a Client to the virtual domain as required.

Once a client is connected to the appropriate domain, the Web Server software delivers the Client the first HTML page of that domain which is traditionally *Index.html* or *Index.htm* and browsing of the specific domain can begin.

Note

Web Server software, can be configured to forward any HTML page (or run a CGI script) when a Client connects.

In case some other Client has already connected to the same Internet Server via the same ISP then the server's IP address will be cached on the ISP's Server.

If this is true, the ISP's Server already knows the Internet Server's unique IP address. Hence when the Client broadcasts a call to the Internet Server the ISP's Server will directly route the call to the appropriate Internet Server.

If a client already knows the IP address of the Internet Server, directly keying in the IP address into the Browser's search window will establish a connection between the Client and the Internet Server in the shortest possible time. For example, 127.45.27.18, (i.e. *the actual IP address of the Internet Server*).

The Structure Of An Internet Address

The structure of an Internet Server's address keyed into a Client's browser software is as follows:

http://www.microsoft.com

where; http is the communication protocol to be used,
www is the notation for World Wide Web,
microsoft is the registered Domain Name associated with the IP address of an Internet server, and
com the Server provides commercial services to Clients who connect to it.

To help speed up access, its IP address can be directly used, i.e. 127.57.13.1 instead of the domain name, *miscrosoft.com*. In this case no name resolution needs to take place.

Note

Only the Domain Name (i.e. microsoft) will be resolved to an explicit IP address by looking up the InterNIC Server. The period used in the Domain address is a parameter delimiter.

http, www, com are all optional information that is built into the Domain address loaded in to the Client's browser.

microsoft.com is the *compulsory segment* of a domain address as it is 'resolved' into a specific and unique IP address that points to a server.

A BRIEF OVERVIEW OF TCP/IP AND ITS SERVICES

TCP/IP is an acronym for *Transmission Control Protocol / Internet Protocol*. TCP/IP is a collection of protocols, applications and services. The protocols in TCP/IP move data from one network layer to another. There are five layers within TCP/IP.

- Application
- Transport
- Internet
- Data Link
- Physical

The Physical Layer

The physical layer is pure hardware in any network infrastructure. This includes the cable, satellite, or any other connection medium, and the network interface card, which transmits electrical signals, and so on.

The Data Link Layer

This is the layer that is responsible for splitting data into packets to be sent across the connection medium such as cables, satellites, and so on. Once the data is on the communication link, the Data Link Layer handles any interference, which may arise due to noise, solar flares, and so on. The Data Link Layer works hard to make sure that the physical link does not garble the electrical signals carrying the data.

The Network Layer

This layer gets packets from the Data Link Layer and sends them to the correct network address. If more than one possible route is available for the data to travel, the network layer figures out the best route. The network layer determines that data is sent to the right address via the most convenient (*need not be the shortest*) route.

The Transport Layer

Though the Network Layer routes data to its destination, it cannot guarantee that the packets holding data will arrive in the correct order or that they won't have picked up any errors during transmission. It is the Transport Layer's job to make sure that the packets have no errors and they are also received in the correct order.

The Application Layer

This is the layer, which contains the application that the user uses to send or receive data. Without this layer the computer and its user would never be able to send data and would not know what to do with data sent by another user.

Internet Protocol

The Internet Protocol is responsible for basic network connectivity. When mapped to the TCP/IP layers, the Internet Protocol or IP works with *The Network Layer*. In networking there has to be a physical location to send data to or receive data from.

To make this happen, every physical location must have a unique network address. This address is called its IP address. Hence, every computer on a TCP/IP network must have an IP address, which is unique to that computer.

This IP address can be compared to a postal address that identifies the exact location of a residence or corporate house. Just as two residences cannot have the same postal address, so also no two computers on a TCP/IP network can have the same IP address.

The Structure of an IP Address

The IP address is a set of numbers separated by periods. An IP address is a 32-bit number, divided into two sections, the network number and the host number. Addresses are written as four fields, eight bits each separated by a period. Each field can be a number ranging from 0 to 255. This method of addressing is called *dotted decimal notation*. An IP address looks like:

field1.field2.field3.field4

All hosts/network interfaces (NIC cards) on the same network use the same network number. Each host/network interface (NIC card) on the same network must have a unique host number.

The four fields of an IP address are clubbed together into two sections, the network number and the host number depending on the type of network the host or the network interface belongs to.

There are three types of networks on the Internet. Table 1.2 gives a classification of the network types and how the fields of an IP address are mapped to the Network section and the Host section of the address.

Network Class	Network Section of the IP Address	Host Section of the IP Address
A	Field1	Field2.Field3.Field4
B	Field1.Field2	Field3.Field4
C	Field1.Field2.Field3	Field4

Table 1.2

TRANSMISSION CONTROL PROTOCOL

TCP/IP uses IP to deliver packets to the upper layer applications and provides a reliable stream of data among computers on the network. Once the packets arrive at the correct IP address, TCP goes to work. TCP's main task is error checking to make sure that the right numbers of packets are received and that they are in proper order. Thus, TCP guarantees that the information received by a computer on a TCP/IP network, is exactly the same information that was sent to it by another computer on the network.

TCP/IP consists of protocols, applications, and services. Protocols enable a server application to offer services, and the client application to use those services. It is possible to design a new protocol and add it to TCP/IP.

The Internet is a large worldwide network of computers, which uses TCP/IP as the underlying communication protocol. Since TCP/IP consists of various services, the Internet is in a position to offer those services to all computers connected to the Internet.

Following is a brief description of some of the commonly used services along with the protocols they use.

World Wide Web

The World Wide Web is a worldwide information service on the Internet. The World Wide Web or the Web, as it is popularly known, uses special software called a Browser (client) and TCP/IP, HTTP and a Web Server to function.

TCP/IP is the communication protocol used by the Internet and is a must for the World Wide Web to function. HyperText Transfer Protocol or HTTP is the protocol used by the WWW service to make communication possible between a Web Server and a Web Browser. A Web Server is a special software, which runs on a computer and responds to requests made by other computers on the network. A Web Browser is simply an application program, which sends request to a Web Server and accepts a response to that request from the Web Server.

FTP

File Transfer Protocol or FTP is not just a *protocol* but also a *service* and an *application*. FTP is especially useful for transferring files between different computers. FTP provides the facility to transfer files between two computers running on different operating systems such as UNIX, MS-DOS and Windows.

FTP As An Application

For two computers to actually make use of the FTP service, both computers require special application software, which understands this service. FTP is an application for copying files. A client application can be run on the local computer to contact the FTP server application on the remote computer. Depending upon what the user wants to do, instructions can be given to the client application, which works with the server application to execute those instructions.

CuteFTP and Reachout are two very popular FTP applications, which provide excellent user interfaces and a wide range of FTP commands and functions. CuteFTP permits the user to log onto a remote computer offering the FTP service, upload or download files between the client computer and the server computer, perform various operations on the files such as delete, rename, change file permissions, and so on and logout from the remote computer when done.

FTP As A Service

FTP is a service for copying files from one computer to another. A connection can be made from one computer (client) to another computer (server) offering this service and files can be sent or received.

FTP As a Protocol

FTP is a protocol for copying files between two computers. The client and the server applications both use it for communication to ensure that the new copy of the file is identical to the original.

TELNET

Telnet is both a TCP/IP application and a protocol for connecting a local computer to a remote computer. The Telnet application acts as a terminal emulator. Whatever commands are typed into the local computer are sent across the network for execution by the remote computer.

To use Telnet, the Telnet application must be given the IP address of the computer to connect to. Once the connection is established with the remote computer, a username and a password must be supplied to access the resources of the remote computer.

In Conclusion

The Internet is a worldwide collection of interconnected computer networks that use TCP/IP and its related services. TCP/IP provides the flexibility to add new protocols and services to the already existing ones. This led to the advent of protocols such as Hyper Text Transfer Protocol (HTTP) and its associated World Wide Web (WWW) service, the File Transfer Protocol (FTP) and its associated FTP services, and so on. The Internet gained popularity primarily due to the advent of the World Wide Web or the Web, as it is popularly known.

Once the Internet's addressing system is understood it is quite simple to link to an Internet Server anywhere on the Internet. Once linked to the appropriate Internet Server, a Client can access all that the Server has to offer with complete freedom.

The Internet really is a rich resource for information and data. Never ending, always changing and completely dynamic.

SELF REVIEW QUESTIONS

FILL IN THE BLANKS

1. A permanent connection to the Internet is obtained by the ISP through its ______.
2. Servers run special software called _____ ______ ______ that allows them to respond to a client's request for information.
3. Each computer that has a permanent IP address, runs Server software and offers information to clients is considered to be a ________ __________.
4. ________ a quasi government body in the U.S.A registers and issues Internet servers their IP addresses.
5. The protocol used to setup communications between a Client and Server on the Internet is __________.
6. ________ is the protocol used by the WWW service to establish a communication between a Web server and a Web Browser.
7. The default HTML page that is delivered to a client connected to a Web Server is ______.

TRUE OR FALSE

8. It is possible for a 'Domain Name' be unknown to an ISP's Internet Server.
9. A single computer having a permanent IP address can host multiple virtual domains on its hard disk drive.
10. TCP/IP is not a connection independent protocol.

2. INTRODUCTION TO HTML

The term **<u>Knowledge is Power</u>** really takes on a special dimension in software. This is one area where information plays a vital and dynamic role. Tried and tested methods of providing information to those who need it, like printed documents bound together in the form of manuals, books and so on, does not really work for software information. This is because this information is very dynamic and it keeps changing and re-changing all the time.

A change in information requires the contents of books, manuals, and so on, to change. This will in turn require complete reprinting of the books and manuals. Reprinting always results in time and cost overheads. Reprinting also results in out dated books and manuals being held in inventory, unable to be used.

To resolve this problem, information needs be stored in such a manner that whenever the information changes, these changes can be incorporated with the least cost and time. A tried and tested method that allows this is to store the information in the form of computer based files. These files could be stored at a central location. Once stored at a central location the files can be accessed when required for reference.

Since these files are stored at a central location on a computer, their access will also require a computer and some sort of network that connects these two computers together.

Thus to provide information to the users:

- Files holding information must be created.
- These files must be stored at a central location on a computer.
- When required the users should be allowed to access these files using their desktop computers.
- A network link must be established between the desktop computer and the computer serving information at a central location.

This introduces **Client / Server** terminology wherein

- The desktop computer requesting for information is termed as the **Client**.
- The computer serving information from a central location is termed as the **Server**.

INFORMATION FILES CREATION

If information has to be stored on a central computer, it must be created first. While being created, information can only be stored in the form of files on the computer. These files are created using special software programs or programming environments.

Files that travel across the largest network in the world, the Internet, and carry information from a **Server** to a **Client** that requested them are called **Web Pages**. The individual who develops these web pages is called **Web Developer**.

WEB SERVER

Web Pages are created using HTML syntax. These pages must be organized and stored at a central computer.

The organization of web pages into directories and files stored on the HDD of a central computer is called **Web Site** creation.

Computers, which store web pages in the form of directories and files and provide these files to be read, are called **Servers**'. They act like service providers that service the need for information.

The Server Computer runs special software called **Web Server** software that allows:

- Web Site Management.
- Accept a client's request for information.
- Respond to a client's request by providing the page with the required information.

Some of the most popular software, which Servers run to allow them to respond to client request for information, is Internet Information Server (**IIS**), Apache Web Server, Netscape Server, and Microsoft Personal Web Server.

Web Server Software stores and manages web pages. When required, the Web Server accepts requests for these Web Pages, retrieves these web pages from its HDD, and sends the page back to the client who requested for it.

WEB CLIENT / BROWSER

To access information stored in the form of web pages, users must connect to a Web Server. Once connected, an interface that displays the contents of the web page is required.

Computers that offer the facility to read information stored in web pages are called **Web Clients**.

Web Clients run special software called a **Browser** that allows them to:

- Connect to an appropriate Server.
- Query the Server for the information to be read.
- Provides an interface to read the information returned by the Server.

Some of the most popular Browser software that clients run to allow them to query Web Servers for information is Netscape Communicator, Internet Explorer.

Understanding How A Browser Communicates With A Web Server

As seen earlier, a Web Server is responsible for sending web pages to a Browser on a client. When a Browser communicates with a Web Server, it results into a four-step HTTP transaction.

As seen in diagram 2.1, a client's Browser retrieves a web page from the server and displays the web page in the Browser. The communication steps between the client and the server can be summarized as follows:

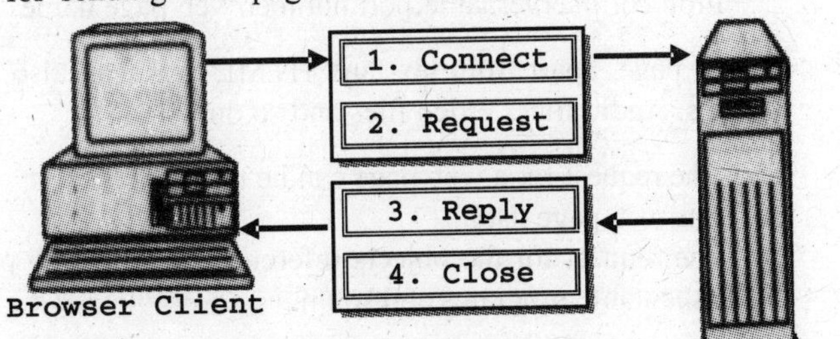

Diagram 2.1

Establish Connection

Before a client and server can exchange information, they must first establish a connection. TCP/IP is used to let computers establish a link between a Web Server and a Web Browser over the Internet.

To communicate with the Web Server, the client machine must be given the IP address of the server along with the sub protocol that must be used i.e. HTTP, FTP etc. The client browser will attempt to locate the server based on the IP address supplied and establish a connection.

A Web Server supports multiple protocols. For example, a Web Server may support two protocols viz. HTTP, FTP.

In such cases, each of the protocols (like HTTP, FTP) can be accessed by specifying protocol name and a specific "port number". Common protocols like HTTP, FTP etc have "well known" port numbers. For example the HTTP protocol by default works on port number 80. Similarly the FTP protocol by default works on port number 21.

If the protocols are configured on default port numbers, the connection to a Web Server can be established by:

Protocol://IP address

For example, if the IP address for the SCT Server is 131.100.2.107 and communication must be established using HTTP then any client attempting to connect would have to pass the IP address as: http://131.100.2.107 to the ISP whose gateway is being used to access the Internet.

Protocols can be configured to run on port numbers other than the default port number. Valid values are 0 to 9999. If a protocol is configured to run on any other port number then the client when trying to establish a communication link with the Web Server must specify the port number along with the protocol name and the IP address.

Thus the complete syntax to access and connect to any server would be:

Protocol://servername:port number.

Client Issues A Request And Server Sends A Response

As seen earlier, each Web Server controls a web site. From amongst the collection of several web pages (i.e., the Web site), one page is treated as a 'Default Web Document'.

When a Browser connects to a Web Server using an appropriate protocol name, IP address and port number, and the Web Server treats this connection to be a request for the 'Default Web Document'. The Web Server then dispatches the 'Default Web Document' to the client who connected.

If the client requires viewing any other web page then the client can specify the web page name (*if known*) along with the connection information. Thus the complete connection and web page information will now be specified as:

Protocol://servername:port number/web page name.

A web page, apart from text and HTML tags, can also include references to external objects like GIF's, JPEG's, Audio files, Video files and so on.

Thus the request for a web page can be two-fold:

- The web page itself.
- The request for the objects referenced by the web page i.e. GIF's, JPEG's, Audio Files, Video Files, Executable programs and so on.

When an appropriately structured, HTTP request, is received from a Browser, the Web Server will try to locate the web page requested. If the Web Page exists, the server responds by providing the page to the browser.

If the Web Page is not found, an appropriate Error Message is sent as a response to the browser request. After sending the web page the Web Server resets the connection with the browser.

After receiving the Web page, the Browser will identify the external objects that are specified in the web page (*if any*) and request the Server to deliver the external objects.

Such a request will result in a connection being re-established with the Web Server and a request being sent by the browser. The Web Server responds to the request being sent by the browser.

Server Terminates The Connection

It is the Server's responsibility to terminate the TCP/IP connection with the Browser after it responds to the Browser's request. However, both the Browser and the Web Server must manage an unexpected closing of a connection as well. In other words, if the user clicks on the Browser's STOP button, the Browser must close the connection.

Also a computer crash by either a Browser or a Web Server must be recognized by the surviving computer, which, in turn, will close the connection.

HYPER TEXT MARKUP LANGUAGE (HTML)

The language used to develop web pages is called **H**yper**T**ext **M**arkup **L**anguage (HTML). HTML is the language interpreted by a Browser. Web Pages are also called HTML documents. HTML is a set of special codes that can be embedded in text to add formatting and linking information. HTML is specified as TAGS in an HTML document (*i.e. the Web page*).

HTML Tags

Tags are instructions that are embedded directly into the text of the document. An HTML tag is a signal to a browser that it should do something other than just throw text up on the screen. By convention all HTML tags begin with an open angle bracket (<) and end with a close angle bracket (>).

HTML tags can be of two types:

Paired Tags

A tag is said to be a *paired* tag if it, along with a companion tag, flanks the text. For example the <B> tag is a paired tag. The <B> tag with its companion tag </B> causes the text contained between them to be rendered in *bold*. The effect of other paired tags is applied only to the text they contain.

In paired tags, the *first* tag (<B>) is often called the *opening tag* and the *second* tag (</B>) is called the *closing tag*.

The opening tag activates the effect and the closing tag turns the effect off.

Singular Tags

The second type of tag is the *singular* or *stand-alone* tag. A *stand-alone* tag does not have a companion tag. For example <BR /> tag will insert a line break. This tag does not require any companion tag.

Note

Some HTML tags require additional information to be supplied to them. For instance, when a picture is placed on the screen, information like the height and width of the picture can be specified.

Additional information supplied to an HTML tag is known as *Attributes* of a tag. Attributes are written immediately following the tag, separated by a *space*. Multiple attributes can be associated with a tag, also separated by a *space*.

The skill in creating an HTML (web) page would lie in knowing the functionality of all HTML tags and tag attributes where applicable. This skill can then be used to format large quantities of textual information as required and have this ready to use on a web site.

The simplest and quickest way to know the functionality of HTML tags would be to learn a few tags (*and their attributes where applicable*) and immediately use these tags in formatting textual information to be used in a web page as part of a web site. Using this technique the HTML tag, its attributes where applicable, and its functionality will immediately become apparent.

Our approach to learning HTML is to create a series of web pages for a fictitious company to be used on its web site. Textual information will be viewed in a browser **without** the HTML tags in place and subsequently **with** the HTML tags in place. The difference in presentation quality of the textual information will be very apparent.

FOCUS 1:

Delta Engineering Pvt. Ltd. is a Company, dealing with manufacture of products like Barbed Wire, Barbed Tapes and so on. This Company is interested in publicity with the widest possible reach and modest investment. The least expensive approach is through the Web! Delta is therefore looking at preparing a *Web Site* to let the World know about itself and main lines of business.

Consider the preparation of a web site for this engineering company. The information being presented on the site is categorized into:

- ❑ The Company Profile
- ❑ The Products manufactured in the Company

The Products manufactured by the Company primarily include:

- ❑ Barbed Wire
- ❑ Barbed Tape
- ❑ Animal Fencing

Information in all these areas needs to be provided to anyone who requires it. The information provided is segregated into four major heads:

- ❑ The Company Profile
- ❑ Barbed Wire
    - Line Wire
    - Barbed Wire
    - Carrying Handles
- ❑ Barbed Tape
    - Short Blade Barbed Tape (SBBT)
    - Medium Blade Barbed Tape (MBBT)
    - Long Blade Barbed Tape (LBBT)
- ❑ Animal Fencing

The creation of the textual content of the Web Site is done in a simple ASCII editor such as **Notepad** and saved as *filename.**html*** file. The file will contain the following textual material created as an ASCII file and saved as indicated above.

After creating this text file, view its contents in a browser, either Internet Explorer or Netscape navigator. The browser used for page testing purposes while creating this book has always been Netscape navigator.

After the text file created has been viewed in a browser a few HTML tags will be added to the material and the file will be re-viewed to register the changes in its presentation. This is the standard learning technique used with all the HTML tags and their attributes where applicable.

```
DELTA ENGINEERING PVT. LTD.
```

PROFILE

Delta Engineering Pvt. Ltd. is a specialist manufacturer of wire and wire products. DEPL established in Mumbai, India is ideally located for shipments to any part of the world. The main items of manufacture, in collaboration with Gulf Fencing Industry (GFI) include protector gabions and protector fencing systems.

Protector fencing systems offer a wide range of solutions for all security problems on any terrain and under extreme climatic conditions. The protector fencing system has been used extensively in Europe, America and the Far East, and this has helped formulate a package especially suited to Middle East requirements.

DEPL is equipped to offer comprehensive packages including design, material and installation.

Products strictly adhere to BS, ASTM and DIN international specifications. Quality control is guaranteed by independent laboratory test certificates from India.

Quality control is implemented without sacrificing economy and efficiency. DEPL is dedicated to technical services and problem solving.

DEPL can provide planning support by offering design, technical specifications, drawings, foundation plans and installation instructions, together with a personalized service. The company's technical sales engineers keep in constant touch with all clients. Utmost importance is given to optimum design, versatility, durability and economy backed by the DEPL guarantee for work undertaken.

Please forward any inquiries to enq_depl@bom2.vsnl.net.in

DELTA ENGINEERING PVT. LTD.
502, 5th Floor, Tejas Building
Andheri (W), Mumbai
INDIA
Telephone : 91-022-8210050

BARBED WIRE

Concertina Barbed Wire in roll form is used in high security areas to deter trespassing men and animals. The effectiveness of this material is proved as it has been in use for more than 75 years during war and peace.

Line Wire:
This is made up of 3.05 mm diameter high carbon steel wire, with a tensile strength of 170 to 180 kg/mm². The wire is drawn and dressed in

such a manner that the coils formed will fall naturally into the specified diameter without forming a figure eight. Line wire is heavy hot dipped galvanized with minimum zinc coating of 185 gm/mm².

Barbed Wire:
This is 2.00mm diameter bright mild steel wire with a tensile strength of 38 to 55kg/mm² conforming to BS 1052. The wire is hot dipped galvanized with a minimum zinc coating of 20 to 50 gm/mm². The barbs are formed with four points. Spacing between the centers of the barbs is every 70mm along the length of the wire. The barbs are firmly secured by indentations made on the wire.

Carrying Handles:
Handles are made of mild steel wire of 3.55mm diameter and are attached to the outer turn of the coil on each side.

BARBED TAPES

Barbed Tapes are used as psychological and physical deterrent against intrusion by personnel and animals. Barbed tape barrier systems are more vicious and difficult to tamper with, providing superior perimeter security. Some of the users are military installations, nuclear energy sites, maximum-security prisons, various petroleum installations, tank farms and other important industrial facilities.

Short Blade Barbed Tape (SBBT):
To give the maximum tensile strength at the time of the breach hard drawn steel cord is used (ES1). For camouflage purposes, a coaltar coating can be applied over the entire surface (ES-1), and to attain the high degree of rust resistance, the core wire is made of galvanized steel (ES-2). Any of the above three options are available to meet your specific requirements. There are several variations in spiral diameter in accordance with the needs of the customers.

Medium Blade Barbed Tape (MBBT):
The specification of the "ivory" tape is similar to those of ES types. However the blades are sharper and have a greater pricking capacity. This can be used for both temporary and permanent security. The life of this tape is more than three times longer than those of ES types. Therefore, "ivory" tape is a more effective choice in terrain, which has heavy rain or in coastal areas.

Long Blade Barbed Tape (LBBT):
This is the most effective psychological and physical deterrent, ever made as a barrier obstacle. It is available in stainless steel (SUS 430) and the core wire can be fabricated from either galvanized carbon steel or stainless steel.

ANIMAL FENCING

```
DEPL's animal fencing system is mainly used as an anti-intrusion
barrier against any farm and other animals.

The most common use is on highways where vast distances are covered at
a very economical cost.

Animal fencing can also be used to enclose areas such as farms, forest
areas and national
parks, where security is not crucial.

This system is easy to install and can be erected in a comparatively
short time.
```

The above textual material can be typed into a file using any ASCII text editor and saved as an HTML file. This HTML file can then be opened in a Web Browser. This file when opened in the Browser will display the output as shown in diagram 2.2.

DELTA ENGINEERING PVT. LTD. --
------ PROFILE --
Delta Engineering Pvt. Ltd. is a specialist manufacturer of wire and wire products. DEPL established in Mumbai, India is ideally located for shipments to any part of the world. The main items of manufacture, in collaboration with Gulf Fencing Industry (GFI) include protector gabions and protector fencing systems. Protector fencing systems offer a wide range of solutions for all security problems on any terrain and under extreme climatic conditions. The protector fencing system has been used extensively in Europe, America and the Far East, and this has helped formulate a package especially suited to Middle East requirements. DEPL is equipped to offer comprehensive packages including design, material and installation. Products strictly adhere to BS, ASTM and DIN international specifications. Quality control is guaranteed by independent laboratory test certificates from India. Quality control is implemented without sacrificing economy and efficiency. DEPL is dedicated to technical services and problem solving. DEPL can provide planning support by offering design, technical specifications, drawings, foundation plans and installation instructions, together with a personalized service. The company's technical sales engineers keep in constant touch with all clients. Utmost importance is given to optimum design, versatility, durability and economy backed by the DEPL guarantee for work undertaken. Please forward any inquiries to enq_depl@bom2.vsnl.net.in DELTA ENGINEERING PVT. LTD. 502,

Diagram 2.2

Output For Focus 1:

The output in diagram 2.2 lacks visual appeal. To increase the present ability of this textual material, it should be well formatted. HTML has a series of formatting tags. HTML tags along with syntax on how to use them are described in the following pages.

COMMONLY USED HTML COMMANDS

The Structure Of An HTML program

Every HTML program has a rigid structure. The entire web page is enclosed within <HTML> </HTML> tags. Within these tags two distinct sections are created using the <HEAD> </HEAD> tags and the <BODY> </BODY> tags. These sections are described below.

Document Head

Information placed in this section is essential to the inner workings of the document and has nothing to do with the content of the document. With the exception of information contained within the <TITLE> </TITLE> tags, all information placed within the <HEAD> </HEAD> tags is not displayed in the browser. The HTML tags used to indicate the start and end of the head section are:

<HEAD><TITLE> . . . </TITLE></HEAD>

Document Body

The tags used to indicate the start and end of the main body of textual information are:

<BODY>

. . .

</BODY>

Page defaults like background color, text color, font size, font weight and so on can be specified as *attributes* of the <BODY> tag. The attributes that the <BODY> tag takes are:

CSS Background Formatting (background-color:)	Set the default background-color property to the background-color of an element. This tag is written in the CSS file.
CSS Background Formatting (background-image :)	Sets the background-image property of an element or of the document. This tag is written in the CSS file.
TEXT	Changes the body text color from its default value to the color specified with this attribute.

Table 2.1

Example:

<BODY STYLE = "background: url(starfield.gif); color: red;">

Note

The **.gif** file "starfield.gif" should be present in the current working directory. If not, a Relative path should be specified to where the **.gif** file exists.

Tip

Specifying a Relative File Path:

Wherever a file name needs to be specified (for instance, *a .gif file needs to be specified with the BACKGROUND attribute*), the specified file must be present in the current working directory. If the file is not in the current working directory, the specified file must include the file path. The file path can be specified relative to the current directory. This is because, by default, the Browser searches for the file only within the current directory.

For example, consider the following directory structure.

```
C:\
|________ boxes.gif
|________ Meher
            |________ try.htm
            |________ texture1.gif
            |________ images
                        |________ stars.gif
```

Consider working with the file *try.htm.* To use all the different **.gif** files as backgrounds, the tag specifications will change as follows:

Use of the file boxes.gif

<BODY STYLE="background: url(../boxes.gif)">

Use of the file texture1.gif

<BODY STYLE="background: url(texture1.gif)">

Use of the file stars.gif

<BODY STYLE="background: url(images/stars.gif)">

TITLES AND FOOTERS

Title

A web page could have a title that describes what the page is about without being too wordy. This can be achieved by using the TITLE tag. Text included between the <TITLE>...</TITLE> tag shows up in the title bar of the browser window.

<TITLE> ... </TITLE>

Footer

Just as a title can be placed in the title bar of the browser window, certain information is commonly placed at the foot of the web page. Copyright information, contact details of the creator of the Web page and so on are the type of information traditionally placed at the foot of the web page. The HTML tags are:

<ADDRESS> . . . </ADDRESS>

This tag should ideally be placed *immediately after* the last line of the textual material of the web page. However, it could also be placed anywhere in the body of the document. The text typed within these tags always appears in *Italics*.

Example:

```
<HEAD><TITLE>This is the title</TITLE></HEAD>
<BODY>
    . . .
    <ADDRESS>This is the footer </ADDRESS>
</BODY>
```

TEXT FORMATTING

Paragraph breaks

A blank line always separates paragraphs in textual material. The tag that provides this functionality is **<P>**. On encountering this tag the browser, moves onto a new line, skipping one line between the previous line and the new line.

Example:

A channel is a dedicated path for data to flow along. It doesn't bother too much about error correction on its own, merely reporting to the processor that the transfer failed. So a channel can be very fast. **<P>** Fiber channel has the above attributes along with those of a network. It lets you transfer data from a source buffer to another buffer at journey's end. It does not care for the contents or the data format.**</P>**

Output:

```
A channel is a dedicated path for data to flow along. It doesn't
bother too much about error correction on its own, merely reporting
to the processor that the transfer failed. So a channel can be very
fast.

Fiber channel has the above attributes along with those of a
network. It lets you transfer data from a source buffer to another
buffer at journey's end. It does not care for the contents or the
data format.
```

Line Breaks

When text needs to start from a new line and not continue on the same line (*without skipping a blank line*), the **
** tag should be used. This tag simply jumps to the start of the next line.

Example:

Silicon Chip Technologies, **
** A/5, Jay Apartments, **
**
Vile Parle (East), **
** Mumbai - 400057.

Output:

```
Silicon Chip Technologies,
A/5, Jay Apartments,
Vile Parle (East),
Mumbai - 400057.
```

Note

Browsers **ignore** multiple consecutive <P> tags, but **recognize** multiple consecutive <BR /> tags.

FOCUS 2:

Using appropriate text formatting and break tags to improve the present ability of the DEPL Web Site.

Code Listing:

```
<HTML>
    <HEAD><TITLE>Delta Engineering Pvt. Ltd.</TITLE></HEAD>
    <BODY STYLE="background: url(images/PINKWHIT.GIF)">
        <P>DELTA ENGINEERING PVT. LTD. </P>
        ------------------------------------------------------------------------------------------<BR />
        PROFILE <BR />
        ------------------------------------------------------------------------------------------<BR />
        Delta Engineering Pvt. Ltd. is a specialist manufacturer of wire and wire products. DEPL
        established in Mumbai, India is ideally located for shipments to any part of the world. The main
        items of manufacture, in collaboration with Gulf Fencing Industry (GFI) include protector gabions
        and protector fencing systems. <P> Protector fencing systems offer a wide range of solutions to all
        security problems on any terrain and under extreme climatic conditions. Protector fencing system
        has been used extensively in Europe, America and the Far East, and this has helped formulate a
        package especially suited to Middle East requirements. </P> DEPL is equipped to offer
        comprehensive packages including design, material and installation. <P> Products strictly adhere
        to BS, ASTM and DIN international specifications. Quality control is guaranteed by independent
        laboratory test certificates from India. </P> Quality control is implemented without sacrificing
        economy and efficiency. DEPL is dedicated to technical services and problem solving. <P> DEPL
        can provide planning support by offering design, technical specifications, drawings, foundation
        plans and installation instructions, together with personalized service. The company's technical
        sales engineers keep in constant touch with all clients. Utmost importance is given to optimum
        design, versatility, durability and economy backed by the DEPL guarantee for work undertaken.
        <P> Please forward any inquiries to enq_depl@bom2.vsnl.net.in </P>
        DELTA ENGINEERING PVT. LTD. <BR />
        502, 5th Floor, Tejas Building, <BR /> Andheri (W), Mumbai <BR /> India <BR />
        Telephone : 91-022-8210050 <BR />
        ------------------------------------------------------------------------------------------<BR />
        BARBED WIRE <BR />
        ------------------------------------------------------------------------------------------<BR />
        Concertina Barbed Wire in roll form is used in high security areas to deter trespassing men and
        animals. The effectiveness of this material is proved as it has been in use for more than 75 years
        during war and peace.
```

<P>Line Wire: **
** This is made up of 3.05mm diameter high carbon steel wire, with a tensile strength of 170 to 180 kg/mm^2. The wire is drawn and dressed in such a manner that the coils formed will fall naturally into the specified diameter without forming a figure eight. Line wire is heavy hot dipped galvanized with minimum zinc coating of 185 gm/mm^2. **</P>**

<P> Barbed Wire: **
** This is 2.00mm diameter bright mild steel wire with a tensile strength of 38 to 55kg/mm^2 conforming to BS 1052. The wire is hot dipped galvanized with a minimum zinc coating of 20 to 50 gm/mm^2. The barbs are formed with four points. Spacing between the centers of the barbs is every 70mm along the length of the wire. The barbs are firmly secured by indentations made on the wire. **</P>**

<P> Carrying Handles: **
** Handles are made of mild steel wire of 3.55mm diameter and are attached to the outer turn of the coil on each side. **</P>**

--**
**

BARBED TAPES **
**

--**
**

<P> Barbed Tapes are used as psychological and physical deterrent against intrusion by personnel and animals. Barbed tape barrier systems are more vicious and difficult to tamper with, providing superior perimeter security. Some of the users are military installations, nuclear energy sites, maximum-security prisons, various petroleum installations, tank farms and other important industrial facilities. **</P>**

<P>Short Blade Barbed Tape (SBBT): **
** To give the maximum tensile strength at the time of the breach hard drawn steel cord is used (ES1). For camouflage purposes, a coaltar coating can be applied over the entire surface (ES-1), and to attain the high degree of rust resistance, the core wire is made of galvanized steel (ES-2). Any of the above three options are available to meet your specific requirements. **</P>**

<P> Medium Blade Barbed Tape (MBBT): **
** The specification of the "ivory" tape is similar to those of ES types. However the blades are sharper and have a greater pricking capacity. This can be used for both temporary and permanent security. The life of this tape is more than three times longer than those of ES types. Therefore, "ivory" tape is a more effective choice in terrain, which, has heavy rain or in coastal areas. **</P>**

<P> Long Blade Barbed Tape (LBBT): **
** This is the most effective psychological and physical deterrent, ever made as a barrier obstacle. It is available in authentic stainless steel (SUS 430) and the core wire can be fabricated from either galvanized carbon steel or stainless steel. **</P>**

--**
**

ANIMAL FENCING **
**

--**
**

<P>DEPL's animal fencing system is mainly used as an anti-intrusion barrier against any farm and other animals. **</P>** The most common use is on highways where vast distances are covered at a very economical cost. **<P>** Animal fencing can also be used to enclose areas such as farms, forest areas and national parks, where security is not crucial. **</P>** This system is easy to install and can be erected in a comparatively short time.

</BODY>

</HTML>

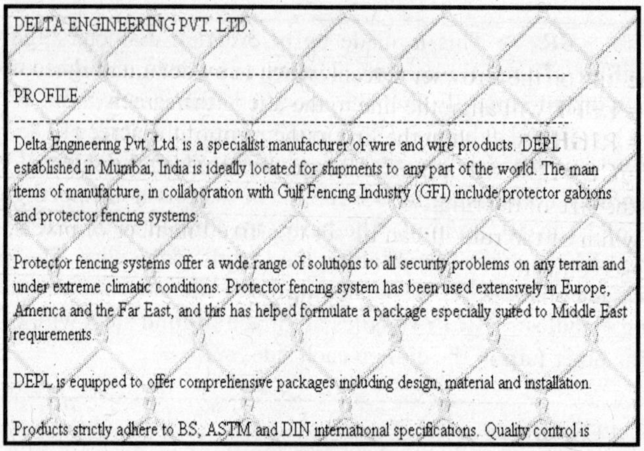

DELTA ENGINEERING PVT. LTD.

PROFILE

Delta Engineering Pvt. Ltd. is a specialist manufacturer of wire and wire products. DEPL established in Mumbai, India is ideally located for shipments to any part of the world. The main items of manufacture, in collaboration with Gulf Fencing Industry (GFI) include protector gabions and protector fencing systems.

Protector fencing systems offer a wide range of solutions to all security problems on any terrain and under extreme climatic conditions. Protector fencing system has been used extensively in Europe, America and the Far East, and this has helped formulate a package especially suited to Middle East requirements.

DEPL is equipped to offer comprehensive packages including design, material and installation.

Products strictly adhere to BS, ASTM and DIN international specifications. Quality control is

Diagram 2.3

Output for Focus 2:

When the web page is viewed in the browser the output shows paragraphs distinctly, but still is not visually attractive. For instance, headings like Profile, Products, and Barbed Wire and so on are emphasized by means of two dashed lines, one above and one below the Heading. This is not a visually pleasing way of laying emphasis on headers.

Headers should preferably be displayed in Bold, Italics and so on. Also, simple dashed lines drawn do not have aesthetic appeal.

EMPHASIZING MATERIAL IN A WEB PAGE

Document pages are usually divided into sections and subsections (i.e. *pages could have headings and sub headings*), which need to be emphasized. HTML provides certain HEADING STYLES and HORIZONTAL RULES, which helps break text into logical sections with visual appeal.

Heading Styles

HTML supports six different levels of headings. The highest-level header format is <H1> and the lowest level is <H6>. All the styles appear in BOLDFACE and the size of the heading depends on the level chosen, i.e. <H1> to <H6>

Example:

```
<H3>The early years</H3>
```

Output:

```
The early years
```

Note

As the number next to <H> (1, 2, . . .) increases, the font size actually decreases.

Drawing Lines

The tag <HR> draws lines and horizontal rules. This tag draws a horizontal line across the whole page, wherever specified. The attributes to the <HR> tag are:

Attributes	Description
ALIGN	Aligns the line on the Browser screen, which is by default, aligned to the center of the screen. **ALIGN = LEFT** will align the line to the left of the screen **ALIGN = RIGHT** will align the line to the right of the screen **ALIGN = CENTER** will align the line to the center of the screen
SIZE	Changes the size of the rule.
WIDTH	Sets the width of the rule. It can be set to a fixed number of pixels, or to a percentage of the available screen width.

Table 2.2

Example:

Welcome to our Web site.
<HR ALIGN="left" WIDTH="10" SIZE="4" />

Output:

▬

TEXT STYLES

Bold

Displays text in BOLDFACE style. The tags used are <B>. . .</B>

Example:

<B>Welcome to our home page!</B>

Output:

Welcome to our home page!

Italics

Displays text in ITALICS. The tags used are between <I>. . .</I>

Example:

<I> Welcome to our home page! </I>

Output:

Welcome to our home page!

Underline

Displays text as UNDERLINED, The tags used are <U> . . . . .</U>

Example:

<U> Welcome to our home page! </U>

Output:

Welcome to our home page!

FOCUS 3:

Emphasize the headings and sub-headings displayed on the DEPL web page.

Code Listing:

```
<HTML>
    <HEAD><TITLE>Delta Engineering Pvt. Ltd.</TITLE></HEAD>
    <BODY STYLE="background: url(images/PINKWHIT.GIF)">
        <H2><I>Delta Engineering Pvt. Ltd.</I></H2>
        <H3>PROFILE</H3>Delta Engineering Pvt. Ltd. is a specialist manufacturer of wire and wire
        products. DEPL established in Mumbai, India is ideally located for shipments to any part of the
        world. The main items of manufacture, in collaboration with Gulf Fencing Industry (GFI) include
        protector gabions and protector fencing systems.
        <P>Protector fencing systems offer a wide range of solutions to all security problems on any
        terrain and under extreme climatic conditions. The protector fencing system has been used
        extensively in Europe, America and the Far East, and this has helped formulate a package
        especially suited to Middle East requirements. </P> DEPL is equipped to offer comprehensive
        packages including design, material and installation.
        <P>Products strictly adhere to BS, ASTM and DIN international specifications. Quality control is
        guaranteed by independent laboratory test certificates from India. </P> Quality control is
        implemented without sacrificing economy and efficiency. DEPL is dedicated to technical services
        and problem solving. <P> DEPL is following quality methods and is accredited with ISO 9002.
        </P> DEPL can provide planning support by offering design, technical specifications, drawings,
        foundation plans and installation instructions, together with a personalized service. The company's
        technical sales engineers keep in constant touch with all clients. Utmost importance is given to
        optimum design, versatility, durability and economy backed by the DEPL guarantee for work
        undertaken. <P> Please forward any inquiries to enq_depl@bom2.vsnl.net.in</P>
        <P><I>DELTA ENGINEERING PVT. LTD. <BR /> 502, 5th Floor, Tejas Building <BR />
        Andheri (W), Mumbai <BR /> India <BR /> Telephone: 91-022-8210050</I>< /P><HR />
        <H3>BARBED WIRE</H3> Concertina Barbed Wire in roll form is used in high security areas
        to deter trespassing men and animals. The effectiveness of this material is proved as it has been in
        use for more than 75 years during war and peace.
        <P><B><I> Line Wire: </I></B><BR /> This is made up of 3.05mm diameter high carbon steel
        wire, with a tensile strength of 170 to 180 kg/mm². The wire is drawn and dressed in such a
        manner that the coils formed will fall naturally into the specified diameter without forming a
        figure eight. Line wire is heavy hot dipped galvanized with minimum zinc coating of 185
        gm/mm².
        <P><B><I> Barbed Wire: </I></B> <BR /> This is 2.00mm diameter bright mild steel wire with
        a tensile strength of 38 to 55kg/mm² conforming to BS 1052. The wire is hot dipped galvanized
        with a minimum zinc coating of 20 to 50 gm/mm². The barbs are formed with four points. Spacing
        between the centers of the barbs is every 70mm along the length of the wire. The barbs are firmly
        secured by indentations made on the wire, so that the barbs do not rotate or slide along the wire.
        The four points of the barbs are formed at the right angles to one another and project outwards
        approximately 12mm from the center of the wire.
        <P><B><I> Carrying Handles: </I></B> <BR /> Handles are made of mild steel wire of 3.55mm
        diameter and are attached to the outer turn of the coil on each side.< /P><HR />

        <H3>BARBED TAPES </H3> Barbed Tapes are used as psychological and physical deterrent
        against intrusion by personnel and animals. Barbed tape barrier systems are more vicious and
        difficult to tamper with, providing superior perimeter security. Some of the users are military
        installations, nuclear energy sites, maximum-security prisons, various petroleum installations, tank
        farms and other important industrial facilities.
        <P><B><I> Short Blade Barbed Tape (SBBT): </I></B></P><BR />
```

```
To give the maximum tensile strength at the time of the breach hard drawn steel cord is used
(ES1). For camouflage purposes, a coaltar coating can be applied over the entire surface (ES-1),
and to attain the high degree of rust resistance, the core wire is made of galvanized steel (ES-2).
Any of the above three options are available to meet your specific requirements.
<P><B><I> Medium Blade Barbed Tape (MBBT): </I></B></P><BR /> The specification of
the "ivory" tape is similar to those of ES types. The blades are sharper and have a greater pricking
capacity. The life of this tape is more than three times longer than those of ES types. Therefore,
"ivory" tape is a more effective choice in terrain which has heavy rain or in coastal areas. The
diameter will be similar to ES type.
<P><B><I> Long Blade Barbed Tape (LBBT): </I></B><BR/> This is the most effective
psychological and physical deterrent, ever made as a barrier obstacle. It is available in authentic
stainless steel (SUS 430) and the core wire can be fabricated from either galvanized carbon steel
or stainless steel.</P><HR/>
<H3>ANIMAL FENCING</H3> DEPL's animal fencing system is mainly used as an anti-
intrusion barrier against any farm and other animals.  <P> The most common use is on highways
where vast distances are covered at a very economical cost.  </P>This system is easy to install and
can be erected in a comparatively short time. <HR />
  </BODY>
</HTML>
```

Output for Focus 3:

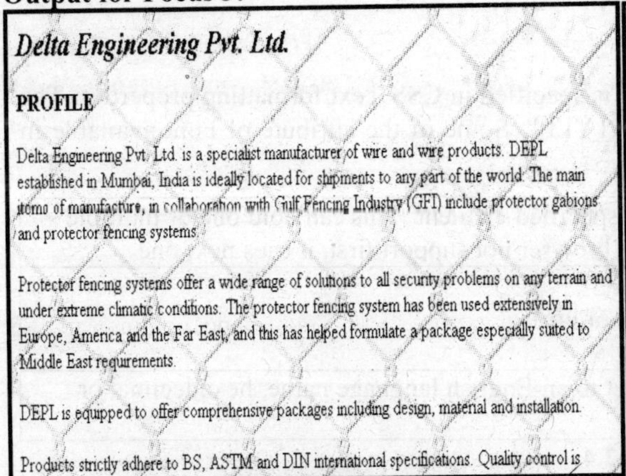

Delta Engineering Pvt. Ltd.

PROFILE

Delta Engineering Pvt. Ltd. is a specialist manufacturer of wire and wire products. DEPL established in Mumbai, India is ideally located for shipments to any part of the world. The main items of manufacture, in collaboration with Gulf Fencing Industry (GFI) include protector gabions and protector fencing systems.

Protector fencing systems offer a wide range of solutions to all security problems on any terrain and under extreme climatic conditions. The protector fencing system has been used extensively in Europe, America and the Far East, and this has helped formulate a package especially suited to Middle East requirements.

DEPL is equipped to offer comprehensive packages including design, material and installation.

Products strictly adhere to BS, ASTM and DIN international specifications. Quality control is

Diagram 2.4.1

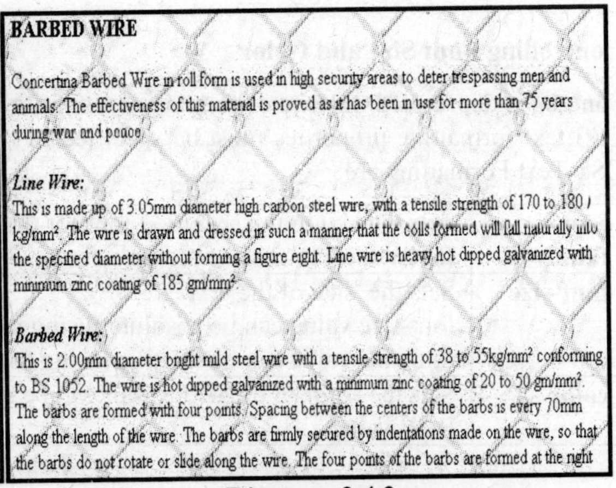

BARBED WIRE

Concertina Barbed Wire in roll form is used in high security areas to deter trespassing men and animals. The effectiveness of this material is proved as it has been in use for more than 75 years during war and peace.

Line Wire:

This is made up of 3.05mm diameter high carbon steel wire, with a tensile strength of 170 to 180 kg/mm². The wire is drawn and dressed in such a manner that the coils formed will fall naturally into the specified diameter without forming a figure eight. Line wire is heavy hot dipped galvanized with minimum zinc coating of 185 gm/mm².

Barbed Wire:

This is 2.00mm diameter bright mild steel wire with a tensile strength of 38 to 55kg/mm² conforming to BS 1052. The wire is hot dipped galvanized with a minimum zinc coating of 20 to 50 gm/mm². The barbs are formed with four points. Spacing between the centers of the barbs is every 70mm along the length of the wire. The barbs are firmly secured by indentations made on the wire, so that the barbs do not rotate or slide along the wire. The four points of the barbs are formed at the right

Diagram 2.4.2

When a text file is formatted as above is viewed in a browser what is seen is visually pleasing. The visual aesthetics of the web page can be further improved by introducing various Fonts, Colors, centering of Text and so on. The following sections illustrate how this Web page can be made visually, further attractive.

OTHER TEXT EFFECTS

Centering (Text, Images etc.)

<CENTER> . . . . </CENTER> tags are used to center everything found between them – text, lists, images, rules, tables or any other page element.

Example:

```
<CENTER> Welcome to our home page! </CENTER>
```

Output:

```
                    Welcome to our home page!
```

Spacing (Indenting Text)

The tag used for inserting blank spaces in an HTML document is <SPACER>. Its attributes are:

TYPE	To specify whether space has to be left horizontally or vertically. **TYPE = "HORIZONTAL"** indicates that horizontal space has to be left. **TYPE = "VERTICAL"** indicates that vertical space has to be left.
SIZE	Indicates the amount of space to be left. Size accepts any integer.

Table 2.3

Note

The SPACER command is understood **only** by the browser Netscape. There are several other techniques that can be used to introduce space in the document (understood by all Browsers). These will be covered in the later Chapters.

Example:

```
Welcome to my site <BR />
<SPACER TYPE = "HORIZONTAL" SIZE = 90>Hope you enjoy it
```

Output:

```
Welcome to my site
               Hope you enjoy it
```

Controlling Font Size and Color

Font tag is deprecated. Instead of font tag now font tag is specified in CSS Text formatting properties. The CSS text formatting properties must be specified in "STYLE". Some of the attribute of Font available in CSS Text Formatting are:

font-family	Sets the text to the specified font for the specified element. This can hold one or multiple font names, In case of multiple fonts, if browser not support first, it tries next one
font-size	Sets the size of the text font-size value can be absolute (using px or em) font-size value can be relative (using %)
color	Sets the color of the text. Color can be set to an English language name, hexadecimal or RGB value

Table 2.4

Example:

<P STYLE="FONT-FAMILY: Comic Sans MS; FONT-SIZE: 10px; COLOR: red; ">Welcome to our home page **</P>**

Output:

Welcome to our home page!

Caution

The FONTFACE attribute can take the name of any font supported by Windows i.e. the font should be present in the directory. C:\Windows\Font\.... . If the font used with this attribute is not available on the computer, the browser uses its own default font. Therefore, it is a good practice to use commonly used fonts, which have a high possibility of being present on every client computer.

FOCUS 4:

One method of making a web site more readable and interesting, to be able to draw the viewer's attention to certain key areas in thc page is by using different Fonts and Colors.

Code Listing:

```
<HTML>
   <HEAD><TITLE> Delta Engineering Pvt. Ltd. </TITLE></HEAD>
   <BODY STYLE="background-image: url(images/pinkwhit.gif);color:#008000;">
      <P STYLE="font-family: Brush Script MT;font-size:30px" ><I>Delta Engineering Pvt. Ltd.
      </I><HR /></P>
      <H3 STYLE="text-align:center;">PROFILE</H3>Delta Engineering Pvt. Ltd. is a specialist manufacturer of wire and wire products. DEPL established in Mumbai, India is ideally located for shipments to any part of the world. The main items of manufacture, in collaboration with Gulf Fencing Industry (GFI) include protector gabions and protector fencing systems. <P STYLE="text-align:center;"> Protector fencing systems offer a wide range of solutions to all security problems on any terrain and under extreme climatic conditions. The protector fencing system has been used extensively in Europe, America and the Far East, and this has helped formulate a package especially suited to Middle East requirements. </P><P STYLE="text-align:center;"> DEPL is equipped to offer comprehensive packages including design, material and installation. </P><P STYLE="text-align:center;"> Products strictly adhere to BS, ASTM and DIN international specifications. Quality control is guaranteed by independent laboratory test certificates from India. <P STYLE="text-align:center;"> Quality control is implemented without sacrificing economy and efficiency. DEPL is dedicated to technical services and problem solving. </P><P STYLE="text-align:center;"> DEPL is following quality methods and is accredited with ISO 9002. </P><P STYLE="text-align:center;"> DEPL can provide planning support by offering design, technical specifications, drawings, foundation plans and installation instructions, together with a personalized service. The company's technical sales engineers keep in constant touch with all clients. Utmost importance is given to optimum design, versatility, durability and economy backed by the DEPL guarantee for work undertaken.</P>
      <P>Please forward any enquiries to enq_depl@bom2.vsnl.net.in</P>
      <P><I><B>DELTA ENGINEERING PVT. LTD.</B><BR />502, 5th Floor, Tejas Building <BR/> Andheri (W), Mumbai <BR/> India <BR/> Telephone : 91-022-8210050</I></P><P><HR><H3 STYLE="text-align:center;">BARBED WIRE</H3> Concertina Barbed Wire in roll form is used in high security areas to deter trespassing men and animals. The effectiveness of this material is proved as it has been in use for more than 75 years during war and peace.</P>
      <P><B><I>Line Wire:</I></B><BR />This is made up of 3.05mm diameter high carbon steel wire, with a tensile strength of 170 to 180 kg/mm². The wire is drawn and dressed in such a manner that the coils formed will fall naturally into the specified diameter without forming a figure eight. Line wire is heavy hot dipped galvanized with minimum inc coating of 185 gm/mm².</P>
      <P><B><I>Barbed Wire:</B></I><BR />This is 2.00mm diameter bright mild steel wire with a tensile strength of 38 to 55kg/mm² conforming to BS 1052. The wire is hot dipped galvanized with a minimum zinc coating of 20 to 50 gm/mm².
```

```
The barbs are formed with four points. Spacing between the centers of the barbs of every 70mm
along the length of the wire. The barbs are firmly secured by indentations made on the wire, so
that the barbs do not rotate or slide along the wire. The four points of the barbs are formed at the
right angles to one another and project outwards approximately 12mm from the center of the
wire.</P>
<P><B><I>Carrying Handles:</I></B><BR />Handles are made of mild steel wire of 3.55mm
diameter and are attached to the outer turn of the coil on each side. </P><HR />
<P><H3 STYLE="text-align:center;">BARBED TAPES</H3>Barbed Tapes are used as
psychological and physical deterrent against intrusion by personnel and animals. Barbed tape
barrier systems are more vicious and difficult to tamper with, providing superior perimeter
security. Some of the users are military installations, nuclear energy sites, maximum-security
prisons, various petroleum installations, tank farms and other important industrial facilities.</P>
<P><B><I>Short Blade Barbed Tape (SBBT):</I></B><BR/> To give the maximum tensile
strength at the time of the breach hard drawn steel cord is used (ES1). For camouflage purposes, a
coaltar coating can be applied over the entire surface (ES-1), and to attain the high degree of rust
resistance, the core wire is made of galvanized steel (ES-2). Any of the above three options are
available to meet your specific requirements.</P>
<P><B><I>Medium Blade Barbed Tape (MBBT):</I></B><BR/> The specification of the
"ivory" tape is similar to those of ES types. The blades are sharper and have a greater pricking
capacity. The life of this tape is more than three times longer than those of ES types. Therefore,
"ivory" tape is a more effective choice in terrain which has heavy rain or in coastal areas. The
diameter will be similar to ES type. </P>
<P><B><I>Long Blade Barbed Tape (LBBT):</I></B><BR/> This is the most effective
psychological and physical deterrent, ever made as a barrier obstacle. It is available in authentic
stainless steel (SUS 430) and the core wire can be fabricated from either galvanized carbon steel
or stainless steel. </P><HR/>
<P><H3 STYLE="text-align:center;">ANIMAL FENCING</H3> DEPL's animal fencing
system is mainly used as an anti-intrusion barrier against any farm and other animals. The most
common use is on highways where vast distances are covered at a very economical cost. Animal
fencing can also be used to enclose areas such as farms, forest areas and national parks, where
security is not crucial. This system is easy to install and can be erected in a comparatively short
time.</P><HR />
</BODY>
</HTML>
```

Diagram 2.5

Output:
The visual aesthetics of this page may be improved upon by using common techniques like HTML **Lists**, Bulleted, Numbered, Unordered and Ordered and so on. The technique (syntax) of using HTML **Lists** is given in the following chapters.

SELF REVIEW QUESTIONS

FILL IN THE BLANKS

1. HTML stands for ____________________.
2. Files that travel across the largest network in the world, the Internet, and carry information from ________ to a ________ that request them are called ____ ________. The person who develops them is called a _____ ________.
3. TCP/IP stands for __________.
4. An HTML document is divided into ________ ________ and the ________ ________ sections.
5. _____ tag starts text from a new line skipping one line in between.

TRUE OR FALSE

6. Some of the most popular software, which Servers run to allow them to respond to client request for information, are Microsoft Internet Explorer, Netscape Navigator, Neo Planet etc.
7. HTML supports 6 different levels of headings.
8. HTML tags are of two types are Paired Tags and Singular Tags.
9. SIZE can take values between 1 & 7.The **.gif** files are specified with BGCOLOR attribute.
10. The tag used for inserting spaces in HTML documents is <MARKER>.

HANDS ON EXERCISES

1. For the screen shown in diagram 2.7 write the HTML code which makes use of:

- The Italics tag
- The Center tag
- The Paragraph tag
- The Break tag
- The Font tag and its attributes

Text Content
Beware of password hackers and crackers!

The threat of hackers and crackers is for real, and is alike for everything for everyone. If the security breach at the Babha Atomic Research Center last year by the hacker group milworm didn't convince you of their capabilities, then consider this: James Davis aka jdavis_4, a resident of www.geocities.com/SiliconValley/Bit/2483 homestead community on the Internet, might just be reading your e-mail in your mailbox right now, or using your account for some benign Internet surfing, or exchanging it with someone else on the Net for more such accounts!
Surprised? Or scared?

Whatever it is, jdevis_4 claims in his home page Free VSNL passwords that he has got exactly 108 working passwords (and growing daily), *36 Satyam, 31 MTNL, 11 WimiNet and 23 online passwords.*

> ***Beware of password hackers and crackers!***
>
> The threat of hackers and crackers is for real, and is alike for everyone. If the security breach at the Bhabha Atomic Research Center last year by the hacker group milwOrm didn't convince you of their capabilities, then consider this: James Davis aka jdavis_4, a resident of www.geocities.com/SiliconValley/Bit/2483 homestead community on the Internet, might just be reading your e-mail in your mailbox right now, or using your account for some benign Internet surfing, or exchanging it with someone else on the Net for more such accounts!
> Surprised? Or scared?
>
> Whatever it is, jdavis_4 claims in his home page-Free VSNL passwords-that he has got exactly 108 working VSNL passwords (and growing daily), *36 Satyam, 31 MTNL, 11 WmiNet and 23 Mantra Online* passwords.

Diagram 2.6: Output of Hands on Exercise

3. LISTS

TYPES OF LISTS

Unordered List (Bullets)

An unordered list starts with the tag **<UL>** and ends with **</UL>**. Each list item starts with the tag <LI>. Attribute and css\style properties, which can be specified with <LI> are

s

css list-style-type	Specifies the type of the bullet. **list-style-type: circle** will give a solid round black bullet **list-style-type: square** will give a solid square black bullet

Table 3.1

Example:

Some of these products include:

```
<UL STYLE="list-style-type: circle;" >
      <LI> Floppies
      <LI> Hard Disks
      <LI> Monitors
</UL>
```

Output:

```
Some of these products include:
•   Floppies
•   Hard Disks
•   Monitors
```

Ordered Lists (Numbering)

An ordered list start with the tag **<OL>** and ends with **</OL>**. Each list items start with the tag <LI>. The attribute and css\style properties, which can be specified with <LI> are

css\style list-style-type	Controls the numbering scheme to be used. **list-style-type:** decimal will give numbers (1, 2 ,3 ,4, 5,etc.) **list-style-type:** lower-alpha will give lower-alpha (a, b, c, d, e, etc.) **list-style-type:** lower-greek will give lower- greek (alpha, beta, gamma, etc.) **list-style-type:** lower-latin will give lower-latin (a, b, c, d, e, etc.) **list-style-type:** lower-roman will give lower-roman (i, ii, iii, iv, v, etc.) **list-style-type:** upper-alpha will give upper-alpha (A, B, C, D, E, etc.) **list-style-type:** upper-latin will give upper -latin (A, B, C, D, E, etc.) **list-style-type:** upper-roman will give upper -roman (I, II, III, IV, V, etc.)
css\style counter-reset	The counter-reset property creates or resets one or more counters.

Table 3.2

Example:

```
Some of these products include:
<OL STYLE="list-style-type: decimal" START="3">
    <LI> Floppies
    <LI> Hard Disks
    <LI> Monitors
</OL>
```

Output:

```
Some of these products include:
3. Floppies
4. Hard Disks
5. Monitors
```

Definition Lists

Definition list values appear within tags <DL> and </DL>. Definition lists consists of two parts:

Definition term	appears after the tag <DT>
Definition description	appears after the tag <DD>

Table 3.3

Example:

```
<DL>
    <DT> Keyboard
    <DD> An input device
    <DT> Printer
    <DD> An output device
</DL>
```

Output:

```
Keyboard
    An input device
Printer
    An output device
```

FOCUS

When a manufacturing company publishes its information on the Web it seeks to draw user attention to its (*list of*) products. Creating such a list can be achieved through the use of Bullets or Numbering. These techniques will be well applied to the *Barbed Wires* and *Barbed Tapes* lists on DEPL's web page to illustrate their use.

Code Listing:

```
<HTML>
    <HEAD><TITLE>Delta Engineering Pvt. Ltd.</TITLE></HEAD>
    <BODY STYLE="background-image: url(images/pinkwhit.gif); color:#008000;">
        <P STYLE="font-family: Brush Script MT;font-size:30px"><I>Delta Engineering Pvt. Ltd.</I><HR/><CENTER><H3>PROFILE</H3>Delta Engineering Pvt. Ltd. is a specialist manufacturer of wire and wire products. DEPL established in Mumbai, India is ideally located for shipments to any part of the world. The main items of manufacture, in collaboration with Gulf Fencing Industry (GFI) include protector gabions and protector fencing systems.</P><P>Protector fencing systems offer a wide range of solutions to all security problems on any terrain and under extreme climatic conditions. The protector fencing system has been used extensively in Europe, America and the Far East, and this has helped formulate a package especially suited to Middle East requirements.</P>
        <P>DEPL is equipped to offer comprehensive packages including design, material and installation.</P><P>Products strictly adhere to BS, ASTM and DIN international specifications. Quality control is guaranteed by independent laboratory test certificates from India.</P><P>Quality control is implemented without sacrificing economy and efficiency. DEPL is dedicated to technical services and problem solving.</P><P>DEPL is following quality methods and is accredited with ISO 9002.</P><P>DEPL can provide planning support by offering design, technical specifications, drawings, foundation plans and installation instructions, together with a personalized service. The company's technical sales engineers keep in constant touch with all clients. Utmost importance is given to optimum design, versatility, durability and economy backed by the DEPL guarantee for work undertaken.</P></CENTER>
        <P>Please forward any enquiries to enq_depl@bom2.vsnl.net.in</P>
        <P><I><B>DELTA ENGINEERING PVT. LTD.</B><BR/>502, 5th Floor, Tejas Building <BR/> Andheri (W), Mumbai <BR/> India <BR/> Telephone: 91-022-8210050</I></P><P><HR/>
        <CENTER><H3>BARBED WIRE</H3></CENTER> Concertina Barbed Wire in roll form is used in high security areas to deter trespassing men and animals. The effectiveness of this material is proved as it has been in use for more than 75 years during war and peace.</P>
        <OL><P><LI><B><I>Line Wire:</I></B><BR />This is made up of 3.05mm diameter high carbon steel wire, with a tensile strength of 170 to 180 kg/mm². The wire is drawn and dressed in such a manner that the coils formed will fall naturally into the specified diameter without forming a figure eight. Line wire is heavy hot dipped galvanized with minimum inc coating of 185 gm/mm².</LI></P>
        <P><LI><B><I>Barbed Wire:</I></B><BR/>This is 2.00mm diameter bright mild steel wire with a tensile strength of 38 to 55kg/mm² conforming to BS 1052. The wire is hot dipped galvanized with a minimum zinc coating of 20 to 50 gm/mm². The barbs are formed with four points. Spacing between the centers of the barbs of every 70mm along the length of the wire. The barbs are firmly secured by indentations made on the wire, so that the barbs do not rotate or slide along the wire. The four points of the barbs are formed at the right angles to one another and project outwards approximately 12mm from the center of the wire.</LI></P>
        <P><LI><B><I>Carrying Handles:</I></B><BR/>Handles are made of mild steel wire of 3.55mm diameter and are attached to the outer turn of the coil on each side.</LI></P></OL></P><P><HR/>
        <CENTER><H3>BARBED TAPES</H3></CENTER> Barbed Tapes are used as psychological and physical deterrent against intrusion by personnel and animals. Barbed tape barrier systems are more vicious and difficult to tamper with, providing superior perimeter security. Some of the users are military installations, nuclear energy sites, maximum-security prisons, various petroleum installations, tank farms and other important industrial facilities.</P><P><UL><P><LI>
```

```
<DT><B><I>Short Blade Barbed Tape (SBBT):</I></B><BR /><DD>To give the maximum tensile strength at the time of the breach hard drawn steel cord is used (ES1). For camouflage purposes, a coaltar coating can be applied over the entire surface (ES-1), and to attain the high degree of rust resistance, the core wire is made of galvanized steel (ES-2). Any of the above three options are available to meet your specific requirements</DD></DT></LI></P>
<P><LI><DT><B><I>Medium Blade Barbed Tape (MBBT):</I></B><BR /><DD>The specification of the "ivory" tape is similar to those of ES types. The blades are sharper and have a greater pricking capacity. The life of this tape is more than three times longer than those of ES types. Therefore, "ivory" tape is a more effective choice in terrain which has heavy rain or in coastal areas. The diameter will be similar to ES type.</DD></DT></LI></P>
<P><LI><DT><B><I>Long Blade Barbed Tape (LBBT):</I></B><BR /><DD>This is the most effective psychological and physical deterrent, ever made as a barrier obstacle. It is available in authentic stainless steel (SUS 430) and the core wire can be fabricated from either galvanized carbon steel or stainless steel.
</DD></DT></LI></P></UL>
<P><HR><CENTER><H3>ANIMAL FENCING</H3></CENTER>DEPL's animal fencing system is mainly used as an anti-intrusion barrier against any farm and other animals.</P> <P> The most common use is on highways where vast distances are covered at a very economical cost. </P> <P> Animal fencing can also be used to enclose areas such as farms, forest areas and national parks, where security is not crucial. </P><P> This system is easy to install and can be erected in a comparatively short time.<HR/>
  </BODY>
</HTML>
```

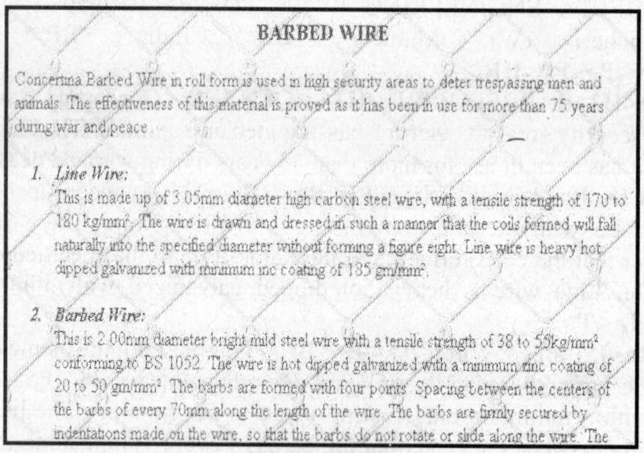

BARBED WIRE

Concertina Barbed Wire in roll form is used in high security areas to deter trespassing men and animals. The effectiveness of this material is proved as it has been in use for more than 75 years during war and peace.

1. *Line Wire:*
   This is made up of 3.05mm diameter high carbon steel wire, with a tensile strength of 170 to 180 kg/mm². The wire is drawn and dressed in such a manner that the coils formed will fall naturally into the specified diameter without forming a figure eight. Line wire is heavy hot dipped galvanized with minimum inc coating of 185 gm/mm².

2. *Barbed Wire:*
   This is 2.00mm diameter bright mild steel wire with a tensile strength of 38 to 55kg/mm² conforming to BS 1052. The wire is hot dipped galvanized with a minimum zinc coating of 20 to 50 gm/mm². The barbs are formed with four points. Spacing between the centers of the barbs of every 70mm along the length of the wire. The barbs are firmly secured by indentations made on the wire, so that the barbs do not rotate or slide along the wire. The

Diagram 3.1

Output For Focus:

The HTML pages of DEPL's site are fairly well laid out, visually. However, it is a well established fact that a large document with vast textual content is not very interesting to the viewer. On the Web, such documents fail to attract viewers. Pictures or images added to web pages definitely serve to attract users.

At the same time, an image can be used very effectively to give information to a user, without having to read lengthy descriptions.

Fortunately, HTML provides techniques by which not only static, but also animated pictures can be placed on a web page. In fact the power of HTML lies in the fact that HTML supports adding Multimedia to the Web Pages.

How Pictures can be added to the Web Page is described in the following chapters.

SELF REVIEW QUESTIONS

FILL IN THE BLANKS

1. TYPE = __________ is the attribute specified with the <LI> tag which will give a solid round black bullet.
2. The __________ attribute specified with the <LI> tag alters the numbering sequence for ordered lists.
3. __________ appears after the <DD> tag of the definition lists.

TRUE OR FALSE

4. Lists are of three types; Ordered lists, Unordered lists and Definition lists .
5. Ordered lists are used for Bullets.
6. START alters the numbering sequence in the middle of an Ordered list.
7. Definition lists consists of two parts; Definition Term and Definition Description

HANDS ON EXERCISE

1. Looking at the Screen given below write the HTML code making use of following tags:

- ❑ Unordered Lists
- ❑ Ordered Lists
- ❑ Definition Lists

Text Content:

//Example on Unordered List//

- Sportstar
- Business Week
- Time

//Example on Ordered List//

iv. Sportstar
v. Business Week
vi. Time

//Example on Definition List//

Sports Magazine
    Sportstar
Business Magazine
    Business Week

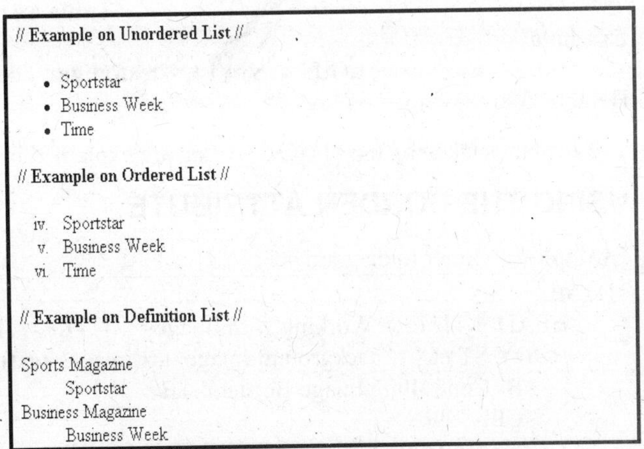

Diagram 3.2: Output of Hands on Exercise

4. ADDING GRAPHICS TO HTML DOCUMENTS

Other than text, HTML allows placing of static and/or animated images in an HTML page. HTML accepts two picture file formats **.gif** and **.jpg**. Using tools such as Gif Constructor or Adobe PhotoShop, images can be created to suit the requirements of a web page and saved in these file formats.

Once an image is ready and stored in the above-mentioned formats, it can be inserted into a web page using the tag <IMG>, which takes the name of the image file (*filename*.gif *filename*.jpg or *filename*.jpeg) as an attribute. In addition, HTML also allows control of the height, width, border and so on, of every image placed on the web Page. The <IMG> tag takes the following attributes:

BORDER	Specifies the size of the border to place around the image. This attribute should be specified in the CSS
WIDTH	Specifies the width of the image in pixels.
HEIGHT	Specifies the height of the image in pixels.
css/style PADDING	Indicates the amount of space to the left, right, top and bottom of the image. This attribute should be specified in the CSS.
ALT	Indicates the text to be displayed in case the Browser is unable to display the image specified in the SRC attribute.
SRC	Specifies the location and name of the image file.

Table 4.1

Example:

```
<IMG src="image1.GIF" STYLE="text-align: center; border-width: 0px; padding: 0px;" Height="57px" Width="447px" />
```

The attributes taken by the <IMG . . . > tag are explained in the following examples.

USING THE BORDER ATTRIBUTE

Example 1: (Refer to diagram 4.1)

```
<HTML>
    <HEAD><TITLE> Working with Images </TITLE></HEAD>
    <BODY STYLE="background-image: url(images/texture1.gif);">
        <B>Controlling Image Borders!</B>
        <CENTER>
            <I>Image Without a BORDER </I><BR/><BR/>
```

```
        <IMG Src = "images/corp.gif" /><BR/><BR/>
            <I>Image With border-width: 3px </I><BR/><BR/>
            <IMG STYLE="border-width:3px;" SRC="images/corp.gif"><BR/>
        </CENTER>
    </BODY>
</HTML>
```

Output For Example 1:

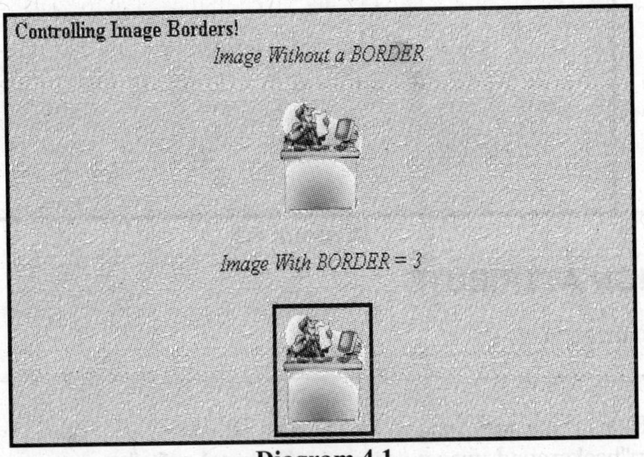

Diagram 4.1

USING THE WIDTH AND HEIGHT ATTRIBUTE

Example 2: (Refer to diagram 4.2)

```
<HTML>
    <HEAD><TITLE> Working with Images </TITLE></HEAD>
    <BODY STYLE="background-image: url(images/texture1.gif); ">
        <CENTER><B>Controlling Image Sizes!</B> <BR/>
            <I>Normal Image Size</I><BR/><BR/>
                <IMG Src="images/computer.gif"><BR />
            <I>Image With Size (Height And Width) Set To 200</I><BR/><BR/>
                <IMG HEIGHT="200" SRC="images/computer.gif" WIDTH="200"><BR/>
        </CENTER>
    </BODY>
</HTML>
```

Output for Example 2:

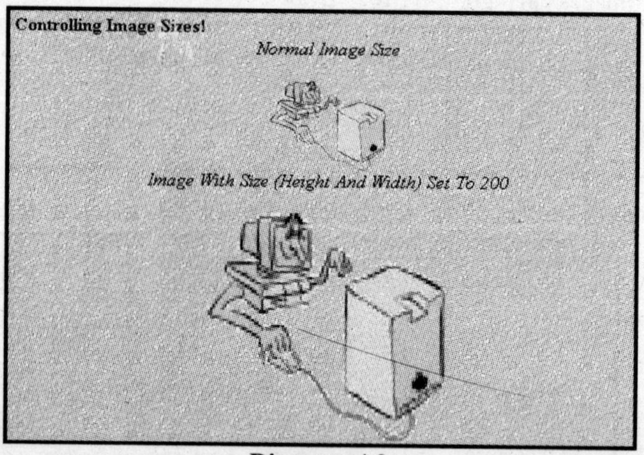

Diagram 4.2

USING THE ALIGN ATTRIBUTE

Example 3: (Refer to diagram 4.3)

```
<HTML>
    <HEAD><TITLE>Working with Images </TITLE></HEAD>
    <BODY STYLE="background-image: url(images/texture1.gif); ">
        <B><I> Image Aligned Left </I></B>
            <IMG STYLE="float: left" SRC="sony-logo.gif"/><BR/><BR/>Silicon Chip Technologies,
            <BR />
            <I> We Specialize In Corporate Training, Software Development And Placements. Our
Training Programs and Software Development include Web Based Commercial Applications and
Commercial Application Development using Databases. </I><BR/><BR/><BR/><BR/>
    <B><I>Image Aligned Right </I></B>
    <IMG STYLE="float: right" SRC="sony-logo.gif" /><BR/><BR/>Silicon Chip Technologies, <BR/>
        <I>We Specialize In Corporate Training, Software Development and Placements. Our Training
Programs and Software Development include Web Based Commercial Applications and Commercial
Application Development using Databases</I>
    </BODY>
</HTML>
```

Output for Example 3:

Diagram 4.3

USING THE ALT ATTRIBUTE

Example 4: (Refer to diagram 4.4)

```
<HTML>
    <HEAD><TITLE> Working with Images </TITLE></HEAD>
    <BODY STYLE="background-image: url(images/texture1.gif); ">
        <B>Use of ALT attribute</B><BR/>
        <CENTER>
            <I>Avaliable Image: javacup.gif</I><BR/><BR/>
            <IMG SRC="images/javacup.gif"><BR/><BR/>
            <I>Unavaliable Image: javac.gif - Without the ALT Attribute </I><BR/><BR/>
            <IMG SRC="images/javac.gif"><BR /><BR />
            <I>Unavaliable Image: javac.gif - With the ALT Attribute set to "Java"</I><BR/><BR/>
            <IMG ALT="The Java Cup" SRC="images/javac.gif"><BR/>
        </CENTER>
    </BODY>
</HTML>
```

Note

The <IMG> tag specifies a file **javac.gif** as the source file. This file is ***not present in the current work directory.***

Therefore, the browser will display an icon indicating the unavailability of the file. If the **Alt** attribute is present along with the <IMG> tag then the text that is specified in the **Alt** attribute is displayed in place of the missing the icon.

Output for Example 4:

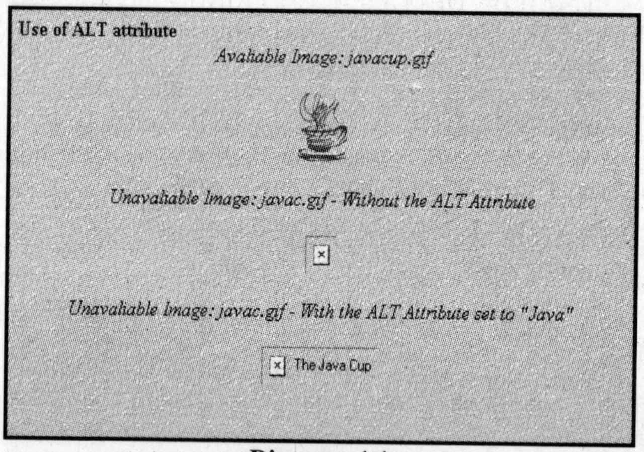

Diagram 4.4

FOCUS: Increase the visual appeal of the web site by replacing or complementing the text with pictures wherever possible. For instance, the Company's Logo can be used at the start of the web page. Each product description can be supplemented with an image.

Code Listing:

```
<HTML>
    <HEAD><TITLE> Delta Engineering Pvt. Ltd. </TITLE></HEAD>
    <BODY STYLE="background-image: url(images/pinkwhit.gif); color:#008000;">
        <P STYLE="font-family: Brush Script MT;font-size:45px" >
            <IMG STYLE="vertical-align:middle;" SRC="images/logo.gif" /><I>Delta Engineering Pvt. Ltd.</I>
        </P>
        <HR/>
        <SPAN STYLE="text-align:center">
        <H3 STYLE="text-align:center;">PROFILE</H3>
        <IMG HEIGHT="57" SRC="images/intro.gif" WIDTH="185" /> <BR/><BR/>Delta Engineering Pvt. Ltd. is a specialist manufacturer of wire and wire products. DEPL established in Mumbai, India is ideally located for shipments to any part of the world. The main items of manufacture, in collaboration with Gulf Fencing Industry (GFI) include protector gabions and protector fencing systems. <P>Protector fencing systems offer a wide range of solutions to all security problems on any terrain and under extreme climatic conditions. The protector fencing system has been used extensively in Europe, America and the Far East, and this has helped formulate a package especially suited to Middle East requirements.</P><P>DEPL is equipped to offer comprehensive packages including design, material and installation.</P><P>Products strictly adhere to BS, ASTM and DIN international specifications. Quality control is guaranteed by independent laboratory test certificates from India.</P><P>Quality control is implemented without sacrificing economy and efficiency. DEPL is dedicated to technical services and problem solving.</P><P>DEPL is following quality methods and is accredited with ISO 9002.</P><P><IMG HEIGHT="57" SRC="images/planning.gif" WIDTH="184" /><BR/>DEPL can provide planning support by offering design, technical specifications, drawings, foundation plans and installation instructions, together with a personalized service. The company's technical sales engineers keep in constant touch with all clients. Utmost importance is given to optimum design, versatility, durability and economy backed by the DEPL guarantee for work undertaken.</P>
        </SPAN>
```

```
<P>Please forward any enquiries to enq_depl@bom2.vsnl.net.in
<P><I><B> DELTA ENGINEERING PVT. LTD.</B><BR/>502, 5th Floor, Tejas Building <BR/> Andheri (W), Mumbai <BR/> India <BR/> Telephone : 91-022-8210050</I></P>
<HR/>
<H3 STYLE="text-align:center;">BARBED WIRE</H3>
<IMG STYLE="text-align:bottom; border:2px solid;" HEIGHT="130" SRC="images/barbed1.jpg" WIDTH="150" /> Concertina Barbed Wire in roll form is used in high security areas to deter trespassing men and animals. The effectiveness of this material is proved as it has been in use for more than 75 years during war and peace.
<OL><P><LI><B><I>Line Wire:</I></B><BR/>This is made up of 3.05mm diameter high carbon steel wire, with a tensile strength of 170 to 180 kg/mm². The wire is drawn and dressed in such a manner that the coils formed will fall naturally into the specified diameter without forming a figure eight. Line wire is heavy hot dipped galvanized with minimum inc coating of 185 gm/mm2.</LI></P>
<P><LI><B><I>Barbed Wire:</I></B><BR/>This is 2.00mm diameter bright mild steel wire with a tensile strength of 38 to 55kg/mm² conforming to BS 1052. The wire is hot dipped galvanized with a minimum zinc coating of 20 to 50 gm/mm². The barbs are formed with four points. Spacing between the centers of the barbs of every 70mm along the length of the wire. The barbs are firmly secured by indentations made on the wire, so that the barbs do not rotate or slide along the wire. The four points of the barbs are formed at the right angles to one another and project outwards approximately 12mm from the center of the wire.</LI></P>
<P><LI><B><I>Carrying Handles:</I></B><BR/>Handles are made of mild steel wire of 3.55mm diameter and are attached to the outer turn of the coil on each side.</LI></P></OL>
<HR/>
<H3 STYLE="text-align:center">BARBED TAPES</H3>
<IMG STYLE="text-align:bottom;border:3px solid;" Height="130" Src="images/barbed.jpg" Width="150" />Barbed Tapes are used as psychological and physical deterrent against intrusion by personnel and animals. Barbed tape barrier systems are more vicious and difficult to tamper with, providing superior perimeter security. Some of the users are military installations, nuclear energy sites, maximum-security prisons, various petroleum installations, tank farms and other important industrial facilities.
<UL><P><LI><DT><B><I>Short Blade Barbed Tape (SBBT):</I></B><BR/>
<DD>To give the maximum tensile strength at the time of the breach hard drawn steel cord is used (ES1). For camouflage purposes, a coaltar coating can be applied over the entire surface (ES-1), and to attain the high degree of rust resistance, the core wire is made of galvanized steel (ES-2). Any of the above three options are available to meet your specific requirements.</DD></DT></LI></P>
<P><LI><DT><B><I>Medium Blade Barbed Tape (MBBT):</I></B><BR/>
<DD>The specification of the "ivory" tape is similar to those of ES types. The blades are sharper and have a greater pricking capacity. The life of this tape is more than three times longer than those of ES types. Therefore, "ivory" tape is a more effective choice in terrain which has heavy rain or in coastal areas. The diameter will be similar to ES type.</DD></DT></LI></P>
<P><LI><DT><B><I>Long Blade Barbed Tape (LBBT):</I></B><BR/>
<DD>This is the most effective psychological and physical deterrent, ever made as a barrier obstacle. It is available in authentic stainless steel (SUS 430) and the core wire can be fabricated from either galvanized carbon steel or stainless steel.</DD></DT></LI></P>
</UL><HR/>
<H3 STYLE="text-align:center;">ANIMAL FENCING</H3>
```

```
        <IMG STYLE="text-align:bottom;border:3px solid;" HEIGHT="130" SRC="images/fence1.jpg"
WIDTH="150" />DEPL's animal fencing system is mainly used as an anti-intrusion barrier against any
farm and other animals. <P> The most common use is on highways where vast distances are covered at a
very economical cost. <P> Animal fencing can also be used to enclose areas such as farms, forest areas
and national parks, where security is not crucial. <P> This system is easy to install and can be erected in a
comparatively short time. <HR/>
        </BODY>
        </HTML>
```

Output:

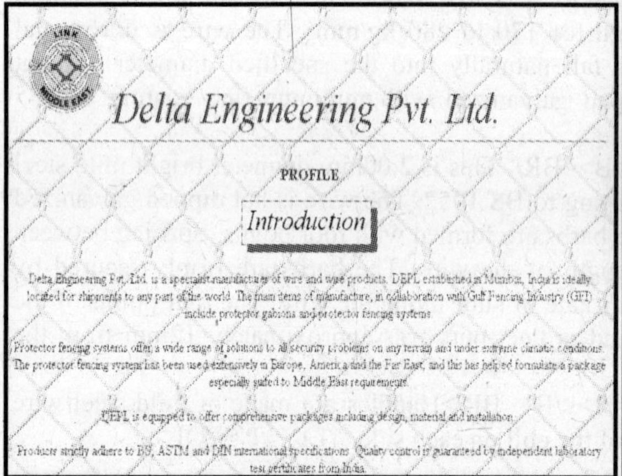

Diagram 4.5.1

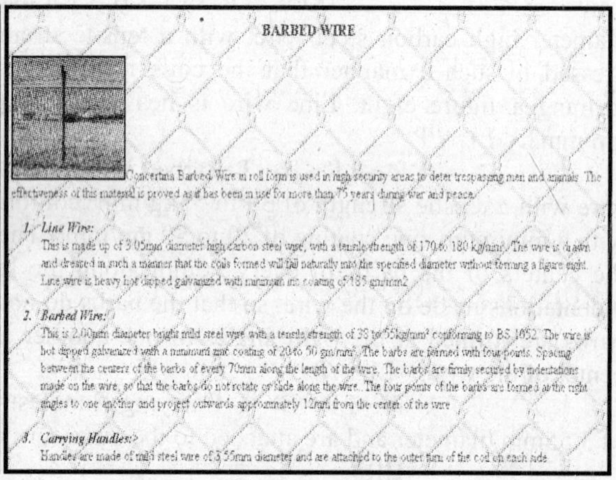

Diagram 4.5.2

The output in diagram 4.5.1 and diagram 4.5.2 displays the same web site, but now with pictures inserted wherever possible. The first page displays the Company Logo and another small picture, which displays the word *Introduction*. The second page shows the picture of a *Barbed Wire*. Similarly, there are pictures for Barbed Tape, Animal Fencing and so on.

Displayed in the second page, the text following the picture starts at the bottom of the picture.

It would be nice to have the whole text about barbed tape appearing exactly besides the picture of barbed tape. To have text aligned starting from the top of the image. The IMG tag attributes can be rewritten as:

```
    <IMG STYLE="text-align:bottom;border:3px solid;" HEIGHT="130" SRC="images/barbed.jpg"
WIDTH="150" />
```

This would display in the browser as seen in diagram 4.6.

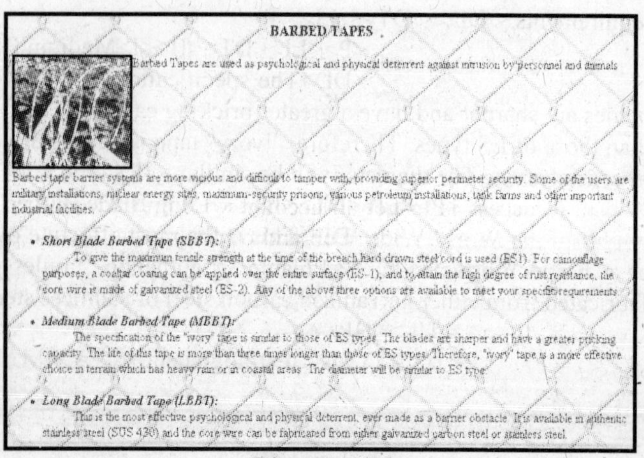

Diagram 4.6

This is because the image and the first line of text are considered to be placed in ***one line.*** To overcome this problem, HTML allows the placement of tables on a web page. Then place the image in one cell of the table, and the text in the adjacent cell. This will make the entire text to appear aligned next to the image.

The width of the table, the number of columns in a table and so on, can be controlled according to requirements. The following chapter deals with how to create tables and place them on a web page together with all the attributes that the <TABLE> tag takes.

SELF REVIEW QUESTIONS

FILL IN THE BLANKS

1. HTML accepts ___________ and ___________ picture formats.
2. An Image can be inserted into the HTML page using ______ tag that takes the name of the image file as an attribute.
3. ____________ and _____________ attributes are used to control the size of the image on the web page.
4. ____________ attribute is used to set a border around the image.
5. The amount of space to the top and bottom of the image is indicated by ____________.
6. The ____________ attribute takes text to be displayed in case the Browser is unable to display the image specified in the SRC attribute.

TRUE OR FALSE

7. HTML allows only static text to be displayed on the page.
8. GIF Constructors or Adobe Photoshop can be used to create .GIF and .JPG picture formats.
9. ALIGN=LEFT indicates the image is aligned to the left with respect to the screen.
10. SRC takes the name of an image file to be displayed as a parameter.

HANDS ON EXERCISE

1. Design a web page using the image files **House.gif**, **Javacup.gif**, and **Computer.gif** according to the following specifications.

- ❑ Use a Border for **House.gif**.
- ❑ Resize the **Height** and **Width** of **Javacup.gif** and **Computer.gif** to 100 pixels each.
- ❑ **Align** the text with respect to the images so as to obtain the output displayed in the diagrams 4.7.1 and 4.7.2.

Text Content

The World Wide Web
The World Wide Web or simply the Web has been a 'Killer App' of the Internet. Certainly its capabilities to display text and graphics provide access to other pages and information has made the fastest growing component of the Internet. Major online services are American Online, CompuServe and Prodigy.

Get Connected
A way to access is to get an account with an Internet Service Provider, or ISP. These accounts include access to the World Wide Web and other Internet resources, and often provide space to store Web pages one will create. A very helpful feature of the web is the capability to move from page to page by selecting specific highlighted words and phrases or images, which are called as links.

Output for Hands On Exercise:

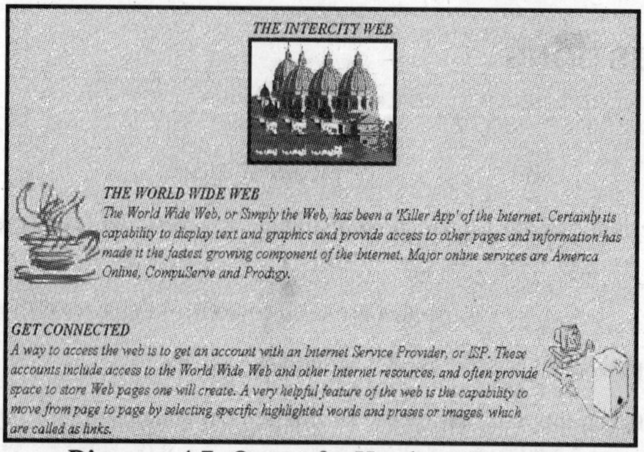

Diagram 4.7: Output for Hands on Exercise.

5. TABLES

INTRODUCTION

A table is a two dimensional matrix, consisting of rows and columns. Tables are intended for displaying data in columns on a web page. All table related tags are included between the <TABLE>...</TABLE> tags. Each row of a table is described between the <TR>...</TR> tags. Each column of a table is described between the <TD>...</TD> tags.

Table rows can be of two types:

- Header Rows: A row that spans across columns of a table is called the Header Row. A table header row is defined using **<TH>...</TH>** tags. The content of a table header row is automatically centered and appears in boldface.
- Data Rows: Individual data cells placed in the horizontal plane creates a data row. There could be a single data cell (i.e. a single column table) or multiple data cells (i.e. a multi column table)

Data cells hold data that must be displayed in the table. A data row is defined using **<TR>...</TR>** tags. Text matter displayed in a data row is left justified by default. Any special formatting like boldface or italics is done by including appropriate formatting tags inside the **<TR>...</TR>** tags. An image can also be displayed in a data cell.

The attributes that can be included in the <TABLE> tag are:

ALIGN	Horizontal alignment is controlled by the ALIGN attribute. It can be set to left, right, center, justify or inherit. This attribute should be used in CSS.
VALIGN	Controls the vertical alignment of cell contents. It accepts the values TOP, MIDDLE or BOTTOM.
WIDTH	Sets the WIDTH to a specific number of pixels or to a percentage of the available screen width. If width is not specified, the data cell is adjusted based on the cell data value.
BORDER	Controls the border to be placed around the table. The border thickness is specified in pixels.
CELLPADDING	This attribute controls the distance between the data in a cell and the boundaries of the cell.
CELLSPACING	Controls the spacing between adjacent cells.
COLSPAN	The COLSPAN attribute inside a <TH> or <TD> tag instructs the browser to make the cell defined by the tag to take up more than one column. The COLSPAN attribute can be set equal to the number of columns the cell is to occupy. This attribute is useful when one *row* of the table needs to be a certain number of **columns** wide.
ROWSPAN	The ROWSPAN attribute works in the same way as the COLSPAN attribute except that it allows a cell to take up more than one row. The attribute can be set by giving a numeric value. For example ROWSPAN = "3".

Table 5.1

The Caption Tag

Often tables need to be given a heading, which gives the reader a context for the information in the tables. Table Headings are called Captions. Captions can be provided to a table by using the <CAPTION>...</CAPTION> tags. This paired tag appears within the <TABLE>...</TABLE> tags. The table caption can be made to appear above or below the table structure with the help of the attribute ALIGN, as explained in table 5.2.

css\style caption-side	It controls placing of the caption with respect to the table. **caption-side :bottom** will place the caption immediately below the table **caption-side :top** will place the caption immediately above the table **caption-side :right** will place the caption immediately right side of the table **caption-side :left** will place the caption immediately left side of the table

Table 5.2

Note:

caption-side is not supported by IE

By passing a row's <TR> tag the VALIGN and ALIGN attributes, vertical or the horizontal alignment can be made identical for every cell in a given row.

By passing the <TH> and/or <TD> tags, VALIGN or ALIGN attributes, vertical or horizontal alignments in both header and data cells can be done. *Any alignment specified at the cell level overrides any default alignments and any alignments specified in a <TR> tag.*

Note

- Alignments specified in <TD> or <TH> apply only to the cell being defined.
- Alignments specified in a <TR> tag apply to all cells in a row, unless overridden by an alignment specification in a <TD> or <TH> tag.

USING THE WIDTH AND BORDER ATTRIBUTE

Example 1: (Refer to diagram 5.1)

```
<HTML>
    <HEAD><TITLE>Table Attributes</TITLE></HEAD>
    <BODY STYLE="background-color: lightgray; " >
        <B>Specifying the BORDER and WIDTH of the Table!</B><BR/><BR/><BR/><BR/>
        <TABLE BORDER="5" WIDTH="50%">
            <CAPTION STYLE="caption-side: bottom;" ><B>Personal Information</B></CAPTION>
                <TR><TH>NAME</TH><TH>AGE</TH></TR>
                <TR ALIGN="CENTER"><TD>Ivan Bayross</TD><TD>57</TD></TR>
                <TR ALIGN="CENTER"><TD>Meher</TD><TD>21</TD></TR>
        </TABLE>
    </BODY>
</HTML>
```

Output For Example 1:

Specifying the BORDER and WIDTH of the Table!

NAME	AGE
Ivan Bayross	57
Meher	21

Personal Information

Diagram 5.1

Note

If the **WIDTH** attribute is associated with the **<TH>** tag then the width of an individual column can be adjusted.

USING THE CELLPADDING ATTRIBUTE

Example 2: (Refer to diagram 5.2)

```
<HTML>
	<HEAD><TITLE>Working With Table</TITLE></HEAD>
	<BODY STYLE="background-color: LIGHTGREY;" >
		<B>Specifying CELLPADDING!</B><BR /> <HR>
		<I>Without Cellpadding</I>
		<TABLE BORDER="1" STYLE="text-align: center" WIDTH="25%" >
			<TR><TH>NAME</TH><TH>AGE</TH></TR>
			<TR ALIGN="center"><TD> Ivan Bayross </TD><TD>57</TD></TR>
			<TR ALIGN="center"><TD> Meher </TD><TD>21</TD></TR>
		</TABLE><HR>
		<I>With Cell padding of 10</I>
		<TABLE STYLE="text-align: center" BORDER="1" CELLPADDING="10"
			WIDTH="25%" >
			<TR><TH>NAME</TH><TH>AGE</TH></TR>
			<TR ALIGN="center"><TD>Ivan Bayross</TD><TD>57</TD></TR>
			<TR ALIGN="center"><TD>Meher</TD><TD>21</TD></TR>
		</TABLE>
	</BODY>
</HTML>
```

Output For Example 2:

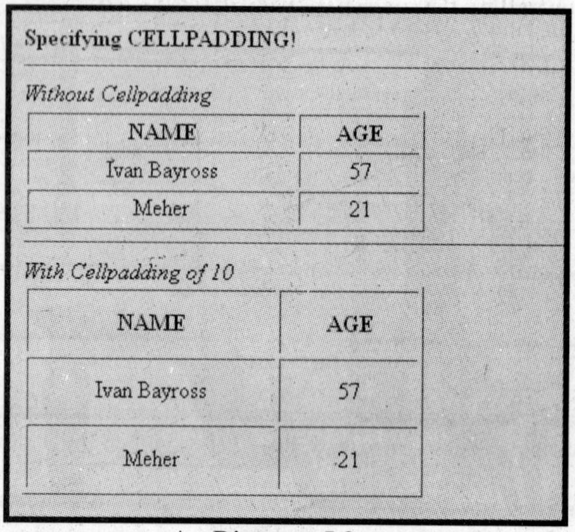

Diagram 5.2

USING THE CELLSPACING ATTRIBUTE

Example 3: (Refer to diagram 5.3)

```
<HTML>
    <HEAD><TITLE>Working with Table</TITLE></HEAD>
    <BODY STYLE="background-color: lightgrey;" >
        <B>Controlling the space between Adjacent Cells!</B><BR/><BR/><HR />
        <I>Without Cellspacing</I>
        <TABLE BORDER="1" STYLE="text-align: center" WIDTH="25%" >
            <TR><TH>NAME</TH><TH>AGE</TH></TR>
            <TR Align="CENTER"><TD>Ivan Bayross</TD><TD>57</TD></TR>
            <TR Align="CENTER"><TD>Meher</TD><TD>21</TD></TR>
        </TABLE><HR />
        <I>With Cellspacing of 10</I>
        <TABLE BORDER="1" STYLE="text-align: center" CELLSPACING ="10" Width="25%">
            <TR><TH>NAME</TH><TH>AGE</TH></TR>
            <TR Align=CENTER><TD>Ivan Bayross</TD><TD>57</TD></TR>
            <TR Align=CENTER><TD>Meher</TD><TD>21</TD></TR>
        </TABLE>
    </BODY>
</HTML>
```

Output For Example 3:

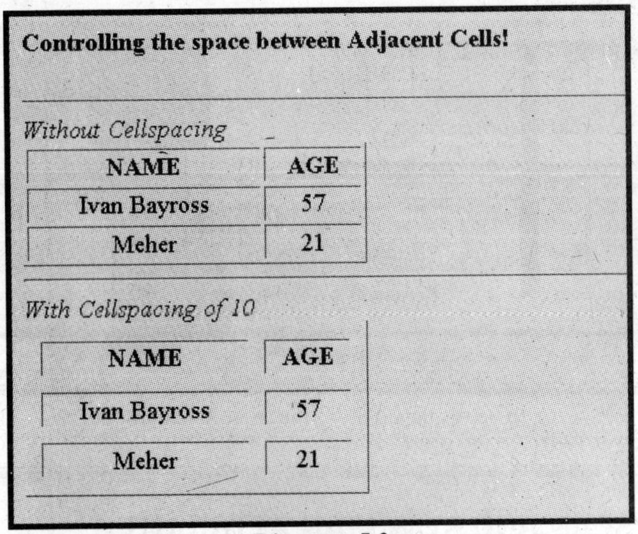

Diagram 5.3

USING THE BACKGROUND-COLOR PROPERTY

Example 4: (Refer to diagram 5.4)

```
<HTML>
   <HEAD><TITLE>Working With Tables</TITLE></HEAD>
   <BODY STYLE="background-color: lightgrey;" >
      <B>Specifying Coloured Table Cells!</B><BR /><BR /><BR /><BR />
      <TABLE Border="1" STYLE="text-align: center" Width="50%">
         <TR><TH STYLE="background-color: GRAY; ">NAME</TH>
            <TH STYLE="background-color: GRAY; "> AGE </TH>
         </TR>
         <TR Align=CENTER>
            <TD STYLE="background-color: BLACK; color: WHITE; ">Ivan Bayross</TD>
            <TD STYLE="background-color: VIOLET; color: RED; ">57</TD>
         </TR><TR Align=CENTER>
            <TD STYLE="background-color: BLUE; color: WHITE;"> Meher </TD>
            <TD STYLE="background-color: RED; color: BLUE; ">21</TD>
         </TR>
         <CAPTION STYLE="caption-side: bottom;" ><B>Personal Information</B></CAPTION>
      </TABLE>
   </BODY>
</HTML>
```

Output For Example 4:

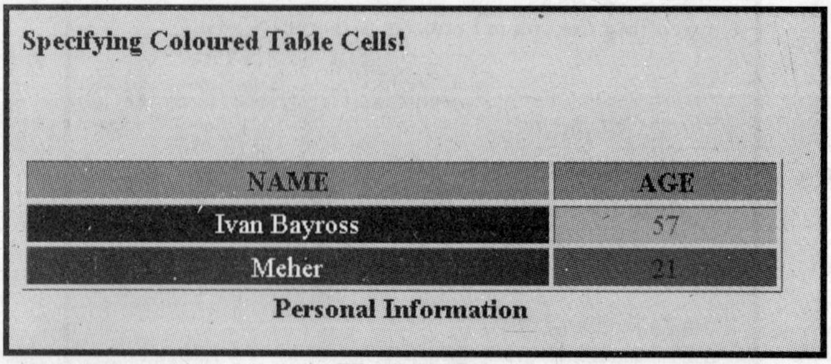

Diagram 5.4

Tip

If the entire table needs to be displayed using the same BackGround Color, the attribute BGColor can be passed to the <TABLE> tag itself.

USING THE COLSPAN AND ROWSPAN ATTRIBUTES

Example 5: (Refer to diagram 5.5)

```
<HTML>
    <HEAD><TITLE>Working With Table</TITLE></HEAD>
    <BODY STYLE="background-color: lightgrey;" >
        <B>Specifying ROWSPAN and COLSPAN Attributes!</B><BR/><BR/><BR/><BR/>
        <CENTER><TABLE Border="1" STYLE="text-align: center" Width="50%" >
        <TR>
            <TH RowSpan="2">NAME</TH><TH ColSpan="3">MARKS</TH>
        </TR>
        <TR>
            <TH>PowerBuilder</TH><TH>VisualBasic</TH><TH>Developer2000</TH>
        </TR>
        <TR ALIGN="CENTER">
            <TD>Ivan Bayross</TD><TD>40</TD><TD>45</TD><TD>40</TD>
        </TR>
        <TR ALIGN="CENTER">
            <TD>Meher</TD><TD>30</TD><TD>30</TD><TD>40</TD>
        </TR><CAPTION ALIGN="bottom"><B><BR />Mark Sheet</B></CAPTION>
        </TABLE></CENTER>
    </BODY>
</HTML>
```

Output For Example 5:

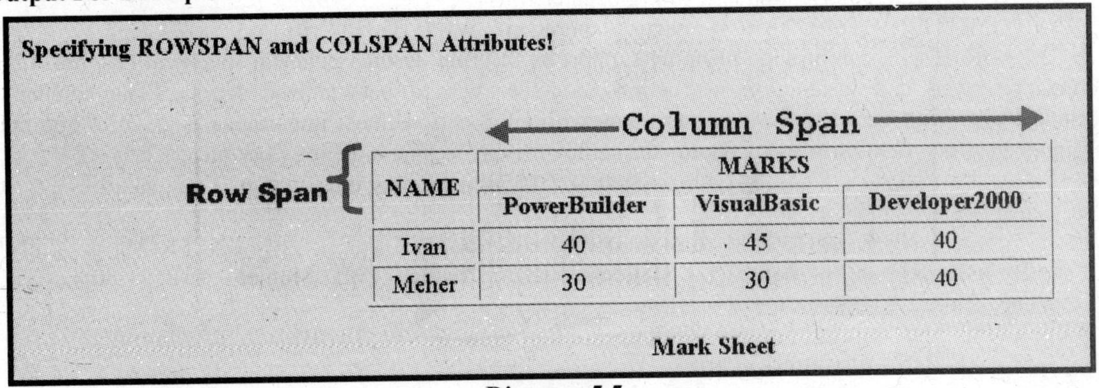

Diagram 5.5

FOCUS: The Management at DEPL has decided that all their product images should be displayed on the Web Site in appropriate web pages. The textual description of each product should come up alongside the image and not below it.

This can be done by the use of tables on the web page.

Code Listing:

```
<HTML>
	<HEAD><TITLE> Delta Engineering Pvt. Ltd. </TITLE></HEAD>
	<BODY STYLE="background-image: url(images/pinkwhit.gif);">
		<P STYLE="font-family:Brush Script MT;font-size:35px;color:#008000;text-align:center;"><IMG Src="images/logo.gif" STYLE="vertical-align: bottom;" /><I>Delta Engineering Pvt. Ltd.</I>
	<BR/><HR/></P>
	<P STYLE="color:#008000;text-align:center;"><B>PROFILE</B></P>
	<P STYLE="text-align:center;"><IMG HEIGHT="57" SRC="images/intro.gif" WIDTH="185" />
<BR/><BR/></P>
	<P STYLE="color:#008000;text-align:center;">Delta Engineering Pvt. Ltd. is a specialist manufacturer of wire and wire products. DEPL established in Mumbai, India is ideally located for shipments to any part of the world. The main items of manufacture, in collaboration with Gulf Fencing Industry (GFI) include protector gabions and protector fencing systems.</P>
	<P STYLE="color:#008000;text-align:center;">Protector fencing systems offer a wide range of solutions to all security problems on any terrain and under extreme climatic conditions. The protector fencing system has been used extensively in Europe, America and the Far East, and this has helped formulate a package especially suited to Middle East requirements.</P>
	<P STYLE="color:#008000;text-align:center;">DEPL is equipped to offer comprehensive packages including design, material and installation.</P>
	<P STYLE="color:#008000;text-align:center;">Products strictly adhere to BS, ASTM and DIN international specifications. Quality control is guaranteed by independent laboratory test certificates from India.</P>
	<P STYLE="color:#008000;text-align:center;">Quality control is implemented without sacrificing economy and efficiency. DEPL is dedicated to technical services and problem solving.</P><P STYLE="color:#008000;text-align:center;">DEPL is following quality methods and is accredited with ISO 9002.</P>
```

```
<P STYLE="color:#008000;text-align:center;">
<IMG HEIGHT="57" SRC="images/planning.gif" WIDTH="184" />
<BR/>DEPL can provide planning support by offering design, technical specifications, drawings, foundation plans and installation instructions, together with a personalized service. The company's technical sales engineers keep in constant touch with all clients. Utmost importance is given to optimum design, versatility, durability and economy backed by the DEPL guarantee for work undertaken.</P>
<P STYLE="color:#008000;">Please forward any enquiries to enq_depl@bom2.vsnl.net.in</P>
<P STYLE="color:#008000;"><I><B>DELTA ENGINEERING PVT. LTD.</B><BR/>502, 5th Floor, Tejas Building <BR/> Andheri (W), Mumbai <BR/> India <BR/> Telephone : 91-022-8210050</I></P><HR/>
<P STYLE="color:#008000;text-align:center;"><B>BARBED WIRE</B></P>
<TABLE Border="0">
<TR><TD>
<IMG Height="130" Src="images/barbed1.jpg" STYLE="border:2px solid; vertical-align: bottom;" Width="150" />
</TD>
<TD>
<SPAN STYLE="color:#008000;" >Concertina Barbed Wire in roll form is used in high security areas to deter trespassing men and animals. The effectiveness of this material is proved as it has been in use for more than 75 years during war and peace. </SPAN>
</TD></TR></TABLE>
<OL>
<LI><P><B><I>Line Wire:</I></B><BR/>This is made up of 3.05mm diameter high carbon steel wire, with a tensile strength of 170 to 180 kg/mm². The wire is drawn and dressed in such a manner that the coils formed will fall naturally into the specified diameter without forming a figure eight. Line wire is heavy hot dipped galvanized with minimum inc coating of 185 gm/mm2.</P></LI>
<LI><P><B><I>Barbed Wire:</B></I><BR/>This is 2.00mm diameter bright mild steel wire with a tensile strength of 38 to 55kg/mm² conforming to BS 1052. The wire is hot dipped galvanized with a minimum zinc coating of 20 to 50 gm/mm². The barbs are formed with four points. Spacing between the centers of the barbs of every 70mm along the length of the wire. The barbs are firmly secured by indentations made on the wire, so that the barbs do not rotate or slide along the wire. The four points of the barbs are formed at the right angles to one another and project outwards approximately 12mm from the center of the wire.</P></LI>
<LI><P><B><I>Carrying Handles:</I></B><BR/>Handles are made of mild steel wire of 3.55mm diameter and are attached to the outer turn of the coil on each side.</P></LI></OL><P><HR/>
<P STYLE="color:#008000;text-align:center;"><B>BARBED TAPES</B></P>
<TABLE Border="0"><TR><TD>
<IMG Height="130" Src="images/barbed.jpg" STYLE="border:3px solid; vertical-align: bottom;" Width="150" />
</TD><TD>
<SPAN STYLE="color:#008000;" >Barbed Tapes are used as psychological and physical deterrent against intrusion by personnel and animals. Barbed tape barrier systems are more vicious and difficult to tamper with, providing superior perimeter security. Some of the users are military installations, nuclear energy sites, maximum-security prisons, various petroleum installations, tank farms and other important industrial facilities.</SPAN>
</TD></TR></TABLE>
<UL>
<LI><DT><P><B><I>Short Blade Barbed Tape (SBBT):</I></B><BR/>
```

```
                    <DD>To give the maximum tensile strength at the time of the breach hard
drawn steel cord is used (ES1). For camouflage purposes, a coaltar coating can be applied over the entire
surface (ES-1), and to attain the high degree of rust resistance, the core wire is made of galvanized steel
(ES-2). Any of the above three options are available to meet your specific requirements.</DD></P></LI>
              <LI><DT><P><B><I>Medium Blade Barbed Tape (MBBT):</I></B><BR/>
                    <DD>The specification of the "ivory" tape is similar to those of ES types. The
blades are sharper and have a greater pricking capacity. The life of this tape is more than three times longer
than those of ES types. Therefore, "ivory" tape is a more effective choice in terrain which has heavy rain or
in coastal areas. The diameter will be similar to ES type.</DD></P></LI>
              <LI><DT><P><B><I>Long Blade Barbed Tape (LBBT):</I></B><BR/>
                    <DD>This is the most effective psychological and physical deterrent, ever made
as a barrier obstacle. It is available in authentic stainless steel (SUS 430) and the core wire can be
fabricated from either galvanized carbon steel or stainless steel.</DD></P></LI>
              </UL><P><HR/>
              <P STYLE="color:#008000;text-align:center;"><B>ANIMAL FENCING</B></P>
              <TABLE Border="0"><TR><TD>
                    <IMG SRC="images/fence1.jpg" STYLE="border:3px solid; vertical-align:
bottom;" Width="150" />
              </TD><TD>
                    <SPAN STYLE="color:#008000;" >DEPL's animal fencing system is mainly
used as an anti-intrusion barrier against any farm and other animals. <P> The most common use is on
highways where vast distances are covered at a very economical cost. </P> <P> Animal fencing can also be
used to enclose areas such as farms, forest areas and national parks, where security is not crucial. </P><P>
This system is easy to install and can be erected in a comparatively short time.</P></SPAN>
              </TD></TR></TABLE><HR/>
       </BODY>
</HTML>
```

Output:

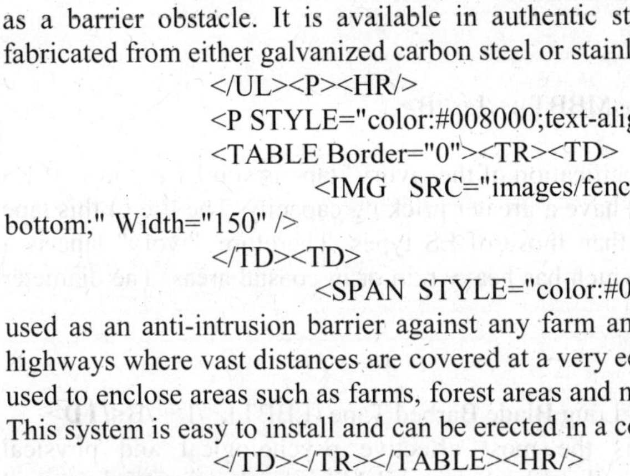

Diagram 5.6

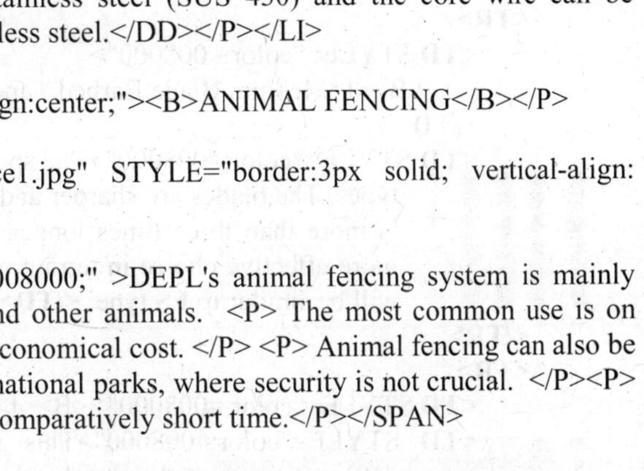

Diagram 5.7

Detailed information about the types of barbed tapes currently represented by means of bullets would now be represented in a tabular format as shown in diagram 5.7.

The output in diagram 5.7 can be achieved by writing the following code.

Code Listing:

```
<P>
    <TABLE Border="4">
        <TR>
            <TD STYLE="color:#008000"><B><I>Short Blade Barbed Tape (SBBT): </I></B><TD>
            <TD STYLE="color:#008000">To give the maximum tensile strength at the time of the
                breach hard drawn steel cord is used (ES1). For camouflage purposes, a coaltar coating
                can be applied over the entire surface (ES-1), and to attain the high degree of rust
                resistance, the core wire is made of galvanized steel (ES-2). Any of the above three
                options are available to meet your specific requirements. </TD>
        </TR>
        <TR>
            <TD STYLE="color:#008000">
                <B><I>Medium Blade Barbed Tape MBBT):</I></B>
            </TD>
            <TD STYLE="color:#008000">The specification of the "ivory" tape is similar to those of ES
                types. The blades are sharper and have a greater pricking capacity. The life of this tape
                is more than three times longer than those of ES types. Therefore, "ivory" tape is a
                more effective choice in terrain which has heavy rain or in coastal areas. The diameter
                will be similar to ES type. </TD>
        </TR>
        <TR>
            <TD STYLE="color:#008000"><B><I>Long Blade Barbed Tape (LBBT):</I></B</TD>
            <TD STYLE="color:#008000">This is the most effective psychological and physical
                deterrent, ever made as a barrier obstacle. It is available in authentic stainless steel
                (SUS 430) and the core wire can be fabricated from either galvanized carbon steel or
                stainless steel.
            </TD>
        </TR>
    </TABLE>
</P>
<HR/>
```

The above HTML code display text in a much more presentable and attractive format. However, it still suffers from a drawback. Consider a user wanting information only about barbed tapes. To reach the required information, the user needs to scroll down the entire text and search for information concerned with barbed tapes.

In other words, the user will have to read the introduction to the company, information about barbed wire and then reach information about barbed tapes. The site is still not very user friendly. To increase user-friendliness, an index would be preferred. The entries in this index would serve as shortcuts to specific information, and would provide the option to access whatever information is relevant.

Such shortcuts are called Hyperlinks. Creation and Use of Hyperlinks are explained in detail in the following chapter.

SELF REVIEW QUESTIONS

FILL IN THE BLANKS

1. A Table is a two dimensional matrix consisting of __________ and __________.
2. Table related tags are included between the ________ and ________ tags.

3. ______________ controls the spacing between adjacent cells in the table.

4. Table rows can be of ______________ and ______________types.

5. The horizontal alignment of the table on the page is controlled by the ______________attribute.

6. The ____________ attribute is used to assign the width of the table.

7. The distance between the data in a cell and the boundaries of the cell is controlled by ______________attribute.

8. The _________ tag indicates a new row of a table.

TRUE OR FALSE

9. The vertical or the horizontal alignment for every cell in a given row is controlled by using the VALIGN and ALIGN attributes in the row's <TR> tag.

10. A table header row is defined with the <TD> and </TD> tag pair.

11. CELLSPACING controls the distance between the data in a cell and the boundaries of the cell.

12. ALIGN=TOP will place the caption immediately above the table.

HANDS ON EXERCISES

1. Create a Web page giving the following train details.

- Train name
- Starting Place
- Destination
- Arrival and Departure time
- Fare

Place a border for the table and use cell padding to present the cell data with clarity. Align the table in the center of the screen. Use a caption saying 'Time Table and Fare list'. Let the output be as shown in the diagram 5.8 below.

Text Content

Name of Train	Place	Destination	Time		Fare
			Arrival	Departure	
Rajdhani Express	Bombay	Delhi	07.30	08.45	Rs. 989.00
Madras Mail	Bombay	Madras	09.00	10.15	Rs. 450.00
Konya Express	Bombay	Bangalore	11.30	12.25	Rs. 645.05
Konkan Express	Bombay	Mangalore	13.30	14.45	Rs. 756.00
Deccan Express	Bombay	Madras	13.30	14.45	Rs. 756.00

Table 5.3: Time Table And Fare List

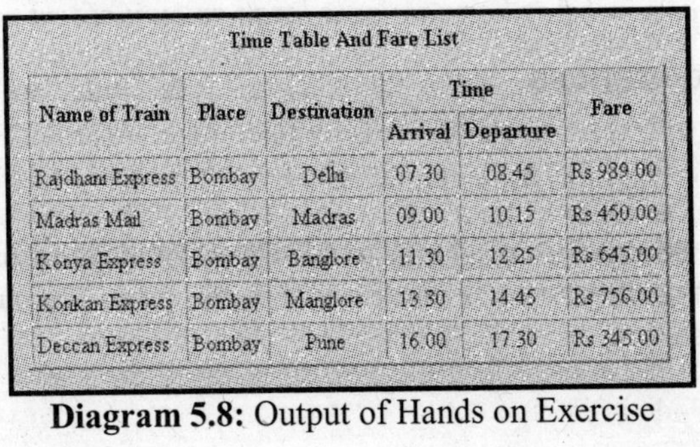

Time Table And Fare List

Name of Train	Place	Destination	Time		Fare
			Arrival	Departure	
Rajdhani Express	Bombay	Delhi	07.30	08.45	Rs 989.00
Madras Mail	Bombay	Madras	09.00	10.15	Rs 450.00
Konya Express	Bombay	Banglore	11.30	12.25	Rs 645.00
Konkan Express	Bombay	Manglore	13.30	14.45	Rs 756.00
Deccan Express	Bombay	Pune	16.00	17.30	Rs 345.00

Diagram 5.8: Output of Hands on Exercise

6. LINKING DOCUMENTS

LINKS

HTML allows *linking* to other HTML documents as well as images. Clicking on a section of text or an image in one web page will open an entire web page or an image. The text or an image that provides such linkages is called *Hypertext,* a *Hyperlink,* or a *Hotspot.*

The browser distinguishes Hyperlinks from normal text. Every Hyperlink,

- ❑ Appears blue in color
  - *The default color setting in a browser for Hyperlink text or image*
  - *The color can be set dynamically via an HTML program if required*
- ❑ The hyperlink text / image is underlined
- ❑ When the mouse cursor is placed over it, the standard arrow shaped mouse cursor changes to the shape of a hand

The blue color, which appears by default, can be over-ridden. To change these link colors, there are three attributes that can be specified with the **<BODY>** tag. These are:

css\style a:link	Changes the default color of a Hyperlink to whatever color is specified with this tag. The user can specify the color name or an equivalent hexadecimal number.
css\style a:active	Changes the default color of a Hyperlink to whatever color is specified with this tag. The user can specify the color name or an equivalent hexadecimal number.
css\style a:visited	Changes the default color of a Hyperlink to whatever color is specified with this tag. The user can specify the color name or an equivalent hexadecimal number.

Table 6.1

Links are created in a web page by using the **<A> . . . </A>** tags. Anything written between the **<A> </A>** tags becomes a hyperlink/hotspot. By clicking on the hyperlink navigation to a different web page or image takes place.

The document to be navigated needs to be specified. By using the HREF attribute of the **<A>** tag the next navigable web page or image can be specified.

Syntax:

<A href = "*filename.htm*">

Hyperlinks can be of two types:

- ❑ Links to an external document
- ❑ Links (jumps) to a specific place within the same document
  Generally done in case of a web page containing a large amount of text

External Document References

Example:

<A href = "details.html">Visit my Home Page</A>

Here, *Visit my Home Page* becomes a *hyperlink*, and links to another document, **details.html**, which is present in the current working directory. If the file is not present in the current directory, *a relative or absolute path can be specified.*

By default, a hyperlink takes a user to the beginning of the new web page. At times, it might be necessary to jump to a *particular location* within the new web page. To enable a jump to a specific location on a web page, *named anchors* can be set up. Anchors target hyperlinks to a specific location point on a web page.

Jumping to a particular location on a web page can be summarized in two steps:

- **Step One:**

Mark the location to be jumped to i.e. Identify the location in a web page to jump to by giving the location a name.

Using the NAME attribute of the <A> tag does this.

Syntax:

<A Name = "*location_name*">

Example:

<A Name = "*point1*">

This identifies a location to be jumped to as *point1*.

- **Step Two:**

While jumping to a specific web page and a specific location on the web page, in addition to the name of the web page to be jumped to, the name of the location on the web page to go to is required.

Hence the web page to jump to, requires a *filename*.htm, together with the name of the location to jump to in the HTML file.

This is done as follows:

Syntax:

<A href = "*file_name*.html # *location_name*"> . . . </A>

Example:

<A href = "details.html# point1 ">Visit My Home Page</A>

Visit my Home Page becomes a Hotspot and leads to a location named *point1* in the file *details.html*.

Internal document references

Sometimes, a jump is required to a different location in the same document. Since the jump has to be targeted to a specific location, the same two steps need to be performed as before, i.e. identify a location with a name and then jump to that location using the name. The only difference is that the *filename*.htm now will be the **current** *filename*.htm.

Syntax:

<A Name="*location_name*">
<A href ="# *location_name*"> . . . </A>

Note

The absence of the *filename*.html before the # symbol indicates that a jump is required within the same document.

Example:

<A Name="*point1*">
<A HREF = "# *point1*"> Visit My Home Page </A>

Visit my Home Page becomes a Hotspot and leads to a location named *point1* in the same document.

Note

Ensure that the named location is specified in the HTML file where a jump is being made.

Hyper Linking To A HTML File (Starting At The Beginning Of The Document)

Example 1:

The Web Page shown in diagram 6.1 presents SCT as an institute for Corporate Training. The subjects, undertaken for Corporate Training are listed, each of which is a Hyperlink, and clicking on the hyperlink will lead to a different document, showing a syllabus for the corresponding subject.

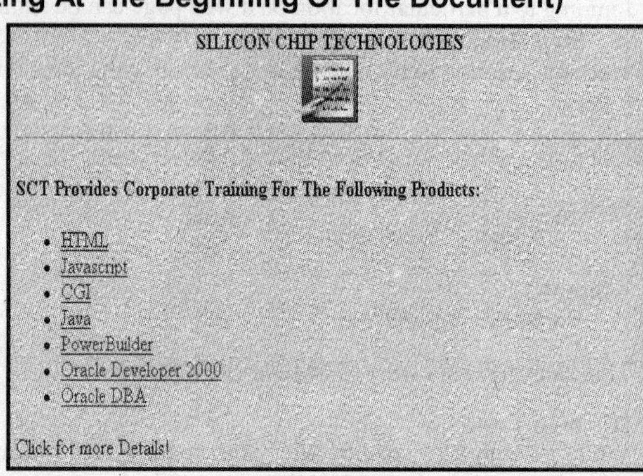

Diagram 6.1

Clicking on *HTML* will show the syllabus of HTML, clicking on *Javascript* will show the syllabus of Javascript, and so on.

The syllabus for each subject is coded within separate files. The HTML syllabus is within a file called *HTMLSyl.html*. Thus, clicking on the *HTML* hyperlink opens a file, *HTMLSyl.html* that gives a listing of the syllabus of HTML.

The file Index.htm is the one that displays the hyperlinks to the syllabi of various subjects.

Code for Index.html

```
<HTML>
	<BODY Background="../images/texture1.gif">
		<SPAN STYLE="font-family: LatinoPalSH; text-align:center;">
			<B>SILICON CHIP TECHNOLOGIES</B><BR/>
			<IMG WIDTH="50" HEIGHT="50" SRC="../images/traing31.gif">
		</SPAN><HR/>
		<H4>SCT Provides Corporate Training For The Following Products :</H4>
		<UL>
			<LI><A href="HTMLSyl.html">HTML</A>
			<LI><A href="JsSyl.html">Javascript</A>
			<LI><A href="CGISyl.html">CGI</A>
			<LI><A href="JvSyl.html">Java</A>
			<LI><A href="PBSyl.html">PowerBuilder</A>
			<LI><A href="OraSyl.html">Oracle Developer 2000</A>
			<LI><A href="DbaSyl.html">Oracle DBA</A>
		</UL><SPACER Size=275>Click for more Details!
	</BODY>
</HTML>
```

Subsequently, when the 'HTML' hyperlink is clicked on the Htmlsyl.html is navigated to.

Code for HTMLSyl.html

```
<HTML>
<BODY STYLE="background-image: url(../images/texture1.gif);"><BR/><B>
        <SPAN STYLE="text-align:center">
        <H3>We Cover The Following Topics . . . </H3><HR/></SPAN><BR/>
                <OL>
                        <SPACER Size = "200"><LI>Text Formatting<BR />
                        <SPACER Size = "200"><LI>Creation Of Lists<BR />
                        <SPACER Size = "200"><LI>Creation Of Tables<BR />
                        <SPACER Size = "200"><LI>Creation Of Graphics<BR />
                        <SPACER Size = "200"><LI>Creation Of Hyperlinks<BR />
                        <SPACER Size = "200"><LI>Creation Of Imagemaps<BR />
                        <SPACER Size = "200"><LI>Creation Of Forms<BR />
                </OL>
        </B></BODY>
</HTML>
```

Similarly, different files can be created for each syllabus and called from the file Index.html. The HTML file names will have to be the same as the ones specified in Index.html.

Linking To A Particular Location In A Separate Document

Example 2:
The Web page shown in diagram 6.2.1 informs a reader about guidelines should be followed while developing web sites. This information is grouped into sections. Clicking on an appropriate section will display specific information.

Information about individual sections is held in one file called as **sections.htm**. Depending upon the section that a reader user clicks on, information about *only that particular section* will be seen on the reader's VDU.

For instance, clicking on **Section 2** will display to the user, the output as shown in diagram 6.2.2.

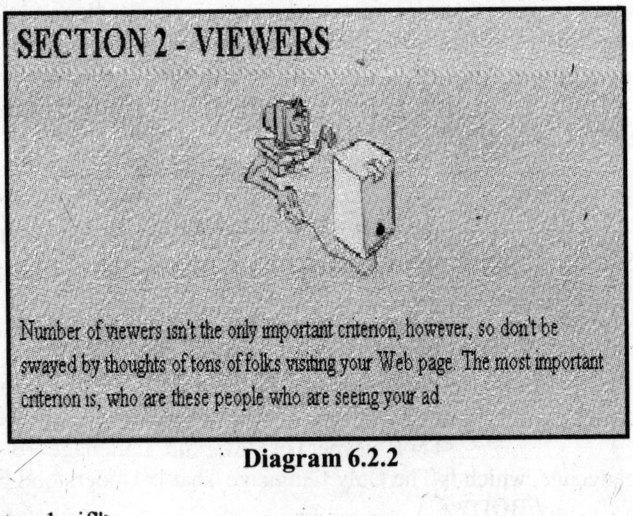

Diagram 6.2.2

Code for Index.html

```
<HTML>
        <HEAD><TITLE>Links To A Particular Location In A Separate Document</TITLE></HEAD>
        <BODY Background = "../images/texture1.gif">
                <SPAN STYLE="font-family: LatinoPalSH; text-align:center;">
                        <H1>Web Guidelines</H1>
                </SPAN>
```

```
            There are several guidelines that can be followed when creating and developing Web
Sites. The user needs to be familiar with the working of the Internet, several terms like Web Server, Web
Pages and so on. Information about hosting a Web Site needs to be understood. These and more
information has been segregated into sections and listed below. Clicking on any of these sections will lead
to a detailed explanation of the section.<BR/><BR/><B>These are References a Section in Another
Document.</B><BR/><BR/><UL>
                        <SPAN STYLE="font-family: LatinoPalSH;">
                              <LI><A HREF = "Sections.html#SECTION1">Section 1</A>
                              <LI><A HREF = "Sections.html#SECTION2">Section 2</A>
                              <LI><A HREF = "Sections.html#SECTION3">Section 3</A>
            </UL></SPAN>
      <BODY>
</HTML>
```

Code for Sections.html

```
<HTML>
      <HEAD>
            <TITLE>Document With Targets For Links To Particular Locations</TITLE>
      </HEAD>
      <BODY STYLE="background-image: url(../images/texture1.gif);">
            <A Name="SECTION1"><H2>SECTION 1 - INTRODUCTION</H2></A>
            <SPAN STYLE="text-align:center">
            <IMG SRC="../images/intro.gif" /></SPAN><BR/> Internet has a growing importance in
today's life. It provides us with a vast variety of information including educational stuff, Political
comments, Current affairs, Technological Advancements, Social and Cultural information etc. Besides it
offers mailing facilities and also provides with facilities wherein a user can demand for anything and be
sure that his requirements will be met.<P>With so much to give, its importance is flashing and more and
more people are attracted towards this giant network.</P>
            <P>Thus, developing information and hosting it on the Web is of prime importance in the
current century.</P><BR/><BR/>
            <A Name="SECTION2"><H2>SECTION 2 - VIEWERS</H2></A>
            <SPAN STYLE="text-align: center">
            <IMG HEIGHT=100 SRC="../images/computer.gif" WIDTH=100 /> </SPAN> <BR/>
Number of viewers isn't the only important criterion, however, so don't be swayed by thoughts of tons of
folks visiting your Web page. <BR /><BR / >
            <A Name="SECTION3"><H2>SECTION 3 - LANGUAGES</H2></A>
            <SPAN STYLE="text-align: center">
            <IMG HEIGHT =150 SRC="../images/corp.gif" WIDTH =150 /></SPAN><BR />
            The Language That Is Used To Develop Web Pages Is Called HTML Which Stands For
            <I><B>HyperText Markup Language</B></I> Which Is A Linking And Formatting
Language, which Is The Only Language That Is Understood By a Browser.
      </BODY>
</HTML>
```

IMAGES AS HYPERLINKS

Just as text can act as a hyperlink, so also images can act as hyperlinks. Anything included within <A>...</A> tags becomes a Hotspot. Thus, an image can be made a Hotspot by enclosing an <IMG> tag within the <A>...</A> tags. The <IMG> tag places the image on the screen, and because the <IMG> tag is enclosed within the <A>...</A> tags, it becomes a Hotspot.

Example:

<A href="details.html"><IMG SRC="mickey.gif" /></A>

Here, the picture mickey.gif acts as a Hotspot, and navigates to a file **details.html**.

Image Maps

When a hyperlink is created on an image, clicking on any part of the image will lead to opening of the document specified in the **<A href ...>** tag. If the image is a large image and there is a need to link multiple documents to the same image, there has to be a technique that divides the image into multiple sections and allows linking of each section to a different document.

The technique that is implemented to achieve this is an **Image Map**. Image maps can be created and applied to an image so specific portions of the image can be linked to a different file/image.

Linked regions of an image map are called **hot regions** and each hot region is associated with a *filename*.htm document that will be loaded into the browser (*navigated to*) when the hot region is clicked.

Creating an image map is a two-step process:

Step One:

Create an image map, i.e. divide the image into various areas. This is done using the <MAP> </MAP> tags. The <MAP> tag takes an attribute, **Name**, via which the map can be referenced in an HTML file.

Syntax:

<MAP Name="map name">

Within the **<MAP>. . . </MAP>** tags the <AREA> tag is specified. This tag defines the specific region within the image. The <AREA> tag takes certain attributes. The attributes are:

Shape	The shape of a region can be one of the following: Rect, Circle, Polygon, Default
Coords	Each of the above shapes takes different coordinate parameters. A **Rectangle** will take four coordinates: **x1, y1, x2, y2** A **Circle** will take three coordinates: **centerx**, **centery** and **radius.** A **Polygon** will take three or more pairs of coordinates denoting a polygonal region. A **Default** shape will not take any parameter and it indicates the portion of the image not specified under any Area tag.
HRef	Takes the name of the .htm file that is linked to the particular area on the image.

Table 6.2

If specific areas within an image have to be linked to different documents, these areas will have to be identified on the image and linked to different documents. These areas can be in the shape of a rectangle, circle or a polygon. For each, coordinates need to be specific to mark an appropriate area on the image. For instance, a rectangle needs 2 points of specification, the upper left corner and the lower right corner. Consider the following image, which offers more knowledge about a company called SCT and provides two options.

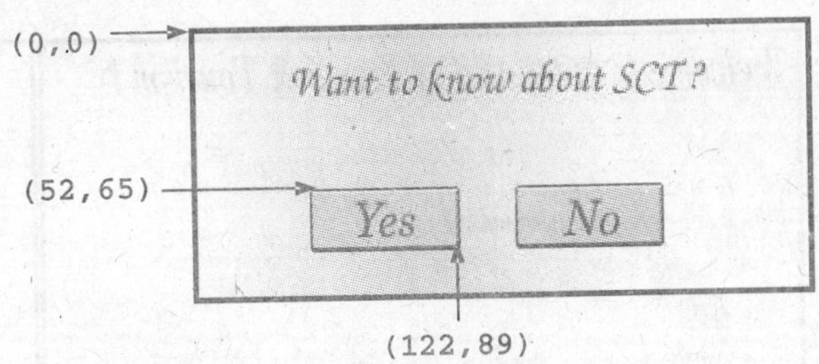

Diagram 6.3

Clicking on **Yes** will display information about SCT and clicking on No could lead back to a start page. Thus, area on the image that displays the buttons Yes and No need to be mapped to two different HTML files. These areas are in the shape of a rectangle and will be identified by means of top/left and bottom/right **coordinates**, i.e. Yes can be marked as (52,65,122,89).

Similarly, the coordinates of No can be obtained and marked.

Example:

```
<MAP Name="Sct_map">
    <AREA Shape="rect" Coords="52,65,122,89" HRef="sct.htm">
    <AREA Shape="rect" Coords="148,65,217,89" HRef="no.htm">
</MAP>
```

Step Two:

Deals with applying the image map to a particular image. For this purpose, the <IMG> tag takes an attribute called **UseMap** that takes the name of the image map as a value, and applies the map specifications to the respective image. The value is always preceded with the # sign.

Syntax:

```
<IMG UseMap = "#map_name">
```

Example:

```
<IMG src="question.gif" UseMap="#Sct_map">
```

Example 3:

To create an HTML web page that offers an opportunity to get information about Travel & Tourism. Clicking on Yes will display the required information. Clicking on No displays another HTML file.

The startup HTML Page should be as shown in diagram 6.4.1.

Clicking on Yes will displays the output as shown in diagram 6.4.2.

Clicking on No will display to the user the output as shown in diagram 6.4.3.

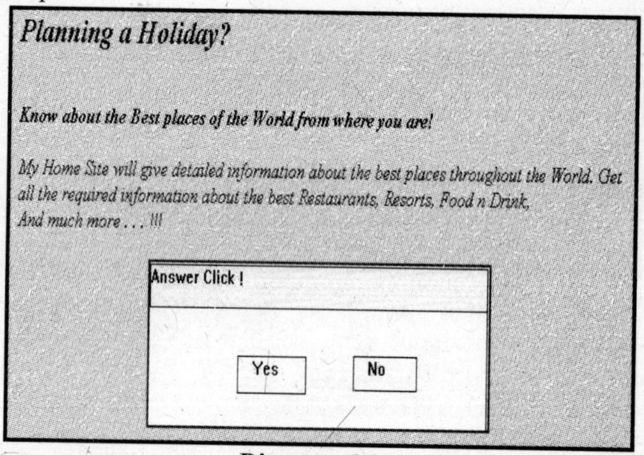

Diagram 6.4.1

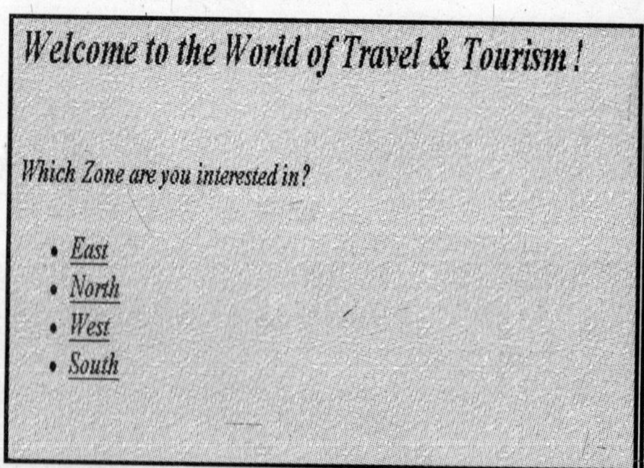

Diagram 6.4.2

Diagram 6.4.3

Code for ImgMap.html

```
<HTML>
        <HEAD><TITLE>Using Image Maps!!</TITLE></HEAD>
        <BODY STYLE="background-image: url(../images/texture1.gif);">
                <MAP Name="Alert_Map">
                        <AREA Shape="Rect" Coords="102,74,164,96" href="Travel.html">
                        <AREA Shape="Rect" Coords="209,74,272,96" href="Missing.html">
                </MAP><BR/>
                <H2><SPAN STYLE="font-style: italic" >Planning a Holiday?</SPAN></H2>
                <BR/>
                <SPAN STYLE="font-weight:bold;" ><I>Know about the Best places of the World from
where you are!<I></SPAN><P><I>My Home Site will give detailed information about the best places
throughout the World. Get all the required information about the best Restaurants, Resorts, Food n
Drink,<BR/>And much more . . . !!!</I><BR/><BR/>
                <SPAN STYLE="text-align: center;" >
                        <IMG src="../images/alert.gif" UseMap="#Alert_Map" />
                </SPAN>
        </BODY>
</HTML>
```

Code for Travel.html

```
<HTML>
        <HEAD><TITLE>Using Image Maps!!</Title></HEAD>
        <BODY STYLE="background-image: url(../images/texture1.gif);"> <BR/>
                <H2><I> Welcome to the World of Travel & Tourism ! </I></H2><BR/>
                <I><B>Which Zone are you interested in?<UL>
                        <LI><A HRef="East.html"> East </A>
                        <LI><A HRef="North.html"> North </A>
                        <LI><A HRef="West.html"> West  </A>
                        <LI><A HRef="South.html"> South </A>
                </UL></B></I>
        </BODY>
</HTML>
```

Code for Missing.html

```
<HTML>
        <HEAD><TITLE>Using Image Maps!!</TITLE></HEAD>
        <BODY STYLE="background-image: url(../images/texture1.gif);">
        <SPAN STYLE="text-align: center;"><BR/><BR/>
                <H2><I>You are missing out on Valuable Information! </I></H2>
                <BR/><BR/><BR/><BR/>
                <H3><I>Anyway, Have A Nice Day!!!</I></H3>
        </SPAN>
        </BODY>
</HTML>
```

FOCUS

Make use of Hyperlinks to provide navigation through the DEPL Web Site. Provide an index, each entry of the index leads to different blocks of information.

This means that the DEPL site information needs to be separated into multiple *filename*.html files. A startup file has to serve as the index. The DEPL is being broken up into five different HTML files described as follows:

File Name	Functionality
Index.html	The first (startup) file. This file has following **4 Hyperlinks** which leads to specific information: ❑ Profile ❑ Barbed Wire ❑ Barbed Tape ❑ Animal Fencing Additionally, these hyperlinks are **images**, not text.
Profile.html	Holds the company profile.
BWire.html	Holds a detailed description about the barbed wire products of the company.
BTape.html	Holds a detailed description about one the barbed tape products of the company.
AniFenc.html	Holds a detailed description about the animal fencing products of the company.

Table 6.3

Code for Index.html

```
<HTML>
        <HEAD><TITLE>Delta Engineering Pvt. Ltd.</TITLE></HEAD>
        <BODY STYLE="background-image: url(../images/pinkwhit.gif);text-align:center;">
                <SPAN STYLE="color: #008000; font-family:brush Script MT; font-size: 30px;">
                <IMG STYLE="vertical-align: bottom;" src="../images/logo.gif" />
                        <I>Delta Engineering Pvt. Ltd.</I><HR/>
                </SPAN>
                <SPAN STYLE="color: #008000; font-size:12px;">
                <BR/>
                <B><I>Delta Engineering Pvt. Ltd. is a specialist manufacturer of wire and wire
products. DEPL established in Mumbai, India is ideally located for shipments to any part of the world. The
main items of manufacture, in collaboration with Gulf Fencing Industry (GFI) include protector gabions
and protector fencing systems.</I></B>
                </SPAN>
                <P>
                <TABLE Width = "90%"><TR>
                <TD ALIGN="CENTER"><A href="Profile.html"><IMG ALT="Profile"
HEIGHT="35" SRC="../images/profile.gif" WIDTH="101" STYLE="border:0px solid" /></A></TD>
                        <TD ALIGN="CENTER"><A href="BWire.html"><IMG ALT="Barbed Wire"
HEIGHT="35" SRC="../images/conwire.gif" WIDTH="101" STYLE="border:0px solid" /></A></TD>
                        <TD ALIGN="CENTER"><A href="BTape.html"><IMG ALT="Barbed
Tapes" HEIGHT="35" SRC="../images/contape.gif" WIDTH="101" STYLE="border:0px solid" />
</A></TD>
                        <TD ALIGN="CENTER"><A href="AniFenc.html"><IMG ALT="Fencing"
HEIGHT="35" SRC="../images/anifenc.gif" WIDTH="101" STYLE="border:0px solid" /></A></TD>
                </TR>
                </TABLE>
                </P>
        </BODY>
</HTML>
```

Output For Index.html:

As seen in the output shown in diagram 6.5.1, there are four pictures at the end of the screen. Each of these is actually a Hyperlink.

- Clicking on **Profile** opens a file called **Profile.html**.
- Clicking on **Concertina Barbed Wire** opens a file called **BWire.html**.
- Clicking on **Concertina Barbed Tape** opens a file called **BTape.html**.
- Clicking on **Animal Fencing** opens a file called **Anifenc.html**.

The code for each of these HTML files along with their what these files should look like when viewed in a browser is given below.

Code For Profile.html

```
<HTML>
    <HEAD><TITLE> Delta Engineering Pvt. Ltd. </TITLE></HEAD>
    <BODY STYLE="background-image: url(../images/pinkwhit.gif);">
        <P STYLE="text-align:center; color: #008000; font-family:Brush Script MT; font-size: 30px;">
            <IMG STYLE="vertical-align:bottom;" SRC="../images/logo.gif" />
                <I>Our Profile</I><BR/><HR Size="3" />
        </P>
        <P STYLE="text-align:center;color: #008000; font-family:Times Roman; font-size: 12px;">
            <IMG HEIGHT="57" SRC="../images/intro.gif" WIDTH="185" /><BR/>
        <P>Delta Engineering Pvt. Ltd. is a specialist manufacturer of wire and wire products. DEPL established in Mumbai, India is ideally located for shipments to any part of the world. The main items of manufacture, in collaboration with Gulf Fencing Industry (GFI) include protector gabions and protector fencing systems.<P>Protector fencing systems offer a wide range of solutions to all security problems on any terrain and under extreme climatic conditions. The protector fencing system has been used extensively in Europe, America and the Far East, and this has helped formulate a package especially suited to Middle East requirements.<P>DEPL is equipped to offer comprehensive packages including design, material and installation.<P>Products strictly adhere to BS, ASTM and DIN international specifications. Quality control is guaranteed by independent laboratory test certificates from India.<P>Quality control is implemented without sacrificing economy and efficiency. DEPL is dedicated to technical services and problem solving.<P>DEPL is following quality methods and is accredited with ISO 9002.<P><IMG HEIGHT="57" SRC="../images/planning.gif" WIDTH="184" /><BR/>DEPL can provide planning support by offering design, technical specifications, drawings, foundation plans and installation instructions, together with a personalized service. The company's technical sales engineers keep in constant touch with all clients. Utmost importance is given to optimum design, versatility, durability and economy backed by the DEPL guarantee for work undertaken.</P><BR/><HR/>
        <SPAN STYLE="color: green; font-family: ZappedChancellorSH; font-size: 14px; ">
            <P><SPACER Type="Horizontal" Size="20">
                Please forward any enquiries to enq_depl@bom2.vsnl.net.in
            <P><I>
                <SPACER Type="Horizontal" Size="120" />
                    <B>DELTA ENGINEERING PVT. LTD.</B><BR/>
                <SPACER Type="Horizontal" Size="120" />502, 5th Floor, Tejas Building,<BR/>
                <SPACER Type="Horizontal" Size="120" />Andheri (W), Mumbai<BR/>
                <SPACER Type="Horizontal" Size="120" />INDIA<BR/>
                <SPACER Type="Horizontal" Size="120" />Telephone : 91-022-8210050
            </I></P>
        </SPAN><HR/>
    </BODY>
```

Output For Profile.html:

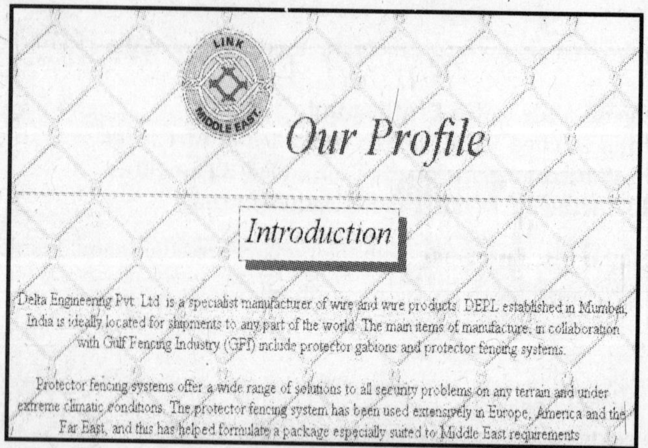

Diagram 6.5.2

Code for BWire.html

```
<HTML>
    <HEAD><TITLE> Delta Engineering Pvt. Ltd. </TITLE></HEAD>
    <BODY STYLE="background-image: url(../images/pinkwhit.gif);">
        <P STYLE="text-align:center; color: #008000; font-family:Brush Script MT; font-size: 30px;"><I>Barbed Wires</I><BR/><HR Size="3" />
        <TABLE CellPadding="20"><TR>
            <TD><IMG STYLE= "vertical-align:bottom;border:2px solid" Height="300" Src="../images/barbed1.jpg" Width="250"></TD>
            <TD><SPAN STYLE="color: #008000; font-family:Comic Sans MS; font-size: 10px;"><B>Concertina Barbed Wire in roll form is used in high security areas to deter trespassing men and animals.<P>The effectiveness of this material is proved as it has been in use for more than 75 years during war and peace.</B></TD>
        </TR></TABLE>
        <P STYLE="color: #008000; font-family:Comic Sans MS; font-size: 10px;">
        <OL>
            <P><B><I><LI>Line Wire:</I></B><BR/>This is made up of 3.05mm diameter high carbon steel wire, with a tensile strength of 170 to 180 kg/mm². The wire is drawn and dressed in such a manner that the coils formed will fall naturally into the specified diameter without forming a figure eight. Line wire is heavy hot dipped galvanized with minimum inc coating of 185 gm/mm2.</P>
            <P><B><I><LI>Barbed Wire:</I></B><BR/>This is 2.00mm diameter bright mild steel wire with a tensile strength of 38 to 55kg/mm² conforming to BS 1052. The wire is hot dipped galvanized with a minimum zinc coating of 20 to 50 gm/mm². The barbs are formed with four points. Spacing between the centers of the barbs of every 70mm along the length of the wire. The barbs are firmly secured by indentations made on the wire, so that the barbs do not rotate or slide along the wire. The four points of the barbs are formed at the right angles to one another and project outwards approximately 12mm from the center of the wire.
            </P>
            <P><B><I><LI> Carrying Handles:</I></B><BR/>Handles are made of mild steel wire of 3.55mm diameter and are attached to the outer turn of the coil on each side.
        </OL></P><HR>
    </BODY>
</HTML>
```

Output For BWire.html:

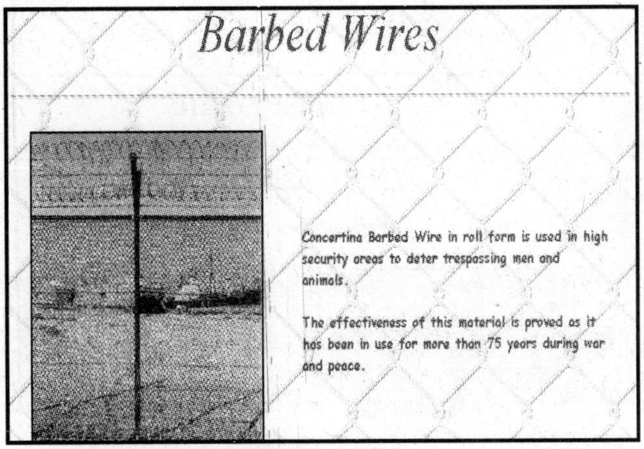

Diagram 6.5.3

Code for BTape.html

```
<HTML>
	<HEAD><TITLE> Delta Engineering Pvt. Ltd. </TITLE></HEAD>
	<BODY STYLE="background-image: url(../images/pinkwhit.gif);">
		<P STYLE="text-align:center; color: #008000; font-family:Brush Script MT; font-size: 30px;"><I>Barbed Tapes</I><BR/><HR Size="3" /><TABLE CellPadding="20"></P><TR>
			<TD><IMG STYLE= "vertical-align:bottom;border:2px solid" HEIGHT="300" SRC="../images/barbed.jpg" WIDTH="280" /></TD>
			<TD><SPAN STYLE="color: #008000; font-family:Comic Sans MS; font-size: 10px;"><B>Barbed Tapes are used as psychological and physical deterrent against intrusion by personnel and animals. Barbed tape barrier systems are more vicious and difficult to tamper with, providing superior perimeter security. Some of the users are military installations, nuclear energy sites, maximum security prisons, various petroleum installations, tank farms and other important industrial facilities.</B></SPAN></TD>
		</TR></TABLE>
		<UL>
			<P STYLE="color: #008000; font-family:Comic Sans MS; font-size: 10px;"><LI><DT><B><I>Short Blade Barbed Tape (SBBT):</I></B></DT><BR/>
			<DD>To give the maximum tensile strength at the time of the breach hard drawn steel cord is used (ES1). For camouflage purposes, a coaltar coating can be applied over the entire surface (ES-1), and to attain the high degree of rust resistance, the core wire is made of galvanized steel (ES-2). Any of the above three options are available to meet your specific requirements.</DD></LI>
			<P><LI><DT><B><I>Medium Blade Barbed Tape (MBBT):</I></B></DT>
			<BR/>
			<DD>The specification of the "ivory" tape is similar to those of ES types. The blades are sharper and have a greater pricking capacity. The life of this tape is more than three times longer than those of ES types. Therefore, "ivory" tape is a more effective choice in terrain which has heavy rain or in coastal areas. The diameter will be similar to ES type.</DD></LI>
			<P><LI><DT><B><I>Long Blade Barbed Tape (LBBT):</I></B></DT>
			<BR/>
			<DD>This is the most effective psychological and physical deterrent, ever made as a barrier obstacle. It is available in authentic stainless steel (SUS 430) and the core wire can be fabricated from either galvanized carbon steel or stainless steel.</DD></LI>
		</UL></P>
```

```
            <HR/>
        </BODY>
</HTML>
```

Output For Btape.html:

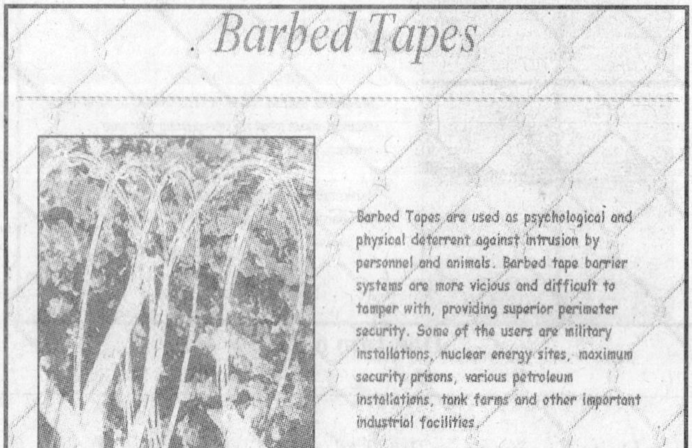

Diagram 6.5.4

Code for AniFenc.html

```
<HTML>
    <HEAD><TITLE> Delta Engineering Pvt. Ltd. </TITLE></HEAD>
    <BODY STYLE="background-image: url(../images/pinkwhit.gif);">
        <P STYLE="text-align:center; color: #008000; font-family:Brush Script MT; font-size:
            30px;"><I>Animal Fencing</I><BR/><HR Size="3" /></P>
        <TABLE CellPadding="20"><TR>
            <TD><IMG STYLE= "vertical-align:bottom;border:2px solid;" HEIGHT="240"
            WIDTH="200" SRC="../images/fence1.jpg" /></TD>
            <TD><SPAN STYLE="color: #008000; font-family:Comic Sans MS; font-size:
            10px;"><B>DEPL's animal fencing system is mainly used as an anti-intrusion barrier against
            any farm and other animals.<P>The most common use is on highways where vast distances
            are covered at a very economical cost.<P>Animal fencing can also be used to enclose areas
            such as farms, forest areas and national parks, where security is not crucial.</P><P>This
            system is easy to install and can be erected in a comparatively short
            time.</P></B></SPAN></TD>
        </TR></TABLE><HR />
    </BODY>
</HTML>
```

Output For AniFenc.html:

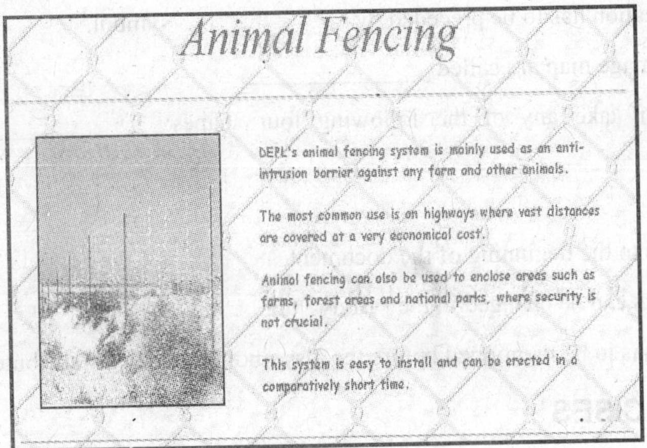

Diagram 6.5.5

The technique of using hyperlinks allows navigation to specific information in a web site. If this technique is incorporated into a web site the facility of navigating to specific information in the site is available. This provides some 'Reader Control' over the site. It is now possible for a reader to view only selective information, without scanning through a large amount of textual matter.

There is still one obvious drawback. Every time a reader clicks on a hyperlink, a new document is opened over the current document. That is, the document containing the Index is hidden, and the reader has to compulsorily click on the browser's **Back** button to reach the Index page.

For a single one level of navigation, it might be feasible to click on the **Back** button. But consider a scenario where the index, opens **File1** (via a hyperlink). Further, File1 consists of a hyperlink, which leads to **File2**. Now, to go back to the Index, the **Back** button will have to be clicked twice. This complexity will increase with the number 'drill down' nested hyperlinks, thereby the reader may lose sight of the index.

To overcome this problem, one approach would be to let the index file always be visible on one side of the screen, no matter what hyperlink is clicked on. In such a case, the remaining part of the screen will display the document asked for.

In other words, the browser screen itself needs to be divided two unique, recognizable sections, one always showing the index, and the other changing its content dynamically, depending on the hyperlink clicked on.

When the browser screen is divided into more than one unique, (HTML) recognizable, section each such section is called a **Frame.**

The following chapter explains how the browser screen can be divided into frames. How hyperlinks in one frame can open different HTML documents in another frame.

SELF REVIEW QUESTIONS

FILL IN THE BLANKS

1. ____________ allows linking to other documents.
2. The __________ color is the default color of a hyperlink.
3. Hyperlinks can be of two types: Links to an _________ document or an ____________ document.

4. ______ ______ enable a jump to a particular location in a document.
5. The name of the location has to be preceded by a _________-__ symbol.
6. Linked regions of image map are called ______________.
7. An image map can take any of the following four shapes: _______, ________, _______ & _________.

TRUE OR FALSE

8. Anchors target links to the beginning of the document.
9. The color of the links can be changed in the <Body> tag.
10. A filename always has to be mentioned before the # symbol in the HREF attribute of a link.

HANDS ON EXERCISES

1. Create a document with two links to an external document. The first link should lead to the beginning of the external document. The second link should lead to a particular section in the external document.

   In the external document specify a link that will lead to a particular section within it.

Text Content:

```
Welcome to our homepage
This page has links to the website of ABC Lever Inc.

For further information click on any of the following:
•  About ABC Lever Inc.
•  Contact information
About us
________________________________________________________________
ABC Lever inc. is a conglomerate that has interests ranging from bodycare
products to toilet soaps.
A couple of years ago we entered the frozen food industry through mergers
and acquisitions.
Last year we started our plant to manufacture salt and this year it is
wheat flour.
Our current turnover is about Rs. 7500 cr and by the next decade we are
looking at a target of 15000 cr.
________________________________________________________________
Contact Us
________________________________________________________________
You can contact us at the following address:
ABC Lever Inc.
101 Maker Chambers III,
Nariman Point,
Mumbai - 21
Tel. 2102011

You can also email us at customersservice@abclever.com
```

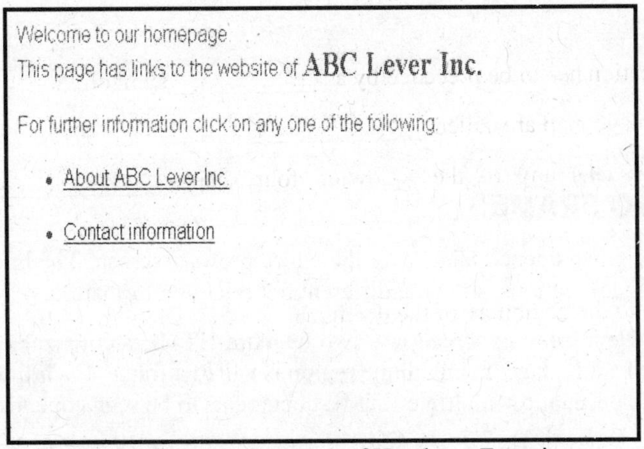

Diagram 6.6.1: Screen 1 of Hands on Exercise.

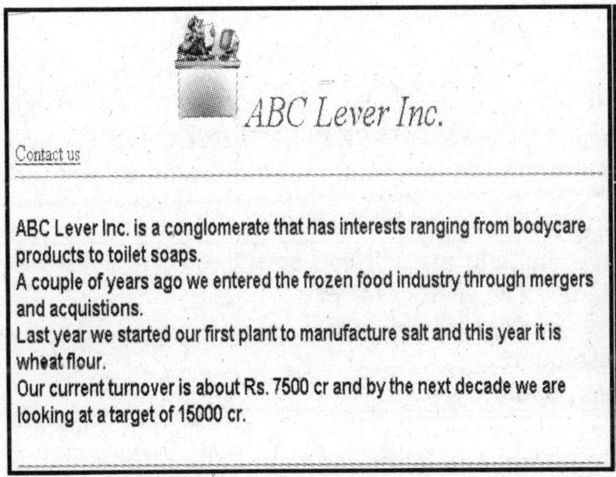

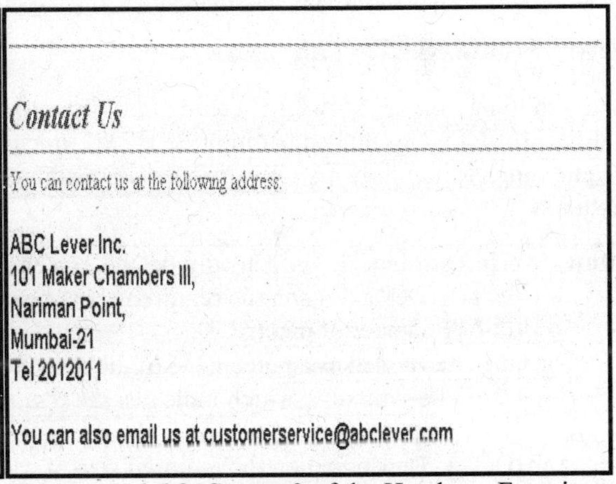

Diagram 6.6.2: Screen 2 of the Hands on Exercise. **Diagram 6.6.3:** Screen 3 of the Hands on Exercise.

7. FRAMES

INTRODUCTION TO FRAMES

Until now each web page when opened takes over the entire browser screen. The browser screen could not be split into separate (unique) sections, showing different but related information.

The HTML tags that divide a browser screen into two or more HTML recognizable unique regions is the <FRAMESET> </FRAMESET> tags. Each unique region is called a frame. Each frame can be loaded with a different document and hence, allow multiple HTML documents to be seen concurrently.

The HTML frame is a powerful feature that enables a web page to be broken into different unique sections that, although related, operate independently of each other.

The <FRAMESET> Tag

The splitting of a browser screen into frames is accomplished with the <FRAMESET> and </FRAMESET> tags embedded into the HTML document. The **<FRAMESET> . . . </FRAMEST>** tags require one of the following two attributes depending on whether the screen has to be divided into rows or columns.

Rows	This attribute is used to divide the screen into multiple rows. It can be set equal to a list of values. Depending on the required size of each row. The values can be: ❑ A number of pixels ❑ Expressed as a percentage of the screen resolution ❑ The symbol *, which indicates *the remaining space*.
Cols	This attribute is used to divide the screen into multiple columns. It can be set equal to a list of values. Depending on the required size of each column. The values can be: ❑ A number of pixels ❑ Expressed as a percentage of the screen resolution ❑ The symbol *, which indicates *the remaining space*.

Table 7.1

Example:

```
<FRAMESET Rows="33%,33%,33%">      -- Divides the browser screen into 3 equal Horizontal sections.
    <FRAMESET Cols="50%,50%">      -- Splits the 1st Horizontal Section into 2 equal Vertical sections.
    </FRAMESET>
    <FRAMESET Cols="50%,50%">      -- Splits the 2nd Horizontal section into 2 equal Vertical sections
    </FRAMESET>
</FRAMESET>
```

The <FRAME> Tag

Once the browser screen is divided into rows (Horizontal Sections) and columns (Vertical Sections), each unique section defined can be loaded with different HTML documents. This is achieved by using the <FRAME> tag, which takes in the following attributes:

SRC="url"	Indicates the URL of the document to be loaded into the frame.
MarginHeight="n"	Specifies the amount of white space to be left at the top and bottom of the frame.
MarginWidth ="n"	Specifies the amount of white space to be left along the sides of the frame
Name="name"	Gives the frame a unique name so it can be targeted by other documents. The name given must begin with an Alphanumeric character
Noresize	Disables the frames resizing capability.
Scrolling	Controls the appearance of horizontal and vertical scrollbars in a frame. This takes the values YES / NO /AUTO.

Table 7.2

Example 1:

```
<HTML>
    <FRAMESET Rows = "30%, *">            -- Divides the screen into 2 rows, one occupying 30%of
                                             the screen, and the other occupying the remaining
                                             space, i.e. 70% of the screen.
        <FRAMESET Cols = "50%, 50%">      -- Divides the 1st row into 2 equal columns, each 50% of
                                             the screen.
            <FRAME Src="File1.html">      -- Loads the 1st frame with file1.html.
            <FRAME Src="File2.html">      -- Loads the 2nd frame with file2.html.
        </FRAMESET>
        <FRAMESET Cols="50%, 50%">        -- Divides the 2nd row into 2 equal columns, 50% of the
                                             screen
            <FRAME Src="File3.html">      -- Loads the 1st frame with file3.html.
            <FRAME Src="File4.html">      -- Loads the 2nd frame with file4.html.
        </FRAMESET>
    </FRAMESET>
</HTML>
```

Output For Example 1:

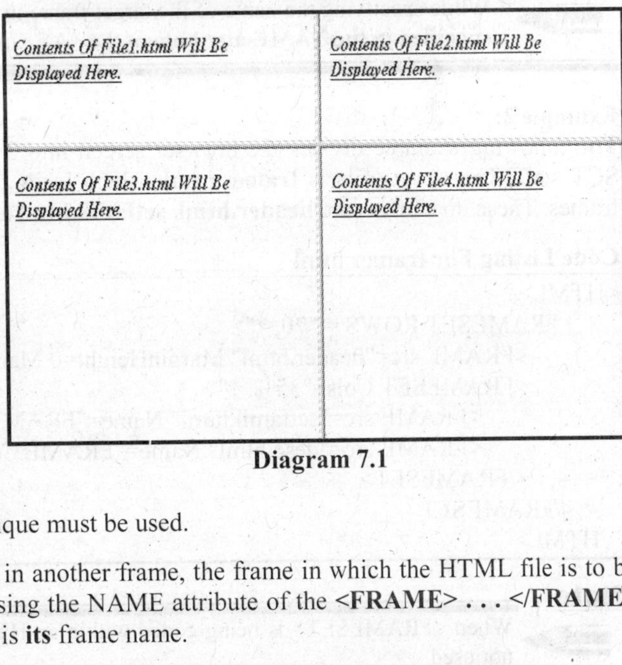

Diagram 7.1

Targeting Named Frames

Whenever a hyperlink, which loads a document in a frame is created, the file referenced in the hyperlink will be opened and will replace the current document that is in the frame.

In a situation where the new document needs to be opened in a different frame while keeping the document from which the new document was navigated open in a different frame, a simple HTML coding technique must be used.

Since the hyperlink must open an HTML file in another frame, the frame in which the HTML file is to be opened needs to be named. This is done by using the NAME attribute of the **<FRAME> . . . </FRAME>** tags. The NAME takes one parameter, which is **its** frame name.

The hyperlink tag will have to be supplied with the following information

1. The *filename*.htm file that has to be opened (*navigated to*).
2. The name of the frame where the *filename*.htm file has to be opened.

The attribute, via which the frame name is specified is the **Target** attribute, which is a part of the <A>...</A> tag. This information is given as:

Target ="<Frame_Name>"

The attribute, via which the HTML file name is specified is the **HRef** attribute which is a part of the <A>...</A> tag. This information is given as:

<A href="index.html" Target="Main">Visit us</A>

Example:

Frame Identification:

```
<FRAMESET Cols = 30%, 70%>
    <FRAME Name="Part">
    <FRAME Name="Main">
</FRAMESET>
```

The above command will divide the browser screen into two vertical frames the first frame called **Part** that will occupy 30% of the browser area and the second frame called **Main** will occupy 70% of the browser area.

Hyperlink Specification:

```
<A href="Index.html" Target="Main">Visit us</A>
```

Here, an HTML file called **Index.html** is loaded into the frame named **Main** when the hyperlink Visit us is clicked.

Note

While specifying the name of the target frame in the TARGET attribute, the **case must be same as specified in the NAME attribute** of the <A> </A> tag.

Example 2:

The following example divides the browser screen into 3 frames. The need is to give information about SCT staff. The startup file is **frames.html,** which loads three different documents in the three different frames. These documents are **header.html, sctfamil.html** and **desc.html.**

Code Listing For frames.html

```
<HTML>
    <FRAMESET ROWS = "70, *">
        <FRAME src="header.html" MarginHeight=0 MarginWidth=0 Name="FRAME1">
        <FRAMESET Cols="35%, *">
            <FRAME src="sctfamil.html" Name="FRAME2">
            <FRAME src="desc.html" Name="FRAME3">
        </FRAMESET>
    </FRAMESET>
</HTML>
```

Note

When <FRAMESET> is being coded within an HTML document, the <BODY> </BODY> tags are not used.

Code Listing For header.html

```
<HTML>
<BODY STYLE="background-image: url(../images/texture1.gif);text-align: center;
font-family: Comic Sans MS;">
<P><BR/>
<H2>The SCT Family</H2></P>
</BODY>
</HTML>
```

Code Listing for sctfamil.html

```
<HTML>
	<BODY STYLE="background-image: url(../images/texture1.gif);text-align: center;">
<BR/><BR/>
	<IMG Height="175" Src="../images/sctfamil.gif" Width="150" />
	</BODY>
</HTML>
```

Code Listing for desc.html

```
<HTML>
	<BODY STYLE="background-image: url(../images/texture1.gif);"><BR/><BR/>
		<B><UL>
			<LI>Mr Ivan Bayross (CEO)</LI>
			<LI>Mrs Cynthia Bayross (MD)</LI>
			<LI>Miss Mita Engineer (GMS)</LI>
			<LI>Mrs Melba Mehta (Sr. Admin Executive)</LI>
			<LI>Miss Vaishali Bhayani (Programmer)</LI>
			<LI>Mr Ajay Lulia (Programmer)</LI>
			<LI>Miss Shilpa Ratwani (Programmer)</LI>
			<LI>Miss Jyoti V. (HR Manager)</LI>
			<LI>Mr Milind Parab (Marketing Executive)</LI>
		</UL></B>
	</BODY>
</HTML>
```

Output For Example 2:

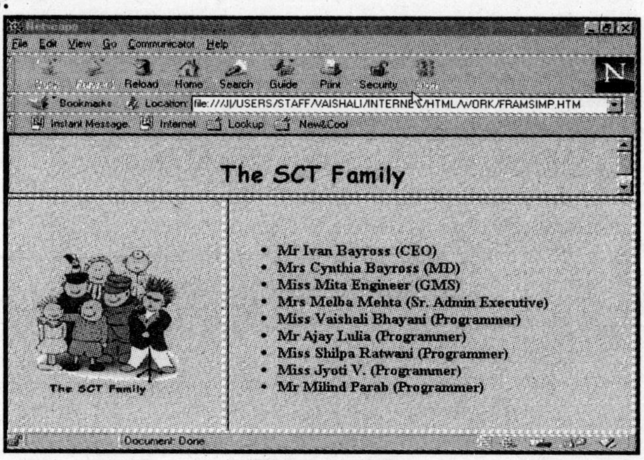

Diagram 7.2

FOCUS

The DEPL site will now have a starting page as a brief introduction of the company, consisting of Logo, Name and what the company does in a few words. The starting page should provide hyperlinks, which give more detailed information about a topic. The Company Logo, Name and the site index must always be visible when the site is navigated through.

This is achieved by the use of frames. Various HTML files required are as listed in table 7.3:

File Name	Functionality
Frames.htm	This file divides the screen into 3 frames as follows: ❑ One frame on top, loaded with the file - Header.htm ❑ Second frame on the left, loaded with the file - *Index.htm* ❑ Third Frame occupying the remaining area on the screen, initially loaded with the file - *Intro.htm*
Header.htm	Displays Header Information like company name and logo.
Index.htm	Provides an Index, consisting of the following 4 *Image Hyperlinks*: ❑ Profile ❑ Barbed Wire ❑ Barbed Tape ❑ Animal Fencing These Hyperlinks, when clicked, open different files in the third frame on the screen.
Profile.htm	Gives the company profile
BWire.htm	Gives a description about the product - Barbed Wires
BTape.htm	Gives a description about the product - Barbed Tapes
AniFenc.htm	Gives a description about the product - Animal Fencing

Table 7.3

Code for Frames.html:

```
<HTML><FRAMESET Rows="30%, *" Framespacing="0">
    <FRAME Name="Header" src="Header.html" FrameBorder="0" Scrolling=NO>
   <FRAMESET Cols="25%, *">
        <FRAME Name="Index" src="Index.html" FrameBorder="0" Scrolling= NO>
        <FRAME Name="Details" src="Intro.html" FrameBorder="0">
   </FRAMESET>
</FRAMESET></HTML>
```

Code listing for Header.html:

```
<HTML>
    <BODY  STYLE="background-image:  url(../images/pinkwhit.gif);text-align:center;font-family:Brush
Script MT;font-size:25px;color:#008000">
        <IMG STYLE="vertical-align:middle;" Src="../images/logo.gif" />
        <SPACER Size="30" />
        <I>Delta Engineering Pvt. Ltd.</I>
    </BODY>
</HTML>
```

Code listing for Index.html:

```
<HTML>
        <BODY STYLE="background-image: url(../images/pinkwhit.gif);">
                <A HRef="Profile.html" Target="Details">
```

```
            <IMG Alt="Profile" Height="35" Src="../images/profile.gif" Style="border:0px solid"
Width="101" /></A><BR/><BR/>
            <A href="BWire.html" Target="Details"><IMG Alt="Barbed Wire" Height="35"
Src="../images/conwire.gif" Style="border:0px solid" Width="101" /></A><BR/><BR/>
            <A href="BTape.html" Target="Details"><IMG Alt="Barbed Tapes" Height="35"
Src="../images/contape.gif" Style="border:0px solid" Width="101" /></A><BR/><BR/>
            <A href="AniFenc.html" Target="Details"><IMG Alt="Fencing" Height="35"
Src="../images/anifenc.gif" Style="border:0px solid" Width="101" /></A>
      </BODY>
</HTML>
```

Code listing for Intro.html:

```
<HTML>
   <BODY STYLE="background-image: url(../images/pinkwhit.gif);">
      <P STYLE="text-align: center; font-family: Brush Script MT; font-size: 22px;color:#008000;">
         <BR/><I>
         Delta Engineering Pvt. Ltd. is a specialist manufacturer of wire and wire products. DEPL
         established in Mumbai, India is ideally located for shipments to any part of the world. The
         main items of manufacture, in collaboration with Gulf Fencing Industry (GFI) include
         protector gabions and protector fencing systems.
      </I>
      </P>
   </BODY>
</HTML>
```

Output For Frame.html:

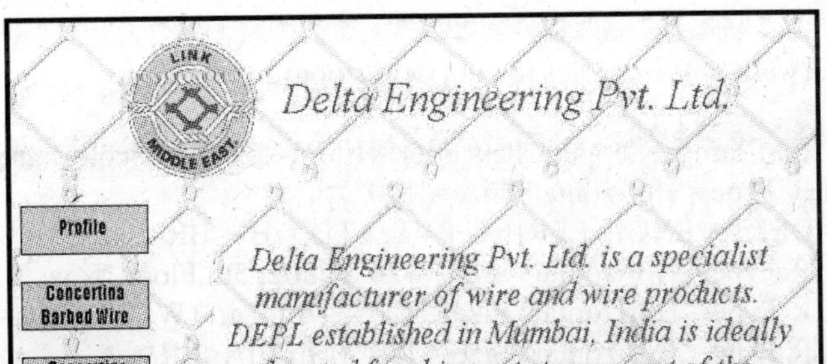

Diagram 7.3.1

Code For Profile.html:

```
<HTML>
   <HEAD><TITLE> Delta Engineering Pvt. Ltd. </TITLE></HEAD>
   <BODY STYLE="background-image: url(../images/pinkwhit.gif);">
      <P STYLE="font-family:Brush Script MT;font-size:30px;color:#008000;"><I>Our Profile</I>
      <BR/><HR Size="3" />
```

```
        <IMG Height="40" Src="../images/intro.gif" Width="120" /><BR/>
        <P STYLE="font-family:Times Roman;font-size: 12px;color: #008000;text-align: center;">Delta
Engineering Pvt. Ltd. is a specialist manufacturer of wire and wire products. DEPL established in Mumbai,
India is ideally located for shipments to any part of the world. The main items of manufacture, in
collaboration with Gulf Fencing Industry (GFI) include protector gabions and protector fencing
systems.</P><P STYLE="font-family:Times Roman;font-size: 12px;color: #008000;text-align:
center;">Protector fencing systems offer a wide range of solutions to all security problems on any terrain
and under extreme climatic conditions. The protector fencing system has been used extensively in Europe,
America and the Far East, and this has helped formulate a package especially suited to Middle East
requirements.</P><P STYLE="font-family:Times Roman;font-size: 12px;color: #008000;text-align:
center;">DEPL is equipped to offer comprehensive packages including design, material and
installation.</P><P STYLE="font-family:Times Roman;font-size: 12px;color: #008000;text-align:
center;">Products strictly adhere to BS, ASTM and DIN international specifications. Quality control is
guaranteed by independent laboratory test certificates from India.</P><P STYLE="font-family:Times
Roman;font-size: 12px;color: #008000;text-align: center;">Quality control is implemented without
sacrificing economy and efficiency. DEPL is dedicated to technical services and problem solving.</P><P
STYLE="font-family:Times Roman;font-size: 12px;color: #008000;text-align: center;">DEPL is following
quality methods and is accredited with ISO 9002.</P><P STYLE="font-family:Times Roman;font-size:
12px;color: #008000;text-align: center;"><IMG Height="40" Src="../images/planning.gif" Width="120"
/><BR/>DEPL can provide planning support by offering design, technical specifications, drawings,
foundation plans and installation instructions, together with a personalized service. The company's
technical sales engineers keep in constant touch with all clients. Utmost importance is given to optimum
design, versatility, durability and economy backed by the DEPL guarantee for work
undertaken.</P><BR/><HR/>
        <P STYLE="font-family:ZappedChancellorSH;font-size: 15px;color: green;">

            <SPACER Type="Horizontal" Size="20" />
                Please forward any enquiries to enq_depl@bom2.vsnl.net.in
            </P>
            <P STYLE="font-family:ZappedChancellorSH;font-size: 15px;color: green;"><I>
                <SPACER Type="Horizontal" Size="120" />
                    <B>DELTA ENGINEERING PVT. LTD.</B><BR/>
                <SPACER Type="Horizontal" Size="120" />502, 5th Floor, Tejas Building,<BR/>
                <SPACER Type="Horizontal" Size="120" />Andheri (W), Mumbai<BR/>
                <SPACER Type="Horizontal" Size="120" />INDIA<BR/>
                <SPACER Type="Horizontal" Size="120" >Telephone : 91-022-8210050
            </I></P>
        <HR/>
    </BODY>
</HTML>
```

Output For Profile.html:

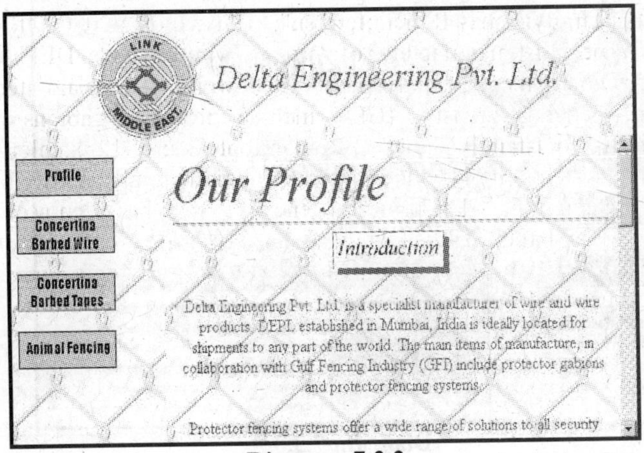

Diagram 7.3.2

Code for BWire.html

```
<HTML>
    <HEAD><TITLE> Delta Engineering Pvt. Ltd. </TITLE></HEAD>
    <BODY STYLE="background-image: url(../images/pinkwhit.gif);">
            <P STYLE="font-family:Brush Script MT;font-size:30px;color:#008000;"><I>Barbed
            Wires</I>
        </P><BR/><HR Size="3" />
        <TABLE CELLPADDING="10"><TR>
            <TD><IMG HEIGHT="200" SRC="../images/barbed1.jpg" style="border:2px solid; vertical-
            align: bottom;" WIDTH="160" /></TD>
            <TD><SPAN STYLE="font-family:Comic Sans MS; font-size:11px; color:#008000;"
            ><B>Concertina Barbed Wire in roll form is used in high security areas to deter trespassing
            men and animals.<P>The effectiveness of this material is proved as it has been in use for
            more than 75 years during war and peace.</B></SPAN></TD>
        </TR></TABLE>
        <OL STYLE="font-family:Comic Sans MS;font-size:11px;color:#008000;" >
            <LI><P><B><I>Line Wire:</I></B><BR/>This is made up of 3.05mm diameter high carbon
            steel wire, with a tensile strength of 170 to 180 kg/mm². The wire is drawn and dressed in
            such a manner that the coils formed will fall naturally into the specified diameter without
            forming a figure eight. Line wire is heavy hot dipped galvanized with minimum inc coating of
            185 gm/mm2.</P></LI>
            <LI><P><B><I>Barbed Wire:</B></I><BR/>This is 2.00mm diameter bright mild steel
            wire with a tensile strength of 38 to 55kg/mm² conforming to BS 1052. The wire is hot dipped
            galvanized with a minimum zinc coating of 20 to 50 gm/mm². The barbs are formed with four
            points. Spacing between the centers of the barbs of every 70mm along the length of the wire.
            The barbs are firmly secured by indentations made on the wire, so that the barbs do not rotate
            or slide along the wire. The four points of the barbs are formed at the right angles to one
            another and project outwards approximately 12mm from the center of the wire.</P></LI>
            <LI><P><B><I>Carrying Handles:</I></B><BR/>Handles are made of mild steel wire of
            3.55mm diameter and are attached to the outer turn of the coil on each side.</P></LI>
        </OL><HR/>
    </BODY>
</HTML>
```

Output For BWire.html:

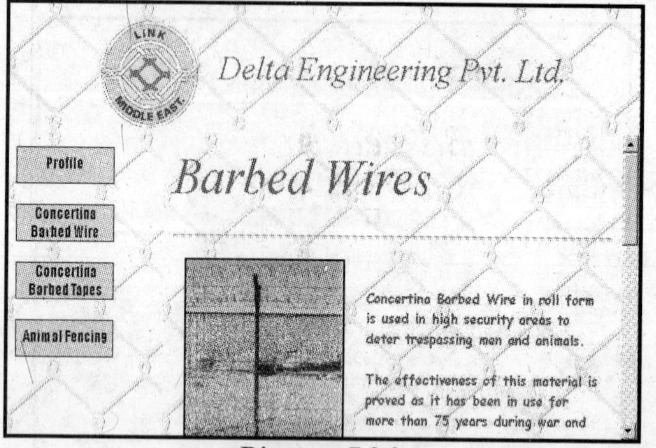

Diagram 7.3.3

Code for BTape.html

```
<HTML>
    <HEAD><TITLE>Delta Engineering Pvt. Ltd.</TITLE></HEAD>
    <BODY STYLE="background-image: url(../images/pinkwhit.gif);">
    <P STYLE="font-family:Brush Script MT;font-size:30px;color:#008000;"><I>Barbed Tapes</I>
        </P><BR/><HR Size="3" />
            <TABLE CellPadding="20"><TR>
            <TD><IMG Height="350" Src="../images/barbed.jpg" style="border:2px solid; vertical-align:
bottom;" Width="200"></TD>
            <TD><SPAN STYLE="font-family:Comic Sans MS;font-size:11px;color:#008000;"
><B>Barbed Tapes are used as psychological and physical deterrent against intrusion by personnel and
animals. Barbed tape barrier systems are more vicious and difficult to tamper with, providing superior
perimeter security. Some of the users are military installations, nuclear energy sites, maximum security
prisons, various petroleum installations, tank farms and other important industrial
facilities.</B></SPAN></TD>
        </TR></TABLE>
        <UL STYLE="font-family:Comic Sans MS;font-size:11px;color:#008000;">
            <LI><DT><P><B><I>Short Blade Barbed Tape (SBBT):</I></B></DT><BR/>
            <DD>To give the maximum tensile strength at the time of the breach hard drawn steel cord is
used (ES1). For camouflage purposes, a coaltar coating can be applied over the entire surface (ES-1), and
to attain the high degree of rust resistance, the core wire is made of galvanized steel (ES-2). Any of the
above three options are available to meet your specific requirements.</DD></P></LI>
            <LI><DT><P><B><I>Medium Blade Barbed Tape (MBBT):</I></B></DT><BR/>
            <DD>The specification of the "ivory" tape is similar to those of ES types. The blades are
sharper and have a greater pricking capacity. The life of this tape is more than three times longer than those
of ES types. Therefore, "ivory" tape is a more effective choice in terrain which has heavy rain or in coastal
areas. The diameter will be similar to ES type.</DD></P></LI>
            <LI><DT><P><B><I>Long Blade Barbed Tape (LBBT):</I></B></DT><BR/>
            <DD>This is the most effective psychological and physical deterrent, ever made as a barrier
obstacle. It is available in authentic stainless steel (SUS 430) and the core wire can be fabricated from
either galvanized carbon steel or stainless steel.</DD></P></LI>
        </UL><HR/>
    </BODY>
</HTML>
```

Output For BTape.html:

Diagram 7.3.4

Code for Anifenc.html

```
<HTML>
	<HEAD><TITLE> Delta Engineering Pvt. Ltd. </TITLE></HEAD>
	<BODY STYLE="background-image: url(../images/pinkwhit.gif);">
	<P STYLE="font-family:Brush Script MT;font-size:30px;color:#008000;">
	<I>Animal Fencing</I>
	</P><BR/><HR Size="3" />
	<TABLE CellPadding="20"><TR>
	<TD><IMG Height="240" Src="../images/fence1.jpg" STYLE="border: 2px solid; vertical-align: bottom;" Width="200" /></TD>
	<TD>
<SPAN STYLE="font-family:Comic Sans MS;font-size:11px;color:#008000;" >
<B>DEPL's animal fencing system is mainly used as an anti-intrusion barrier against any farm and other animals.<P>The most common use is on highways where vast distances are covered at a very economical cost.<P>Animal fencing can also be used to enclose areas such as farms, forest areas and national parks, where security is not crucial.</P><P>This system is easy to install and can be erected in a comparatively short time.</P></B></SPAN></TD>
	</TR>
</TABLE><HR>
	</BODY>
</HTML>
```

Output:

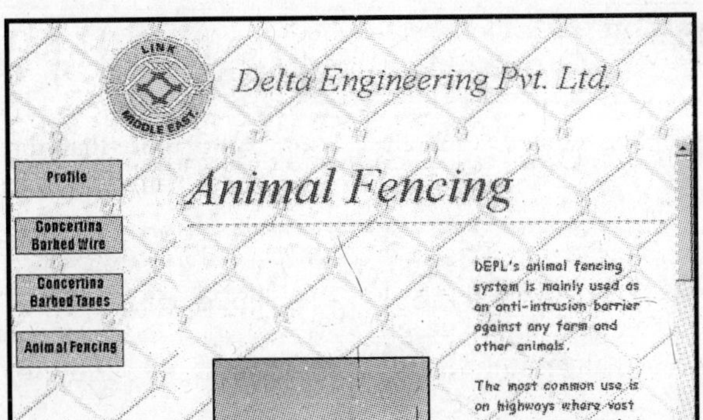

Diagram 7.3.5

SELF REVIEW QUESTIONS

FILL IN THE BLANKS

1. ______________ enable a Web page to be broken into different sections.
2. The splitting of a page into frames can be accomplished by using the ____________ tag.
3. Once the screen is divided into different sections, each section can be loaded with a different HTML document using the __________ tag.
4. The ________ attribute of the <FRAME> tag contains the URL of the document to be loaded into the frame.
5. The ________ attribute of the <FRAME> tag disables the user's ability to resize the frame.
6. The __________ attribute controls the appearance of horizontal and vertical scrollbars in a frame.
7. A frame is identified using the ________ attribute of the <FRAME> tag.

TRUE OR FALSE

8. The browser window cannot be split into separate little sections, showing different but related information.
9. By default, a user cannot resize a frame.
10. The TARGET attribute in the <A>...</A> tag specifies the name of the Target frame.

HANDS ON EXERCISES

1. Create a specimen of a corporate web page. Divide the browser screen into two frames. The frame on the left will be a menu consisting of hyperlinks. Clicking on any one of these links will lead to a new page, which must open in the target frame, which is on the right hand side.
2. Create two links, the first link that will open a page that displays the company profile, its business and its products. The second link will display the contact address of the company.

Text Content:

```
Welcome to our homepage
This page has links to the website of ABC Lever Inc.

For further information click on any of the following:
•  About ABC Lever Inc.
•  Contact information

About us
________________________________________________________________
ABC Lever inc. is a conglomerate that has interests ranging from bodycare
products to toilet soaps.
A couple of years ago we entered the frozen food industry through mergers
and acquisitions.
Last year we started our plant to manufacture salt and this year it is
wheat flour.
Our current turnover is about Rs. 7500 cr and by the next decade we are
looking at a target of 15000 cr.
```

```
Contact Us
-------------------------------------------------------------
You can contact us at the following address:
ABC Lever Inc.
101 Maker Chambers III,
Nariman Point,
Mumbai - 21
Tel. 2102011

You can also email us at customersservice@abclever.com
```

Output:

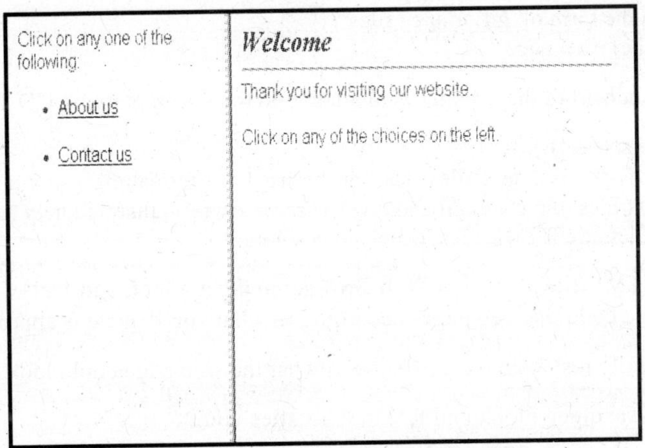

Diagram 7.4.1: Screen 1 of the Hands on Exercise.

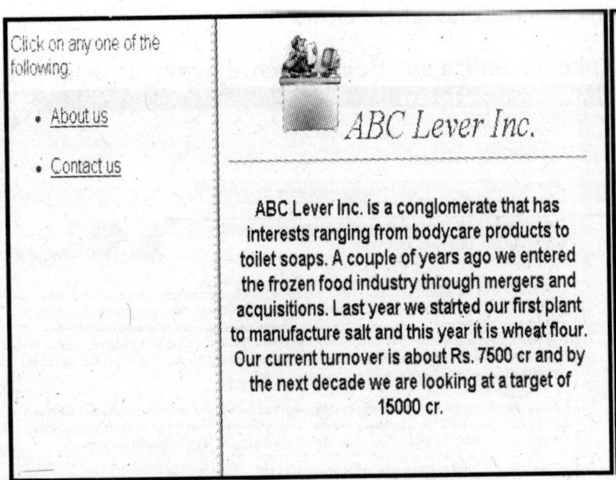

Diagram 7.4.2: Screen 2 of the Hands on Exercise.

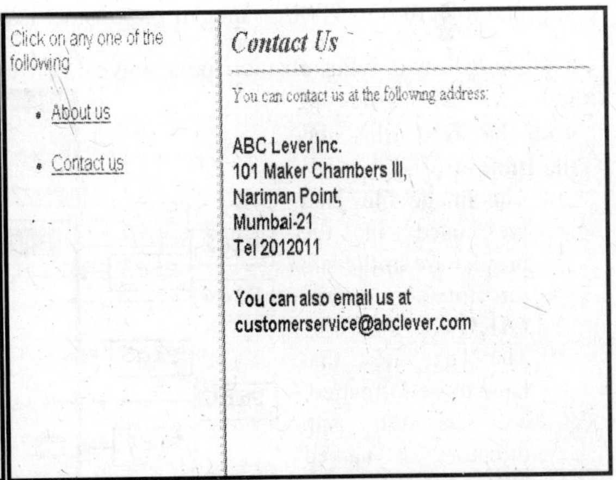

Diagram 7.4.3: Screen 3 of the Hands on Exercise.

A - PROJECTS IN HTML

Project Specifications For The First Project In HTML

Since the learning of HTML is completed, it is time to consolidate this learning by building a small web site. The structure of web site is given in the following pages. This is a description of how the pages of this web site will be navigated through starting from the traditional first page, index.html.

Each web page called from index.html is described in complete detail.

- ❑ Textual content
- ❑ Simple visuals in the form of .gif or .jpeg files
- ❑ The look and feel of each page

The files required to construct these pages is available on the accompanying CD-ROM for immediate use.

There are two unique sets of files:

- ❑ One set of files, is the raw text files that can be used for formatting using appropriate HTML tags. In addition to the text files, there are .gif and .jpg (*where necessary*) that will help build the web site.
- ❑ The other set of files, are HTML files, which are a solution.

If required run the HTML files first in a Web Browser and get a look and feel of what the project could be like. Once this is done code the web pages according to what you believe is appropriate.

Each HTML file is really just a simple guideline to what the web page could look like.

Feel free to improvise and get a look and feel that satisfies you.

For your guidance:
A broad idea of the HTML pages of the project is given in the diagrams below.

The images and links of each page have been explicitly indicated. Below each diagram is a table that indicates the names of both the **Text** files and the **Images** used.

- ❑ The image files that are used in the project are in the sub directory named **GIFJPG**.
- ❑ The Text files, that have to be formatted, are in the sub directory named **TEXTFILES**.

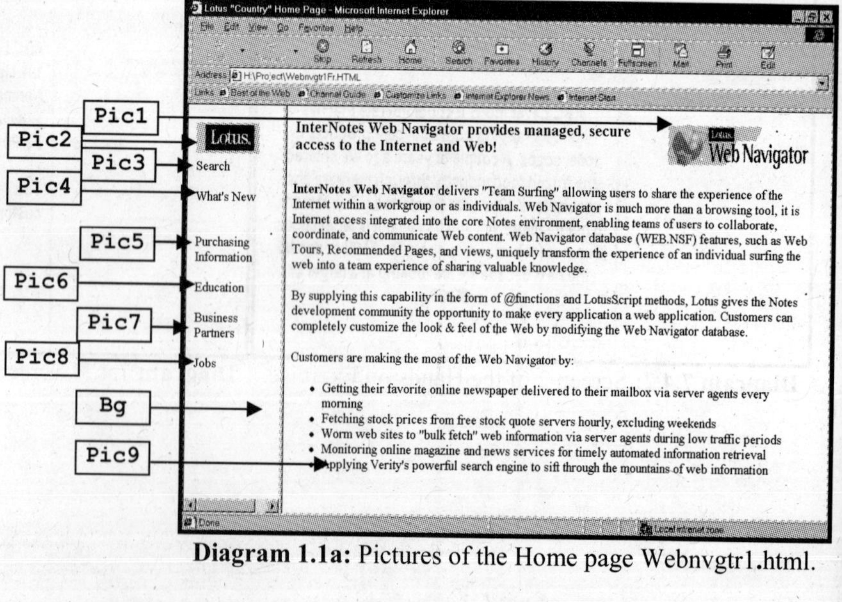

Diagram 1.1a: Pictures of the Home page Webnvgtr1.html.

Output For The Project's Home Page

The **Home page** objects and their corresponding file names:

Bg	yellban1.gif	Pic1	1e2_0.gif	Pic2	ylotus1.gif	Pic3	ysearch.gif	Pic8	yjobs.gif
Pic4	ywhatnew.gif	Pic5	ybuy.gif	Pic6	yeducat.gif	Pic7	ypartner.gif	Pic9	white2.gif

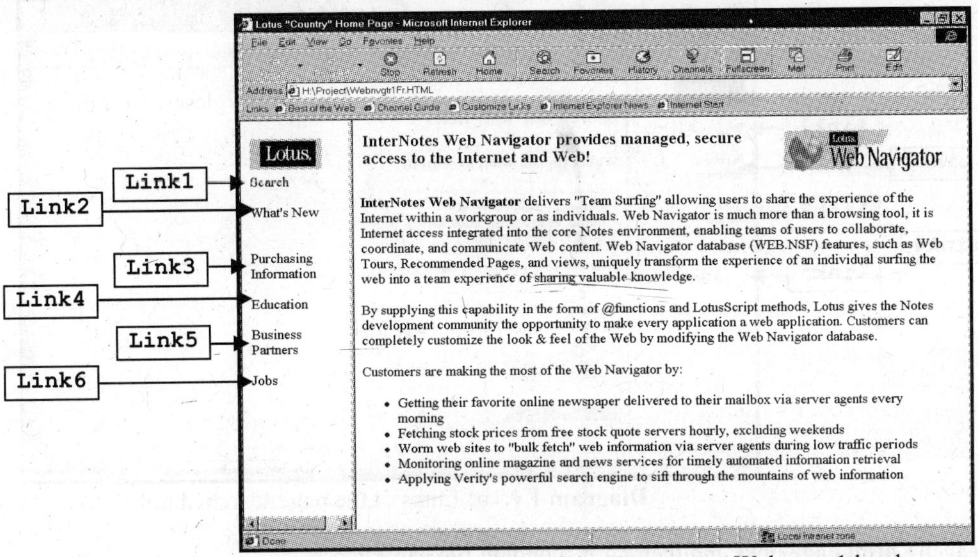

Diagram 1.1b: Links of the Home page Webnvgtr1.html.

The **Home page** links and their corresponding file names:

Link1	search1.html	Link2	whatsnew1.html	Link3	buylots1.html
Link4	laec1.html	Link5	partners1.html	Link6	strategy1.html

Output For search1.html called from the Home page[Search]

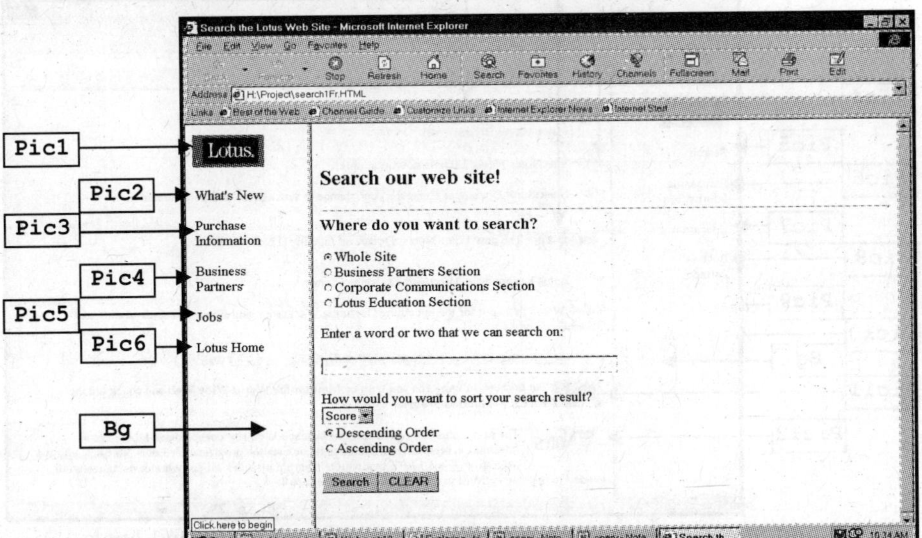

Diagram 1.1.1a: Pictures of the page search1.html.

The **search1.html page** objects and their corresponding file names:

Bg	purpband.gif	Pic1	plotus1.gif	Pic2	pwhatnew.gif	Pic3	pbuy.gif
Pic4	ppartner.gif	Pic5	pjobs.gif	Pic6	phome.gif		

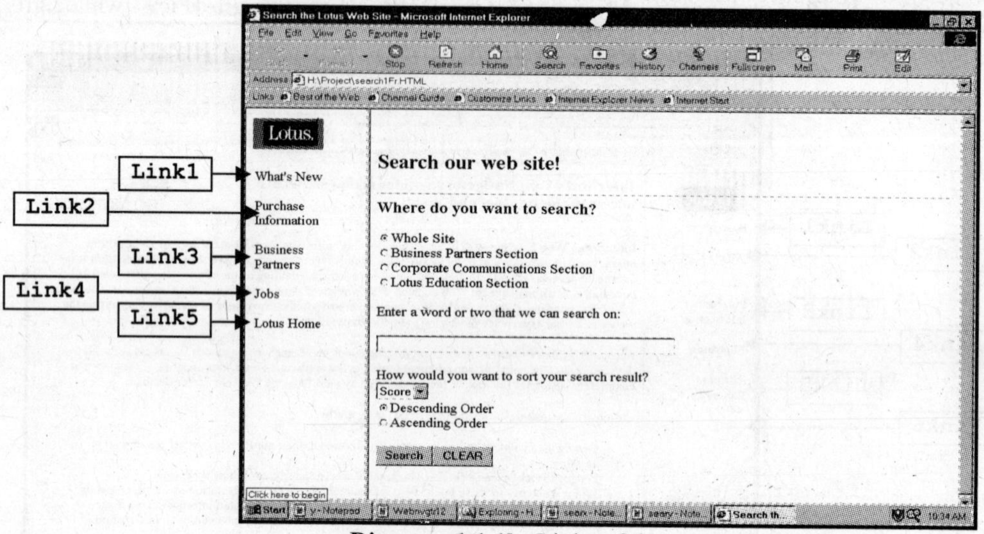

Diagram 1.1.1b: Links of the page search1.html.

The **search1.html page** links and their corresponding file names:

Link1	whatsnew1.html	Link2	buylots1.html	Link3	partners1.html
Link4	strategy1.html	Link5	webnvgtr1.html		

Output for whatsnew1.html called from the Home page[What's New]

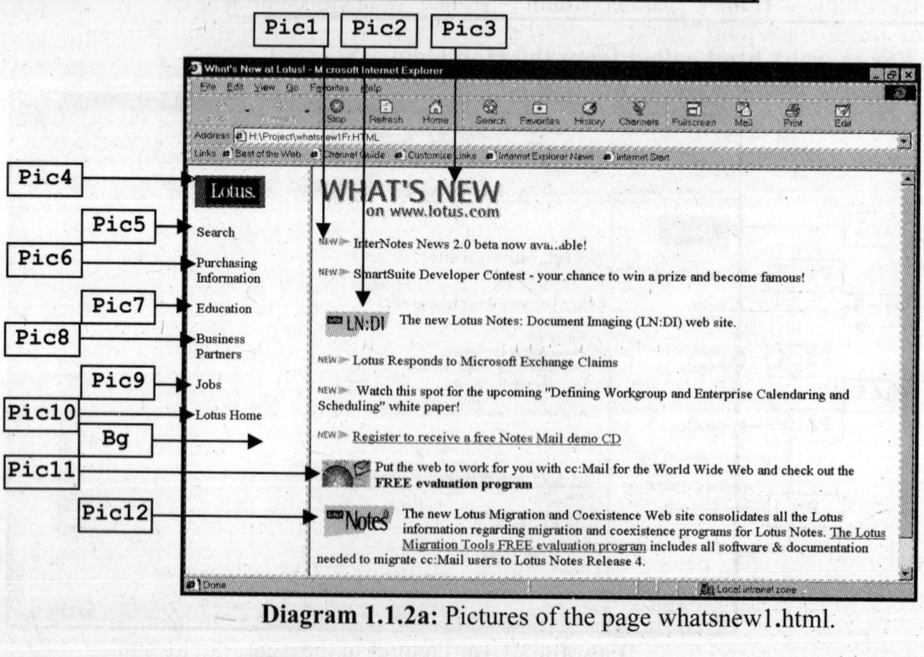

Diagram 1.1.2a: Pictures of the page whatsnew1.html.

The **whatsnew1.html page** objects and their corresponding file names:

Bg	purpband.gif	Pic1	genrcnew1.gif	Pic2	Lndinew.gif	Pic3	newtxt.gif	Pic4	plotus1.gif
Pic5	psearch.gif	Pic6	pbuy.gif	Pic7	yeducat.gif	Pic8	ppartner.gif	Pic9	pjobs.gif
Pic10	phome.gif	Pic11	ccwbsmal.gif	Pic12	notesnew.gif				

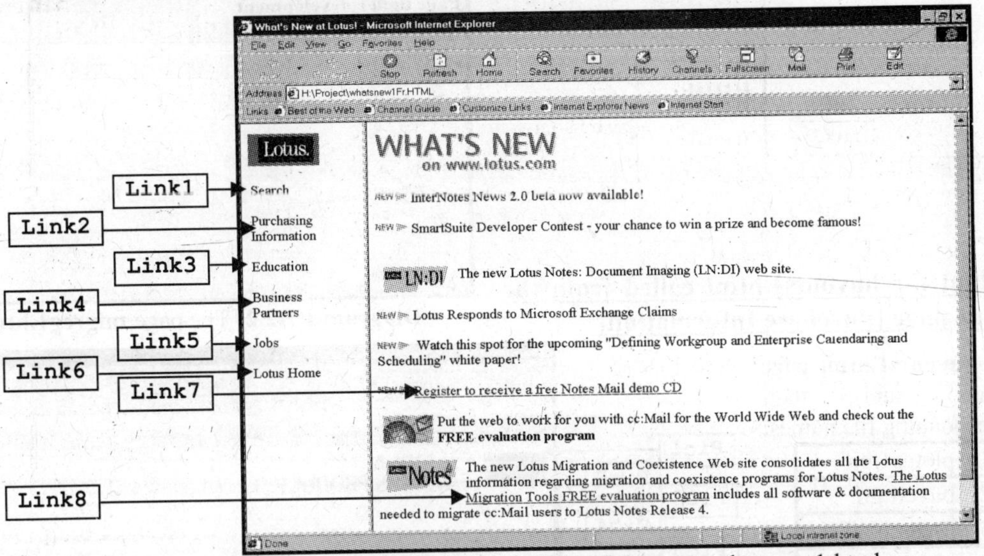

Diagram 1.1.2b: Links of the page whatsnew1.html.

The **whatsnew1.html page** links and their corresponding file names:

Link1	search1.html	Link2	buylots1.html	Link3	laec1.html	Link4	partners1.html
Link5	strategy1.html	Link6	webnvgtr1.html	Link7	notesmai1.html	Link8	migreg1.html

Output for notesmail.html called from Link7 on the whatsnew1.html page

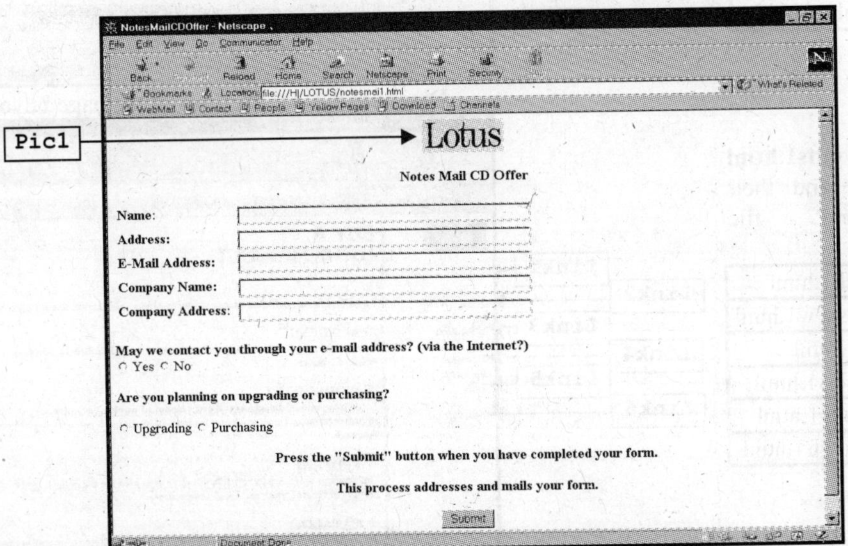

Diagram 1.1.2.1: Picture of the page **notesmail.html**.

The **notesmail.html page** object and it's corresponding file name:

Pic1	4ae_0.gif

Output for migreg1.html called from Link8 on the whatsnew1.html page

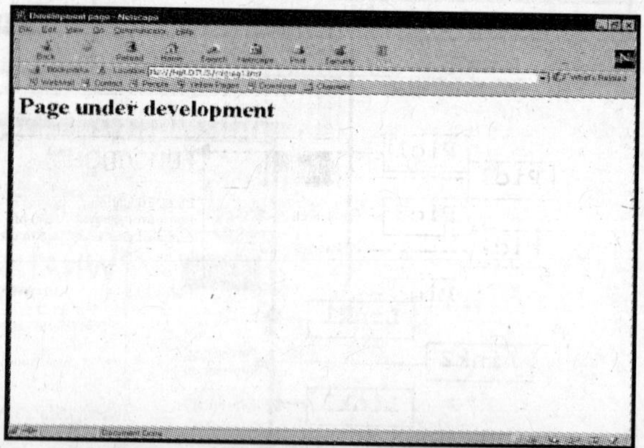

Diagram 1.1.2.2: The page **migreg1.html**.

Output for buyouts1.html called from the Home page [Purchase Information]

The **buyouts1.html** page objects and their corresponding file names:

Pic1	plotus1.gif
Pic2	buytxt.gif
Pic3	psearch.gif
Pic4	pwhatnew.gif
Pic5	yeducat.gif
Pic6	ppartner.gif
Pic7	pjobs.gif
Pic8	phome.gif
Pic9	nobull.gif
Bg	purpband.gif

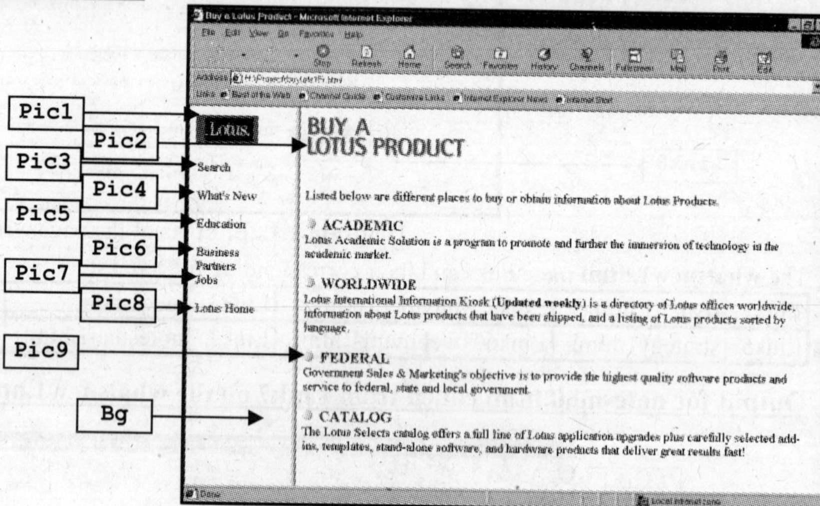

Diagram 1.1.3a: Pictures of the page buyouts1.html.

The **buyouts1.html page** links and their corresponding file names:

Link1	search1.html
Link2	whatsnew1.html
Link3	laec1.html
Link4	partners1.html
Link5	strategy1.html
Link6	webnvgtr1.html

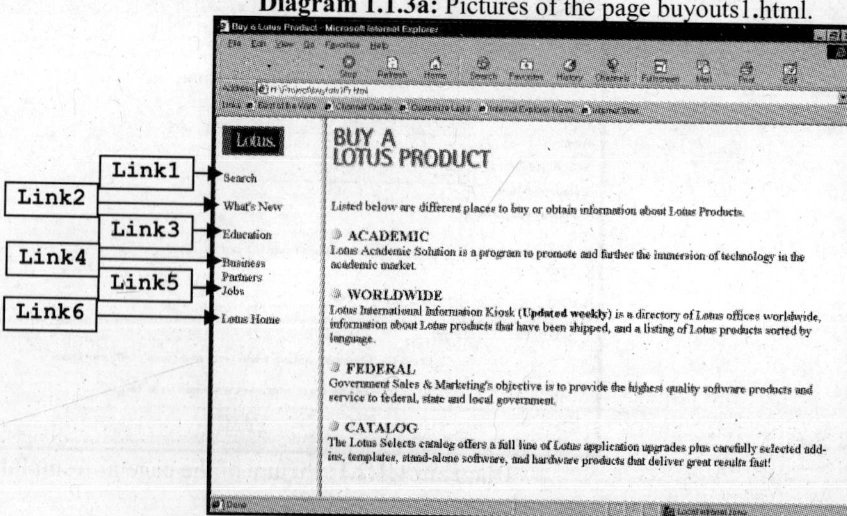

Diagram 1.1.3b: Links of the page buyouts1.html.

Output for laec1.html called from the Home page [Education]

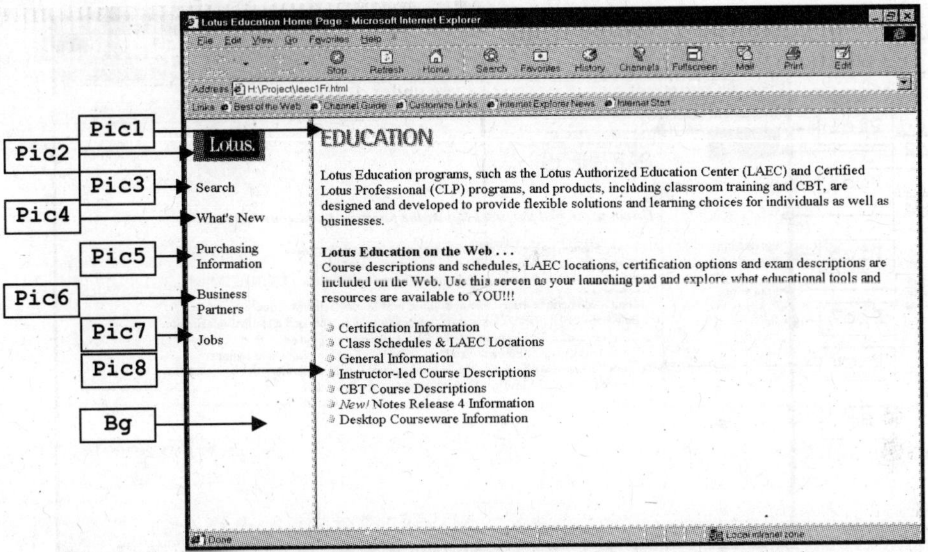

Diagram 1.1.4a: Pictures of the page laec1.html.

The **laec1.html page** objects and their corresponding file names:

Bg	purpband.gif	Pic1	edutxt.gif	Pic2	plotus1.gif	Pic3	psearch.gif	Pic5	pbuy.gif
Pic4	pwhatnew.gif	Pic6	ppartner.gif	Pic7	pjobs.gif	Pic8	nobull.gif		

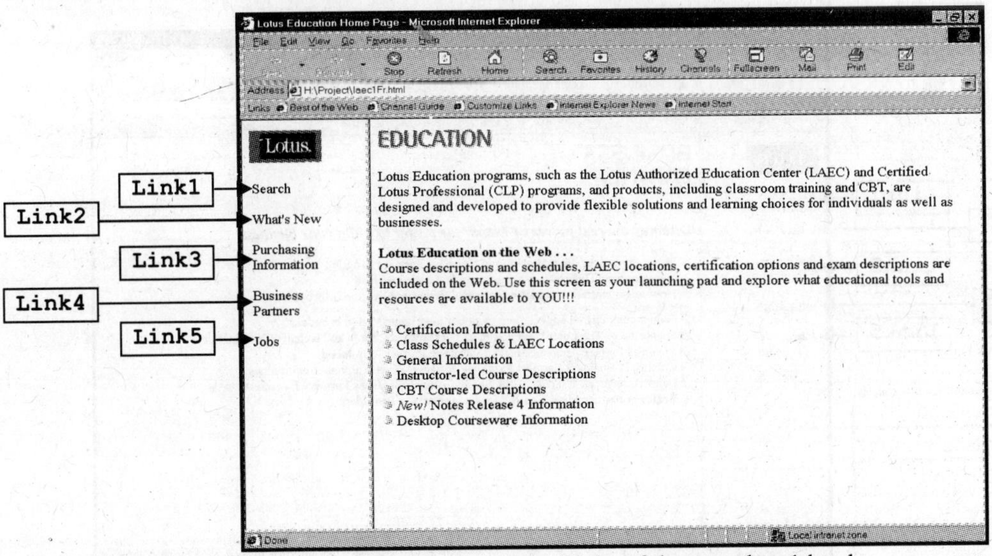

Diagram 1.1.4b: Links of the page laec1.html.

The **laec1.html page** links and their corresponding file names:

Link1	search1.html	Link2	whatsnew1.html	Link3	buylots1.html
Link4	partners1.html	Link5	strategy1.html		

Output for partners1.html called from the Home page [Business Partners]

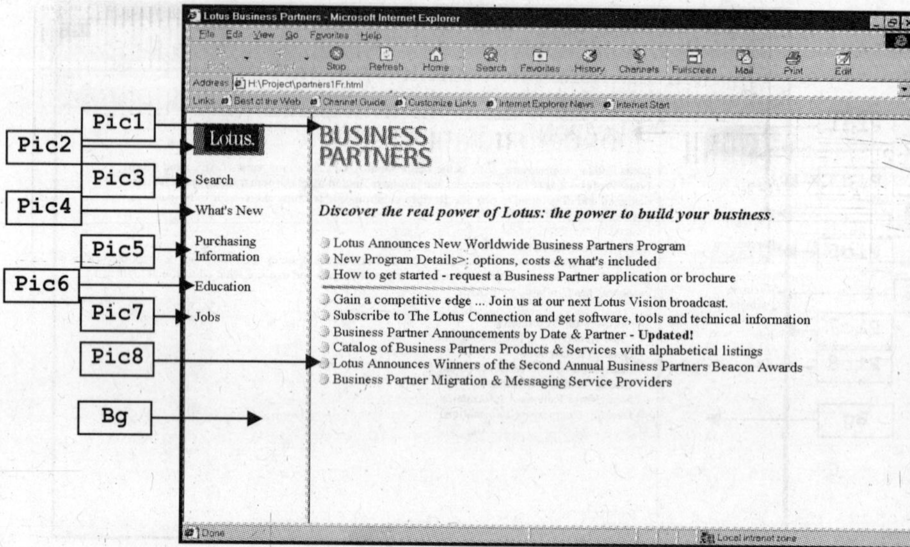

Diagram 1.1.5a: Pictures of the page partners1.html.

The **partners1.html page** objects and their corresponding file names:

Bg	purpband.gif	Pic1	bptxt.gif	Pic2	plotus1.gif	Pic3	psearch.gif	Pic5	pbuy.gif
Pic4	pwhatnew.gif	Pic6	yeducat.gif	Pic7	pjobs.gif	Pic8	nobull.gif		

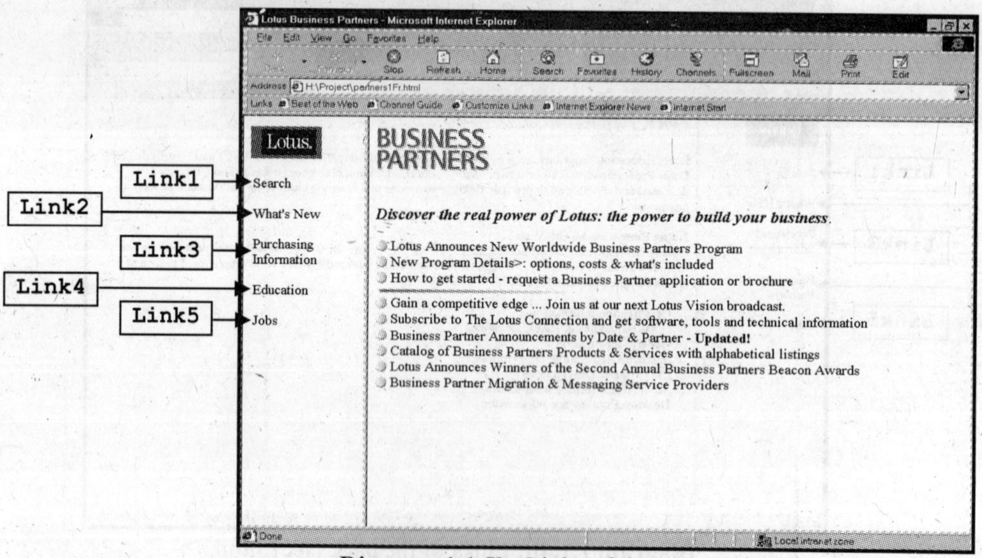

Diagram 1.1.5b: Links of the page partners1.html.

The **partners1.html page** links and their corresponding file names:

Link1	search1.html	Link2	whatsnew1.html	Link3	buylots1.html
Link4	laec1.html	Link5	strategy1.html		

Output for strategy1.html called from the Home page [Jobs]

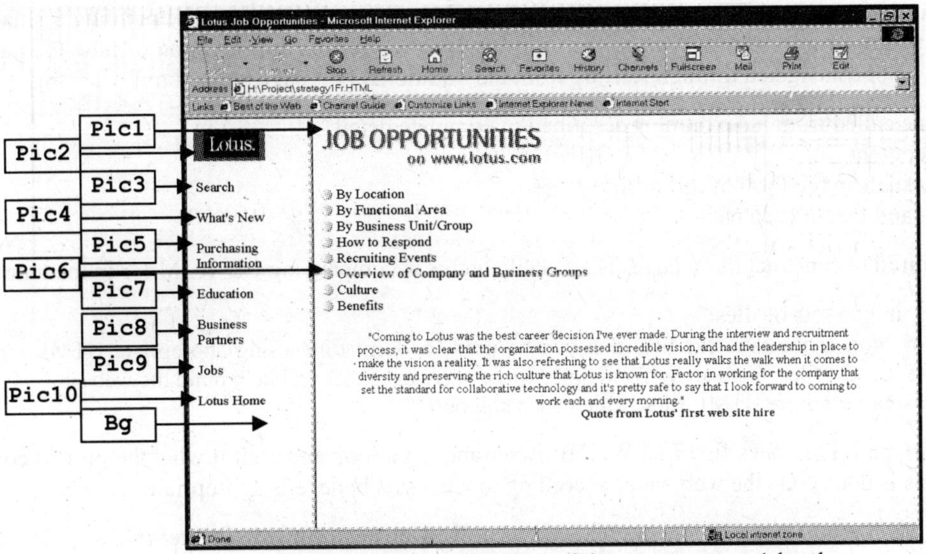

Diagram 1.1.6a: Pictures of the page strategy1.html.

The **strategy1.html page** objects and their corresponding file names:

Bg	purpband.gif	Pic1	jobtxt.gif	Pic2	plotus1.gif	Pic3	psearch.gif
Pic4	pwhatnew.gif	Pic5	pbuy.gif	Pic6	nobull.gif	Pic7	yeducat.gif
Pic8	ppartner.gif	Pic9	pjobs.gif	Pic10	phome.gif		

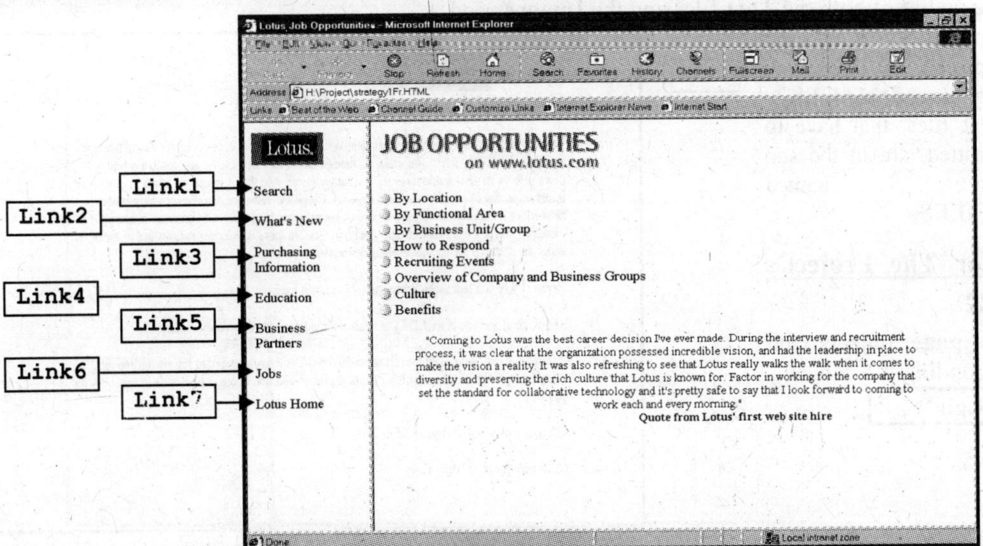

Diagram 1.1.6b: Links of the page strategy1.html.

The **strategy1.html page** links and their corresponding file names:

Link1	search1.html	Link2	whatsnew1.html	Link3	buylots1.html	Link4	laec1.html
Link5	partners1.html	Link6	strategy1.html	Link7	webnvgtr1.html		

Project Specifications For The Second Project In HTML

Since the learning of HTML is completed, it is time to consolidate this learning by building a small web site. The structure of web site is given in the following pages. This is a description of how the pages of this web site will be navigated through starting from the traditional first page, index.html.

Each web page called from index.html is described in complete detail.

- ❑ Textual content
- ❑ Simple visuals in the form of .gif or .jpeg files
- ❑ The look and feel of each page

The files required to construct these pages is available on the accompanying CD-ROM for immediate use.

There are two unique sets of files:

- ❑ One set of files, is the raw text files that can be used for formatting using appropriate HTML tags. In addition to the text files, there are .gif and .jpg (*where necessary*) that will help build the web site.
- ❑ The other set of files, are HTML files, which are a solution.

If required run the HTML files first in a Web Browser and get a look and feel of what the project could be like. Once this is done code the web pages according to what you believe is appropriate.

Each HTML file is really just a simple guideline to what the web page could look like.

Feel free to improvise and get a look and feel that satisfies you.

For your guidance:

A broad idea of the HTML pages of the project is given in the diagrams below.

The images and links of each page have been explicitly indicated. Below each diagram is a table that indicates the names of both the **Text** files and the **Images** used.

- ❑ The image files that are used in the project are in the sub directory named **IMAGES**.
- ❑ The Text files, that have to be formatted, are in the sub directory named **TEXTFILES**.

Output For The Project's Home Page

The **Home page** objects and their corresponding file names:

Pic1	Book.gif

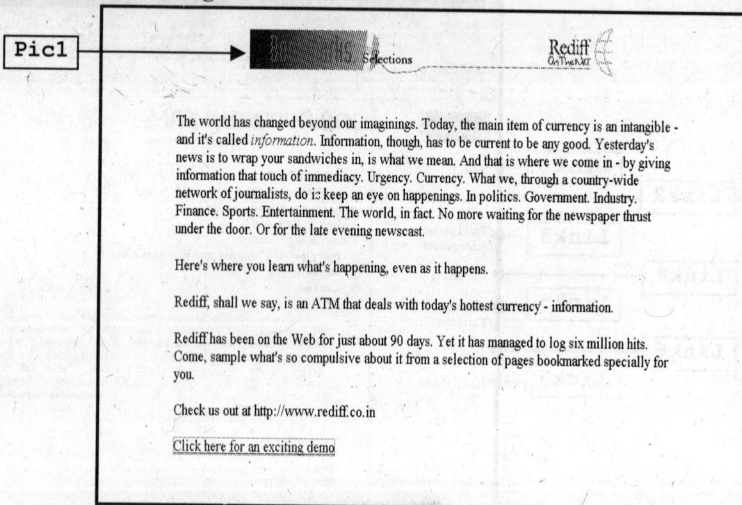

Diagram 2.1.1a: Pictures of the Home page Intro.htm.

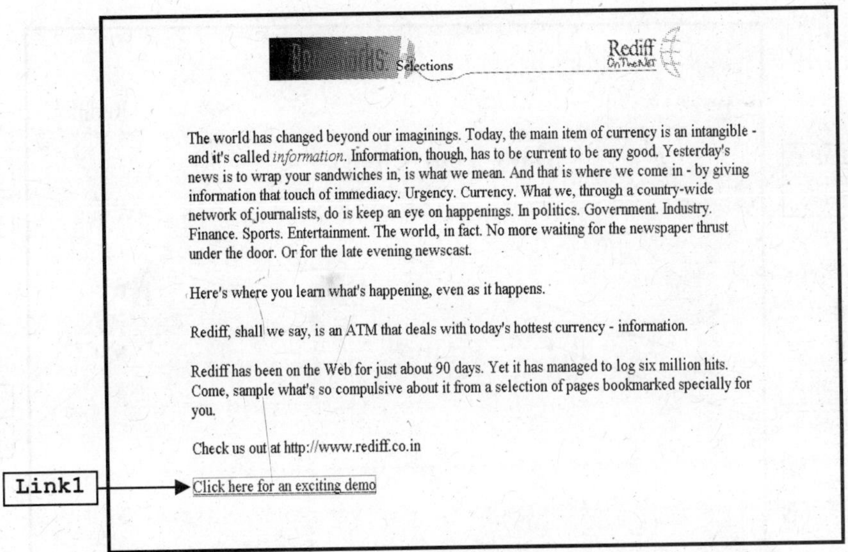

Diagram 2.1.1b: Links of the Home page Intro.html

The **Home page** link and it's corresponding file name:

Link1	2ndhome.htm

Output For 2ndhome.htm called from the Home page[Click here for an exciting demo]

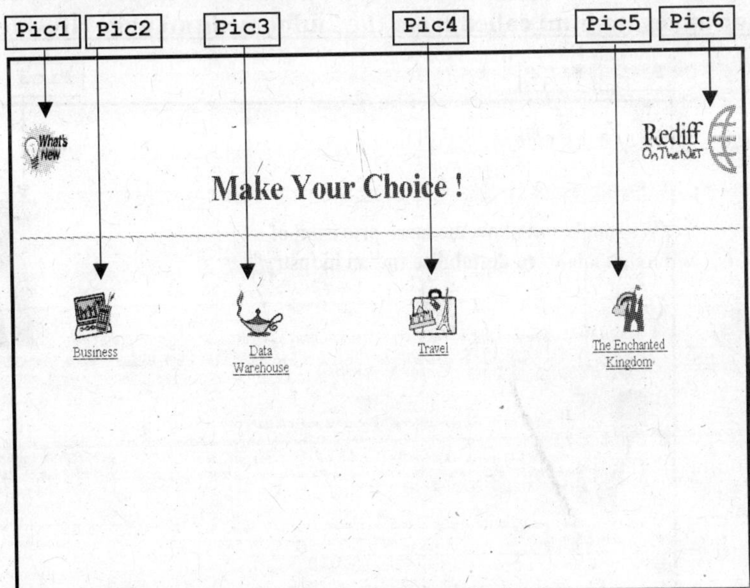

Diagram 2.1.2a: Pictures of the page 2ndhome.htm.

The **2ndhome.html page** objects and their corresponding file names:

Pic1	whatsne2.gif	Pic2	business2.gif	Pic3	archive2.gif
Pic4	travel2.gif	Pic5	kids2.gif	Pic6	logo1.gif

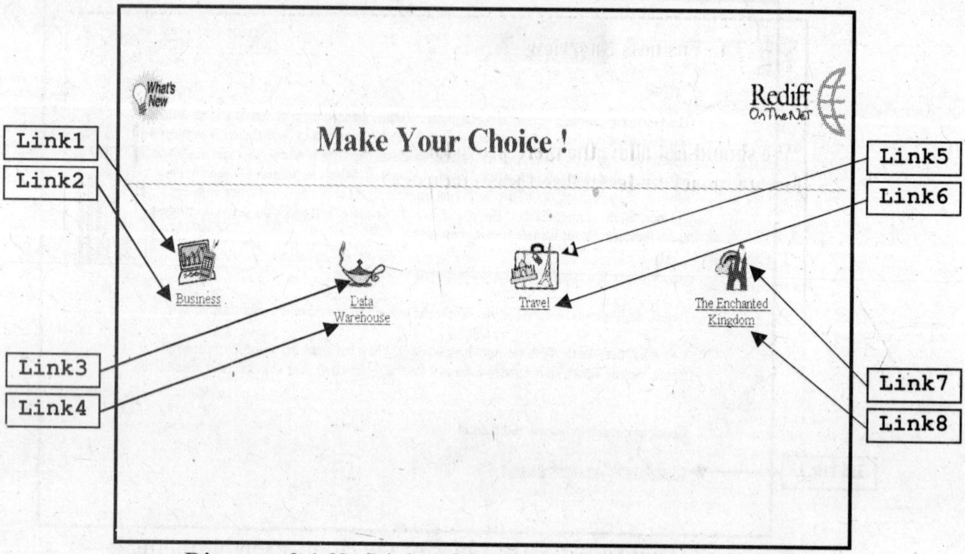

Diagram 2.1.2b: Links of the Home page 2ndhome.html

The **2ndhome.html page** links and their corresponding file names:

Link1	malegam.html	Link3	fintabl2.html	Link5	ladakh.html	Link7	aquarium.html
Link2	malegam.html	Link4	fintabl2.html	Link6	ladakh.html	Link8	aquarium.html

Output For malegam.html called from the 2ndhome.html page [Business]

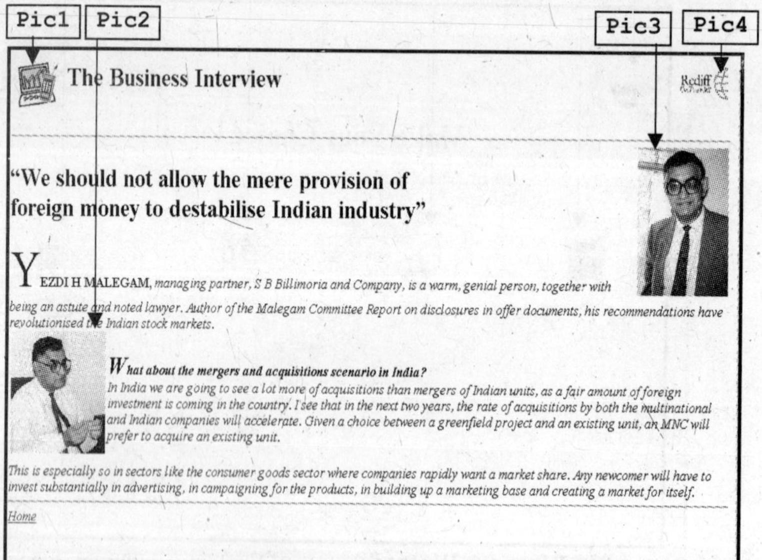

Diagram 2.2.1a: Pictures of the page malegam.html.

The **malegam.html page** objects and their corresponding file names:

Pic1	business2.gif	Pic2	malegama.jpg	Pic3	malegam.jpg	Pic4	logo1.gif

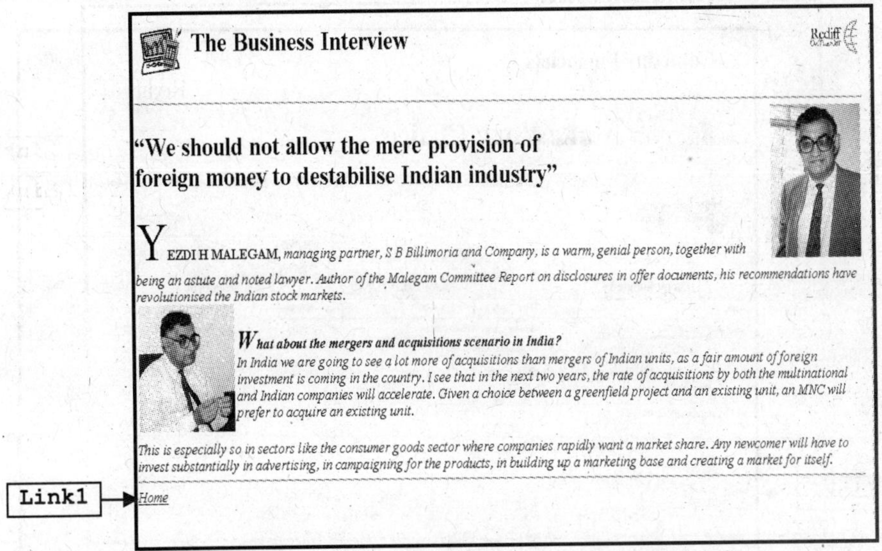

Diagram 2.2.1b: Links of the page malegam.htm.

The **malegam.html page** link and it's corresponding file name:

Link1	2ndhome.html

Output For fintabl2.html called from the 2ndhome.html page [Data Warehouse]

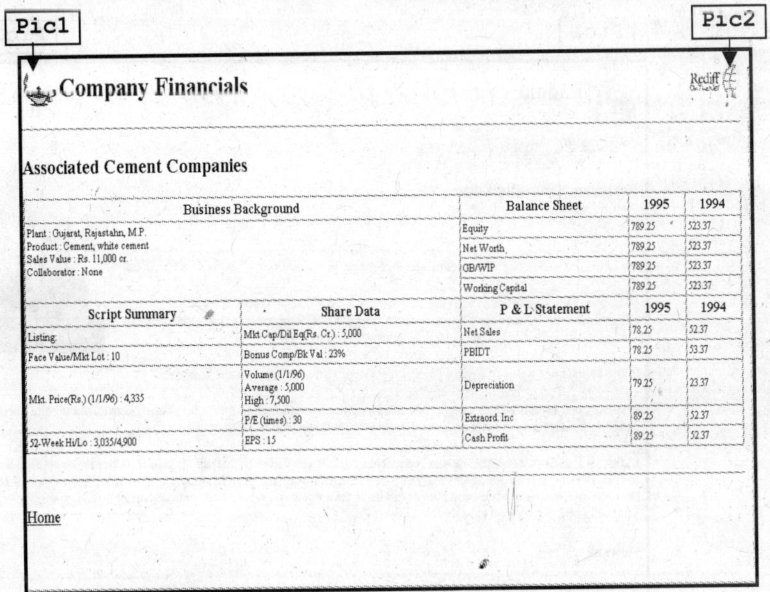

Diagram 2.2.2a: Pictures of the page fintabl2.htm.

The **fintabl2.html page** objects and their corresponding file names:

Pic1	archive2.gif	Pic2	logo1.gif

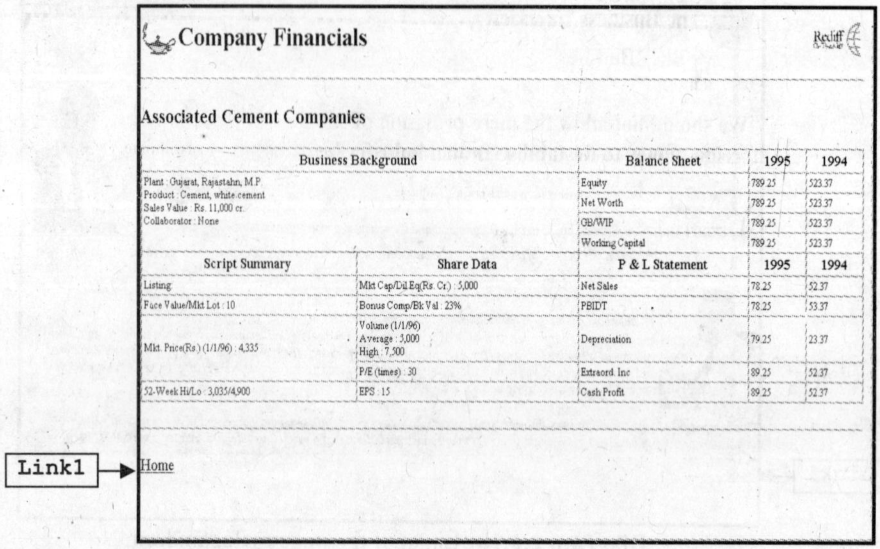

Diagram 2.2.2b: Links of the page fintabl2.htm.

The **fintabl2.html page** link and it's corresponding file name:

Link1	2ndhome.html

Output For ladakh.html called from the 2ndhome.html page [Data Warehouse]

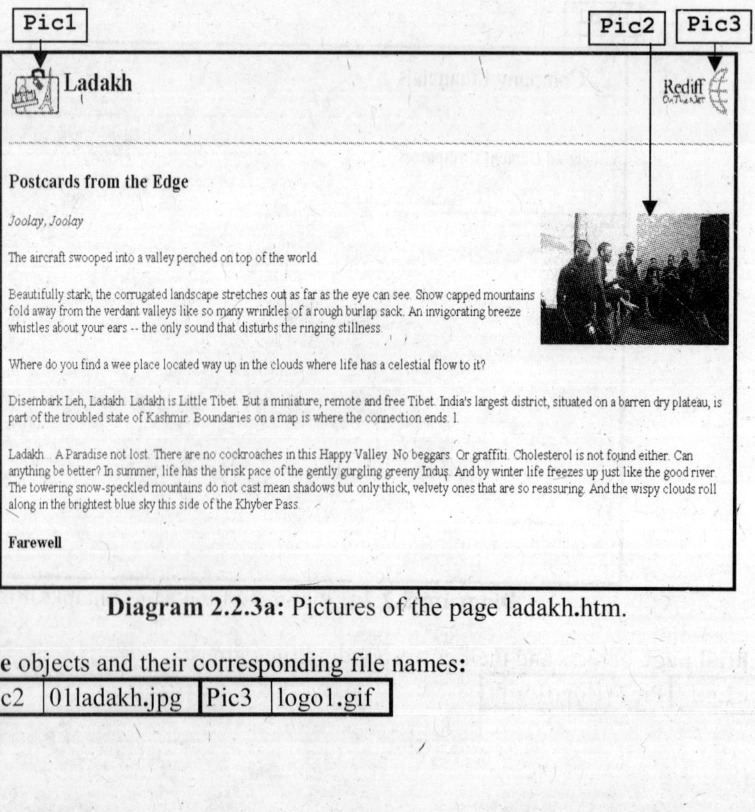

Diagram 2.2.3a: Pictures of the page ladakh.htm.

The **ladakh.html page** objects and their corresponding file names:

Pic1	travel2.gif	Pic2	01ladakh.jpg	Pic3	logo1.gif

Output For aquarium.html called from the 2ndhome.html page [The Enchanting Kingdom]

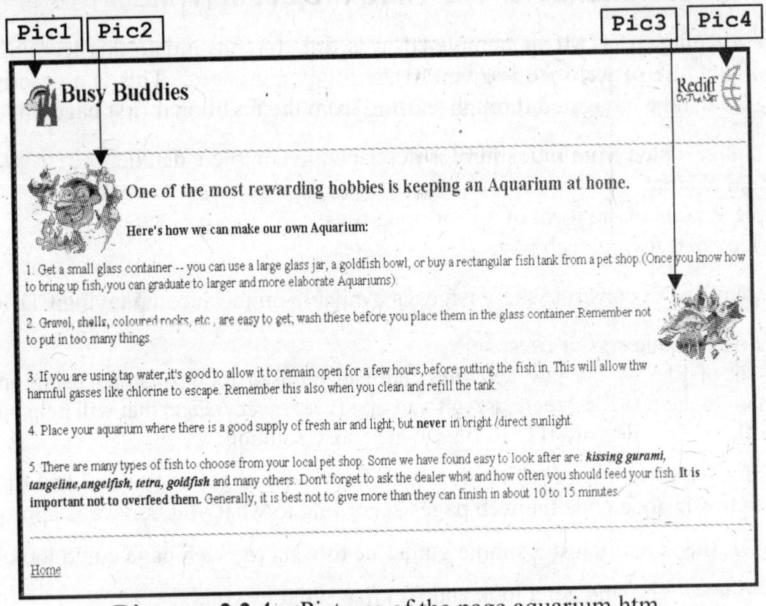

Diagram 2.2.4a: Pictures of the page aquarium.htm.

The **aquarium.html page** objects and their corresponding file names:

Pic1	kids2.gif	Pic2	aqua1.jpg	Pic3	aqua2.jpg	Pic4	logo1.gif

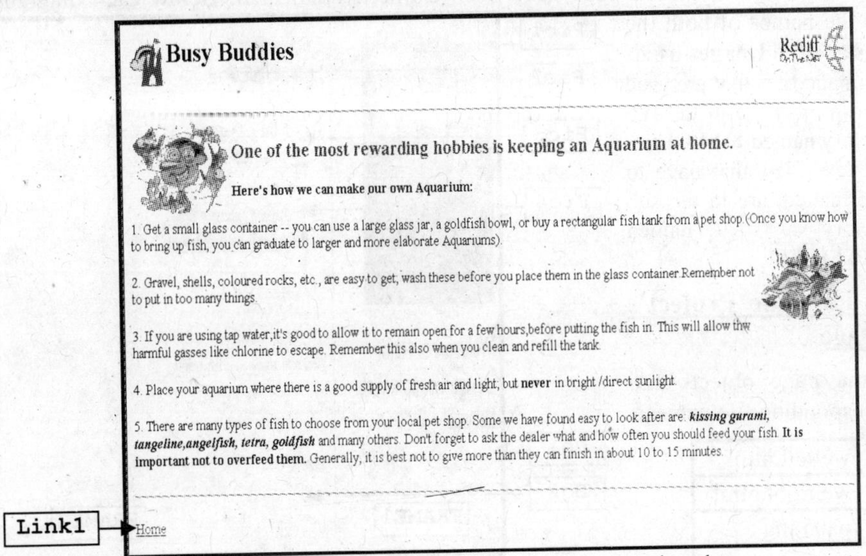

Diagram 2.2.4b: Links of the page aqurium.htm.

The **aquarium.html page** link and it's corresponding file name:

Link1	2ndhome.html

Project Specifications For The Third Project In HTML

Since the learning of HTML is completed, it is time to consolidate this learning by building a small web site. The structure of web site is given in the following pages. This is a description of how the pages of this web site will be navigated through starting from the traditional first page, index.html.

Each web page called from index.html is described in complete detail.

- Textual content
- Simple visuals in the form of .gif or .jpeg files
- The look and feel of each page

The files required to construct these pages is available on the accompanying CD-ROM for immediate use.

There are two unique sets of files:

- One set of files, is the raw text files that can be used for formatting using appropriate HTML tags. In addition to the text files, there are .gif and .jpg (*where necessary*) that will help build the web site.
- The other set of files, are HTML files, which are a solution.

If required run the HTML files first in a Web Browser and get a look and feel of what the project could be like. Once this is done code the web pages according to what you believe is appropriate.

Each HTML file is really just a simple guideline to what the web page could look like.

Feel free to improvise and get a look and feel that satisfies you.

For your guidance:
A broad idea of the HTML pages of the project is given in the diagrams below.

The images and links of each page have been explicitly indicated. Below each diagram is a table that indicates the names of both the **Text** files and the **Images** used.

- The image files that are used in the project are in the sub directory named **IMAGES**.
- The Text files, that have to be formatted, are in the sub directory named **TEXTFILES**.

Output For The Project's Home Page

The **Home page** objects and their corresponding file names:

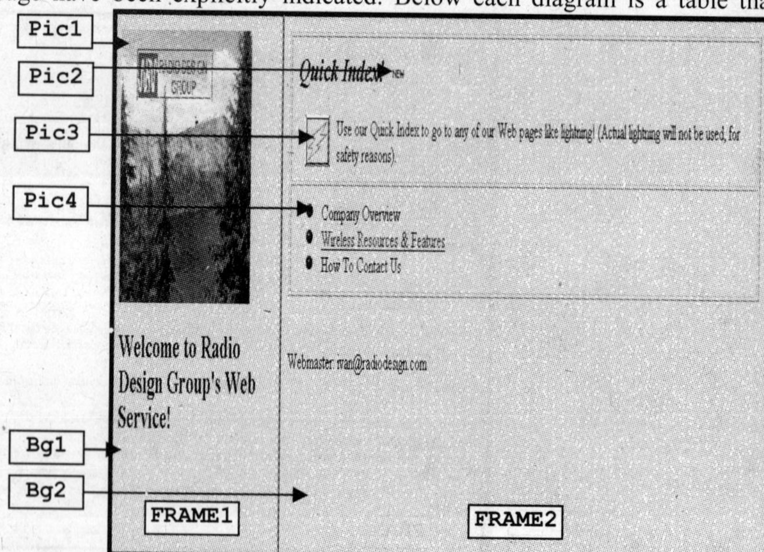

Diagram 3.1a: Pictures of the Home page welfrm.htm.

Frame1	welleft.html
Frame2	welright.html
Bg1	pa05.jpg
Bg2	pa05.jpg
Pic1	rdglogo.jpg
Pic2	new.gif
Pic3	ltngbutn.gif
Pic4	blueb.gif

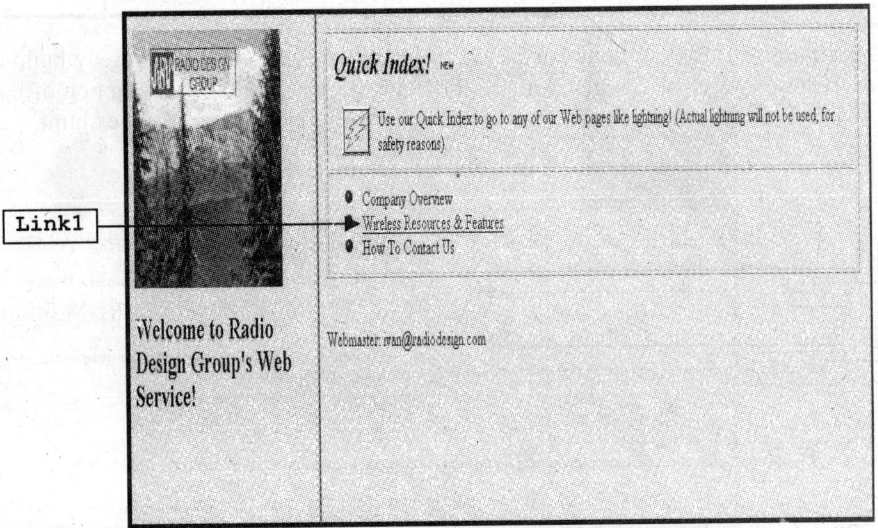

Diagram 3.1b: Link of the Home page welright.html in the right side frame for welfrm.html.

The **Home page** link and it's corresponding file name:

Link1	hwitwrks1.html

Output For hwitwrks1.html called from the Home page [Wireless Resource & Features]

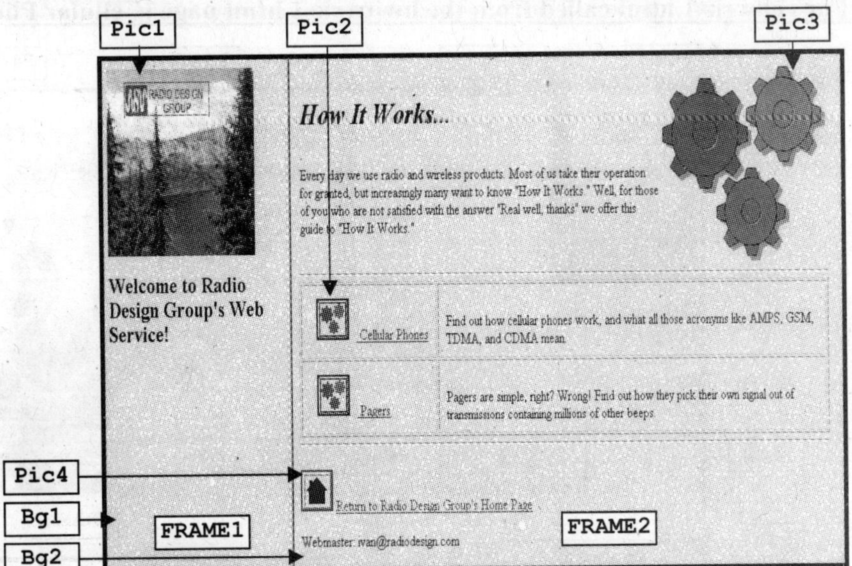

Diagram 3.2a: Pictures of the page hwitwrks1.htm in the right side frame for welfrm.htm.

The **hwitwrks1.html page** objects and their corresponding file names:

Frame1	welleft.html	Bg1	pa05.jpg	Pic1	rdglogo.jpg	Pic3	gears.gif
Frame2	welright.html	Bg2	pa05.jpg	Pic2	gearbutn.gif	Pic4	house.gif

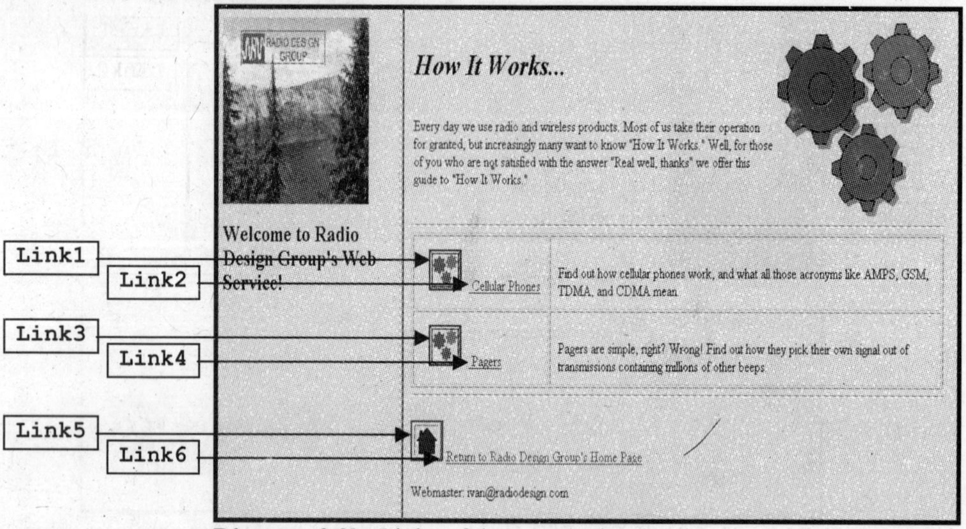

Diagram 3.2b: Links of the page hwitwrks1.htm in the right side frame for welfrm.htm.

The **hwitwrks1.html page** links and their corresponding file names:

Link1	cellwrks1.html	Link3	pgrwrks1.html	Link5	welright.html
Link2	cellwrks1.html	Link4	pgrwrks1.html	Link6	welright.html

Output For cellwrks1.html called from the hwitwrks1.html page [Cellular Phones]

Diagram 3.3a: Pictures of the page cellwrks1.htm in the right side frame for welfrm.htm.

The **cellwrks1.html page** objects and their corresponding file names:

Frame1	welleft.html	Bg1	pa05.jpg	Pic1	rdglogo.jpg	Pic3	blueb.gif	Pic5	house.gif
Frame2	welright.html	Bg2	pa05.jpg	Pic2	redlogo.gif	Pic4	mancell.jpg		

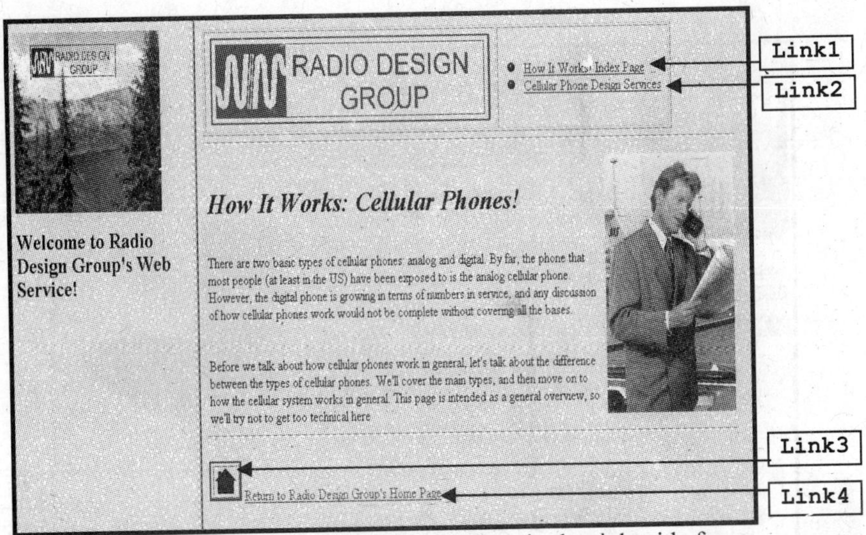

Diagram 3.3b: Links of the page cellwrks1.htm in the right side frame for welfrm.htm.

The **cellwrks1.html page** links and their corresponding file names:

Link1	hwitwrks1.html	Link2	pager1.html	Link3	welright.html	Link4	welright.html

Output For pgrwrks1.html called from the hwitwrks1.html page [Cellular Phones]

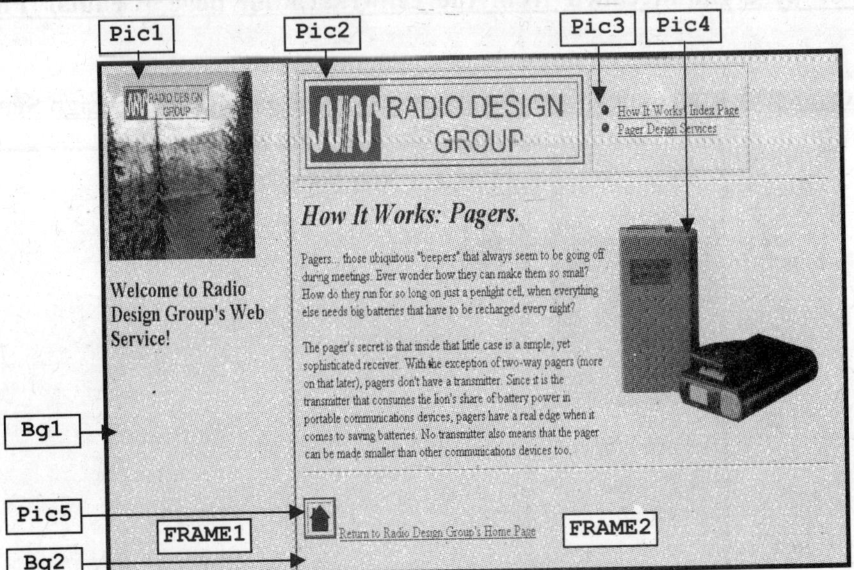

Diagram 3.4a: Pictures of the page pgrwrks1.htm in the right side frame for welfrm.htm.

The **pgrwrks1.html page** objects and their corresponding file names:

Frame1	welleft.html	Bg1	pa05.jpg	Pic1	rdglogo.jpg	Pic3	blueb.gif	Pic5	house.gif
Frame2	welright.html	Bg2	pa05.jpg	Pic2	redlogo.gif	Pic4	pager.gif		

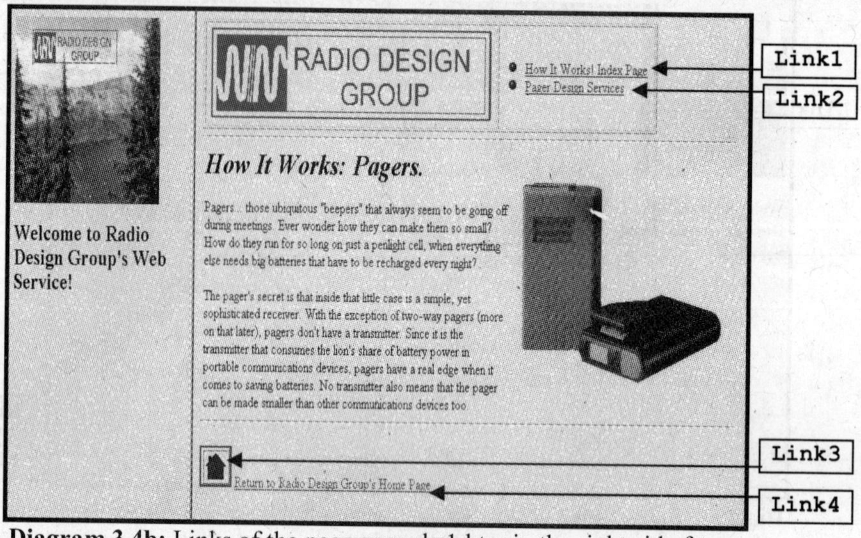

Diagram 3.4b: Links of the page pgrwrks1.htm in the right side frame for welfrm.htm.

The **pgrwrks1.html page** links and their corresponding file names:

Link1	hwitwrks1.html	Link2	pager1.html	Link3	welright.html	Link4	welright.html

<u>Output For pager1.html called from the cellwrks1.html page [Cellular Phones Design Services]</u>

OR

<u>Output For pager1.html called from the pgrwrks1.html page [Pager Design Services]</u>

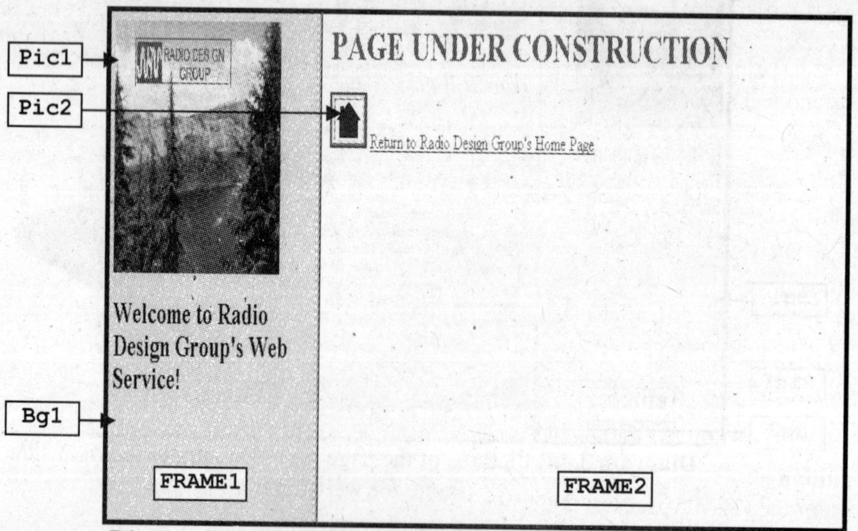

Diagram 3.5a: Pictures of the page pager1.htm in the right side frame for welfrm.htm.

The **pager1.html page** objects and their corresponding file names:

Frame1	welleft.html	Frame2	welright.html	Bg1	pa05.jpg	Pic1	rdglogo.jpg	Pic2	house.gif

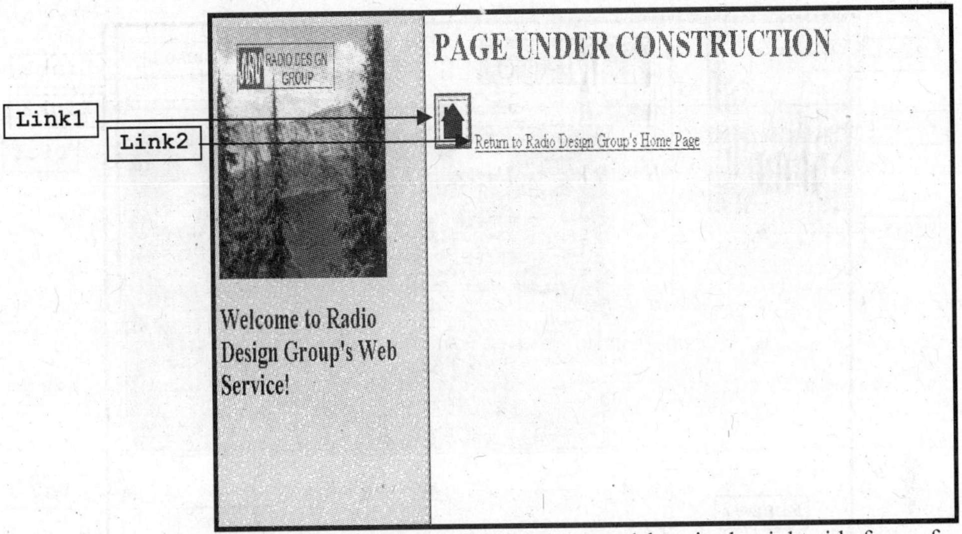

Diagram 3.5b: Links of the page pager1.htm in the right side frame for welfrm.htm.

The **pager1.html page** links and their corresponding file names:

Link1	welright.html	Link2	welright.html

Project Specifications For The Fourth Project In HTML

Since the learning of HTML is completed, it is time to consolidate this learning by building a small web site. The structure of web site is given in the following pages. This is a description of how the pages of this web site will be navigated through starting from the traditional first page, index.html.

Each web page called from index.html is described in complete detail.

- Textual content
- Simple visuals in the form of .gif or .jpeg files
- The look and feel of each page

The files required to construct these pages is available on the accompanying CD-ROM for immediate use.

There are two unique sets of files:

- One set of files, is the raw text files that can be used for formatting using appropriate HTML tags. In addition to the text files, there are .gif and .jpg (*where necessary*) that will help build the web site.
- The other set of files, are HTML files, which are a solution.

If required run the HTML files first in a Web Browser and get a look and feel of what the project could be like. Once this is done code the web pages according to what you believe is appropriate.

Each HTML file is really just a simple guideline to what the web page could look like.

Feel free to improvise and get a look and feel that satisfies you.

For your guidance:
A broad idea of the HTML pages of the project is given in the diagrams below.

The images and links of each page have been explicitly indicated. Below each diagram is a table that indicates the names of both the **Text** files and the **Images** used.

- The image files that are used in the project are in the sub directory named **IMAGES**.
- The Text files, that have to be formatted, are in the sub directory named **TEXTFILES**.

Output For The Project's Home Page

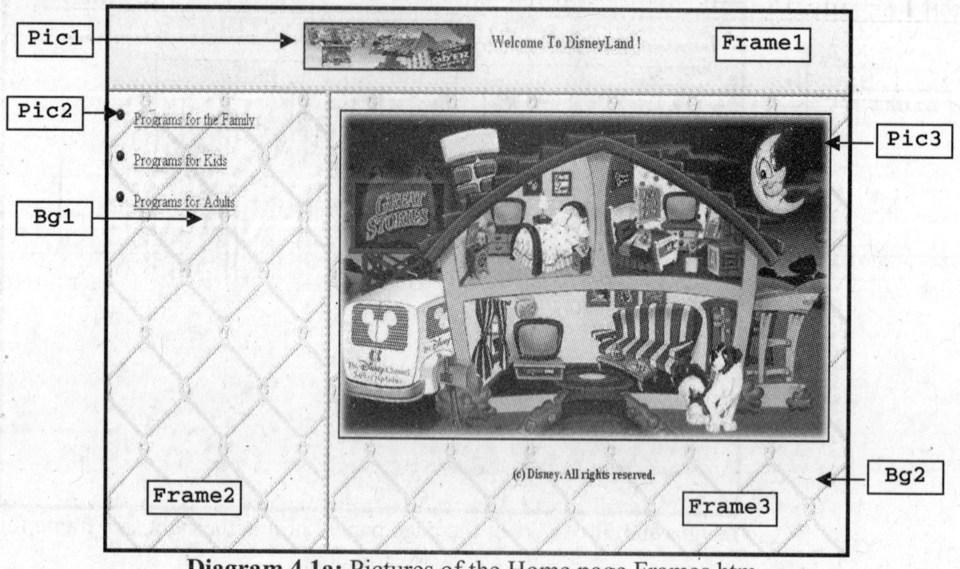

Diagram 4.1a: Pictures of the Home page Frames.htm.

The **Home page** objects and their corresponding file names:

Bg1	pinkwhit.gif	Pic1	blueb.gif	Pic2	blueb.gif	Pic3	house_sp.gif
Bg2	pinkwhit.gif	Frame1	Head.html	Frame2	Index.html	Frame3	Home.html

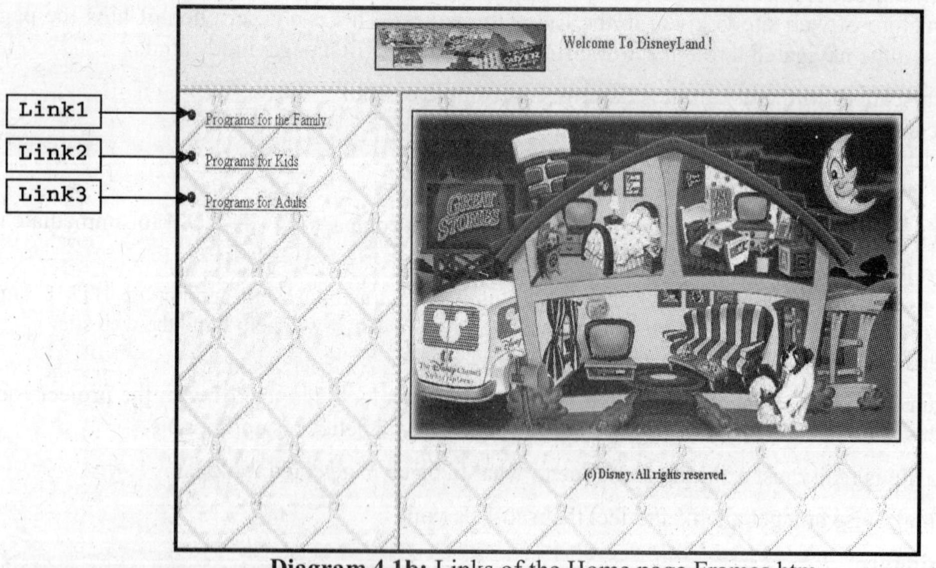

Diagram 4.1b: Links of the Home page Frames.htm.

The **Home page** links and their corresponding file names:

Link1	index18.html	Link2	index19.html	Link3	Index20.html

Output For index18.html called from the Home page [Programs for the Family]

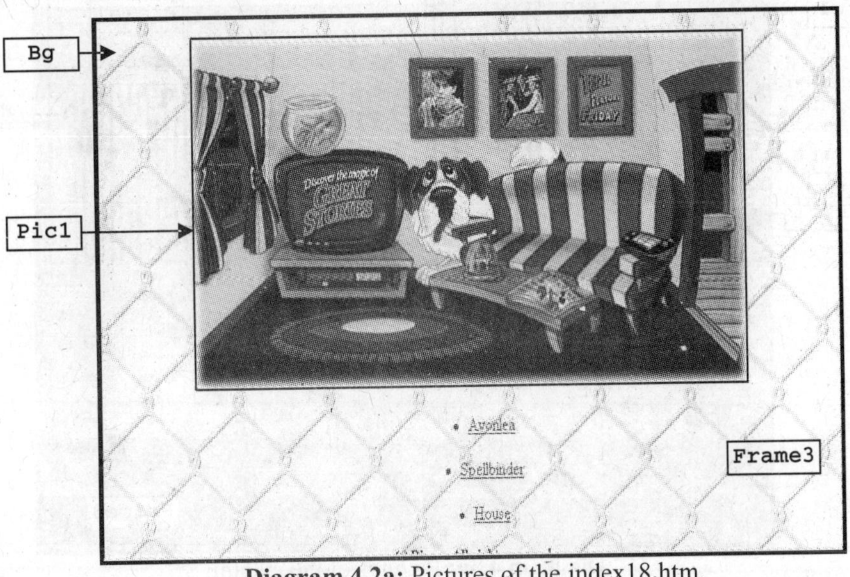

Diagram 4.2a: Pictures of the index18.htm.

The **Home page** objects and their corresponding file names:

Bg	pinkwhit.gif	Pic1	family_r.jpg

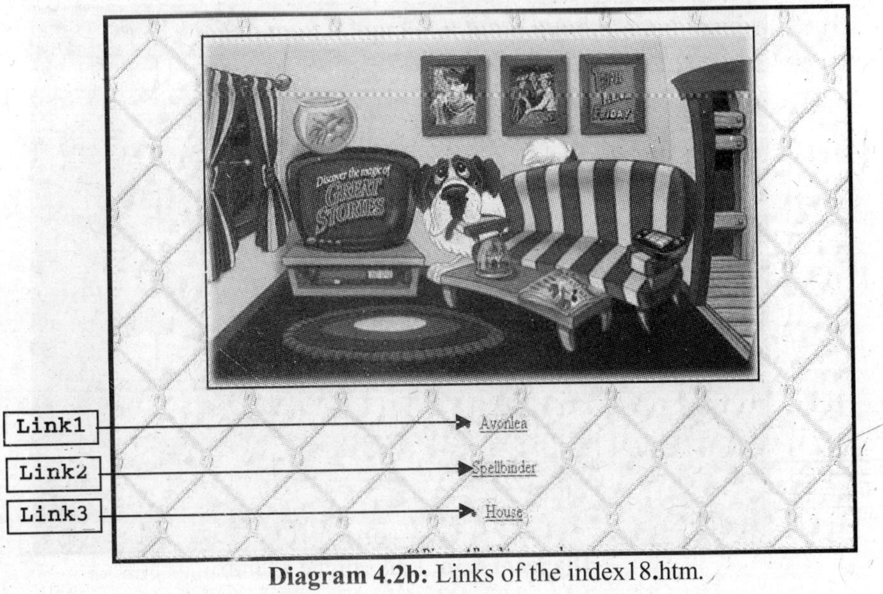

Diagram 4.2b: Links of the index18.htm.

The **Home page** links and their corresponding file names:

Link1	av.html	Link2	sb.html	Link3	home.html

Output For av.html called from the index18.html page [Avonles]

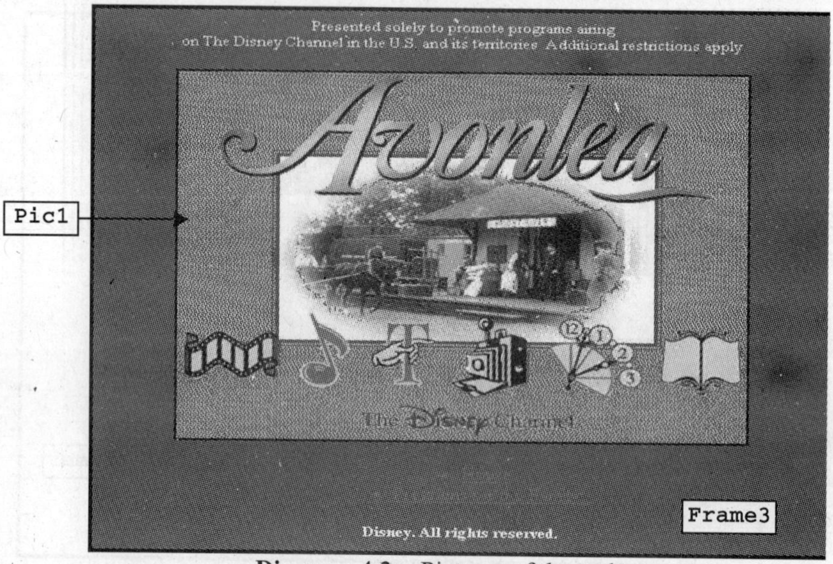

Diagram 4.3a: Pictures of the av.htm.

The **av.html page** objects and their corresponding file names:

Pic1	av2h.gif

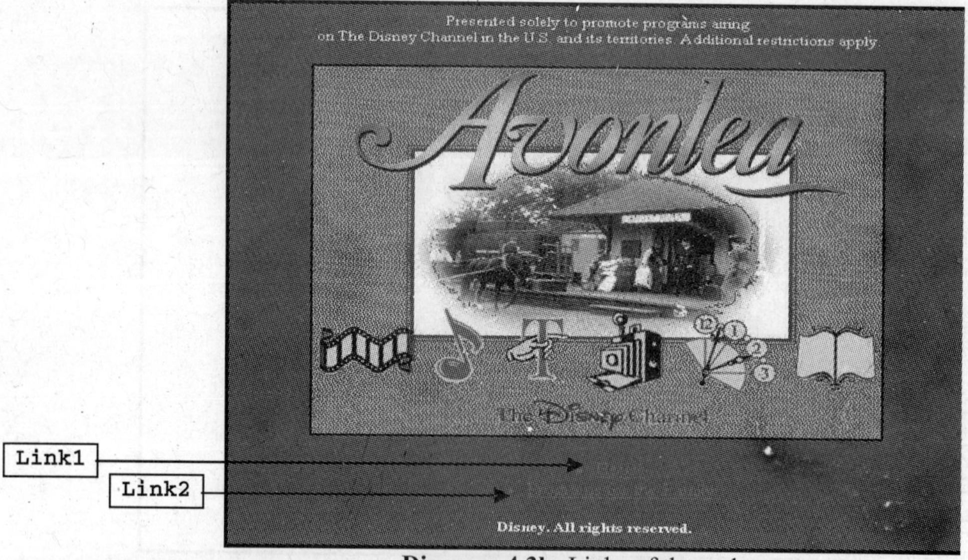

Diagram 4.3b: Links of the av.htm.

The **av.html page** links and their corresponding file names:

Link1	home.html	Link2	index18.html

Output For sb.html called from the index18.html page [Spellbinder]

Diagram 4.4a: Pictures of the sb.htm.

The **sb.html page** objects and their corresponding file names:

Pic1	sb2h.gif

Diagram 4.4b: Links of the sb.htm.

The **sb.html page** links and their corresponding file names:

Link1	home.html	Link2	index18.html

Output For index19.html called from the Index page [Programs for Kids]

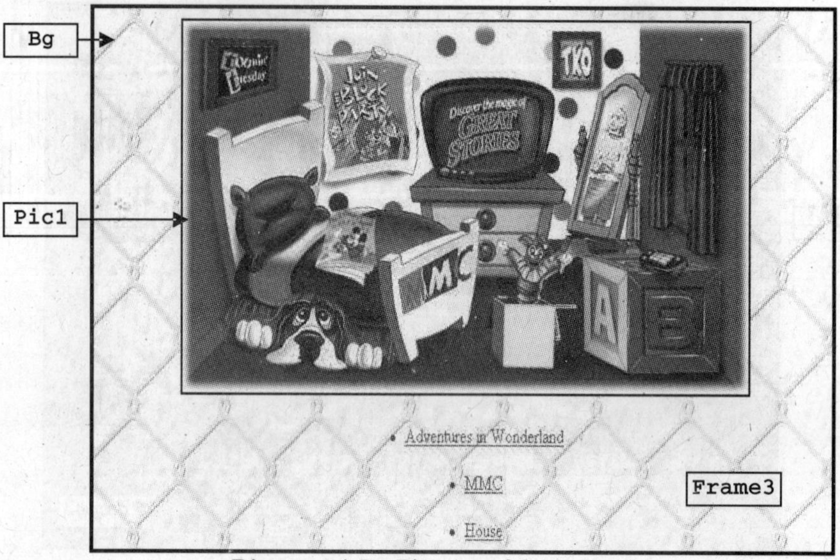

Diagram 4.5a: Pictures of the index19.htm.

The **index19.html page** objects and their corresponding file names:

Bg	pinkwhit.gif	Pic1	kids_roo.jpg

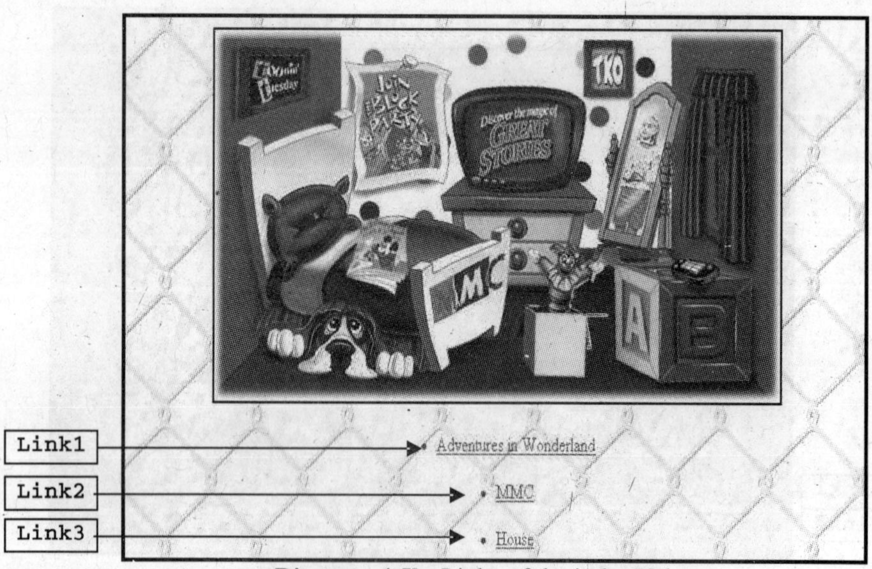

Diagram 4.5b: Links of the index19.htm.

The **index19.html page** links and their corresponding file names:

Link1	ad.html	Link2	mm.html	Link3	home.html

Output For ad.html called from the index19.html page [Adventures in Wonderland]

Diagram 4.6a: Pictures of the ad.htm.

The **ad.html page** objects and their corresponding file names:

Pic1	ad2h.gif

Diagram 4.6b: Links of the ad.htm.

The **ad.html page** links and their corresponding file names:

Link1	home.html	Link2	index19.html

Output For mm.html called from the index19.html page [MMC]

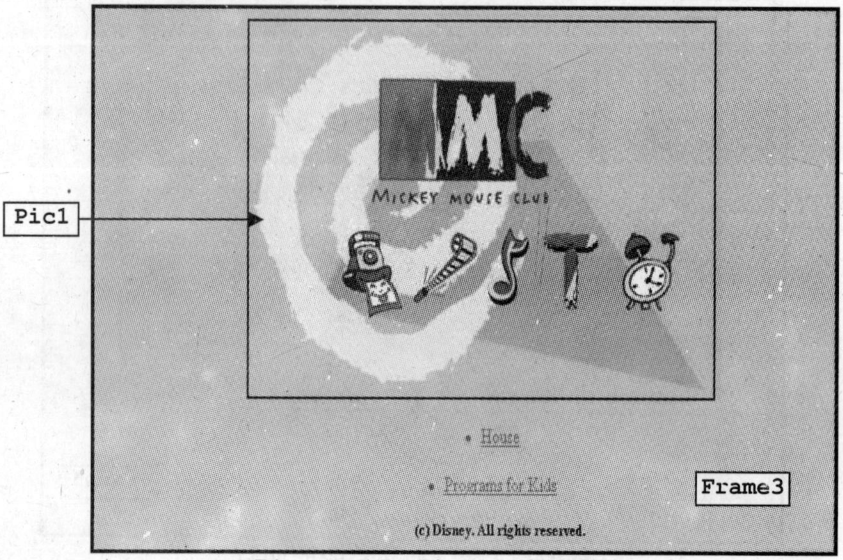

Diagram 4.7a: Pictures of the mm.htm.

The **mm.html page** objects and their corresponding file names:

Pic1	mm2h.gif

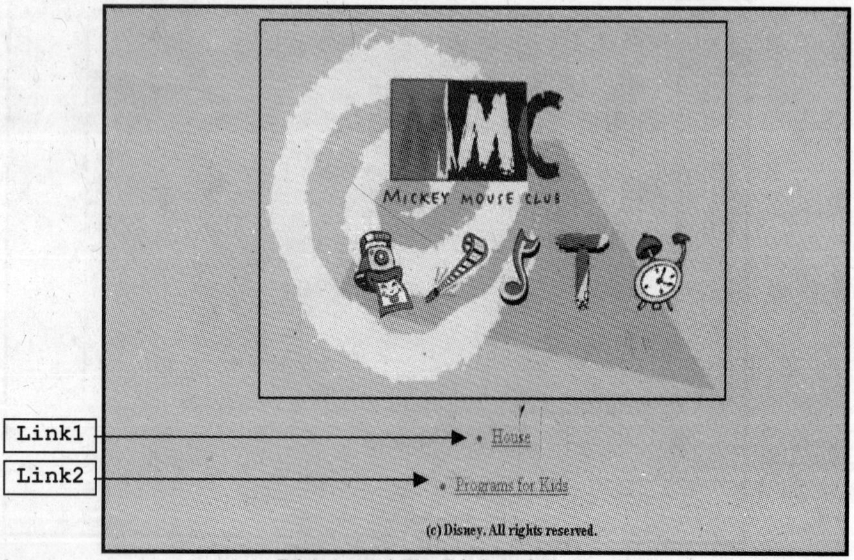

Diagram 4.7b: Links of the mm.htm.

The **mm.html page** links and their corresponding file names:

Link1	home.html	Link2	index19.html

Output For index20.html called from the Index page [Programs for Adults]

Diagram 4.8a: Pictures of the index20.htm.

The **index20.html page** objects and their corresponding file names:

Bg	pinkwhit.gif	Pic1	adult_ro.jpg

Diagram 4.8b: Links of the index20.htm.

The **index20.html page** links and their corresponding file names:

Link1	bh.html	Link2	al.html	Link3	home.html

Output For bh.html called from the index20.html page [The Best of Hollywood]

Diagram 4.9a: Pictures of the bh.htm.

The **bh.html page** objects and their corresponding file names:

Pic1	bh2h.gif	Pic2	bhlines2h.gif

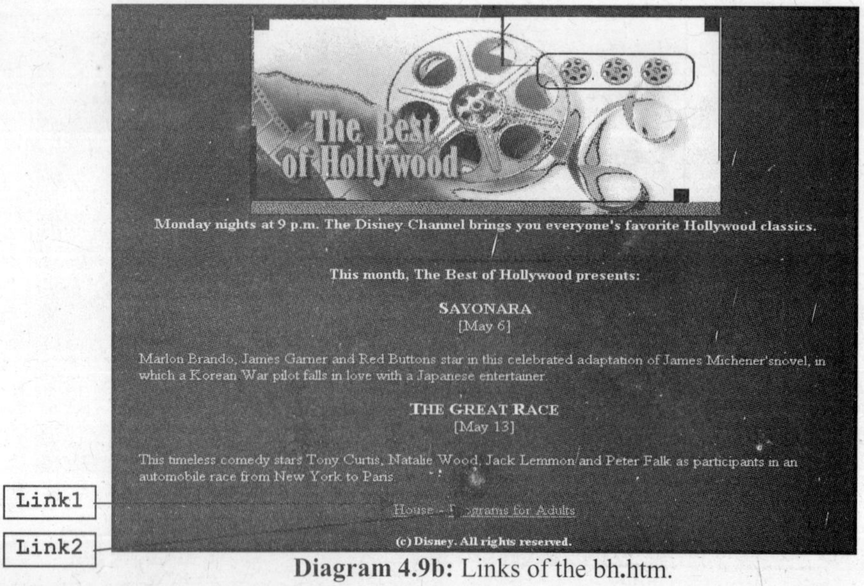

Diagram 4.9b: Links of the bh.htm.

The **bh.html page** links and their corresponding file names:

Link1	home.html	Link2	index20.html

Output For al.html called from the index20.html page [The American Legacy]

Diagram 4.10a: Pictures of the al.htm.

The **al.html page** objects and their corresponding file names:

Pic1	al2h.gif	Pic2	allines2h.gif

Diagram 4.10b: Links of the al.htm.

The **al.html page** links and their corresponding file names:

Link1	home.html	Link2	index20.html

Output For home.html called from the all page [Programs for the Family]

Diagram 4.11: Pictures of the home.htm.

The **home.html page** objects and their corresponding file names:

Bg	pinkwhit.gif	Pic1	house_sp.gif

ANSWERS TO SELF REVIEW QUESTIONS

1. INTERNET BASICS

FILL IN THE BLANKS

1. Gateway
2. Web Server Software
3. Physical Domain
4. InterNIC
5. TCP/IP
6. HTTP
7. Index.html

TRUE OR FALSE

8. True
9. True
10. False

2. INTRODUCTION TO HTML

FILL IN THE BLANKS

1. Hyper Text Markup Language
2. Server, Client, Web Pages, Web Developer
3. Transmission Control Protocol/Internet Protocol
4. <HEAD> </HEAD>, <BODY> </BODY>
5. <P>

TRUE OR FALSE

6. False
7. True
8. True
9. True
10. False
11. False

3. LISTS

FILL IN THE BLANKS

1. FILLROUND
2. START
3. Definition Description

TRUE OR FALSE

4. True
5. False
6. False
7. True

4. ADDING GRAPHICS TO HTML DOCUMENTS

FILL IN THE BLANKS

1. .GIF and .JPG
2. <IMG>
3. WIDTH and HEIGHT
4. BORDER
5. VSPACE
6. ALT

TRUE OR FALSE

7. False
8. True
9. True
10. True

5. TABLES

FILL IN THE BLANKS

1. Rows, Columns
2. <Table>, </Table>
3. CELLSPACING
4. Header, Data
5. ALIGN
6. WIDTH
7. CELLPADDING
8. <TR>

TRUE OR FALSE

9. True
10. False
11. False
12. True

6. LINKING DOCUMENTS

FILL IN THE BLANKS

1. Hyperlinks
2. Blue
3. External, Internal
4. Named Anchors
5. #
6. Hot regions
7. Rectangle, circle, polygon & default

TRUE OR FALSE

8. False
9. True
10. False

7. FRAMES

FILL IN THE BLANKS

1. Frames
2. <FRAMESET>
3. <FRAME>
4. SRC
5. NORESIZE
6. SCROLLING
7. NAME

TRUE OR FALSE

8. False
9. False
10. True

SOLUTIONS TO HANDS ON EXERCISES

2. INTRODUCTION TO HTML

```
<HTML>
    <HEAD><TITLE>Password hackers and crackers! </TITLE></HEAD>
    <BODY BGColor="Beige">
        <H2><I><CENTER>Beware of password hackers and crackers!</CENTER></I></H2><HR/>
        <H4>The threat of hackers and crackers is for real, and is alike for everyone. If the security breach
        at the Bhabha Atomic Research Center last year by the hacker group milwOrm didn't convince
        you of their capabilities, then consider this: James Davis aka jdavis_4, a resident of <B><FONT
        Face="Comic Sans MS" Color=RED> www.geocities.com/SiliconValley/Bit/2483 </B></FONT>
        homestead community on the Internet, might just be reading your e-mail in your mailbox right
        now, or using your account for some benign Internet surfing, or exchanging it with someone else
        on the Net for more such accounts!<BR /> Surprised? Or scared? <P>Whatever it is, jdavis_4
        claims in his home page-Free VSNL passwords-that he has got exactly 108 working VSNL
        passwords (and growing daily), <I>36 Satyam, 31 MTNL, 11 WmiNet and 23 Mantra Online</I>
        passwords.</H4>
    </BODY>
</HTML>
```

3. LISTS

```
<HTML>
    <HEAD><TITLE>Lists</TITLE></HEAD>
    <BODY>
    // <B>Example on Unordered List</B> //
        <UL TYPE=FILLROUND>
            <LI>Sportstar
            <LI>Business Week
            <LI>Time
        </UL>
    // <B>Example on Ordered List</B> //
        <OL TYPE="i" START=4>
            <LI> Sportstar
            <LI> Business Week
            <LI> Time
        </OL>
    // <B>Example on Definition List</B> //
        <DL>
            <DT>Sports Magazine<DD>Sportstar
            <DT>Business Magazine<DD>Business Week
            <DT>General Magazine<DD>Time
        </DL>
    </BODY>
</HTML>
```

4. ADDING GRAPHICS TO HTML DOCUMENTS

```
<HTML>
    <HEAD><TITLE>WORLD WIDE WEB</TITLE></HEAD>
    <BODY BackGround="../images/texture1.gif">
        <CENTER><B><I>THE INTERCITY WEB</I></B><BR/>
            <IMG Src="../images/House.GIF" Border="4"><BR/><BR/></CENTER>
        <IMG Align=LEFT Height=100 Src="../images/Javacup.GIF" Width="100">
        <B><I>THE WORLD WIDE WEB</I></B><BR/>
        <I>The World Wide Web, or Simply the Web, has been a 'Killer App' of the Internet. Certainly its
        capability to display text and graphics and provide access to other pages and information has made
        it the fastest growing component of the Internet. Major online services are America Online,
        CompuServe and Prodigy.</I><BR/><BR/><BR/>
        <IMG Align="RIGHT" Height="100" Src="../images/Computer.GIF" Width="100">
        <B><I>GET CONNECTED</I></B><BR/>
        <I>A way to access the web is to get an account with Internet Service Provider, or ISP. These
        accounts include accounts include access to the World Wide Web and other Internet resources,
        and often provide space to store Web pages one will create. A very helpful feature of the web is
        the capability to move from page to page by selecting specific highlighted words and prases or
        images, which are called as links.</I><BR/><BR/><BR/>
    </BODY>
</HTML>
```

5. TABLES

```
<HTML>
    <HEAD><TITLE>Table Test</TITLE></HEAD>
    <BODY BackGround="../images/texture1.gif">
        <TABLE Align=CENTER Border=2 CellPadding=3 >
        <CAPTION><B>Time Table And Fare List</B><CAPTION><TR>
            <TH RowSpan=2>Name of Train</TH>
            <TH RowSpan =2>Place</TH>
            <TH RowSpan =2>Destination</TH>
            <TH ColSpan=2> Time</TH>
            <TH RowSpan =2>Fare</TH>
        </TR><TR><TH>Arrival</TH><TH>Departure</TH></TR><TR>
            <TD>Rajdhani Express</TD>
            <TD Align=CENTER>Bombay</TD>
            <TD Align=CENTER>Delhi</TD>
            <TD Align=CENTER>07.30</TD>
            <TD Align=CENTER>08.45</TD>
            <TD Align=RIGHT>Rs 989.00</TD>
        </TR><TR>
            <TD>Madras Mail</TD>
            <TD Align=CENTER>Bombay</TD>
            <TD Align=CENTER>Madras</TD>
            <TD Align=CENTER>09.00</TD>
            <TD Align=CENTER>10.15</TD>
            <TD Align=RIGHT>Rs 450.00</TD>
        </TR><TR>
```

```
        <TD>Konya Express</TD>
        <TD Align=CENTER>Bombay</TD>
        <TD Align=CENTER>Banglore</TD>
        <TD Align=CENTER>11.30</TD>
        <TD Align=CENTER>12.25</TD>
        <TD Align=RIGHT>Rs 645.00</TD>
    </TR><TR>
        <TD>Konkan Express</TD>
        <TD Align=CENTER>Bombay</TD>
        <TD Align=CENTER>Manglore</TD>
        <TD Align=CENTER>13.30</TD>
        <TD Align=CENTER>14.45</TD>
        <TD Align=RIGHT>Rs 756.00</TD>
    </TR><TR>
        <TD>Deccan Express</TD>
        <TD Align=CENTER>Bombay</TD>
        <TD Align=CENTER>Pune</TD>
        <TD Align=CENTER>16.00</TD>
        <TD Align=CENTER>17.30</TD>
        <TD Align=RIGHT>Rs 345.00</TD>
    </TR></TABLE>
  </BODY>
</HTML>
```

6. LINKING DOCUMENTS

Code For Menu.html:

```
<HTML>
    <BODY>
            <span style="color:Green; font-family:Arial, Helvetica, sans-serif">Welcome to our
homepage.<BR/> This page has links to the website of </span>
            <span style="color:Brown; font-family:Arial, Helvetica, sans-serif; font-size:12pt;"><B>
ABC Lever Inc.</B></span>
            <P>
            <span style="color:Green; font-family:Arial, Helvetica, sans-serif;">
                    For further information click on any one of the following:
                    <UL>
                            <LI><A href="AboutUs.html">About ABC Lever Inc.</A></LI>
                            <LI><A href="AboutUs.html#SECTION 1">
                                    Contact information</A></LI>
                    </UL>
            </span>
            </P>
    </BODY>
</HTML>
```

Code for AboutUs.html

```
<HTML>
        <HEAD><TITLE> ABC Lever Inc. </TITLE></HEAD>
        <BODY>
                <CENTER>
                <span style="color:Brown; font-family:Arial, Helvetica, sans-serif; font-size:15pt">
                        <IMG Align="BOTTOM" Src="../images/corp.gif" /><I>ABC Lever Inc.</I>
                </span>
                </CENTER>
                <A href="#SECTION 1">Contact us</A><HR/><BR/>
                <span style="color:Blue; font-family:Arial, Helvetica, sans-serif; font-
size:"><P><B>ABC Lever Inc. is a conglomerate that has interests ranging from bodycare products to
toilet soaps.<BR/>A couple of years ago we entered the frozen food industry through mergers and
acquistions.<BR/>Last year we started our first plant to manufacture salt and this year it is wheat
flour.<BR/>Our current turnover is about Rs. 7500 cr and by the next decade we are looking at a target of
15000 cr.</B></P></span>
                <HR/>
                <P><A Name="SECTION 1"><span style="color:Green; font-family:Arial, Helvetica,
sans-serif; font-size:12pt;"><B><I>Contact Us </I></B></span></A></P>
                <HR/>
                <span style="color:RED; font-family:Arial, Helvetica, sans-serif">You can contact us at
the following address:</span>
                <P><span style="color:Blue; font-family:Arial, Helvetica, sans-serif"><B> ABC Lever
Inc.<BR/>
                        101 Maker Chambers III,<BR/>Nariman Point,<BR/>Mumbai-21<BR/>Tel
2012011
                        <P>You can also email us at
customerservice@abclever.com</P></B></span></P>
        </BODY>
</HTML>
```

7. FRAMES

Code for Handsonframe.html

```
<HTML>
    <HEAD><TITLE> Hands on</TITLE></HEAD>
    <FRAMESET Cols = "35%,*">
        <FRAME Name="First" Src="Menu.html">
        <FRAME Name="Second" Src="Desc.html">
    </FRAMESET>
</HTML>
```

Code for Menu.html

```
<HTML>
        <BODY>
                <SPAN STYLE="color:Green; font-family:Arial, Helvetica, sans-serif">
                        Click on any one of the following:
```

```
        <UL>
                <LI><A href="AboutUs.htm" Target="Second">About us</A></LI>
                <LI><A href="Contact.htm" Target="Second">Contact us</A></LI>
        </UL>
        </SPAN>
    </BODY>
</HTML>
```

Code for Desc.html

```
<HTML>
    <HEAD><TITLE> Welcome</TITLE></HEAD>
    <BODY>
        <SPAN STYLE="color:Brown; font-family:Arial, Helvetica, sans-serif; font-size:12pt">
                <B><I>Welcome</I></B>
        </SPAN>
        <HR/>
        <SPAN STYLE="color:Green; font-family:Arial, Helvetica, sans-serif; font-
size:10pt;">Thank you for visiting our website.</SPAN>
        <P>Click on any of the choices on the left.</P>
    </BODY>
</HTML>
```

Code for AboutUs.html

```
<HTML>
  <HEAD><TITLE>ABC Lever Inc.</TITLE></HEAD>
  <BODY>
  <CENTER>
    <SPAN STYLE="color:Brown; font-family:Arial, Helvetica, sans-serif; font-size:12pt">
        <IMG Align="Bottom" Src="../images/corp.gif" /><I>ABC Lever Inc.</I></SPAN>
    <HR/><BR/>
    <SPAN STYLE="color:Brown; font-family:Arial, Helvetica, sans-serif; font-size:10pt">
        <B>ABC Lever Inc. is a conglomerate that has interests ranging from bodycare products to
toilet soaps. A couple of years ago we entered the frozen food industry through mergers and acquisitions.
Last year we started our first plant to manufacture salt and this year it is wheat flour. Our current turnover
is about Rs. 7500 cr and by the next decade we are looking at a target of 15000 cr.</B>
    </SPAN>
  </CENTER>
  </BODY>
</HTML>
```

Code for Contact.html

```
<HTML>
    <HEAD><TITLE>Contact Us </TITLE></HEAD>
    <BODY><span style="color:Brown; font-size:12pt"><B><I>Contact Us </I></B></span><HR/>
    <span style="color:Green; font-size:12pt">You can contact us at the following
address:</span><span style="color:Blue; font-size:12pt"><P><B>ABC Lever Inc.<BR/></B></P>101
Maker Chambers III,<BR/>Nariman Point,<BR/>Mumbai-21<BR/>Tel 2012011<P>You can also email us
at customerservice@abclever.com</P></B></span>
    </BODY>
</HTML>
```

SECTION - II: JavaScript

8. INTRODUCTION TO JAVASCRIPT

JAVASCRIPT IN WEB PAGES

Today's web sites need to go much beyond HTML. There is a definite need to allow users, browsing through a web site, to actually interact with the web site. The web site must be intelligent enough to accept users input and dynamically structure web page content, tailor made, to a user's requirements.

This may be as simple as ensuring a web page delivered to a user, having a background color that the user is comfortable with or as complex as delivering a web page with special textual formatting for a user with visual disabilities.

Users, who browse through a web site today, prefer to choose to view what interests them. Hence even the **content** of a web page needs to be dynamic, based on what a user wishes to see.

This requires a web site development environment that will allow the creation of **Interactive** web pages. These web pages will accept input from a user. Based on the input received return customized web pages, both in content and presentation, to the user.

In the absence of any user input the web site must be intelligent enough to return a default web page containing predetermined information and text formatting.

This calls for a web site development environment with coding techniques capable of accepting a client's requests and processing these requests. The result of the processing being passed back to the client via standard HTML pages.

The need to return standard HTML pages, that map to a user's input, is due to the fact that browsers use HTTP to communicate with a web server and are designed to interpret and render HTML on a client's machine.

Capturing user requests is traditionally done via a **Form**. Hence the web site development environment needs to have the facilities to create forms.

After a form captures user input, the form must have a *built in* technique for sending the information captured back to the web server for processing. Processing user requests is generally done via scripts (*small programs*) that are based on the server.

The web site development environment should also provide the facility for **Validating** user input. Invalid user input, will either cause data to be sent back from the web server to the browser, which is not what the user wants or give rise to an error message being sent back to the browser from the web server. Neither of which would really attract repeat visits to the web site.

Hence, the web site development environment must also facilitate coding which runs in a browser at client side for data validation. Most development environments offer standard constructs for data validation. Standard programming constructs are:

- ❑ Condition checking constructs
- ❑ Case checking constructs
- ❑ Super controlled Loop constructs

Additionally, all development environments provide syntax to create and use memory variables, constants, and functions.

If the development environment is object oriented it will provide an object hierarchy to work with. An **O**bject **O**riented **P**rogramming (OOP) environment always offers event driven programming. This means that the programming environment will recognize object based events and allow the connection of code snippets to these events. When an event occurs, the code snippets will execute.

All these facilities and more are available in JavaScript.

Netscape and JavaScript

JavaScript is a scripting language (*web site development environment*) created by Netscape hence JavaScript works best with the Netscape suite of Client and Server products.

The Netscape client **browser** product is called Netscape Communicator. The default scripting language that Netscape Communicator understands is JavaScript.

One Netscape server product, from its suite of server products, is Netscape Commerce Server. The default scripting language that Netscape Commerce Server understands is JavaScript.

Database Connectivity

Netscape has a product called **Live Wire**, which permits server side, JavaScript code, to connect to **R**elational **D**ata**B**ase **M**anagement **S**ystems (RDBMS). RDBMS such as Oracle, MS SQL Server, MySQL, mSQL and a host of other widely used relational databases, which generally use ANSI SQL as their natural language. **Live Wire** database drivers also support a number of non-relational databases.

Client side JavaScript

Client-side JavaScript is traditionally embedded into a standard HTML program. JavaScript is embedded between the **<SCRIPT> . . . </SCRIPT>** HTML tags. These tags are embedded within the **<HEAD> . . . </HEAD>** or **<BODY> . . . </BODY>** tags of the HTML program.

JavaScript is embedded into an HTML program because JavaScript uses the *filename*.html and the HTTP protocol to transport itself from the web server to the client's browser where the JavaScript executes and processes client information.

Only a browser that is JavaScript enabled will be able to interpret JavaScript code. Netscape Communicator does this best as JavaScript is the natural language of Netscape Communicator.

Microsoft's Internet Explorer also interprets JavaScript. However, Internet Explorer latest releases support an old version of JavaScript. Hence, the total functionality of the latest release of JavaScript as is available in Netscape Communicator is not available in Internet Explorer.

Note

The default scripting language of Internet Explorer is VB Script. Netscape Communicator does not support VB Script.

Capturing User Input

Web site interactivity starts from being able to capture user input. The **<FORM> . . . </FORM>** HTML tags can be used to create a user **Request-form**. Between these HTML tags the HTML **<INPUT> </INPUT>** tags can be used to instantiate HTML objects in the HTML form to facilitate the capture of user data.

The HTML objects used in HTML form creation are **Text**, **TextArea**, **Radio Buttons**; **Push Buttons**, **Check Boxes** and so on. These will be passed as **values** to the TYPE attribute of the **<INPUT> . . . </INPUT>** tags as will be seen in later chapters. Once the HTML form has been coded in *filename*.html JavaScript can be embedded in the same HTML file to make it interactive and facilitate client side data validation and/or processing.

The concept being that standard HTML form objects are used to *capture* user input while client side, JavaScript (*embedded in the HTML file*) is used to *validate* and/or *process* such user input. The application of *validation rules* to the data captured by HTML form objects and *error handling* is conveniently done using JavaScript which executes in the client's browser.

Once user input passes the validation tests applied, and/or has been processed appropriately by client side, JavaScript, the form data captured will have to be passed backward to the web server from where the HTML file originated.

At the web server an appropriate program (*written in JavaScript, VB Script, CGI-PERL, Java and so on*) will accept this user input. Based on user input information will be assembled on the web server, converted to an HTML file (*page*) and returned to the user. Such an HTML page is created on **Demand**.

An HTML file (*page*) created on demand, based on user input, is a dynamically created HTML page. This then is a clear indication of a dynamic and interactive web site.

HTML itself is static. HTML allows a very minimum interaction with users by providing hyperlinks. Truly interactive pages as described above, cannot be created using standard HTML **Tags** alone. Embedding JavaScript in an HTML program does this

For instance, a Web Site can be created and hosted on a web server to take orders for products. Typically, an HTML form is used to capture '*User orders for products*'. At the same time, form data (*the user order's*) validation must be done. For example:

- ❑ Orders should be accepted only for products which are available
- ❑ Any quantity ordered should not exceed the quantity currently available
- ❑ The order date should be set to the current date
- ❑ The quantity required cannot be left blank
- ❑ The place of delivery (*address*) cannot be left blank

HTML alone cannot do any of this. At the maximum, HTML can provide an elegant interface for capturing **Order** information. HTML (as mentioned earlier) does not provide any techniques for validating user entries. This makes it necessary to introduce client side JavaScript in the HTML (*page*) program, which extends the functionality of the web page by introducing client side data processing.

JAVASCRIPT

JavaScript is an object-oriented language that allows creation of interactive Web Pages. JavaScript allows user entries, which are loaded into an HTML form to be processed as required. This empowers a web site to return site information according to a user's requests.

JavaScript offers several advantages to a Web developer such as a short development cycle, ease of learning, small size scripts and so on. The strengths of JavaScript can be easily and quickly used to extend the functionality of HTML pages, already on a web site.

The Advantages Of JavaScript

An Interpreted Language: JavaScript is an interpreted language, which requires no compilation steps. This provides an easy development process. The syntax is completely interpreted by the browser just as it interprets HTML tags.

Embedded Within HTML: JavaScript does not require any special or separate editor for programs to be written, edited or compiled. It can be written in any text editor like Notepad, along with appropriate HTML tags, and saved as *filename.html.* HTML files with embedded JavaScript commands can then be read and interpreted by any browser that is JavaScript enabled.

Minimal Syntax - Easy to Learn: By learning just a few commands and simple rules of syntax, complete applications can be built using JavaScript.

Quick Development: Because JavaScript does not require time-consuming compilations, scripts can be developed in a short period of time. This is enhanced by the fact that many GUI interface features, such as alerts, prompts, confirm boxes, and other GUI elements, are handled by client side JavaScript, the browser and HTML code.

Designed for Simple, Small Programs: It is well suited to implement simple, small programs (*for example, a unit conversion calculator between miles and kilometers, or pounds and kilograms*). Such programs can be easily written and executed at an acceptable speed using JavaScript. In addition, they can be easily integrated into a web page.

Performance: JavaScript can be written such that the HTML files are fairly compact and quite small. This minimizes storage requirements on the web server and download time for the client.

Additionally, because JavaScript programs are usually included in the same file as the HTML code for a web page, they require fewer separate network accesses.

Procedural Capabilities: Every programming language needs to support facilities such as Condition checking, Looping and Branching. JavaScript provides syntax, which can be used to add such procedural capabilities to web page (*filename*.html) coding.

Designed for Programming User Events: JavaScript supports Object/Event based programming. JavaScript recognizes when a form **Button** is pressed. This event can have suitable JavaScript code attached, which will execute when the **Button Pressed** event occurs.

JavaScript can be used to implement context sensitive help. Whenever an HTML form's **Mouse** cursor **Moves Over** a button or a link on the page a helpful and informative message can be displayed in the status bar at the bottom of the browser window.

Easy Debugging and Testing: Being an interpreted language, scripts in JavaScript are tested line by line, and the errors are also listed as they are encountered, i.e. an appropriate error message along with the line number is listed for every error that is encountered. It is thus easy to locate errors, make changes, and test it again without the overhead and delay of compiling.

Platform Independence / Architecture Neutral: JavaScript is a programming language that is completely independent of the hardware on which it works. It is a language that is understood by any JavaScript enabled browser. Thus, JavaScript applications work on any machine that has an appropriate JavaScript enabled browser installed. This machine can be anywhere on the network.

Since each browser is for a specific platform, JavaScript interpretation will be with respect to the specific platform. The browser will add whatever platform specific information is required to the JavaScript while it interprets the code. Thus, JavaScript is truly platform independent. A JavaScript program developed on a Unix machine will work perfectly well on a Windows machine.

The fact that a platform specific browser, maintained at the client end, does the interpretation of JavaScript, relieves the developer of the responsibility of maintaining multiple source code files for multiple platforms.

WRITING JAVASCRIPT INTO HTML

JavaScript syntax is embedded into an HTML file. A browser reads HTML files and interprets HTML tags. Since all JavaScripts need to be included as an integral part of an HTML document when required, the browser needs to be informed that specific sections of HTML code is JavaScript. The browser will then use its built-in JavaScript engine to interpret this code.

The browser is given this information using the HTML tags **<SCRIPT> . . . </SCRIPT>**. The <SCRIPT> tag marks the beginning of a snippet of scripting code. The paired </SCRIPT> marks the end of the snippet of scripting code.

Like most other HTML tags, the <SCRIPT> tag takes in an optional attribute, as listed below:

Attributes	Description
Language	Indicates the scripting language used for writing the snippet of scripting code. If left undefined Netscape Communicator will assume JavaScript. If left undefined Internet Explorer will assume VB Script

Table 8.1

Syntax:

```
<SCRIPT LANGUAGE= "JavaScript">
    // Javascript code snippet written here
</SCRIPT>
```

BASIC PROGRAMMING TECHNIQUES

JavaScript offers the very same programming capabilities found in most programming languages. Creating variables, constants, programming constructs, user defined functions and so on.

All these programming techniques can be used in JavaScript embedded in any HTML program. These are the techniques that make JavaScript an exciting programming language that extends the functionality of HTML and makes web pages interactive.

The **<HEAD> . . . </HEAD>** tags make an ideal place to create JavaScript variables and constants and so on. This is because the head of an HTML document is always processed before the body. Placing JavaScript memory variables, constants and user defined JavaScript functions in this section of an HTML document will cause them to be defined (*by the JavaScript interpreter*) before being used. This is important because any attempt to use a variable (*or any other JavaScript object*) before it is defined, results in an error.

Variables are used to store values that can be used in other parts of a program. Variables always have a name associated with them via which they can be referenced later. When naming variables, it is good programming practice to structure a descriptive name.

Variable names can begin with an uppercase letter (A through Z), lowercase letter (a through z), and underscore character (_) or dollar sign character ($). The remaining characters can consist of letters, the underscore character, the dollar sign character or digits 0 to 9. Variable names are **case sensitive**.

Caution

STOP The dollar sign ($) character is reserved for machine generated code and should not be used in scripts. In particular it should not be used in scripts that will be run by earlier browsers that are not fully ECMAScript-compatible.

If two words are used to name a variable then it is a programming convention to start the first letter of the first word in lower case and the first letter of the second word in uppercase for example, *variableName*.

JavaScript does not allow the data type of the variable to be declared when a variable is created. The same variable may be used to hold different types of data at different times when the JavaScript code snippet runs.

Data Types And Literal

JavaScript supports four primitive types of values and supports complex types such as arrays and objects. Primitive types are types that can be assigned a single literal value such as number, string or boolean value. Literals are fixed values, which *literally* provide a value in a program.

The primitive data types that JavaScript supports are:

Number

Consists of integer and floating point numbers and the special **NaN** (*not a number*) value.

Integer literals can be represented in JavaScript in decimal, hexadecimal, and octal form.

Note

Hexadecimal and octal integers are converted to decimal before they are displayed.

Floating-point literals are used to represent numbers that require the use of a decimal point, or very large or very small numbers that must be written using exponential notation. A floating-point number must consist of either a number containing a decimal point or an integer followed by an exponent.

For example, 33, 12.10, -35.8, 2E3, 0x5F

Boolean

Consists of the logical value *true* and *false*.

JavaScript supports a pure Boolean type that consists of the two values *true* and *false*. Logical operators can be used in Boolean expressions.

JavaScript automatically converts the Boolean values *true* and *false* into 1 and 0 when they are used in numerical expressions.

Note

Values 1 and 0 are not considered Boolean values in JavaScript.

String

Consists of string values that are enclosed in single or double quotes.

JavaScript provides built-in support for strings. A string is a sequence of zero or more characters that are enclosed by double (“) or single (‘) quotes. If a string begins with a double quote it must end with a double quote. If a string begins with a single quote it must end with a single quote.

For example, "Rahul", '24, Sanjay Nagar, Bangalore'

Note

If a string has to include quote character in the string the quote character must be preceded by the backslash (\) escape character.

Null

Consists of a single value, *null*, which identifies a null, empty or nonexistent reference.

The null value is common to all JavaScript types. It is used to set a variable to an initial value that is different from other valid values. Use of the null value prevents the sort of errors that result from using un-initialized variables. The null value is automatically converted to default values of other types when used in an expression.

Type Casting

In JavaScript variables are loosely cast. The type of a JavaScript variable is **implicitly defined** based on the **literal** values that are assigned to it from time to time.

For instance, combining the string literal "Total amount is " with the integer literal 1000 results in a string with the value "Total amount is 1000". By contrast, adding together the numeric literal 10.5 and the string "20" results in the floating point integer literal 30.5. This process is known as **type casting**.

Creating Variables

In order to make working with data types convenient, variables are created. In JavaScript variables can be created that can hold any type of data.

In order to use a variable, it is good programming style to declare it. Declaring a variable tells JavaScript that a variable of a given name exists so that the JavaScript interpreter can understand references to that variable name throughout the rest of the script.

Although it is possible to declare variables by simply using them, declaring variables helps to ensure that programs are well organized and helps keep track of the scope of the variables. Variables can be declared using **var** command.

Syntax:

var <variable name> = *value*;

Examples:

```
var first_name;
var last_name = "Shah";
var phone = 6128879;
```

The equal sign (=) used in assigning a value to a variable is known as an *assignment* operator.

Note

Like properties and method names in JavaScript, variable names are case sensitive.

Incorporating Variables In A Script

Example 1:
The following illustrates incorporating variables in a script.

```
<HTML>
    <HEAD>
        <SCRIPT Language = "JavaScript">
            var name = prompt("Enter your name", "Name");
        </SCRIPT>
    </HEAD>
```

```
    <BODY>
        <SCRIPT Language = "JavaScript">
            document.write("<H2> Hello " + name  + "</H2>");
        </SCRIPT>
    </BODY>
</HTML>
```

The JavaScript **prompt()** method picks up a string (i.e *User Name*) from the user which is then assigned to the variable *name.* The JavaScript code **document.write()** embedded in the **<BODY> . . . </BODY>** tags writes the contents of the variable *name* to the client browser.

Since the **<HEAD> . . . </HEAD>** section of the HTML program is interpreted first a 'User Name' is picked up first before anything is displayed in the client browser.

The JavaScript Array

Arrays are JavaScript objects that are capable of storing a sequence of values. These values are stored in indexed locations within the array. The length of an array is the number of elements that an array contains. The individual elements of an array are accessed by using the name of the array followed by the *index value* of the array element enclosed in square brackets.

Note

The array element index starts with **0**. Hence the last array element index number is **one less** that the length of the array.

An array must be declared before it is used. An array can be declared using any one of the following techniques.

```
arrayName = new Array(Array length)
arrayName = new Array( )
```

In the first example the array size is explicitly specified. Hence this array will hold a pre-determined set of values. The second example creates an array of the size 0.

Note

JavaScript automatically extends the length of any array when new array elements are initialized.

Example:

```
cust_Orders = new Array( )
cust_Orders[50] = "Lion Pencils"
cust_Orders[100] = "Steadler eraser"
```

When JavaScript encounters the reference to order [50], in the above example, it will extend the size of the array cust_Orders to 51 and initialize order[50]. When JavaScript encounters the reference to order [100], in the above example, it will extend the size of the array cust_Orders to 101 and initializes order[100].

Even if an array is initially created of a fixed length it may still be extended by referencing elements that are outside the current size of the array. This is done in the same manner as with zero-length arrays.

Dense Arrays

A dense array is an array that has been created with each of its elements being assigned a specific value. Dense arrays are used exactly in the same manner as other arrays. They are declared and initialized at the same time.

Listing the values of the array elements in the array declaration creates dense arrays. For example a dense array can be created as:

arrayName = new Array(value**0**, value**1**, **. . .** , value**n**)

In this array, since the element count starts from 0 to *n*, the array length is *n*+1.

Since array is a JavaScript object, arrays have several methods associated with them via which the array and its element content can be manipulated.

Join() returns all elements of the array joined together as a single string. This takes one argument; a string to be used as a separator between each element of the array in the final string. If the argument is omitted, join() uses a comma-space as the separator.

Reverse() reverses the order of the elements in the array.

Example 2:
An array is used with hard coded values. Displaying the values of the array elements in the browser makes use of an array's **join()** method to print the array elements in a single line.

```
<HTML>
    <HEAD><TITLE>Viewing the array elements of a JavaScript Array</TITLE></HEAD>
    <BODY>
        <SCRIPT LANGUAGE = "JavaScript">
        <!-- Begin Hiding JavaScript -->
            friends = new Array(5);
            friends[0] = "Ananth";
            friends[1] = "Cedric";
            friends[2] = "Ketan";
            friends[3] = "Rohan";
            friends[4] = "Leela";
            document.write(friends[0] + "<BR/>");
            document.write(friends[1] + "<BR/>");
            document.write(friends[2] + "<BR/>");
            document.write(friends[3] + "<BR/>");
            document.write(friends[4] + "<BR/>");
            join_crit= friends.join();
            document.write(join_crit);
        // End hiding JavaScript -->
        </SCRIPT>
    </BODY>
</HTML>
```

The Elements Of An Array

JavaScript does not place any restrictions on the values assigned to the elements of an array. These values could be of different types or could refer to other arrays or objects.

Example:

multiTypeArray = new Array("Val**1**", "Val**2**", 1, 2, true, false, null, new array(3, 4))

The array named multiTypeArray has a length of eight and its elements are:

multiTypeArray[0] = "Val**1**"
multiTypeArray[1] = "Val**2**"
multiTypeArray[2] = 1

multiTypeArray[3] = 2
multiTypeArray[4] = true
multiTypeArray[5] = false
multiTypeArray[6] = null
multiTypeArray[7] = *a new dense array consisting of the values of 3,4*

The last element of the array, multiTypeArray, contains a dense array as its value. The two elements of this array can be accessed using a <u>second set of subscripts</u>:

num1 = multiTypeArray[7][0];
num2 = multiTypeArray[7][1];

The JavaScript Array and its length Property

JavaScript arrays are implemented as objects. *Objects* are named collections of data that have **properties** and whose values may be accessed via **methods**. A *property* returns a value that identifies some aspect of the state of an object. *Methods* are used to read or modify the data contained in an object's property.

The length of an array is a property of an array. Access to any JavaScript object's property is done by using **objectname.propertyname**.

For example, to find out the length of the multiTypeArray:

myvar = multiTypeArray.length;

The length of the multiTypeArray will be assigned to the variable *myvar*. By accessing the contents of myvar the length of (*no. of elements in multiTypeArray*) the multiTypeArray can be determined.

OPERATORS AND EXPRESSIONS IN JAVASCRIPT

An *operator* is used to transform one or more values into a single resultant value. The values to which the operator is applied is referred to as *operands*. A combination of an operator and its operands is referred to as an *expression*.

Expressions are evaluated to determine the value of the expression. This is the value that results when an operator is applied to its operands.

Note

For some operators, such as multiplication (*) the *order* of the operands do not matter. For example, A*Y = Y*A is *true* for all integers and floating point numbers.

Other operators such as string concatenation (+), the order of the operands matter. For example, "ab" + "cd" is not the same as "cd" + "ab".

Arithmetic Operators

Arithmetic operators are the most familiar operators because they are used every day to solve common math calculations. The arithmetic operators that JavaScript supports are;

Operator	Description	Operator	Description
+	Addition	-	Subtraction or Unary negation
*	Multiplication	/	Division
%	Modulus	++	Return the value then Increment
--	Return the value then Decrement		

Table 8.2

Note

The % (modulus) operator calculates the remainder by dividing two integers. For example, 17 % 3 = 2 because 17/3 = 5 with a remainder of 2.

An operator requiring a single operand is referred to as a **Unary** operator and one that requires two operands is a *binary* operator.

The above standard arithmetic operators are binary operators. In addition to these binary operators, there are unary arithmetic operators. They are (++) and (--).

Both these increment and decrement operators can be used in two different ways. Before the operand or after the operand. For example, ++x increments x by **one** and returns the result, while x++ returns x and then increments the value of x by one. Similarly, --x decreases the value of x by **one** before returning a result, while x-- returns the value of x before decreasing its value by one.

Example:

```
X = 3;
Y = ++X;
Z = X++;
```

In these lines of code, X is first assigned the value of 3, which is then increased to 4 and assigned to Y. The new value of 4 is assigned to Z, and then the value of X is increased to 5. Finally, X is 5, Y is 4 and Z is 4.

Logical Operators

Logical operators are used to perform Boolean operators on Boolean operands **AND, OR, NOT**. The logical operators supported by JavaScript are:

Operator	&&	||	!
Description	Logical AND	Logical OR	Logical NOT

Table 8.3

Comparison Operators

Comparison operators are used to compare two values. The comparison operators supported by JavaScript are:

Operator	**Description**
==	Equal
!=	Not Equal
<	Less than
>	Greater than

Operator	**Description**
===	Strictly Equal
!==	Strictly Not Equal
<=	Less than or equal to
>=	Greater than or equal to

Table 8.4

Note

The equal (==) and not equal (!=) operators perform type conversions before testing for equality. For example, "5" == 5 evaluate to **true**.

The strictly equal (===) and the strictly not equal (!===) do not perform type conversions before testing for equality. For example, "5" === 5 will return the value **false**.

String Operators

String operators are those operators that are used to perform operations on strings. Currently JavaScript supports only the **string concatenation** (+) operator.

This operator is used to join two strings. For example, "pq" + "ab" produces "pqab".

Assignment Operators

The assignment operator is used to update the value of a variable. Some assignment operators are combined with other operators to perform a computation on the value contained in a variable and then update the variable with the new value. Some of the assignment operators supported by JavaScript are:

Operator	Description
=	Sets the variable on the left of the = operator to the value of the expression on its right
+=	Increments the variable on the left of the += operator by the value of the expression on its right. When used with strings, the value to the right of the += operator is appended to the value of the variable on the left of the += operator
- =	Decrements the variable on the left of the - = operator by the value of the expression on the right
* =	Multiplies the variable on the left of the * = operator by the value of the expression on its right
/ =	Divides the variable on the left of the /= operator by the value of the expression on its right
% =	Takes the modulus of the variable on the left of the % = operator using the value of the expression on its right

Table 8.5

The Conditional Expression Ternary Operator

JavaScript supports the conditional expression operator. They are ? and : The conditional expression operator is a ternary operator since it takes three operands, a condition to be evaluated and two alternative values to be returned based on the truth or falsity of the condition.

Syntax:

```
condition ? value1 : value2
```

The condition expressed must return a value true or false. If the condition is true, value1 is the result of the expression, otherwise value2 is the result of the expression.

Special Operators

JavaScript supports a number of special operators that do not fit into the operator categories covered above.

The delete Operator

The delete operator is used to delete a property of an object or an element at an array index.

Example:
To delete the **sixth** element of myArray.

```
delete myArray[5]
```

The new Operator

The new operator is used to create an instance of an object type.

Example:

To create a new JavaScript object of the type array and assign this array to a context area in memory called myArray.

```
myArray = new Array( )
```

The void Operator

The void operator does not return a value. It is typically used in JavaScript to return a URL with no value.

JAVASCRIPT PROGRAMMING CONSTRUCTS

Most programming languages support a common (**core**) set of constructs. Languages only differ in the syntax used for structuring these constructs.

Languages may also differ in the degree to which they support programming features such as **O**bject **O**riented **P**rogramming, abstract data definition, inference rules and list processing.

JavaScript provides a complete range of basic programming constructs. While it is not an object oriented programming environment JavaScript is an **object-based** language.

The constructs provided by JavaScript are as follows:

Construct / Statement	**Purpose**	**Example**
Assignment	Assigns the value of an expression to a variable.	x = y + z
data declaration	Declares a variable and optionally assigns a value to it.	var myVar = 10

if	Program execution depends upon the value of returned by the condition. If the value returned is True the program executes else the program does not execute.	**if**(x > y) {
		z = X;
		}

while	Repeatedly executes a set of statements until a condition becomes false	**while**(x != 7) {
		x %= n - n
		}

switch	Selects from a number of alternatives	**switch**(val) {
		case 1:
		// First alternative
		break;
		case 2:
		// Second alternative
		break;
		default
		// Default action
		}

for	Repeatedly executes a set of statements until a condition becomes false	**for**(i = 0; i < 7; ++i) {
		document.write(x[i]);
		}

do while	Repeatedly executes a set of statements while a condition is true	**do** {
		// Statements
		} **while**(i > 0)

label	Associates a label with a statement	LabelName: Statement

Table 8.6

Construct / Statement	Purpose	Example
break	Immediately terminates a do while or for loop construct	**if**(x > y) **break**
continue	Immediately terminates the current iteration of a do, while or for construct	**if**(x > y) **continue**
function call	Invokes a function	x = **abs**(y)
return	Returns a value from a function call	**return** x*y

with	Identifies the default object	**with**(Math) {
		d = PI * 2 * r;
		}

delete	Deletes an object property or an array element	**delete** a[5]
Method invocation	Invokes a method of an object	document.write("Hello")

Table 8.6 (continued)

CONDITIONAL CHECKING

The if - then - else Statement

The conditional construct in JavaScript offers a simple way to make a decision in a JavaScript program. The conditional construct in JavaScript will either return a **True** or a **False** depending upon how the **condition** evaluated.

Using the **if-else** construct the flow of the JavaScript program can be altered i.e. the **if** condition determines which section of the program code will be executed based on whether the condition evaluates to **TRUE** or **FALSE.**

Syntax:

```
if(condition) {
  // JavaScript code
}
```

If the **condition** evaluation returns **True** the JavaScript code is *executed* if the evaluation returns **False** this section of JavaScript code will be *skipped.*

Example:

```
var day = "Saturday"
if (day == "Saturday") {
    document.writeln("It's the weekend");
    alert("It's the weekend");
}
```

Immediate if (Conditional expression)

A conditional expression can evaluate to either **True** or **False** based on the **evaluation** of the condition. The structure of a conditional expression is:

Syntax:

```
(condition) ? value1: value2
```

where, **condition** is an expression that can be evaluated to a boolean value. Based on the result, the whole expression evaluates to either **value1** (true condition) or **value2** (false condition).

Example:

```
var day = "Saturday"
    (day == "Saturday") ? "Weekend!" : "Not Saturday"
```

This expression will evaluate to:

"Weekend!"	where **day** holds Saturday!	(Condition TRUE)
"Not Saturday!"	if day holds any other string	(Condition FALSE)

SUPER CONTROLLED - ENDLESS LOOPS

Looping refers to the ability of a block of code to repeat itself. This repetition can be for a predefined number of times or it can go until certain conditions are met. For instance, a block of code needs to be executed till the value of a variable becomes 20 (Conditional Looping), or a block of code needs to be repeated 7 times.

For this purpose, JavaScript offers 2 types of loop structures:

- **for Loops** - These loops iterate a specific number of times as specified.
- **while Loops** - These are Conditional Loops, which continue until a condition is met.

For Loop

The **for** loop is the most basic type of loop and resembles a for loop in most other programming languages, including ANSI 'C'.

Syntax:

```
for(expression1; condition; expression2) {
// JavaScript commands
}
```

where, **expression1** sets up a counter variable and assigns the initial value. The declaration of the counter variable can also be done here itself, **condition** specifies the final value for the loop to fire (i.e. the loop fires till **condition** evaluates to true), **expression2** specifies how the initial value in **expression1** is **incremented**.

Example:
The following block prints numbers from 10 to 1 on the VDU screen (Reverse Order).

```
for (var num = 10; num >=1; num--)
{
    document.writeln(num);
}
```

While Loop

The **while** loop provides a similar functionality. The basic structure of a **while** loop is:

Syntax:

```
while (condition) {
// JavaScript commands
}
```

Where, the *condition* is a valid JavaScript expression that evaluates to a Boolean value. The JavaScript commands execute as long as the condition is **true.**

Example:
The following block prints numbers from 1 to 10 on the screen.

```
var num = 1;
while (num <= 10)
{
    document.writeln(num);
    num++;
}
```

FUNCTIONS IN JAVASCRIPT

Functions are blocks of JavaScript code that perform a specific task and **often** return a value. A JavaScript function may take zero or more parameters. Parameters are a standard technique via which control data can be passed to a function. Control data passed to a function, offers a means of controlling what a function returns.

Built-in Functions

JavaScript provides several built-in functions that can be used to perform explicit type conversions. Some of them are **eval()**, **parseInt()** and **parseFloat()**.

The **eval()** function can be used to convert a string expression to a numeric value.

Example:
The following results in the value 105 being assigned to the variable grand_Total.

```
var grand_Total = eval("10 * 10 + 5");
```

Note

Even if the string value passed as a parameter to **eval()** does represent a numeric value the use of **eval()** results in an error being generated.

The **parseInt()** function is used to convert a string value to an integer. The **parseInt()** function returns the first integer contained in a string or 0 if the string does not begin with an integer.

Example:
The following results in the integer 123 being assigned to the variable string2Num.

```
var string2Num = parseInt("123xyz");
```

The following results in "**NaN**" (Not a Number) being assigned to the variable string2Num.

```
var string2Num = parseInt("xyz");
```

The **parseFloat()** function returns the first floating point number contained in a string or 0 if the string does not begin with a valid floating point number.

Example:
The following results in the float 1.2 being assigned to the variable string2Num.

```
var string2Num = parseFloat("1.2xyz");
```

The following results in "**NaN**" (Not a Number) being assigned to the variable string2Num.

```
string2Num = parseInt("xyz");
```

USER DEFINED FUNCTIONS

Functions offer the ability to group together JavaScript program code that performs a specific task into a single unit that can be used repeatedly whenever required in a JavaScript program.

A user defined function first needs to be declared and coded. Once this is done the function can be invoked by calling it using the name given to the function when it was declared.

Functions can accept information in the form of arguments and can return results.

Appropriate syntax needs to be followed for declaring functions, invoking them, passing them values and accepting their return values.

Declaring Functions

Functions are declared and created using the **function** keyword. A function can comprise of the following:

- A name for the function
- A list of parameters (arguments) that will accept values passed to the function when called
- A block of JavaScript code that defines what the function does

Syntax:

```
function function_name(parameter1, parameter2, . . . ){
// Block of JavaScript code
}
```

A **function_name** is case sensitive, can include underscores (_), and has to start with a letter. The list of **parameters** passed to the function appears in parentheses and commas separate members of the list.

Note

Defining a function does not execute the JavaScript code that makes up the function.

Place Of Declaration

Functions can be declared anywhere within an HTML file. Preferably, functions are created within the **<HEAD>...</HEAD>** tags of the **HTML** file. This ensures that all functions will be *parsed* before they are invoked or called. If the function is called before it is declared and parsed, it will lead to an error condition, as the function has not been evaluated and the 'Browser' does not know that it exists.

Note

The term **parsed** refers to the process by which the JavaScript interpreter evaluates each line of script code and converts it into a pseudo-compiled bytecode, before attempting to execute it. At this time, syntax errors and other programming mistakes that would prevent the script from running are trapped and reported.

Passing Parameters

Values can be passed to function parameters when a 'parameterized' function is called. Values are passed to the function by listing them in the parentheses following the function name. Multiple values can be passed, separated by commas provided that the function has been coded to accept multiple parameters.

Both JavaScript built-in functions and user-defined functions can accept parameters, process them and return values. During declaration, a function needs to be informed about the number of values that will be passed.

Example:

<u>Function Declaration:</u>

```
function printName(user){
        document.write("<HR/>Your Name is <B><I>");
        document.write(user);
        document.write("</B></I><HR/>");
}
```

where, **printName** is a function, which has a parameter called **user**. The parameter user can be passed a value at the time of invoking the function. Within the function, reference to **user** will then refer to the **value** passed to the function.

<u>Function Call:</u>

<u>A static value passed:</u>

printName("Bob"); (will cause the string "Bob" to be assigned to the parameter **user**.)

<u>A Variable Passed:</u>

var user = "John";
printName(user); (will cause the value "John" to be assigned to the parameter **user**.)

Note

- Both variables and literals can be passed as arguments when calling a function.
- If a variable is passed to the function, changing the value of the parameter within the function <u>does not change the value of the variable passed to the function.</u>
- Parameters exist only for the life of the function.

Example 3:

Once an HTML page completes loading it greets a user with a message 'Welcome'. When a user leaves this page, the 'Good-bye' alert dialog box is displayed.

```
<HTML>
   <HEAD>
      <TITLE>Creating and Using User Defined Functions</TITLE>
      <SCRIPT Language="JavaScript">
         var name = "";
         function hello()
         {
            name = prompt('Enter Your Name:', 'Name');
            alert('Greetings ' + name + ', Welcome to my page!');
         }
         function goodbye()
         {
            alert('Goodbye ' + name + ', Sorry to see you go!');
         }
      </SCRIPT>
   </HEAD>
   <BODY onLoad="hello();" onUnload="goodbye();">
      <IMG SRC="images/Pinkwhit.gif" />
   </BODY>
</HTML>
```

Variable Scope

The parameters of a function are local to the function. They come into existence when the function is called and cease to exist when the function ends. For instance, in the example **printName(), user** exists only within the function **printName()** - it cannot be referred to or manipulated outside the function.

Also, any variable declared using **var** variable-name *within* the function would have a scope limited to the function.

If a variable is declared outside the body of the function, it is available to all statements within the JavaScript.

If a *local variable* is declared within a function has the same name as an existing *global variable*, then within the function code, that variable name will refer to the *local variable* and **not** the global variable. It is as though the global variable does not exist with respect to the JavaScript code within the function.

Return Values

As with some JavaScript built-in functions, user defined functions can return values. Such values can be returned using the **return** statement. The return statement can be used to return any valid expression that evaluates to a single value.

Example:

```
function cube(number) {
    var cube = number * number * number;
    return cube;
}
```

where, **cube** is a function, which accepts a parameter *number*, calculates its cube, assigns this calculation to a variable **cube** and returns the value of cube.

This function can also be written as follows:

```
function cube(number) {
    return number * number * number;
}
```

Recursive Functions

Recursion refers to a situation, wherein *functions call themselves*. In other words, there is a call to a specific function from within the same function. Such functions are known as Recursive Functions.

Example:

The following JavaScript function is an example of a Recursive Function that calculates the factorial of a number. (A factorial is a mathematical function. For example, factorial 5 is equal to 5*4*3*2*1)

```
function factorial(number) {
    if(number>1) {
        return number * factorial(number-1);
    }
    else {
        return number;
    }
}
```

This function receives a number as an argument and relies on the fact that the factorial of a number is the number multiplied by the factorial of one less than the number.

The function applies the formula and returns the number multiplied by the factorial of one less than the number.

Note

Recursive functions are powerful, but can lead to infinite recursions. Infinite recursions occur when the function is designed in such a way as to call itself without being able to stop.

It is important to note that the function **factorial()** prevents infinite recursions because the **if-else** construct ensures that eventually the function will stop calling itself once the number passed to the function is equal to one. Additionally, if the function is *initially* called with a value *less than two*, no recursion will take place at all.

PLACING TEXT IN A BROWSER

Using JavaScript a string can be written to the browser from within an HTML file. The **document** object in JavaScript has a **method** for placing text in a browser. This method is called **write()**. Methods are called by combining the object name with the method name:

Object-name.Method-Name

The **write()** method accepts a string value passed to it within its parentheses. The string value can then be written to the browser. The **write()** method accepts this string and places it in the current browser window. For example:

document.write("Test");

The string "Test" will be placed in the browser.

Example 4:
The following example illustrates how JavaScript code places text in the browser window using document.write().

```
<HTML>
    <HEAD><TITLE>Outputting Text </TITLE></HEAD>
    <BODY><CENTER><BR/><BR/>
        <IMG HEIGHT="100" SRC="sony-logo.gif" WIDTH="100"/>Silicon Chip Technologies.<BR/>
        <SCRIPT Language = "Javascript">
            document.write("<BR/><BR/>");
            document.write('<IMG HEIGHT="100" SRC="sony-logo.gif" WIDTH="100"/>');
            document.write("<B>Silicon Chip Technologies.</B> <BR/>");
        </SCRIPT>
    </CENTER></BODY>
</HTML>
```

Output For Example 4:
(Refer to diagram 8.1)

Diagram 8.1

DIALOG BOXES

JavaScript provides the ability to pickup user input or display small amounts of text to the user by using dialog boxes. These dialog boxes appear as separate windows and their content depends on the information provided by the user. This content is independent of the text in the HTML page containing the JavaScript script and does not affect the content of the page in any way.

There are three types of dialog boxes provided by JavaScript:

The Alert Dialog Box

The simplest way to direct small amounts of textual output to a browser's window is to use an alert dialog box. The JavaScript **alert()** method takes a string as an argument and displays an alert dialog box in the browser window when invoked by appropriate JavaScript.

The alert dialog box displays the string passed to the **alert()** method, as well as an OK button. The JavaScript and the HTML program, in which this code snippet is held, will not continue processing until the OK button is clicked.

The alert dialog box can be used to display a cautionary message or display some information. For instance:

- A message is displayed to the user when incorrect information is keyed in a form
- An invalid result is the output of a calculation
- A warning that a service is not available on a given date/time

Syntax:

alert("<Message>");

Example:

alert("Click OK to continue");

Example 5:

The following example shows an alert dialog box, welcoming a user. As soon as the OK button is clicked, an image is displayed in the browser. This illustrates that all background processing **stops** until an **alert** has been responded to.

```
<HTML>
        <HEAD><TITLE>Example</TITLE></HEAD>
        <BODY><SCRIPT Language="Javascript">
                alert("Welcome To My Web Site!");
                document.write('<IMG SRC="Images/welcome.gif"/>');
        </SCRIPT></BODY>
</HTML>
```

Output For Example 5:

(Refer to diagram 8.2)

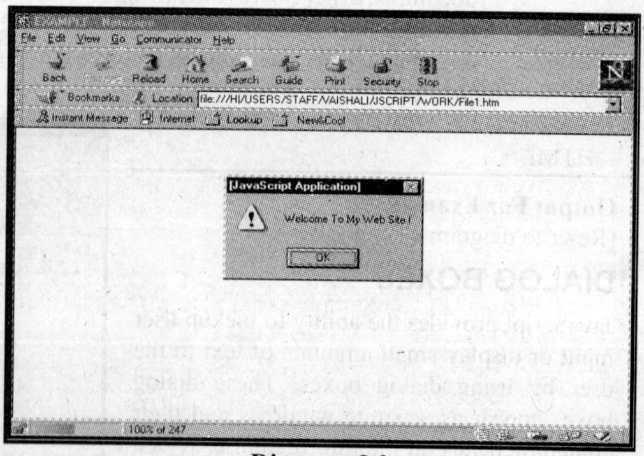

Diagram 8.2

The Prompt Dialog Box

As seen, the alert dialog box simply displays information in a browser and does not allow any interaction. The addition of the `OK` button provides some very minimal control over form events *i.e.* program execution halts completely until some user action takes place (*clicking on the* `OK` *button*).

An alert dialog box, cannot be used to customize any web page output based on user input, which is what user interaction requires.

JavaScript provides a prompt dialog box for this. The **prompt()** method instantiates the prompt dialog box which displays a specified message. In addition, the prompt dialog box also provides a single data entry field, which accepts user input. Thus, a prompt dialog box:

- Displays a predefined Message
- Displays a textbox and accepts user input
  - Can pass what the user keyed into the textbox back to the JavaScript
- Displays the `OK` and the `Cancel` buttons

The prompt dialog box also causes program execution to halt until user action takes place. This could be the `OK` button being clicked, or the `Cancel` button being clicked, which causes the following action to take place.

- Clicking on the `OK` button causes the text typed inside the textbox to be passed to the program environment (i.e. *JavaScript*)
- Clicking on the `Cancel` button causes a NULL value to be passed to the environment.

When the **prompt()** method is used to instantiate and use a dialog box the method requires two blocks of information:

- A message to be displayed as a prompt to the user
- Any message to be displayed in the textbox (*this is optional*)

Syntax:

```
prompt("<Message>", "<Default value>");
```

Example:

```
prompt("Enter your favorite color:", "Blue");
```

The value that the user keys into the textbox on the prompt dialog box is accepted and can be stored in a variable.

Example 6:

The following example shows a welcoming image on the screen. Asks the user for a name. Then displays the name keyed into the prompt dialog box along with a Greeting message.

```
<HTML>
    <HEAD><TITLE>Example </TITLE></HEAD>
    <BODY>
        <SCRIPT LANGUAGE="JavaScript">
            document.write('<IMG Src="Images/welcome.gif"/>');
            document.write("<H1>Greetings</H1>");
            document.write(prompt("Enter Your Name: ", "Name"));
            document.write(" Welcome to My HomePage!</H1>");
        </SCRIPT>
    </BODY>
</HTML>
```

Output For Example 6: (Refer to diagram 8.3)

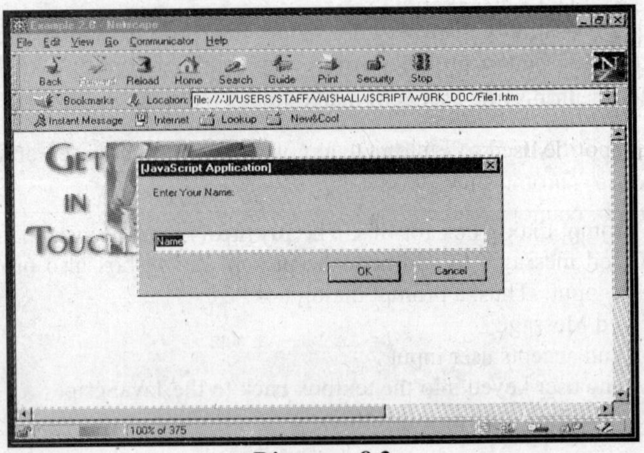

Diagram 8.3

The Confirm Dialog Box

JavaScript provides a third type of a dialog box, called the confirm dialog box. As the name suggests, this dialog box serves as a technique for confirming user action. The confirm dialog box displays the following information:

- A pre-defined message
- `Ok` and `Cancel` button

The confirm dialog box, causes program execution to halt until user action takes place. User action can be either the `OK` button being clicked, or the `Cancel` button being clicked, which causes the following action to take place.

- Clicking on the `OK` button causes TRUE to be passed to the program which called the confirm dialog box.
- Clicking on the `Cancel` button causes FALSE to be passed to the program which called the confirm dialog box.

Display of a confirm dialog box thus requires only one block of information:
A pre-defined message to be displayed

Syntax:

confirm("<Message>");

Example:

confirm("Are you sure you want to exit out of the system");

Example 7:
The following JavaScript example asks a question and accepts an answer. The user is given three chances. The second and third chance to provide an answer can be accepted or rejected, if accepted the program prompts for an answer again.

```
<HTML>
    <HEAD>
        <TITLE> Confirm Method </TITLE>
        <SCRIPT LANGUAGE="JavaScript">
            var question = "What is 10+10 ?";
            var answer = 20;
            var correct = '<IMG SRC="images/man2.gif"/>';

            var incorrect ='<IMG Src="images/man1.gif"/>';
            var Response = prompt(question,"0");
            for(count = 0; count < 3; count++) {
                if(Response != answer) {
                    confirm("Wrong, Press OK For Another Chance");
                    Response = prompt(question,"0");
                    if(count == 1)
                    {
                        alert("Better Luck Next Time");
                    }
                }

                else {
                    alert("Great!! You Are Right");
                    count = 3;
                }
            }
            var output = (Response == answer) ? correct : incorrect;
            document.write("<BR/>");
            document.write(output);
        </SCRIPT>
    </HEAD>
    <BODY></BODY>
</HTML>
```

Output:

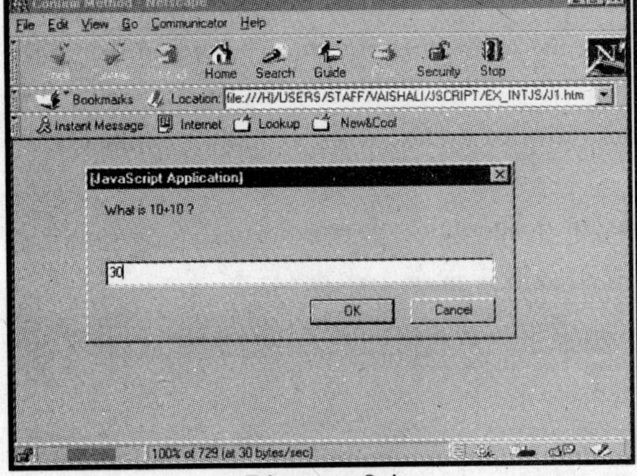

Diagram 8.4

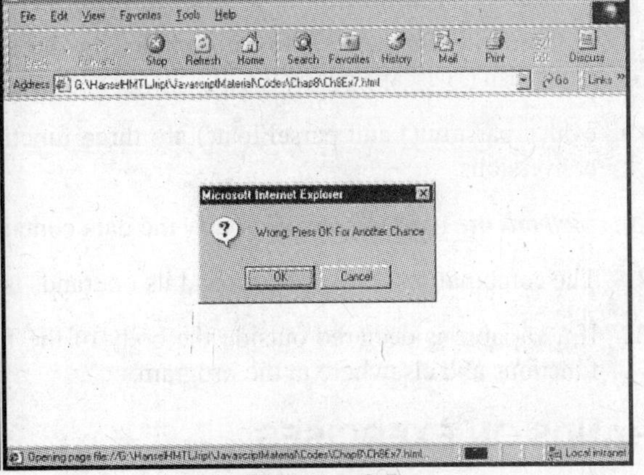

Diagram 8.5

SELF REVIEW QUESTIONS

FILL IN THE BLANKS

1. Capturing user requests is traditionally done via a ______.
2. JavaScript is a scripting language created by ______.
3. JavaScript is embedded between the ____________ HTML tags.
4. A user request form can be created with the ____________ HTML tags.
5. __________ are used to store values that can be used in other parts of a program.
6. The __________ is reserved for machine generated code and should not be used in scripts.
7. In JavaScript, variable is ________ ________ based on the ________ value that is assigned to it.
8. A ________ is a sequence of zero or more characters that are enclosed by double (") or single (') quotes.
9. _________ are block of JavaScript code that perform a specific task and return a value.
10. ________ are JavaScript objects that are capable of storing a sequence of values.
11. A ________ array is an array that has been created with each of its elements being assigned a specific value.
12. __________ are named collections of data that have properties and may be accessed via methods.
13. The __________ operator calculates the remainder by dividing two integers.

TRUE OR FALSE

14. JavaScript is not an interpreted language.
15. A JavaScript program developed on a Unix machine will work perfectly well on a Windows machine.
16. The <BODY></BODY>HTML tags make an ideal place to create JavaScript variables and constants and so on.
17. JavaScript does not allow the data type of the variable to be declared when a variable is created.
18. If the quote character is to be included in the string, the quote character must be preceded by the frontslash (/) escape character.
19. eval(), parseInt() and parseFloat() are three functions provided by JavaScript to perform explicit type conversions.
20. *Methods* are used to read or modify the data contained in an object.
21. The combination of an operator and its operands is referred to as an *expression*.
22. If a variable is declared outside the body of the function, it is available throughout a script inside all functions and elsewhere in the program.

HANDS ON EXERCISES

1. Write a JavaScript code block using arrays and generate the current date in words, this should include the day, the month and the year. The output should be as follows, **Saturday, January 01, 2000**.

2. Write a JavaScript code block, which checks the contents entered in a form's Text element. If the text entered is in the lower case, convert to upper case. Make use of function *toUppercase()*.

3. Write a JavaScript code block, which validates a username and password against hard coded values.

   If either the name or password field is not entered display an error message showing: "You forgot one of the required fields. Please try again."

   In case, the fields entered do not match the hard coded values, display an error message showing: "Please enter a valid username and password"

   If the fields entered match, display the following message: "Welcome (username)"

9. THE JAVASCRIPT DOCUMENT OBJECT MODEL

INTRODUCTION

An HTML page is rendered (*painted*) in a browser. The browser assembles all the elements (*objects*) contained in the HTML page, downloaded from the web server, in its memory. Once done the browser then renders (*paints*) these objects in the browser window. Once the HTML page is rendered (*painted*) in the browser window, the browser can no longer recognize individual HTML elements (*objects*).

To create an interactive web page it is imperative that the browser continues to recognize individual HTML objects even after they are rendered in the browser window. This allows the browser to access the properties of these objects using the built-in methods of the object. Once the properties of an object are accessible then the functionality of the object can be controlled at will.

JavaScript enabled browsers are capable of recognizing individual objects in an HTML page, after the page has been rendered in the browser, because the JavaScript enabled browser recognizes and uses the **D**ocument **O**bject **M**odel (i.e *the DOM*).

Using the Document Object Model (DOM) JavaScript enabled browsers identify the collection of web page objects (*web page elements*) that have to be dealt with while rendering an HTML based, web page in the browser window.

The HTML objects (i.e. *the collection of web page elements*), which belong to the DOM, have a *descending* relationship with each other.

The topmost object in the DOM is the **Navigator** (i.e. <u>*the browser*</u>) itself. The next level in the DOM is the browser's **Window**. The next level in the DOM is the **Document** displayed in the browser's window.

Should the document displayed in the browser's window have an HTML **Form** coded in it, then the next level in the DOM is the **Form** itself.

The DOM hierarchy continues downward to encompass individual elements on a **FORM**, such as Text boxes, Labels, Radio buttons, Check boxes, Push buttons and so on, which belong to the form.

JavaScript's object hierarchy is mapped to the DOM, which in turn is mapped to the web page elements in the browser window. Hence, when a web page is rendered in a JavaScript enabled browser window, JavaScript is capable of uniquely identifying each element in the web page, because major elements of a web page are bound to the DOM.

The DOM that JavaScript recognizes is described in diagram 9.1.

JavaScript's DOM is referred to as an ***instance hierarchy***.

The Navigator – i.e. Netscape Navigator, Internet Explorer, Opera, Mosaic and so on.

```
Window
 |-> Document
    |-> Anchor
    |-> Link
    |-> Form
       |-> textbox
       |-> textarea
       |-> radiabutton
       |-> checkbox
       |-> select
       |-> button
```

Diagram 9.1: JavaScript's DOM.

Instance

No HTML object is registered in the DOM by a JavaScript enabled browser unless they are assembled in memory prior being rendered in the browser window.

What this means is, if a document does not have any **Anchors** described in it the **Anchors** object will exist but it will be empty. If the document does not have any **Links** described in it the **Links** object will exist but it will be empty.

Hierarchy

All objects on a web page are not created equal. Each exists in a set relationship with other objects on the web page. From diagram 9.1 the navigator occupies the topmost slot in the DOM followed by the Window object and so on.

Below the Window is the **Document** object. Below the document object three other objects exist. They are the **Anchor**, **Link** and **Form** objects. Individual form elements are found under the **Form** object.

In addition to the DOM, other objects currently recognized by a JavaScript enabled browser are *Plug-ins*, *Applets* and *Images*. Hence using a JavaScript enabled browser and JavaScript most of the major web page objects are accessible.

However, every single element of a web page rendered in the browser window, is **not** part of the DOM.

For example, HTML tags such as **<HEAD> . . . </HEAD>** or **<BODY> . . . </BODY>** are not part of the DOM. Presentation styles, headings, body text, H1 to H6 and so on are **not** part of the DOM hence **not** recognized by JavaScript.

Diagram 9.1 shows web page objects that are part of the DOM.

JavaScript however, recognizes presentation styles, headings, body text, H1 to H6 and so on, when **J**ava**S**cript assisted **S**tyle **S**heets [JSSS] are in a web page. JSSS is usually between the **<HEAD> . . . </HEAD>** HTML tags in a web page.

THE JAVASCRIPT ASSISTED STYLE SHEETS DOM [JSSS DOM]

JSSS use JavaScript syntax to control a document's presentation style. When a JSSS is embedded in an HTML page within the **<HEAD> . . . </HEAD>** tags, then the JavaScript DOM picks up a whole new set of objects, which **add** to the standard DOM objects already recognized by JavaScript. The additional objects brought into the DOM by JSSS are shown in diagram 9.2.

Objects added to the DOM by the use of JSSS are:

```
|-> Document
   |-> Tags
   |    |-> P
   |    |-> DIV
   |    |-> SPAN
   |    |-> H1 through H6
   |->classes
   |    |-> Tag Names
   |-> IDS
```

Diagram 9.2: JSSS's DOM.

By extending the DOM recognized by JavaScript by embedding JSSS in a web page, developers of web pages can access every element of a web page whether this element appears on the page when it is rendered in a client browser or not.

By accessing appropriate properties of the **Navigator** object, (i.e. *the Browser*), the topmost object in the DOM, JavaScript can recognize the browser type (i.e. *Netscape Navigator, Internet Explorer, Opera, Mosaic and so on*) and subsequently dispatch all HTML pages to the browser from the web server, with a **style** based on this knowledge. This is where the power of JavaScript really becomes visible in providing finely tuned web page content to a client's browser.

Since JavaScript understands the DOM and can extend the DOM with the use of JSSS in a web page JavaScript understands **Objects**.

All **objects** have:

- **Properties** that determine the functionality of the object
- **Methods** that allow access to these properties
- **Events** that allow JavaScript code snippets to be connected to the object by being mapped to appropriate JavaScript event handlers.

Hence when a pre-determined event occurs the code snippet will execute. This is the traditional Object, Event driven, Code execution model of any object based programming environment.

Using appropriate JavaScript code snippets, which reference the properties of an object via its built-in methods, developers of web pages can actually control the functionality of any HTML object in the DOM (*or extended DOM*) while the HTML program executes (i.e. *at run time*).

JavaScript can access the methods of all objects belonging to the DOM and JSSS DOM. Hence using JavaScript, truly interactive web pages can be created.

Note

JavaScript is an **object-based** programming language it is **not** fully object oriented. It does not fully support basic object oriented programming capabilities such as classification, inheritance, encapsulation and information hiding.

JavaScript features are geared towards providing developers the capability to quickly generate scripts that will execute in the context of a web page within a JavaScript enabled browser **or** on a web server that understands JavaScript.

Although JavaScript does not provide all of the features of a full object oriented programming language, it does provide a suite of object-based features that are especially tailored to Browser or Server side scripting.

These features include the recognition of a number of predefined browser and server objects. JavaScript has the ability to control the behavior of these objects through their properties and methods.

In the following chapters the focus will be only on **browser** side JavaScripting. The browser in which JavaScript code snippets will always run correctly will be Netscape Communicator as JavaScript is a Netscape product. JavaScript is the natural language of Netscape Communicator.

UNDERSTANDING OBJECTS IN HTML

HTML can be used to create a Graphical User Interface (GUI) in a web page. HTML is capable of accessing and using a number of objects that actually belong to the operating system (i.e. Windows). One such object is a *textbox*. A 'textbox' is used in an HTML form to accept user input.

The text box is an object, which belongs to the DOM. JavaScript recognizes a text box. JavaScript facilitates access to all the *methods* of a *textbox*. One of the methods of the textbox permits access to the contents of the text box. Hence, JavaScript can process the contents of any textbox in an HTML form.

Properties Of HTML Objects

Just like real world objects, HTML objects have a number of **properties** that determine the behavior of that object. An object's properties can be referenced as:

ObjectName.PropertyName

For example, a *textbox* can have properties like *name, size* and so on.

Methods Of HTML Objects

As seen, properties determine the state of an object. While building interactive web pages an object's properties need to be set dynamically, *i.e. when the object is being used*. Thus all object based programming environments **must** have facilities to *set* or *get* the value of object properties. This allows program code to control the state of the object at run time.

Methods of an object are used to *set* or *get* a value of an object's property. Thus determining how an object behaves. An object's methods can be referenced as:

ObjectName.MethodName

Using JavaScript it is possible to use an object's built-in methods and manipulate the object's properties at run time. This gives a great deal of creative control to web page developers when web pages have to be created on demand.

Once JavaScript code accepts client side input and / or reads a client's browser parameters, on demand web pages can be structured and sent to the browser from a web server.

BROWSER OBJECTS

When any JavaScript enabled browser loads a web page, the browser automatically creates a number of JavaScript objects that map to the DOM (*or JSSS DOM*). It is the DOM, which provides JavaScript access to the HTML objects that are contained in the web page.

The JavaScript code snippets imbedded as part of the web page itself (i.e. embedded within the <SCRIPT> </SCRIPT> tags of *filename*.html) makes use of these objects to interact with the HTML objects in the web page.

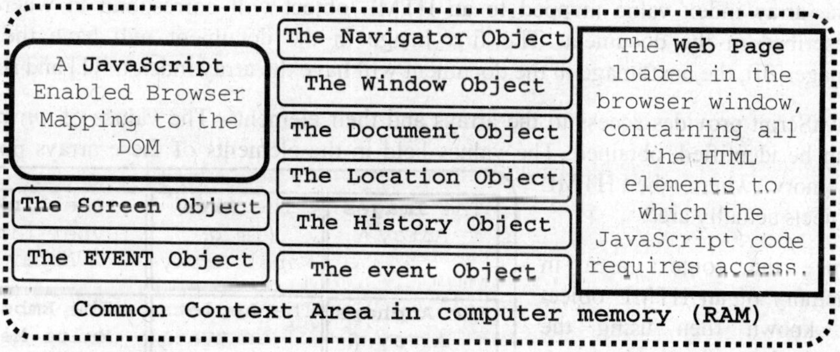

Diagram 9.3

The JavaScript objects created by [Netscape Communicator] are listed below:

Object Name	Its Use
navigator	To access information about the browser that is executing the current script.
window	To access a browser *window* or a *frame* within the window. The window object is assumed to exist and does not require the **window** prefix when referring to its properties and methods.
document	To access the document currently loaded into a window. The document object refers to an HTML document that provides content, that is, one that has HEAD and BODY tags.
location	To represent a URL. It can be used to create a URL object, access parts of a URL, or modify an existing URL.
history	To maintain a history of the URL's accessed within a window.
event	To access information about the occurrence of an event.
EVENT	The EVENT (*capitalized*) object provides constants that are used to identify events.
screen	To access information about the size and color depth of a client computer's screen in which the current browser is running.

Table 9.1

How A JavaScript Enabled Browser Handles The Document Object

Any document (i.e. *the HTML page*) can contain various HTML objects such as:

- Images
- Image Maps
- Hyperlinks
- Frames
- Anchors
- Applets
- Multimedia objects such a audio files, streaming video files
- A Form with various form elements

The browser creates one array in memory per HTML object in the document, thus registering each of these HTML objects.

If these HTML objects are actually contained in the HTML page then these arrays will hold indexed elements, which will point to the context area in memory where the HTML object are. Otherwise the array will exist, but will be empty (i.e. *have no elements in it*).

If there are multiple, similar HTML objects in the document (i.e *multiple images*) each array will have multiple (*indexed*) elements.

The array index value mapped to an HTML object will correspond to where the HTML object was described in the document. The first image in the document will have the array index as [0] (i.e. Images[0]), the next image in the document will have the array index of [1] and so on.

JavaScript provides access to the arrays and their elements. The values of *any/all* elements of each array can be identified, obtained. The values held in the elements of these arrays point to the context area in memory where the HTML objects actually are.

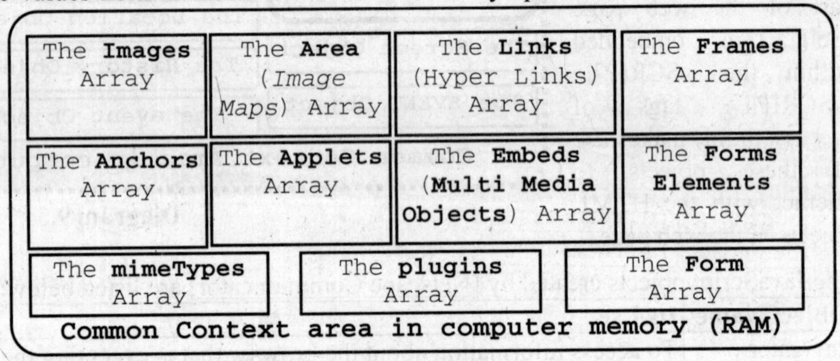

Diagram 9.4

Once the context area in memory of an HTML object is known then using the **Methods** of the object, specific object **Properties** can be set using JavaScript. Thus the functionality of an HTML object can be controlled while the HTML page is running in the browser.

The JavaScript arrays [created by Netscape Communicator] are listed below:

Image/Images Array	To access an image that is embedded in an HTML document. The **images array** is used to access all image objects in a document.
Link / Links Array	To access a text or image-based source anchor of a hypertext link. The **links array** is used to access all link objects within a document.
Area	To access an **area** within a client-side image map.
Frame / Frames Array	To access an HTML frame. The **frames array** is used to access all frames within a window.

Table 9.2

The JavaScript arrays [created by Netscape Communicator] are listed below: (Continued)

Anchor/Anchors array	To access the target of a hyperlink. The **anchors array** is used to access all anchor objects within a document.
Applet/Applets array	To Access a Java applet. The **applets array** being used to access all the applets in a document.
Embed / Embeds array	To access an embedded object. The **embeds array** provides access to all the embedded objects in a document.
MimeType / MimeTypes array	To access information about a particular MIME type supported by a browser. The **mimeTypes array** is an array of all the mimeType objects supported by a browser.
Plugin / Plugins array	To access information about a particular browser plug-in. The **plugins array** is an array of all plug-ins supported by a browser.
Form / Forms array	To access an HTML form. The **forms array** is used to access all forms within a document.

Table 9.2 (Continued)

The JavaScript **form elements** array [created by Netscape Communicator]:

elements	Access to all the form elements in the form.
text	To access a text field of a form.
textarea	To access a text area of a form.
radio	To access a set of radio buttons on the form or to access an individual radio button within the set.
checkbox	To access a checkbox on a form.
button	To access a form button that is not a reset or submit button.
submit	To access a submit button on a form.
reset	To access a reset button on a form.
select	To access a select list of a form.
option	The option object is used to access the elements of a select list.
password	To access a password field on a form.
hidden	To access a hidden object on a form.
fileupload	To access a file upload element of a form.

Table 9.3

THE WEB PAGE HTML OBJECT HIERARCHY

This is an *instance hierarchy*. This means if a web page does not have a specific HTML object defined in it the array associated with that specific HTML object will exist, but will have no elements.

Access To Elements Of A Web Page

Conceptually once a web page is rendered (*painted*) in a browser window it is completely static.

For any program code to be able to interact with the web page, each element of the web page would have to be held in memory, with a unique name. The unique name translates to a context area in memory where the web page element resides.

Hence, while a web page is being assembled in memory (RAM) prior being rendered (*made visible*) in the browser's window, a JavaScript enabled browser creates several arrays as described earlier. These arrays hold references to individual web page objects in their (*indexed*) elements.

Referencing an appropriate element in its associated array provides access to each element of a web page. Hence, using JavaScript web page elements can be updated or processed. Once processed, the web page can be re-rendered in the browser. When re-rendered in the browser changes made to the web page elements will be visible.

If updation or processing of any web page element is done, *based on client input*, the web page is then an *interactive* web page.

How A Web Page Element Is Manipulated

HTML tags are used to create (*instantiate*) objects in a web page. For example, <INPUT Type="TEXT"> will instantiates a text box on the web page when encountered in HTML code.

Each HTML object instantiated in a web page has **properties** and **methods** that allow access to the object's properties. Each HTML object has an **event** or several **events** bound to the object when the object was created. Thus an HTML object can recognize a specific event when it occurs.

Once the HTML object recognizes that an event has occurred this knowledge has to be passed to JavaScript so that JavaScript also recognizes that the 'event' occurred. To facilitate this JavaScript provides a number of named JavaScript 'Event Handlers'. The names of these event handlers are descriptively bound to an HTML object's event name.

Example:
A **Change** event is recognized by a text box when its contents change. JavaScript provides an event handler called **onChange** that is internally bound to the **Change** event of the text box. The **Change** event of the text box talks to the **onChange** event handler of JavaScript. The **onChange** event handler of JavaScript can then execute an appropriate JavaScript code snippet. For example:

```
<INPUT Type="TEXT" onChange="<myFunction>">
```

Here the JavaScript function **myFunction** is bound to the JavaScript event handler onChange. The assignment operator (=) does this binding.

The JavaScript, onChange event handler, is bound to the HTML object **TEXT** by being passed as one of its attributes.

Hence, as soon as the **Change** event of the text box occurs the JavaScript event handler onChange is invoked.

Since the JavaScript function myFunction is bound to the JavaScript event handler onChange, as soon as the onChange event handler is invoked the JavaScript code in myFunction executes.

HANDLING (WEB PAGE) EVENTS USING JAVASCRIPT

A web page event could be associated with the action of the mouse cursor on the web page. Such as:

- A mouse-click on an object in a web page
- The movement of the mouse cursor across a web page
- The mouse cursor hovering at a specific place on a web page and so on

These will be events recognized by the Window object of the DOM.

Other web page events could be the opening or closing of a Window, the loading of an image in a web page and so on.

JavaScript's approach to working with web page elements is a multi step process:

- ❑ Identify a web page object
- ❑ Choose an appropriate event associated with the object
- ❑ Have a standard method of connecting an object's event and JavaScript code snippets. JavaScript **event handlers** mapped to an object's **events** do this.

JavaScript has several named event handlers that are mapped to an HTML object's events. To work with JavaScript it is necessary to understand how to use JavaScript 'Event Handlers' correctly.

JavaScript, event handlers, can be divided into two types **Interactive** and **Non Interactive**.

An interactive event handler depends on user interaction with an HTML page. For example, the JavaScript **onMouseOver** event handler is an interactive event handler. This requires the user to move the mouse cursor over a web page.

A JavaScript, non-interactive, event handler, does not need user interaction to be invoked. For example the JavaScript 'onLoad' event handler is a non-interactive event handler as it automatically executes whenever a form is loaded into a web page.

Table 9.4 details JavaScript event handlers that descriptively bound to HTML object events. As long as the HTML object has an associated event, JavaScript provides an associated, named, event handler.

Named JavaScript Event Handlers

JavaScript Event Handler	Will Be Called When
onAbort	The loading of an image is aborted as a result of user action
onBlur	A document, window, frame set, or form element loses current input focus.
onChange	A text field, text area, file-uploaded field or selection is modified and loses the current input focus.
onClick	A link, client-side image map area or document is clicked
onDblClick	A link, client-side image map area or document is double clicked
onDragDrop	A dragged object is dropped in a window or frame
onError	An error occurs during loading of an image, window or frame
onFocus	A document, window, frame set, or form element receives the current input focus
onKeyDown	The user presses a Key
onKeyPress	The user presses and releases a Key
onKeyUp	The user releases a Key
onLoad	An image, document or frame set is loaded
onMouseDown	The user presses a mouse button
onMouseMove	The user moves the mouse
onMouseOut	The mouse is moved out of a link or an area of a client side image map
onMouseOver	The mouse is moved over a link or an area of a client side image map
onMouseUp	The user releases a mouse button
onReset	The user resets a form by clicking on the form's reset button
onResize	The user resizes a window or frame
onSelect	Text is selected in a text field or a text area
onSubmit	The user presses a form's submit button
onUnload	The user exits a document or frame set

Table 9.4

The naming convention followed by Java Script makes it easy to identify a JavaScript event handler. The JavaScript, event handler's name, simply has the string '*on*' added to the HTML object's event name (e.g. *on**MouseOver***).

Example:

<A HRef=http://www.sctindia.com onMouseOver="*<JavaScript code snippet itself>* **or** *<A call to a* JavaScript *function>*">`Text associated with the Link`</A>

Tip

Here, the **onMouseOver** JavaScript event handler is bound to the hyperlink <A> . . . </A> HTML tag. When the mouse cursor moves over the hyperlink its **MouseOver** event occurs. When **MouseOver** event occurs a call is made to the JavaScript event handler **onMouseOver**. When the JavaScript **onMouseOver** event handler is invoked a JavaScript code snippet can execute directly or a JavaScript function can be called.

Note

If a JavaScript code snippet is directly passed as a value to an HTML attribute **and** is enclosed in **double quotes** ("), then double quotes (") cannot be used within the enclosed JavaScript code. Replacing these double quotes with single quotes (') where necessary.

To use the JavaScript DOM and manipulate its objects properties will help in raising this basic comfort level to a confidence level required for coding in JavaScript.

To achieve this several examples which use the HTML **<FORM> . . . </FORM>** tags along with their attributes mapped to JavaScript code will be used.

SELF REVIEW QUESTIONS

FILL IN THE BLANKS

1. Using the ________ ________ ________ JavaScript enabled browsers identify the collection of web page objects that have to be dealt with while rendering an HTML based web page in the browser window.
2. ________ ________ ________ use JavaScript to control a document's presentation style
3. ________ of an object are used to set or get a value of an object's property.
4. JavaScript event handlers can be divided into two types ________ and ________.
5. ________ object is used to access information about the browser that is executing the current script

TRUE OR FALSE

6. If the document does not have any links described in it, the Link object does not exist.
7. JavaScript 'onLoad' event handler is an interactive event handler as it automatically executes whenever a form is loaded into a web page.
8. The browser creates one array in memory per HTML object in the document.

HANDS ON EXERCISES

1. Create a Web page using two image files, which switch between one another as the mouse pointer moves over the images. Use the onMouseOver and onMouseOut event handlers. The output is as shown in the diagrams 9.5 and 9.6.

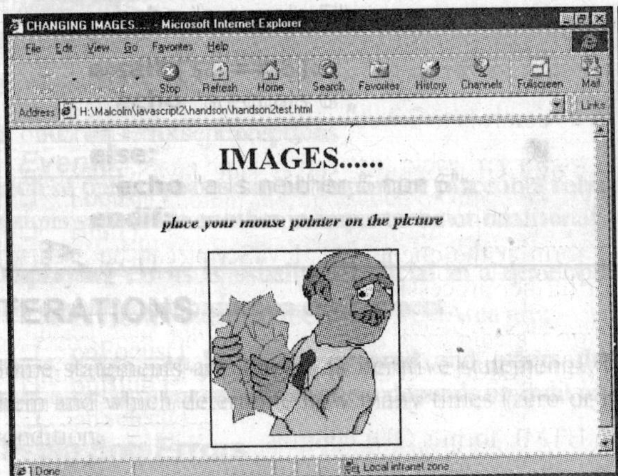

Diagram 9.5: Output for Hands on Exercise.

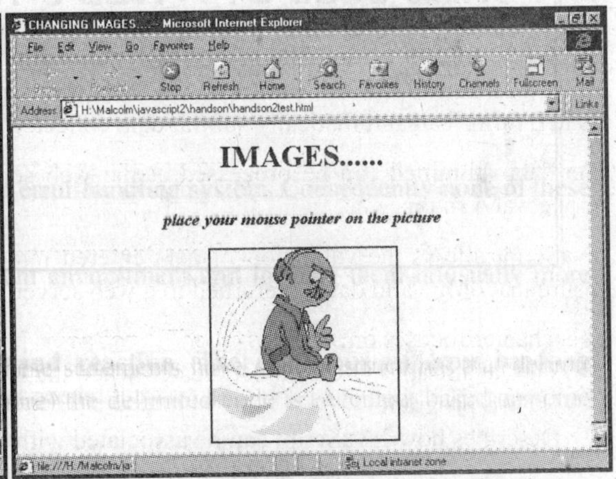

Diagram 9.6: Output for Hands on Exercise.

10. FORMS USED BY A WEB SITE

An HTML form provides data gathering functionality to a web page. This is very useful if the web site is used to advertise and sell products. HTML forms provide a full range of GUI controls. Additionally, HTML forms can automatically submit data collected in its controls to a web server.

The data submitted can be processed at the web server by CGI programs, server side JavaScripts, Java Servlets and so on.

JavaScript allows the validation of data entered into a form at the client side. JavaScript can be used to ensure that only valid data is returned to a web server for further processing.

This chapter focuses on:

- ❑ The JavaScript FORM object created when the HTML <FORM> </FORM> tags are encountered in an HTML program.
- ❑ Describes how JavaScript can be associated with an HTML form's GUI controls.

After working through chapter examples the following will be understood:

- ❑ The properties and methods of the JavaScript FORM object and it's associated GUI controls.
- ❑ How JavaScript is used to handle form related events and perform (*client side - in the browser window*) local processing of form data.

THE FORM OBJECT

When creating an interactive web site for the Internet it is necessary to capture user input and process this input. Based on the result of this processing, appropriate information from a web site can be dispatched to be viewed. Both the capturing of user input and the rendering of appropriate web pages takes place in the client side, browser's window.

Traditionally, user input is captured in a **Form**. HTML provides the **<FORM> ... </FORM>** tags with which an HTML form can be created to capture user input.

As soon as the **<FORM> ... </FORM>** tags are encountered in an HTML program by a JavaScript enabled browser, the browser creates a '*forms array*' in memory. This array tracks the number of form objects described in the HTML program.

Each form object in the HTML page will be described between its own <FORM> **...** </FORM> HTML tags. Should there be multiple forms (i.e. multiple occurrences of the <FORM> **...** </FORM> tags) described in the HTML page then the forms array will have multiple (*indexed*) elements, each holding a reference to an HTML form object.

The first form object described in the HTML file being held as array index[0], the second form object described in the HTML file being held in the array index[1] and so on. By referencing a specific index number of the forms array a specific form object can be accessed. The JavaScript **forms array** also holds information about each object used within the **<FORM> ... </FORM>** tags.

Common HTML objects used between the **<FORM> ... </FORM>** tags are **Text**, **TextArea**, **Radio Buttons**, **Buttons**, **Check Boxes** and so on. An HTML form is used extensively in creating interactive web pages. Using the associated arrays created by a JavaScript enabled browser and JavaScript code, all form elements (*objects contained in the form*) are accessible. Once accessible their properties can be manipulated so as to control the functionality of the form at run time.

There are two forms in the HTML file; **Form1** and **Form2**. Refer to diagram 10.1. These will be held in the first two elements of the Forms array. **Form1** will be an address, which points to where the Form elements array is located.

Form1 in the Forms array, will be a reference to the context area where the elements of Form1 are located. Form1 has three form elements.

Form2 in the Forms array, is a reference to the context area where the elements of Form2 are located. Form2 has five form elements.

To understand this model, let us write a JavaScript procedure that will read the elements of the Form object's array, and return the number of actual form objects held.

Once the reference to the form's elements are known let us write a JavaScript procedure that will read the each Form's Element array and return the names of the form elements held in the array. The elements held in each of the arrays must be exactly the same as the elements described between the **<FORM>...</FORM>** tags in the HTML file running in the browser.

Forms Object's (Array)

Index	Value
0	Form1
1	Form2

Form1.Elements

Index	Value
0	Form1.Element1
1	Form1.Element2
2	Form1.Element3

Form2.Elements

Index	Value
0	Form2.Element1
1	Form2.Element2
2	Form2.Element3
3	Form2.Element4
4	Form2.Element5

Diagram 10.1: The Form Element's Array

Exercise 1:

Focus: Count the number of elements in a Form's, elements array. Check the number returned against the number of form elements described between the **<FORM>...</FORM>** tags in the HTML page that is running in the Browser. Recognize that the number of elements in the elements array match the number of elements described between the <FORM>**...**</FORM> tags in the HTML page exactly.

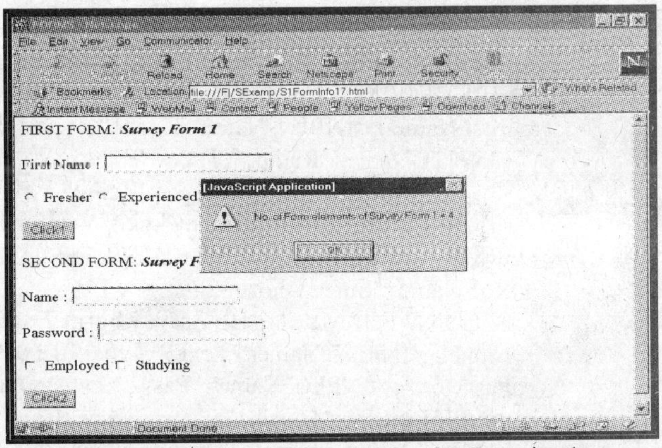

Diagram 10.2.1: First message for Exercise 1.

The diagram 10.2.1 shows an Alert box that displays a message indicating the number of form elements of implemented by the First Form in the HTML file. Refer to the HTML and JavaScript code described in Exercise 1.

Pop up an Alert that displays the individual form elements of the array and recognize that these are the same as are specified between the <FORM>**...**</FORM> tags in the HTML program

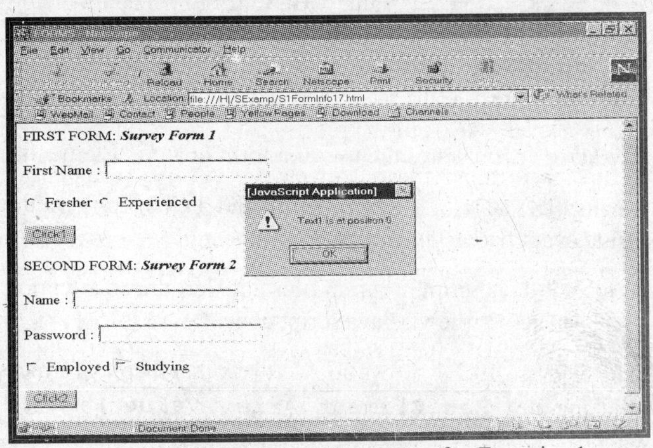

Diagram 10.2.2: Second message for Exercise 1.

The diagram 10.2.2 shows an Alert box displaying a message that the Textbox named **Text1** of the First Form is at position **0** in the Elements array.

The Code Listing For Exercise 1:

```
<HMTL>
  <HEAD><TITLE>FORMS</TITLE>
<!-- The code allows to access the Form objects Elements Array //-->
  <SCRIPT Language="JavaScript">
    function Ver(form1) {
      v = form1.elements.length;
      if (form1.elements[3].name == "Button1") {
        alert('First form name : ' + document.forms[0].name);
        alert('No. of Form elements of ' + document.forms[0].name + ' = ' + v);
      }
      else if (form1.elements[4].name == "Button2") {
        alert('Second form name : ' + document.forms[1].name);
        alert('No. of Form elements of ' + document.forms[1].name + ' = ' + v);
      }
      for(i=0; i < v; i++)
        alert(form1.elements[i].name + ' is at position ' + i);
    }
  </SCRIPT></HEAD>
  <BODY>
    <FORM Name="Survey Form 1">
      FIRST FORM: <I><B>Survey Form 1 </B></I><BR/><BR/>
      First Name : <INPUT Name="Text1" Type="Text" Value="" /><BR/><BR/>
      <INPUT Name="Radio1" Type="Radio" Value="" /> Fresher
      <INPUT Name="Radio2" Type="Radio" Value="" /> Experienced<BR/><BR/>
      <INPUT Name="Button1" onClick="Ver(form)" Type="Button" Value="Click1" />
    </FORM>
    <FORM Name="Survey Form 2">
      SECOND FORM: <I><B> Survey Form 2 </B></I><BR/><BR/>
      Name : <INPUT Name="Text2" Type="Text" Value="" /> <BR/><BR/>
      Password : <INPUT Name="Pass2" Type="Password" Value="" /> <BR/><BR/>
      <INPUT Name="Check1" Type="CheckBox" Value="" /> Employed
      <INPUT Name="Check2" Type="CheckBox" Value="" /> Studying <BR/><BR/>
      <INPUT Name="Button2" onClick="Ver(form)" Type="Button" Value="Click2" />
    </FORM>
  </BODY>
</HTML>
```

Exercise 2: Illustrates the use of a form object's Elements array

Focus: The state of a Radio button and a Checkbox on the HTML form can be programmatically changed using event based JavaScript, *i.e. on the clicked event of a command button.*

When the JavaScript program runs an Alert draws attention to the fact that the Checkbox, **checked** property has been set to true via JavaScript code.

The diagram 10.3.1 shows an Alert box that displays a message indicating that the Checkbox is checked, on clicking the `Set Element Array Value` button.

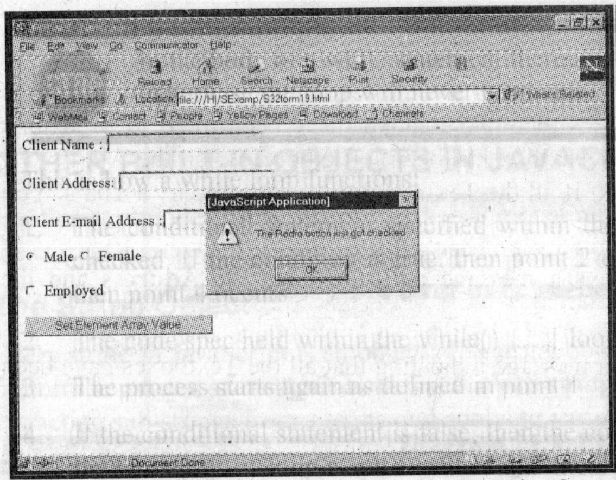

Diagram 10.3.1: First message for Exercise 2.

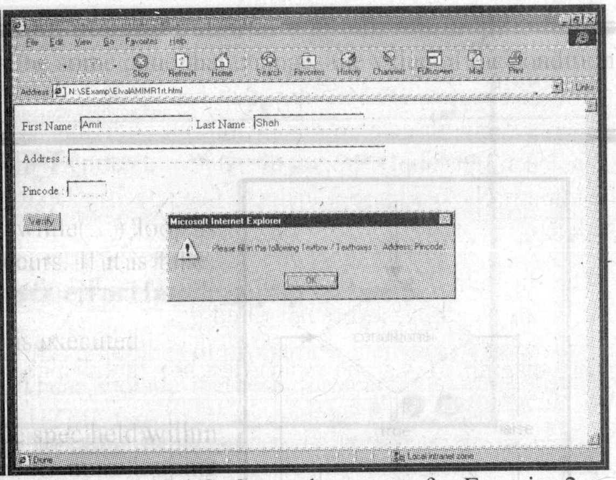

Diagram 10.3.2: Second message for Exercise 2.

On clicking the first Alert's **OK** button, another Alert pops up that displays a message indicating that the Radio button is checked, when the same 'Set Element Array Value' button was clicked.

Conceptually, without clicking on the HTML form objects their 'Checked' properties have been set. This illustrates how JavaScript code can access a form's element via the form elements array and manipulate an element's properties.

As soon as the elements properties change the Browser will display the object with its changed property in the HTML page. <u>Refer to the HTML and JavaScript code described in Exercise 2.</u>

The Code Listing For Exercise 2:

```
<HMTL>
   <HEAD><TITLE>FORMS</TITLE>
<!-- The code allows to access the Form objects Elements Array //-->
   <SCRIPT Language='JavaScript'>
      function Chk(f1) {
         f1.Check.checked=true;
         alert("The Checkbox just got checked");
         f1.Check.checked=false;
         f1.Radio[0].checked=true;
         f1.Radio[1].checked=false;
         alert("The Radio button just got checked");
      }
   </SCRIPT></HEAD>
   <BODY><FORM>
      Client Name : <INPUT Name="Text" Type="Text" Value="" /><BR/><BR/>
      Client Address : <INPUT Name="Text1" Type="Text" Value="" /> <BR/><BR/>
      Client E-mail Address : <INPUT Name="Text2" Type="Text" Value="" /><BR/><BR/>
      <INPUT Name="Radio" Type="radio" Value="" /> Male
      <INPUT Name="Radio" Type="radio" Value="" /> Female<BR/><BR/>
      <INPUT Name="Check" Type="CheckBox" Value="" /> Employed <BR/><BR/>
      <INPUT Name="Bt" onClick="Chk(this.form)" Type="Button"
            Value="Set Element Array Value"
   </FORM></BODY>
</HTML>
```

Exercise 3:

Focus: Create a HTML form that has a number of Textboxes. When the form runs in the Browser fill the Textboxes with data. Write JavaScript code that verifies that all Textboxes have been filled. If a Textbox has been left empty, popup an Alert indicating which Textbox has been left empty. When the Alert's OK button is clicked on, Set focus to that specific Textbox. If all the Textboxes are filled, display a Thank You alert.

The diagram 10.4.1 shows an Alert box that displays a message indicating that the **Address** and the **Pincode** Textboxes were not filled in.

The diagram 10.4.2 shows an Alert box that displays a message indicating that all the Textboxes have been filled.

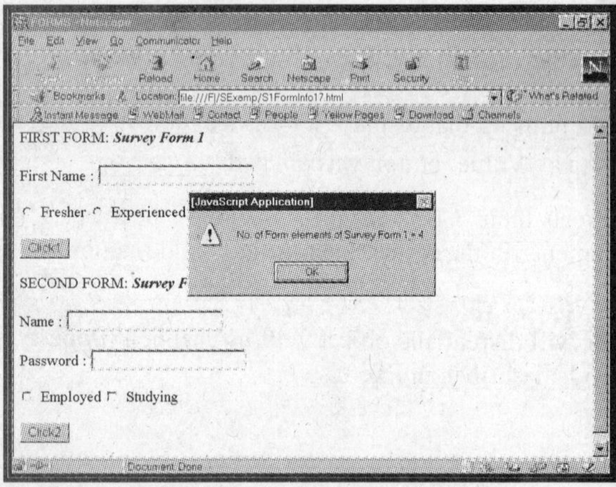

Diagram 10.4.1: First message for Exercise 1.

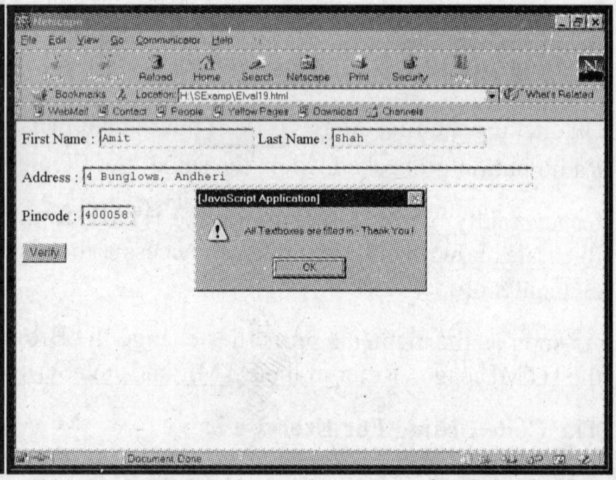

Diagram 10.4.2: Second message for Exercise 3.

This is a simple exercise, which illustrates how JavaScript code can be used to validate data that is entered in a Form.

Based on this concept, business rules can be implemented in any HTML form using JavaScript.

Thus data being entered into an HTML form can be validated on the client's machine before being dispatched to a web server for further processing. <u>Refer to the HTML and JavaScript code described in Exercise 3.</u>

The code listing for Exercise 3:

```
<HTML>
    <HEAD><SCRIPT LANGUAGE="JAVASCRIPT">
        function verifyData() {
            a=0;    r="";
            for (i=0; i<=4; i++) {
                if (document.forms[0].elements[i].value == "") {
                    a=1;
                    r = r + " " + document.forms[0].elements[i].name + ";" ;
                }
                else if ((i > 3)&&(a==0)) {
                    alert("All Textboxes are filled in - Thank You !");
                }
```

```
            }
            for (i=0; i<=4; i++) {
                if (document.forms[0].elements[i].value == "") {
                    alert("Please fill in the following Textbox / Textboxes :- " + r);
                    document.forms[0].elements[i].focus( );
                    break;
                }
            }
        }
    </SCRIPT></HEAD>
    <BODY><FORM>
        First Name : <INPUT Name="Firstname" Type="Text" Size=20 />
        Last Name : <INPUT Name="Lastname" Type="Text" Size=20 />
        <P>Address : <INPUT Name="Address" Type="Text" Size=60 /></P>
        <P>Pincode : <INPUT Name="Pincode" Type="Text" Size=6 /></P>
        <INPUT Name="act" onClick="verifyData( )" Type="button"Value="Verify" />
    </FORM></BODY>
    <SCRIPT Language="JavaScript">
        document.forms[0].Firstname.focus( );
    </SCRIPT>
</HTML>
```

The Form Object's Methods

HTML forms can be made up of a variety of HTML elements that accept user input. The <FORM> </FORM> HTML tags enclose the HTML elements that make up the form. Once a JavaScript enabled browser encounters these tags in an HTML file the JavaScript enabled browser creates a **form object** in memory, which is held as an element of the forms array. The form object has properties like **Name, Method** and **Action**.

Method

The **Method** property of a form is used to specify the method used to send data captured by various form elements back to the web server. The method used can be either **Get** or **Post**.

The **Get** method sends the data captured by form elements to the web server encoded into a URL, which points to a web server. The data captured in form elements is appended to the URL.

This technique is used when there is a small amount of data being sent back to the web server. The maximum amount of data that can be sent back to the web server using this method is 1024 bytes.

The **Post** method sends the data captured by form elements back to the web server as a separate bit-stream of data. When there is a large amount of data to be sent back to the web server, this is the method used.

If the method attribute is not specified within the <FORM> </FORM> tags, the default method used by the browser to send data back to the web server is the ***Get*** method, *i.e. as an encoded URL.*

Action

The **Action** attribute of the **<FORM>...</FORM>** tags points to the URL (*address*) of a program on the web server that will process the form data captured and being sent back. The server side program that processes this data can be written in any scripting language that the web server understands.

Commonly used web server side scripting languages are:

- JavaScript - (*used with the Netscape suite of web servers*)
- VB Script and ASP - (*used with the Microsoft suite of web servers*)
- Perl, ANSI C - (*used with the Unix based suite of web servers*) and so on.

HTML elements used to capture form data are specified as attributes of the **<INPUT>...</INPUT>** tags used within the **<FORM>...</FORM>** tags.

The HTML form elements that can be specified as attributes to the <INPUT> tag are:

Form Elements	Description & Syntax
Text	A text field (<INPUT Type="**Text**">)
Password	A password text field in which each keystroke appears as an asterisk(*) (<INPUT Type="**Password**">)
Button	A new element that provides a button other than a submit or reset button (<INPUT Type="**Button**">)
Checkbox	A checkbox (<INPUT Type="**Checkbox**">)
Radio	A radio button (<INPUT Type="**Radio**">)
Reset	A reset button (<INPUT Type="**Reset**">)
Submit	A submit button (<INPUT Type="**Submit**">)
Select	A selection list (<SELECT><OPTION>option1</OPTION> <OPTION>option2</OPTION></SELECT>)
TextArea	A multi line text entry field (<TEXTAREA>Default Text</TEXTAREA>)
Hidden	A field that may contain a value but is not displayed within a form (<INPUT Type="**Hidden**">)

Table 10.1

Each of these form elements can be named. Once named, their names can then be used for referencing them in JavaScript. 'Name' is a property associated with every HTML object used in a form.

There are several other Properties and Methods associated with each of these form objects. These Properties and Methods, along with the objects with which they are associated is summarized as follows:

Properties Of Form Elements

Form Element Name	Property Name	Description
Text Password TextArea Button Radio CheckBox Select Submit Reset Hidden Fileupload	Name	Indicates the name of the object. This name can be used for referencing the object in future, when required.

Table 10.2: Properties Of Form Elements

Form Element Name	Property Name	Description
Text	Value	Indicates the current value of the element.
Password		
TextArea		
Button		
Radio		
CheckBox		
Submit		
Reset		
Hidden		
Fileupload		
Select		It contains any value indicated in the option tag.
Text	DefaultValue	Indicates the default value of the object.
Password		
TextArea		
Radio Button	Checked	Indicates the current status of the object, whether checked or unchecked.
Check Box		
Radio Button	DefaultChecked	Indicates the default status of the element.
Check Box		
Radio	Length	Indicates the number of radio buttons in a group.
Radio Button	Index	Indicates the index value of the currently selected radio button.
Select		Contains the index value in the current option of the options array.
	Text	Contains the value of the text displayed in the menu for the specific option
	SelectedIndex	Contains the index number of the currently selected option.
	DefaultSelected	Indicates whether the option is selected by default in the option tag.
	Selected	Indicates the current status of the option.

Table 10.2: Properties Of Form Elements (Continued)

Methods of Form Elements

Form Element Name	Method Name	Description
Text	onFocus()	Fires when the form cursor enters into an object.
Password		
TextArea		
Text	onBlur()	Fires when the form cursor is moved away from an object.
Password		
TextArea		
Text	onSelect()	Fires when text is selected in an object.
Password		
TextArea		
Text	onChange()	Fires when text is changed in an object.
Password		
TextArea		
Button	onClick()	Fires when an object is clicked on.
Radio		
Checkbox		
Submit		
Reset		

Table 10.3: Methods Of Form Elements

The Text Element

Text elements are data entry fields used in HTML forms. Text fields accept a single line of text entry.

Properties

The text object has the following properties:

- name
- value

Methods

The text object has the following methods:

- focus()
- blur()
- select()
  (Selects the text in the data entry field, i.e. causes the text to be highlighted).

Events

- Focus()
- Blur()
- Select()
- Change()

JavaScript provides the following event handlers for the text object's events:

- onFocus()
- onBlur()
- onSelect()
- onChange()

Syntax:

<INPUT Name="`<NameOfTheObject>`**" Type="Text" Value="**`<DefaultValue>`**">**

Example:

<INPUT Name="txt_age" Type="Text" Value="18">

This places a **Text** field (i.e. a single line text edit area) within an HTML form, which can be referenced by the name **txt_age**. The text field will immediately display the value **18**.

The Password Element

The password element is a unique type of text entry field. All keystrokes for this field are displayed as an asterisk [*]. This makes the password element ideal for accepting input of confidential information, such as a password, bank account number or a personal identification number.

Properties

The password object has the following properties:

- defaultValue
- name
- value

Methods

The password object has the following methods:

- focus()
- blur()
- select()
  (Selects text in the password element, i.e. causes selected text to be highlighted).

Events

The password object has the following methods:

- Focus()
- Blur()
- Select()
- Change()

JavaScript provides the following event handlers for the password object's events:

- onFocus()
- onBlur()
- onSelect()
- onChange()

Syntax:

<INPUT Name="`<NameOfTheObject>`**" Type="Password" Value="**`<DefaultValue>`**">**

Example:

<INPUT Name="txt_usr_pswd" Type="Password" Value="">

This places a **Password** field within an HTML form, which can be referenced by the name **txt_user_name**.

The Button Element

An HTML button element is a commonly used form object. It is generally used to trigger appropriate form level processing.

Properties

- name
- value

Method

- click()

Event

- click()

JavaScript provides the following event handler for the button object's event:

- onClick().

Syntax:

<INPUT Name="`<NameOfTheObject>`**" Type="Button" Value="**`<ButtonLabel>`**">**

Example:

<INPUT Name="btn_check" Type="Button" Value="Verify...">

This places a **Button** on the HTML form named **btn_check**. The button will display the text **Verify...** on its face as a label.

Exercise 4:

Focus: Develop a HTML Page, which accepts:

- Any mathematical expression
- Evaluates the expression
- Displays the result of the evaluation

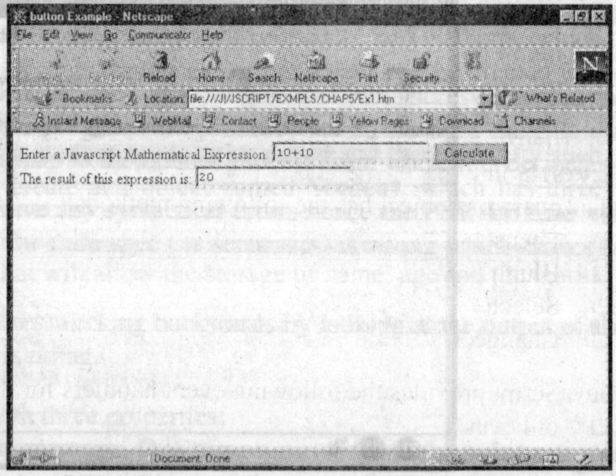

Diagram 10.5: Output for Exercise 4.

To achieve this a form is created which has two **Text** objects and one **Button** object as shown in diagram 10.5. The first **Text** object is used to accept a mathematical expression for evaluation. When the **Button** object (Calculate) is clicked on, the second **Text** object will display the output of the evaluation of the expression entered into the first **Text** object. Refer to the HTML and JavaScript code described in Exercise 4.

The Code listing for Exercise 4:

```
<HTML>
    <HEAD><TITLE>Using Text and Button objects in an HTML Form</TITLE>
    <SCRIPT Language="JavaScript">
        function calculate(form) {
            form.results.value = eval(form.entry.value);
        }
    </SCRIPT></HEAD>
    <BODY><FORM>Enter a Javascript Mathematical Expression:
        <INPUT Type="Text" Name="entry" Value="" />
        <INPUT Type="button" Value="Calculate" onClick="calculate(this.form);" /><BR/>
        The result of this expression is:
        <INPUT Type="Text" Name="results" onFocus="this.blur();" />
    </FORM></BODY>
</HTML>
```

When this program is executed in a JavaScript enabled browser, the used defined JavaScript function **calculate()** is registered by the browser first as it is written between the **<HEAD>... </HEAD>** tags.

The lines of code between the <FORM> </FORM> tags creates a form as seen in diagram 10.5. Enter an expression in the first 'Text' object on the form for evaluation and with the mouse cursor click on the button 'Calculate'.

When the button Calculate is clicked on its **click()** event fires. This in turn will activate the JavaScript event handler **onClick**. This invokes the function **calculate()**.

The function **calculate()** evaluates the expression entered in the first **Text** object and displays its output in the second **Text** object on the form.

The Submit (Button) Element

The submit button is a special purpose button. The submit button submits the **current** data held in **each** data aware, form element to a Web Sever for further processing.

Properties

The submit button is associated with 2 properties:

- name
- value

Method

The submit button's method is:

- click()

Event

The submit button's event is:

- click()

JavaScript provides the following event handler for the Submit button's event:

- onClick().

Example:

```
<INPUT Name="btn_submit" Type="Submit" Value="SUBMIT DATA">
```

This will place a **Submit** button on an HTML form, named **btn_submit**. The Submit button will display **SUBMIT DATA**. When this button is pressed the contents of each data aware, form element will be sent back to a web server for further processing.

Note

There is no example to the functionality of the HTML **submit** button at this stage since this material is only focused on client side JavaScript exclusively.

In subsequent chapters where PERL CGI programming is covered the **GET** and **POST** methods of the **Form** object will be covered with appropriate examples.

The Reset (Button) Element

Properties

The reset button has 2 properties, (*the same as the button*):

- name
- value

Methods

The reset button has only one method associated with it:

- click()

Events

The reset button has only one event associated with it:

- click()

The reset button's JavaScript event handler is:

- onClick( )

Example:

```
<INPUT Name="btn_reset" Type="Reset" Value=" RESET FORM ">
```

This places a **Reset** button on the HTML form, named **btn_reset**. When this button is pressed each data aware form object will be reset to their default values. All user-input values will be initialized.

The Submit and Reset buttons are usually used together on an HTML form. The Submit button will cause the contents of all the data aware form elements to be dispatched to the web server for further processing. The Reset button will empty the contents of the form objects so that the form is ready for reuse.

Note

It is good programming practice to simulate the reset button in a form's unLoad() event.

This will ensure that whenever a form is closed its fields will be emptied so that the next time the form is opened, its form elements will be empty, ready for reuse.

Exercise 5: To illustrate how the **Reset** button on a form functions.

Focus: Create a form having Textboxes, Radio buttons, a Checkbox and a Reset button as shown in diagram 10.6.1. On clicking the Reset button, the entire form is reset (i.e. cleared). Refer to the HTML and JavaScript code described in Exercise 5.

When the Reset button is clicked the form will appear as in diagram 10.6.2.

The diagram 10.6.2 shows an Alert box that displays a message indicating that all the form elements have been cleared.

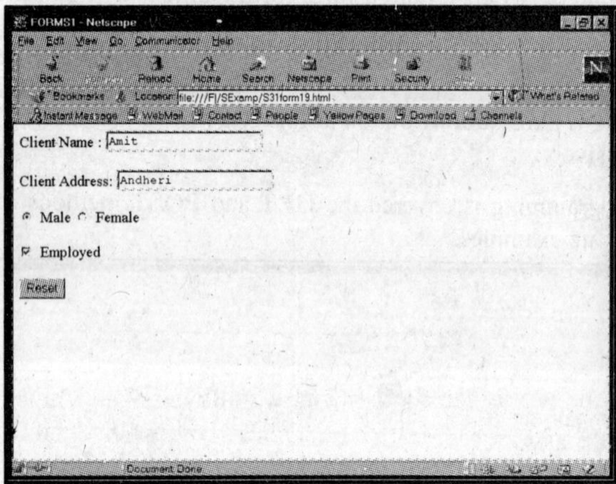

Diagram 10.6.1: First message for Exercise 5.

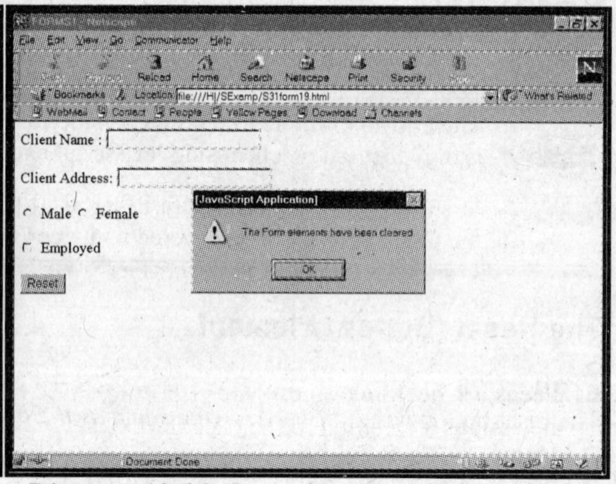

Diagram 10.6.2: Second message for Exercise 5.

The code listing for Exercise 5:

```
<HTML>
   <HEAD><TITLE>FORMS1</TITLE>
<!-- Using Reset Button //-->
   <SCRIPT>
      function func(f1) {    alert("The Form Elements have been cleared");        }
   </SCRIPT></HEAD>
   <BODY><FORM onReset="func(this.form)">
      Client Name : <INPUT Name="Text1" Type="Text" Value="" /><BR/><BR/>
      Client Address : <INPUT Name="Text2" Type="Text" Value="" /><BR/><BR/>
      <INPUT Type="Radio" Name="Radio" Value="" />Male
      <INPUT Type="Radio" Name="Radio" Value="" />Female<BR/><BR/>
```

```
    <INPUT Type="CheckBox" Name="Check" Value="" />Employed<BR/><BR/>
    <INPUT Name="Rst" Type="Reset" Value="Reset" />
  </FORM></BODY>
</HTML>
```

The Checkbox Element

A checkbox is an HTML form object that behaves as a toggle switch. This means a checkbox can be in either one of two states, either **checked** or **unchecked**. A checkbox is used to return a single specific value to a web server. Either **T** or **F** or **1** or **0** can be returned depending upon whether the checkbox is checked or unchecked. Based on the value returned from the HTML form, a web server script can decide what further proccssing the web server should do.

Properties

- name
- value
- checked

Method

- click()

Event

- click()

A checkbox's JavaScript event handler is:

- onClick()

Syntax:

<INPUT Name="`<NameOfTheObject>`**" Type="checkbox" Value="**`<Yes/No>`**"** CHECKED>

Example:

<INPUT Name="Employed" Type="Checkbox" VALUE="Yes" CHECKED>

This places a **Checkbox** on an HTML form, which can be referenced by the name **Employed**. The Value attribute assigns a meaning to the checkbox. This is the value that is returned if the check box is **Checked**.

The checkbox is checked on (*i.e. marked checked*) by default. Hence, if the check box is not unchecked and the form is submitted to a web server this check box will automatically return the value **Yes**.

Exercise 6:

Focus: Develop a HTML Page, which uses two text fields and a checkbox. The **first** text object accepts a numeric value. Depending on the **checked** or **unchecked** state of the **checkbox**, the **second** text object displays:

Checkbox is **not** checked	**Double** the numeric value entered
Checkbox **is** checked	The **square** of the numeric value entered

If the **second** text object is loaded with a numeric value depending on the **checked** or **unchecked** state of the **checkbox**, the **first** text object displays:

Checkbox is **not** checked	**Half** the numeric value entered
Checkbox **is** checked	The **square root** of the numeric value entered

Whenever the state of the checkbox is changed, recalculation and display of values takes place appropriately. The diagram 10.7 shows a form created to perform mathematical calculations as specified above. Refer to the HTML and JavaScript code described in Exercise 6.

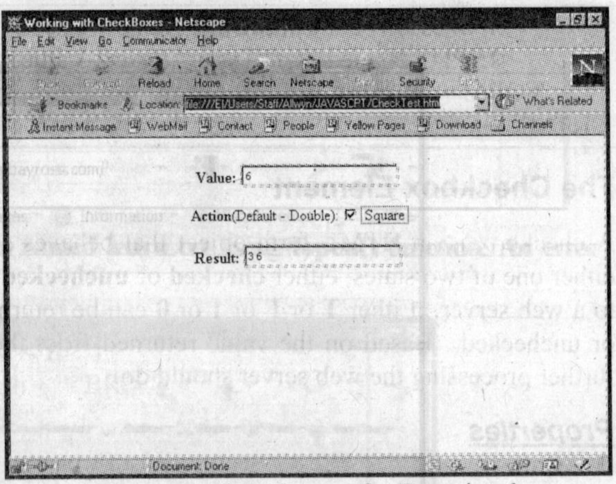

Diagram 10.7: Output for Exercise 6.

The Code Listing for Exercise 6:

```
<HTML>
    <HEAD><TITLE>Working with Check
            Boxes</TITLE>
    <SCRIPT>
        function calculate(form, callingField) {
            if (callingField == "result") {
                if(form.square.checked) {
                    form.entry.value = Math.sqrt(form.result.value);
                }
                else {    form.entry.value = form.result.value/2;        }
            }
            else {
                if(form.square.checked) {
                    form.result.value = form.entry.value * form.entry.value;
                }
                else {  form.result.value = form.entry.value * 2;   }
            }
        }
    </SCRIPT></HEAD>
    <BODY><FORM><CENTER><BR/>
        <B>Value:</B>
        <INPUT Name="entry" onChange="calculate(this.form, this.name);" Type="Text" Value="0" />
        <BR/><BR/><B>Action</B>(Default - Double):
        <INPUT Name="square" onClick="calculate(this.form, this.name);" Type="Checkbox" />Square
        <BR/><BR/><B>Result:</B>
        <INPUT onChange="calculate(this.form, this.name);" Name="result" Type="Text" Value=0 />
    </CENTER></FORM></BODY>
</HTML>
```

Analysis

This example illustrates the use of the **onClick** event handler of a check box. If the check box is *checked* or *not* passes an appropriate Boolean value back to the JavaScript, user defined, function **calculate()**. Depending upon this value a decision is made.

A checkbox named **square** is placed on the HTML form it can be **checked** or **unchecked**.

If a value is placed in the **first** text field on the form and the checkbox is *checked*, the *square* of the value in the first text field will be displayed in the **second** text field. If the checkbox is unchecked *double* the numeric value of the first text field will be displayed in the second text field.

If a value is placed in the **second** text field on the form and the checkbox is checked, the *half* the value held in the second text field will be displayed in the **first** text field. If the checkbox it is unchecked then the *square root* of the value in the second text field will be displayed in the first text field.

The *onClick* event handler of the *checkbox* ensures that when checkbox is clicked, to change (*toggle*) its state, all values are recalculated.

The onChange event handler of the *text boxes* ensures that when the values in the text fields change, the form is recalculated.

The Radio Element

The radio button element has two states and can toggle between them. The one special exception is that when several radio buttons are combined into a radio (button) group only a single radio button can be selected at any given time. Giving the **same name** to all the radio buttons places them in the same radio group.

Properties

- checked
- index
- length
- name

Method

- clicked( )

Event

- clicked()

A radio button's JavaScript event handler is:

- onClicked( )

Syntax:

```
<INPUT Type="Radio" Name="<RadioGroupName>" Value="<1/0>"
    CHECKED="CHECKED" />
```

Example:

```
<INPUT Type="Radio" Name="Numbers" Value="1" Checked="Checked" >1<BR/>
<INPUT Type="Radio" Name="Numbers" Value="2" >2<BR/>
<INPUT Type="Radio" Name="Numbers" Value="3" >3<BR/>.
```

This places three *radio buttons* on the HTML form, belonging to the same radio group called '*Numbers*'. The first radio button will be set as *active* as soon as the HTML page is visible.

Exercise 7:

Focus: An HTML form displays two text boxes and two radio buttons. The first text box accepts a numeric value. If the **first** radio button if active, **double** the number entered in the first text field will be displayed in the second text field. If the **second** radio button is active the **square** of the number entered in the first field will be displayed in the second text field.

Whenever the radio buttons are toggled, recalculation takes place and the output is displayed appropriately.

The diagram 10.8 show a form created to perform mathematical calculations as specified above. Refer to the HTML and JavaScript code described in Exercise 7.

The Code Listing for Exercise 7:

```
<HTML>
    <HEAD><TITLE> Working with Radio
            Buttons </TITLE>
    <SCRIPT>
        function calculate(form) {
            if(form.elements[1].checked) {
                form.result.value =
                        form.entry.value
                        * 2;
            }
            else {
                form.result.value =
form.entry.value * form.entry.value;
            }
        }
    </SCRIPT></HEAD>
    <BODY><FORM><CENTER><BR/>
        <B>Value:</B>
        <INPUT Name="entry" Type="Text" Value="0" /><BR/><BR/><SPACER Size="190" />
        <B>Action:<B><BR/><SPACER Size="225">
        <INPUT Name="action1" onClick="calculate(this.form);" Type="Radio" Value="twice" />
        Double
        <BR/><SPACER Size = "225" />
        <INPUT Name="action1" onClick="calculate(this.form);" Type="Radio" Value="square" />
        Square<BR/><BR/>
        <B>Result:</B>
        <INPUT Name="result" onFocus="this.blur();" Type="Text" />
    </CENTER></FORM></BODY>
</HTML>
```

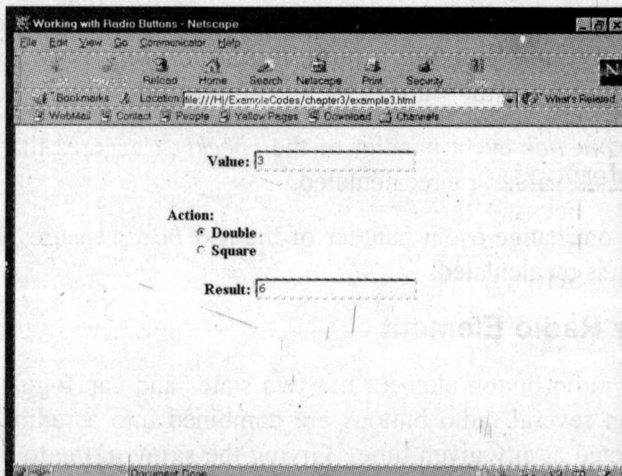

Diagram 10.8: Output for Exercise 7.

Analysis

This example illustrates the use of the *onClick* and *onChange* event handlers.

Two radio buttons are displayed. These radio buttons belong to the same radio group because each of the radio buttons has been given the same **name** as specified in the <INPUT> tag. Each radio button is named *square*.

In the above example, if the first radio button is checked, the program will double the numeric value held in the first text field. On checking the second radio button, the program will square the value held in the first text box. In either case the results of this processing will be displayed in the second text box.

The *onClick* event handler in the radio button ensures that when radio buttons are toggled, the recalculation takes place.

The *onChange* event handler in the text boxes ensures that when changes to values in the text boxes takes place, recalculation is done.

The TextArea Element

The textArea form element provides a way to create a custom sized, multiple line, text entry object, which can be placed on an HTML form.

Properties
- defaultChecked
- name
- value

Methods:
- Focus()
- Blur()
- Select()

Events:
- Focus()
- Blur()
- Select()

The Javacript eventhandlers of a TextArea are:
- onFocus()
- onBlur()
- onSelect()

Syntax:
```
<INPUT TYPE="TextArea" Name="<MyTextArea>" Row="10" Cols="25">
    <H2>Enter Data Here</H2></TEXTAREA>
```
This will place a textArea object on a form. It can be referenced by the name *MyTextArea*. The textarea can accommodate 25 characters per line and 10 such lines inside its user defined boundaries. The boundaries are set by the values passed to the ROW and COLS attributes of the TextArea object.

The Select And Option Elements

A Select object on an HTML form appears as drop down list or a scrollable list of selectable items. To conserve form space, the scrollable list of selectable items is used.

The list of items to choose from is described between the **<SELECT>...</SELECT>** tags using the **<OPTION>** tag. The <OPTION> tag is not a paired tag.

Example:
```
<SELECT Name="Items">
    <OPTION SELECTED> French Fries
    <OPTION>Hamburgers
    <OPTION>Hot Dogs
</SELECT>
```

This will place a Select object on an HTML form. The select object can be referenced by the name "Items". There will be three choices French Fries, Hamburgers, and Hot Dogs available in the select object. Using the <SIZE> attributes the number of items visible in a select list can be controlled.

If the <SIZE> attribute is set to a value less than the actual choices available in the select list a scrollable list will be created.

The following code snippet will display a drop down list on an HTML form, which displays 2 items and has a vertical scrollbar.

Example:

```
<SELECT Name = "Items" Size="2">
    <OPTION SELECTED>French Fries</ OPTION>
    <OPTION>Hamburgers</ OPTION>
    <OPTION>Hot Dogs</ OPTION>
    <OPTION>Ice Cream Cones</ OPTION>
    <OPTION>Salads</ OPTION>
</SELECT>
```

Using a Select object, only **one** item can be chosen, from the list of items.

Multi Choice Select Lists

To use a Select object, from which multiple choices can be made from within the list the **MULTIPLE** attribute must be set in the select object.

```
<SELECT Name = "Items"  Size ="2" MULTIPLE>
    <OPTION SELECTED>French Fries</ OPTION>
    <OPTION>Hamburgers</ OPTION>
    <OPTION>Hot Dogs</ OPTION>
    <OPTION>Ice Cream Cones</ OPTION>
    <OPTION >Salads</ OPTION>
</SELECT>
```

Selection lists are accessible in JavaScript through the *Select* object. When the <SELECT> </SELECT> HTML tags is encountered in an HTML page a JavaScript enabled browser's creates an array in memory that holds the items available in the list.

In each of the sample code snippets an array of the name *Items* is created in memory. This array has an array index which starts with '0' (i.e. *zero*). The value of any element in the array can be obtained in JavaScript by using:

```
memvarname="arrayname.indexvalue"
```

Properties

- ❑ selectedIndex
- ❑ defaultSelected
- ❑ index
- ❑ selected
- ❑ text
- ❑ value

Methods

- ❑ Blur
- ❑ Focus
- ❑ Change

Events

- ❑ Blur()
- ❑ Focus()
- ❑ Change()

JavaScript Event handlers bound to these events:

- ❑ onBlur()
- ❑ onFocus()
- ❑ onChange()

Exercise 8: Illustrate the use of Select and Option elements on a HTML form.

Focus: The form consists of a two Multiple choice lists and one single choice list.

- The first Multiple choice list displays the Major dishes available.
- The second Multiple choice list displays the Starters available.
- The single choice list displays the Miscellaneous (Milkshakes, Soft drinks, Softy) available.

The selected items from all the lists should be captured and displayed in a Text Area along with their respective costs. On clicking the 'Total Cost' button, the total cost of all the selected items is calculated and displayed at the end in the Text Area. A 'Clear' button is provided to clear the Text Area.

The diagram 10.9 shows a form that displays the basic form elements required to capture data in a commercial application as specified above.

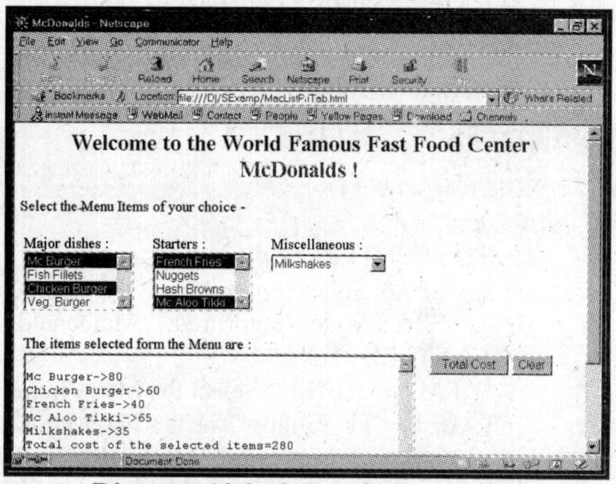

Diagram 10.9: Output for Exercise 8.

The code listing for Exercise 8:

```
<HTML>
    <HEAD><TITLE>McDonalds</TITLE>
    <SCRIPT Language="JavaScript">
        var m;
        function pick(F1) {
            var z=" ";
            for(j=0; j<3; j++) {
                for(i=0; i<F1.elements[j].length; i++) {
                    if (F1.elements[j][i].selected) {
                        var y=F1.elements[j].options[i].value;
                        z=z + "\n" + y;
                        F1.elements[3].value=z;
                    }
                }
            }
            m=z;
        }
        function cal(F1) {
            var d=0;
            for(j=0; j<3; j++) {
                for(i=0; i<F1.elements[j].length; i++) {
                    if (F1.elements[j][i].selected) {
                        var y=F1.elements[j].options[i].value;
                        s=new String(y);
                        var a=s.indexOf(">");
                        var b=s.substring(a+1,a+3);
                        c=parseInt(b);
```

```
                    d=d+c;
                }
            }
        }
        p="Total cost of the selected items=" + d;
        m=m + "\n" + p;
        F1.elements[3].value=m;
    }
    function clr(F1) {
        F1.elements[3].value=" ";
    }
</SCRIPT></HEAD>
<BODY>
    <H2><CENTER>
        <SPAN Style="color: blue; ">Welcome to the World Famous Fast Food Center </SPAN>
        <SPAN Style="color: red;">McDonalds !</SPAN>
    </CENTER></H2>
    <FORM Name="F1">Select the Menu Items of your choice - <BR/><BR/>
    <TABLE><TR valign="Top"><TD>Major dishes :<BR/>
        <SELECT Name="s1" MULTIPLE onBlur="pick(this.form)">
            <OPTION Value="Mc Burger->80" SELECTED> Mc Burger</OPTION>
            <OPTION Value="Fish Fillets->70"> Fish Fillets</OPTION>
            <OPTION Value="Chicken Burger->60"> Chicken Burger</OPTION>
            <OPTION Value="Veg. Burger->45"> Veg. Burger</OPTION>
        </SELECT><BR/><BR/>
    </TD><TD></TD><TD></TD><TD>
        Starters :<BR/>
        <SELECT Name="s2" MULTIPLE onBlur="pick(this.form)">
            <OPTION Value="French Fries->40"> French Fries</OPTION>
            <OPTION Value="Nuggets->50">Nuggets</OPTION>
            <OPTION Value="Hash Browns->55">Hash Browns</OPTION>
            <OPTION Value="Mc Aloo Tikki->65">Mc Aloo Tikki</OPTION>
        </SELECT><BR/><BR/>
    </TD><TD></TD><TD></TD><TD>
        Miscellaneous :<BR/>
        <SELECT Name="s3" onBlur="pick(this.form)">
            <OPTION Value=" ">'Check these out'
            <OPTION Value="Milkshakes->35">Milkshakes</OPTION>
            <OPTION Value="Soft drinks->20">Soft drinks</OPTION>
            <OPTION Value="Softy->25">Softy</OPTION>
        </SELECT><BR/><BR/>
    </TD><TD></TD><TD></TD></TR></TABLE><BR/>
    <TABLE><TR valign="Top"><TD>
        The items selected form the Menu are :
        <TEXTAREA Name="TA1" Rows="10" Cols="50"></TEXTAREA><BR/><BR/>
    </TD><TD></TD><TD></TD><TD>
        <BR/><Input Type="button" Value="Total Cost" onClick="cal(this.form)" />
        <Input Type="button" Value="Clear" onClick="clr(this.form)" />
```

```
    </TD></TR></TABLE>
  </FORM></BODY>
</HTML>
```

OTHER BUILT-IN OBJECTS IN JAVACRIPT

JavaScript provides a few other objects that are not related to the current window or the document loaded in the current window. These objects are used quite extensively for data processing in JavaScript.

The String Object

Every string in JavaScript is an object. The string object has a number of properties, methods, which helps perform a variety of manipulations on a given string. These include methods for searching for a string, extracting sub-strings from a string and applying various HTML tags to string contents and so on.

Properties

The string object has only one property:

Property	Description
Length	An integer value indicating the number of characters in the string.

Table 10.4

Methods

The flexibility and power of the string object rests in the wide variety of methods available to manipulate the contents of the string. Some of the methods available for string manipulation are as follows:

Method	Description
big( )	Surrounds the string with the HTML big tag
blink( )	Surrounds the string with the HTML blink tag
bold( )	Surrounds the string with the HTML bold tag
charat( )	Given an index as an argument, returns the character at the Specified index
italics( )	Surrounds the string with the HTML <I> tag.
tolowercase( )	Makes the entire string lowercase.
touppercase( )	Makes the entire string uppercase.
substring( )	Given two indexes, returns the substring starting at the first index and ending with the character before the last index. If the second index is greater, the substring with the second index and ends with the character before the first index; if the two indexes are equal, returns the empty string.

Table 10.5

Example:

If a variable named **sample contains** a value **"Hello"**, then:

sample.substring(0,3)	returns	Hel
sample.toLowercase()		hello
sample.CharAt(3)		l
sample.italics()		*Hello*

sample.substring(2,4)	returns	ll
sample.toUpperCase()		HELLO
sample.bold()		**Hello**

The Math Object

The **math** object provides methods and properties to move beyond simple arithmetic manipulations offered by arithmetic operators.

Among the features offered by the **math** object are several special values such as pi, natural logarithms, common square roots, trigonometric methods, rounding methods, an absolute value method, and more.

Properties

Property	Description
E	Euler's constant – the base of natural logarithms.
LN10	The natural logarithms of 10(roughly 2.302).
LN2	The natural logarithms of 2 (roughly 0.693).
PI	The ratio of the circumference of a circle to the diameter of the same circle (roughly 3.1415).

Table 10.6

Methods

Method	Description
abs( )	Calculates the absolute value of a number.
ceil( )	Returns the next integer greater than or equal to a number.
cos( )	Calculates the cosine of a number.
floor( )	Returns the next integer less than or equal to a number.
pow( )	Calculates the value of one number to the power of a second number – takes two arguments.
random( )	Returns a random number between zero and one.
sin( )	Calculates the sine of a number.
sqrt( )	Calculates the square root of a number.
tan( )	Calculates the tangent of a number.

Table 10.7

Example:

abs(-15)	returns	15	ceil(15.45)	returns	16
tan(45)		1	pow(2,2)		4

The Date Object

The Date object enables JavaScript programmers to create an object that contains information about a particular date and provides a set of methods to work with that information. To create an instance of the date object, use the keyword **new** as follows:

var my_date = **new Date(<parameters>);**

The parameter, if left empty, indicates today's date & time. The parameter could be any specific date format.

Methods

The date object provides the following methods:

Method	Description
getDate( )	Returns the day of the month as an integer from 1 to 31
setDate( )	Sets the day of the month based on an integer argument from 1 to 31
getHours( )	Returns the hours as an integer from 0 and 23
setHours( )	Sets the hours based on an argument from 0 to 23
getTime( )	Returns the number of milliseconds since 1 January 1970 at 00:00:00.
setTime( )	Sets the time based on an argument representing the number of milliseconds since 1 January 1970 at 00:00:00.

Table 10.8

Exercise 9:

Focus: Write JavaScript code to display the current date and time in a Browser.

The diagram 10.10 shows a form created to display the current date and time in a Browser as specified above. Refer to the HTML and JavaScript code described in Exercise Nine.

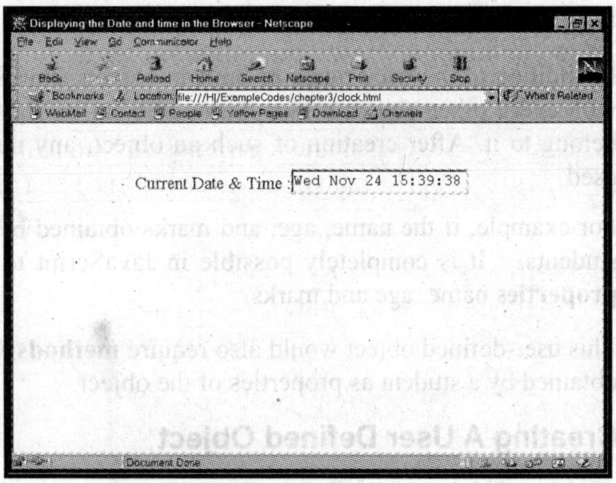

Diagram 10.10: Output for Exercise 9.

The code listing for Exercise 9:

```
<HTML>
    <HEAD>
        <TITLE>Displaying the Date and time in
                the Browser</TITLE>
    </HEAD>
    <BODY>
        <SCRIPT Language="JavaScript">
        function begin(form) {
            form_name = form;
            time_out=window.setTimeout("display_date()",500)
        }
        function display_date() {
            form_name.date.value=new Date();
            time_out=window.setTimeout("display_date()",1000)
        }
        function display_clock() {
            document.write('<CENTER><SPAN Style="color:red;font-size:14px;" >
            <FORM Name=time_form><BR/> <BR/> Current Date & Time :')
            document.write('<INPUT Name="date" Size="19" Value=""
            /></FORM></SPAN></CENTER>')
            begin(document.time_form);
        }
        display_clock();
        </SCRIPT>
    </BODY>
</HTML>
```

Other JavaScript objects can be summarized as follows:

Name	Description
String	The string object enables programs to work with and manipulate strings of text, including extracting substrings and converting text to upper or lowercase characters
Math	The math object provides methods to perform trigonometric functions (sine and tangent) as well as general mathematical functions, such as square roots.
Date	With the date object, programs can work with the current date or create instances for specific dates. The object includes methods for calculating the difference between two dates and working with times.

Table 10.9

USER DEFINED OBJECTS

In addition to the wide range of built-in objects, JavaScript permits the creation of user defined objects. As with every other object, a user-defined object will also be associated with properties and methods, which belong to it. After creation of such an object, any number of instances of this object can be created and used.

For example, if the name, age, and marks obtained by a student needs to be stored and there are fifty such students. It is completely possible in JavaScript to create and object named **Student,** which has three **properties** name, age and marks.

This user-defined object would also require **methods** that will allow the storage of name, age and the marks obtained by a student as properties of the object.

Creating A User Defined Object

A user-defined object called **student** is to be created with three properties:

- Name
- Age
- Marks

The object **student** also will include a method **insert()**.

Just as variables are named containers of data in traditional languages, similarly properties are named containers used to hold data, such as numbers or text in an object oriented approach.

Properties

The properties of the object student can be referenced as:

- Student.Name
- Student.Age
- Student.Marks

Methods

The methods of the object student can be referenced as:

- Student.insert()

Example:

```
function student(name, age, marks) {
    this.name = name;
    this.age = age;
    this.marks = marks;
}
```

This creates an object called student with three properties, name, age and marks.

Note

- **this:** refers to the current object in focus. For example, **this.name** will refer to the name of the current object.
- **Parent:** refers to the parent of the current object.

Instances

In object oriented programming, once an object is defined and created, any number of copies of the object can be created and used to store information. If there are fifty students whose data has to be maintained then 50 copies of the object **student** must be created to store the information of the fifty students.

Every new copy of the object is called an **Instance** of the object. The process of creating an instance of an object is termed as **Instantiation** of the object.

Example:

```
student1 = new student("Anil",10,75);
student2 = new student("Chhaya",9,82);
```

Objects Within Objects

Just as objects consist of properties and methods, they can also consist of other objects. For instance, the marks of a student will further depend on the marks of individual subjects Science, Math and English. Hence, another object can be created called as **Marks**, which has three properties:

- English
- Science
- Math

This object can now be included in the student object, where marks is no more a singular property, but an **object** called **Marks**, which consists of three individual properties English, Science and Math.

In such a case, a new instance of the object **Marks** must be created first, and this new instance must be included in the object **student**. The properties of this compound object can now be referenced as:

- Student.Name
- Student.Age
- Student.Marks.English
- Student.Marks.Science
- Student.Marks.Maths

Example:

Creating the Marks object:

```
function Marks(English, Science, Math) {
    this.Math = Math;
    this.English = English;
    this.Science = Science;
}
```

Creating the Student object:

```
function Student(name, age, marks) {
    this.name = name;
    this.age = age;
    this.marks = marks;
}
```

The technique of creating an object instance embedded in another object is as follows:

```
anilGrade = new marks(75, 80, 77);
chhayaGrade = new marks(82, 88, 75);
student1 = new student("Anil", 10, anilGrade);
student2 = new student("Chhaya", 9, chhayaGrade);
```

Under these circumstances the property marks of the object student actually holds another object 'anilGrade' or 'chhayaGrade' which in turn hold marks for Math, English or Science.

To access the Math marks of Anil the technique would be:

```
myvar = student1.anilGrade.Math
```

The variable **myvar** will now hold the Math marks obtained by Anil.

Example10:
This example illustrates opening a new window when a link on a web page is clicked. The new window opened, is closed by placing a button on the new window and writing JavaScript code in the **onClick** event of the button

```
<HTML>
    <HEAD><SCRIPT>
        function makeNewWindow() {
            var newwindow = prompt("Enter the document to go to in format http://www.url.com", "");
            if (!(newwindow == null || newwindow == "" )) {
                window.open(newwindow , "", "status, menubar=yes,resizable=no, toolbar=no")
            }
            else {
                var blankwindow=window.open("" ,"", "status, menubar=yes,resizable=no, toolbar=no")
                var windowcontent="<HTML><BODY Style='background-color:#FFFFFF'><H1>
                New window</H1>"
                windowcontent += "<FORM><INPUT Name=close onClick=window.close()"
                windowcontent += " Type=Button Value=Close /></FORM></BODY></HTML>"
            blankwindow.document.write(windowcontent)
            }
        }
    </SCRIPT></HEAD>
    <BODY><FORM>
        <INPUT Name="open" onClick="makeNewWindow()" Type="button" Value="Open URL">
    </FORM></BODY>
</HTML>
```

Example 11:
This example illustrates an application with two frames. The top frame contains entry fields for the background color, text color, link color, active link color and visited link color and a button to enable users to test their color combinations. When the user presses the button, the script loads a simple document using specified colors, into the lower frame.

The Parent Frameset for the Color Tester:

```
<HTML>
    <HEAD><TITLE>Example 11 On Document Object</TITLE></HEAD>
    <FRAMESET Rows="45%,*">
        <FRAME Src="pick.html">
        <FRAME Name="output" Src="blank.html">
    </FRAMESET>
</HTML>
```

Pick.html file

```
<HTML>
    <HEAD><SCRIPT Language="JavaScript">
    <!-- HIDE FROM THE BROWSERS
        function display(form) {
            doc = open(" ","output");
            doc.document.write('<BODY Style="background-color:'+ form.bg.value
            +';color:'+form.fg.value+'"');
            doc.document.write('" Link="' + form.link.value + '" ALink="'+ form.alink.value);
```

```
        doc.document.write('" VLink="'+ form.vlink.value + '">');
        doc.document.write("<H1>This is a Test</H1>You Have Selected These Colors<BR/>");
        doc.document.write('<A HRef="# ">This is a Test Link</A></BODY>');
        doc.document.close();
    }
  // STOP HIDING SCRIPT -->
  </SCRIPT></HEAD>
  <BODY><CENTER><SCRIPT Language="JavaScript">
  <!-- HIDE FROM OTHER BROWSERS
    document.write('<H1>The Color Picker</H1><FORM Method=POST>');
    document.write('Enter Colors:<BR/>');
    document.write('Background: <INPUT Name="bg" Type=Text Value="' + document.bgColor +
                '" /><BR/>');
    document.write('Text: <INPUT Name="fg" Type=Text Value="' + document.fgColor + '"
                /><BR/>');
    document.write('Link: <INPUT Name="link" Type=Text Value="' + document.linkColor + '"
                /><BR/>');
    document.write('Active Link: <INPUT Name="alink" Type=Text Value="' +
                document.alinkColor + '" /><BR/>');
    document.write('Followed Link: <INPUT Name="vlink" Type=Text Value="' +
                document.vlinkColor + '" /><BR/>');
    document.write('<INPUT onClick="display(this.form);" Type=Button Value="Test" />');
    document.write('</FORM>');
    display(document.forms[0]);
  // STOP HIDING FROM OTHER BROWSERS -->
  </SCRIPT></CENTER></BODY>
</HTML>
```

Example 12:
This example illustrates the use of the History object. Using this object we can navigate through the previous or next pages opened in the browser.

```
<HTML>
  <BODY><FORM>
    <INPUT Name="back" onClick="history.back()" Type="Button" Value="Back" />
    <INPUT Name="forward" onClick="history.forward()" Type="Button" Value="Forward" />
  </FORM></BODY>
</HTML>
```

Example 13:
Capture and displays the properties of the browser using the navigator object.

```
<HTML>
  <HEAD><TITLE>Displaying A Browser's Attributes</TITLE>
  <SCRIPT language="JavaScript">
  <!--
    function displayNavigatorProperties() {
    // to avoid "document.write" every where below
      with(document) {
        write("<B>appName:</B>")
        writeln(navigator.appName + "<BR/>")
```

```
        write("<B>appVersion:</B>")
        writeln(navigator.appVersion + "<BR/>")
        write("<B>appCodeName:</B>")
        writeln(navigator.appCodeName + "<BR/>")
        write("<B>platform:</B>")
        writeln(navigator.platform + "<BR/>")
        write("<B>useragent:</B>")
        writeln(navigator.useragent + "<BR/>")
        write("<B>language: </B>")
        writeln(navigator.language + "<BR/>")
        write("<B>Number of mimeTypes: </B>")
        writeln(navigator.mimeTypes.length + "<BR/>")
        write("<B>Number of plugins:</B>")
        writeln(navigator.plugins.length)
    }
}
function displayExplorerProperties() {
    with(document) {
        write("<B>appName:</B>")
        writeln(navigator.appName + "<BR/>")
        write("<B>appVersion:</B>")
        writeln(navigator.appVersion + "<BR/>")
        write("<B>appMinorVersion:</B>")
        writeln(navigator.appMinorVersion + "<BR/>")
        write("<B>appCodeName:</B>")
        writeln(navigator.appCodeName + "<BR/>")
        write("<B>platform:</B>")
        writeln(navigator.platform + "<BR/>")
        write("<B>cpuClass:</B>")
        writeln(navigator.cpuClass + "<BR/>")
        write("<B>useragent:</B>")
        writeln(navigator.useragent + "<BR/>")
        write("<B>cookieEnabled:</B>")
        writeln(navigator.cookieEnabled + "<BR/>")
        write("<B>browserLanguage:</B>")
        writeln(navigator.browserLanguage + "<BR/>")
        write("<B>userLanguage:</B>")
        writeln(navigator.userLanguage + "<BR/>")
        write("<B>systemLanguage:</B>")
        writeln(navigator.systemLanguage + "<BR/>")
        write("<B>onLine: </B>")
        writeln(navigator.onLine + "<BR/>")
        write("<B>Number of mimeTypes: </B>")
        writeln(navigator.mimeTypes.length + "<BR/>")
        write("<B>Number of plugins:</B>")
        writeln(navigator.plugins.length)
        write("<B>userProfile: </B>")
        writeln(navigator.userProfile)
    }
}
```

```
        function displayBrowserProperties() {
            if(navigator.appName=="Netscape")
                displayNavigatorProperties()
            else
                if(navigator.appName=="Microsoft Internet Explorer")
                    displayExplorerProperties()
        }
        displayBrowserProperties()
    //-->
    </SCRIPT></HEAD>
</HTML>
```

SELF REVIEW QUESTIONS

FILL IN THE BLANKS

1. HTML provides _________ and _________ tags with which an HTML form can be created to capture user input.
2. The form tag has two properties namely ___________ and ___________.
3. The method property is used to specify the method used to send data, which can be _________ or _________.
4. The _________ attribute of the < FORM> tag points to the URL of a program on the web server that will process the form data.
5. Various form elements can be specified as attributes of the ___________ tag.
6. The _________ button sends the current information held in each field of the form to the web server for further processing.
7. To have a select object from which multiple choices can be made from a list the ___________ attribute must be set in the select object.
8. ___________ is the only property of the string object.
9. The _________ object provides methods and properties to move beyond simple arithmetic manipulations offered by arithmetic operators.

TRUE OR FALSE

10. As soon as the <FORM></FORM> tags are encountered by the browser, the browser creates an array called form1 in the absence of a Form name being specified in the HTML code.
11. The Post method sends data captured by the form elements to the web server, encoded as part of the URL that points to the web server.
12. Text fields accept a single line of text entry.
13. The Select object allows multiple choices from a list of choices that are offered.
14. Date object enables the creation of an object that contains information about a particular date.
15. In addition to the wide range of built-in objects, JavaScript permits the creation of user defined objects.

HANDS ON EXERCISES

1. Create a web page, which accepts user information and user comments on the web site. Design the web page using form elements and check if all the Text fields have being entered with data else display an alert. Obtain an output as shown in the diagrams 10.11.1, 10.11.2 and 10.11.3.

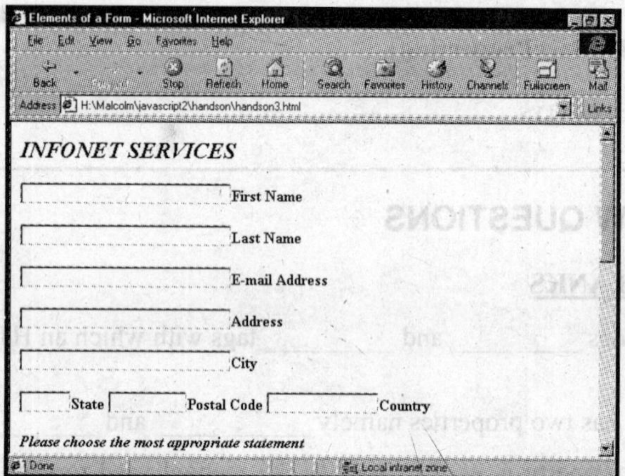

Diagram 10.11.1: Hands On Exercise output part 1.

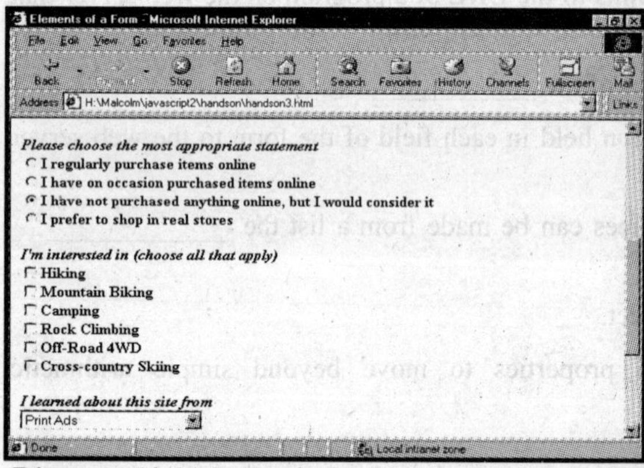

Diagram 10.11.2: Hands On Exercise output part 2.

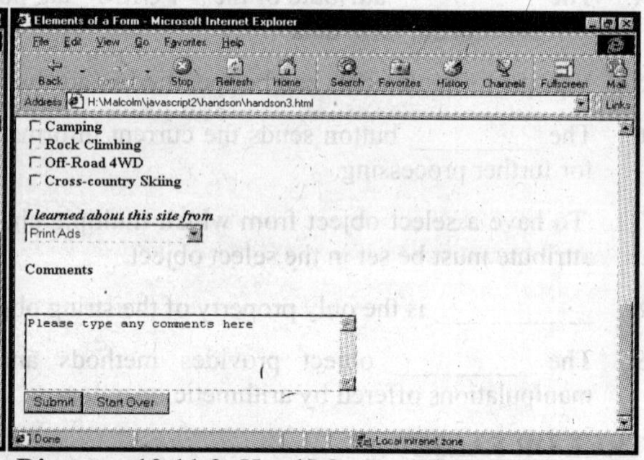

Diagram 10.11.3: Hands On Exercise output part 3.

11. COOKIES

WHAT ARE COOKIES

One of the challenges of writing applications for the World Wide Web has been inability of the web to maintain state. That is, after a user sends a request to the server and a web page is returned, the server forgets all about the user and the page that has been downloaded. If the user clicks on a link, the server doesn't have background information about what page the user is coming from, and more importantly, if the user returns to the page at a later date, there is no information available to the server about the user's previous actions on the page.

Maintaining state can be important to developing complex interactive applications. However, browsers address this problem with **cookies**, which is a method of storing information locally in the browser and sending it to the server whenever the appropriate pages are requested by the user.

The term *cookies* has no special significance. It is just a name in the same way Java is just a name for Sun's object-oriented programming language.

When a user requests a page, an HTTP request is sent to the server. The request includes a header that defines several pieces of information, including the page being requested.

The server returns an HTTP response that also includes a header. The header contains information about the document being returned, including its MIME type. These headers all contain one or more fields of information in a basic format.

FieldName: Information

Cookie information is shared between the client browser and a server using fields in the HTTP headers. When the user requests a page for the first time, a cookie (or more than one cookie) can be stored in the browser by a **set-cookie** entry in the header of the response from the server. The set-cookie field includes the information to be stored in the cookie along with several optional pieces of information including an expiry date, path, and server information and if the cookie requires security.

Then, when the user requests a page in the future, if a matching cookie is found among all the stored cookies, the browser sends a cookie field to the server in a request header. The header will contain the information stored in that cookie.

The set-cookie and cookie fields use a syntax to transfer significant information between client and server.

SETTING A COOKIE

Syntax:

Set-cookie: NAME=value ; EXPIRES=date; PATH=path; DOMAIN=domain; SECURE

The **NAME=value** is the only required piece of information that must be included in the set-cookie field. All other entries are optional.

Name	Description
NAME = value	Specifies the name of the cookie.
PATH = path	Specifies the path portion of the URLs for which the cookie is valid. If the URL matches both the PATH and the DOMAIN, then the cookie is sent to the server in the request header. (If left unset, the value of the PATH is the same as the document that set the cookie)

Table 11.1

Name	Description
EXPIRES = date	Specifies the expiry date of the cookie. After this date the cookie will no longer be stored by the client or sent to the server (DATE takes the form Weekday, DD-MON-YY HH:MM:SS GMT- dates are only stored in Greenwich Mean Time). By default the value of expires is set to the end of current Navigator session.
DOMAIN= domain	Specifies the domain portion of the URLs for which the cookie is valid. The default value for this attribute is the domain of the current document setting the cookie.
SECURE	Specifies that the cookie should only be transmitted over a secure link (i.e. to HTTP servers using the SSL protocol-known as HTTPS servers)

Table 11.1 (Continued)

Example:
This example illustrates the use of cookies. While the user traverses from page to page, the information entered by the user in any page is stored in cookies at the client side and made available to the user whenever the user returns to any page previously visited.

```
<HTML>
   <HEAD><SCRIPT>
      function newcookie(cookiename, value) {
         document.cookie = cookiename + "=" + value;   }
      function getCookie(cookiename) {
         var cookiefound = false;
         var start = 0;
         var end = 0;
         var cstring = document.cookie;
         var clength = 0;
         while (clength <= cstring.length) {
            start = clength;
            end = start + cookiename.length;
            if (cstring.substring(start, end) == cookiename) {
               cookiefound = true;
               break;
            }
            clength++;
         }
         if (cookiefound) {
            start = end + 1;
            end = document.cookie.indexOf(";", start);
            if (end < start) {
               end = document.cookie.length;
               var contents = document.cookie.substring(start, end);
               return contents;
            }
            else {
               var contents = document.cookie.substring(start, end);
               return contents;
            }
         }
      }
   </SCRIPT>
   </HEAD>
```

```
<BODY ><SCRIPT>
    var thisCookie = ((document.cookie !== "") && (document.cookie != null));
    var cfirst_name = (thisCookie) ? getCookie("first_name") : "";
    var cmiddle_name = (thisCookie) ? getCookie("middle_name") : "";
    var clast_name = (thisCookie) ? getCookie("last_name") : "";
    document.write('<FORM>');
    document.write('<TABLE Border="0" CellPadding="4" CellSpacing="4" Width = 100%>');
    document.write('<TR><TD ColSpan="2"><B> Personal Details (<SPAN Style="color: Red"> *
                </SPAN> indicates Required)</B> </TD></TR>');
    document.write('<TR>');
    document.write('<TD Width="25%"> First Namc <SPAN Style="color: Red">
                 * </SPAN></TD>');
    document.write('<TD Width="75%"><INPUT Name="first_name"
                onBlur="newcookie(this.name, this.value);" Size="20" Type="Text" Value="' +
                cfirst_name + '" /></TD></TR>');
    document.write('<TR><TD Width="25%"> Middle Name </TD>');
    document.write('<TD Width="75%"><INPUT Name="middle_name"
                onBlur="newcookie(this.name, this.value);" Size="20" Type="Text" Value="' +
                cmiddle_name + '" /></TD></TR>');
    document.write('<TR>');
    document.write('<TD Width="25%"> Last Name <SPAN Style="color: Red">
                 * </SPAN></TD>');
    document.write('<TD Width="75%"><INPUT Name="last_name"
                onBlur="newcookie(this.name, this.value);" Size="20" Type="Text" Value="' +
                clast_name + '" /></TD>');
    document.write('</TR></TABLE><BR />');
    document.write('<CENTER>');
    document.write('<INPUT Typc="Submit" Value"–"Done" />');
    document.write('<INPUT Type="Reset" Value="Reset" />');
    document.write('</CENTER>');
    document.write('</FORM>');
</SCRIPT></BODY>
</HTML>
```

SELF REVIEW QUESTIONS

FILL IN THE BLANKS

1. Information can be stored locally in the browser which can be sent to the server whenever required by using ____________.
2. Cookie information is shared between the client browser and the server using fields in the ________ headers.
3. When the user requests a page for the first time a cookie can be stored in the browser by a __________ entry in the header of the response from the server.
4. If a matching cookie is found among all the stored cookies, the browser sends a cookie field to the server in a ______________.
5. The _________ attribute specifies that the cookie should be transmitted only over a secure link.

TRUE OR FALSE

6. The name Cookie has a special significance with respect to object oriented programming language.
7. The set-cookie field includes the information to be stored in the cookie along with several optional piece of information.

B - PROJECTS IN JAVASCRIPT

Project Specifications For The First Project In JavaScript – Guest Book

Since the learning of Java Script has now been completed, it is time to consolidate this learning by building a small guest book.

A Guest Book is used to store any comments that a visitor to the site may have regarding the site. The comments (if applicable) help improve the functionality of the site.

The structure of the guest book is given in the following pages along with html source code. This is a description of how the guest book will be used by the person signing-in. The java script code working with Html which provides for various client side data capture validations.

The guest book is a html document with:
- ❑ Simple visuals in the form of .gif or .jpeg files.
- ❑ Java Script embedded HTML code.

The files required to construct these pages is available on the accompanying CD-ROM for immediate use.

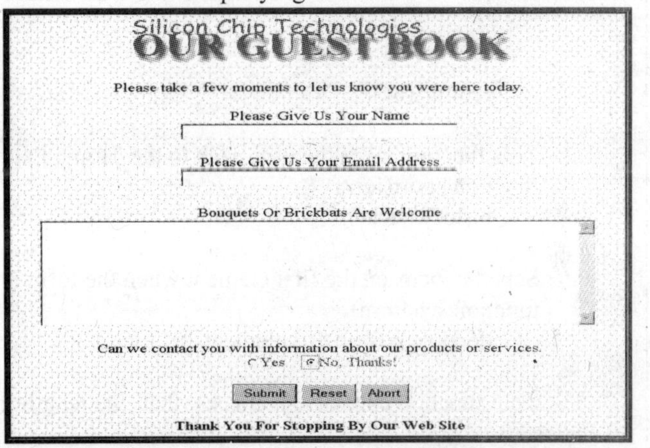

Diagram B.1: The User Interface For Guest book

If required run the HTML files first in a web browser and get a look and feel of what the project could be like. Once this is done, code the web pages according to what you believe is appropriate.

For a visitor to leave comments about the site, or comments in general, the HTML form used in diagram B.1 is used. This is the guest book page.

This form captures the following:
- ❑ Visitors Name (Not compulsory)
- ❑ Emailid (Mandatory)
- ❑ A visitors Comments (Mandatory)

Feel free to improvise and get a look and feel that satisfies you.

Each HTML file is really just a simple guideline to what the web page could look like.
Java script is added to perform simple client side validations.

For your guidance:
- ❑ The source code is provided in the document file.

Client Side Validations

The Client side validations to be coded in Java script are as follows
- ❑ Emailid, General Comments, cannot be left empty
- ❑ The Emailid needs to be scanned for the presence of an '@' and '.' symbol.
- ❑ The length of the Name and Emailid fields cannot exceed 30 characters.

```
<HTML>
    <HEAD><TITLE>SCT'S GUEST BOOK</TITLE>
    <SCRIPT Language = "Javascript">
    <!-- The function verify() checks whether appropriate information is filled in all the elements. If any
element is left empty, an alert() box is displayed informing the user to fill in the empty element The code
also scans the Emailid for the presence of an '@' and a '.' symbol. -->
        function verify(form) {
            for (i=1; i<=2; i++) {
                if (document.forms[0].elements[i].value == "") {
                    alert("Please fill in the " + document.forms[0].elements[i].name + " field");
                    document.forms[0].elements[i].focus( );
                    return (false);
                }
                if(document.forms[0].elements[1].value != "") {
                    pass = document.forms[0].elements[1].value.indexOf('@',0);
                    pass1 = document.forms[0].elements[1].value.indexOf('.',0);
                    if((pass==-1) || (pass1==-1)) {
                        alert("Not a valid Email address");
                        document.forms[0].elements[1].focus();
                        return (false);
                    }
                }
            }
            return(true);
        }
    <!-- This function takes the user back to the 'Home Page' from the current page -->
        function abort(form) {
            history.back();
        }
    <!-- Sets the focus on the first element when the form is loaded -->
        function set(form) {
            document.forms[0].elements[0].focus( );
        }
    <!-- The function checklen() checks that the length of name and email addresses does not exceed
30 characters -->
        function checklen(form) {
            for (i=0; i<=1; i++) {
                val=document.forms[0].elements[i].value;
                len=val.length;
                if (len > 30) {
                    alert ("Value exceeds 30 characters");
                    document.forms[0].elements[i].value="";
                    document.forms[0].elements[i].focus();
                }
            }
        }
    </SCRIPT></HEAD>
    <BODY Style="background: url(images/grid1.gif);color:green;" onLoad="set(this.form)">
        <CENTER><IMG Src="images/Gestbk.gif" Alt="gestbk.gif" /></CENTER>
        <P><CENTER>Please take a few moments to let us know you were here today.</P>
```

```
    <P><FORM Action = "" Method="POST" onSubmit=" return verify(this.form)"></P>
        <P>Please Give Us Your Name<BR/>
        <INPUT Type="text" Name="name" Size="40" onBlur="checklen(this.form)" /><BR/>
        <P>Please Give Us Your Email Address<BR/>
        <INPUT Type="text" Name="emailid" Size="40" onBlur="checklen(this.form)"
        /><BR/></P>
        <P>Bouquets Or Brickbats Are Welcome<BR/>
        <TEXTAREA Name="request" Rows="8" Cols="65"></TEXTAREA></P>
        <P>Can we contact you with information about our products or services.<BR/><BR/>
        <INPUT TYPE="radio" NAME="moreinfo" VALUE="y" />
        <SPAN Style="color: Blue">Yes</SPAN><IMG Src="images/shim.gif" Width="20"
        Height="10" />
        <INPUT TYPE="radio" NAME="moreinfo" VALUE="n" Checked="True" />
        <SPAN Style="color: Red">No, Thanks!</SPAN></P>
        <P><INPUT Type="Submit" Value="Submit"><INPUT Type="Reset" Value="Reset" />
        <INPUT Type="Button" Value="Abort" onClick = "abort(this.form)" /></P>
  </FORM>
  <P><B>Thank You For Stopping By Our Web Site</B></P></CENTER>
  </BODY>
</HTML>
```

Project Specifications For The First Project In JavaScript – Pen Pals

Since the learning of Java Script has now been completed, it is time to consolidate this learning by building a page, which offers free hosting of pen pal information. Java Script will then be used to validate data captured by this page.

Using this service, visitors can post their Name, Emailid, Sex, Date of birth, Interests and Hobbies on the Web Site. Other visitors who find compatible information in the Pen pals list would email the registrant. This could become the start of a lasting friendship.

The structure of the pen pal page is given in the following pages along with the html source code. This is a description of how the Pen Pal page is to be used by the person visiting the page. The java code working within html provides for data capture validations.

Other visitors can then refer to these pages and email of individuals who's Age, Sex, Interests and other criteria are interesting. To post Pen Pal Information on a Web Site a simple form needs to be filled in with details as shown in diagram B.2.

Diagram B.2: The User Interface For Pen Pals

The Pen Pal page is a html document with:

- Simple visuals in the form of .gif or .jpeg files.
- Java script embedded HTML code.

The files required to construct these pages is available on the accompanying CD-ROM for immediate use.

If required run the HTML files first in a web browser and get a look and feel of what the project could be like. Once this is done, code the web pages according to what you believe is appropriate.

Pen Pal information is hosted for free on our website to visitors to the website.

For a visitor to leave his/her information on a site. The HTML form used in diagram 1 is used. This is the Pen Pal page.

The form captures the following:

- Visitors Name (Mandatory)
- Emailid (Mandatory)
- The visitors D.O.B in DD/MM/YYYY (Mandatory)
- Textbox to retrieve users hobbies and interests (Not Compulsory)

Feel free to improvise and get a look and feel that satisfies you.

Each HTML file is really just a simple guideline to what the web page could look like. Java script is added to perform simple client side validations.

For your guidance:

- The source code is provided in the document file.

Client Side Validations:

The Client Side validations to be coded in Java script are as follows:

- Name, Email id, Sex, DOB entries, cannot be left empty
- The Email id needs to be scanned for the presence of an '@' and '.' sign
- The length of the Name and Email id fields cannot exceed 30 characters
- Ensure that the date is keyed in as "DD/MM/YYYY".

```
<HTML>
    <HEAD><TITLE>SCT's PEN PAL</TITLE>
    <SCRIPT Language = "Javascript">
<!-- The function verify() checks whether appropriate intervention is filled in all the form elements. If any element is left empty an alert() box is displayed informing the user to fill in all the empty elements. The code also searches the emailed for the presence of an '@' and a '.' symbol -->
            function verify() {
                for (i=0; i<=7; i++) {
                    if (document.forms[0].elements[i].value == "") {
                        alert("Please fill in the " +
                        document.forms[0].elements[i].name + " field");
                        document.forms[0].elements[i].focus( );
                        return (false);
                    }
                    if(document.forms[0].elements[1].value != "") {
                        pass = document.forms[0].elements[1].value.indexOf('@',0);
                        pass1 = document.forms[0].elements[1].value.indexOf('.',0);
                        if((pass==-1) || (pass1==-1)) {
                            alert("not a valid email address");
                            document.forms[0].elements[1].focus();
                            return (false);
                        }
                    }
                }
```

```
            return(true);
    }
    <!-- The function checkdate() checks whether the date is between (1-31) whether the month is
entered as a number and is between (1-12) whether the year entered is within 1995 -->
            function checkdate() {
                    year=document.forms[0].elements[6].value;
                    if (year>1995) {
                            alert("Enter proper year (till 1995)");
                            document.forms[0].elements[6].focus();
                            return(false);
                    }
                    monval=document.forms[0].elements[5].value;
                    dtval=document.forms[0].elements[4].value;
                    if ((dtval > 31) || (dtval < 1)) {
                            alert("Enter proper date");
                            document.forms[0].elements[4].focus();
                            return(false);
                    }
                    if (isNaN(monval) != true) {
                            if ((monval > 12) || (monval < 1)) {
                                    alert("Enter proper month");
                                    document.forms[0].elements[5].focus();
                                    return(false);
                            }
                    }
                    else {
                            alert("Enter the month number");
                            document.forms[0].elements[5].focus();
                            return(false);
                    }
                    return (true);
            }
    <!-- The function checklen() checks whether the length of name and email address does not
exceed 30 characters -->
            function checklen() {
                    for (i=0; i<=1; i++) {
                    val=document.forms[0].elements[i].value;
                    len=val.length;
                    if (len > 30) {
                            alert ("Value exceeds 30 characters");
                            document.forms[0].elements[i].value="";
                            document.forms[0].elements[i].focus();
                    }
            }
    }
    <!-- The function takes the user to the previous page -->
            function abort(form) {
                    history.back();
            }
    <!-- Sets the focus on the first field when the form is loaded -->
```

```
            function set(form) {
                    document.forms[0].elements[0].focus();
            }
        </SCRIPT></HEAD>
        <BODY Background="images\Grid1.gif" onLoad="set(this.form)">
            <CENTER><IMG SRC="images\Penpals.gif" /></CENTER>
            <CENTER>
            <FORM Action="" Method="POST" onSubmit="return verify()">
                    <P>Please enter your name<BR/>
                    <INPUT Type="text" Name="name" Size="40" onBlur="checklen()"
                    /><BR/></P>
                    <P>Please enter your E-Mail address<BR/>
                    <INPUT Type="Text" Name="emailid" Size="40" onBlur="checklen()"
                    /><BR/></P>
                    <P>Please indicate your Sex<BR/>
                    <INPUT Type="Radio" Name="sex" Value="m" checked />Male
                    <IMG Src="images/Shim.gif" Height="1" Width="5" />
                    <INPUT Type="Radio" Name="sex" Value="f" />Female<BR/></P>
                    <P>Please enter your DOB as DD/MM/YYYY<BR/>
                    <INPUT Type="Text" Name="day" Size="2" />
                    <IMG Src="images/Shim.gif" Height="1" Width="2" />
                    <INPUT Type="Text" Name="month" Size="2" />
                    <IMG Src="images/Shim.gif" Height="1" Width="2" />
                    <INPUT Type="Text" Name="year" Size="4" /></P>
                    <P>Tell us about your hobbies and interests in the 'Text-Box' below<BR/>
                    We'll keep your Penpal info posted for <B>One Year</B> from today</P>
                    <P><TEXTAREA NAME="request" ROWS="8" COLS="65"
                    onFocus="checkdate()">
                    </TEXTAREA></P>
                    <P>Can we contact you with information about our products or services.<BR/>
                    <INPUT Type="Radio" Name="moreinfo" Value="y" />
                    <SPAN Style="color: blue;">Yes</SPAN><IMG Src="images\shim.gif"
                    Width="20" Height="10" />
                    <INPUT Type="Radio" Name="moreinfo" Value="n" Checked="True" />
                    <SPAN Style="color: Red;">No, Thanks!</SPAN></P>
                    <P><CENTER><INPUT Type="Submit" Value="Submit" Name="Submit" />
                    <INPUT Type="Reset" Value="Reset" Name="Reset" />
                    <INPUT Type="Button" Value="Abort" Name="At" onClick =
                    "abort(this.form)" />
            </CENTER></P></FORM>
            <P><B>Thank You For Stopping By Our Web Site</B></P></CENTER>
        </BODY>
</HTML>
```

Project Specifications For The First Project In JavaScript – Registration Form

Since the learning of Java Script has now been completed, it is time to consolidate this learning by building a Registration form page.

This Registration page is used to register visitors and provide access to a number of services provided by the Web Site. To register a simple form as show in diagram B.3 is used.

The structure of the registration page is given in the following pages along with html source code. The Java script code working within html, which provides for various client side data capture validations.

This captures two different blocks of information. The first block of information is associated with the visitors Login ID and Password that will be used when access to the sites services will be required in future. The second block of information captured, will be the services that the visitor wishes to sign up for.

The Registration page is a html document with:

- Simple visuals in the form of .gif or .jpeg files.
- Java Script embedded HTML code.

The files required to construct these pages is available on the accompanying CD-ROM for immediate use..

If required run the HTML files first in a web browser and get a look and feel of what the project could be like. Once this is done, code the web pages according to what you believe is appropriate.

Feel free to improvise and get a look and feel that satisfies you.

Each HTML file is really just a simple guideline to what the web page could look like.
Java script is added to perform simple client side validations.

Diagram B.3: The User Interface For Registration Form

For your guidance:

- The source code is provided in the document file.

Client Side Validations

The Client side validations to be coded in Java script are as follows

- The Login name, Password, Confirm Password cannot be left empty.
- The Emailid needs to be scanned for the presence of an '@' and '.' symbol.
- The Password and the Confirm Password has to be the same.
- The length of the Name and Emailid fields cannot exceed 30 characters.

```
<HTML>
        <HEAD><TITLE>SCT'S GOODIES SIGN UP FORM</TITLE>
        <SCRIPT Language="JavaScript">
        <!-- Declaration of Variables  -->
                var valueofpass1="";
                var valueofpass2="";
                var whitespace = " \t\n\r";
```

```
<!-- Function to check whether the value in a Text Field is Null -->
        function isEmpty(s) {
                return ((s == null) || (s.length == 0))
        }
        <!-- Function to check whether the value in a Text Field is a WhiteSpace -->
        function isWhitespace (s) {
                var i;
        <!-- Is empty? -->
                        if (isEmpty(s)) return true;
<!-- Search through string's' characters one by one until we find a non-whitespace character. -->
                for (i=0; i < s.length; i++) {
                <!-- Check that current character isn't' whitespace.-->
                        var currchar = s.charAt(i);
                        if (whitespace.indexOf(currchar) == -1)
                                return false;
                        }
        <!-- All characters are whitespace. -->
                return true;
        }
<!-- Function to ensure that the email address is in proper format. -->
        function isEmail (eadd) {
                if (isEmpty(eadd))
    <!-- Is s whitespace? -->
                        if (isWhitespace(eadd)) return false;
<!-- There must be >= 1 character before @, so we start looking at c    haracter position 1 (i.e. second
character) -->
                                var i = 1;
                                var sLength = eadd.length;
                        <!-- look for @ -->
                                while ((i < sLength) && (eadd.charAt(i) != "@")) {
                                        i++;
                                }
                                if ((i >= sLength) || (eadd.charAt(i) != "@"))
                                        return false;
                                else
                                        i += 2;
                        <!-- look for period -->
                                while ((i < sLength) && (eadd.charAt(i) != ".")) {
                                        i++;
                                }
                                <!--There must be at least one character after the period-->
                                if ((i >= sLength - 1) || (eadd.charAt(i) != "."))
                                        return false;
                                else
                                        return true;
                                }
```

```
<!-- Function to check whether the value in Password contains Alphabets and
Characters-->
        function isCharsInBag (string, bag) {
            var i;
<!-- Search through string 's' characters one by one. If character is in bag, append to returnString. -->
            for (i=0; i < string.length; i++) {
                var charval = string.charAt(i);
                if (bag.indexOf(charval) == -1)    return false;
            }
            return true;
        }
            <!-- Function to check whether the Password contains atleast one number -->
            function isNumberInPass (string, bag) {
            var i, flag;
            flag=0;
<!-- Search through string's' characters one by one. If character is in bag, append to return String. -->
            for (i=0; i < string.length; i++) {
                var charval = string.charAt(i);
                if (bag.indexOf(charval) == -1) {
                    continue;
                }
                else {
                    flag=1;
                    break;
                }
            }
            if(flag == 1) {    return true;        }
            else {   return false;      }
            return false;
        }
<!-- Function to check the values entered in all the elements of the formCalled on the clicked event of the
Submit button -->
        function verify() {
            var flag =0;
            <!-- Begining the check for Email address, Password and Confirm Password -->
                var loginName = document.forms[0].elements[0].value;
                var email = document.forms[0].elements[1].value;
                var passwd = document.forms[0].elements[2].value;
                var confPasswd = document.forms[0].elements[3].value;

                <!-- Check to see if the Login name field is left blank -->
                if (loginName == "") {
                    alert("Please fill in the login name");
                    document.forms[0].elements[0].focus( );
                    return false;
```

```
<!-- Check to see if the Email Address field is left blank -->
        else if (email == "") {
                alert("Please fill in the email address");
                document.forms[0].elements[1].focus( );
                return false;
        }
<!-- Check to see if the Email Address filled is valid or not-->
        else if (!isEmail(email)) {
                alert("Please enter the Email address in the proper Format");
                document.forms[0].elements[1].focus( );
                return false;
        }
<!-- Check to see if the password field is left blank -->
        else if ( passwd == "" ) {
                alert("Please fill in the Password");
                document.forms[0].elements[2].focus( );
                return false;
        }
<!-- Check to see if the length of the password entered is less than 5 -->
        else if ( passwd.length < 5 ) {
                alert( "Password must be 5 or more characters." );
                document.forms[0].elements[2].focus( );
                return false;
        }
<!-- Check to see if the length of the password entered is  more than 8 -->
        else if (passwd.length > 8 ) {
                alert( "Password must be 8 or less characters." );
                document.forms[0].elements[2].focus( );
                return false;
        }
<!-- Check to see if the password field is contain other than alphabate or number -->
        else if (!isCharsInBag(passwd,
                "abcdefghijklmnopqrstuvwxyzABCDEFGHIJKLMNOPQRS
                TUVWXYZ0123456789")) {
                alert( "Password must only contain alphabets and number");
                document.forms[0].elements[2].focus( );
                return false;
        }
<!-- Check to see if the length of the password entered should have atleast one numeric character -->
        else if ( !isNumberInPass( passwd, "0123456789")) {
                alert( "Password must have atleast one number.");
                document.forms[0].elements[2].focus( );
                return false;
        }
```

```
<!-- Check to see if the Confirm password is entered or not -->
                    else if ( confPasswd == "" ) {
                            alert("Please fill in the Confirm Password");
                            document.forms[0].elements[3].focus( );
                            return false;
                    }
<!-- Check to see if the password and Confirm password is not match or not  -->
                    else if (document.forms[0].elements[2].value
                     != document.forms[0].elements[3].value) {
                      alert( "Your passwords do not match. Please retype and try again.");
                            return false;
                    }

                    <!-- Check to see if atleast one is checkbox checked or not-->
                    for (j=4; j<=5; j++) {
                            if(document.forms[0].elements[j].checked) {
                                    break;
                            }
                    else if (j>=5) {
                            alert("Atleast Check on One of Our Services");
                            document.forms[0].elements[j].focus();
                            return (false);
                    }
            }
            return(true);
    }
<!-- Function called on the Clicked event of the Abort button -->
    function Abort() {
            history.back();
    }
</SCRIPT></HEAD>
<BODY Style="background-image: url(images/Grid1.gif);text-align:center;">
    <IMG Src="images/RegGoodies.gif" />
    <FORM Action="" Method="post" onSubmit="return verify()">
            <TABLE Align="center" Border="0" CellPadding="0" CellSpacing="0"
            Size="800">
            <TBODY><TR>
                    <TD Align="right"><B>Login Name:</B></TD>
                    <TD><INPUT Name="LoginName" /></TD>
            </TR><TR>
                    <TD Align="right"><B>E-Mail Address:</B></TD>
                    <TD><INPUT Name="Email:" /></TD>
            </TR><TR>
                    <TD Align="right"><B>Password:</B></TD>
                    <TD><INPUT Name="Passwd1" Type="password" /></TD>
            </TR><TR>
                    <TD Align="right"><B>Confirm Password:</B></TD>
```

```
                <TD><INPUT Name="Passwd2" Type="password" /></TD>
                </TR></TBODY></TABLE>
                <P>
                <TABLE Align="center" Border="0" CellPadding="0" CellSpacing="0"
                        Size="800" Style="color:red;font-family:verdana;font-size:10px;">
                <TBODY><TR><TD>
                        <B>PASSWORD RULES:</B></FONT>
                </TD></TR><TR><TD>
                        A Password's minimum length is five characters
                </TD></TR><TR><TD>
                        A Password's maximum length is eight characters
                </TD></TR><TR> <TD>
                        A Password should have at least one digit included
                </TD></TR><TR> <TD>
                        Other than Alphabets and Digits no other values are allowed
                </TD></TR></TBODY></TABLE>
                <P>
                <IMG Height="40" Src="images\Shim.gif" Width="1" />
                        <IMG Src="images/SeleGoodies.gif" />
                <IMG Height="30" Src="images\Shim.gif" Width="1" />
                </P>
                <TABLE Align="center" Border="0" CellPadding="0"
                        CellSpacing="0" Size="800">
                <TBODY><TR>
                        <TD><IMG Height=5 Src="images/Shim.gif" width="10" /></TD>
                        <TD><B>Pen Pals</B>
                        <IMG Height="1" src="images/Shim.gif" Width="3" />
                                <INPUT type="checkbox" Name="PenPals"
                                value="y" /></TD>
                        <TD><IMG Height=5 Src="images/Shim.gif" width="10" /></TD>
                        <TD><B>News Letter</B>
                                <IMG Height="1" src="images/Shim.gif" Width="3" />
                                <INPUT type="checkbox" Name="NewsLtr" value="y" />
                        </TD>
                        <TD><IMG Height="5" src="images/Shim.gif" Width="10" /></TD>
                </TR></TBODY></TABLE>
                <IMG Height="30" src="images/Shim.gif" Width="1" />
                <P>
                        <INPUT Type="submit" Value="Submit" />
                        <INPUT Type="reset" Value="Reset" />
                        <INPUT onClick="Abort()" Type="button" Value="Abort" />
                </P>
        </FORM>
    </BODY>
</HTML>
```

ANSWERS TO SELF REVIEW QUESTIONS

8. INTRODUCTION TO JAVASCRIPT

FILL IN THE BLANKS

1. Form
2. Netscape
3. <SCRIPT></SCRIPT>
4. <FORM></FORM>
5. Variables
6. ($) character
7. implicitly defined, literal
8. string
9. Functions
10. Arrays
11. dense
12. Objects
13. %(modulus)

TRUE OR FALSE

14. False
15. True
16. False
17. True
18. False
19. True
20. True
21. True
22. True

9. OBJECTS IN JAVASCRIPT

FILL IN THE BLANKS

1. Document Object Model
2. JavaScript Assisted Style Sheets
3. Method
4. Interactive, Non Interactive
5. Navigator

TRUE OR FALSE

6. False
7. False
8. True

10. FORMS OF A WEB SITE

FILL IN THE BLANKS

1. <FORM> and </FORM>
2. Method and Action
3. Get or Post
4. Action
5. <INPUT>
6. Submit
7. <MULTIPLE>
8. Length
9. Math

TRUE OR FALSE

10. True
11. False
12. True
13. False
14. True
15. True

11. COOKIES

FILL IN THE BLANKS

1. Cookie
2. HTTP
3. set-cookie
4. Request header
5. SECURE

TRUE OR FALSE

6. False
7. True

SOLUTIONS TO HANDS ON EXERCISES

8. INTRODUCTION TO JAVASCRIPT

1. Creating a JavaScript code block using arrays to generate the current date in words, (in the format: Saturday, January 01, 2000).

```
<HTML>
    <HEAD><TITLE> Date validations </TITLE><SCRIPT>
        var monthNames = new Array(12);
        monthNames[0]= "January";
        monthNames[1]= "February";
        monthNames[2]= "March";
        monthNames[3]= "April";
        monthNames[4]= "May";
        monthNames[5]= "June";
        monthNames[6]= "July";
        monthNames[7]= "August";
        monthNames[8]= "September";
        monthNames[9]= "October";
        monthNames[10]= "November";
        monthNames[11]= "December";
        var dayNames = new Array(7) ;
        dayNames[0]= "Sunday";
        dayNames[1]= "Monday";
        dayNames[2]= "Tuesday";
        dayNames[3]= "Wednesday";
        dayNames[4]= "Thursday";
        dayNames[5]= "Friday";
        dayNames[6]= "Saturday";
        function customDateString (m_date) {
            var daywords = dayNames[m_date.getDay()];
            var theday = m_date.getDate();
            var themonth = monthNames[m_date.getMonth()];
            var theyear = m_date.getYear();
            return daywords + ",  " + themonth + " " + theday + ", " + theyear;
        }
    </SCRIPT></HEAD>
    <BODY><H1>WELCOME!</H1>
        <SCRIPT>document.write(customDateString( new Date()))</SCRIPT>
    </BODY>
</HTML>
```

2. Creating a JavaScript code block, which checks the contents entered in a form's Text element. If the text entered is in the lower case, convert to upper case.

```
<HTML>
    <HEAD><SCRIPT Language="JavaScript">
        function checkData(column_data) {
            if ( column_data != "" && column_data.value != column_data.value.toUpperCase() ) {
                column_data.value = column_data.value.toUpperCase()
            }
        }
    </SCRIPT></HEAD>
    <BODY><FORM><B>Field 1:</B> 
        <INPUT TYPE="text" NAME="collector" SIZE=10 onChange="checkData(this)"><BR>
        <B>Field 2:</B> <INPUT TYPE="text" NAME="dummy" SIZE=10>
    </FORM></BODY>
</HTML>
```

3. Creating a JavaScript code block, which validates a username and password against hard coded values.

```
<HTML>
    <HEAD><TITLE>Password Validation</TITLE>
    <SCRIPT language="JavaScript">
    <!--
        var userpassword = new Array(4);
        userpassword[0]= "Allwyn";
        userpassword[1]= "allwyn";
        userpassword[2]= "Rohan";
        userpassword[3]= "rohan";
        function checkOut() {
            var flag =0;
            var flag1 =0;
            var i =0;
            var j =0;
            for (x=0; x<document.survey.elements.length; x++) {
                if (document.survey.elements[x].value == "") {
                    alert("You forgot one of the required fields. Please try again");
                    return;
                }
            }
            var user= document.survey.elements[0].value;
            var password = document.survey.elements[1].value;
            while(i<=3) {
                if(userpassword[i] == user) {
                    j=i;
                    j++;
                    if(userpassword[j] == password) {
                        flag=1;
                        break;
                    }
                }
```

```
            i+=2;
        }
        if(flag == 0) {
            alert("Please enter a valid user name and password");
            return;
        }
        else {
            alert("Welcome !!\n" + document.forms[0].Username.value);
        }
        return;
    }
    //-->
    </SCRIPT></HEAD>
    <BODY><FORM Action="" Method="POST" onSubmit="return checkOut(this.form)"
                Name="survey" >
        <INPUT Type="TEXT" Name="Username" Size="15" MaxLength="15">User Name<BR>
        <INPUT Type="PASSWORD" Name="Pasword" size="15">Password<BR>
        <INPUT Type="SUBMIT" Value="Submit">
        <INPUT Type="RESET" Value="Start Over">
    </FORM></BODY>
</HTML>
```

9. OBJECTS IN JAVASCRIPT

1. **Creating a Web page using two image files, which switch between one another as the mouse pointer moves over the images.**

```
<HTML>
    <HEAD><TITLE>CHANGING IMAGES....</TITLE><SCRIPT>
        if(document.images)   rollover="yes";
        else       rollover="no";
        if(rollover=="yes") {
            img1on = new Image();
            img1off = new Image();
            img1on.src="Images/man1.gif";
            img1off.src="Images/man2.gif";
        }
        function imageSwitchOn(imagename) {
            if(rollover=="yes") {
                imageOn=eval(imagename + "on.src");
                document [imagename].src = imageOn;
            }
        }
        function imageSwitchOff(imagename) {
            if (rollover=="yes") {
                imageOff=eval(imagename + "off.src");
                document [imagename].src = imageOff;
            }
        }
    </SCRIPT></HEAD>
```

```
    <BODY><CENTER>
        <H1>IMAGES......</H1><BR>
        <H3><I>place your mouse pointer on the picture</I></H3>
        <A onMouseOver="imageSwitchOn('img1')" onMouseOut="imageSwitchOff('img1')">
            <IMG Alt="space" Height=200 Name="img1" Src="Images/man2.gif" Width=200></A>
    </CENTER></BODY>
</HTML>
```

10. FORMS OF A WEB SITE

1. **Creating a Web page, which accepts user information and user comments on the web site to check if all thc Tcxt fields have being entered with data else display an alert.**

```
<HTML>
    <HEAD><TITLE>Elements of a Form</TITLE>
    <SCRIPT language="JavaScript">
    <!--
        function checkOut() {
            for (x=0; x<document.survey.elements.length; x++) {
                if (document.survey.elements[x].value == "") {
                    alert("Sorry, you forgot one of the required fields. Please try again.");
                    break;
                }
            }
            return false;
        }
    //-->
    </SCRIPT></HEAD>
    <BODY bgcolor="lightyellow"><H2><I>INFONET SERVICES</I></H2>
        <FORM NAME="survey" onSubmit="return checkOut(this.form)">
            <INPUT Name="firstname" Size="30" Type="TEXT" MaxLength="30">
            <B>First Name</B><BR><BR>
            <INPUT Type="TEXT" Name="lastname" Size="30"><B>Last  Name</B><BR><BR>
            <INPUT Type="TEXT" Name="emailaddr" Size="30"><B>E-mail Address</B><BR><BR>
            <INPUT Type="TEXT" Name="address" Size="30"><B>Address</B><BR><BR>
            <INPUT TYPE="TEXT" NAME="city" SIZE="30"><B>City</B><BR><BR>
            <INPUT NAME="state" SIZE="6"><b>State</b>
            <INPUT NAME="zip" SIZE="10"><b>Postal Code</b>
            <INPUT NAME="country" SIZE="15"><b>Country</b>
            <P><B><I>Please choose the most appropriate statement</I></B><BR>
            <INPUT Type="RADIO" Name="buying" Value="regular">
                <B>I regularly purchase items online</B><BR>
            <INPUT Type="RADIO" Name="buying" Value="sometimes">
                <B>I have on occasion purchased items online</B><BR>
            <INPUT Type="RADIO" Name="buying" Value="might" CHECKED>
                <B>I have not purchased anything online, but I would consider it</B><BR>
            <INPUT Type="RADIO" Name="buying" Value="willnot">
                <B>I prefer to shop in real stores</B>
            <P><B><I>I'm interested in (choose all that apply)</I></B><BR>
            <INPUT TYPE="CHECKBOX" NAME="hiking" VALUE="hiking"><B>Hiking</B><BR>
```

```
        <INPUT Type="CHECKBOX" Name="mbiking" Value="mbiking">
            <B>Mountain Biking</B><BR>
        <INPUT Type="CHECKBOX" Name="camping" Value="camping">
            <B>Camping</B><BR>
        <INPUT Type="CHECKBOX" NAME="rock" Value="rock">
            <B>Rock Climbing</B><BR>
        <INPUT Type="CHECKBOX" Name="4wd" Value="4wd">
            <B>Off-Road 4WD</B><BR>
        <INPUT Type="CHECKBOX" Name="ccskiing" Value="ccskiing">
            <B>Cross-country Skiing</B>
        <P><B><I>I learned about this site from</I></B><BR>
        <SELECT NAME="referral">
            <OPTION VALUE="print" SELECTED>Print Ads
            <OPTION VALUE="visit"> In-Store Visit
            <OPTION VALUE="rec"> Friend's Recommendation
            <OPTION VALUE="internet"> Sources on the Internet
            <OPTION VALUE="other"> Other
        </SELECT>
        <P><H4>Comments</H4><BR>
        <TEXTAREA Name="comments" Cols="40" Rows="5">
            Please type any comments here</TEXTAREA><BR>
        <INPUT Type="SUBMIT" Value="Submit">
        <INPUT Type="RESET" Value="Start Over">
    </FORM>
  </BODY>
</HTML>
```

SECTION - III: Dynamic Hyper Text Markup Language

12. DYNAMIC HTML

First Impression - Did the initial page grab attention?
Interface Design - Is the menu interface interactive enough and visually interesting?
Corporate Mildew - Is the site trapped in a web of corporate look, feel and canned marketing speak?
Coriolis Effect - Does the site generate enough currents of interest based on design and content for the user to comeback?

The above points emphasize the requirements of a good web site.

DHTML is a new and emerging technology that has evolved to meet the increasing demand for eye-catching and mind-catching web sites.

DHTML combines HTML with Cascading Style Sheets (CSSs) and Scripting Languages. HTML specifies a web page's elements like table, frame, paragraph, bulleted list, etc. Cascading Style Sheets can be used to determine an element's size, color, position and a number of other features. Scripting Languages (JavaScript and VBScript) can be used to manipulate the web page's elements so that styles assigned to them can change in response to a user's input.

CASCADING STYLE SHEETS

Style Sheets are powerful mechanism for adding styles (e.g. fonts, colors, spacing) to Web documents. They enforce standards and uniformity throughout a web site and provide numerous attributes to create dynamic effects. With Style Sheets, text and image formatting properties can be predefined in a single list. HTML elements on a web page can then be bound to the style sheet. The advantages of a Style Sheet includes the ability to make global changes to all documents from a single location. Style Sheets are said to Cascade when they combine to specify the appearance of a page.

The Style assignment process is accomplished with the **<STYLE>...</STYLE>** tags. The syntax for making the assignment is simple. Between the <STYLE>...</STYLE> HTML tags, specific style attributes are listed. The <STYLE>...</STYLE> tags are written within the <HEAD>...</HEAD> tags.

Syntax:

```
<STYLE Type="text/css">
    tag {attribute:value; attribute:value ... }
    ...
</STYLE>
```

Note

In the <STYLE> tag, the expression "Type = text/css" indicates that the style sheet conforms to CSS syntax

The attributes that can be specified to the **<STYLE>** tag are Font Attributes, Color and Background Attributes, Text Attributes, Border Attributes, Margin Attributes and List Attributes.

Font Attributes

Attributes	Values
font-family	A comma-delimited sequence of font family names (serif, sans-serif, cursive)
font-style	Normal, italic or oblique
font-weight	Normal, bold, bolder, lighter, or one of the nine numerical values (100, 200, 300, 400, 500, 600, 700, 800, 900)
font-size	A term that denotes absolute size (xx-small, x-small, small, medium, large, x-large, xx-large), relative size (larger, smaller), a number (of pixels), percentage (of the parent element's size)

Table 12.1

Use Of Font Attributes

Example 1: (Refer to diagram 12.1)

```
<HTML>
    <HEAD><TITLE> Working with
            Style Sheets using Font
            Attributes </TITLE>
    <STYLE Type = "text/css">
        H1{font-family:arial, helvetica}
        P{font-size:12pt; font-style:italic}
    </STYLE></HEAD>
    <BODY>
        <H1>Silicon Chip
            Technologies</H1>
        <P>Silicon Chip Technologies, a
            private limited company, was
            founded in December 1989.
        <P>The vision of this company is to provide any corporate client a single entity which addresses
            all their Software Development, Technical and User Documentation, Training and Manpower
            Recruitment needs.
    </BODY>
</HTML>
```

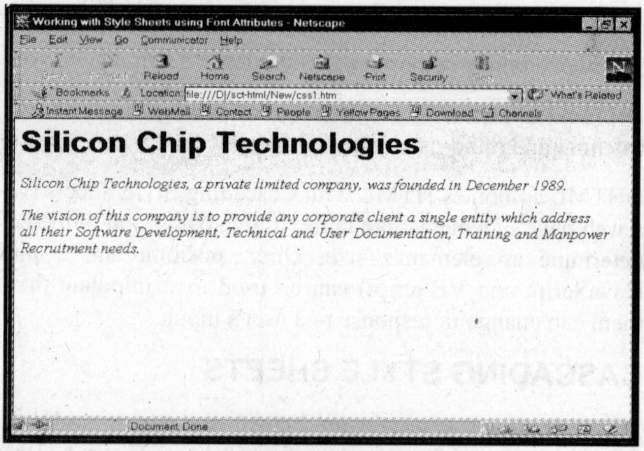

Diagram 12.1

Color And Background Attributes

Attributes	Values
color	Sets an element's text-color. *A color name or a color code*
background-color	Specifies the color in an element's background. *A color name or a color code*
background-image	Sets the background image. *A URL or none*
background-repeat	With a background image specified, sets up how the image repeats throughout the page. *repeat-x*(repeats horizontally), *repeat-y*(repeats vertically), *repeat*(both), *no-repeat*

Table 12.2

Use Of Color And Background Attributes

Example 2: (Refer to diagram 12.2)

Diagram 12.2

```
<HTML>
    <HEAD><TITLE> Working with Style
            Sheets using Color and
            Background
            Attributes</TITLE>
    <STYLE Type = "text/css">
        H1 {font-family:arial, helvetica;
            font-size:26pt; background-
            image:url(images/sct-logo.gif)}
        H2 {font-family:arial, helvetica;
            font-size:26pt; background-
            image:url(images/sct-logo.gif);
            background-repeat:no-repeat}
        P {font-size:12pt; font-style:italic;
            font-weight:bold;
            color:#23238e; background-color:red; background-position:bottom-left}
    </STYLE></HEAD>
    <BODY>
        <B><U>With background repeat</U></B>
        <H1> Silicon Chip Technologies</H1>
        <P>A private limited company, which was founded in December 1989. The vision of this
        company is to provide any corporate client a single entity which addresses all their Software
        Development, Technical and User Documentation, Training and Manpower Recruitment needs.
        </P><BR />
        <B><U>With background no-repeat</U></B>
         <H2> Silicon Chip Technologies</H2>
    </BODY>
</HTML>
```

Text Attributes

Attributes	Values
text-decoration	Adds decoration to an element's text. *None, underline, overline, line-through, blink*
vertical-align	Determines an element's vertical position, *Basline, sub, super, top, text-top, middle, bottom, text-bottom,* also *percentage of the element's height*
text-transform	Applies a transformation to the text.*Capitalize* (puts the text into initial caps), *uppercase, lowercase* or *none*
text-align	Aligns text within an element. *Left, right, center, or justify*
text-indent	Indents the first line of text. *A percentage of the element's width, or a length*

Table 12.3

Tip

Length values can be positive or negative, have a numerical value, and are followed by a unit of measurement. Note that while length values can be either positive or negative, many properties cannot have negative length units.

There are two basic kinds of length unit, **relative** and **absolute**. As aril of thumb, **absolute** units should be used only when the physical characteristics of the output device are known.

The units of measurement are:

Unit Name	Abbreviation	Explanation	Relative
Em	Em	the height of a font	yes
Ex	Ex	height of the letter x in a font	yes
Pica	Pc	1 pica is 12 points	no
Point	Pt	1/72 of an inch	no
Pixel	Px	one dot on a screen	yes
Millimeter	Mm	printing unit	no
Centimeter	Cm	printing unit	no
Inch	In	printing unit	no

Table 12.4

Use of Text Attributes

Example 3: (Refer to diagram 12.3)

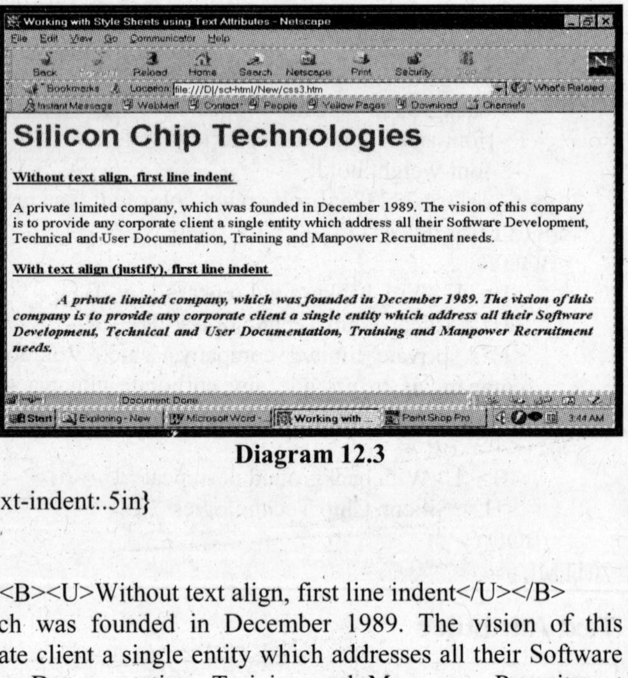

Diagram 12.3

```
<HTML>
    <HEAD><TITLE> Working with Style
            Sheets using Text Attributes
            </TITLE>
    <STYLE Type = "text/css">
        H1 {font-family:arial, helvetica;
            font-size:26pt; text-
            decoration:blink; color:red}
        P {font-size:12pt; font-style:normal;
            font-weight:bold;
            color:#23238e;}
        H6 {font-size:12pt; font-style:italic;
            font-weight:bold;
            color:#23238e; text-align:justify; text-indent:.5in}
    </STYLE></HEAD>
    <BODY>
        <H1>Silicon Chip Technologies</H1><B><U>Without text align, first line indent</U></B>
        <P>A private limited company, which was founded in December 1989. The vision of this
            company is to provide any corporate client a single entity which addresses all their Software
            Development, Technical and User Documentation, Training and Manpower Recruitment
            needs.</P>
        <B><U>With text align (justify), first line indent</U></B>
        <H6>A private limited company, which was founded in December 1989. The vision of this
            company is to provide any corporate client a single entity which addresses all their Software
            Development, Technical and User Documentation, Training and Manpower Recruitment
            needs.</H6>
    </BODY>
</HTML>
```

Border Attributes

Attributes	Values
border-style	*Solid, double, groove, ridge, inset, outset*
border-color	A *color name* or *color code*
border-width	*Thin, medium, think* or *length*
border-top-width	*Thin, medium, think* or *length*
border-bottom-width	*Thin, medium, think* or *length*
border-left-width	*Thin, medium, think* or *length*
border-right-width	*Thin, medium, think* or *length*
border-top	Specifies width, color and style
border-bottom	Specifies width, color and style
border-left	Specifies width, color and style
border-right	Specifies width, color and style
border	Sets all the properties at once

Table 12.5

Use Of Border Attributes

Example 4: (Refer to diagram 12.4)

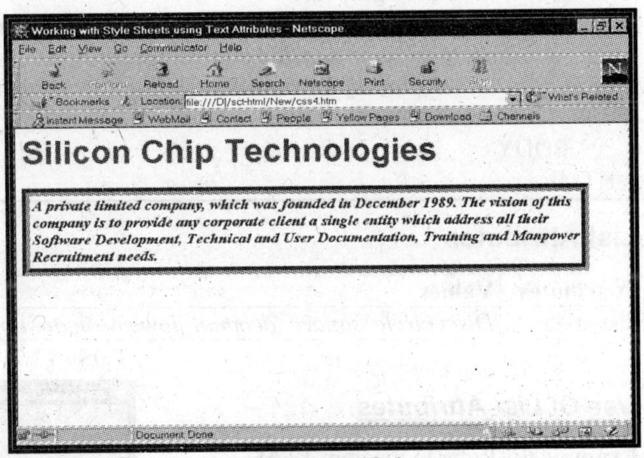

Diagram 12.4

```
<HTML>
    <HEAD><TITLE>Working with Style
            Sheets using Border
            Attributes </TITLE>
    <STYLE Type = "text/css">
        H1 {font-family:arial, helvetica;
            font-size:26pt; color:red}
        P {font-size:12pt; font-style:italic;
            font-weight:bold;
            color:#23238e; border-
            color:#23238e; border-
            style:groove; border-
            width:thick}
    </STYLE></HEAD>
    <BODY><H1> Silicon Chip Technologies</H1>
        <P>A private limited company, which was founded in December 1989. The vision of this
            company is to provide any corporate client a single entity which addresses all their Software
            Development, Technical and User Documentation, Training and Manpower Recruitment
            needs.</P>
    </BODY>
</HTML>
```

Margin Related Attributes

Attributes	Values
margin-top	*Percent, length* or *auto*
margin-bottom	*Percent, length* or *auto*
margin-left	*Percent, length* or *auto*
margin-right	*Percent, length* or *auto*
margin	*Percent, length* or *auto*

Table 12.6

Use Of Margin Attributes

Example 5: (Refer to diagram 12.5)

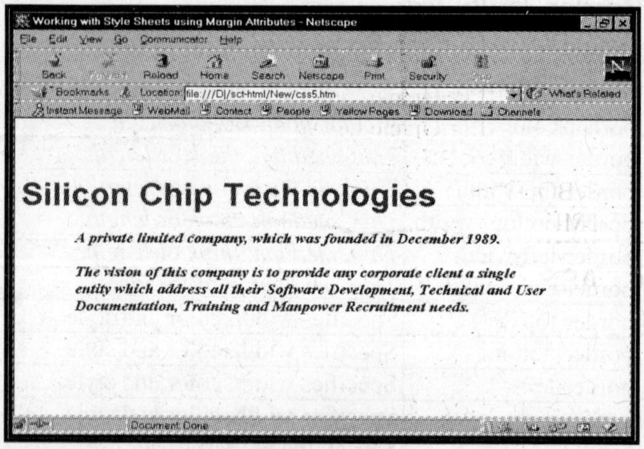

Diagram 12.5

```
<HTML>
    <HEAD><TITLE> Working with Style
Sheets using Margin Attributes</TITLE>
    <STYLE Type = "text/css">
        BODY {margin-top:10%}
        H1   {font-family:arial, helvetica;
            font-size:26pt; color:red}
        P  {font-size:12pt; font-style:italic;
            font-weight:bold;
            color:#23238e;           margin-
            left:15%; margin-right:15%}
    </STYLE> </HEAD>
    <BODY><H1>Silicon Chip
            Technologies</H1>
        <P>A private limited company, which was founded in December 1989. The vision of this
            company is to provide any corporate client a single entity which addresses all their Software
            Development, Technical and User Documentation, Training and Manpower Recruitment
            needs.</P>
    </BODY>
</HTML>
```

List Attributes

Attributes	Values
list-style	*Disc, circle, square, decimal, lower-roman, upper-roman, lower-alpha, upper-alpha, none*

Table 12.7

Use Of List Attributes

Example 6: (Refer to diagram 12.6)

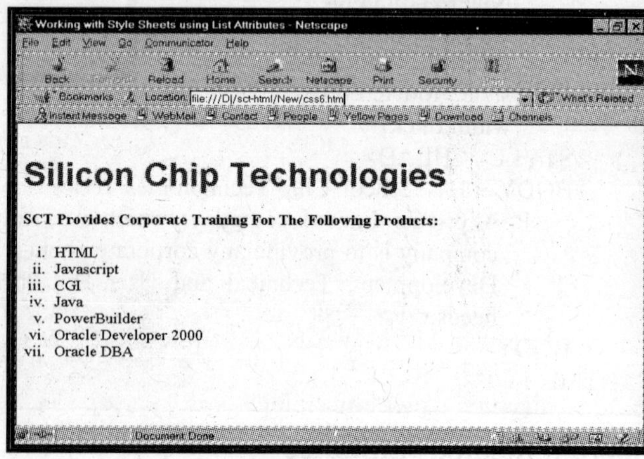

Diagram 12.6

```
<HTML>
    <HEAD><TITLE> Working with Style
            Sheets using List Attributes
            </TITLE>
    <STYLE Type = "text/css">
        BODY {margin-top:5%}
        H1   {font-family:arial, helvetica;
            font-size:26pt; color:red}
        UL {list-style-type:lower-roman}
    </STYLE></HEAD>
    <BODY><H1>Silicon Chip
            Technologies</H1>
        <H4>SCT Provides Corporate Training For The Following Products:</H4>
        <B><UL>
            <LI> HTML
            <LI> Javascript
            <LI> CGI
```

```
            <LI> Java
            <LI> PowerBuilder
            <LI> Oracle Developer 2000
            <LI> Oracle DBA
        </UL></B>
    </BODY>
</HTML>
```

CLASS

The control over page design that style sheet gives is exciting, but can be heavy handed. Its great to be able to change every paragraph, but what if only one paragraph, or a few paragraphs need to be changed?

A particular paragraph may need to look different from other paragraphs. It's probably because the content of the paragraph is in some way different from other paragraphs on the page. Think of a question and answer page. Questions in bold, while the answers are in plain text. The appearance of a paragraph is a function of the content of the paragraph.

Style sheets support classes or sets of style changes for a document. A class can be defined to change the style in a specific way for any element it is applied to, and classes can be used to identify logical sets of style changes that might be different for different HTML elements. The style changes can be applied directly to each HTML element or applied to part of a document with the <SPAN> </SPAN> tags. If any element is made a member of a class by inserting *Class = ClassName* into its opening tab, it conforms to that class specification.

In the example above, there are two classes of paragraph - question and answer. So in the style sheet there need to be two statements, one which affects only paragraphs of *class* question, and one which only affects paragraphs of *class* answer.

In a style sheet, class is defined by a dot followed by the name of the class i.e. **.class-name**.

Use Of Class

Example 7: (Refer to diagram 12.7)

```
<HTML>
    <HEAD><TITLE> Working with
            Class </TITLE>
    <STYLE Type = "text/css">
        P {font-size:12pt; font-
          weight:bold; text-align:justify;
          margin-left:10%; margin-
          right:10%}
        .question {color:brown; font-
                style:italic}
        .answer {color:#23238e}
    </STYLE></HEAD>
    <BODY>
        <P class="question"> How to
          create style sheet to alter an
          HTML element ? </P>
```

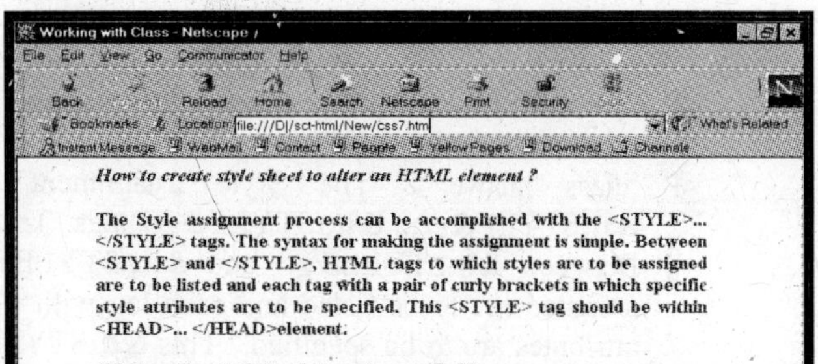

Diagram 12.7

```
        <P class="answer"> The Style assignment process can be accomplished with the
           &lt;STYLE&gt;...&lt;/STYLE&gt; tags. The syntax for making the assignment is simple.
           Between &lt;STYLE&gt; and &lt;/STYLE&gt;, HTML tags to which styles are to be
           assigned are to be listed and each tag with a pair of curly brackets in which specific style
           attributes are to be specified. This &lt;STYLE&gt; tag should be within &lt;HEAD&gt;...
           &lt;/HEAD&gt;element.</P>
        <P class='question'> What are the attributes that can be specified ? </P>
        <P class='answer'> The attributes that can be specified are, Font Attributes, Color and Background
           Attributes, Text Attributes, Border Attributes, Margin Attributes and List Attributes.</P>
    </BODY>
</HTML>
```

USING THE <SPAN>...</SPAN> TAG

SPAN is an HTML element that plays a prominent role in style sheets. In the body of the document, **<SPAN>...</SPAN>** is used to set the boundaries of the rule's styling specifications.

Use Of SPAN Tags

Example 8: (Refer to diagram 12.8)

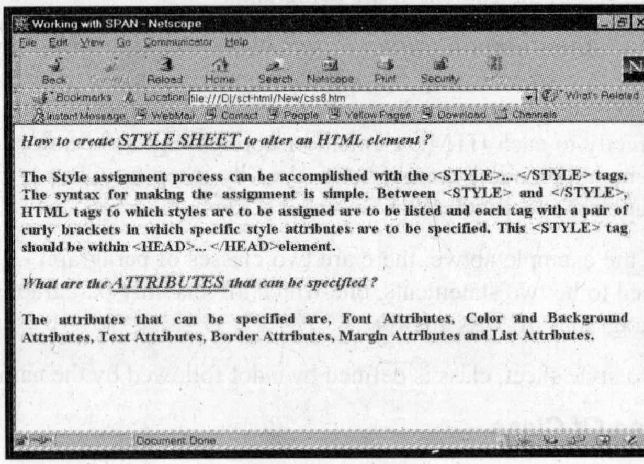

Diagram 12.8

```
<HTML>
    <HEAD><TITLE>Working with
            SPAN</TITLE>
    <STYLE Type = "text/css">
        P {font-size:12pt;font-
           weight:bold; text-align:justify}
        .question {color:brown; font-
           style:italic}
        .answer {color:#23238e}
        .big {font-size:14pt; text-
           decoration:underline; text-
           transform:uppercase; color:red}
    </STYLE></HEAD>
    <BODY>
        <P class="question"> How to create <SPAN class="big"> style sheet </SPAN> to alter an HTML
           element ?</P>
        <P class="answer"> The Style assignment process can be accomplished with the
           &lt;STYLE&gt;...&lt;/STYLE&gt; tags. The syntax for making the assignment is simple.
           Between &lt;STYLE&gt; and &lt;/STYLE&gt;, HTML tags to which styles are to be
           assigned are to be listed and each tag with a pair of curly brackets in which specific style
           attributes are to be specified. This &lt;STYLE&gt; tag should be within &lt;HEAD&gt;...
           &lt;/HEAD&gt;element.</P>
        <P class='question'> What are the <SPAN class="big"> attributes </SPAN> that can be
           specified?</P>
        <P class='answer'> The attributes that can be specified are, Font Attributes, Color and Background
           Attributes, Text Attributes, Border Attributes, Margin Attributes and List Attributes.</P>
    </BODY>
</HTML>
```

Tip

To protect browsers that do not support <STYLE> element, insert comment tags around the declarations within the style element.

```
<STYLE Type = "text/css">
<!--
  /* declaration */
  -->
</STYLE>
```

EXTERNAL STYLE SHEETS

External Style Sheets are composed of standard text, which consists of a series of entries, each composed of a selector and a declaration. The selector indicates the HTML element(s) affected by the properties in the declaration. These external style sheets are then saved as a file with extension .css, which can be linked, to a web page via the **<LINK>** tag.

```
<LINK Rel=stylesheet HRef="<StyleSheet File Name>">
```

Use Of External Style Sheet

Example 9: (Refer to diagram 12.9)

Code for mystyle.css:

```
P {font-size:12pt;font-weight:bold; text-
   align:justify}
.question {color:brown;  font-style:italic}
.answer {color:#23238e}
.big {font-size:14pt; text-
      decoration:underline; text-
      transformation:uppercase; color:red}
```

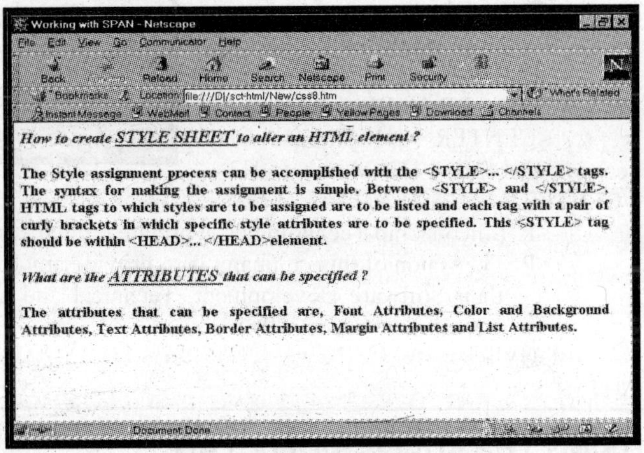

Diagram 12.9

Code for the HTML page:

```
<HTML>
   <HEAD><TITLE> Working with
            External Style Sheet </TITLE>
   <LINK Rel="stylesheet" HREF="mystyle.css"></HEAD>
   <BODY>
      <P class="question">How to create <SPAN class="big"> style sheet </SPAN> to alter an HTML
         element?</P>
      <P class="answer"> The Style assignment process can be accomplished with the
         &lt;STYLE&gt;...&lt;/STYLE&gt; tags. The syntax for making the assignment is simple.
         Between &lt;STYLE&gt; and &lt;/STYLE&gt;, HTML tags to which styles are to be
         assigned are to be listed and each tag with a pair of curly brackets in which specific style
         attributes are to be specified.  This &lt;STYLE&gt; tag should be within &lt;HEAD&gt;...
         &lt;/HEAD&gt;element.</P>
      <P class='question'> What are the <SPAN class="big"> attributes </SPAN> that can be
         specified?</P>
      <P class='answer'> The attributes that can be specified are, Font Attributes, Color and Background
         Attributes, Text Attributes, Border Attributes, Margin Attributes and List Attributes.</P>
   </BODY>
</HTML>
```

Tip

Style information can be associated with the web page in several ways:

- By embedding the style information directly through a STYLE attribute
- <H1 STYLE = text-align:center> Inline Style Sheet </H1>
- By embedding the style information directly through a <STYLE> header
- By embedding the style information directly through <LINK> element

Example 10: (Refer to diagram 12.10)

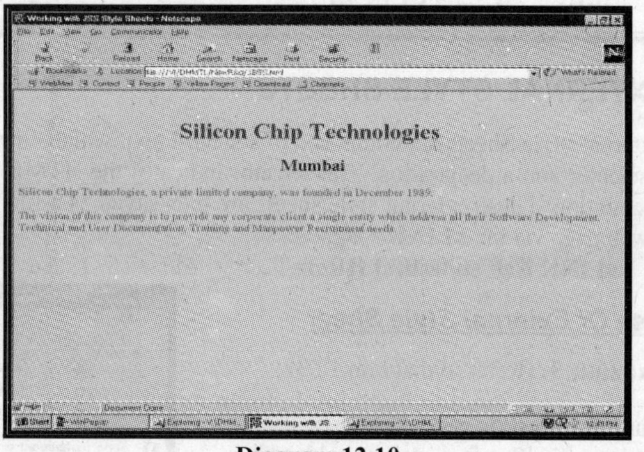

Diagram 12.10

```
<HTML>
   <HEAD><TITLE> Working with Cascading Style Sheets </TITLE>
   <STYLE Type="text/css">
      BODY {background-Color: 'cyan';}
      H1 {Color: red;}
      H2 {Color: blue;}
      P {Color: green;}
   </STYLE></HEAD>
   <BODY><BR /><BR />
      <CENTER><H1>Silicon Chip Technologies</H1><H2>Mumbai</H2>
</CENTER>
      <P>Silicon Chip Technologies, a private limited company, was founded in December 1989.</P>
      <P>The vision of this company is to provide any corporate client a single entity which address all
         their Software Development, Technical and User Documentation, Training and Manpower
         Recruitment needs.</P>
   </BODY>
</HTML>
```

USING THE <DIV>...</DIV> TAG

A web page can be divided into segments or divisions called **DIV**s. Each segment starts with <DIV> and ends with </DIV>. These segments can be positioned anywhere on the page. The <DIV> tag has a 'position' attribute that can take one of the two values, **Absolute** or **Relative**. **Absolute** positions the segment with respect to the top/left edge of the browser window. In contrast with Absolute, *Relative* positions the segment in relation to other elements on the page.

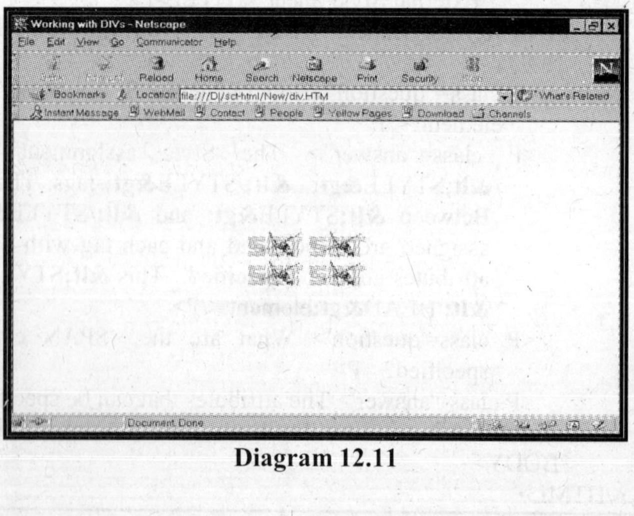

Diagram 12.11

Use Of DIVs

Example 11: (Refer to diagram 12.11)

```
<HTML>
    <HEAD><TITLE> Working with DIVs </TITLE></HEAD>
    <BODY>
        <DIV ID="box1" Style="background-color:red; position:absolute; left:300; top:150; width:50">
            <IMG Src="images/SCT-LOGO.gif"></DIV>
        <DIV ID="box2" Style="background-color:red; position:absolute; left:380; top:150; width:50">
            <IMG Src="images/SCT-LOGO.gif"></DIV>
        <DIV ID="box3" Style="background-color:red; position:absolute; left:300; top:190; width:50">
            <IMG Src ="images/SCT-LOGO.gif"></DIV>
        <DIV ID="box4" Style="background-color:red; position:absolute; left:380; top:190; width:50">
            <IMG Src="images/SCT-LOGO.gif"></DIV>
    </BODY>
</HTML>
```

These images are actually put in four different segments.

This example shows when the mouse cursor is placed on the first picture, the second picture becomes invisible and viceversa. If the mouse is on neither of the pictures both the pictures are visible.

Use Of The DIV Tag And Visibility Property

Example 12: (Refer to diagram 12.12.1)

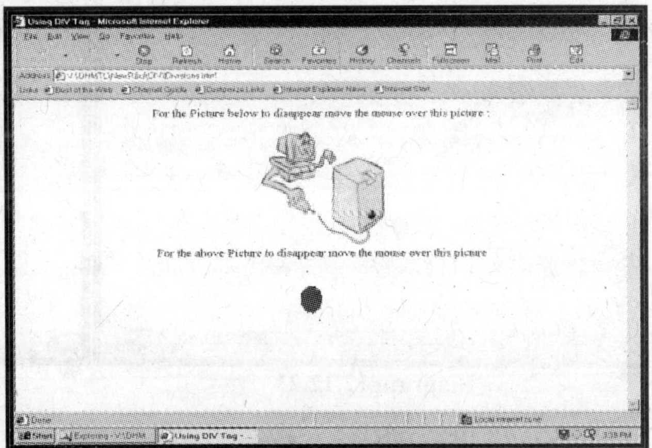

Diagram 12.12.1

```
<HTML>
    <HEAD><TITLE>Using DIV
            Tag</TITLE> </HEAD>
    <BODY><SCRIPT
Language="Javascript">
        function computer_onmouseover()
{
            text1.style.visibility = "visible";
            computer.style.visibility =
"visible";
            text2.style.visibility = "hidden";
            balloon.style.visibility =
"hidden";
        }
        function everyone_onmouseout() {
            text1.style.visibility = "visible";
            computer.style.visibility = "visible";
            text2.style.visibility = "visible";
            balloon.style.visibility = "visible";
        }
        function balloon_onmouseover() {
            text1.style.visibility = "hidden";
            computer.style.visibility = "hidden";
            text2.style.visibility = "visible";
```

```
            balloon.style.visibility = "visible";
        }
    </SCRIPT>
    <DIV Style="visibility:visible;text-align:center;" onmouseover="computer_onmouseover();"
            onmouseout="everyone_onmouseout();">
        <SPAN ID="text1" Style="color:blue;font-family:sans-serif;">For the Picture below to disappear
            move the mouse over this picture</SPAN>
        <P><IMG ID="computer" Src="Images/computer.gif" Height="200" Width="200" />
    </DIV><DIV Style="visibility:visible;text-align:center;" onmouseover="balloon_onmouseover();"
            onmouseout="everyone_onmouseout();">
        <SPAN ID="text2" Style="color:blue;font-family:sans-serif;">For the above Picture to disappear
            move the mouse over this picture</SPAN>
        <P><IMG ID="balloon" Src="Images/balloon.gif" Height="200" Width="200" /></DIV>
    </BODY>
</HTML>
```

When the mouse is not on any of the pictures, the output of above example is as shown in diagram 12.12.1

When the mouse is on the first picture, the output of above example is as shown in diagram 12.12.2 and when the mouse is on the second picture, the output is as shown in diagram 12.12.3.

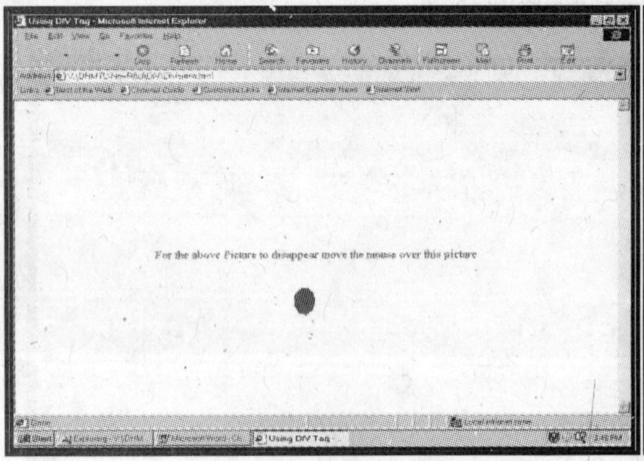

Diagram 12.12.2

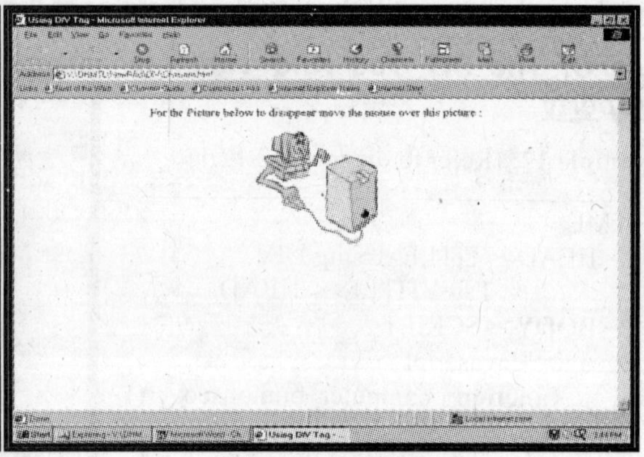

Diagram 12.12.3

TO MOVE FORWARD

In the topics discussed so far, information flows only in one direction from the web server to the browser. Web pages can be created with well-formatted page contents, which would attract visitors to the web site. This would still be incomplete if a Web site cannot process the feedback form and store the information in a Database or some text file for some future reference. Feedback on a web site leads to constant improvement of the site. Based on the data stored, dynamic Web pages can be created by reading the data that is stored in the Database, which also enhances the Web site.

The next chapters describes how to create interactive web pages that obtain information from viewers through forms, validate this using JavaScript and then store it in Database or a File using Server side code. The Server side code can be developed using languages like PHP, ASP, Java and so on. Further chapters are going to take an interesting look at **PHP** (i.e. The **P**HP **H**ypertext **P**rocessor scripting language).

SELF REVIEW QUESTIONS

FILL IN THE BLANKS

1. ______ _________ are powerful mechanism for adding styles (e.g. fonts, colors, spacing etc) to web documents.
2. The advantages of style sheets include the ability to make ________ changes to all documents from a single location.
3. The Style assignment process can be accomplished with the _________ and ________ tag.
4. The <STYLE> tag should be within the___________ and _________element.
5. ___________ attribute sets an element's text-color.
6. __________ attribute aligns the text within an element to the right.
7. In the body of a document, ______ and _______ tags are used to set the boundaries of the rule's styling specifications.
8. ________________ attribute is used to set the color of the border.
9. External Style Sheets can be saved as file using _______ extensions, which can be linked to web pages by the _________ tag.
10. Style Sheets support _________, which are sets of style changes for a document.

TRUE OR FALSE

11. BACKGROUND-REPEAT: repeat-x will repeat the image specified vertically.
12. Text-indent is used to indent the first line of text encountered.
13. <DIV>...</DIV> are used to divide a web page into segments which can be positioned anywhere on the page.

HANDS ON EXERCISES

1. Design a web page for CYBERSHOP INC, using style sheets with the following specifications:

- Define a style class '.Maxx' with the following attributes: {font-size:120%; color:'green'; font-weight:bold; font-family:cursive}
- Use the defined Style class wherever the text 'CYBERSHOP INC' appears on the web document.
- Use unordered listing giving the list of services offered by CYBERSHOP INC.
- Define three segments using <DIV>...</DIV> tags with background colors Blue, Green and Goldenrod positioned accordingly with the given text. Obtain an output as shown in the diagram 12.13.

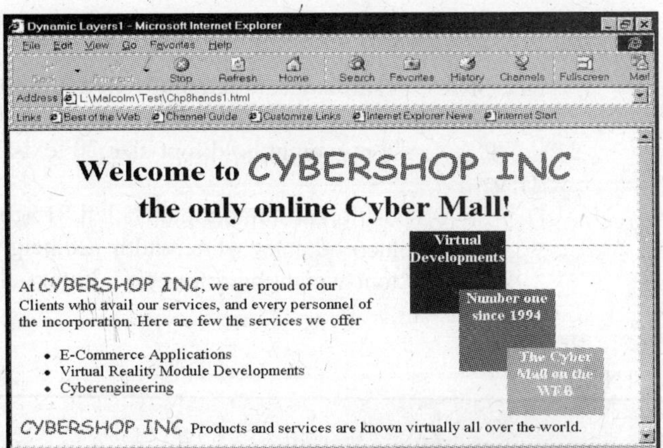

Diagram 12.13: Output of Hands on Exercises .

SOLUTIONS TO HANDS ON EXERCISES

12. DYNAMIC DHTML

1. **Designing a web page for CYBERSHOP INC using style sheets:**

```
<HTML>
    <HEAD>
        <TITLE>Dynamic Layers 1</TITLE>
        <STYLE Type="text/css">
            .Maxx{font-size:120%;color:green;font-weight:bold;font-family:cursive}
        </STYLE>
    </HEAD>
    <BODY Style="background-color:#ffffcc">
        <H1 Style="text-align:center">Welcome to <A Class="Maxx">CYBERSHOP INC</A><BR>the
            only online Cyber Mall!</H1><HR>
        <P Style = "margin-right:40%">At <A Class="Maxx"> CYBERSHOP INC</A>, we are proud of
            our Clients who avail our services, and every personnel of the incorporation.  Here are few
            the services we offer:<UL>
            <LI>E-Commerce Applications</LI>
            <LI>Virtual Reality Module Developments</LI>
            <LI>Cyberengineering</LI>
        </UL></P>
        <A Class="Maxx">CYBERSHOP INC</A>
        Products and services are known virtually all over the world.
        <DIV Style="position:absolute;top:40%;left:65%;background-color:blue;
            color:white;width:120;height:110;z-index:0">
            <P Style="font-weight:bold;font-size:20;text-align:center">Virtual Developments</P>
        </DIV>
        <DIV Style="position:absolute;top:60%;left:73%;background-
            color:green;color:white;width:120;height:110;z-index:1">
            <P Style="font-weight:bold;font-size:20;text-align:center">Number one since 1994</P>
        </DIV>
        <DIV Style="position:absolute;top:80%;left:81%;background-
            color:goldenrod;color:white;width:120;height:90;z-index:2">
            <P style="font-weight:bold;font-size:20;text-align:center">The Cyber Mall on the WEB</P>
        </DIV>
    </BODY>
</HTML>
```

ANSWERS TO SELF REVIEW QUESTIONS

12. DYNAMIC DHTML

FILL IN THE BLANKS

1. Style Sheets
2. Global
3. <STYLE> and </STYLE>
4. <HEAD> and </HEAD>
5. Color
6. Text-Align:Right
7. <SPAN> and </SPAN>
8. Border-color
9. .CSS extension and <LINK> tag
10. Classes

TRUE OR FALSE

11. False
12. True
13. True

SECTION - IV: Setting Up The PHP Framework

13. INTRODUCING PHP

PHP - A Server Side Scripting Language

To introduce the element of dynamism to an HMTL page, page content must be extracted from a database table, formatted using HTML as desired, bound to a Cascading Style Sheet and dispatched to a Browser that requests the page. This technique ensures that HTML page content can vary in real time whenever the database table content is updated. PHP does this kind of Web server side work effortlessly.

Since the PHP script executes on the Web server and produces pure HTML as its output the PHP script is completely opaque to the requesting Browser. The Web server always dispatches pure HTML codespec to the Browser which is the output of the PHP script. PHP scripts are therefore Browser neutral. Since the PHP script is never dispatched to a Browser, the script cannot be captured via a Browser's **View Source** capabilities. PHP is quite unlike JavaScript. JavaScript can be read / copied / altered using a Browser's View Source capabilities.

PHP is a **parsed** language. It requires a PHP environment to execute in. Every time a client browser requests a page delivered by PHP code, the Web server invokes the PHP program delivers this to the PHP parser which executes the PHP statements to produce the desired HTML output. Fortunately, this is a really fast process.

Additionally using PHP, JavaScript can be embedded within HTML code spec.

PHP does consume a lot of Web server resources because everything is executed at the Web server. With many concurrent Browser requests, which in turn invoke large complex PHP scripts, the Web server might get stressed out to deliver.

The HTML code spec delivered by or simply embedded in PHP code spec continues to remain static.

Some PHP attributes are:

- PHP stands for Hypertext Preprocessor
- PHP is a Web server-side scripting language
- PHP scripts are executed at the Web server. Their output, which is pure HTML is returned to the requesting Browser
- PHP can connect natively to many database engines such as (MySQL, Oracle, Postgre, SQLite, and so on)
- PHP is Open Source Software (OSS)
- PHP is totally free of cost to download and use

The cost benefits of using PHP when compared to any 'Paid for' development environment are obvious. A huge number of interactive, E-commerce, driven websites are crafted today using PHP.

What Is A PHP File?

A PHP file is group of grammatically correct PHP sentences, placed one below the other, created using an ASCII editor by a programmer. PHP file content is a mixture of PHP syntax, embedded with standard HTML codespec. When this combination codespec is interpreted by the PHP runtime at the Web server, it instructs the Web server exactly what to do to deliver a well formatted HTML page to the requesting Browser.

- PHP files can contain body text, HTML tags, with HTML styling commands or a binding to an external CSS file and/or JavaScript or a binding to an external JavaScript file
- After PHP files are processed, their output which is pure HTML is returned to the Browser
- PHP filenames usually have the extension of .php, .php3 or .phtml

Why PHP?

- PHP runs perfectly on different operating systems such as Windows, Linux, Unix and so on
- PHP is compatible with almost all Web servers used today (Apache, IIS and so on)
- PHP is FREE to download from the official PHP resource: http://www.php.net
- PHP is easy to learn and runs efficiently and swiftly on any compatible Web server

There is extensive help for PHP available starting with its excellent manual (also freely downloadable). if stuck, there are a huge number of PHP forums on the Internet where questions are answered for free. Multiple web sites provide excellent PHP tutorials. Finally there are a number of PHP IDE's available today either for free download and use or for modest fees.

Extending PHP is pretty easy. PHP is a full-fledged development environment consisting of a several megabytes of source code.

A PHP learning method that's fun and possibly gives the best end results, especially to experienced application developers is 'Learn by doing'.

This mapped to the tons of Internet PHP material available today, including free PHP libraries for download and use, helps make PHP an exciting, simple to use, satisfying, Internet enabled, programming environment.

INSTALLING THE FRAMEWORK

Web servers are computers linked by the Internet. They host websites, serving web site pages to requesting Browsers. When multiple web sites are hosted on and delivered by a single web server the service provided is referred to as web (site) hosting.

Every web server has a unique address called its **ip**. A Web server's ip permits it to be found on the really immense network called the Internet. The **ip** (**i**nternet **p**rotocol) is a numeric value, expressed as XXX.XXX.XXX.XXX. Four sets of significant numbers with each set of three numbers separated from the other using a period (eg. 192.168.0.101).

This address (the **ip**) is always mapped to a more human friendly address, such as www.ivanbayoss.com or www.ivansmusings.com, called domain names, via special computers located on the Internet called **D**omain **N**ame **S**ervers (DNS).

Website hosting companies rent out space on their Web server's hard disk drive, to people or businesses, in which they set up their websites (i.e. Their domains). The Web server, which runs specific Web server software (i.e. Apache, IIS) on it, is quite capable of locating a unique domain from among the multiple domains on its hard disk, whenever a Browser requests for access to a specific domain's resources.

To connected to and be recognized on the Internet, the computer on which the hard disk resides, is assigned a **unique IP** address by an **I**nternet **S**ervice **P**rovider (ISP) which is the company that provides the connection (or pipeline) to the Internet.

This unique ip identifies this specific computer on the Internet. When a website's address like www.ivanbayross.com is keyed into a Browser's address bar and **GO** is clicked the Browser blindly broadcasts a request on the Internet requesting for the **ip** bound to the website's address.

The browser's blind broadcast includes its own computer's ip. DNS servers located on the Internet, whose sole job is to return an ip to any Browser's blind request for one, respond. The Browser now has the ip of the computer which is actually hosting the website. From that moment onwards, the Browser will broadcast its request for web site resources using the specific ip returned by the DNS servers. Now two computers can communicate on the Internet because the requesting computer has a specific ip to communicate with, and in its request it includes its own ip to link back to.

When the request reaches its destination, the web server that hosts the www.ivanbayross.com website, immediately returns an HTML page to the client machine that attempted contact. This HTML page travels back via the Internet to the requesting computer. The client computer receives the HTML page. Its browser interprets the HTML code. Then renders the HTML code for display on the computer's VDU.

The more powerful the Web server, the faster it can serve website pages (i.e. the faster it can respond to Browser requests). Slower, less powerful web servers may result in a frustrating lag time for viewers.

High incoming traffic can also slow Web servers that are not powerful enough to handle the high volumes of data being exchanged. This lag time is of grave concern to E-Commerce web sites.

Most website hosting companies have a page dedicated to sharing technical information about their Web server(s), which generally includes processor speed, cache, capacity, network configuration, Internet pipeline band width and other details.

In theory, Web servers are connected to the Internet 24/7, 365 days a year. In actual fact Web servers can experience some downtime due to maintenance or technical issues. Web servers with a consistent record of an uptime of 99.5% are considered reliable as a hosting site.

In this material the following two web servers will be focused on:

- Microsoft - **I**nternet **I**nformation **S**erver
- Open Source - Apache Web Server

Internet Information Server

Microsoft **I**nternet **I**nformation **S**erver (IIS), is a set of **Internet-based services** run on the Microsoft Windows O/s. It is the world's second most used web server, in terms of overall websites.

Originally, it was supplied as part of the M.S. Server O/s editions (i.e. M.S. Windows NT 4.0) IIS was upgraded with NT 4.0's subsequent service packs and option packs. Eventually, as IIS matured, it was integrated into M.S. Windows 2000 and M.S. Windows 2003 Server O/s.

IIS is also bundled with Windows XP. This is a **limited feature version** of **I**nternet **I**nformation **S**erver. This version allows the setting up of a virtual directory and can be successfully used as an **Intranet** server for any organization. Windows XP Professional is <u>not</u> a server class operating system hence IIS has limited functionality which prevents users from doing a lot of stuff that can be done with a **full server version** of IIS. However, even the limited functionality still allows a lot of Web server type work to be done via a computer running Windows XP as its operating system.

The following material provides step by step information for setting up IIS on Windows XP (Professional). Once done, this setup of IIS can provide a good practice environment to learn how IIS is managed. With this knowledge one should be able to configure IIS on Windows 2003 which is a full fledged server O/s.

Installing IIS

IIS is **not installed** by default when the Windows XP Professional O/s is installed. IIS has to be installed separately. This requires the Windows XP Professional, setup CD-ROM.

Steps for setting up IIS on Windows XP Professional:

1. Click **Start → Control Panel →** 

(Add or Remove Programs). Refer to diagram 13.1

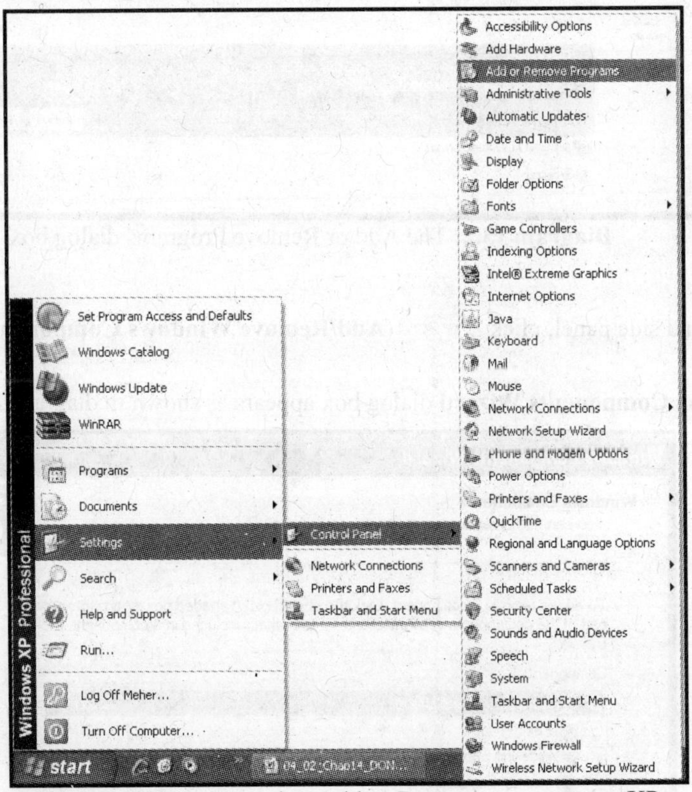

Diagram 13.1: Accessing Add or Remove programs on XP

2. The **Add or Remove Programs** dialog box appears as shown in diagram 13.2

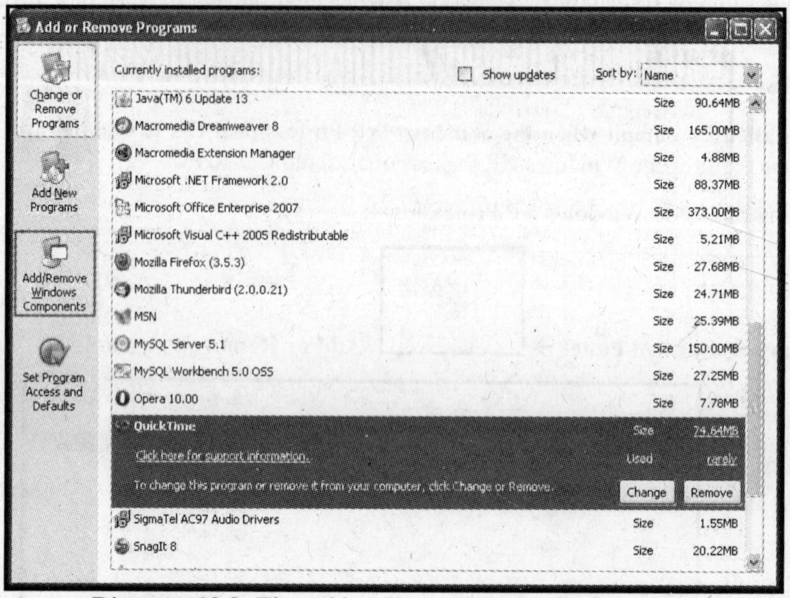

Diagram 13.2: The Add or Remove Programs dialog box

3. In the left hand side panel, click  **(Add/Remove Windows Components)** as shown in diagram 13.2

4. The **Windows Components Wizard** dialog box appears as shown in diagram 13.3

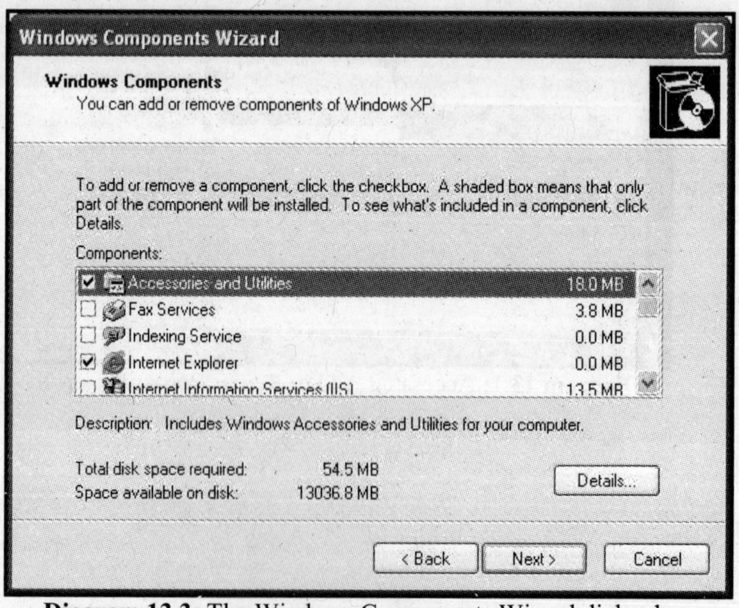

Diagram 13.3: The Windows Components Wizard dialog box

5. Select the check box adjacent **Internet Information Services (IIS)** as shown in diagram 13.4. The check box turns gray  indicating that some of IIS sub-components are **not selected** for installation

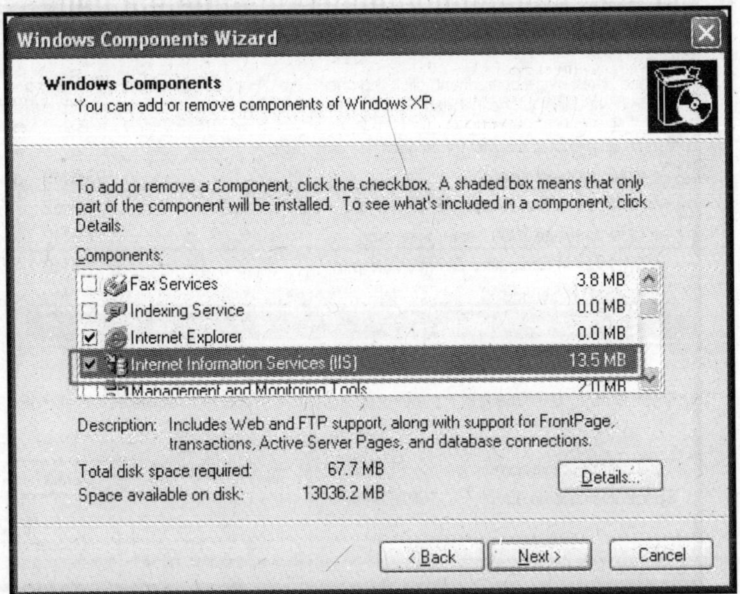

Diagram 13.4: Internet Information Services (IIS) option selected

6. Click . The **Internet Information Services (IIS)** dialog box appears as shown in diagram 13.5. This dialog box displays all of the sub components that can be installed with IIS

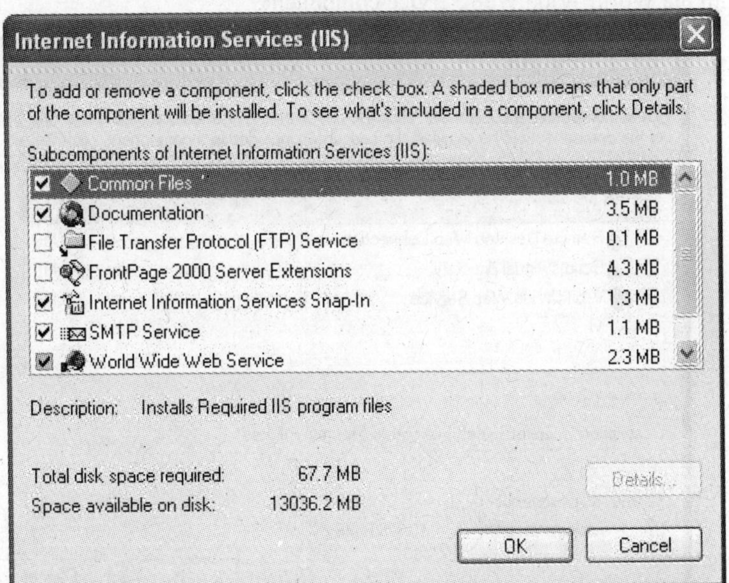

Diagram 13.5: Internet Information Services dialog box

7. Select the check box adjacent to **File Transfer Protocol (FTP) Service** and **Frontpage 2000 Server Extensions** as shown in diagram 13.6

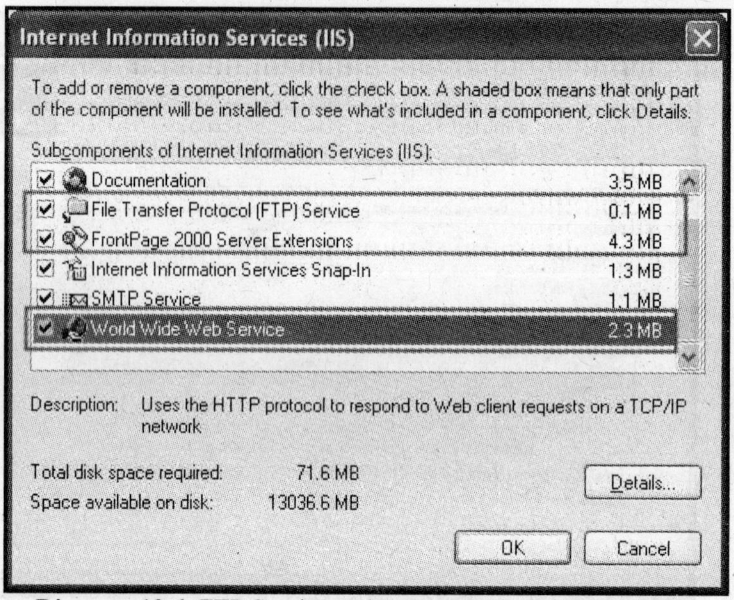

Diagram 13.6: FTP Service and Frontpage Extensions selected

8. Next select **World Wide Web Service** and click Details... . The **World Wide Web Service** dialog box appears as shown in diagram 13.7. This dialog box displays all the sub-components that can be installed with the World Wide Web Service component

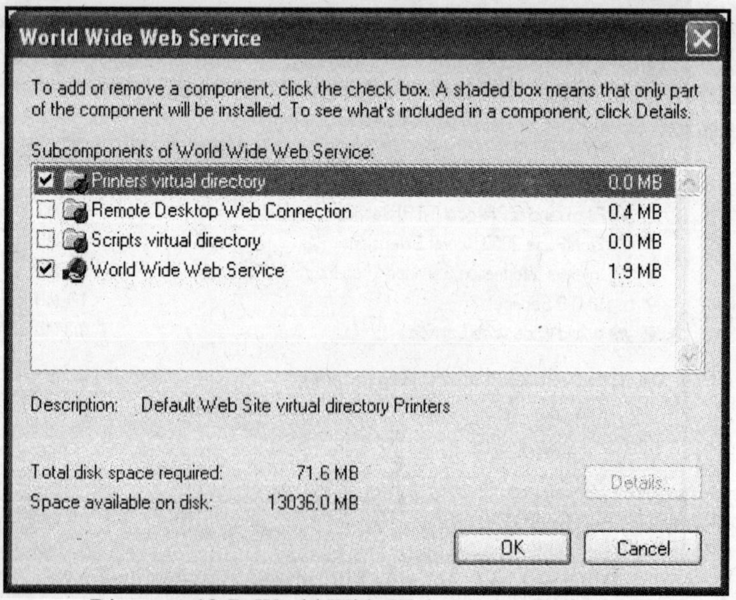

Diagram 13.7: World Wide Web Service dialog box

9. Select the check box adjacent to **Remote Desktop Web Connection** and **Scripts virtual directory** as shown in diagram 13.8

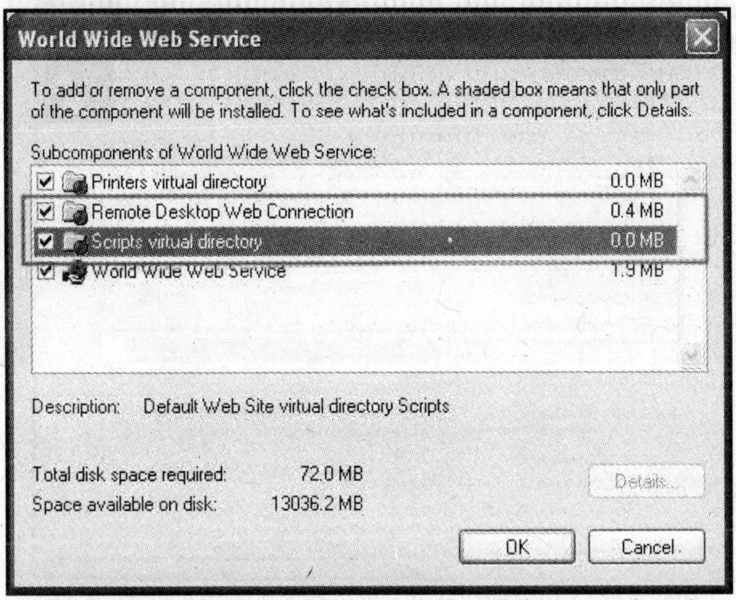

Diagram 13.8: Remote desktop and Virtual directory selected

10. Click OK to return to **Internet Information Services (IIS)** dialog box as shown in diagram 13.9. The check box color of the World Wide Web Service changes from gray to white. This indicates that **all** its sub-components are now selected for installation

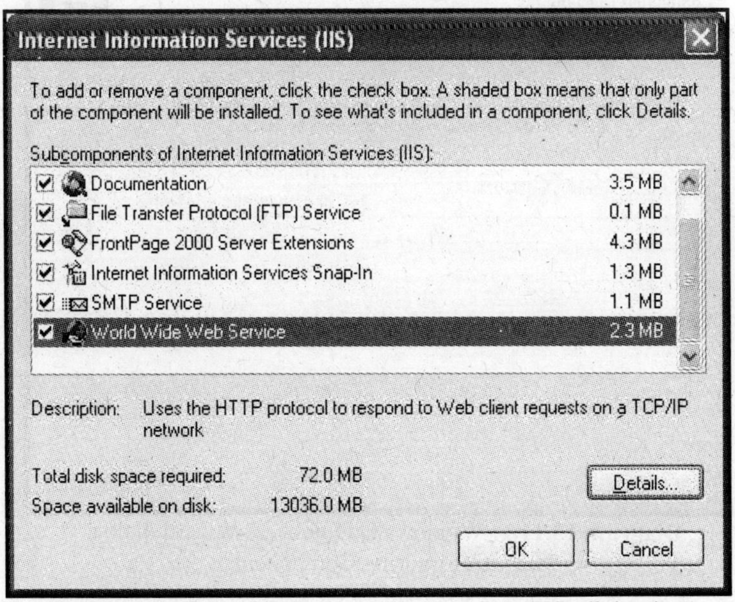

Diagram 13.9: Internet Information Services (IIS) dialog box

11. Click 

in the **IIS** dialog box to return to the **Windows Components Wizard** dialog box. As shown in diagram 13.10

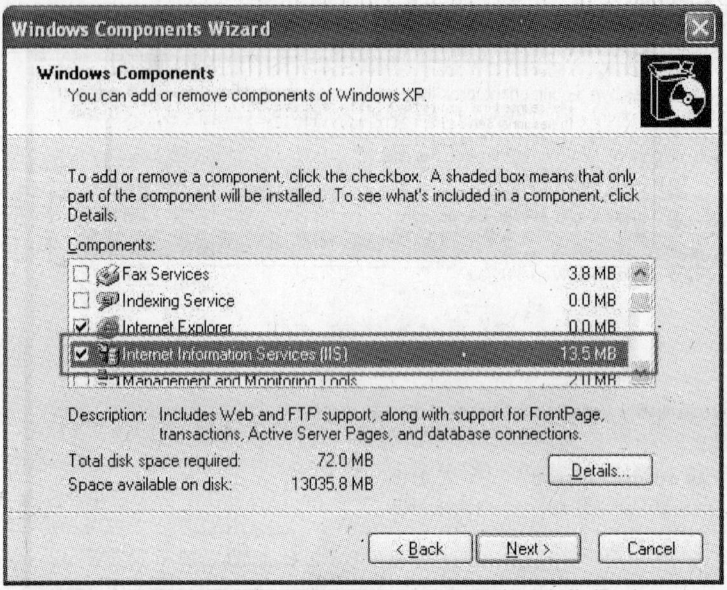

Diagram 13.10: Windows Components Wizard dialog box

12. Click 

to commence installing IIS as shown in diagram 13.11.1

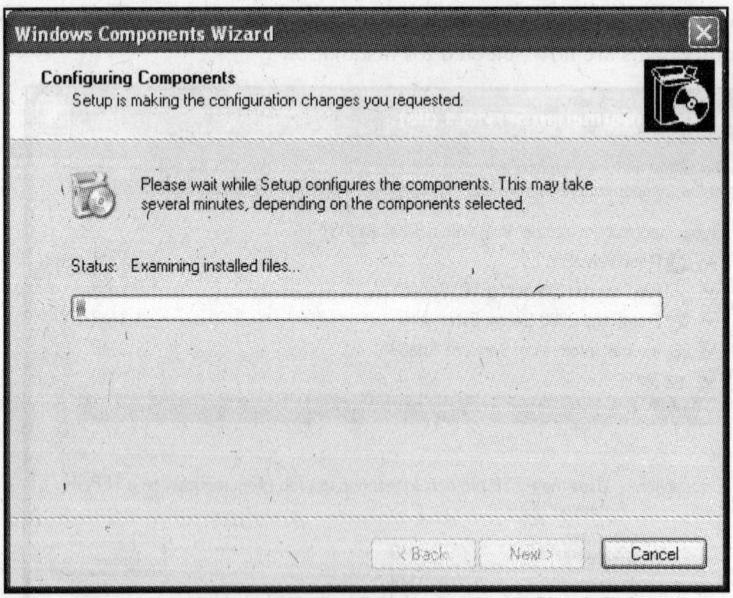

Diagram 13.11.1: Windows Components Wizard dialog box - Configuring Components

13. This process usually requires files from the Windows XP Professional CD-ROM. The CD-ROM is asked for by the configuration wizard via an **Insert Disk** dialog box which prompts for the **Windows XP Professional Service Pack 2 CD** as shown in diagram 13.11.2

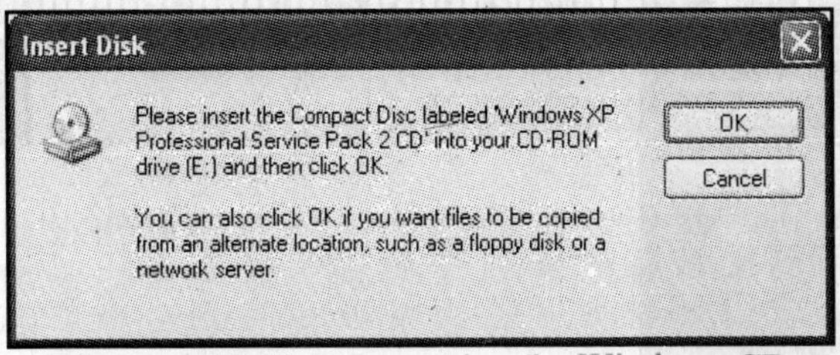

Diagram 13.11.2: Prompting for Windows CD

14. Insert this CD-ROM and click . Windows Components Wizard will automatically resume configuring and installing IIS as shown in diagram 13.12

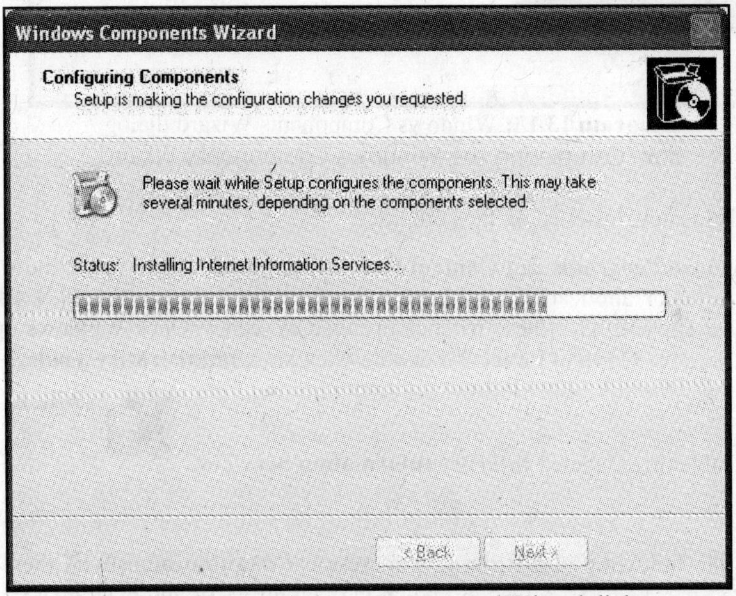

Diagram 13.12: Windows Components Wizard dialog box- Configuring Components - Installing IIS

15. Once the installation process of IIS is complete, the **Windows Components Wizard** dialog box appears indicating the successful completion of configuring and installing components. As shown in diagram 13.13

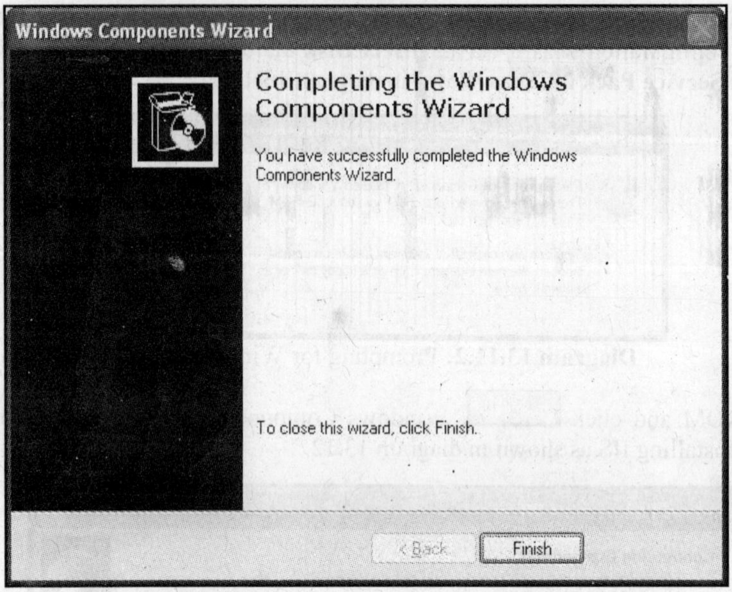

Diagram 13.13: Windows Components Wizard dialog box- Completing the Windows Components Wizard

16. Click . IIS is now installed on the computer.

Close the **Add or Remove Programs** and **Control Panel**. It's a good idea to run Windows Update at this juncture. IIS being a major application may have several patches released by M.S. running Windows Update will ensure that IIS will have these patches installed as well. Once Windows update completes, reboot the machine. Open the **Control Panel** and double-click on **Administrative Tools**.

A new icon will be visible there labeled **Internet Information Services**.

Testing IIS

Test IIS by entering the following in a Browser's address bar. http://localhost and then clicking the GO button or pressing the Enter key. If a screen as shown in diagram 13.14 and diagram 13.15 is displayed in the Browser IIS was successfully installed.

Diagram 13.15, shows the documentation of the IIS.

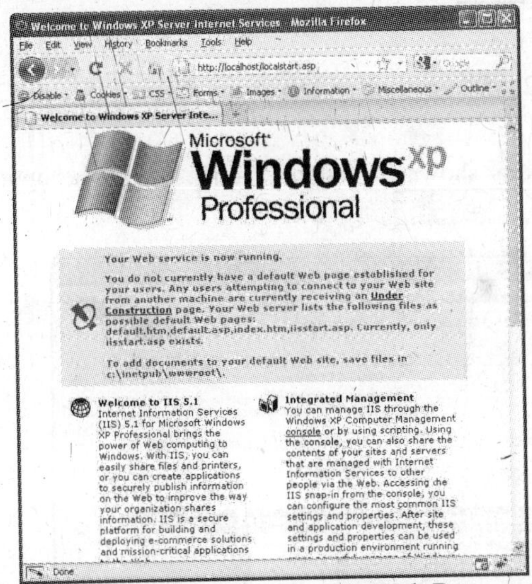

Diagram 13.14: IIS testing via Web Browser

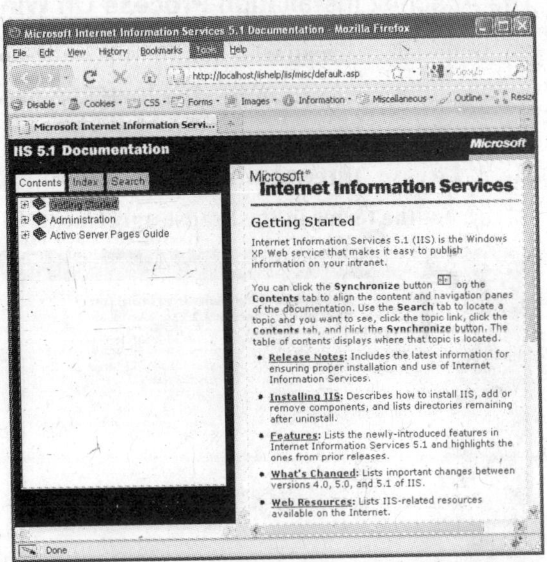

Diagram 13.15: IIS Documentation

APACHE

Apache is an open source, public-domain Web server. The name APACHE evolved from **A PAtCHy** s**E**rver.

Currently there are two versions of Apache available. The first is 1.3.X.XX-X the most popular and tried and tested and completely stable. Apache.org, the Apache website indicates that there will be no enhancements made to 1.3.X.XX-X only bug fixes will be done.

The second is 2.0.X.XX, which is the latest version of Apache, which is being constantly being **bug fixed** and **enhanced** (when creating this material). Either version can be used as a full-fledged production grade Web Server when required.

Apache is a freely available Web server. It can be downloaded from http://www.apache.org for free. Apache software has the largest market share of the Web server market (this includes parked web sites without any real content). Apache is IIS's main competitor.

Downloading Apache2

The Apache2 installable for Windows XP or Vista can be obtained **http://httpd.apache.org/download.cgi**. In the **Downloads** section please choose the **latest stable version** of Apache.

Note

Apache 2.0 add-in modules are **not compatible** with Apache 1.3 modules. If third party add-in modules are currently being run using Apache 1.3, obtain new modules written for Apache 2.0 from that third party before attempting to upgrade from Apache 1.3 to Apache 2.0.

The Apache2 Installation Process On Windows XP

1. Double click the **apache_2.0.54-win32-x86-no_ssl** file
2. The **Welcome screen** of Apache HTTP Server 2.0.54 appears as shown in diagram 13.16. Click Next >
3. A **License Agreement** screen of Apache appears as shown in diagram 13.17. Select the option **I accept the terms in the license agreement.** Click Next >

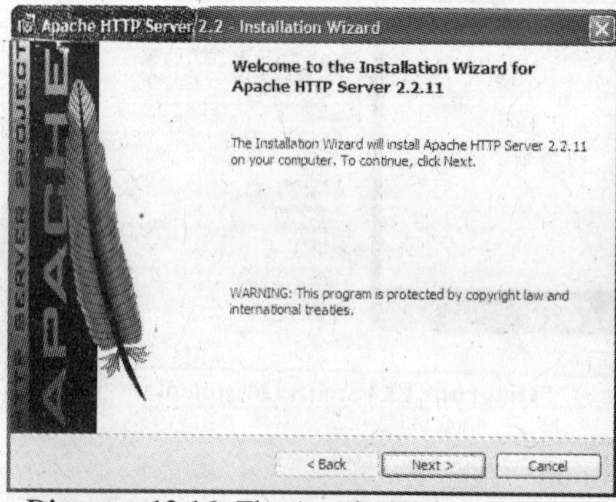

Diagram 13.16: The Apache Welcome Screen

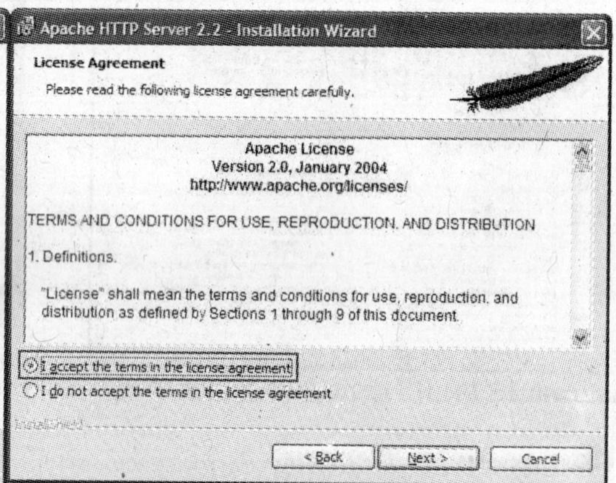

Diagram 13.17: The License Agreement Screen

4. A brief introduction of Apache HTTP Server is displayed as shown in the diagram 13.18. Click Next >
5. The installation wizard prompts for server details such as the domain name, server name and the email address of administrator as shown in diagram 13.19. Fill in the appropriate details and click Next >

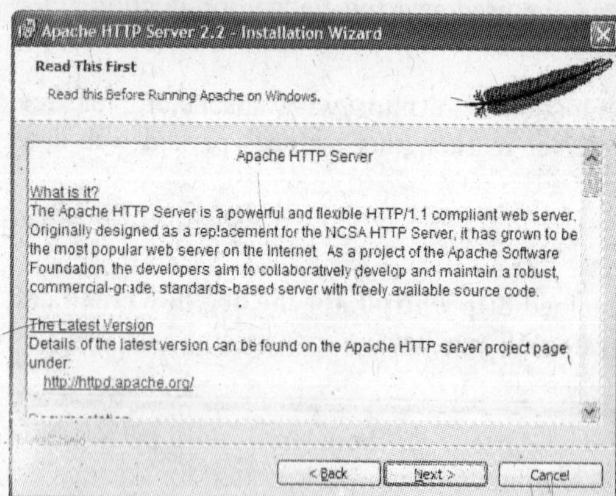

Diagram 13.18: An introduction to Apache Server

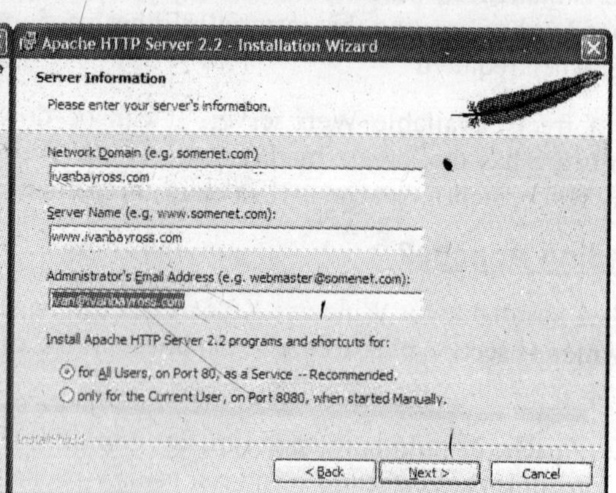

Diagram 13.19: Server Information

For Example:

Network Domain:	ivanbayross.com
Server Name:	www.ivanbayoss.com
Administrator's Email Address:	ivan@ivanbayross.com

Please enter your data as appropriate.

If any of this information required is left blank, the installation wizard will popup errors as shown in diagrams 13.20.1, 13.20.2, 13.20.3.

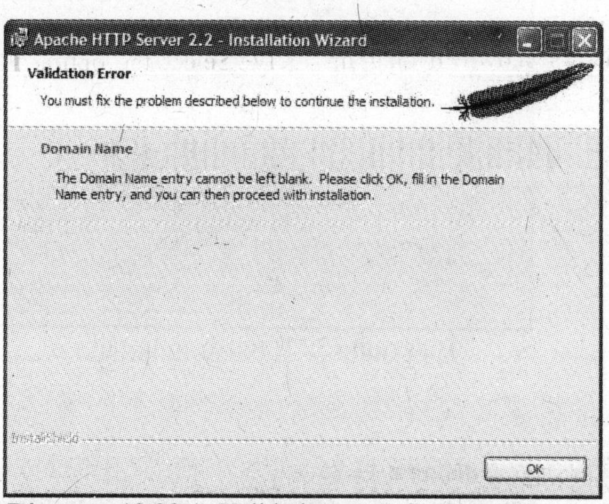

Diagram 13.20.1: Validation error for Domain name

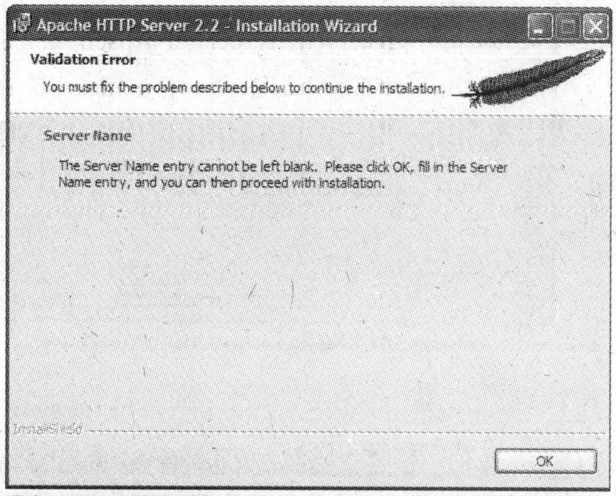

Diagram 13.20.2: Validation error for Server name

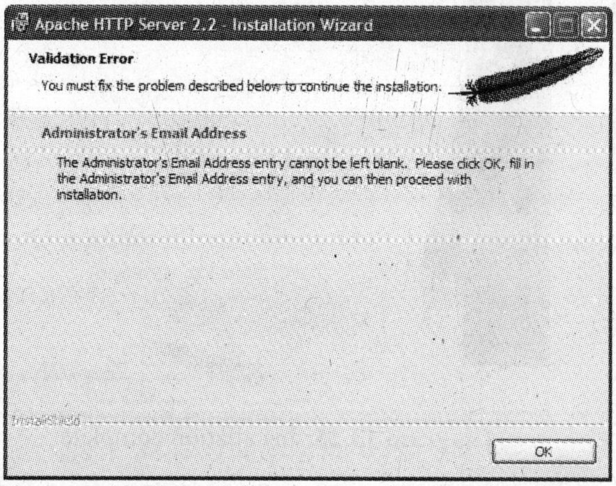

Diagram 13.20.3: Validation error for Email Address

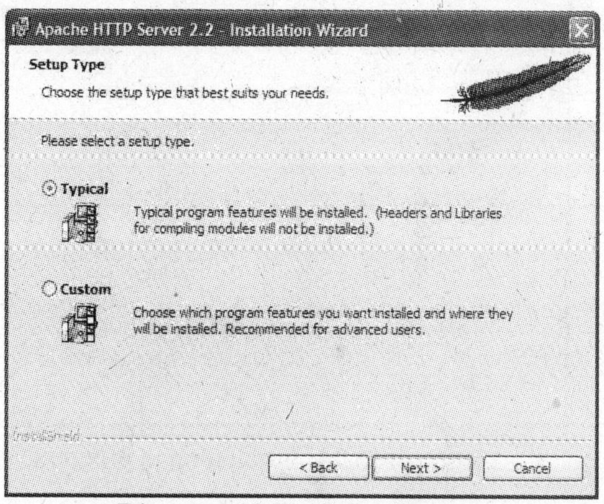

Diagram 13.21: Setup Type

6. If no errors are encountered the wizard proceeds by prompting for the setup type as shown in diagram 13.21. Select the setup type as **Typical.** Click [Next >]
7. The wizard will now prompt for the destination folder as shown in the diagram 13.22. Change the path if required. Click [Next >]
8. Finally the wizard displays the screen as shown in the diagram 13.23. Click [Install] to start Apache's installation process

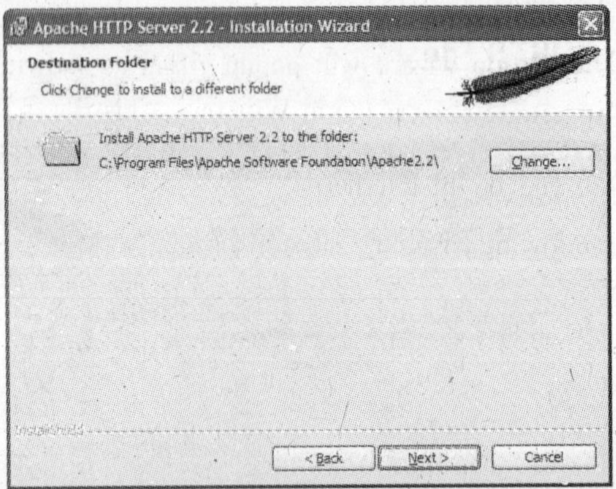

Diagram 13.22: Destination folder

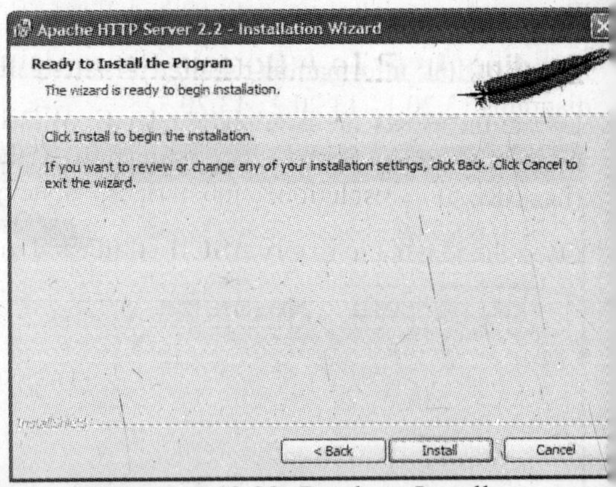

Diagram 13.23: Ready to Install

9. The installation displays a progress bar as shown in diagram 13.24
10. Click Finish to complete the installation as seen in diagram 13.25

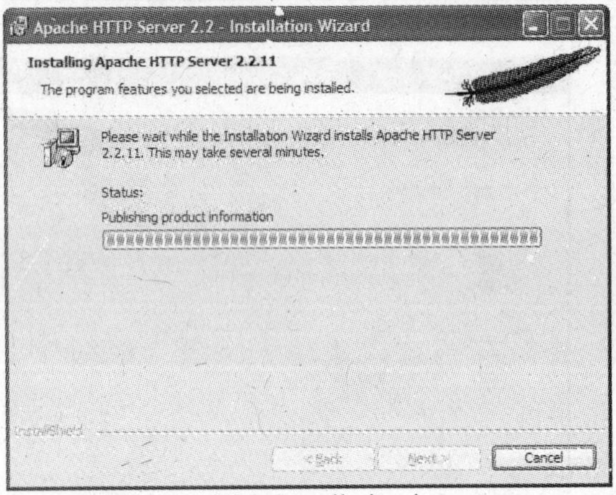

Diagram 13.24: Installation in progress

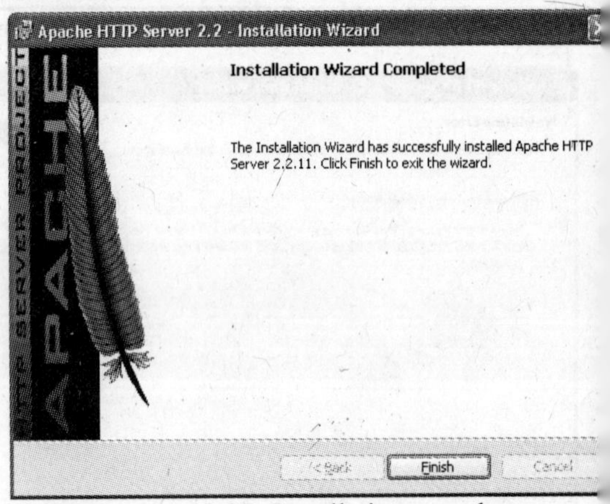

Diagram 13.25: Installation complete

This concludes Apache's installation process on the computer's HDD.

Apache now needs to be configured so that it knows every virtual domain created under it.

Configuring APACHE Web Server

When testing web pages created they have to be placed in a virtual domain under Apache. Once done the web pages can be tested using a Browser and keying in the URL of the virtual domain in its Address bar.

This approach empowers web site developers to physically check and see what the web pages they created look like and how they behave, prior being mounted on the Internet.

To achieve this do the following:

Locate the **httpd.conf** file and set the **server name:**

1. In Windows edit the **C:\Program Files\Apache Software Foundation\Apache2.2\conf\httpd.conf** file. Locate the Apache directive ServerName by searching for it and change it to read:

```
ServerName 192.168.0.4
```

Where 192.168.0.4 is the ip of the computer on which Apache is running.

Binding An IP To A Domain Name Using The HOSTS File:

Locate the **Hosts** file available under **C:\WINDOWS\system32\drivers\etc** in Windows. This file is first referred to by any Browser to obtain the **ip** of the URL entered into its address bar.
(i.e. URL to ip resolution, a job normally done by DNS servers on the Internet)

Open the **Hosts** file in **any ASCII editor** and make the following any entry, structured as follows:

```
IP. Address    Hostname
```

(A **Tab** separates the two entries)- for example:

```
192.168.0.4    www.ivanbayross.com
```

(The URL entered against this ip can be any name of choice)

Due to this entry in the HOSTS file, from now on, when **www.ivanbayross.com** is keyed into a Browser's address bar, it will automatically direct the request to Apache web server is running on the computer whose **ip** is 192.168.0.4. This computer must have the virtual domain named **www.ivanbayross.com** hosted on it.

Creating Virtual Domains Under Apache

When Apache is installed on a M.S. Windows XP / Vista computer the Apache installer places Apache's file structure in:

C:\Program Files\ Apache Software Foundation\Apache2.2

Apache's index file, which is displayed when http://localhost is typed into a Browser window and the Go button or the Enter key is pressed, resides in:

C:\Program Files\ Apache Software Foundation\Apache2.2\htdocs

If you do not want Apaches default index page to be displayed when http://localhost is typed in a Browser's address bar and the **Go** button or the **Enter** key is pressed, simply create your own HTML file, name it index.html and place this in:

C:\Program Files\ Apache Software Foundation\Apache2.2\htdocs

Now if you enter http://localhost in a Browser's address bar and press Go or the Enter key your HTML page will be rendered in the Browser's window. This is an indication that Apache is working perfectly. Having said that, it's definitely not good practice to place all your website's resources within the folder that Apache uses for its own resources i.e.:

C:\Program Files\ Apache Software Foundation\Apache2.2\htdocs

It's good programming practice to keep your website's resources separate from Apache's internal resources. All that is required is that you create a separate folder, anywhere on your hard disk and place your website resources within that folder.

For example: **d:\mysite**
Now all that remains is that Apache needs to be informed that the folder**d:\mysite** is where you've loaded all your website's resources. You do this by creating a **Virtual Domain** under Apache and binding this domain to the folder where your website's resources are placed. To create a virtual domain you have to make changes within Apache's **httpd.conf** file. Apache's httpd.conf file is resides in:

C:\Program Files\ Apache Software Foundation\Apache2.2\conf

Navigate to that folder and the first thing to do is to make a copy of Apache's httd.conf file and save this within Apache's conf folder i.e. **httpd_copy.conf**. This way if you've made some errors when adding a virtual domain to the httpd.conf file and Apache stops working, all you have to do is to overwrite Apache's httpd.conf file with the copy you've made, then ensure that the file is re-named httpd.conf and Apache should start up again.

NOTE

In case you do not keep a copy of Apache's httpd.conf and you've damaged the original httpd.conf file you have to re-install Apache from scratch, to get a working copy of Apache web server.

Now open the httpd.conf file in your favorite ASCII editor, (Notepad would do just fine). Scroll right down to the end of the httpd.conf file and you will notice Apache's virtual domain example. The code there should look something like:

```
#NameVirtualHost *:80
#VirtualHost example:
# Almost any Apache directive may go into a VirtualHost container.
# The first VirtualHost section is used for requests without a known
# server name.
#<VirtualHost>
# ServerAdmin webmaster@dummy-host.example.com
# DocumentRoot /www/docs/dummy-host.example.com
# ServerName dummy-host.example.com
# ErrorLog logs/dummy-host.example.com-error_log
# CustomLog logs/dummy-host.example.com-access_log common
# </VirtualHost>
#
```

The **NameVirtualHost** and **VirtualHost** directives are what we are interested in. Simply copy the whole lot from **# NameVirtualHost** to and paste this below the original code. Then **delete** the # which appears before each entry as shown below. *Please notice the section where the # are **not deleted**.*

```
#NameVirtualHost *:80
# VirtualHost example:
# Almost any Apache directive may go into a VirtualHost container.
# The first VirtualHost section is used for requests without a known
# server name.
<VirtualHost *:80>
ServerAdmin webmaster@dummy-host.example.com
DocumentRoot /www/docs/dummy-host.example.com
ServerName dummy-host.example.com
ErrorLog logs/dummy-host.example.com-error_log
CustomLog logs/dummy-host.example.com-access_log common
</VirtualHost>
```

Next:
Change

NameVirtualHost *:80

To read as:

NameVirtualHost 127.0.0.1:80

Notice that the # has been deleted

And

The local host ip **127.0.0.1** has replaced the * in this entry
Now let's take a look at the <VirtualHost</VirtualHost> XML segment.

```
<VirtualHost 127.0.0.1:80>
ServerAdmin ivan@ivanbayross.com
DocumentRoot d:\mysite
ServerName www.mysite.com
ErrorLog d:\mysite\errors\errorlog
</VirtualHost>
```

Notice that the:

ServerAdmin has a legitimate Email ID bound to it.
DoumentRoot has the physical path to your websites resources
ServerName can have any name bound to it, I've chosen *www.mysite.com*
ErrorLog has the path to where Apache can keep its error log file

NOTE

Do not forget to create the folder **d:\mysite\errors**. Then using Notepad create an empty file named **errorlog** within this folder. *Please notice the absence of any file extension.*
Save the httpd.conf you've been editing and re-start Apache.

To restart Apache simply **right** click on the icon in the task bar and a popup window will appear as shown in diagram 13.26.

Diagram 13.26

Click on Open Apache Monitor and a popup window will appear as shown in diagram 13.27

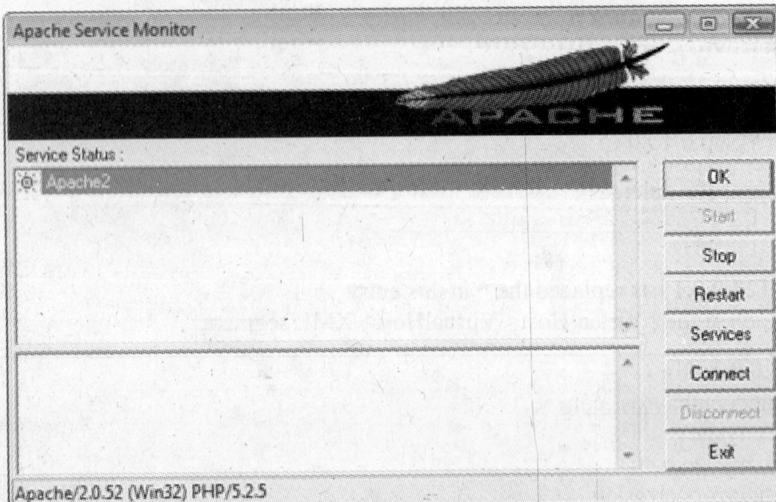

Diagram 13.27 Restarting Apache

Simply click the Restart button. If all is well Apache will startup perfectly. There's a few more steps to be carried out to check is you've created the Virtual domain correctly, they are:

Making an entry in the **hosts** file. Using the file Browser navigate to the folder

C:\Windows\System32\drivers\etc

Within this folder there will be a file called **hosts**.

NOTE:

If you have never used the hosts file ever before then you will find a file called **hosts.sam** or **hosts.tmp** in this folder. Copy this file to a file named **hosts** and you are done.

Then **edit** the contents of **hosts** as indicated below.

```
# Copyright (c) 1993-2006 Microsoft Corp.
#
# This is a sample HOSTS file used by Microsoft TCP/IP for Windows.
#
# This file contains the mappings of IP addresses to host names. Each
# entry should be kept on an individual line. The IP address should
# be placed in the first column followed by the corresponding host name.
# The IP address and the host name should be separated by at least one
# space.
#
# Additionally, comments (such as these) may be inserted on individual
# lines or following the machine name denoted by a '#' symbol.
#
# For example:
#
# 102.54.94.97 rhino.acme.com # source server
# 38.25.63.10 x.acme.com # x client
```

NOTE

Between the ip and the site name you must use the **Tab** key.

```
# For example:
# 102.54.94.97 rhino.acme.com # source server
# 38.25.63.10 x.acme.com # x client host
127.0.0. www.mysite.com
```

Save hosts and exit.

Finally place a unique index.html file within the folder d:\mysite. Now when you enter the URL in the Browser address bar: **http://www.mysite.com** Apache will display the contents of the index.html file you've place in the folder d:\mysite. If all this works perfectly then you can build the rest of your website within the folder d:\mysite

14. SETTING UP AND CONFIGURING PHP TO WORK UNDER APACHE AND IIS

This is a guide to getting PHP up and running under Apache on Windows XP.

DOWNLOADING PHP

PHP the programming environment is free. Its binaries and source code are located at www.php.net.

PHP can be downloaded from http://www.php.net. The site displays a page as shown in diagram 14.1. Click the hotspot **downloads** as shown in diagram 14.1.

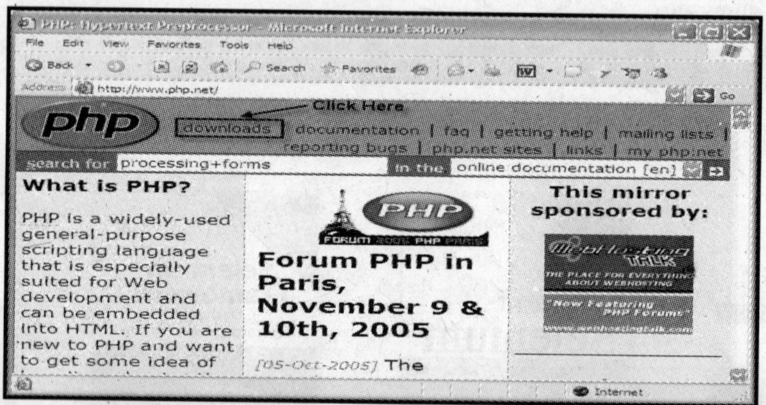

Diagram 14.1: Clicking Downloads at http://www.php.net

On clicking **downloads** a page as shown in diagram 14.2 is rendered in the Browser window.

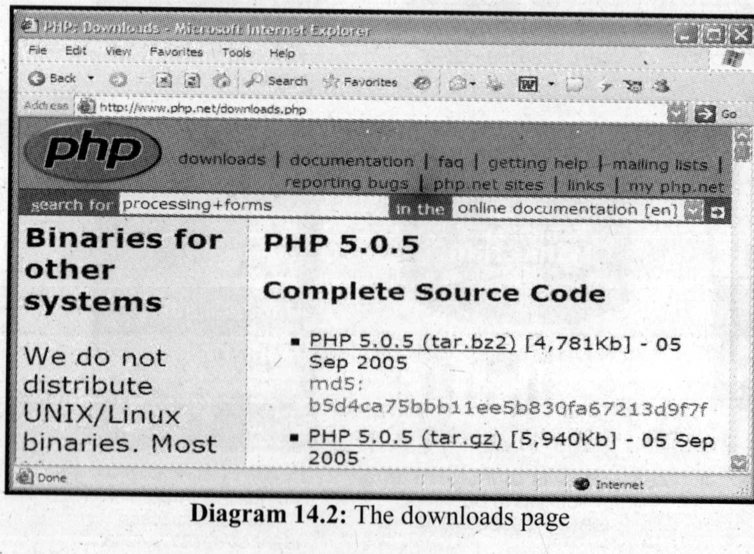

Diagram 14.2: The downloads page

Downloading PHP For Windows

Scroll **half way** down the page till a heading **Windows Binaries** is reached. Click on the topmost link **PHP X.X.ORC1 zip package** as indicated in diagram 14.3.1. This is the latest PHP production level, Windows binary currently available.

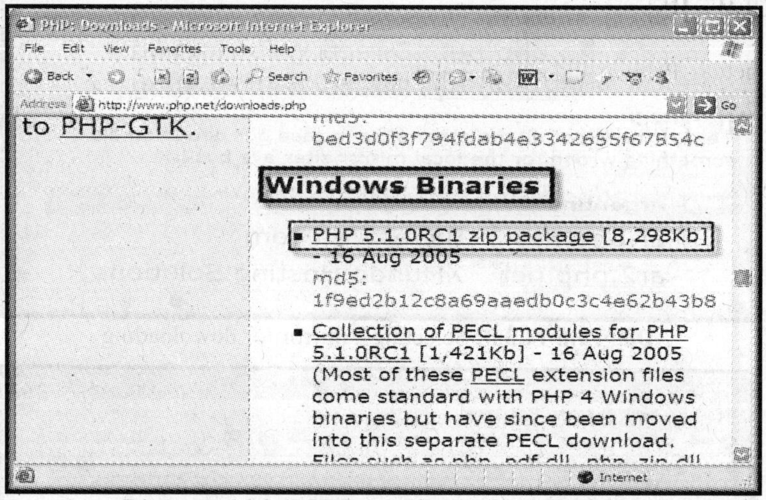

Diagram 14.3.1: PHP 5.1.ORC1 zip package link

On clicking this link, a page with the heading **Choose a mirror site for download** will be rendered in the Browser as shown in diagram 14.3.2.

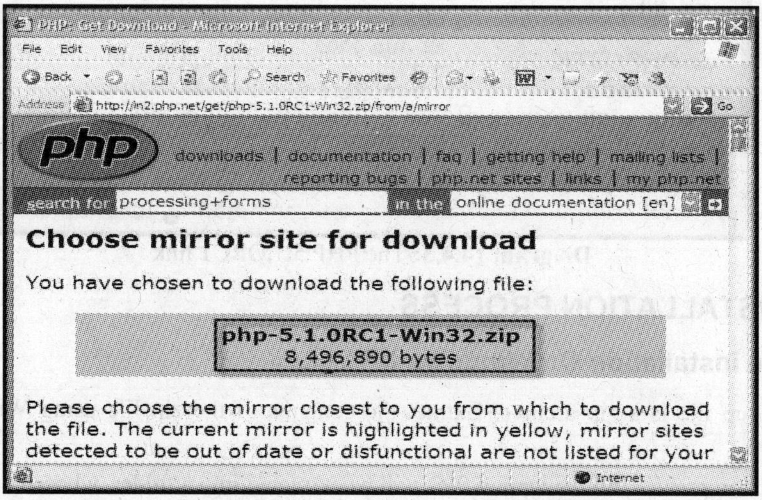

Diagram 14.3.2: Choose a mirror page

Choose any suitable mirror site (here an Indian mirror has been chosen). A link **in.php.net** as shown in diagram 14.3.3 will be displayed. On clicking **in.php.net** link PHP 5.X will be downloaded.

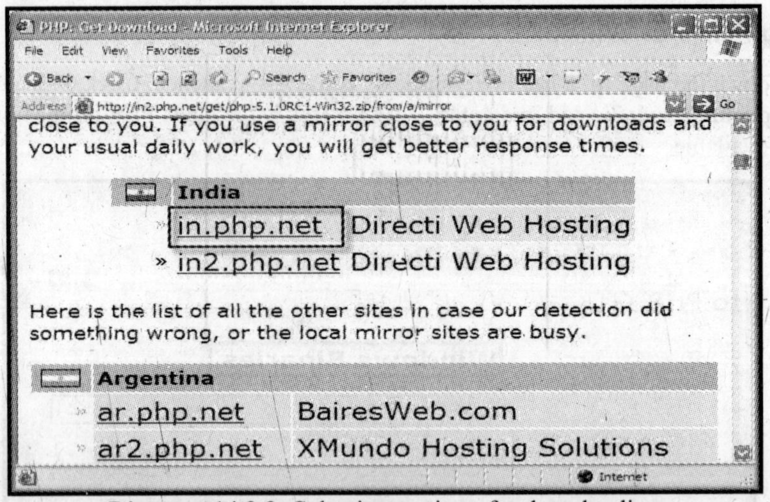

Diagram 14.3.3: Selecting a mirror for downloading

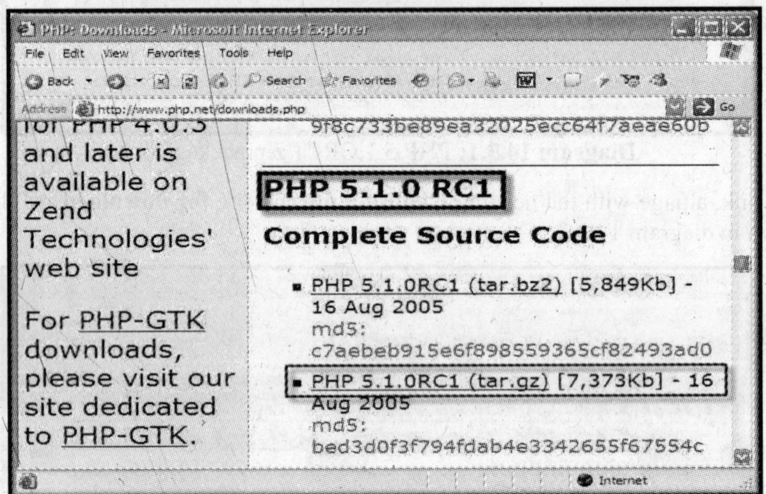

Diagram 14.4.3: The PHP 5.1.ORC1 link

THE PHP INSTALLATION PROCESS

PHP / Apache Installation On Windows XP

1. The PHP setup file is a zip archive. Extract the contents of the zip file using Winzip or any other archiving tool
2. In the extraction process, all the zipped files will be extracted into a folder, whose name is based on the version of PHP that was downloaded. For example, if **php-5.1.0RC1-Win32.zip** was downloaded and extracted to **C:**, then a folder would be created called **C:\php-5.1.0RC1-Win32** in which all files extracted from this archive will reside
3. Next rename the folder **php-5.1.0RC1-Win32** to **php** (Refer to diagram **14.7.1**)

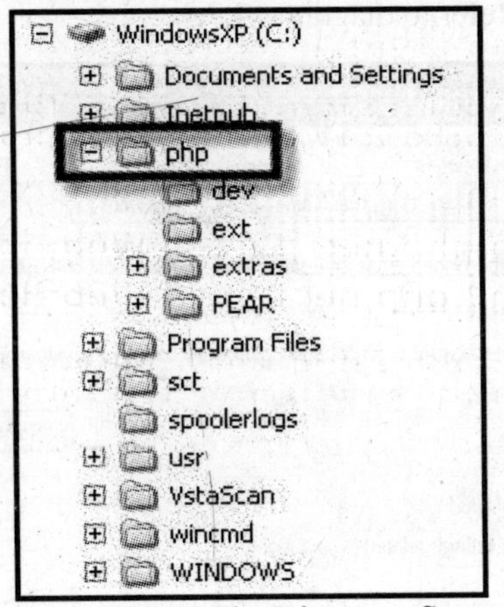

Diagram 14.7.1: The Directory Structure

4. To integrate **PHP** with **Apache2** there are three options available:
   a. Copy the file named **php5ts.dll** available under **c:\php** to the Windows system directory
   b. Copy the file named **php5ts.dll** to the web server's directory
   c. Add the PHP directory i.e. **c:\php** to the PATH variable

   The use of the third option is recommended, as this option will help when upgrading to a newer version of PHP in future.

Add **c:\php** to the PATH variable as follows:

   a. Select **Start → Control Panel → System**. **System Properties** dialog box appears as shown in diagram 14.7.2

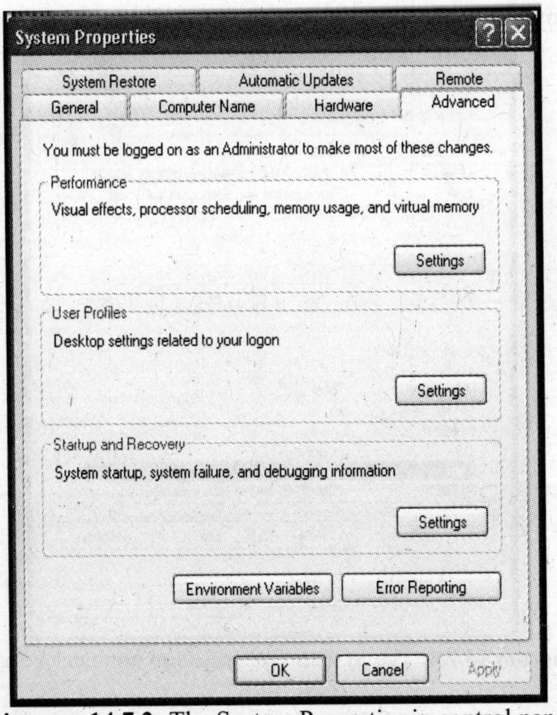

Diagram 14.7.2: The System Properties in control panel

b. Select the **Advanced** tab. Refer to diagram 14.7.3

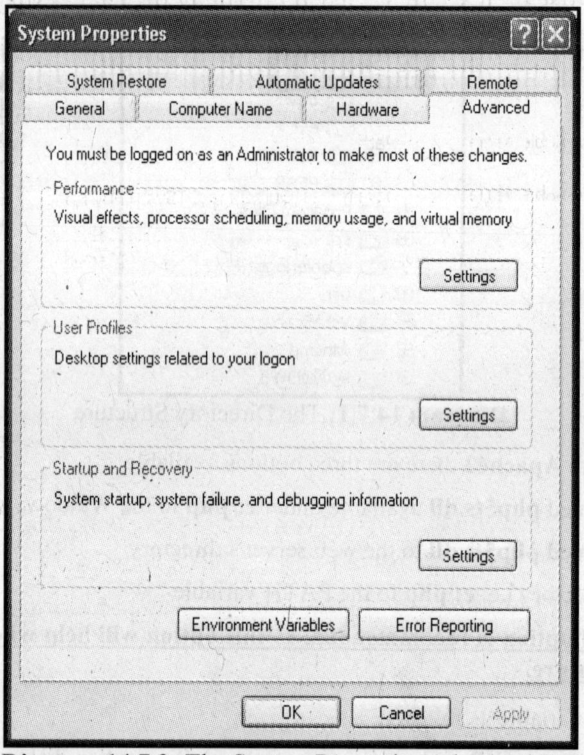

Diagram 14.7.3: The System Properties Advanced Tab

c. Click the **Environment Variables** button. This pops up a window as shown in diagram 14.7.4

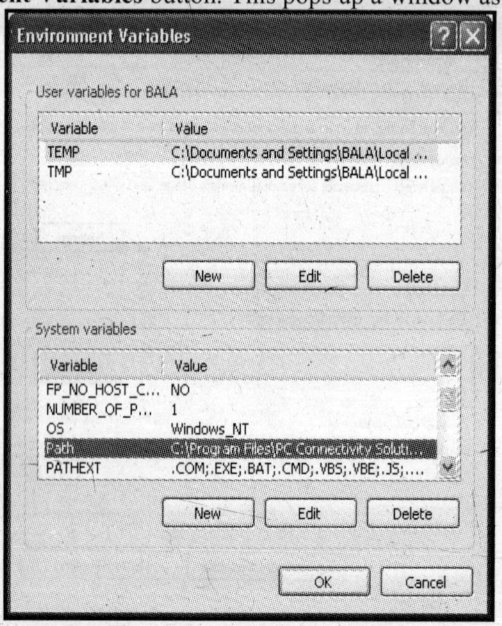

Diagram 14.7.4: The System Properties Environment Variables

d. **Select the** Path **variable under** System variables **section and click** Edit**. This pops up a window, in the text box** Variable value **add** ;C:\php **at the end of the path as shown in diagram 14.7.5**

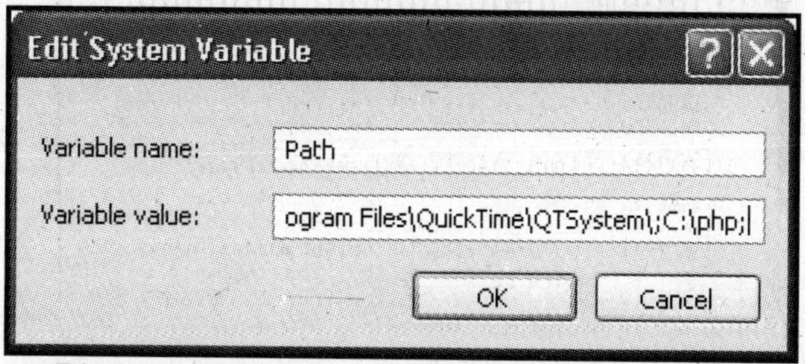

Diagram 14.7.5: The Edit System variable window

e. Click **OK** to apply these settings

5. The next step is to set up a valid configuration file for PHP i.e. **php.ini**. There are two **ini files** distributed in the zip file i.e. **php.ini-dist** and **php.ini-recommended**. Use the **php.ini-recommended**, as it is optimized with the default settings for performance and security
6. Copy the chosen ini-file (i.e. **php.ini-recommended**) to the windows directory (i.e. c:\windows **or** c:\winnt as the case may be) directory and rename it to **php.ini**

Note

If the file system in use is NTFS on Windows NT, 2000, XP or 2003, make sure that the user running the web server has read permissions to the **php.ini**.

PHP is now setup on the Windows system.

PHP Installation On Linux

Login as root.

Erasing An Older Version

All flavors of Linux normally are installed with some stable version of PHP. If a new install of PHP is required on Linux, then do check to find out what version of PHP currently exists on the Linux flavor in use. Hence, prior installing the latest version of PHP it is good to check for the existence of the version of PHP already installed when Linux was installed. This can be done as follows: (Refer to diagram 14.8.1)

<System Prompt> rpm -q php

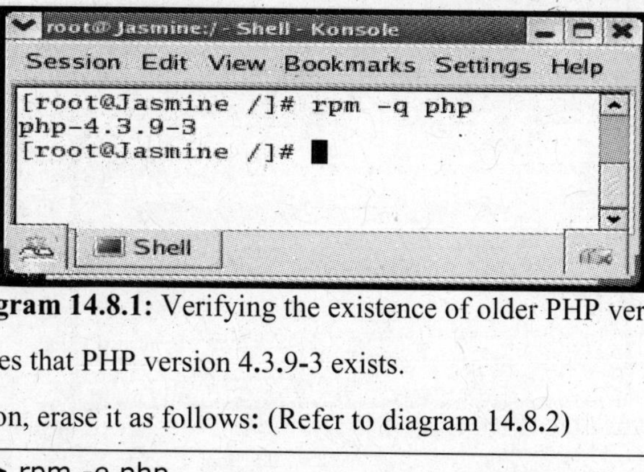

Diagram 14.8.1: Verifying the existence of older PHP version

The above diagram indicates that PHP version 4.3.9-3 exists.

Since this is an older version, erase it as follows: (Refer to diagram 14.8.2)

<System Prompt> rpm -e php

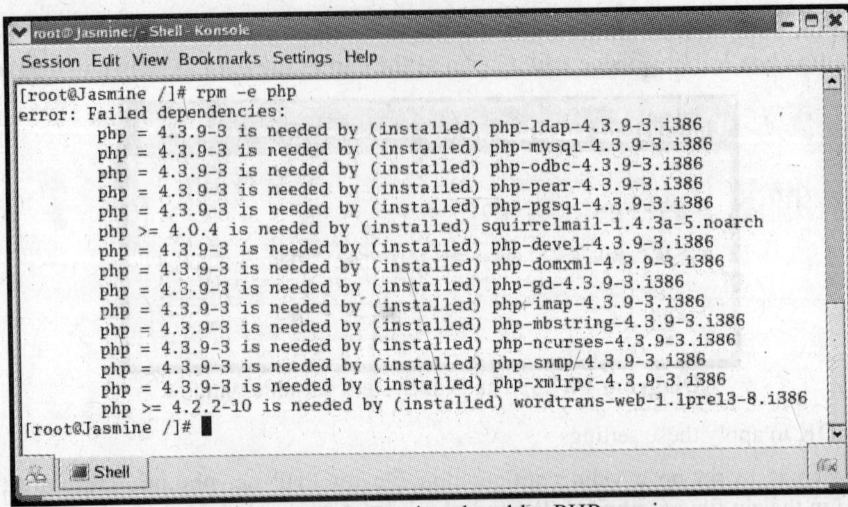

Diagram 14.8.2: Erasing the older PHP version

The above diagram shows a list of dependencies, which exist as a support system to the current PHP version. These **need to be** uninstalled (erased) prior uninstalling (erasing) PHP.

Erase these dependencies as: (Refer to diagram 14.8.3)

```
<System Prompt> rpm -e php-ldap
<System Prompt> rpm -e php-mysql
<System Prompt> rpm -e php-odbc
<System Prompt> rpm -e php-pgsql
<System Prompt> rpm -e php-devel
<System Prompt> rpm -e php-domxml
<System Prompt> rpm -e php-gd
<System Prompt> rpm -e php-imap
<System Prompt> rpm -e php-mbstring
<System Prompt> rpm -e php-ncurses
<System Prompt> rpm -e php-snmp
<System Prompt> rpm -e php-xmlrpc
<System Prompt> rpm -e squirrelmail
<System Prompt> rpm -e wordtrans-web
<System Prompt> rpm -e php-pear --nodeps
<System Prompt> rpm -e php
```

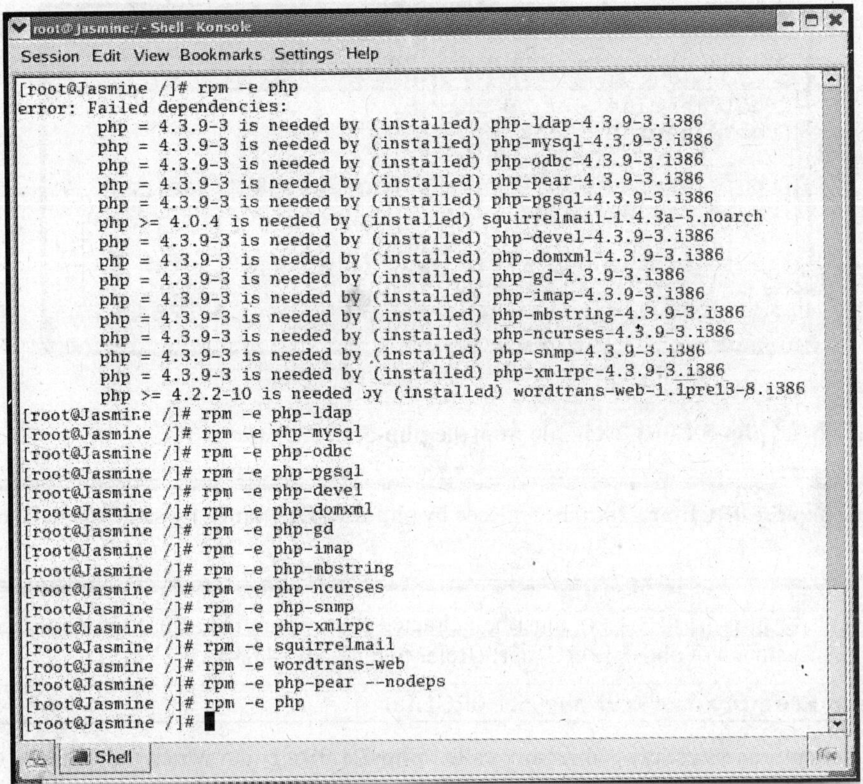

Diagram 14.8.3: Erasing the older PHP version

If any of the listed dependencies indicate they **are required**, then skip the erasing of that particular dependency and finally erase PHP as follows:

```
<System Prompt> rpm -e php --nodeps
```

`i.e. two hyphens followed by nodeps`

In the above command, **--nodeps** instructs the rpm package manager to ignore the existence of the dependencies and erase the current version of PHP.

Installing PHP From Its Source File

It is always advisable to install PHP using its latest source (i.e. tarball). This provides access to quicker releases updates instead of waiting for some entity to release an rpm for a particular flavor of Linux.

1. Make a directory **/php**. Copy the downloaded file **php-5.1.0RC1.tar.gz** here
2. Unzip the file as: (Refer to diagram 14.8.4)

```
<System Prompt> gunzip php-5.1.ORC1.tar.gz
```

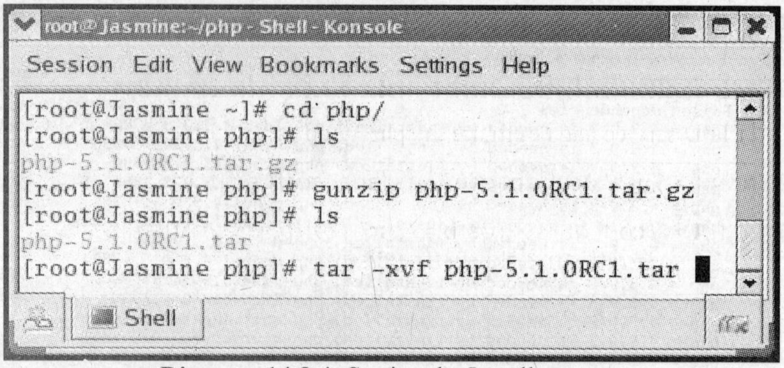

Diagram 14.8.4: Staring the Install process

3. This will extract **php-5.1.0RC1.tar** file from the **php-5.1.0RC1.tar.gz** file

TIP

The **php-5.1.0RC1.tar.gz** will be replaced by **php-5.1.0RC1.tar** in the same sub directory.

4. The contents of **php-5.1.0RC1.tar** must be extracted after which the actual install process can begin. To extract the content of php-5.1.0RC1.tar: (Refer to diagram 14.8.4)

```
<System Prompt> tar -xvf php-5.1.0RC1.tar
```

5. The extraction process creates a directory called **php-5.1.0RC1** into which the contents of the tar file are extracted. This is just one level below the **/php** subdirectory. Change to this sub-directory: (Refer to diagram 14.8.5)

```
<System Prompt> cd php-5.1.0RC1
```

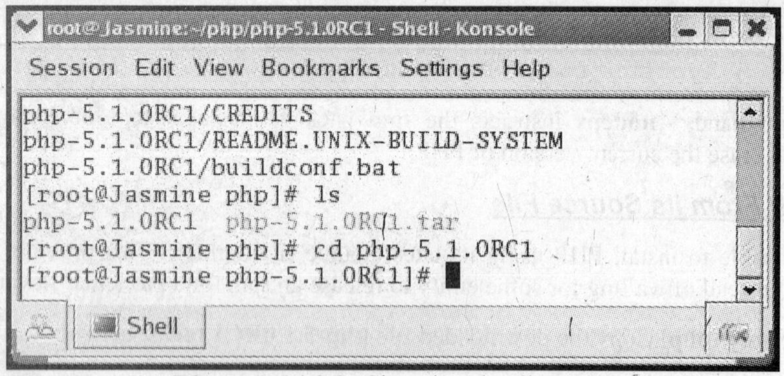

Diagram 14.8.5: Changing the directory

The Configure Command

Make sure that apache is stopped before proceeding with PHP Installation.

Stop the Apache2 HTTPD service and configure the php setup as: (Refer to diagram 14.8.6)

```
<System Prompt> /usr/local/apache2/bin/apachectl stop

<System Prompt>./configure --prefix=/usr/local/php5 --with-zlib
                --with-mysql --with-mysqli
                --with-oci8=/u01/app/oracle/product/10.1.0/Db_1
                --with-sqlite
                --with-pdo-mysql --with-pdo-oci --with-pdo-sqlite
                --with-xmlrpc
                --with-apxs2=/usr/local/apache2/bin/apxs
```

In the above command:

1. **--prefix** argument sets the installation path for the PHP 5.0 binaries
2. **--with-zlib** argument enables to transparently read and write gzip .gz compressed files. *In this material this is enabled to allow Simple Machines forum run smoothly*
3. **--with-mysql** argument activates the regular MySQL extension. In PHP 5.0, this is not active by default (as it is in PHP 4.0) and must be explicitly named in **configure** to be activated

CAUTION

To enable the mysql extension, the MySQL Database Engine (at least the client .rpm) installation is a must. The installation steps are available in Chapter 11: MySQL In Action

4. **--with-mysqli** argument activates the new MySQL Improved extension (for MySQL 4.1.2+ only)
5. **--with-oci8=/u01/app/oracle/product/10.1.0/Db_1** line should point to the location of the database client software i.e. **$ORACLE_HOME** directory, in Oracle terms. This option actually adds Oracle support to PHP. In short PHP will be built using Oracle support

CAUTION

To enable the oci8 extension, the Oracle Database Engine (at least the client version) installation is a must. The installation steps are available in Book's accompanied CDROM

6. **--with-sqlite** argument activates the regular SQLite extension. In PHP 5.0, this is not active by default and must be explicitly named in configure to be activated
7. **--with-xmlrpc** argument activates the PEAR (for MySQL 4.1.2+ only). If PEAR is not needed while installing PHP then **--without-pear** argument has to be given while configuring
8. **--with-pdo-mysql** argument activates the PDO (PHP 5.1 Data Object) extension, which provides a data access abstraction layer for MySQL Db engine
9. **--with-pdo-oci** argument activates the PDO (PHP 5.1 Data Object) extension, which provides a data access abstraction layer for Oracle Db engine
10. **--with-pdo-sqlite** argument activates the PDO (PHP 5.1 Data Object) extension, which provides a data access abstraction layer for SQLite Db engine

11. **--with-apxs2** argument tells PHP where to find Apache 2.0 and its apxs script (used to handle extensions). This is pointed to **/usr/local/apache2/bin/apxs** assuming apache web server's **apxs** script rests here

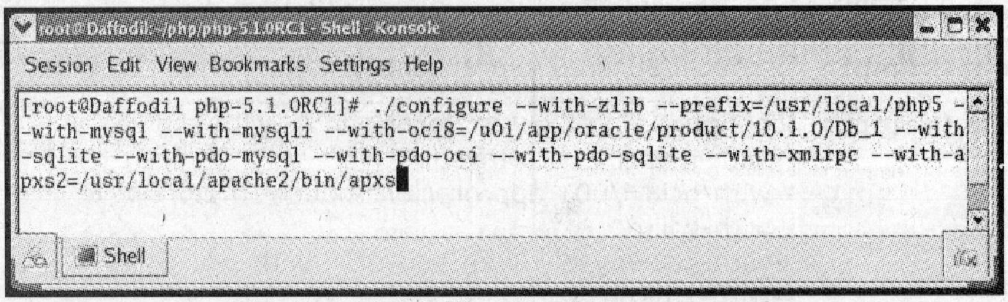

Diagram 14.8.6: The **./configure** command.

NOTE

If an error is generated which indicates that the apxs script cannot be found, look for it on the system (i.e. use **Find Files**) and if found, note down the path to the file. Then provide the full path such as: **--with-apxs2=/path-to-apxs**

Make sure to specify the **version of apxs** that is actually installed on the system and **NOT** the one that is in the apache source tarball.

If an error appears about **apxs** and the help screen from apxs is displayed, then **recompile** Apache and **ensure** that **--enable-module=so** is specified to the **configure** command.

The Make Command

The configuration routine commences. The time taken depends upon the amount of free memory available and the processor speed. After the configuration runs successfully execute the command **make:** (Refer to diagram 14.8.7)

```
<System Prompt> make
```

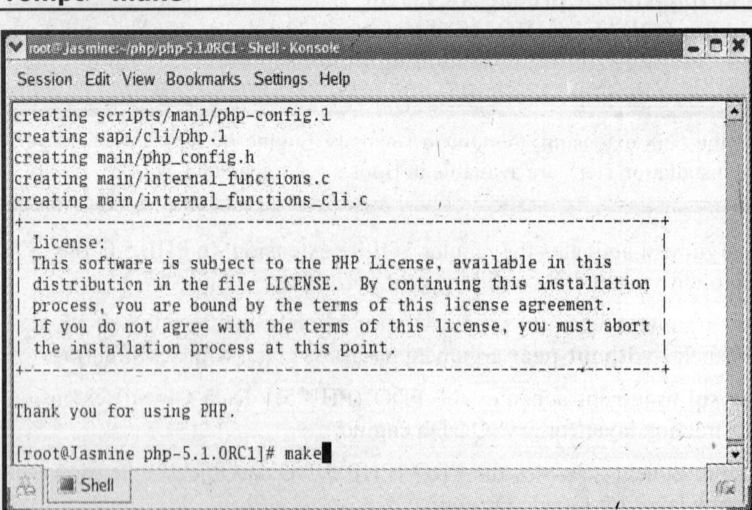

Diagram 14.8.7: The **make** command.

The Make Install Command

Next run the command **make install:** (Refer to diagram 14.8.8)

```
<System Prompt> make install
```

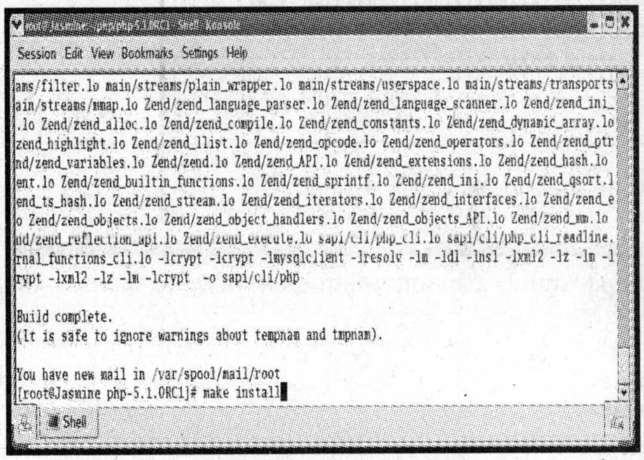

Diagram 14.8.8: The **make install** command

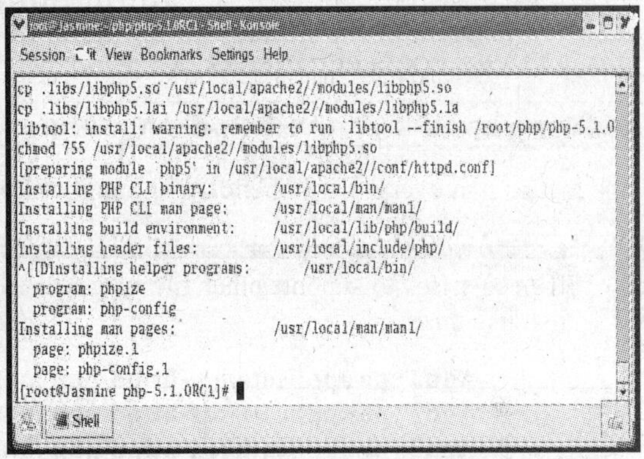

Diagram 14.8.9: The **make install** completes

The next step is to set up a valid configuration file for PHP i.e. **php.ini**. There are two **ini** files distributed in the source file (.tar.gz) as shown in diagram 14.8.10 i.e. **php.ini-dist** and **php.ini-recommended**. Use the file **php.ini-recommended**.

```
<System Prompt> cp php.ini-recommended /usr/local/php5/lib/php.ini
```

This will create a local copy of the PHP configuration file.

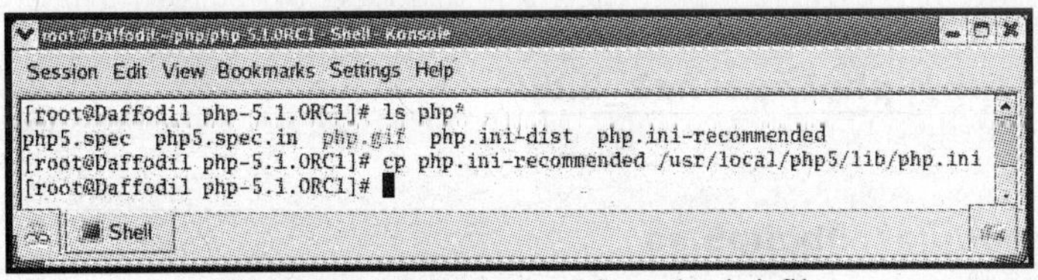

Diagram 14.8.10: Copying php.ini file

The **php.ini-recommended** file has a simpler layout, contains fewer settings and allows PHP to run faster. This completes the installation of PHP on Linux.

Binding The PHP Installation With Apache2

Apache does not know that PHP is just installed. Therefore Apache needs to be informed where to find PHP.

This is done via Apache's httpd.conf file. Apache reads this file and understands what modules need to be loaded and where these modules are located.

NOTE

It is not mandatory to have Apache web server installed in order to test .php scripts. These scripts can simply be run using the interpreter **php.exe**. This can be accomplished by appending the .php script file as a command line argument to **php.exe** interpreter.

There are **two ways** to configure Apache to use PHP 5.

One is to configure it to load the PHP interpreter as an Apache module.

The other is to configure it to run the PHP interpreter as a CGI binary.

TIP

It is recommended that PHP is loaded as a module in Apache, since it runs more efficiently that way, unless there is a specific reason for running PHP as a CGI binary.

Edit Apache's **httpd.conf** file. Make sure the **PHP mime type** is specified and **uncommented**. The line should look like this: (Refer to diagram 14.9.1 and diagram 14.9.2)

```
AddType application/x-httpd-php .php
```

This line means that every file that ends with .php will be processed as a PHP file.

TIP

If need arises to support other file types, like .php3, .html, .asp and .phtml, simply add them to the list, like this:

AddType application/x-httpd-php .php3
AddType application/x-httpd-php .phtml
AddType application/x-httpd-php .html
AddType application/x-httpd-php .asp

NOTE

The **httpd.conf** file is usually available under **C:\Program Files\Apache Software Foundation\Apache2.2\conf** on Windows and under **/usr/local/apache2/conf** on Linux.

Ensure that the PHP module is loaded by adding the following line in the httpd.conf file

On Windows: Refer to diagram 14.9.1.

```
LoadModule php5_module "c:/php/php5apache2_2.dll"
```

On Linux: Refer to diagram 14.9.2.

```
LoadModule php5_module   modules/libphp5.so
```

This line tells Apache from where to load the **.dll** file in case of Windows or the **.so** file in case of Linux which is required to execute PHP. This line enables loading the PHP module dynamically into Apache. Usually in Linux the PHP source installer automatically inserts this line. If this line does not exist then insert it manually in the httpd.conf file.

NOTE

In the Apache 1.3.X, **AddModule** directive was used instead of **LoadModule**. In case of Apache 1.3.X, search for the block AddModule statement. Add the following line after the last AddModule statement:

AddModule mod_php5.c

mod_php5.c file is not available anywhere in the file system. It only specifies the order in which the Apache Web server enables the various modules.

If Apache 2.X is used, **then do not insert** the AddModule directive. It's no longer needed in that version. Apache 2.X has its own internal method of determining the correct order of loading the modules.

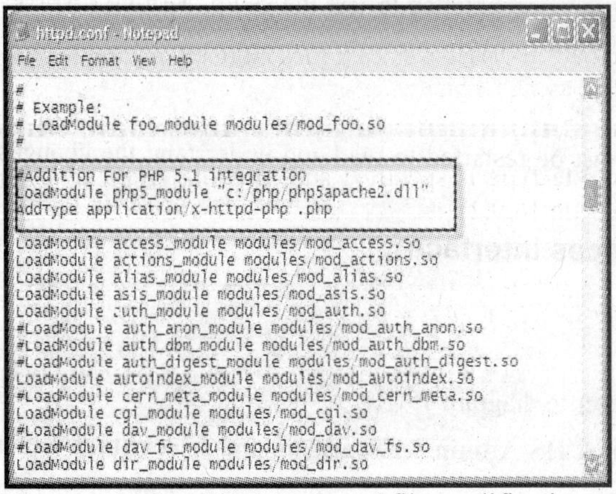

Diagram 14.9.1: The **httpd.conf** file modification on Windows

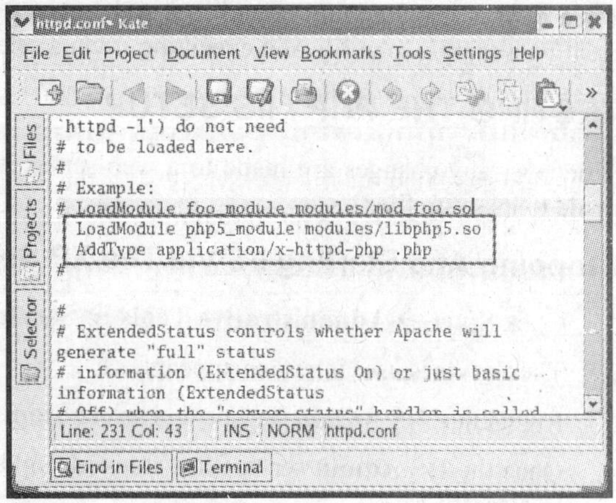

Diagram 14.9.2: The **httpd.conf** file modification on Linux

Restart Apache server. PHP files should be able to be served up now.

15. TESTING THE PHP / WEB SERVER SETUP

Once PHP is installed and bound to a web server, it is a good practice to test the setup. Testing involves creating a sample .php file and executing it via a selected web server.

TESTING THE PHP / IIS SETUP

Whenever any changes are made to a web server it must be restarted to read and understand the changes made to its setup files.

Stopping And Starting IIS Via The XP Services Interface

1. Click **Start → Administrative Tools → Services**
2. The **Services** user interface appears
3. Right click **IIS Admin** service and select **Stop**. Refer to diagram 15.1.1
4. Once the **IIS Admin** service has stopped, right click **IIS Admin** service again and select **Start**. Refer to diagram 15.1.2

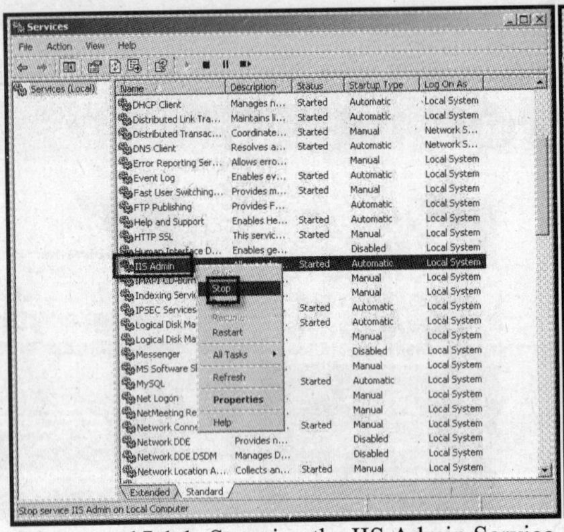

Diagram 15.1.1: Stopping the IIS Admin Service

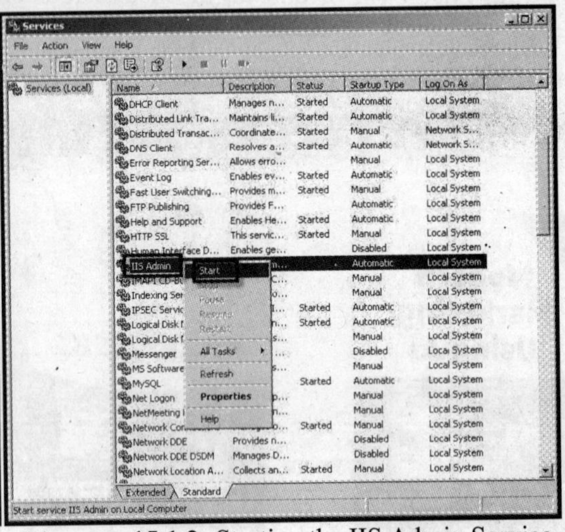

Diagram 15.1.2: Starting the IIS Admin Service

Stopping And Starting IIS Via The Command Prompt

1. Open a **Command Prompt** window
2. Type the following command to stop the **IIS** service: (Refer to diagram 15.2.1)

```
<System Prompt> Net stop iisadmin
```

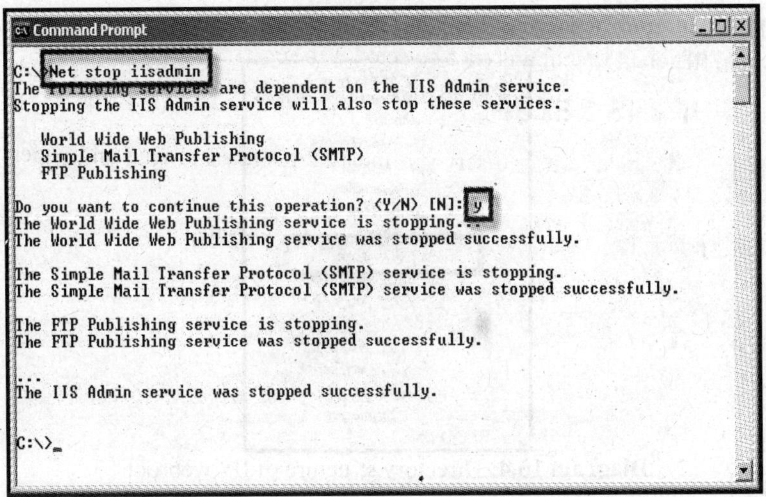

Diagram 15.2.1: Stopping the IIS Admin service

3. If the IIS Admin service is stopped, the following child services need to be stopped as well, **World Wide Web**, **SMTP** and **FTP**. Hence a prompt will be displayed for each. To stop the child services, press **'Y'** and then **Enter**. The World Wide Web, SMTP and the FTP service will stop and only then the IIS Admin service will be stopped

4. Type the following command to start the World Wide Web service: (Refer to diagram 15.2.2)

```
<System Prompt> Net start iisadmin
```

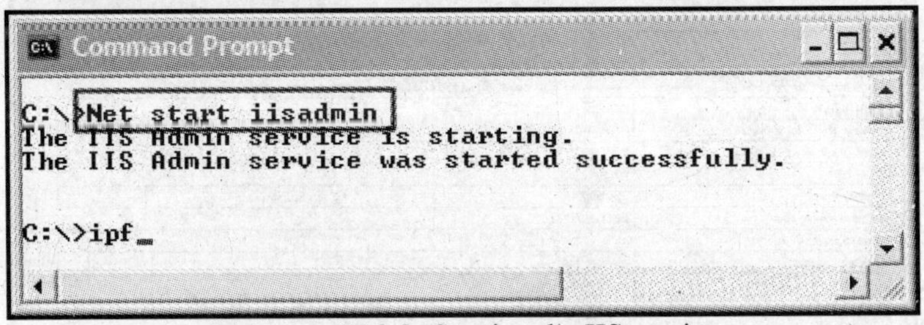

Diagram 15.2.2: Starting the IIS service

Testing The PHP Installation

To test whether PHP has been successfully setup and integrated with IIS create a simple script named phpinfo.php that contains the following code: (Refer to diagram 15.3)

```
<?php
    phpinfo();
?>
```

Diagram 15.3: The phpinfo.php file in Notepad

Place phpinfo.php in **c:\Inetpub\wwwroot** directory. Refer to diagram 15.4.

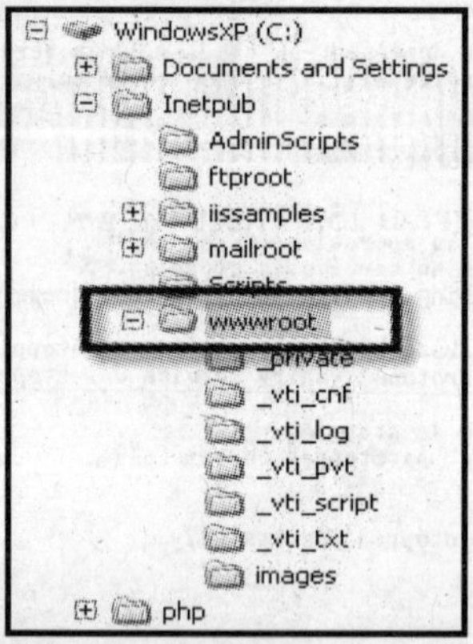

Diagram 15.4: Directory structure of IIS webroot

Examine the output of this script in a Web browser by pointing to **http://localhost/phpinfo.php**. If PHP was successfully setup then a screen similar to that shown in diagram 15.5 appears.

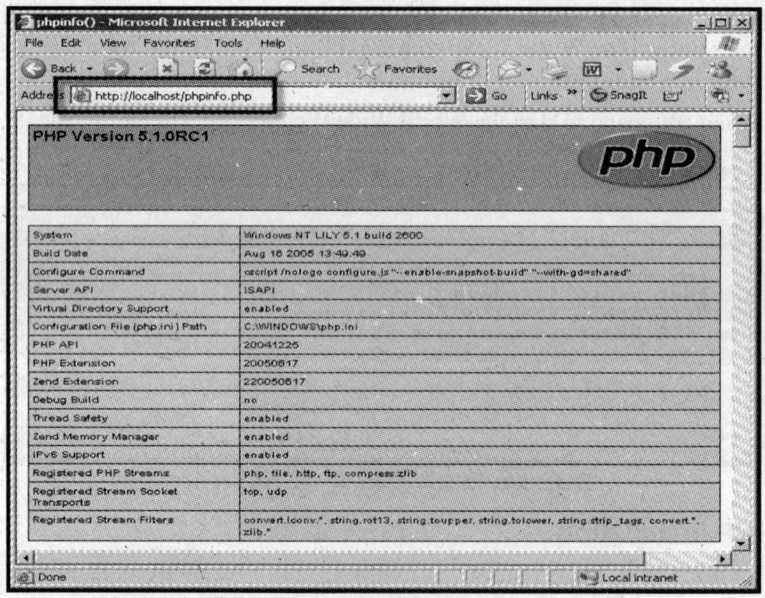

Diagram 15.5: PHP Version displayed in Web browser

TESTING THE PHP / APACHE SETUP

Testing PHP / Apache On Windows

Registering Changes Made In The httpd.conf of Apache2

After making any changes to the **httpd.conf** ensure that Apache is restarted to register the new changes with Apache. Do this by using the icon on the task bar: (Refer to diagram 15.6)

Diagram 15.6: Restarting Apache2

To test whether PHP has been successfully setup and integrated with Apache2 create a simple script named phpinfo.php that contains the following code: (Refer to diagram 15.7)

```
<?php
    phpinfo();
?>
```

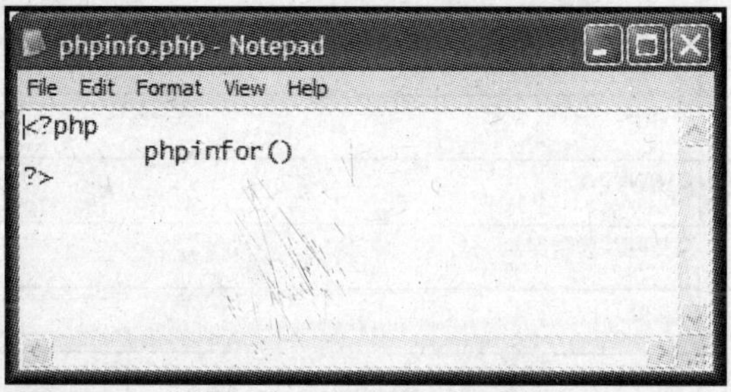

Diagram 15.7: The phpinfo.php file in Notepad

Place this file in Apache's default document root directory i.e. **C:\Program Files\Apache Software Foundation\Apache2.2\htdocs**. Examine the output of this script in a Web browser by pointing to **http://127.0.0.1/phpinfo.php**. If PHP setup is successful then a screen similar to that shown in diagram 15.8 will be displayed.

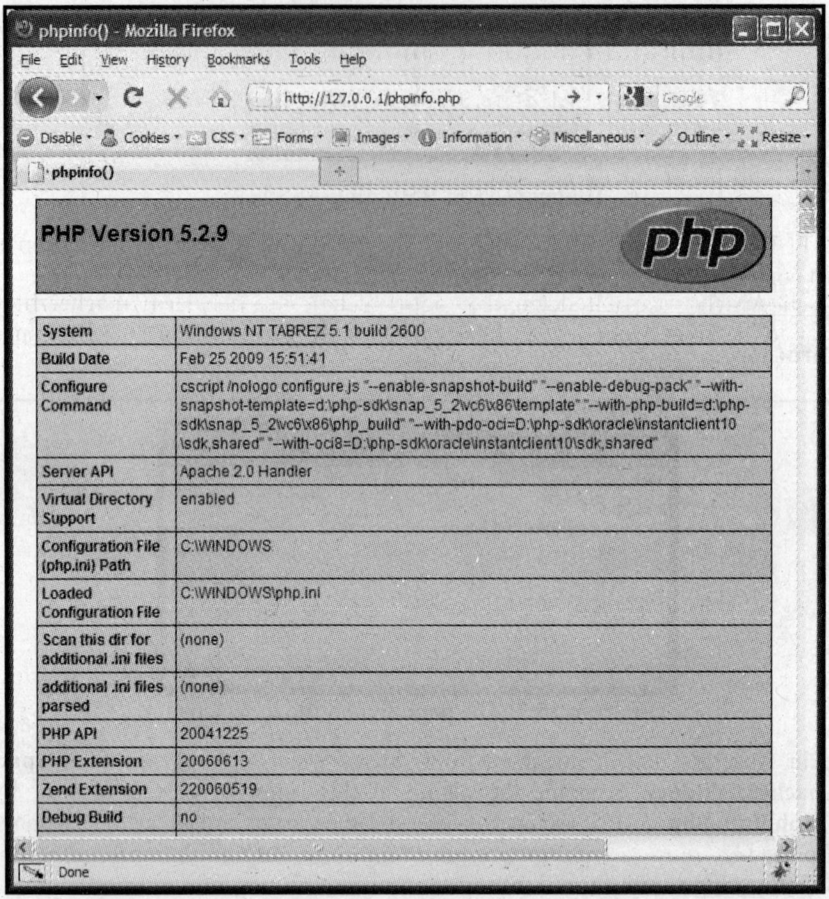

Diagram 15.8: PHP Version Info displayed via Web Bowser

Testing PHP / Apache On Linux

Registering Changes Made In The httpd.conf of Apache2

Restart the Apache2 HTTPD service **or** simply stop and start it using the parameter **stop** and **start:**

```
<System Prompt> /usr/local/apache2/bin/apachectl restart
```

To test whether PHP has been successfully setup and intergrated with Apache2 create a simple script named phpinfo.php that contains the following code: (Refer diagram 15.9)

```
<?php
    phpinfo();
?>
```

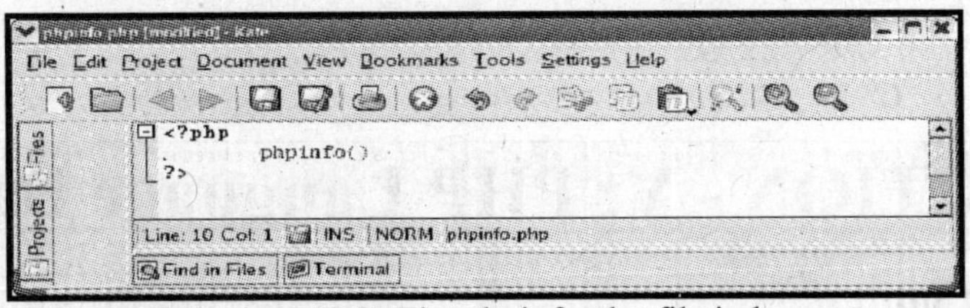

Diagram 15.9: The phpinfo.php file in kate

Place this file in Apache's default document root directory i.e. **/usr/local/apache2/htdocs** directory. Examine the output of this script in a Web browser by pointing to **http://127.0.0.1/phpinfo.php**. If PHP setup is successful then a screen similar to that shown in diagram 15.10 appears.

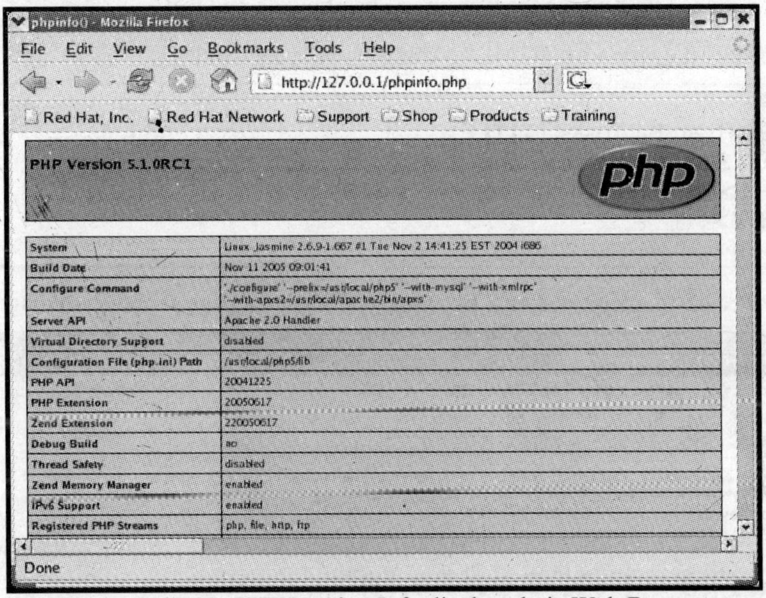

Diagram 15.10: PHP Version Info displayed via Web Browser

SECTION - V: PHP Language Basics

16. PHP & HTML

A website is collection of documents containing marked up content created using **H**yper **T**ext **M**arkup **L**anguage (i.e. HTML). When a site visitor looks at these website documents using a Browser, the Browser reads the HTML code and based on the instructions contained there, creates a page and displays it in the visitors Browser window, thus giving the web site a specific look and feel.

For example, consider the following HTML code spec (staticpage.html):

```
<HTML>
   <TITLE>Ivan Bayross</TITLE>
   <BODY STYLE="background-color:blue;color:red;">
      <H1>Learning PHP for Beginners</H1>
   </BODY>
</HTML>
```

The above code spec when interpreted by a Browser will display a page as shown in diagram 16.1.

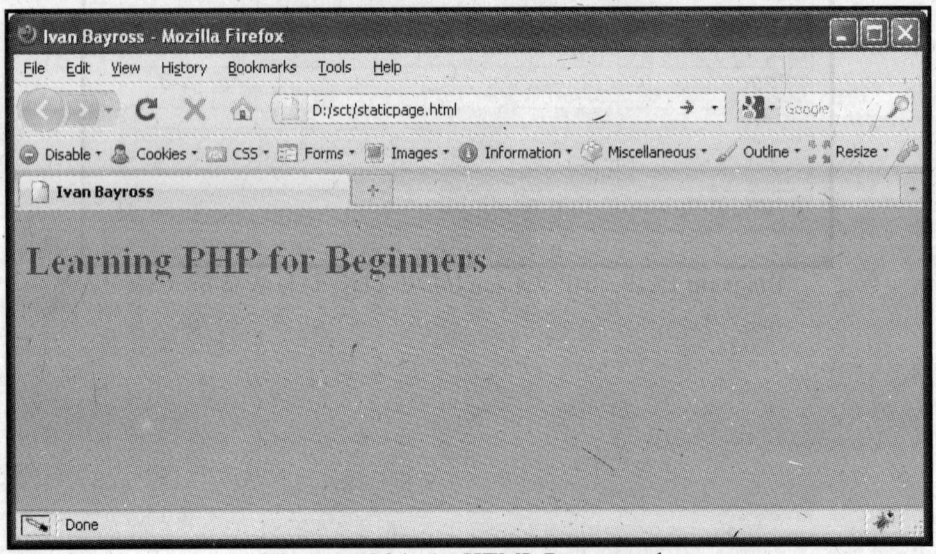

Diagram 16.1: An HTML Page sample

The above HTML code spec is static. If the site visitor were to reload such a static page, they would see exactly the same content every time. Usually on static pages the contents are written directly by the author who owns the page. When the visitor goes to the site, that code is downloaded into the Browser interpreted and displayed.

In contrast to a static website, a dynamic website is one whose page content changes each time a visitor enters (or re-enters) to site or reloads / refreshes a page from the site.

For example, consider the following code spec (dynamicpage.php):

```
<HTML>
  <TITLE>Ivan Bayross </TITLE>
  <BODY STYLE="background-color: 00FFFF; color:red;">
     <?php
        $websites = array("Creating Website using HTM",
           "Creating Website using PHP", "Creating Website using Wordpress",
            "Creating Website using Joomla");
        $item = rand(0, sizeof($websites)-1);
     ?>
     <H1>
        <?php
           echo $websites[$item]
        ?>
     </H1>
  </BODY>
</HTML>
```

When the above code spec is displayed in a Browser the **page contents will change** (i.e. dynamically) every time the page is reloaded (i.e. refreshed) as shown in diagram 16.2.1, diagram 16.2.2, diagram 16.2.3 and diagram 16.2.4.

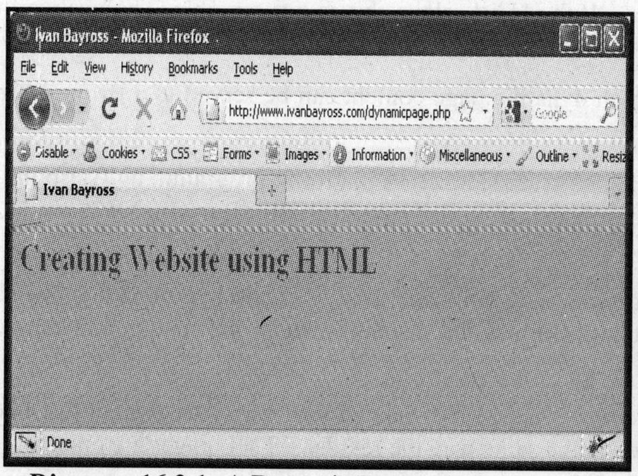

Diagram 16.2.1: A Dynamic Page sample Executed **First** Time

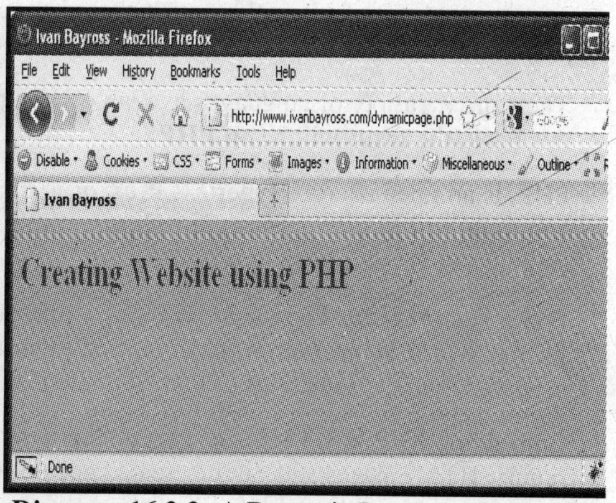

Diagram 16.2.2: A Dynamic Page sample Execute **Second** Time

This is because here an array is being used as a datastore. Each time a client Browser hits the website, new content is picked up from the array, formatted using HTML markup and displayed in the Browser that requested the page. Here, the look and feel of the page is constant while its content keeps changing, thus building the personality of the web site. This is what dynamic websites do. Normally, an RDBMS table is used to store page content rather than an array. Here the array was used only to demonstrate a point.

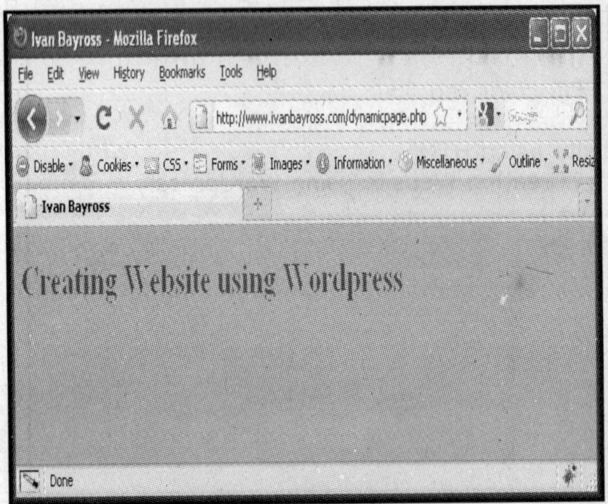

Diagram 16.2.3: A Dynamic Page sample Executed **Third** Time

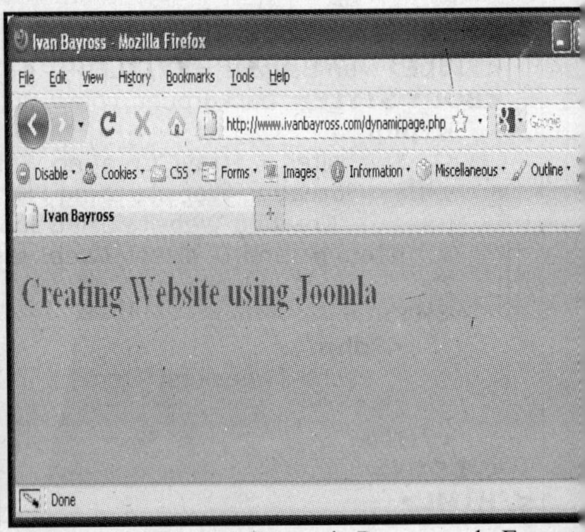

Diagram 16.2.4: A Dynamic Page sample Execut **Four** Time

The above example illustrates how PHP can be instrumental in loading the same HTML page (i.e. a constant look and feel) with content that changes. With HTML alone this is not possible. The change in page content is seen every time the Reload/Refresh button of the Browser is clicked.

There are a variety of languages available via which dynamic page content can be served to a Browser. In this book, the focus will be on **PHP**.

PHP, is an open source **H**ypertext **P**re**P**rocessor i.e. a server side, cross platform, programming (scripting) language, extensively used at the web server to process data provided by an HTML form which was used to capture and validate such data.

Hyper**T**ext **M**arkup **L**anguage (HTML) is the programming language used to create hypertext documents for the **W**orld **W**ide **W**eb. HTML is used to structure (format and display) textual information and can be used to define the semantics of textual document.

Embedding PHP in HTML can generate dynamic web pages. PHP enabled web pages are treated just like regular HTML pages and can be created and edited in the same way the regular HTML pages are created.

This dynamic behavior does not require any additional software to be run on the user machine accessing it. This is because the dynamic content is processed at the web server and then sent to the requester's Browser as pure HTML, which every Browser on earth understands.

A static web page is created simply by embedding HTML code in a text based document. Creating a dynamic web page is similar, except PHP code is embedded in HTML code spec. This makes PHP, an HTML, embedded scripting language. HTML being used to determine the formatting and display of text and pictures and PHP for dynamically determining which text and pictures will be delivered to a Browser.

For example, consider the earlier PHP code spec rendering dynamic contents:

```
<HTML>
  <TITLE>Ivan Bayross </TITLE>
  <BODY STYLE="background-color: 00FFFF; color:red;">
     <?php
        $websites = array("Creating Website using HTML",
           "Creating Website using PHP", "Creating Website using Wordpress ",
           "Creating Website using Joomla");
        $item = rand(0, sizeof($websites)-1);
     ?>
     <H1>
        <?php
           echo $websites[$item]
        ?>
     </H1>
  </BODY>
</HTML>
```

In the above code spec, notice that PHP code is **separated** from HTML code with the symbols **<?php** (LESS-THAN sign followed by a question mark and the word php) and **?>** (a question mark followed by a GREATER-THAN sign).

<?php indicates the start of a PHP block or code and tells the web server that all statements that follow until ?> are PHP statements.

The following examples are valid ways to indicate the start and end of a PHP code block:

```
<?php
        //<Some valid PHP syntax>
?>
```

OR

```
<SCRIPT LANGUAGE="php">
        //<Some valid PHP syntax>
</SCRIPT>
```

Caution

The start and end of the code must be with the same tag. For example the code cannot start with **<?php** and end with **</SCRIPT>**.

PHP runs at the web server, which means that the web server executes the embedded PHP code **first** and then sends the output of the PHP code, as pure HTML code, back to the Browser that requested it. The result is a webpage with dynamic content.

The above can be verified by viewing the source code of the HTML page when it is displayed in the Browser. This can be done using the View Source Option (available as a menu item in all web Browsers). This source code will contain no PHP code segments at all. It is now pure HTML code.

View the page source of every page of the earlier examples i.e. the **output** of dynamicpage.php, diagram 16.3.1, diagram 16.3.2, diagram 16.3.3 and diagram 16.3.4 (using the Browser's view source option) and be assured that the output of a PHP program processed at the Web server and delivered to a client Browser is indeed, pure HTML.

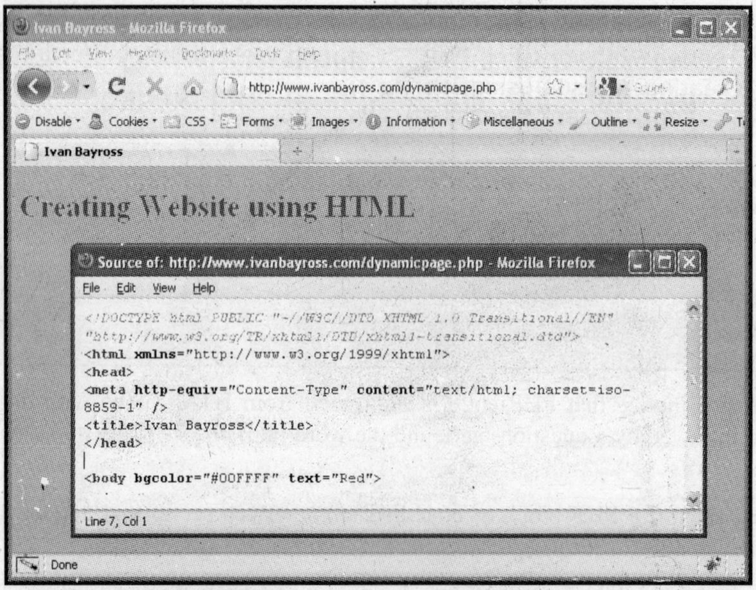

Diagram 16.3.1: Source Code generated on **First** execution

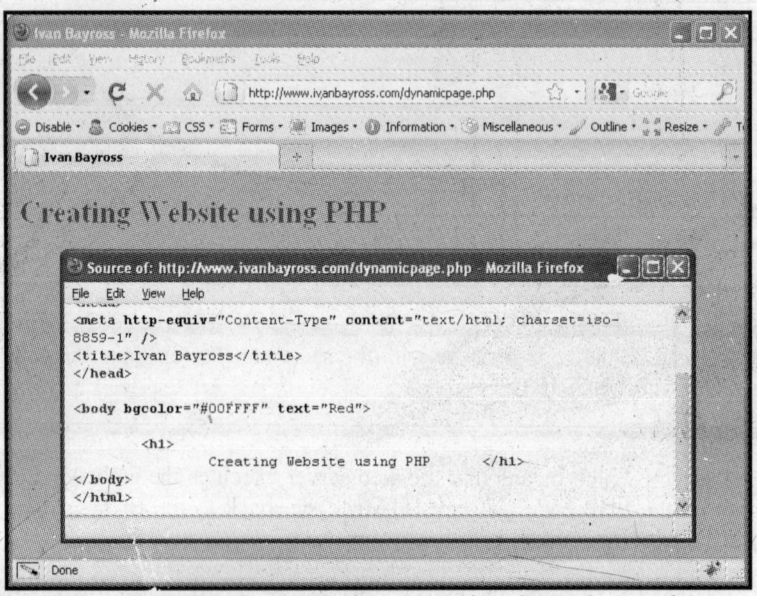

Diagram 16.3.2: Source Code generated on **Second** execution

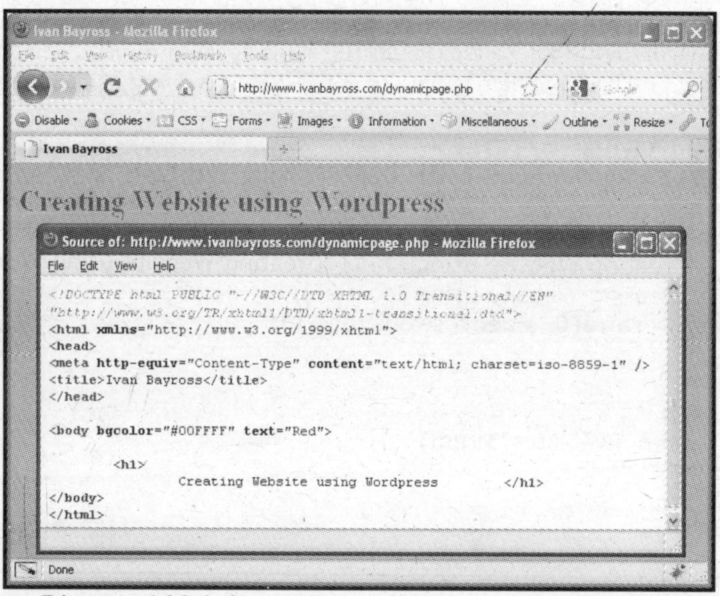

Diagram 16.3.4: Source Code generated on **Third** execution

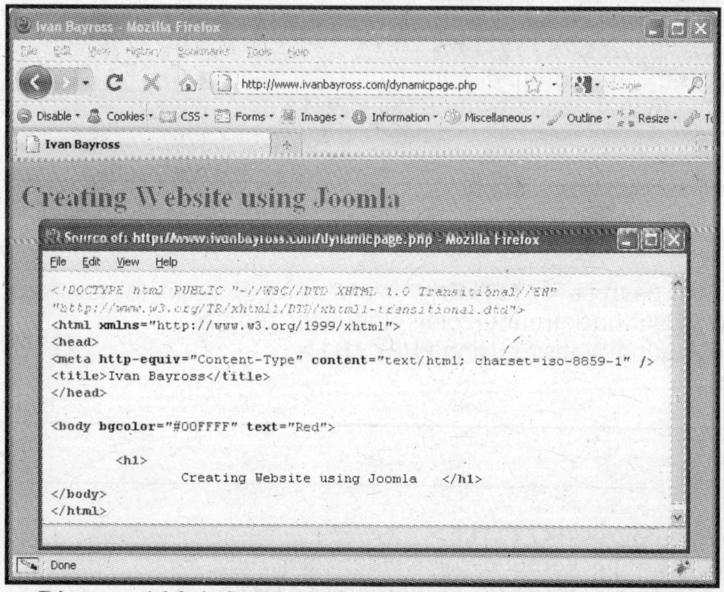

Diagram 16.3.4: Source Code generated on **Fourth** execution

Notice the swapping between PHP and HTML code spec:

PHP code spec:

```
<HTML>
    <TITLE>Ivan Bayross </TITLE>
    <BODY STYLE="background-color: 00FFFF; color:red;">
        <?php
            $websites = array("Creating Website using HTML",
                "Creating Website using PHP", "Creating Website using Wordpress",
                "Creating Website using Joomla");
            $item = rand(0, sizeof($websites)-1);
        ?>
        <H1>
            <?php
                echo $websites[$item]
            ?>
        </H1>
    </BODY>
</HTML>
```

HTML code spec (source code):

```
<HTML>
    <TITLE>Ivan Bayross </TITLE>
    <BODY STYLE="background-color:blue;color:red;">
        <H1>Creating Website using HTML</H1>
    </BODY>
</HTML>
```

OR

```
<HTML>
    <TITLE>Ivan Bayross </TITLE>
    <BODY STYLE="background-color:blue;color:red;">
        <H1>Creating Website using PHP</H1>
    </BODY>
</HTML>
```

OR

```
<HTML>
    <TITLE>Ivan Bayross </TITLE>
    <BODY STYLE="background-color:blue; color:red;">
        <H1>Creating Website using Wordpress</H1>
    </BODY>
</HTML>
```

OR

```
<HTML>
    <TITLE>Ivan Bayross </TITLE>
    <BODY STYLE="background-color:blue;color:red;">
        <H1>Creating Website using Joomla</H1>
    </BODY>
</HTML>
```

This is because the web server **replaces** the PHP code with the content that the code has generated within appropriate HTML tags that will decide it's look and feel in a Browser.

GETTING STARTED

Writing PHP

Writing PHP doesn't need any special software, except for a text editor like Notepad in Windows or Kate in Linux (i.e. pure ASCII editors).

Naming Files

In order to save a PHP script to hard disk, the **filename** must end in <*filename*>**.php**. Like HTML, php files are saved as plain text.

Comments

It is good programming practice to use comment tags embedded within code to describe what the script is doing. Comments help in understanding the code when maintaining it at a later date.

PHP provides the following ways to set comments:

- // at the beginning of each line (i.e. a single line comment)

```
<?php
    // Declaring a variable named $websites.
    $websites= array("Creating Website using HTML", "Creating Website using PHP",
               "Creating Website using Wordpress", "Creating Website using Joomla");
    $item = rand(0, sizeof($websites)-1);
?>
```

- /* and */ to comment out several lines (i.e. a multi line comment)

```
<?php
    /* Declaring a variable named $websites.
       Using the array() function an array is formed to hold three
strings. */
    $websites = array("Creating Website using HTML", "Creating Website using PHP",
               "Creating Website using Wordpress", "Creating Website using Joomla");
    $item = rand(0, sizeof($websites)-1);
?>
```

- # at the beginning of each line (i.e. a single line comment)

```
<?php
    # Declaring a variable named $websites.
    $websites = array("Creating Website using HTML", "Creating Website using PHP",
               "Creating Website using Wordpress", "Creating Website using Joomla");
    $item = rand(0, sizeof($websites)-1);
?>
```

Caution

The comment will not be displayed when the code is executed.

The Semicolon

The semicolon (;) signifies the end of a PHP statement and should never be forgotten. There should be a semicolon after each line of PHP code.

Delivering Text As Output

To output (i.e. send) text in a PHP script to a Browser the commands **print** or **echo** can be used.

The print statement is used in the following way:

```
print("Hello Mr. Ivan Bayross!");
```

print is the command which tells the PHP interpreter what to do. This is followed by the information to be printed, which is contained within brackets and inside double quotes.

The **echo** statement is used in the following way:

```
echo "Hello Mr. Ivan Bayross!";
```

echo is another command which tells the PHP interpreter what to do. This is followed by the information to be printed, which is contained within double quotes.

White Space

White spaces between lines of PHP code embedded in HTML are ignored by the PHP interpreter. This means it is absolutely fine to have one line of PHP code, followed by several blank lines before the next line of PHP code.

The following is an example of PHP code embedded in an HTML document: (myfirst.php)

```
<HTML>
    <HEAD>
        <TITLE>Ivan Bayross</TITLE>
    </HEAD>
    <BODY>
        My first PHP codespec embedded with HTML codespec <BR />
        <?php
            print "<H1> Hello Mr. Ivan Bayross </H1>";
            //Leaving some blank lines after the PHP code
            print "<H2> Hello everyone nice to see you</H2>";
        ?>
    </BODY>
</HTML>
```

In this code spec, PHP code is embedded in HTML. Every time the PHP interpreter encounters the open PHP tag **<?php**, it runs the enclosed code up to the closing PHP tag **?>**.

The PHP code is replaced with appropriate HTML tags and content (i.e. its output) that is passed as HTML via the web server to the web Browser that requested it. The blank lines (white spaces) left are completely ignored. Hence, running the above PHP code spec would produce an output as shown in diagram 16.4.

Running the PHP Script - myfirst.php

Create the file using any ASCII editor and save it as myfirst.php. Save myfirst.php in the web server's document **root** folder. The next step is to open the file in a web Browser using its URL.

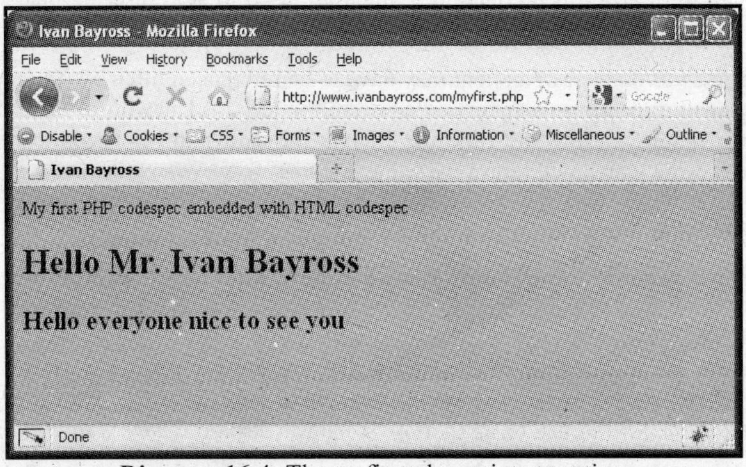

Diagram 16.4: The myfirst.php script at runtime

The above diagram shows the output of the PHP script when it runs on the web server and delivers its output to the Browser.

Here, the URL of myfirst.php is entered in the address bar of the Web Browser and 

is clicked.

17. THE BASICS OF PHP

All programming environments are built around syntax, some of which is used to declare and initialize variables. Variables are user defined containers which are used to store user defined values for later use. PHP permits the creation and use of different variables.

For example, the passport number of a client may have to be referenced often by program code, it would be nice to define **ppno** (i.e. passport number) as a variable once, load it with a value and just refer to its contents, whenever required. Now any time the client's passport number needs to be referenced simply refer to the variable **ppno** which will return the value it stores.

DATA TYPES

PHP has several types of variables. All hold a specific class of information, **except one**.

The PHP variable types are:

- **String** - Strings are a sequence of characters that are always internally NULL terminated. String variables hold characters. Usually a set of characters such as "S", "Ivan", "PHP is my favorite language" and so on. Strings can be as short or as long as desired. *There is **no limit** to size*
- **Integer** - Integer variables hold whole numbers, either positive or negative such as 1, -50, 22937932 and so on. *There is a **maximum limit** to the size of integers*. Any numbers lower than -2147483647 and higher than 2147483647 are automatically converted to floats as this data type can hold a much larger range of values
- **Float** - Float variables hold fractional numbers as well as very high integer numbers such as 3.5, 1.00000001, 2147483647000 and so on
- **Boolean** - Boolean variables hold **TRUE** or **FALSE**. Behind the scenes these are just integers. PHP considers the number **0** to be **FALSE** and **<u>everything else</u>** to be **<u>TRUE</u>**
- **Array** - Arrays are a special variable type, which hold multiple values. They are a great way of storing variables that are related such as colors, days of the week, members of a team or items in a shopping basket
- **Object** - Object variables are complex variables that have their own functions (i.e. methods) for accessing and/or manipulating their content
- **Resource** - Resource variables are variables that hold anything that is **not** PHP data. This could be picture data loaded from a file, the result of an SQL query and so on. A Resource type variable is used like any other variable with the key difference being that they should be freed up by the user when not required

VARIABLES

Variables are nothing but identifiers which point to a memory location (RAM) in which data is stored. Variables in PHP are quite different from compiled languages such as C and Java. This is because PHP variables are **weakly typed**. This means that when a PHP variable is being defined their data type is not declared prior their use. A PHP variable takes its data type from the user defined value that is being stored in it. As a result, a PHP variable can change its type (based on the user value, data type), **as often as needed**.

A PHP variable must be named / declared starting with the **$** character followed by a letter. The rest of the variable name can consist of a mix of both alphabets and numbers.

The following are three examples of valid names for variables:

- $city
- $address2
- $age_30

The _ (underscore) character can also be used in variable names. It is used as a **replacement for space**. Space is a **character** that **cannot** be used when naming a PHP variable.

The following characters are **not allowed** in a variable name and cause errors if used:

*	(asterix)
+	(plus)
#	(hash)
@	(at the rate)
-	(minus)
&	(ampersand)
£	(pound)

Tip

There is no limit on the size of variables in PHP.

Once a variable is named, **it is empty** until assigned a value. To assign a value to variable:

```
$city = 'Mumbai';
```

Everything inside the single quotes will be assigned to the variable named **city**. The **named variable** is on the **left** side of = (**i.e.** the assignment operator) and the **value** to be held by the variable is on its **right**.

Tip

PHP does not require variables to be declared before being initialized. They can simply be populated with a value and put into action whenever and whereever required.

Similarly, numeric values can be assigned.

```
$age = 24;
```

Here, **$age** is assigned a value of **24.** The only difference is that the value 24 is passed **without** quotation marks.

NOTE

Variables declared **without a dollar sign will not work**. This is a common mistake by new PHP programmers!

Different types of values can be assigned to variables. Integer and String types have already been demonstrated.

Irrespective of the value a variable holds in the future, PHP takes care of integer and string conversions **on the fly**. Hence, the same variable can hold different types of user values, at different instances in time.

One thing that causes many hours of hair pulling and anguish is case sensitivity **as PHP is case sensitive**.

Example:

```
<?php
    $Name = "Ivan Bayross";
    echo $name;
?>
```

In the above example a variable named **$Name** is declared. The value **Ivan Bayross** has been assigned but while accessing the value held by the variable, the variable name is **misspelled** (i.e. is in lowercase). This example when run displays the following error on the VDU screen:

```
Notice: Undefined variable: name on line 3
```

Numbers

It's really simple to deal with numbers in PHP. Just use them as required. All the normal rules about number precedence apply.

```
$x = 5;
$y = 10;
$z = 2 + 3 * $x + 5 * $y; // This is evaluated as 2+(3*5)+(5*10) = 67
echo $z;
```

When a variable is referenced by its name, PHP knows that it's the value held in the variable that must be processed and not the variable itself. This is **automatically** done **before** a new value is stored in the variable on the **left** hand side of the assignment operator. Hence, something like this can be done:

```
$x = 8;
$y = 4;
$x = (2 * $x + 5)/$y;     // Evaluated as $x = (2* 8 + 5)/4 = 5.25
```

Strings

When assigning a String value to a variable it **must be** enclosed in quotes. Either single quotes (') or double quotes (") can be used. There is a **vital** difference between the two types of quotes.

The following code demonstrates this difference:

```
$firstName = 'Ivan';
$wishing = "Hello everyone, my first name is $firstName. <BR />";
echo $wishing;
$lastName = 'Bayross';
$greeting = ' Hello everyone, my last name is $lastName.';
echo $greeting;
```

This code produces the following output:

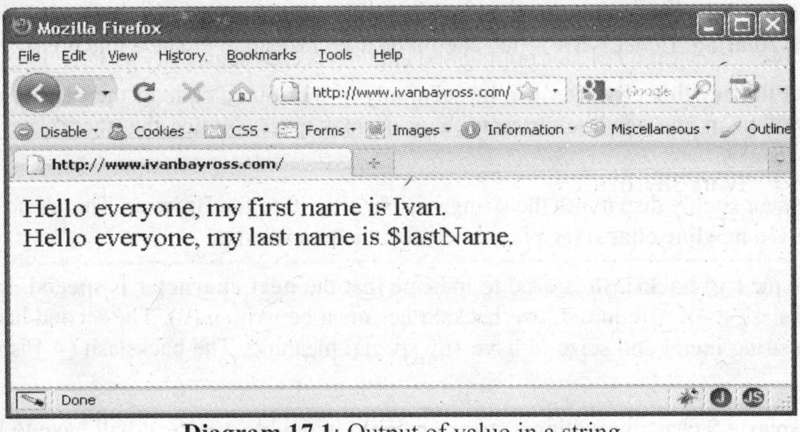

Diagram 17.1: Output of value in a string

When **double quotes** are used, PHP performs **variable expansion**, this means that PHP substitutes the value of **$firstName** wherever a reference to **$firstName** is encountered.

The result is that the string stored in the variable **$wishing** is **Hi, my first name is Ivan**.

When a value is assigned to the variable **$greeting** and **single quotes** are used then PHP does not perform any variable expansion and hence **$greeting** ends up with **Hello, my last name is $lastName**. This means that anything enclosed in **single quotes** is treated as a **string constant** and is not changed in anyway by PHP when processed.

Double quotes are also used for expanding other **special characters**, such as the **newline** character (**\n**).

The following code:

```
<?php
    echo "Ivan\nBayross";
?>
```

Will look like this when the source of the web page is displayed: (Refer to diagram 17.1.1 and diagram 17.1.2)

The following diagrams depict the new line character application at runtime along with the source code.

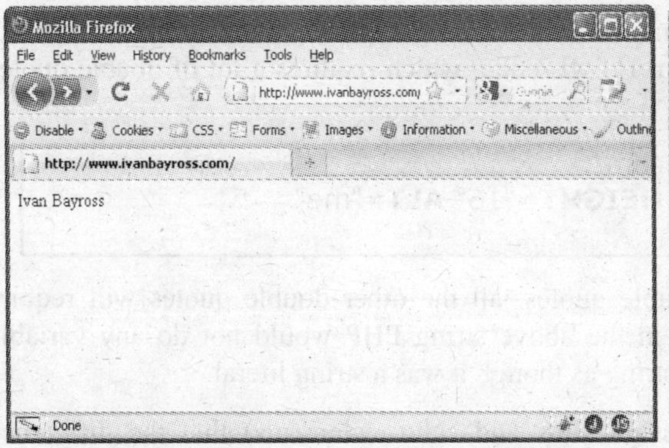

Diagram 17.1.1: Output of echo.php in Web browser

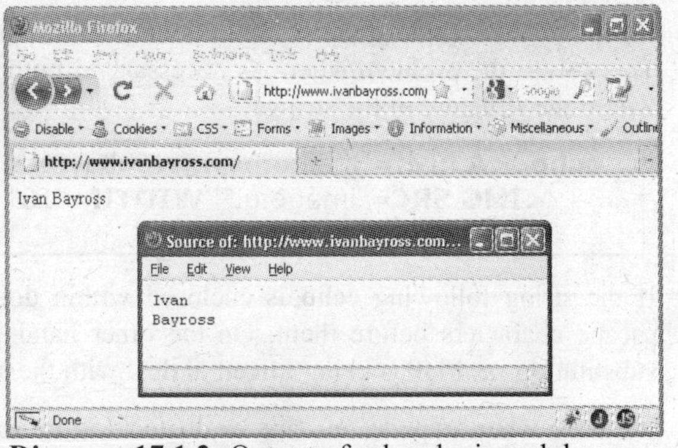

Diagram 17.1.2: Output of echo.php in web browser and in View source

However, browsers usually do not render the newline character while displaying the output. The newline character passed to the **echo** or **print()** function **is sent to the browser as string information and not formatting information**. Hence <**BR** /> tag should be used instead to create a line break in HTML.

This means that the **newline** character can be seen only in the source code of the PHP based page because the Web browser treats the newline character as a normal space. **Notice** that there's **no space before** or **after** the **\n** character.

The **echo** statement simply dispatches the string, visible after it, to the Browser. There's no trace of the PHP code, but there is a **newline character** placed between the two words.

This is because the (\ ) **backslash** is used to indicate that the **next character is special.** In PHP code spec if a single backslash itself is required, two backslashes must be written (\\). The second backslash will then be treated as a string literal and seize to have any special meaning. The backslash (\ ) is called an **escape character**.

Similarly to display a **$** character within a string enclosed in double quotes, it will have to be preceded by a backslash. This is because PHP looks for a variable, since all variables start with a **$**.

This string will give a little problem:

```
$name = "Ivan Bayross is a Professor" residing in Mumbai";
```

If tried out, an error pops up. That's because the parser expects the string to stop after the second double quote, just after the word **Professor**. The rest of the line is ignored by the PHP parser. The following string is correct:

```
$name = "Ivan Bayross is a \"Professor \" residing in Mumbai";
echo $name;
```

This code produces the following output:

```
Ivan Bayross is a "Professor" residing in Mumbai
```

The same applies if single quotes were used throughout the string.

Another way to resolve this issue is to enclose the string within **single quotes** and then use as many double quotes within the string as required.

Or

Do the inverse, enclose the string in double quotes and use as many single quotes in the string as required. This solves the problem when it's necessary to output HTML code, which requires a lot of double quotes within the structure of the string:

```
echo '<A href="mailto:ivan@ivanbayross.com">
    <IMG SRC="image.gif" WIDTH="16" HEIGHT="16" ALT="me"
    BORDER="0"></A>';
```

If the string following **echo** is enclosed within double quotes, all the other double quotes will require escape characters before them. On the other hand, in the above string PHP would not do any variable substitution i.e. PHP is being forced to deal with the string as though it was a string literal.

It's only when expressions are evaluated (as in assignments and echo statements) that the difference between single and double quotes come into the picture. After the assignment is done, no one can tell how the string was produced.

Consider the following example:

```
$fullname = 'Ivan Bayross is a ';
$profession = "Programmer";
$var1 = "$fullname $profession ";
$var2 = 'Ivan Bayross is a Programmer';
```

Variables **$var1** and **$var2** will both contain the string **Ivan Bayross is a Programmer** after evaluation, PHP will not make any distinction between the values stored in the two variables.

Joining Strings

To concatenate (add together) strings use the (**.**) period character (**i.e.** a dot **or** full stop).

```
$fullname = 'Ivan Bayross is a';
$profession = 'Programmer';
$data = $fullname.$profession;
```

Now **$data** will contain the string **Ivan Bayross is aProgrammer**. That's probably not what is wanted. It would be nice with a space between the words **a** and **Programmer**. To do this, execute the following code:

```
$data = $fullname . ' ' . $profession;
```

Notice that the **space** between the variable **$name** and the dot is ignored, it's the **string with the space (within single quotes) that's important**.

This could be solved using variable substitution. It is often easier to read, just remember to use double quotes around the string. This PHP code gives the same results as concatenating two variables using a period:

```
$data = "$fullname $profession ";
```

When using variable substitution a tiny problem will be encountered. The problem occurs with substitution of a variable in a string, which requires having text immediately after the variable. The variable name has to be **delimited** somehow.

Using curly braces is the solution as shown:

```
$noun = 'car';
echo "A $noun, two ${noun}s";
```

The above code shows playing around with English words in plural form. The first occurrence of **$noun** is substituted correctly, even when it is followed immediately by a comma because a comma cannot be a part of a name. But certainly there can be a variable called $nouns, so curly braces are used to indicate that the variable called **$noun** is being referenced and not some nonexistent variable called **$nouns**.

Variable Scope

Each variable has an area (in program memory) in which it exists, known as its scope, which means a domain in which the variable (and therefore its value) can be accessed. In other words, variables have the scope of the page in which they reside.

For example if a variable named **$myVar** is defined on a page, any code spec belonging to the rest of the page can access **$myVar**, but other pages code spec cannot.

All of this becomes interesting when user defined functions are used. Functions have their own scope, which means that variables used within a function are not available outside the run of the function. Variables defined outside a function are in turn not accessible to function code spec. For this reason, a variable inside a function can have the same name as one outside it and PHP will treat both as different variables and they can each hold different values. This is puzzling for most first time programmers.

It is technically possible for a PHP script to have several variables called **$a** in existence during program execution, however there's only one **$a** active at any specific instance in time.

The reason why the scope of a variable is so important is because it prevents crucial variables from being manipulated unexpectedly. If a variable is available in the main part of the program and accidentally the same variable is modified inside a function, the program may not run the way it is expected to. Here's how to correctly use the scoping rules in PHP which in turn controls the visibility of PHP variables.

All variables set **outside** a function or an object are considered **global**. This means, they are accessible from anywhere in the PHP script.

Consider the following example:

```
<?php
    function function()
    {
        global $myVar;
    }
    $myVar = 35;
    // Function call.
    function();
?>
```

In the above example, **$myVar** inside the function is the same as **$myVar** outside it.

This further means that the function **$myVar** already has a value of 35 and if that value changes inside the function, the external **$myVar**'s value will also change.

Example:

```
<?php
    // A global scope variable
    $MyGlobalScpVar = 35;
    // Defining a function
    function function()
    {
        echo $MyGlobalScpVar;
    }
    // Calling a function
    function();
?>
```

The above example when put into action will not produce any output because the **echo** statement refers to the local version of the **$MyGlobalScpVar** variable and it has not been assigned a value within this scope.

This behavior is very much different from **C** where global variables are automatically available to functions unless specifically overridden by a local definition. This usually causes problems when programmers inadvertently change a global variable. In PHP global variables must be declared **global inside a function** if they are going to be used in that function.

Example:

```
<?php
    $var1 = 85;
    $var2 = 50;

    function MySum()
    {
        global $var1, $var2;
        $var2 = $var1 + $var2;
    }
    MySum();
    echo "The Sum is:", $var2;
?>
```

Output: (Refer to diagram 17.2)

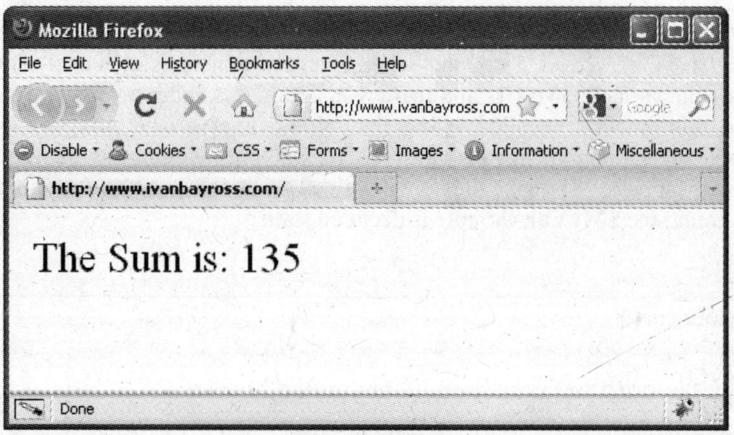

Diagram 17.2

When run the above example will display the result as **135**. This is because **$var1** and **$var2** are now declared global within the function. All references made to either of these variables will point to the global version.

NOTE

There is no limit to the number of global variables that can be manipulated by a function.

Alternatively the same can be achieved by using the special PHP defined **$GLOBALS** array.

Example:
The previous example can be rewritten as:

```
<?php
    $var1 = 85;
    $var2= 50;

    function MySum()
    {
        $GLOBALS["var2"] =
                $GLOBALS["var1"] + $GLOBALS["var2"];
    }
```

```
    MySum();
    echo "The Sum is:", $var2;
?>
```

The **$GLOBALS** array is an associative array with the name of the global variable being the key and the contents of that variable being the value of the array element.

Another important feature of variable scoping is the static variable. A static variable exists only in a local function scope, but it does not lose its value when program execution leaves this scope.

Example:

```
function MyCounter()
{
    $MyCtr = 0;
    echo $MyCtr;
    $MyCtr++;
}
```

This function should have served as a counter wherein every time it is executed it will increment the counter value held by the variable **$MyCtr** and thereby maintain this value for future executions. However, currently every time this function is called, it sets the value of the variable **$MyCtr** to **0** and displays 0 (zero). The **$MyCtr++**, which increments the variable serves no purpose since as soon as the function exits, the **$MyCtr** variable disappears. To make the above defined function serve the actual purpose and not lose track of the current count, the **$MyVar** variable is declared static.

Example:

```
function MyCounter()
{
    static $MyCtr = 0;
    echo $MyCtr;
    $MyCtr++;
}
```

Now, every time the **MyCounter()** function is called it will print the value of **$MyCtr** and increment it.

Variable Variables

Variable variables allow accessing the contents of a variable without knowing its name directly. This is like indirectly referencing a variable.

Consider the following code spec:

```
<?php
    $book = PHP For Beginners;
    $name = "book";
?>
```

There are two ways to retrieve the value of **$book:**

- Use **print $book**, which is quite straightforward

Or

- Use **print $$name** (Note the use of **two dollar** signs when using the variable variables technique)

By using **$$name**, PHP will look up the contents of **$name**, convert it to a string, then look up the variable of the same name and return its value.

In the above example, **$name** contains the string **book** and so PHP will look up the variable named **$book** and output its value in this case will be **5.1**.

Example:

```
<?php
    $book = "PHP For Beginners";
    $name = "book";
    $php = "name";
    $language = "php";
    print "Chapter in 4 in 1 HTML Book<BR />";
    print $book. "<BR />";
    print $$name . "<BR />";
    print $$$php . "<BR />";
    print $$$$language . "<BR />";
?>
```

Output: (Refer to diagram 17.3)

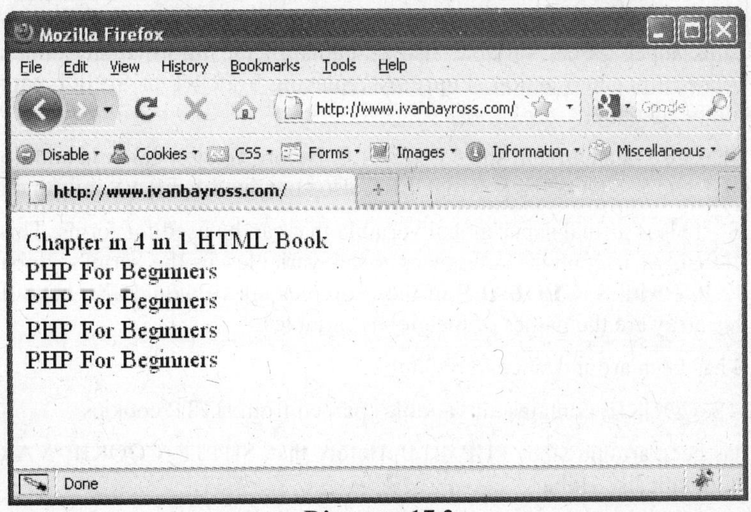

Diagram 17.3

PHP Superglobals

Superglobals are variables that are automatically available throughout all program code, in all scopes. These variables require no declaration they can simply be accessed. Super global variables provide:

- Useful information about the environment
- Allow access to HTML form variables or parameters
- Access to cookies stored on a client
- Keeping track of sessions and file uploads

They are as follows:

- **$_GET** - $_GET is used for data passed using the HTTP GET method, which includes variables passed as part of the URL

  For example: www.sharanamshah.com/index.php?book=PHP&cat=linux

  The GET method is conventionally used when the processing script has no lasting observable effect, such as changing a value in a database table. $_GET has been around since PHP 4.1.0. Before that, $HTTP_GET_VARS was used though this was not automatically global
- **$_POST** - The HTTP POST method is very similar to the $_GET. It is conventionally used when the contents of an HTML form are going to change values in a database table or make some other permanent change

  $_POST has been around since PHP 4.1.0. Before that, $HTTP_POST_VARS was used though this was not automatically global
- **$_REQUEST** - $_REQUEST holds variables provided to the script via the GET, POST and COOKIE input mechanisms. The presence and the order of variable inclusion in this array are defined according to the PHP **variables_order** configuration directive. It is preferable to use this specific super global variable, if it is not known how the variables are being passed (i.e. which method GET or POST is being used) for a particular script

  Additionally, this super global variable also contains all the information contained in $_COOKIE. $_REQUEST can be put into action simply by replacing $_POST or $_GET with $_REQUEST and the result would be identical

  $_REQUEST has also been around since PHP 4.1.0. Before version 4.3.0, in addition to the contents of $_POST, $_GET and $_COOKIE, $_REQUEST also contained $_FILES information
- **$_GLOBALS** - This is a final super global variable that can be used for forms. This would mean it is a super super global, as it contains references to all variables in the script's global scope. Replacing $_POST or $_GET with **$_GLOBALS** in the examples above would also have the identical results. The keys of this array are the names of the global variables

  $_GLOBALS has been around since PHP 3.0.0
- **$_COOKIE** - $_COOKIE contains all variables passed from HTTP cookies

  $_COOKIE has been around since PHP 4.1.0. Before that, $HTTP_COOKIE_VARS was used though this was not automatically global
- **$_FILES** - $_FILES holds variables provided to the script via HTTP post file uploads to provide feedback to the script

  $_FILES has also been around since PHP 4.1.0. Before that, $HTTP_POST_FILES was used though this was not automatically global

- **$_ENV** - $_ENV holds variables provided to the script via the environment. Analogous to the old $HTTP_ENV_VARS array, which is still available, **but deprecated**
- **$_SESSION** - $_SESSION holds variables which are currently registered to a script's session

  $_SESSION, as with most of the super global variables, has been around since PHP 4.1.0. Before that, $HTTP_SESSION_VARS was used though this was not automatically global
- **$_SERVER** - Variables set by the web server or otherwise directly related to the execution environment of the current script

  $_SERVER has also been around since PHP 4.1.0. Before that, $HTTP_SERVER_VARS was used though this was not automatically global

CONSTANTS

A constant, like variable, is a temporary placeholder in memory that holds a value. Unlike variables, the value of a constant never changes.
For example **PI** (3.14) or the value of **midnight** (12:00 am) are examples of constants applicable in **a** real life scenario.

When a constant is declared, the **define()** function is used and requires the name of the constant and the value that is required to be assigned to that constant. The names for constants have the same rules as variables except that they **do not** have the leading dollar sign.

Unlike variables, constants, once defined are globally accessible. Constants need not be declared again and again in each new function and PHP file.

After a constant is created, using that constant is similar to using a variable. However, unlike variables, a script cannot change the value of a constant. Attempting to do so will generate an error.

Constants make it easy to write or maintain the code. Since the value of the constant is set when it is created, the same can be modified if desired. The rest of the script using the value held by the constants will not need any modifications to reflect the new value.

By convention, the constant name is **always in uppercase**. String values must be enclosed in quotation marks. Although they can be created anywhere in the script, it is considered good practice to put them at the beginning of the script.

A constant may be a string, an integer or a floating point value.

Syntax:

```
define("<ConstantName>", <Expr> [, <CaseSensitive>])
```

Where,

- **ConstantName** is the name of the constant
- **Expr** is any valid PHP expression excluding arrays and objects
- **CaseSensitive** is a Boolean (TRUE/FALSE) and is **optional**. The default is **TRUE**

Example:

```
<?php
    define("STRCONSTANT", "This is a String Constant");
    define("INTCONSTANT", 2000);
    define("FLTCONSTANT", 3500.25);

    echo STRCONSTANT;
    echo '<BR />';
    echo INTCONSTANT;
    echo '<BR />';
    echo FLTCONSTANT;
    echo '<BR />';
?>
```

Output: (Refer to diagram 17.4)

Diagram 17.4

Since constants are never preceded by a **$** (dollar sign), PHP cannot determine when a constant is being used. Hence, it is not possible to embed a constant within a string.

Example:

```
define(AUTHORS, "Ivan Bayross");
echo "This book is authored by AUTHORS";
```

Output:

```
This book is authored by AUTHORS
```

Now separate the constant from the string with the concatenation operator.

Example:

```
define("AUTHORS", "Ivan Bayross");
echo "This book is authored by " . AUTHORS;
```

Output:

```
This book is authored by Ivan Bayross
```

PHP is bundled with some system defined constants that can be put to use in any PHP script. The most commonly used are:

__FILE__	The filename of the current script
__LINE__	The current line number
PHP_VERSION	The PHP version number
PHP_OS	The operating system running PHP
TRUE	The value TRUE (1)
FALSE	The value FALSE (0 or an empty string)
NULL	No value

HERE DOCUMENTS

HERE documents use a special form of I/O redirection to feed a command list to an interactive program or command.

They are a way of including large blocks of text (code spec) instead of using multiple statements.

The following example uses several **echo** statements.

Example:

```
<?php
    echo "Ivan Bayross has authorized the following books:" ;
    echo "<OL>";
    echo "<LI>The Chronicles Of Java On Linux";
    echo "<LI>Four in One HTML Book";
    echo "<LI>Moving From Windows To Linux";
    echo "<LI>Using L.A.M.P.P. (Linux Apache MySQL PHP PERL) On Linux";
    echo "</OL>";
?>
```

The following example using **here documents** technique clubs all the echo statements.

Example:

```
<?php
$hereMessage = <<<EOF
Ivan Bayross has authorized the following books:
<OL>
    <LI>The Chronicles Of Java On Linux
    <LI> Four in One HTML Book
    <LI> Moving From Windows To Linux
    <LI> Using L.A.M.P.P. (Linux Apache MySQL PHP PERL) On Linux
</OL>
EOF;
echo ($hereMessage);
?>
```

Output: (Refer to diagram 17.5)

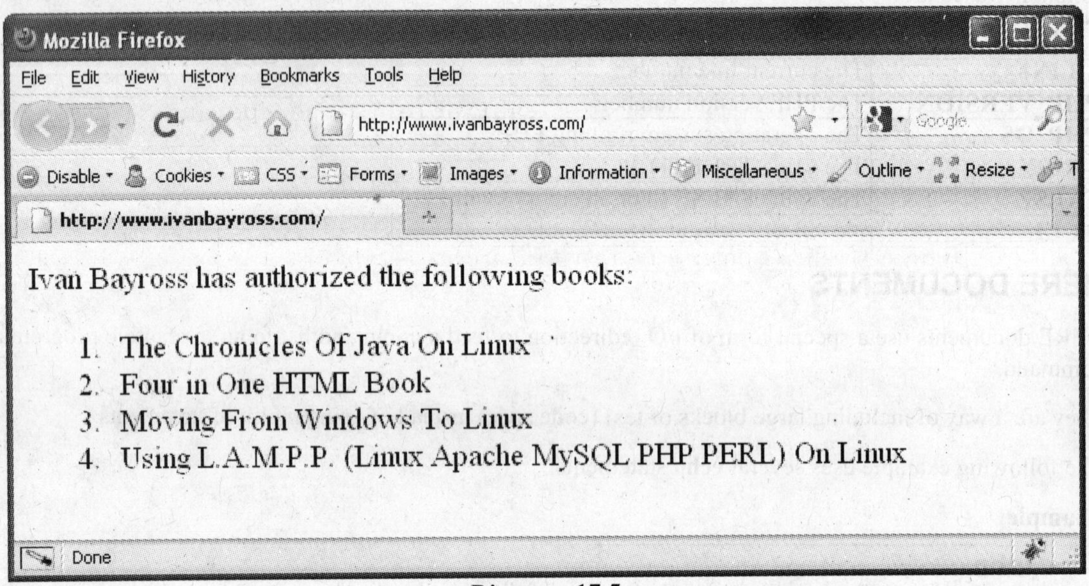

Diagram 17.5

In the above code spec, **EOF** is a string that delineates (frames) the command list. This can be any sequence of alphanumeric characters and/or underscores, although it **must not begin** with a number or an underscore. The special symbol <<< designates the limit string.

The text of the **here** document then begins on the next line. To tell PHP that it has reached the end of the here document, simply include a line beginning with the final delimiter which was declared at the beginning (in this case **EOF**).

TIP

The text within a here document is interpreted according to the same substitution rules as a double-quoted string, so variables and escape characters can also be included.

OPERATORS

An operator is any symbol used to perform an operation on a value. In PHP, operators can easily be grouped by function.

Operators are indispensable components of PHP. They are used for simple purposes such as assigning values to variables, working with strings, working with numbers, controlling program flow and so on.

PHP operators can be classified into the following areas:

- Unary operators
- Binary operators
- Ternary operator

Unary Operators

Unary Operators work on only one operand

Negation Operators

Negation operators are placed before the operand. For example:

```
!$variable
```
```
    // where! is the operator and $variable is the operand
```

Operator	Meaning	Description
!	Logical Negation	True if the operand evaluates to false. False if the operand evaluates to true.
~	Bitwise Negation	In case of a numeric operand, the bitwise negation of its bitwise representation (floating-point values are first converted to integers). In case of strings, a string of equal length, in which each character is the bitwise negation of its corresponding character in the original string.

Example:

```
<?php
    $num1 = 102.52;
    $num2 = 80;
    $num3 = (~$num1) + (!$num2);
    echo "The sum of Bitwise number 102.52 and Logical number 80 is " . $num3;
?>
```

Output: (Refer to diagram 17.6)

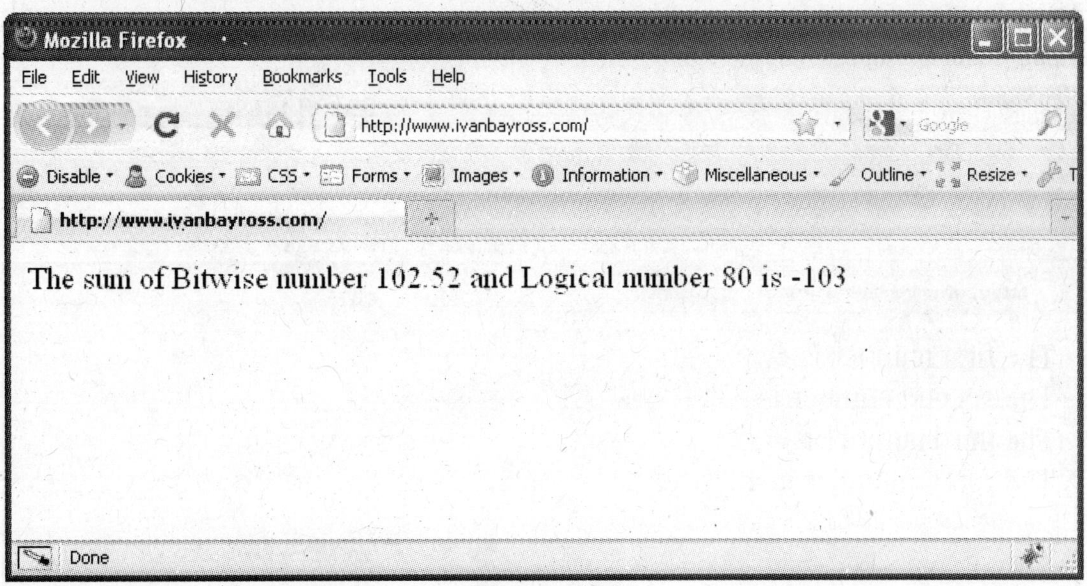

Diagram 17.6

Increment / Decrement Operators

Increment/decrement operators are unique in the sense that they operate only on variables and not on any value. The reason for this is that in addition to calculating the result value, the value of the variable itself changes as well.

Example	Description	Result	Value of the Variable
$variable++	Post increment	$variable is incremented by 1	The previous value of $variable
++$variable	Pre increment	$variable is incremented by 1	The new value of $variable (incremented value)
$variable--	Post decrement	$variable is decremented by 1	The previous value of $variable
--$variable	Pre decrement	$variable is decremented by 1	The new value of $variable (decremented value)

Example:

```
<?php
    $num1 = 5;
    $num2 = $num1++;
    // Post increment, $num2 is assigned $num1's original value
    print "The first number is " . $num1 . "<BR />";
    // This will print the value of $num1, which is now 6
    print "The second number is " . $num2 . "<BR />";
    // This will print the value of $num2, which is the original value of $num1 i.e. 5
    $num3 = 5;
    $num4 = --$num3;
    // Pre decrement, $num4 is assigned $num3's incremented value
    print "The third number is " . $num3 . "<BR />";
    // This will print the value of $num3, which is now 4
    print "The fourth number is " . $num4;
    // This will print the value of $num4, which is same as the value of $num3 i.e. 4
?>
```

Output: (Refer to diagram 17.7)

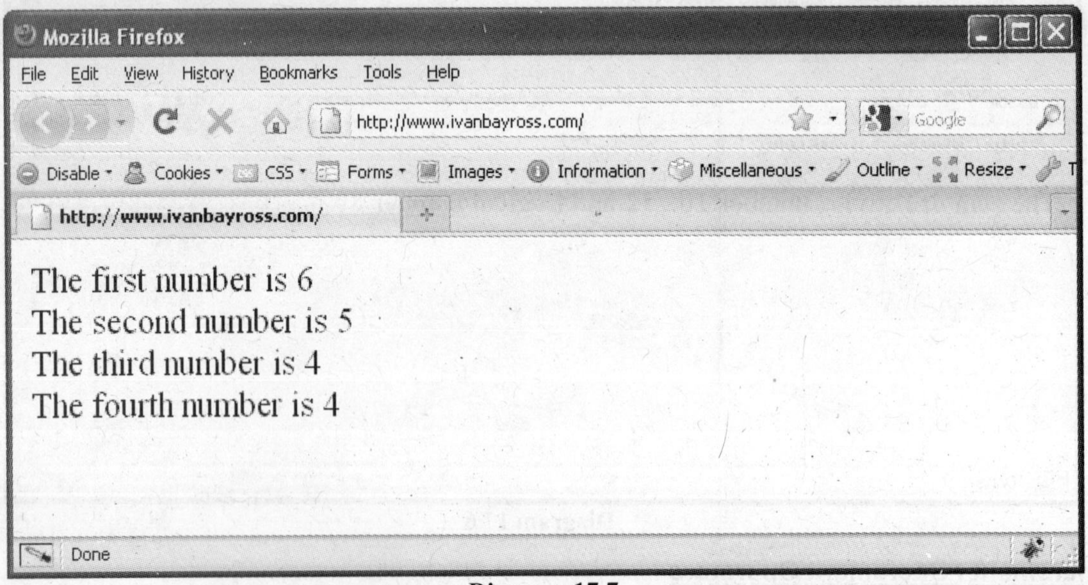

Diagram 17.7

Pre-increment and Post-decrement operators also function in the same manner.

TIP

Strings (when not numeric) are incremented in a different way. If the last letter is alphanumeric, it is incremented by 1. If it was 'z', 'Z' or '9', it is incremented to 'a', 'A' or '0' respectively and the next alphanumeric is also incremented in the same way. If there is no next alphanumeric, one is added to the beginning of the string as 'a', 'A' and '1' respectively. **Non-numeric strings cannot be decremented.**

Cast Operators

PHP provides a C like way to force a type conversion of a value by using the cast operators. The operand appears on the right side of the cast operator and its result is the converted type according to the following table.

Operator	Changes Type To
int or integer	Integer
float, real or double	Floating point
string	String
bool or boolean	Boolean
array	Array
object	Object

The casting operators change the type of a value and not the type of a variable.

Example:

```
<?php
    $numStr = "15.65 Rupees";
    $numDec = 10.54;

    $numInt = (int) $numStr;
    echo "After casting $numStr to Integer the result is " . $numInt ."<BR />";

    $numInt = (int) $numDec;
    echo "After casting $numDec to Integer the result is " . $numInt . "<BR />";
?>
```

Output: (Refer to diagram 17.8)

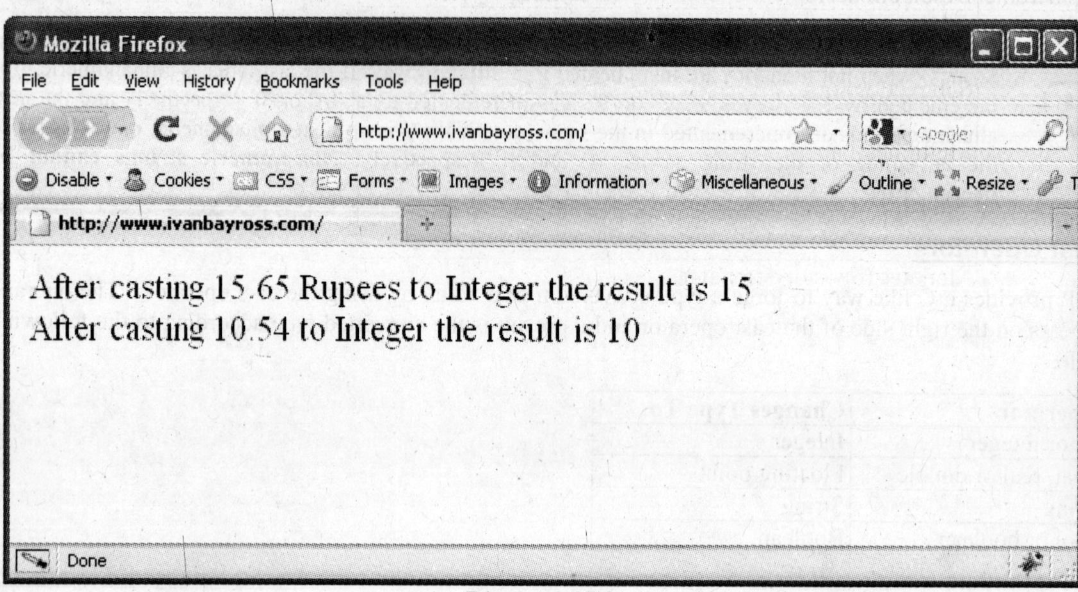

Diagram 17.8

Binary Operators

PHP can only perform binary operations on two operands that have the same type. However, if the two operands have different types, PHP automatically converts one of them to the other's type, according to the following rules:

Type Of One Operand	Type Of Other Operand	Conversion Performed
Integer	Floating Point	The integer operand is converted to a floating-point number.
Integer	String	The string is converted to a number. If the converted string's type is real, the integer operand is converted to a real as well.
Real	String	The string is converted to a real

Numeric Operators

If one or both of the operands are Strings, Booleans, Nulls or Resources, they are automatically converted to their numeric equivalents before the calculation is performed.

Operator	Description	Example	Result
+	Addition	x=3 x+3	6
-	Subtraction	x=3 5-x	2
*	Multiplication	x=5 x*5	25
/	Division	20/2 7/2	10 3.5
%	Modulus (division remainder)	5%3 7%2	2 1
++	Increment	x=8 x++	9
--	Decrement	x=8 x--	7

Example:

```
<?php
    $number = 150 + 150;
    print "Addition of two numbers is: ";
    print $number . "<BR />";

    $num = 50 * 50;
    print "Multiplication of two numbers is: ";
    print $number . "<BR />";

    $num = 50 * 50 - 150;
    print "Multiplication and Subtraction of numbers are: ";
    print $number . "<BR />";
?>
```

Output: (Refer to diagram 17.9)

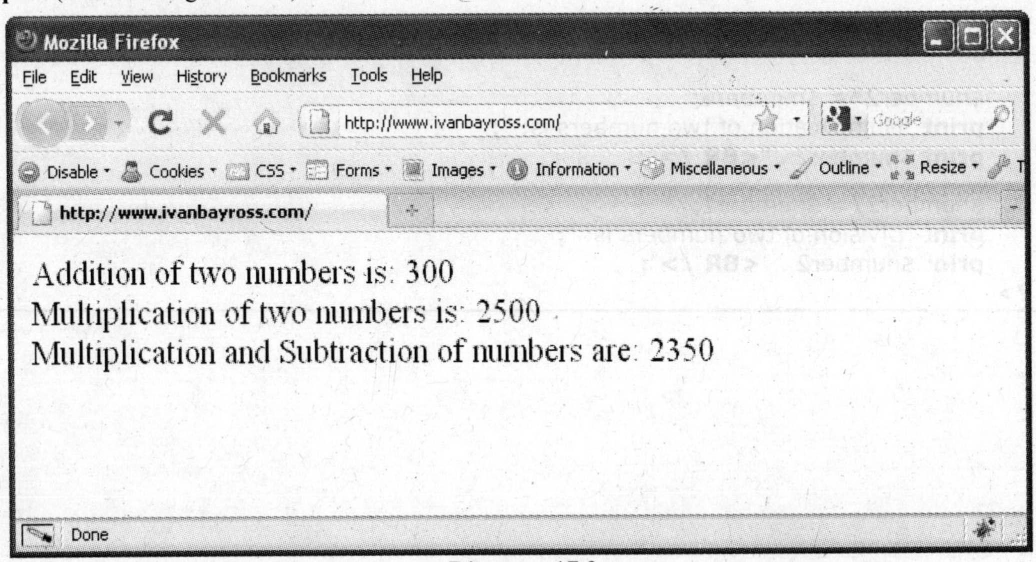

Diagram 17.9

Assignment Operators

Assignment operator enables writing a value to a variable. The first operand (the one on the left of the assignment operator) must be a variable. The value of an assignment is the final value assigned to the variable. This operator can be used to assign strings, integers even the results of functions

Example:

```
$var = 5;
// Assigning value 5 to the variable $var
$var = 'Ivan Bayross';
// Assigning value Ivan Bayross to the variable $var
$var = MyFunction();
// Assigning value returned by the function MyFunction() to
   the variable $var
```

In addition to the regular assignment operator =, several other assignment operators are composites of an operator followed by an equal sign. These composite operators apply the operator taking the variable on the left as the first operand and the value on the right as the second operand and assign the result of the operation to the variable on the left.

Operator	Example	Is The Same As
=	x=y	x=y
+=	x+=y	x=x+y
-=	x-=y	x=x-y
*=	x*=y	x=x*y
/=	x/=y	x=x/y
%=	x%=y	X=x%y

Example:

```
<?php
   $number1 = 40;
   $number2 = $num1;
   print "Second Number is: ";
   print $number2 . "<BR />";

   $number2*= $number1;
   print "Multiplication of two numbers is: ";
   print $number2 . "<BR />";

   $number2/= $number1;
   print "Division of two numbers is: ";
   print $number2 . "<BR />";
?>
```

Output: (Refer to diagram 17.10)

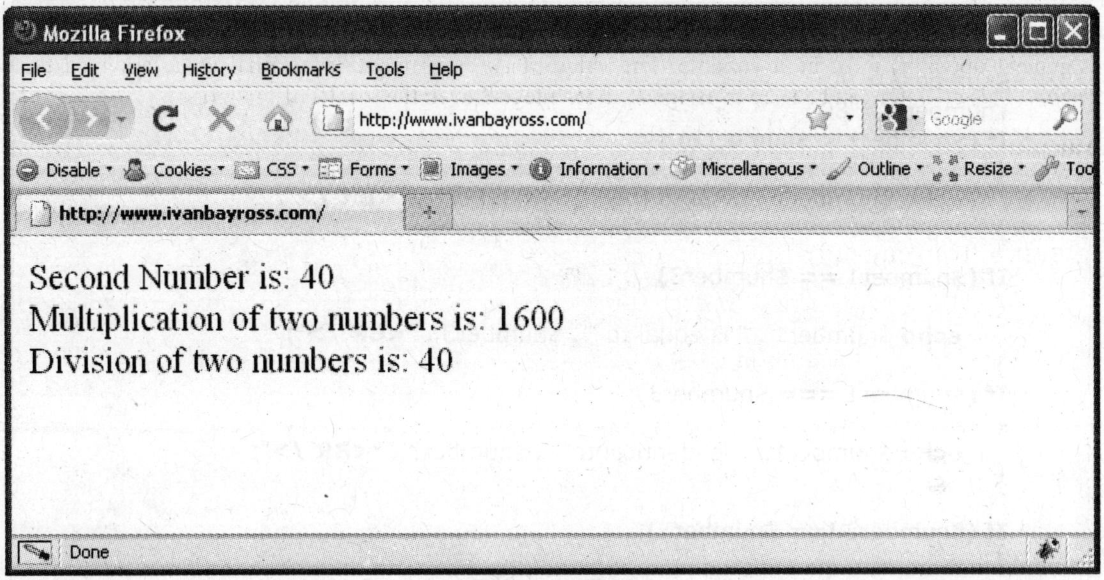

Diagram 17.10

Concatenation Operator

The concatenation operator (.) concatenates two strings. This operator works only on strings. Thus, any non-string operand is first converted to string. The following example would deliver **The Month is 10:**

```
$month = 10;
print "The Month is " . $month;
```

The integer **$month** is internally converted to a string **10** before it is concatenated with the string's prefix, **The Month is**.

Comparison Operators

Comparison operator determines the relationship between two operands. When both operands are Strings, the comparison is performed lexicographically. The comparison results in a Boolean value.

A number of different comparison operators are available to compare the value held in one variable against the value, which is held in another:

Operator	Meaning	Example
==	Is equal to	3==9 returns false
!=	Is not equal to	3!=9 returns true
<	Is less than	3<9 returns true
<=	Is less than or equal to	3<=9 returns true
>	Is greater than	15>18 returns false
>=	Is greater than or equal to	15>=18 returns false
===	Is identical to	3==="3" returns false
!==	Is not identical to	8!=="8" returns true

Example:

```
<?php
    $number1 = 80;
    $number2 = 90;
    $number3 = '80';
    If ($number1 < $number2)
    {
        echo $number1 . " is less than " . $number2 . "<BR />";
    }

    If ($number1 == $number3)
    {
        echo $number1 . " is equal to " . $number3 . "<BR />";
    }
    If ($number1 === $number3)
    {
        echo $number1 . " is identical to " . $number3 . "<BR />";
    }

    If ($number2 !== $number3)
    {
        echo $number2 . " is not identical to " . $number3;
    }
?>
```

Output: (Refer to diagram 17.11)

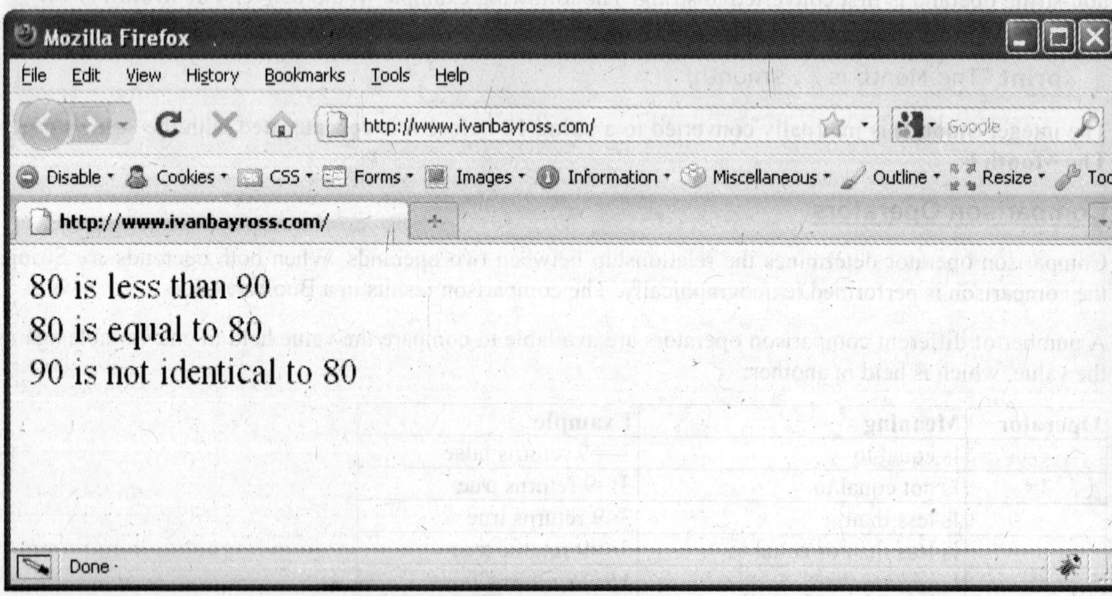

Diagram 17.11

Logical Operators

Logical operators first convert their operands to Boolean values and then perform their respective comparison.

Operator	Description	Example
&&, and	The first **and** the second is true	(15!=18) && (15==18) returns false
||, or, ||	The first **or** the second or both are true	(25!=28) || (25==28) returns true
!	Not	!(25==28) returns true

Example:

```
<?php
    $number1 = 40;
    $number2 = 2;
    $number3 = 20;

    If ((($number1/$number2) && ($number1/$number3) || ($number2 *
$number3 = $number1))
    {
        echo $number1 . " is divisible by " . $number2 . " and " . $number3;
    }
?>
```

Output: (Refer to diagram 17.12)

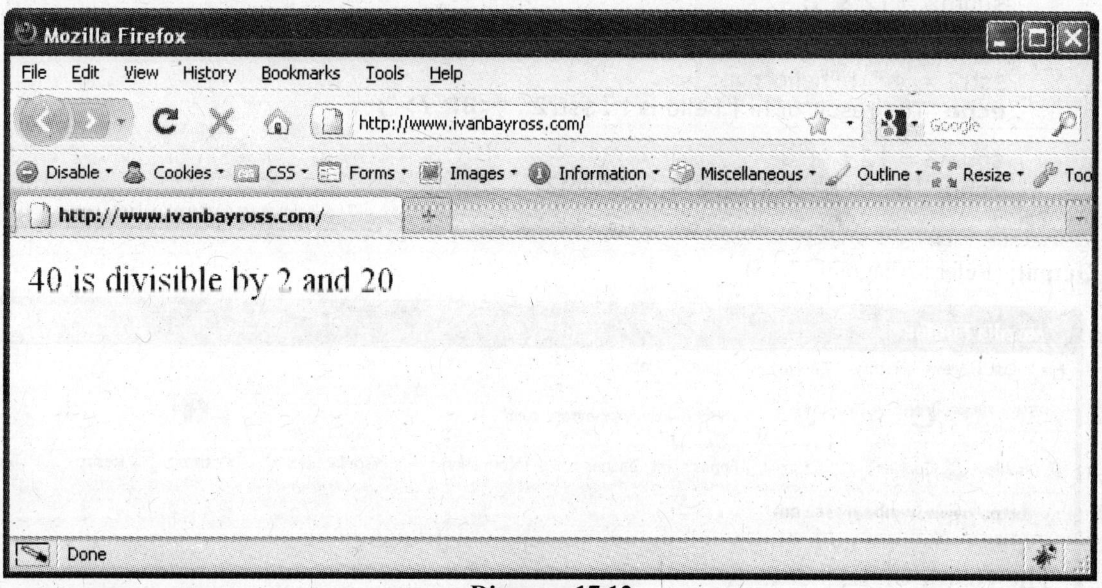

Diagram 17.12

Bitwise Operators

Bitwise operators perform an operation on the bitwise representation of their arguments. Unless the arguments are strings, they are converted to their corresponding integer representation and the operation is then performed. In case both arguments are strings, the operation is performed between corresponding character offsets of the two strings (i.e. each character is treated as an integer).

Operator	Meaning	Description
&	Bitwise AND	The **&** (bitwise AND) operator compares all the bits in operand one against all the bits on operand two, then returns a result with all the joint bits set.
¦, or, |	Bitwise OR	The | (bitwise OR) operator compares all the bits in operand one against those in operand two and returns a result with all the bits set in either of them.
^	Bitwise XOR (Exclusive OR)	The ^ (bitwise XOR) operator compares all the bits in operand one against those in operand two and returns a result with all the bits set in either of them but **not both**.

Example:

```
<?php
    $num1 = 12 ^ 9;
    echo "The result of 12 ^ 9 is " . $num1 . "<BR />";

    $str1 = "hi" & "hello";
    echo "The result of hi & hello is " . $str1 . "<BR />";

    $num2 = 12 & 9;
    echo "The result of 12 & 9 is " . $num2 . "<BR />";

    $str2 = "hi" | "hello";
    echo "The result of hi | hello is " . $str2 . "<BR />";

    $num3 = 12 | 9;
    echo "The result of 12 | 9 is " . $num2;
?>
```

Output: (Refer to diagram 17.13)

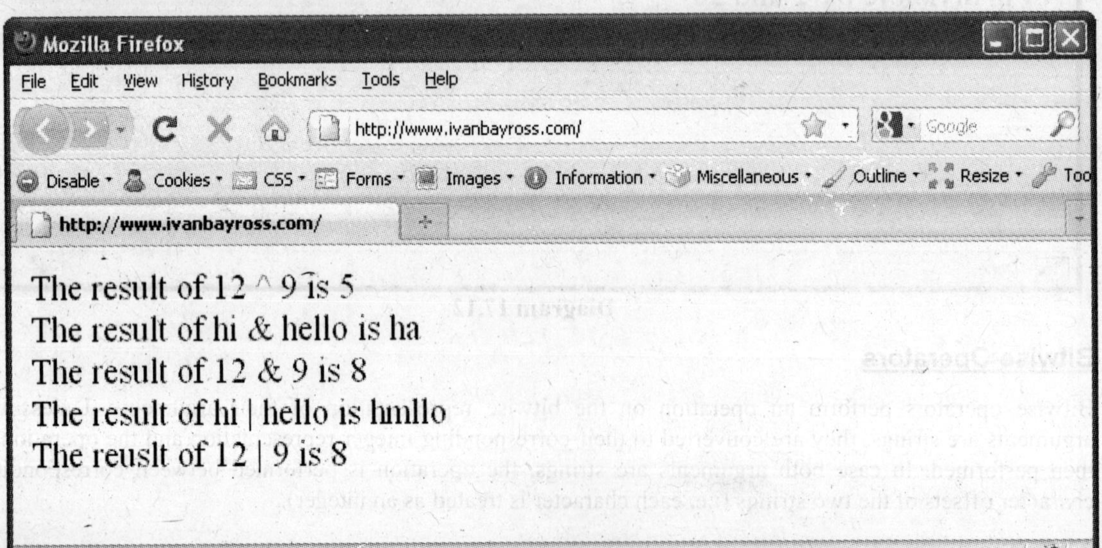

Diagram 17.13

Ternary Operator

One of the most elegant operators is the '**... ? ... :**' operator. Its syntax is:

```
<Truth_Expr> ? <Expr1> : <Expr2>
```

The operator evaluates **Truth_Expr** and checks whether it is true. If it is, the value of the expression evaluates to the value of Expr1 (Expr2 is not evaluated). If it is false, the value of the expression evaluates to the value of Expr2 (Expr1 is not evaluated).

For example, the following code snippet checks whether **$num** is set and displays a message accordingly:

```
$number = 40;
$message = isset($number) ? "$number is set" : "$number is not set";
print $message;
```

This example prints the following:

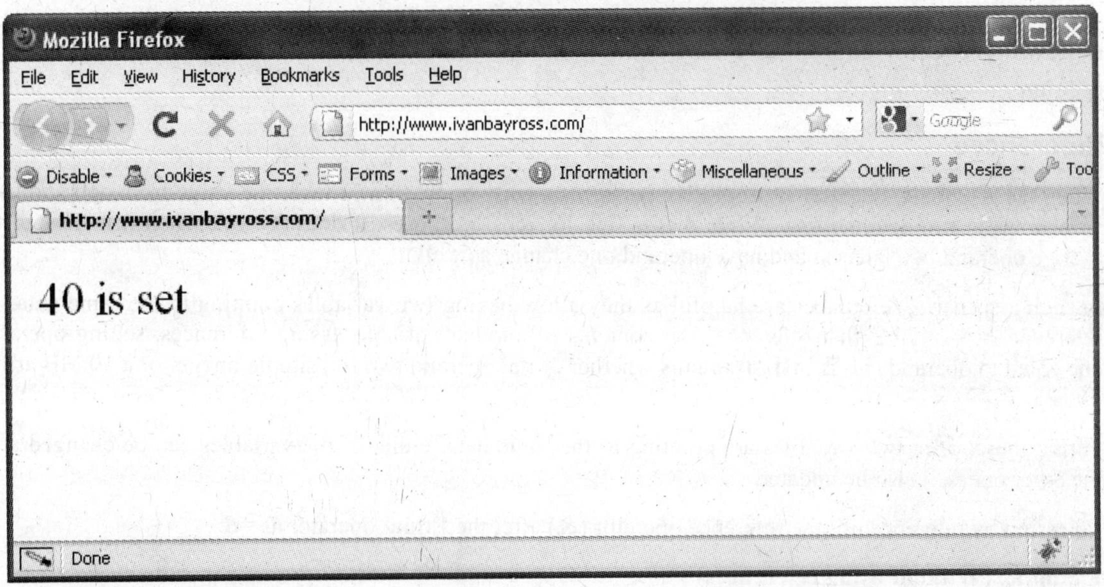

Operator Precedence

The precedence of an operator specifies how tightly it binds two expressions together.

For example:

```
$x = 9 + 1 * 10
```

Because people read left to right, it might be assumed that **$x** equals **100** evaluated as Nine plus one, times ten equals hundred, however, because of operator precedence, this is totally wrong. The multiplication operator has higher precedence than the addition operator, so that calculation would be performed first as One times ten, plus nine, equals nineteen.

Parentheses may be used to force precedence, if necessary.

```
$x = (9 + 1) * 10
```

Since the first part of the above equation is surrounded, it would be calculated first and **$x** would equal **100**.

The following depicts an idea of how various operators rank. Operators listed in the same row have equal precedence.

Highest Precedence

- * / %
- + - .
- < <= > >=
- &&
- ||
- AND
- XOR

Lowest Precedence

- OR

References

When the = (equals) operator is used, PHP performs a **copy operation**. It takes the value from operand two and copies it into operand one. While this is fine for most purposes, it doesn't work when it is desired to change operand two later on and have operand one change as well.

In such a scenario, references are helpful as they allow having two variables pointing to the same data. A reference is a variable that references the contents of another variable. Using references, setting operand one equal to operand two is **instantaneous** whether or not operand two is a simple integer or a 10 MB array of data.

Furthermore, once two variables are pointing to the same data, either of the variables can be changed and the other one will also be updated.

To assign by reference use the reference operator (**&**) after the **Equal** operator as **=&**.

Example: (<u>Without using references</u>)

```
<?php
    $a = 400;
    $b = $a;
    print "The value of a is " . $a . "<BR />";
    print "The value of b is " . $b . " <BR />";
    ++$a;
    print "The increment value of a is " . $a . "<BR />";
    print "The increment value of b is " . $b . "<BR />";
    ++$b;
    print "The increment value of a is " . $a . "<BR />";
    print "The increment value of b is " . $b . "<BR />";
?>
```

Output: (Refer to diagram 17.14.1)

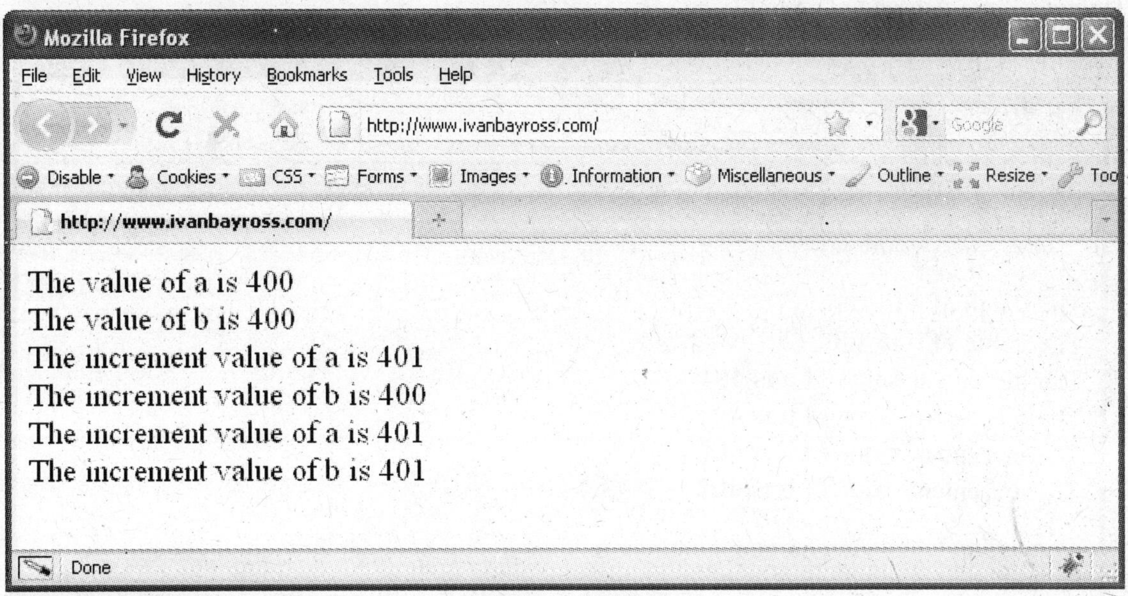

Diagram 17.14.1

Example: (Using references)

```
<?php
    $a = 400;
    $b =& $a;
    print "The value of a is " . $a . "<BR />";
    print "The value of b is " . $b . " <BR />";

    ++$a;
    print "The increment value of a is " . $a . "<BR />";
    print "The increment value of b is " . $b . "<BR />";

    ++$b;
    print "The increment value of a is " . $a . "<BR />";
    print "The increment value of b is " . $b . "<BR />";
?>
```

Notice that the third line in the above code has changed. Instead of simply assigning the value of variable **$a** to the variable **$b**, the **=&** (reference) operator is now used to set the variable **$a** as a reference to the variable **$b**. The difference will be noticed when the code spec is re-executed after making the above change (in the third line).

Output: (Refer to diagram 17.14.2)

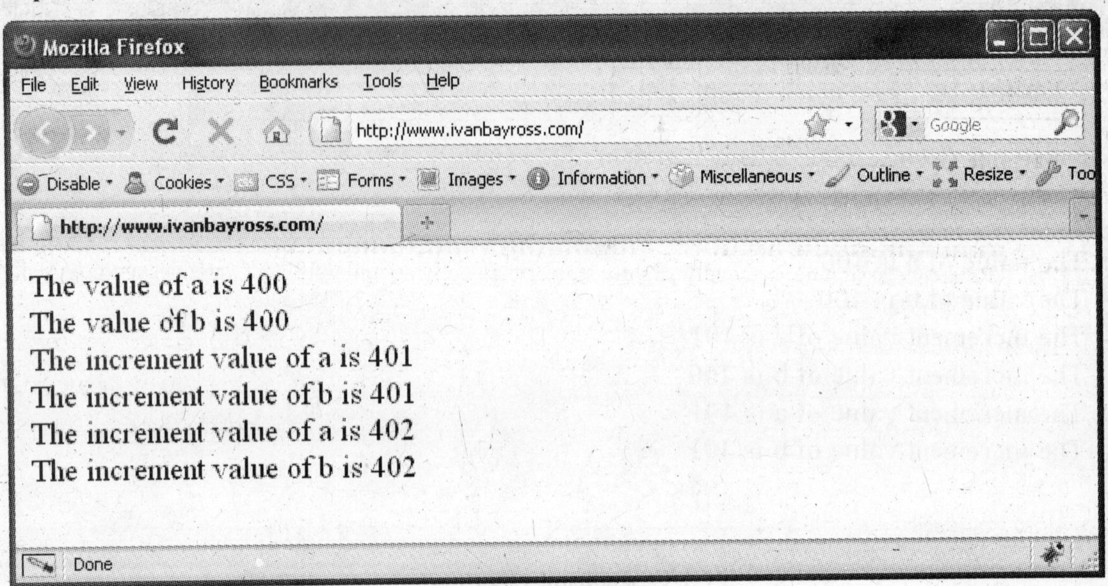

Diagram 17.14.2

Here the reference operator is used to make **$b** point to the same value as **$a**, as can be seen in the first two **print** statements. After incrementing **$a**, both variables are printed out again and both are **101**, as expected. Finally, to prove that the relationship is two-way, **$b** is incremented and again both **$a** and **$b** have been updated. Here, PHP references permit binding two separate variables together, thus allowing modification to both at once

In the first example, the variable **$a** is assigned a value **100**. This is followed by creation of a second variable **$b** which is assigned the same value held by the variable **$a**, using the assignment operator as:

```
$b = $a;
```

The most important point to notice here is that the second variable **$b** was created and thereby is completely independent of the first variable **$a**.

In contrast, the second example created a reference to the variable **$a** and called it **$b**. When this is done, a second variable is not created, but rather a single variable is given another variable name.

The following diagram depicts the above explained scenario.

The First Example:

```
$b = $a;
```

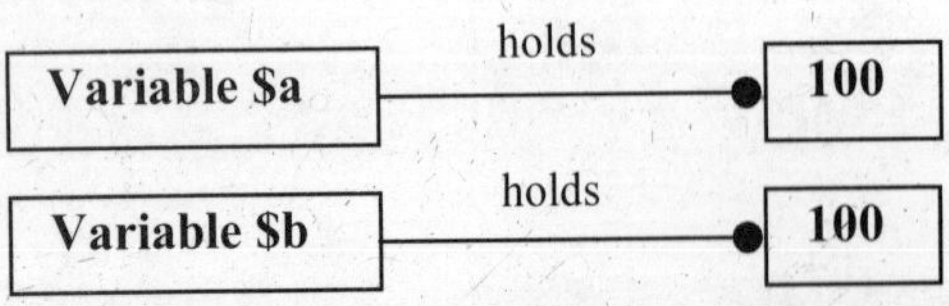

The Second Example:

```
$b =& $a;
```

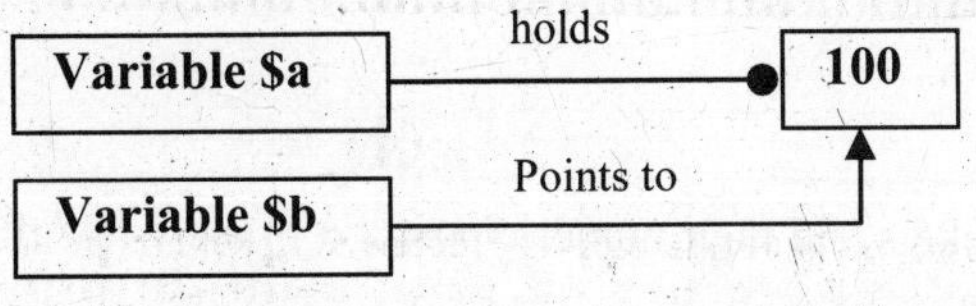

TIP

Reference assigning is actually slightly slower than copy assigning if large variables are not used, so it is best to stick with normal copy assigning unless there is a good reason to switch.

When it comes to functions, references can also be used to allow a function to work directly on a variable rather than on a copy.

ARRAYS

An array is a type of variable that allows:

- Associating one value directly to another value

OR

- Organizing a set of data in form of a list or something much similar to a table

An array is a collection of key/value pairs. This means that it maps keys (or indexes) to values. Array indexes can be either integers or strings whereas values can be of any type (including other arrays).

An array can hold a number of different values at the same time.

For example, if the following data has to be stored using PHP:

- Using MySQL 5 For Professionals
- Application Development With PHP And Oracle On Linux
- Using PHP 5.1 For Professionals

Using standard variables technique:

```
<?php
    $MyBook1 = "The Chronicles Of Java On Linux";
    $MyBook2 = "Four in One HTML Book";
    $MyBook3 = "Using L.A.M.P.P. (Linux Apache MySQL PHP PERL) On Linux";
?>
```

The above shown method of storing the values is usable, but not at all efficient. In such scenarios, an array always proves useful.

Syntactically an array is almost identical to any other variable in PHP as follows:

- Same rules are followed in terms of variable names
- Can be referenced in the same way as any other variable

However an array differs from a normal variable when:

- It is being created
- It is being accessed

Array Creation:

To store the above said values into an array use square brackets and their numeric position in the array after the array name as follows:

```
<?php
    $MyBook[0] = "The Chronicles Of Java On Linux";
    $MyBook[1] = "Four in One HTML Book ";
    $MyBook[2] = "Using L.A.M.P.P. (Linux Apache MySQL PHP PERL) On Linux ";
?>
```

Now an array has been created and its first three slots have been filled. Notice that the numbering starts at **zero** and **not** at **one**.

Alternatively, PHP also provides a function that allows creating an array.

The above data can be inserted into an array using the function **array()** as:

```
<?php
    $MyBook = array(0=>" The Chronicles Of Java On Linux",
                    1=>"Four in One HTML Book",
                    2=>"Using L.A.M.P.P. (Linux Apache MySQL PHP PERL) On Linux ");
?>
```

The result of the above exercise is a single variable named **$MyBook** that contains an indexed list of all three books (data entered in the earlier example).

Array Data Retrieval:
Recall the values held in the array named **MyBook** as follows:

```
echo $MyBook[0] . "<BR />";
echo $MyBook[1] . "<BR />";
echo $MyBook[2] . "<BR />";
```

Notice that the retrieval of data from an array looks very similar to retrieval of values from a normal variable, except when dealing with an array, brackets **[]** are used along with a reference to the index (such as **[2]**) of the value that is to be retrieved.

If it is not important as to which slots data is assigned in the array, then use a pair of empty brackets after its name when loading it with data as follows:

```
<?php
    $MyBook[] = "The Chronicles Of Java On Linux";
    $MyBook[] = "Four in One HTML Book";
    $MyBook[] = " Using L.A.M.P.P. (Linux Apache MySQL PHP PERL) On Linux ";
?>
```

The above code spec has filled the first three slots of the array, which are numbered 0, 1 and 2. When this has to be retrieved specify whicn slot to access. This kind of approach is usually taken when data has to be appended into an array but it is not known what the next index number in the array is.

Array slots can also be identified by **name**. These are called Associative arrays. They are identical to any other type of array with one major difference i.e. their index values.

In Associative arrays, index values are not limited to simple integer values but can also be strings. Declaring and working with Associative arrays is identical to working with any other type of array. The following example makes the code spec more readable and easy to understand by the use of associative arrays as follows:

```
$personal_data['first name'] = 'Ivan';
$personal_data['post'] = 'Professor';
$personal_data['last name'] = 'Bayross';
$personal_data['age'] = 65;
echo 'Hi ' . $personal_data['first name'] .
    '! We know that you are ' . $personal_data['age'] . ' years old.';
```

The PHP parser will ignore all whitespace and the result is:

```
Hi Ivan! We know that you are 65 years old.
```

This is often the easiest way to deal with associative arrays. Another possibility is to use variable substitution with curly braces like this:

```
echo "Hi {$personal_data['first name']}! " .
    "We know that you are {$personal_data['age']} years old.";
```

This code gives the same result. More complex expressions can be used inside such a set of curly braces. This includes accessing elements in multidimensional arrays and object properties.

TIP

It is recommended to use descriptive names for the slots in the arrays. It makes the code spec clear and helps to indicate what the different slots are intended for.

CONDITIONAL STATEMENTS

The linear, hierarchic, top down, execution of a program, is controlled by 'Control Structures' embedded within program code. PHP code often has to do several things, this means that PHP code has to have decision making abilities, based on the decision made, the PHP code will do some work **or** otherwise do something else entirely. PHP provides programmers with conditional statements to achieve this.

There are two types of conditional statements:

- **if (...else) statement** - This statement is used, if a block of code must test a specific condition, if the condition tested returns a 'TRUE' then the code executes. If the condition tested returns 'FALSE' another block of code executes
- **switch statement** - This statement is used to choose and execute **one** code block from among multiple code blocks for execution

The if Statement

if statements are the most common conditional statements and they exist in most programming languages. Use the if-statement to execute different code snippets of PHP code in a program, based on what is returned (i.e. either **TRUE** or **FALSE**) when a condition is evaluated.

Syntax:

```
if (<Condition>)
    <Code Block To Be Executed If Condition Returns TRUE>;
else
    <Code Block To Be Executed If Condition Returns FALSE>;
```

The following example will give the output **Both the strings are equal** as the str1 holds the string **Welcome** is equal to str2 that also holds the string **Welcome** otherwise returns **Both the strings are not equal:**

```
<?php
    $str1="Hi";
    $str2="Hi";

    if ($str1 == $str2)
        echo "Both the strings are equal";
    else
        echo "Both the strings are not equal";
?>
```

Output: (As shown in diagram 17.15)

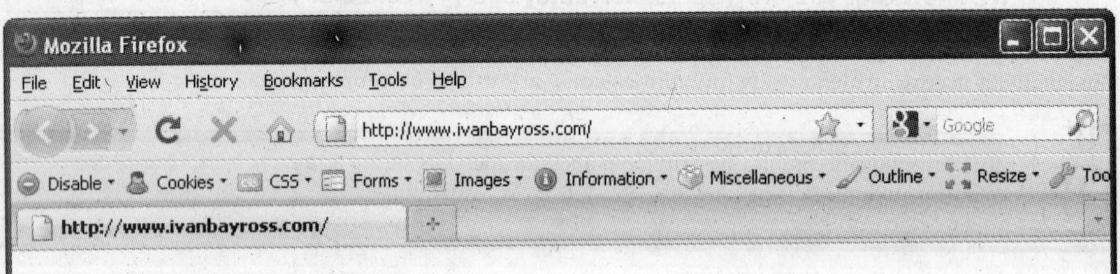

Diagram 17.15

In the above example, there are two variables i.e. **str1** and **str2** holding the value **Hi**. If the **str1** holding the value **Hi** is equal to the value of **str2** then appropriate message is displayed.

Executing Multiple Statements

Example:
When multiple lines of code require execution, when a condition is TRUE, these lines should be enclosed within **curly** brackets. Consider the following code:

```php
<?php
    $month = date("M");

    if ($month == "Oct")
    {
    // Starting the code block
        echo "The month is October<BR />";
        echo "Its Diwali";
    // Ending the code block
    }

    else
    {
    // Starting the code block
        echo "The month is not October<BR />";
        echo "It is " . $month;
    // Ending the code block
    }
?>
```

Output: (As shown in diagram 17.16.1 and diagram 17.16.2)

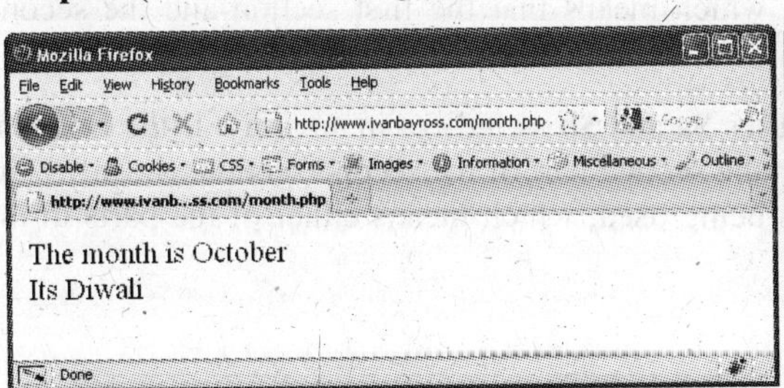

Diagram 17.16.1: Multi-line output when the condition is satisfied

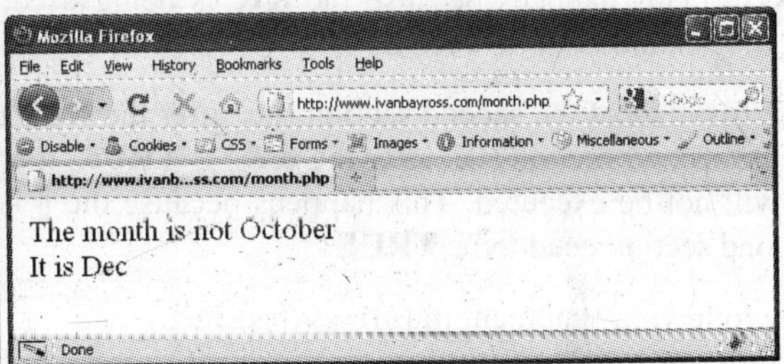

Diagram 17.16.2: Multi-line output when the condition is not satisfied

In the above example, the current month is assigned to the variable **$month**, then a check is made as to whether variable **$month** holds value **Oct** (i.e. whether the current month is October). When the month is October, the **if** statement returns **TRUE**. This allows the code block immediately following the **if** statement to be executed.

If any other month is assigned to **$month**, the **if** statement returns **FALSE**. This causes the code block immediately following the **else** statement to be executed.

However, as multiple statements have to be executed, the **if / else** statements are followed by opening curly braces { (indicating the start of the code block). The statements that should be executed are placed after the opening curly braces. Finally, the closing curly braces } (indicating the end of the code block) are placed.

The pair of curly braces {} after the condition, contains the code block that should be executed when condition returns **TRUE**. Similarly, the pair of curly braces {} after the **else** clause, contains the code block that should be executed when the condition returns **FALSE**.

All kinds of statements can be used between the parenthesis and the curly braces. PHP is a language where almost every statement has a value. A value can be used together with other values to build complex expressions.

Take an assignment for example. The statement **$b** = **$a**, indicates that **$b** now holds the value held by **$a**. This means that this value can be used in another assignment, like this:

```
$c = ($b = $a);
```

The assignment in the parenthesis has the value of **$a**, which is then assigned to **$c**. The parenthesis can actually be dropped and the result will be the same. All three variables have the value of **$a**. This explains the following statement:

```
/* Initializing counters: */
    $i = $j = $k = $l = 0;
```

Using comparison operators any kind of Boolean expression can be constructed. Take for example the following **if** statement:

```
if ($a <= $b && ($array[$a] <= $array[$b] || $array[$a+$b] > $array[$a-$b]))
{
    /* This is a comment, it won't be executed */
}
```

This **if** statement, first tests to see if the value held by variable **$a** is smaller or equal to the value held by variable **$b**. If **TRUE**, the first part of the second section (i.e. after the **&&**) is executed to see if it is also **TRUE**. This happens because the **&&** is being used, which means that the first section and the second section should both be **TRUE**.

The first part of the second section (i.e. after the **&&**) uses **$a** and **$b** as indices in an array. If the first part of the second section (i.e. after the **&&**) is **TRUE**, then the second part of the second section, (i.e. after the ||) will not be executed. This happens because the || is being used, which means either of the parts in the second section need to be **TRUE**.

The following statement illustrates the same:

```
mysql_connect() or die('Could not connect to the MySQL database!');
```

The function **mysql_connect()** tries to connect to a MySQL database engine. This returns **TRUE** if it is able to make a connection. PHP evaluates the line as a Boolean expression. That means it starts by executing **mysql_connect()**. If that returns **TRUE** then PHP skips the next statement because the **or** (||) operator is used. If the first statement fails, the second statement is executed which halts program processing with the user defined error message.

The elseif Clause

The **elseif** construct can be used to conduct a series of conditional checks and only execute the code following the first condition that is met. The last **elseif** could be substituted with an **else** because if **$num** is not negative and not zero, it must be positive.

Consider the following code:

```
<?php
    $m=date("M");
    if ($m=="Jan")
                { print "It is January.";      }
    else    {  if ($m=="Feb")
                { print "It is February.";     }
```

```
    else    {   if ($m=="Mar")
                    {   print "It is March.";         }
    else    {   if ($m=="Apr")
                    {   print "It is April.";         }
    else    {   if ($m=="May")
                    {   print "It is May.";           }
    else    {   if ($m=="Jun")
                    {   print "It is June.";          }
    else    {   if ($m=="Jul")
                    {   print "It is July.";          }
    else    {   if ($m=="Aug")
                    {   print "It is August.";        }
    else    {   if ($m=="Sep")
                    {   print "It is September.";     }
    else    {   if ($m=="Oct")
                    {   print "It is October.";       }
    else    {   if ($m=="Nov")
                    {   print "It is November.";      }
    else            {   print "It is December.";      }
            }   }   }   }   }   }   }   }   }         }
?>
```

The objective of the above code is to identify the current month of the machine serving PHP pages. The technique used is a very crude manner of working with the nested **if** statements.

The code block starts by extracting the month and storing it into the variable **$m**. A check is made if the extracted month is **January**. If the condition returns **TRUE**, a message indicates that the month is **January**. If the condition returns **FALSE**, the code block specified under the **else** clause is executed.

The code block under the **else** clause consist of a nested **if** statement. This **if** statement checks whether the extracted month is **February**. Depending on the value returned by the condition, an appropriate code block is executed (i.e. either a message indicating the month or an **else** clause).

The code block for the inner **else** clause is another set of **if** statements. Thus the level of nested **if** statements increases to check for all possible values for the variable **$m**.

The end result is a code, which is difficult to manage, basically because PHP insists that every code block beginning with an opening curly brace be terminated with a closing curly brace.

Another method for achieving the same functionality is the use of the **elseif** clause. The **elseif** clause allows working with nested if statements in a slightly more intelligent way.

Syntax:

```
if (<Condition>)
    <Code Block To Be Executed If Condition Returns TRUE>;
elseif (<Condition>)
    <Code Block To Be Executed If Second Condition Returns TRUE>;
else
    <Code Block To Be Executed If BOTH Conditions Returns FALSE>;
```

The following code, would replace the above example:

```
<?php
    $m=date("M");
    echo "Hi Everyone<BR />";

    if ($m=="Jan")
    {
        print "It is January.";
    }
    elseif ($m=="Feb")
    {
        print "It is February.";
    }
    elseif ($m=="Mar")
    {
        print "It is March.";
    }
    elseif ($m=="Apr")
    {
        print "It is April.";
    }
    elseif ($m=="May")
    {
        print "It is May.";
    }
    elseif ($m=="Jun")
    {
        print "It is June.";
    }
    elseif ($m=="Jul")
    {
        print "It is July.";
    }
    elseif ($m=="Aug")
    {
        print "It is August.";
    }
    elseif ($m=="Sep")
    {
        print "It is September.";
    }
    elseif ($m=="Oct")
    {
        print "It is October.";
    }
    elseif ($m=="Nov")
    {
        print "It is November.";
    }
    else
```

```
    {
        print "It is December.";
    }
?>
```

Output: (As shown in diagram 17.17)

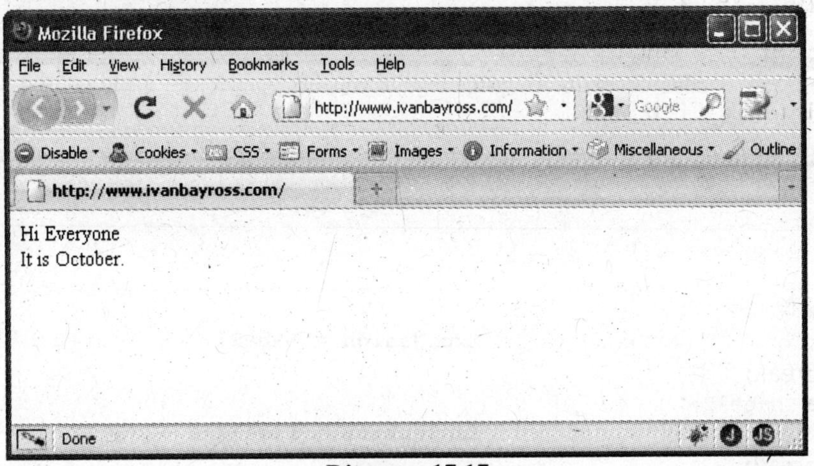

Diagram 17.17

NOTE

The braces could be avoided if only one line of code has to be executed for a condition. Even though there is only the tiniest fraction of a speed difference between using braces and not using braces, it's usually down to a readability issue.

The same effect can be achieved by having lots of **if** statements as shown below:

```
<?php
    $m=date("M");
    if ($m=="Jan")   {   print "It is January.";     }
    if ($m=="Feb")   {   print "It is February.";    }
    if ($m=="Mar")   {   print "It is March.";       }
    if ($m=="Apr")   {   print "It is April.";       }
    if ($m=="May")   {   print "It is May.";         }
    if ($m=="Jun")   {   print "It is June.";        }
    if ($m=="Jul")   {   print "It is July.";        }
    if ($m=="Aug")   {   print "It is August.";      }
    if ($m=="Sep")   {   print "It is September.";   }
    if ($m=="Oct")   {   print "It is October.";     }
    if ($m=="Nov")   {   print "It is November.";    }
    if ($m=="Dec")   {   print "It is December.";    }
?>
```

However, the use of the **elseif** clause is a slightly neater way of working with nested **if** statements. The downside of this system is that the **$m** variable needs to be checked repeatedly.

The switch Statement

The switch statement is usually used to elegantly replace lengthy if / elseif statements. **Switch** statements are used to control program flow by testing a single variable against multiple values.

When the same variable is checked for different possible values, it is advisable to use the **switch** statement, (i.e. if only one of many code blocks have to be selected for execution).

The **switch** statement is given an expression. This expression is then compared to all possible case expressions listed in its body. On a successful match, the code block placed under that particular case expression is executed, after which the code spec terminates because of the explicit **break;** mentioned in each case section.

TIP

The match is done internally using the regular equality operator (==) and not the identical operator (===).

Syntax:

```
switch (<Expression>)
{
    case <Label1>:
        <Code To Be Executed If Expression = Label1>;
        break;
    case <Label2>:
        <Code To Be Executed If Expression = Label2>;
        break;
    default:
        <Code To Be Executed If Expression Is Different From Both Label1
        And Label2>;
}
```

In **Switch** statement, the **case** keyword is a label as it marks a point in the code to do something. Specifically it marks the point in the code to begin executing statements if the value of the expression being evaluated by the switch statement is equal to the value immediately following the case keyword or if the expression following the case keyword evaluates to TRUE. The **colon** marks the end of the label. **The entire label should be on one line.**

Since expressions are allowed in case labels, other conditions can also be tested, such as greater than and less than relationships. When using expressions, the expression used for testing against must be repeated in the case statement.

NOTE

If an expression successfully evaluates to the values specified in more than one case statement, only the first one encountered will be executed. Just after a match is made, PHP stops looking for more matches.

In switch statement the **default** keyword is a catch-all case that marks the point to begin execution of none of the conditions being tested for are met. It is similar to the last else statement in a long elseif code block.

TIP

The **default** keyword should always appear at the end of the switch statement, since it will always be executed if no previous match has been made.

Example:

The following code spec obtains the functionality of the nested **if** statements, by using the **switch** statement:

```
<?php
    $m=date("M");
    switch ($m)
    {
        case "Jan":
            print "It is January.";
            break;
        case "Feb":
            print "It is February.";
            break;
        case "Mar":
            print "It is March.";
            break;
        case "Apr":
            print "It is April.";
            break;
        case "May":
            print "It is May.";
            break;
        case "Jun":
            print "It is June.";
            break;
        case "Jul":
            print "It is July.";
            break;
        case "Aug":
            print "It is August.";
            break;
        case "Sep":
            print "It is September.";
            break;
        case "Oct":
            print "It is October.";
            break;
        case "Nov":
            print "It is November.";
            break;
        case "Dec":
            print "It is December.";
            break;
        default:
            print "None of the months are valid.";
    }
?>
```

Output: (Refer to diagram 17.18)

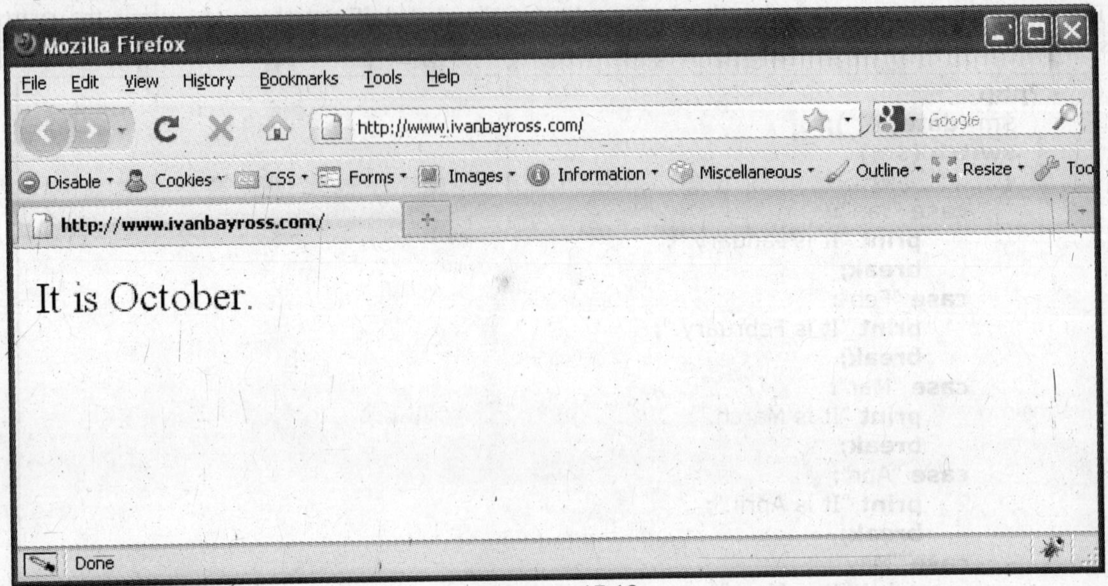

Diagram 17.18

The code block starts by extracting the month and storing it into the variable **$m**. A check is made to identify the value stored in **$m**. When the first case clause is encountered and the value stored in the variable matches the value following the case keyword (in this case 'Nov'), the block of code immediately after the first **case** clause is executed.

If there is no match, the control is directly passed to the next **case** clause. The code block placed between the failed **case** clause and the next are ignored. If all case clauses fail, the code block under the **default** clause gets executed.

Sometimes, it is possible that the argument in a **switch** statement satisfy two of more conditions. In such situations, the **break** keyword is used to restrict PHP from execution of all **case** clauses having their conditions satisfied. When the control comes across the **break** keyword, the remaining code block held within the condition gets ignored and the control is placed on the next statement.

PHP offers an alternative syntax for some of its control structures i.e. **if** and **switch**. In each case, the basic form of the alternate syntax is to change the opening brace to a colon (:) and the closing brace to **endif;** or **endswitch;** respectively.

Example:

```
<?php
    if ($str == "Hello World"):
?>
    str is equal to Hello World
<?php
    endif;
?>
```

In the above example, the HTML block **str is equal to Hello World** is nested within an **if** statement written in the alternative syntax. The HTML block would be displayed only if **$str** is equal to **Hello World**.

The alternative syntax applies to else and elseif as well. The following is an **if** structure with **elseif** and **else** in the alternative format:

```
<?php
    if ($a == 5):
        echo "a equals 5";

    elseif ($a == 6):
        echo "a equals 6";

    else:
        echo "a is neither 5 nor 6";
    endif;
?>
```

ITERATIONS

Some statements are known as iterative statements. These statements have control structures that delimit them and which determine how many times (zero or more) the delimited code is executed, based on some condition.

Iteration (a Loop) in PHP is used to execute the same block of code a pre-specified number of times.

Looping

A loop can be thought of as something that is wrapped around the PHP code spec, to make it happen again and again.

Often when developing an application, to execute the same block of code, a specific number of times, a Loop statement is used in the code spec.

In PHP the following Loop statements are available:

- **for** - loops through a block of code a specified number of times
- **while** - loops through a block of code as long as a specified condition is TRUE
- **do...while** - loops through a block of code **at least once** and then repeats the loop as long as a specified condition is TRUE
- **foreach** - loops through the elements of an array. Works only on arrays. Will throw an error when used with a variable of a different data type **or** an un-initialized variable

The for loop

The **for** loop statement is a repetition statement designed to be used when executing a code block a specific number of times.

The **for** loop is a special kind of loop covering the following tasks:

- Set a counter variable to some initial value
- Check to see if the conditional statement is true
- Execute the code spec held within the loop
- Increment a counter at the end of each iteration through the loop

The **for** loop allows defining these tasks in one simple line of code.

Syntax:

```
for (<Initialization>; <Condition>; <Increment>)
{
    <Code To Be Executed>;
}
```

Where,

- The **initialization** state of the variable to be tested. Normally done as an assignment, although the assigned value can be from any source, literal or variable
- The **condition** to be tested for. The statement keeps processing as long as it remains true
- The **increment** by which the variable being tested changes

Notice how all the above defined tasks of the loop are taken care of in the for loop statement. Each step is separated by a semicolon (;) Initialization, Condition and the Increment. A semicolon is needed because these are separate expressions.

However, notice that a semicolon is not needed after the Increment expression.

In brief, the **for** statement takes **three parameters**. The first is for initializing its variables, the second holds the condition to be checked and the third contains the increment required to implement the loop.

TIP

If more than one variable is included in either the initialization or the increment section, then they should be separated by a comma. The condition must evaluate either to **TRUE** or **FALSE** only.

NOTE

A **for** loop is usually used when the exact number of times a block of code must execute is known in advance.

The for-loop works by first initializing a **control variable**, then performs a conditional test, if the test returns TRUE, the code block is executed. After the code executes, the variable initialized is incremented, the condition is reevaluated and then the main code is executed again. This goes on until the **control variable** holds a value equal to the number of times the loop must run, then the loop exits.

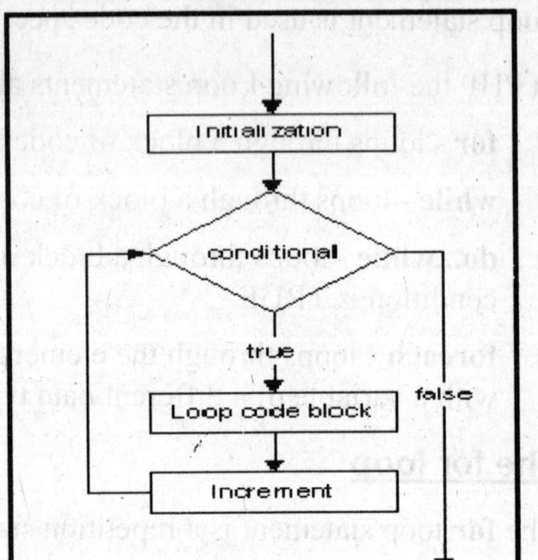

Diagram 17.19

Example:

```
<?php
    for ($ctr = 1; $ctr <= 5; $ctr++)
    {
        echo "The for loop has been executed $ctr time(s)<BR />";
    }
?>
```

Output: (Refer to diagram 17.20)

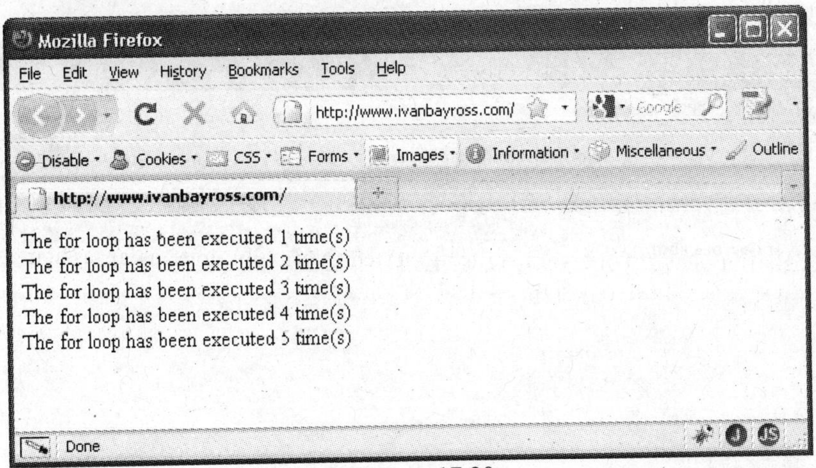

Diagram 17.20

The **for** loop first assigns a starting value **1** to **$ctr**, then it checks to see if **$ctr** is smaller than or equal to **5** and if it is, the **echo** statement is executed. At the end of an iteration (i.e. one pass of the loop) the **$ctr++** statement is executed.

The statement **$ctr++** is shorthand for **$ctr=$ctr+1**, which simply **increments** the variable **$ctr** by **1**. Similarly, **$ctr--** will **decrement** the variable **$ctr** by **1**.

The main code is executed while **$ctr** is less than or equal to **5**, the **for** loop simply prints the numbers from **1** to **5** on a web page.

Example:

```
<?php
    for ($a=1, $b=10; $a<5; $a++, $b+=5)
    {
        $c = $a + $b;
        echo "a: " . $a." . <BR /> b: " . $b." . <BR /> c: " . $c . "<BR /> <BR />";
    }
?>
```

Output: (Refer to diagram 17.21)

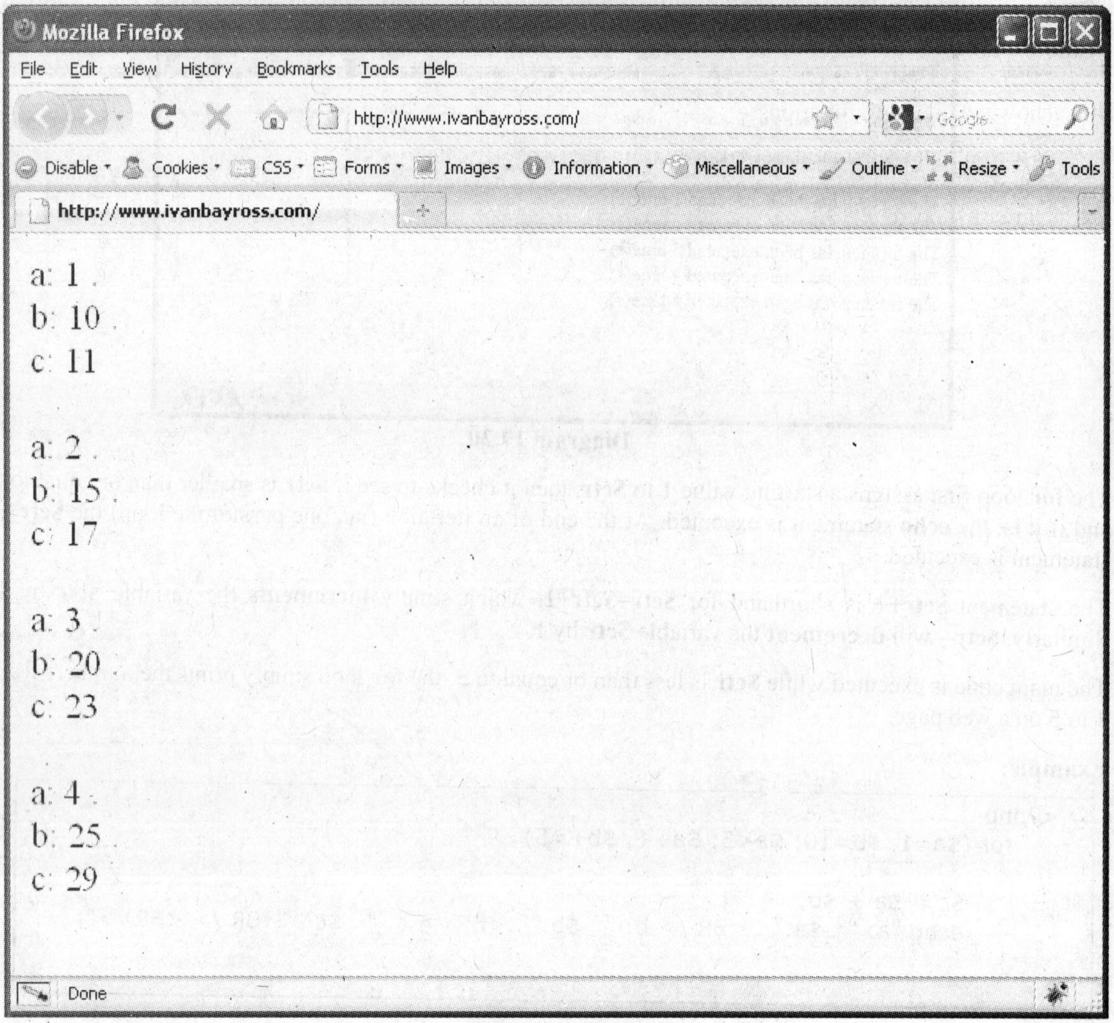

Diagram 17.21

The while loop

The WHILE loop is quite easy to set up and use. A WHILE loop will, as the name suggests, execute a piece of code until a certain condition is met.

The function of a while loop is to do a task over and over as long as the specified conditional statement is true. This logical check (i.e. the condition) is the same as the one that appears in a PHP **if** statement to determine if it is true or false.

Syntax:

```
while (<Some Condition Which Is True>)
{
    <Code To Be Executed>;
}
```

Caution

In the body of a while statement there must be some code that changes the value of the condition. Otherwise the loop will never terminate.

This is how a while loop functions:

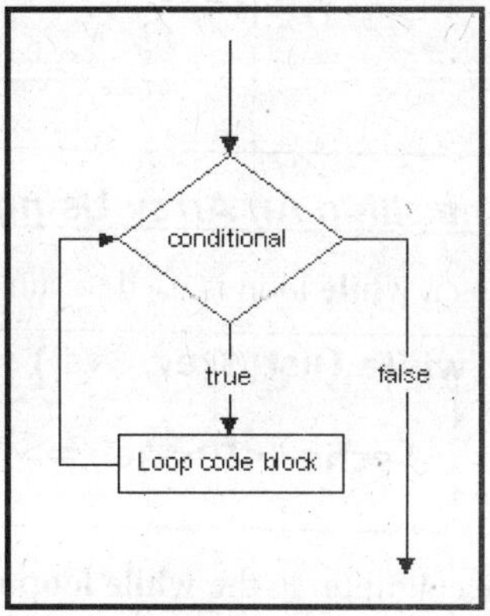

Diagram 17.22

1. The conditional statement specified within the while(...) loop is checked. If the condition is true, then point 2 occurs. If it is false, then point 4 occurs
2. The code spec held within the while() {...} loop is executed
3. The process starts again as defined in point 1
4. If the conditional statement is false, then the code spec held within the while() {...} loop is not executed and there is no more looping that takes place. The code spec (if any) following the while loop is then executed

Example:

The following code, demonstrates a loop that will continue to run as long as the variable **$ctr** is less than **11**. The variable **$ctr** will be incremented by **1** each time the loop runs:

```
<?php
    $ctr=1;
    echo "The multiples of the number 25 upto 10 times are:<BR />";
    while($ctr < 11)
    {
        echo "25 x $ctr  = " . ($ctr*25) . "<BR />";
        $ctr++;
    }
?>
```

Output: (Refer to diagram 17.23)

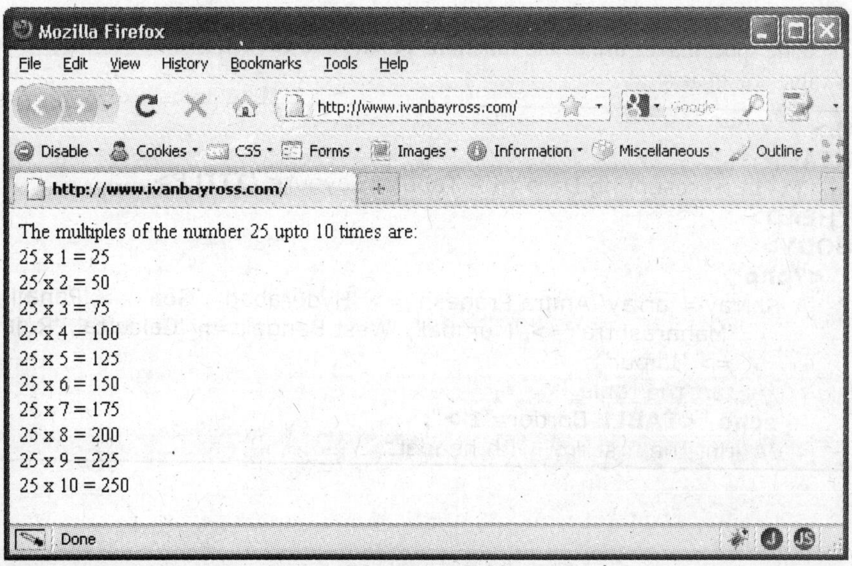

Diagram 17.23

Similarity between the **for** and **while** loops:

for LOOP	while LOOP

for (a; b; c)
{
d;
}
	a;
	while (b)
	{
	d;
	c;
	}

Controlling An Array Using A WHILE Loop

Often a **while** loop is used to run though an array as shown below:

```
while (list($key, $val) = each($array))
{
    echo "<P>$key => $val</P>\n";
}
```

The condition in the **while loop** uses several functions and an assignment. Each time the function **each()** is called, it returns an array with the key and value from **$array**. When there are no elements left in **$array**, **each()** returns false. This is what makes the whole condition false and makes the while loop stop.

The **list()** function can be used on the left side of an assignment to extract values from an array. Use **list()** like this, although it would be much easier to assign the variables one at a time:

```
list($a, $b, $c, $d) = array(1, 2, 3, 4);
// $a == 1, $b == 2, $c == 3, $d == 4
```

So the condition in the while loop prepares **$key** and **$val** for the body of the loop. When all key-value pairs have been examined, the loop terminates because **each()** return false, **while** then becomes the value of the assignment and therefore the value of the condition.

After an array has been run through like this, **each()** will return **false** if used on the same array. Call **reset($array)** to make **each()** start from the beginning again.

Example:
The following code spec, makes use of the functions **reset()** and **each()**, which will build a table that shows the keys and values of an array:

```
<HTML>
    <HEAD>
        <TITLE>Presenting Data In A Tabular Layout</TITLE>
    </HEAD>
    <BODY>
        <?php
            $array = array('Andra Pradesh' => 'Hyderabad', 'Goa' => 'Panaji',
                'Maharashtra' => 'Mumbai', 'West Bengal' => 'Calcutta', 'Rajasthan'
                => 'Jaipur');
            // Start the table
            echo "<TABLE Border='1'>";
            // Print the first row with headers
```

```
            echo "<TR>";
            echo "<TH>Countries</TH>";
            echo "<TH>Capitals</TH>";
            echo "</TR>";
            // Ensures that the each() function begins from the start:
            reset($array);

            while (list($key, $value) = each($array))
            {
                // Printing a single row
                echo "<TR>";
                echo "<TD>$key</TD>";
                echo "<TD>$value</TD>";
                echo "</TR>";
            }
            // Ending the table
            echo "</TABLE>";
        ?>
    </BODY>
</HTML>
```

Output: (Refer to diagram 17.24)

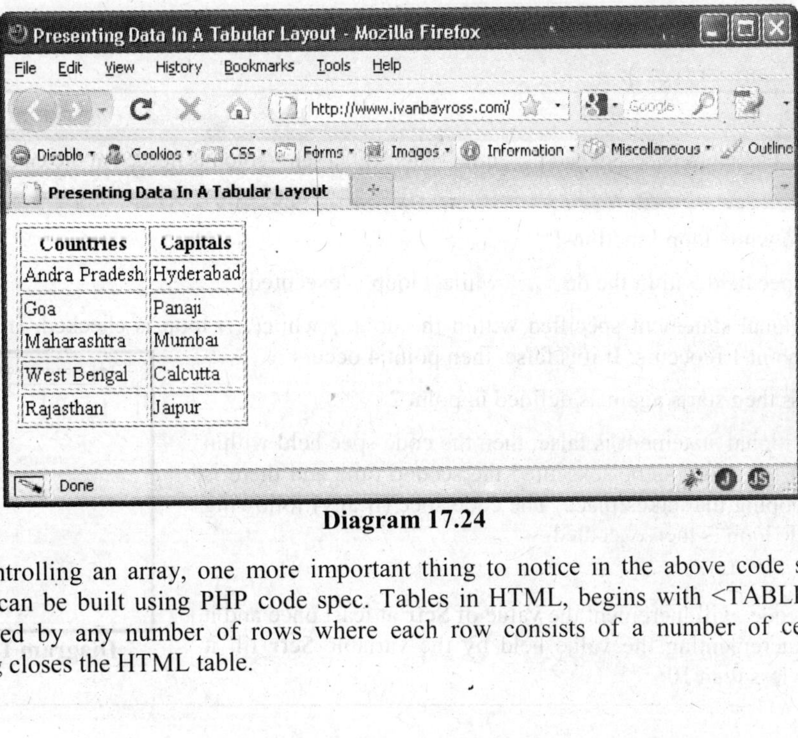

Diagram 17.24

Other than controlling an array, one more important thing to notice in the above code spec is the way HTML tables can be built using PHP code spec. Tables in HTML, begins with <TABLE> opening tag. This is followed by any number of rows where each row consists of a number of cells. Finally the </TABLE> tag closes the HTML table.

The do...while Statement

A do while loop to some extent is a modified version of the while loop.

In case of a while loop, the conditional statement is first checked and if it evaluates to true then the code spec held within the while loop is executed. If the conditional statement is false then the code within the loop is not executed.

On the other hand, the code spec held within the do while loop is executed at least once. This is because the conditional statement is not checked until after the contained code has been executed.

TIP

If the code spec is needed to always run at least once, regardless of the value of its conditional expression use a **do ... while** statement.

A **do ... while** statement is like a **while** statement in **reverse**. First it runs the block of code and then it evaluates the conditional expression. If the conditional expression is true, then it loops back to the beginning of the statement and starts again.

Syntax:

```
do
{
    <Code To Be Executed>;
} while (<Condition>);
```

NOTE

Since the brackets do not end the entire statement, a semi-colon is needed at the end.

This is how a do while loop functions:

1. The code spec held within the do {...} while() loop is executed
2. The conditional statement specified within the do { } while(...) loop is checked. If the condition is true, then point 1 reoccurs. If it is false, then point 4 occurs
3. The process then starts again as defined in point 2
4. If the conditional statement is false, then the code spec held within the while() {...} loop is not executed the second time and there is no more looping that takes place. The code spec (if any) following the do while loop is then executed

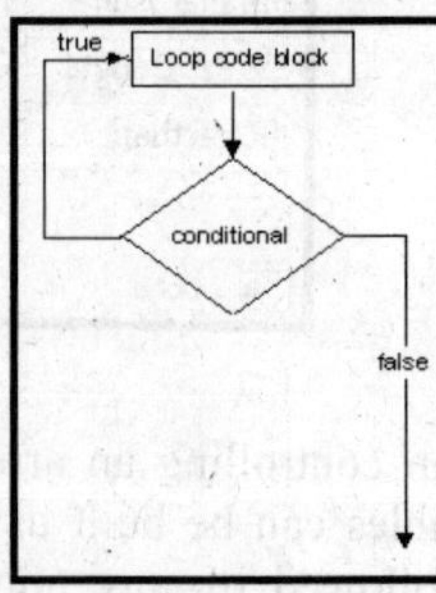

Diagram 17.25

Example:

The following code, will increment the value of **$ctr** at least once and it will continue incrementing the value held by the variable **$ctr** till it reaches a value less than 10:

```
<?php
    $ctr=0;
    echo "The multiples of the number 40 upto 10 times
            are:<BR />";
    do
    {
        $ctr++;
```

```
        echo "40 x $ctr = " . ($ctr*40) . "<BR />";
    } while ($ctr < 10);
?>
```

Output: (Refer to diagram 17.26)

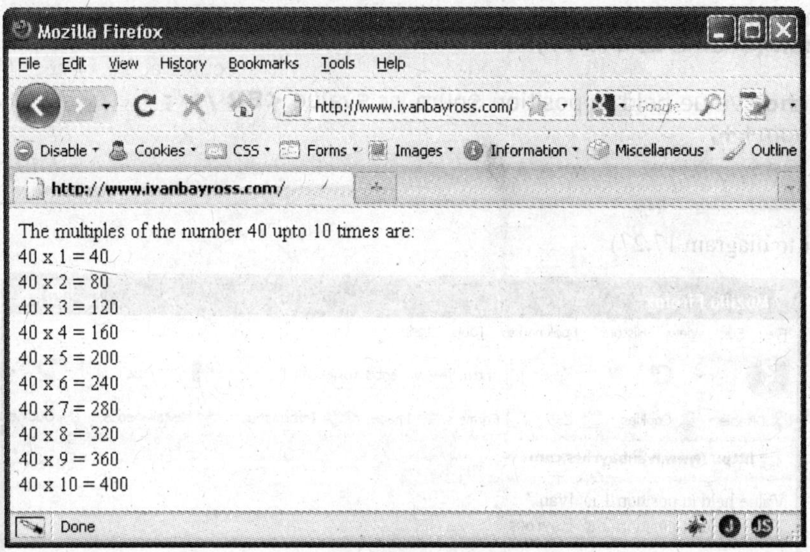

Diagram 17.26

The foreach loop

The **foreach** loop allows iterating over each element of an array. The **foreach** loop provides an easy way to iterate through arrays. The **foreach** works only on arrays and will throw an error when used on a variable with a different data type **or** an un-initialized variable.

The **foreach** loop has two kinds of syntax, one for arrays and one more specifically for associated arrays.

Syntax:

```
foreach (<array_expression> as <$value>)
    <Statement>
```

This loops over the array given by **array_expression**. On each loop, the value of the current element is assigned to **$value** and the internal array pointer is advanced by one.

OR

```
foreach (<array_expression> as $key => $value)
    <Statement>
```

This does the same thing, except that the current element's key will be assigned to the variable **$key** on each pass of the loop.

NOTE

When the **foreach** loop first starts executing, the internal array pointer is automatically **reset** to the first element of the array. This means that **reset()** need not be called before a **foreach** loop.

Example:
The following code spec is an example that demonstrates using value only:

```
<?php
    $name = array('Ivan', 'Bayross');
    $num = 1;
    foreach ($name as $value)
    {
        echo "Value held in position $num is: $value.<BR />";
        $num++;
    }
?>
```

Output: (Refer to diagram 17.27)

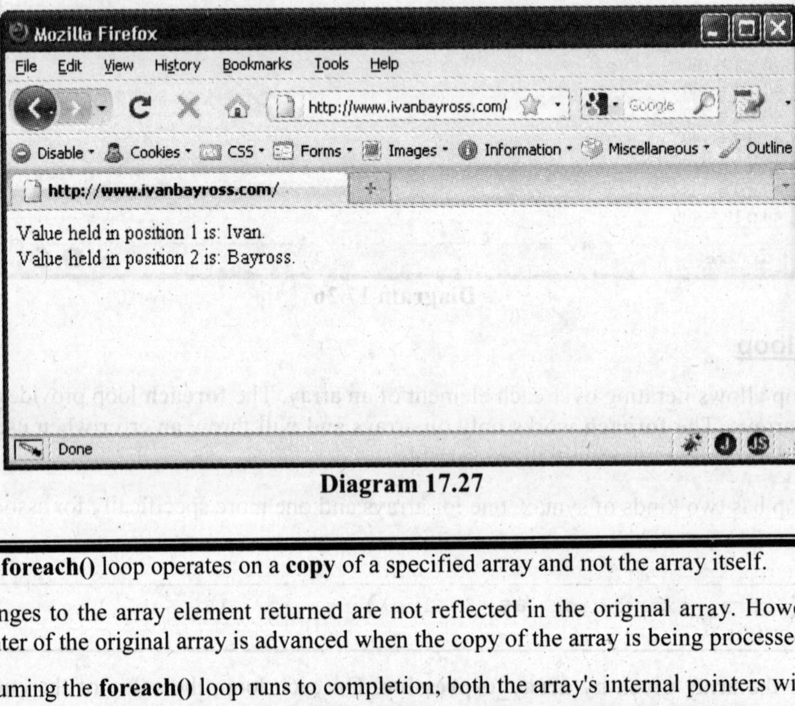

Diagram 17.27

NOTE

The **foreach()** loop operates on a **copy** of a specified array and not the array itself.

Changes to the array element returned are not reflected in the original array. However, the internal pointer of the original array is advanced when the copy of the array is being processed.

Assuming the **foreach()** loop runs to completion, both the array's internal pointers will be at their end.

Example:
The following code spec, is an example that demonstrates using key and value:

```
<?php
    $name = array("First Name" => 'Ivan', "Last Name" => 'Bayross');
    $num = 1;
    foreach ($name as $name => $value)
    {
        echo "The name-value pair on position $num is: \$name[$name] =>
                  $value.<BR />";
        $num++;
    }
?>
```

Output: (Refer to diagram 17.28)

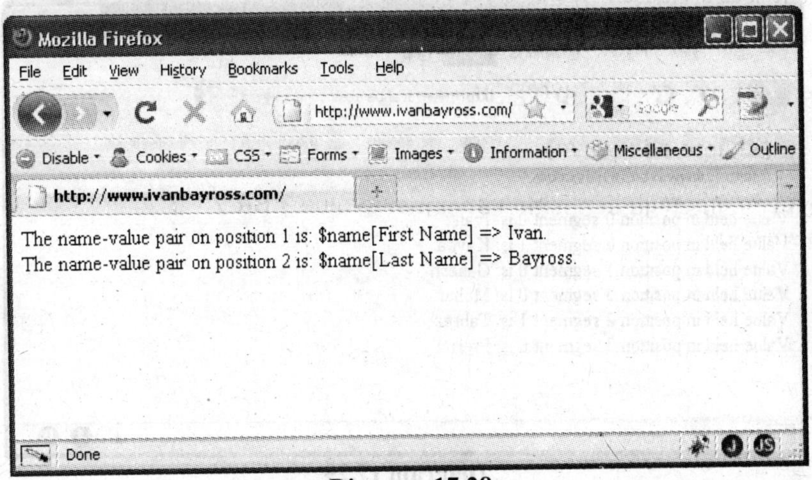

Diagram 17.28

The following code spec, is an example that demonstrates using **foreach()** loop with multi-dimensional arrays:

```
<?php
    $staff [0][0] = "Ivan";
    $staff [0][1] = "Kavita";
    $staff [1][0] = "Ganesh";
    $staff [2][0] = "Meher";
    $staff [2][1] = "Tabrez";
    $staff [3][0] = "Prerna";
    $ctr1 = 0;
    foreach ($staff as $value1)
    {
        $ctr2 = 0;
        foreach ($value1 as $value2)
        {
            echo "Value held in position $ctr1 segment $ctr2 is: $value2<BR />";
            $ctr2++;
        }
        $ctr1++;
    }
?>
```

Output: (Refer to diagram 17.29)

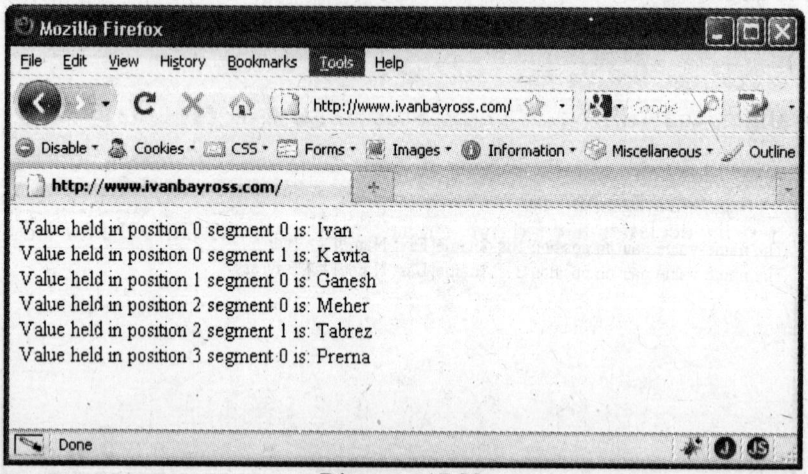

Diagram 17.29

Infinite loops

Loops can be very handy, but also very dangerous. Infinite loops are loops that fail to exit, causing them to execute until power to the computer is stopped. This is caused when no matter what occurs during the loop, the condition will never become false and therefore the loop never exits. Relying on user input to terminate a loop is also possible.

TIP

The most popular way is to break out of the loop and/or exit the script entirely from within the loop whenever a condition is matched up.

Caution

While learning PHP, it is best to steer clear of infinite loops, as they can really cause problems.

Using **Ctrl + C** to terminate PHP operation is restricted to command line execution of the script only.

Example:

```
<?php
    while(1)
    {
        print "In loop!\n";
    }
?>
```

As **1** evaluates to true, the loop will continue forever.

Usually it is preferred to write infinite loops as shown below:

```
<?php
    for (;;)
    {
        print "In loop!\n";
    }
?>
```

In the above example, the declaration, condition and action parts are missing in the **for** loop meaning that it will always loop.

Special Loop Keywords

There are two special keywords that are used with loops and they are **break** and **continue**.

NOTE

The **break** keyword has been used while working with case switching. It is used there to exit a switch/case block and it has the same effect with loops.

break accepts an optional numeric argument which tells it how many nested enclosing structures are to be broken out of.

continue accepts an optional numeric argument which tells it how many levels of enclosing loops it should skip to the end of.

When used inside loops in order to manipulate the loop behavior, **break** causes PHP to exit the loop and **continue** causes PHP to skip the remaining code block in the current loop iteration and go onto the next iteration.

Example:

```
<?php
    for ($i = 0; $i < 12; $i++)
    {
        if ($i == 5)
        {
            echo("Loop continued at $i<BR />");
            continue;
        }
        if ($i == 10)
        {
            echo("Loop terminated at $i<BR />");
            break;
        }
        echo("Number $i<BR />");
    }
?>
```

Output: (Refer to diagram 17.30

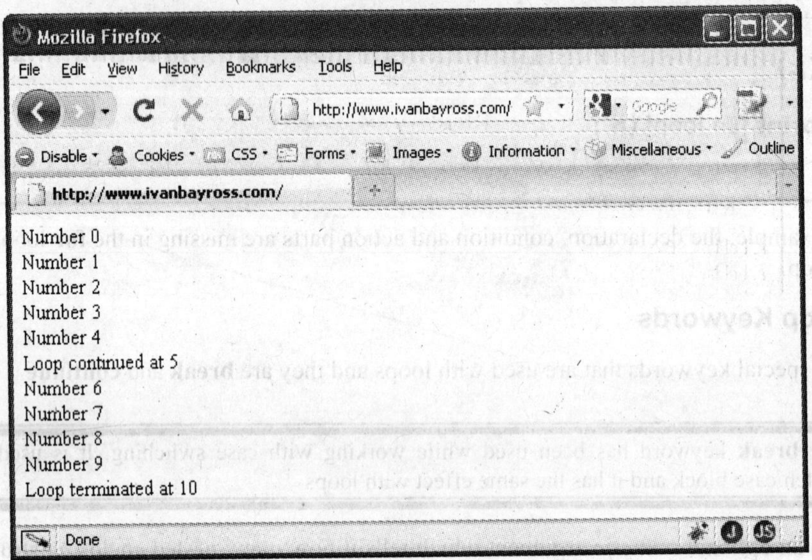

Diagram 17.30

In the above example, a **for** loop iterates through the first four rounds. While in the **fifth** round the first **IF** condition becomes **TRUE** (i.e. **$i** holds **5**). At this moment a message stating Loop continued at 5 is displayed and since **continue** is encountered thereafter, the message that should have appeared as Number 5 is skipped and the loop iterates to the next round. While in the **eighth** round the loop terminates based on the second **IF** condition evaluating to **TRUE** which instructs the loop to exit using the **break** keyword.

Loops Within Loops

Loops can be stacked up by having one loop inside the body of another. These are called nested loops.

Example:

```
<?php
    for ($a = 1; $a < 3; $a++)
    {
        for ($b = 1; $b < 5; $b = $b + 2)
        {
            for ($c = 5; $c > 3; $c--)
            {
                echo ("A holds: $a, B holds: $b, C holds: $c<BR />");
            }
        }
    }
?>
```

Output: (Refer to diagram 17.31)

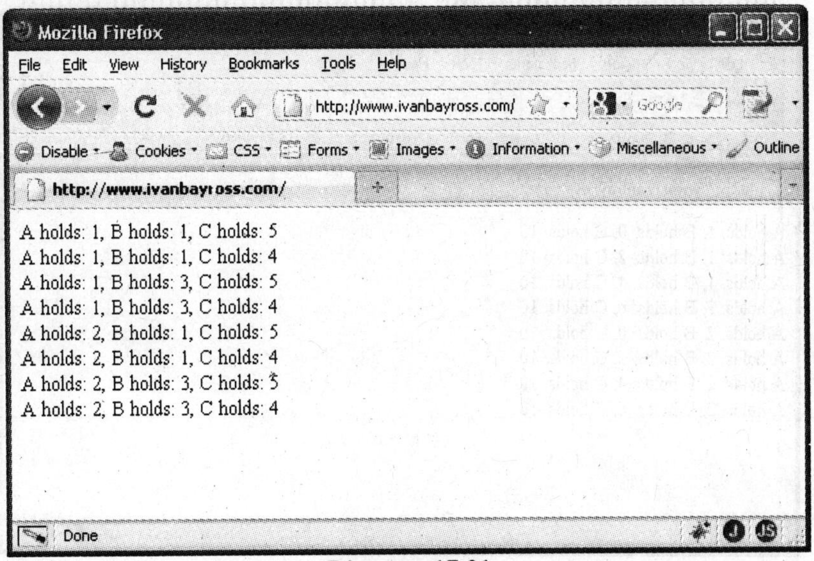

Diagram 17.31

In the above example, the outer loop starts first and completes last. It iterates **twice**.

The middle loop iterates **four** times, but it runs twice, i.e. once for each iteration made by the outer loop.

The inner loop iterates **twice**, but runs eight times, i.e. once for each iteration made by the middle loop.

In this situation, using break is a little more complicated, as it only exits the closest loop.

Example:

```
<?php
    for ($a = 1; $a < 3; $a++)
    {
        for ($b = 0; $b < 7; $b = $b + 2)
        {
            for ($c = 10; $c > 8; $c--)
            {
                echo ("A holds: $a, B holds: $b, C holds: $c<BR />");
                break;
            }
        }
    }
?>
```

Output: (Refer to diagram 17.32)

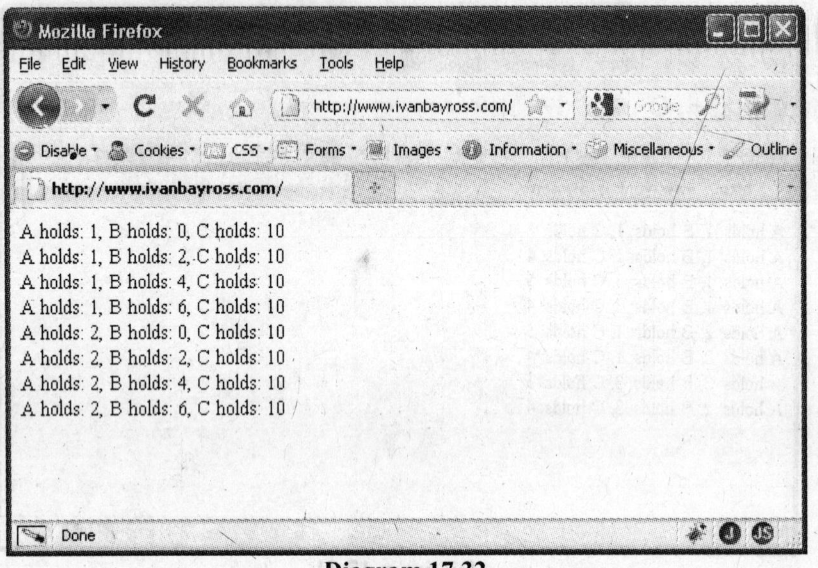

Diagram 17.32

As seen, the inner most loop only loops once because of **break**. However, the other loops execute several times.

More control can be exercised by specifying a number after break, such as **break 2** to break out of two loops or switch/case statements.

Example:

```
<?php
    for ($a = 1; $a < 3; $a++)
    {
        for ($b = 0; $b < 7; $b = $b + 2)
        {
            for ($c = 10; $c > 8; $c--)
            {
                echo ("A holds: $a, B holds: $b, C holds: $c<BR />");
                break 2;
            }
        }
    }
?>
```

Output: (Refer to diagram 17.33)

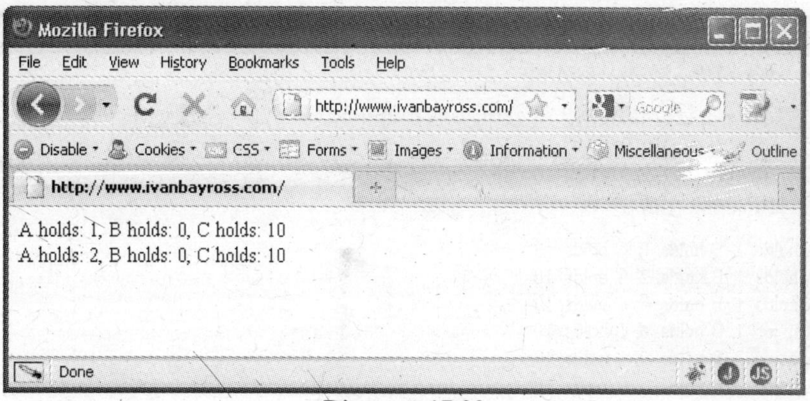

Diagram 17.33

This time the loop only executes twice, because the inner most loop calls **break 2**, which breaks out of the nner most loop and the one above, so only the outer most loop will iterate. Even **break 3** can be used, neaning break out of all three loops and continue normally.

<u>t is important to remember that "break" works both on loops and switch/case statements.</u>

Example:

```
<?php
    for ($a = 1; $a < 3; $a++)
    {
        for ($b = 0; $b < 7; $b = $b + 2)
        {
            for ($c = 10; $c > 8; $c--)
            {
                switch($c)
                {
                    case 10:
                        echo ("A holds: $a, B holds: $b, C holds: $c<BR />");
                        break 2;
                    case 9:
                        echo ("A holds: $a, B holds: $b, C holds: $c<BR />");
                        break 3;
                }
            }
        }
    }
?>
```

Output: (Refer to diagram 17.33)

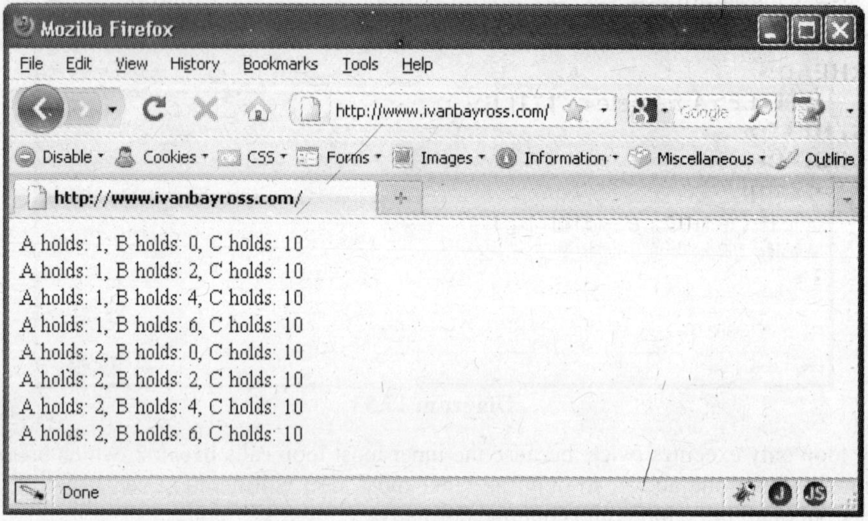

Diagram 17.33

break 2 will break out of the switch/case block and also out of the **$c** loop, whereas **break 3** will break ou of those two and also the **$b** loop. To break out of the loops entirely from within the switch/case statement **break 4** is required.

Mixed-Mode Processing

A key concept in PHP is that the PHP parsing mode can be toggled whenever and as often as wanted and i can even be done from inside a code block. Here is a basic PHP script:

```
<HTML>
    <HEAD>
        <TITLE>A Sample</TITLE>
    </HEAD>
    <BODY>
        <?php
            if ($temp1 == $temp2)
            {
                print "Some PHP Process";
                print "Some PHP Process";
                ...
                print "Some PHP Process";
                print "Some PHP Process";
            }
        ?>
    </BODY>
</HTML>
```

As seen, there are a lot of **print** statements that will only be executed if the variable **$temp1** is the same a variable **$temp2**. The output is encapsulated inside **print** statements. Since PHP allows Mixed Mod Processing, the PHP code block can be terminated using **?>** whilst keeping the **if** statement code block ope (This means that the if statement's closing braces } is still open).

Consider the sample shown below:

```
<HTML>
    <HEAD>
        <TITLE>A Sample</TITLE>
    </HEAD>
    <BODY>
        <?php
            if ($temp1 == $temp2)
            {
        ?>
        Some PHP Process
        Some PHP Process
        ...
        Some PHP Process
        Some PHP Process
        <?php
            }
        ?>
    </BODY>
</HTML>
```

The **Some PHP Process** lines are only sent to output if **$temp1** is equal to **$temp2**, but the PHP mode is terminated using ?> to print it out.

The PHP mode is then reentered to close the **if** statement and continue.

```
<?php
    }
?>
```

This makes the whole script easier to read.

HANDS ON EXERCISES

1. Create and display Names of Fruit (using an array). Refer to diagram 17.34

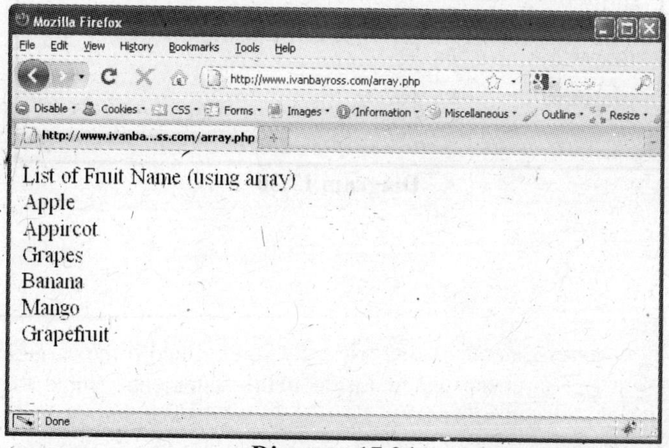

Diagram 17.34

2. Display current date, month, year and day of the week of the machine.

3. Display current day of week(using **ifelse()** condition) as shown in the diagram as shown in diagram 17.35

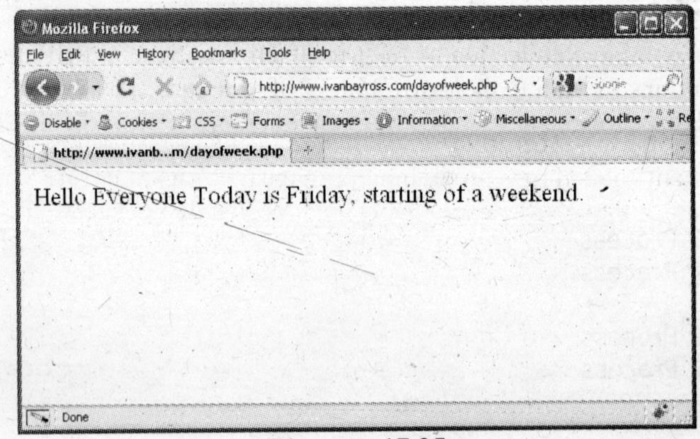

Diagram 17.35

4. Display Fruits Name and their prices in a Tabular Layout (using **key and value pairs)** as shown in the diagram 17.36

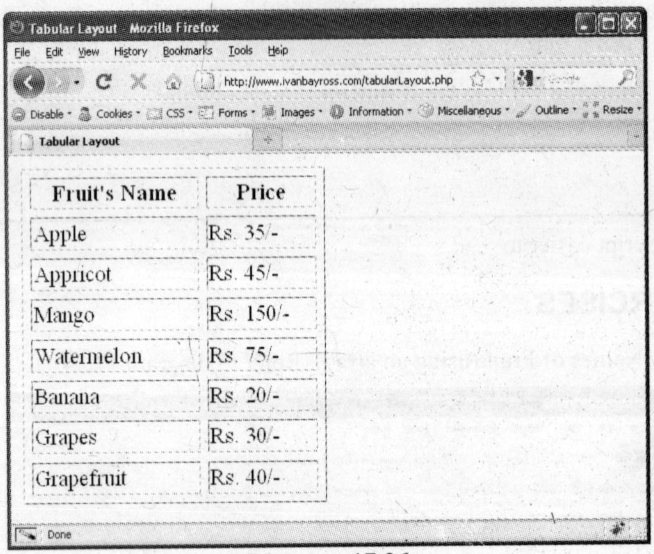

Diagram 17.36

18. FUNCTIONS

PHP draws its power from a large collection of built-in functions. Several PHP developers have extended the PHP core set of functions by adding their own library of functions, usually available for free download or very modestly priced.

Functions are an important tool in any programming language. Functions are code snippets that accept values and produce results, although there are some functions that do not need to be supplied with values to produce a result. Functions are used in situations where the same code snippet is repeated across scripts or even in the same script. The block of code held by the function is not immediately executed, but is called by a script as and when it must be executed.

Functions can either be built-in or user-defined. PHP has several built-in functions. A common one being the **print()** function. In the examples demonstrated earlier, the **print()** function was extensively used to output strings to a Web-browser.

Example:

```
print("Ivan Bayross stays in Mumbai");
```

The values passed to a function prior its code execution are called **arguments**. When arguments are passed to functions they reside in the function's pre-created **parameters**. In general, the arguments passed to a function are included within its parentheses.

For some of PHP's built in functions, the programmer can choose to use **or** ignore the parentheses while passing it as an argument. The **print()** function is one such function.

```
print "Ivan Bayross stays in Mumbai";
```

works just as well as:

```
print("Ivan Bayross stays in Mumbai");
```

A primary advantage of user-defined functions is code reusability. If functions were avoided in an application, the same code snippet would have numerous repetitions, irrespective of whether it is being called within a single **or** in multiple PHP file(s).

USER-DEFINED FUNCTIONS

Writing user-defined functions is as simple as using the function command as:

```
function myFunction()
{
    // Some PHP Code spec
}
```

While creating a function, a **unique** function name follows the **function** keyword (in this case **myFunction**). A pair of opening and closing parentheses follows the function name. If arguments were to be accepted, the variables acting as the function's parameter holders must be mentioned within the parentheses. The actual function code, called the function's **signature**, which follows is enclosed within curly braces.

A basic user defined function example will look like:

```
function Hi()
{
    print("Hi Ivan Bayross! How are you doing today.<BR />");
}
```

The above function simply prints the text **Hi Ivan Bayross! How are you doing today.** in a Browser. It can be called just like a regular PHP function from within any HTML page:

```
<HTML>
    <BODY>
        <?php
        /* Defining the function Hi */
            function Hi()
            {
                print("Hi Ivan Bayross! How are you doing today.<BR />");
            }
        /* Calling the function defined above */
            Hi();
        ?>
    </BODY>
</HTML>
```

Save the above code snippet and run the file using a Web Browser to get the output as shown in diagram 18.1.

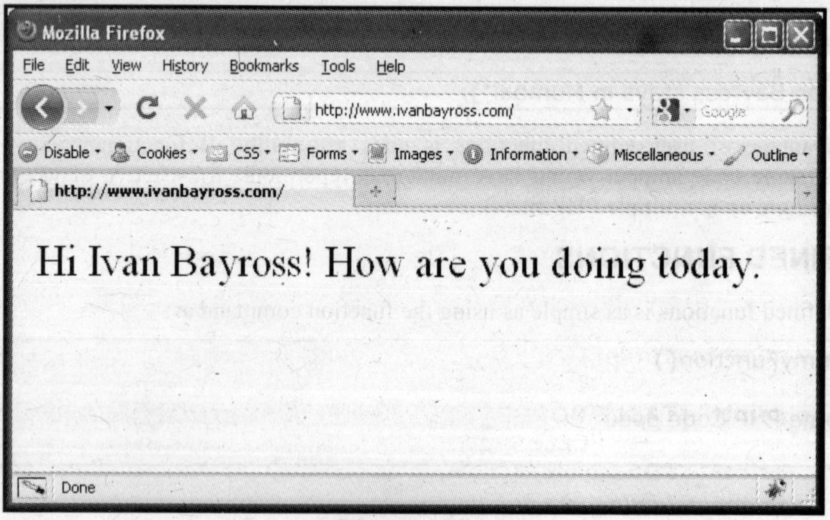

Diagram 18.1

Functions With Arguments

The following example illustrates a function that has a variable to capture an argument passed to it when it is invoked and returns data by its assignment to another variable. For instance, the function **myTable()** creates a single row of data in a table and the data which is passed to it when invoked (i.e. its argument) is displayed in the table cell:

```
function myTable($text)
{
    print("<TABLE BORDER=0 CELLPADDING=0 CELLSPACING=0><TR>");
    print("<TD>$text</TD>");
    print("</TR></TABLE>");
}
```

In this case, the function can be invoked as:

```
myTable("Ivan Bayross stays in Mumbai");
```

Functions With Multiple Arguments

Different functions would require different arguments. Functions can also take multiple arguments. Each argument will be separated from the other by a **comma**. Functions can also be executed without any arguments, in which case only the parenthesis is required after the function name. It all depends on the function and what it does.

Example:

The function **myTable()**, defined earlier, can be extended to allow the user to change the Border, CellPadding and CellSpacing values as:

```
function myTable($text, $border="0", $cellpadding ="0" , $cellspacing="0")
{
    print("<TABLE BORDER=$border CELLPADDING=$cellpadding
                CELLSPACING=$cellspacing><TR>");
    print("<TD>$text</TD>");
    print("</TR></TABLE>");
}
```

The **myTable()** function would then be called as:

```
<HTML>
    <BODY>
        <?php
        /* Defining the function, which will create a single row single column table and
populate it */
            function myTable($text, $border="0", $cellpadding="0", $cellspacing ="0")
            {
                print("<TABLE BORDER=$border CELLPADDING=$cellpadding
                        CELLSPACING=$cellspacing ><TR>");
                print("<TD>$text</TD>");
                print("</TR></TABLE>");
            }
        /* Calling the myTable() function defined above */
            myTable("Ivan Bayross is a Professor", 0, 1, 1);
```

```
    ?>
  </BODY>
</HTML>
```

Save the above code snippet and run the file using a Web Browser to get an output as shown in diagram 18.2.

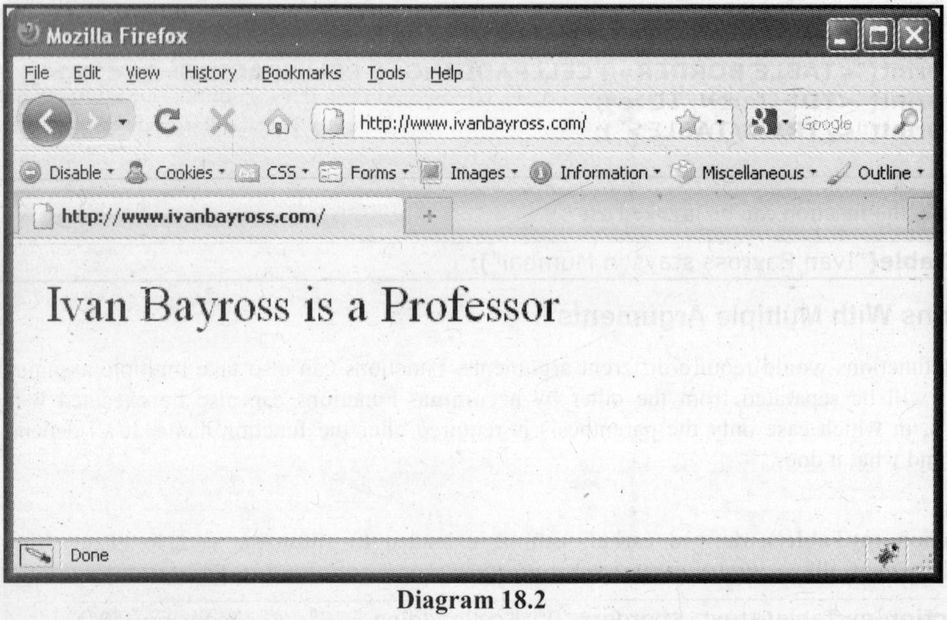

Diagram 18.2

In the above example, **myTable()** assigns **$border**, **$cellpadding** and **$cellspacing** a default value of **0** so that if **no values are passed** to the function when invoked, the default values will be considered. In the above call to **myTable()**, a string **Ivan Bayross is a Professor** is passed as the text to be displayed in the table along with a **Border** of **0** and a **CellPadding** and **CellSpacing** of **1**.

Example:

Functions can be used to return data as well as to receive it. A function can calculate **car mileage** based on the number of kilometers run **and** the litres of fuel consumed. This will require these two values passed as arguments when the function is called. The result of the calculation can be assigned to a variable as:

```
$mileage = calculate_mileage($kms, $litres);
```

The above code spec calls the function **calculate_mileage()** with two parameters. These parameters must be loaded with appropriate values (as arguments) when the function is called that can be stored. After performing the calculation, **calculate_mileage()** will return the result in a variable **$mileage**.

The above function called **calculate_mileage(**$kms, $litres**)** must receive the two numbers as its arguments. It will then return the result as output after processing them. Write the function as:

```
function calculate_mileage($kms, $litres)
{
    $result = $kms/$litres;
    return($result);
}
```

Use the function **calculate_mileage()** in the code spec as:

```
$mileage = calculate_mileage(300, 30);
```

Only a single **value** can be returned from a function. This is done by using the **return** statement. Any variable can be returned, as long as it is just one variable. The variable returned can be an integer, a string, a database connection and so on. The **return** keyword loads the function's return variable with a value to be returned, then exits the function immediately. Only **return();** can also be used which means exit without sending a value back.

In this case, the value of **$mileage** will be **10**. The function divides the number of kilometers by the litres of fuel consumed received as input, assigns that value to **$result**. The **return** command returns the value of **$result** to the caller of the function.

Example:
The following example of function accepts one argument i.e. **$num** and returns its square. After defining the function, the function is called:

```
<?php
    function square($num)
    {
        return ($num * $num);
    }
    print 'The square of 40 is ' . square(40);
?>
```

Output: (Refer to diagram 18.3)

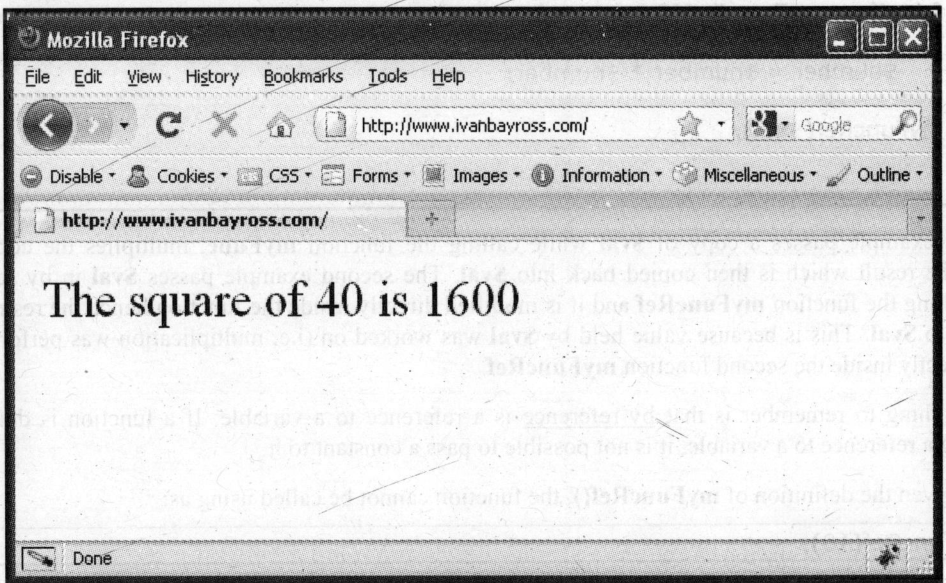

Diagram 18.3

Functions Accepting And Returning Values By Reference

Values can also be returned by their reference via a function. Functions can accept parameters by reference and also return values by reference. This is done with the reference operator **&**.

Marking a variable as **passed by reference** is done within the function definition, not in the function call as:

```
function cal(&$num1, &$num2)
{
}
```

is correct

where as

```
$mynum = cal(&5, &10);
```

is wrong.

This means that if there is a function being used frequently across the project edit the function definition to make it accept variables by reference. Passing by reference is often a good way to make scripts shorter and easier to read. However a script's performance **can deteriorate** by doing this.

Consider the following code:

```
<?php
    ...
    function myFunc($number)
    {
        return ($number * $number);
    }
    $val = myFunc($val);
    ...
    function myFuncRef(&$number)
    {
        $number = $number * $number;
    }
    myFuncRef($val);
    ...
?>
```

The first example passes a copy of **$val** while calling the function **myFunc**, multiplies the copy, then returns the result which is then copied back into **$val**. The second example passes **$val** in by reference while calling the function **myFuncRef** and it is modified directly inside the function hence the result is not returned to **$val**. This is because value held by **$val** was worked on (i.e. multiplication was performed on **$val**) directly inside the second function **myFuncRef**.

One key thing to remember is that by reference is a reference to a variable. If a function is defined as accepting a reference to a variable, it is not possible to pass a constant to it.

That is, given the definition of **myFuncRef()**, the function cannot be called using as:

```
myFuncRef(10);
```

as **10** is not a variable, so it cannot be treated as a reference.

Another thing about user defined functions and by reference is how to **return** a function's value by reference. To specify a function that returns a value by reference, place the ampersand **&** (i.e. reference operator) before the function name and specify that the result of the function is to be returned by a reference to it, as opposed to using a copy of the value.

This means that a copy to the variable is not returned, but the physical address of the variable is returned instead, which enables changing it from within the calling scope.

```
...
function &myRefFunc($number)
{
    return $number * $number;
}
$val =& myRefFunc(10);
...
```

To return a variable by-reference, define the function as such by placing an **&** sign in front of the function's name and in the caller's code. Assign the return value by reference to **$value1**:

```
<?php
    function &GlobalVariable($str)
    {
        return $GLOBALS[$str];
    }
    $number = 30;
    $value1 =&GlobalVariable("number");
    print $value1 . "<BR />";
    $value1 = 40;
    print $number. "<BR />";
    $value1 = $value1 + 35;
    print $number;
?>
```

Output: (Refer to diagram 18.4)

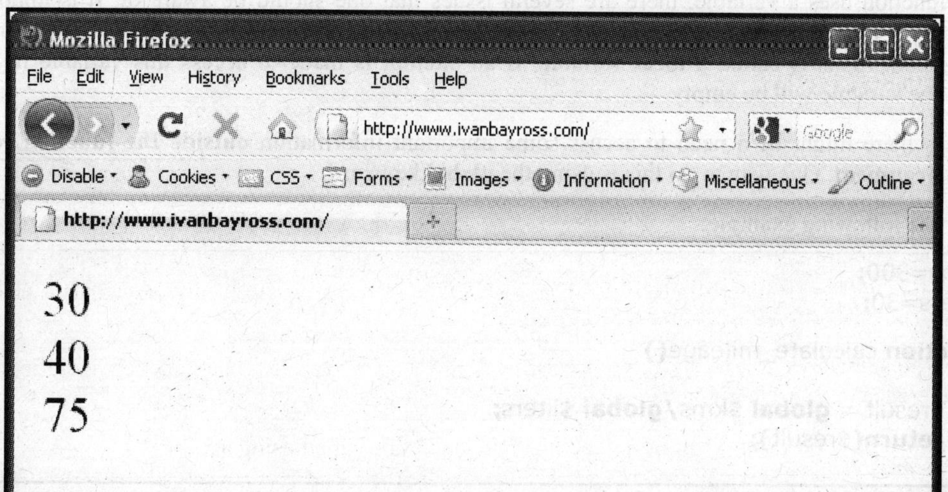

Diagram 18.4

$number was successfully modified by modifying **$value1** because it is a reference to the global variable **$number**. It is not recommended to use this kind of method for returning values by reference. But if it is used, it should be used with precaution, because if assigning by reference is overlooked, the by-reference returned value would lead to bugs that are really difficult to track down.

Functions Accepting And Returning Values By Value

From the previous example it can be seen that the **return** statement is used to return values from functions. The return statement returns values by value, which means that a copy of the value is created and is returned to the caller of the function.

Example:

```
<?php
    function GlobalValue($name)
    {
        return $GLOBALS[$name];
    }
    $number = 150;
    $value1 = GlobalValue("num");
    print $value1;
?>
```

This code prints the number **150**. However, making changes to **$value1** before the print statement only affects **$value1** and not the global variable **$number**. This is because its value was returned by the **GlobalValue()** by value and **not by reference**.

Accessing Global Variables Within A Function

When a function uses a variable, there are several issues that one should be aware of. It is important to know that if a variable is declared inside a function, that variable will only be available to the rest of that function's code. This is called a **local** variable. If an attempt is made to access this variable in another function, the variable will be empty.

Sometimes there might be a need to access some important information **outside the function without using an argument**. One way to do this is using the **global** keyword.

Consider the following example:

```
$kms=300;
$liters=30;

function calculate_mileage()
{
    $result = global $kms/global $liters;
    return($result);
}
```

The previous script is expanded here. The above function definition uses **global** to inform the function that the **$kms** and **$liters** variable has been declared outside it. If the **global** statement is not applied, the function will have returned to **zero**, because **$kms** and **$liters** would have been **NULL**.

The function would simply not know the value of these variables if it is not informed that these variables are assigned outside the function.

Be very careful while using a global statement, because if these values (held by the variables used with global statement) are modified within a function, the original values will be modified as **PHP uses the variable itself and not a copy** when used with global statement.

Globalizing Functions

For small applications, such as a one-page site, functions can be placed at the top of the PHP file i.e. before the rest of the code spec. For larger applications and multi-page sites, it might be prudent to consider putting all the functions in a special file. These functions can then be made available to the code spec using the PHP built-in **include()** in each of the Web pages that require those functions.

This technique gives functions portability thereby reducing the size of the web application. It also helps program execution and code reuse by consolidating all the **functions** in one file.

Consider the following file named, functions.php, which holds the following code spec:

```
<?php
    /*
        Date      :- 05th October 2009
        Author    :- Ivan Bayross
        Filename :- functions.php
        Purpose  :- Holds all the common functions used across the application.
    */
    // Defining the function, which will calculate mileage.
    function calculate_mileage($kms, $liters)
    {
        $result = $kms/$liters;
        return($result);
    }
//Defining the function, which will create a single row single column table and populate it.
    function myTable($text, $border="0", $cellp="0", $cells="0")
    {
        print("<TABLE BORDER=$border CELLPADDING=$cellp
                    CELLSPACING=$cells><TR>");
        print("<TD>$text</TD>");
        print("</TR></TABLE>");
    }
?>
```

The following file named helpPage.php will include the function.php file as:

```
<?
/*
        Date      :- 05th October 2009
        Author   :- Ivan Bayross Shah
        Filename :- helpPage.php
        Purpose  :- Displays Help information. Control is shifted to this page when the user
                    selects HELP
*/
/* A variable named $author is defined to store the name of the user who designed/coded
the page. */
```

```
        $author = "Ivan Bayross";
/* A variable named $helppage is defined to store the name of the HTML page that will serve
help on demand. */
        $helppage ="help_page.html";
/* The functions.php file is included to make available the functions defined. */
        include "../includes/functions.php";
        ...
    ?>
```

Some PHP applications use filenames such as **functions.inc**, which omits the .php extension. This kind of extension will make the file vulnerable. The .php extension is used to keep the **code spec private**. If visitors load the **functions.php** file directly, nothing will be rendered on screen however, if they load a file called **functions.inc**, the entire source code is rendered, which could give out sensitive information such as path locations, passwords, database information and so on.

Functions In Files

In PHP it is also possible to use an **entire file** as a function. This makes it possible to save functions in different files and then use them in different scripts. This helps expand the concept of **code-reuse**. This can be done using a pre-defined PHP function **include()**. This function can use a value returned from an external file, instead of calling a function declared in the same file.

The following is a file days.php, which is used within the file script.php. The days.php file includes the following code spec:

```
    <?php
        return (time() - mktime(0, 0, 0, 1, 21, 2595))/96400;
    ?>
```

The script.php file uses it as:

```
    <?php
        $days = include('days.php');
        echo "Value returned by days.php: $days\n";
    ?>
```

Output: (Refer to diagram 18.5)

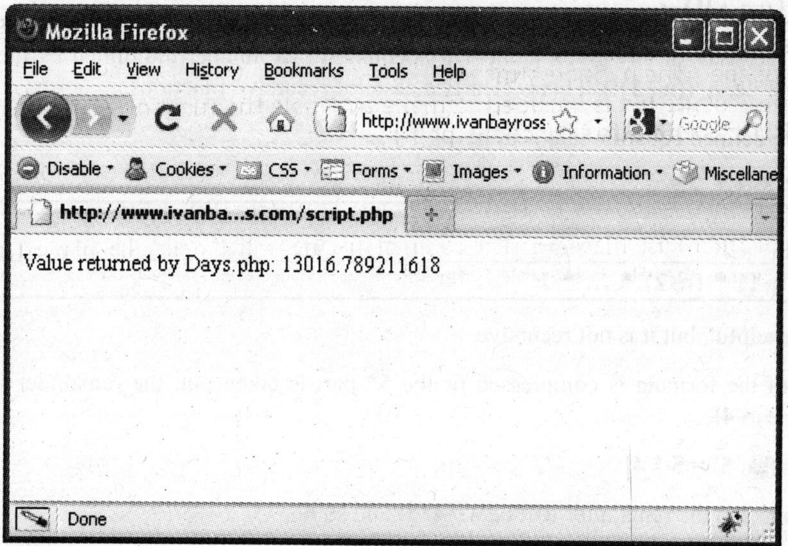

Diagram 18.5

This will work just like any other code spec, except that code has been re-used from source based in an external file.

Recursion

A recursive function is one that calls an instance of the same function from within itself. There are times when this type of recursion can overcome problems and handle scenarios that would otherwise be impossible.

Calculating factorials is a commonly cited example.

The factorial of 7 = 7 * 6 * 5 * 4 * 3 * 2 * 1 or 5040 and is usually represented as 7!.

The basic calculation:
Factorial 7 (7!) = 7 * 6 * 5 * 4 * 3 * 2 * 1
Therefore,
Factorial 7 (7!) = 5040

Answer these:
What is factorial 8
How does it relate to 7!

Solution:
Factorial 8 (8!) = 8 * 7!
This means that once the factorial of 7 is calculated, it is simply a matter of multiplying the result by 8 to get 8!

This further means:
Factorial 8 (8!) = 8 * 5040(- This is 7!)
Therefore,
Factorial 8 (8!) = 40320

The equation to calculate factorial can be represented as:

```
n! = n * ((n - 1)!)
```

This means the factorial for any given number **n** is equal to that number multiplied by the factorial of the number one lower i.e. **n*((n - 1)!)**. This is clearly a case for recursive functions.

Putting the above defined equation into action:

```
5! = 5 * 4 * 3 * 2 * 1
```

OR

```
n! = n * (n-1) * (n-2) * ... * 1
```

This equation is helpful, but it is not recursive.

If the last part of the formula is compressed or the **5*** part is taken out, the remainder will be **4*3*2*1** which is the same as **4!**.

This thus means that **5! = 5 * 4!**

Again do the same and the remainder will be **4!=4*3!** and so on.

One interesting thing is that of **0!=1**. **0!=1** will become an **exit** condition in the equation later.

The above defined scenario indicates the need of a function that will accept an integer and if that integer is not 0 or 1, will call the function again by passing in the same number it accepted minus 1 as a function argument, then multiply that result by itself.

Example:

```
<?php
    function factorial( $n )
    {
        if ($n == 0 || $n == 1)
        {
            // $n == 0 or $n == 1 is the exit conditions
            return 1;
        }
        else
        {
            // Next line contains recursive call
            return ($n * factorial($n-1));
        }
    }
    echo factorial(6);
?>
```

Output: (Refer to diagram 18.6)

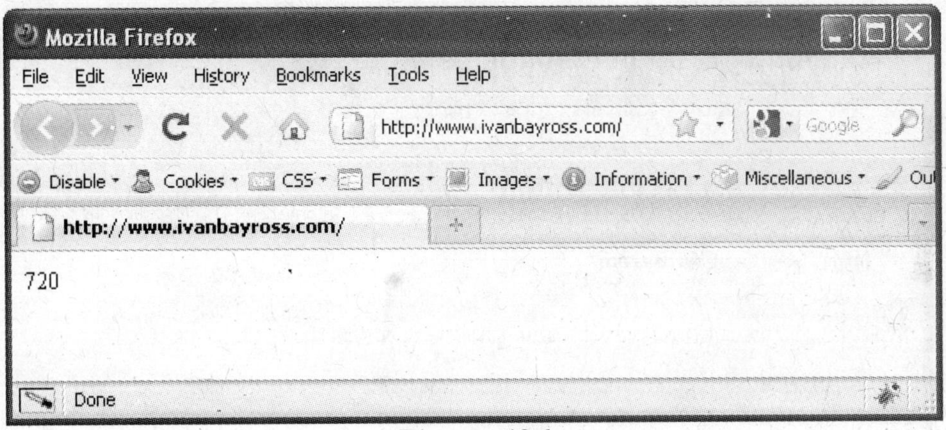

Diagram 18.6

In the above example, two conditions are defined:

- If **n = 1** or **n = 0**, then the function will return **1**
- If **n > 1**, then the function will return **n*(n-1)!**

A recursive factorial function calculates and produces the same value as an iterative function can. Recursive functions are often regarded as more elegant than alternative implementations and they are usually shorter and simpler. For example, above function coded without recursion would be as follows:

Example:

```
<?php
    function factorial( $n )
    {
        $temp_result = 1;
        if ($n == 0 || $n== 1)
        {
            // $n == 0 or $n == 1 is the exit condition
            return 1;
        }
        else
        {
            // Next line contains non-recursive solution
            for($i = 1; $i <= $n; $i++)
                $temp_result *= $i;
            return $temp_result;
        }
    }
    echo factorial(6);
?>
```

Output: (Refer to diagram 18.7)

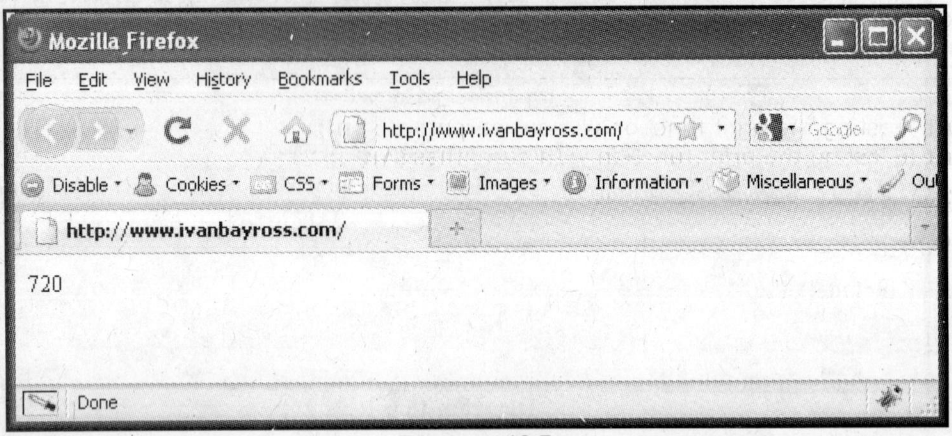

Diagram 18.7

Anonymous Functions

PHP also allows generating of anonymous functions, called **lambda** functions. These functions **do not have names**. They are assigned directly to variables and called by the variable name. This allows the creation of transient functions without worrying about having to give them a new function name, each time they are created.

Use **create_function()** to create an anonymous function. It takes two strings as arguments. One represents the parameter list of the function, exactly as it would appear between the parentheses in a normal function definition. The other is a string, which contains the actual body of the function. This technique is best used with short functions.

Example:

```
$Multiply = create_function('$a, $b', 'return $a*$b;');
$Result = $Multiply($x, $y);
```

Anonymous functions **do have names**, but they are **randomly** generated strings, which minimizes the chance of the **create_function()** accidentally producing two functions with the same name.

The ability to create anonymous functions exists in PHP primarily for interacting with functions that expect other functions as their arguments. It makes coding easier. Most such functions are very contextual and tend to require variations, if not within the execution of the same script, then certainly between executions.

BUILT-IN FUNCTIONS

One of the things that make PHP so easy to use is the wealth of built-in functions. These functions act as tools to simplify and speed up many of the everyday tasks required during the creation of a full-fledged application.

There are built in PHP functions for working with just about everything an application requires such as strings, arrays, databases, dates and times, email ID's, numbers, even functions for working with other functions and so on. It is impossible to cover all of built in PHP functions in this material hence a few of the important functions will be introduced and elaborated on.

print()

The function **print()** basically accepts a string as an argument and outputs this to a Browser. It works with or without parentheses as shown below:

```
...
print "Testing the print function without parenthesis\n";
print ("Testing the print function with parenthesis\n");
...
```

include()

The function **include()** allows embedding one file inside another.

To understand how it works, first create a text file and write some text in it as:

```
This is testing the use of Include() function created by Ivan Bayross.
```

Next, create a PHP file and place the following code spec in it:

```
<?php
    include "textInclude.txt";
?>
```

NOTE

Just as in the **print()** function, the parentheses for the **include()** function are optional.

CAUTION

Make sure both files are saved to the same directory on the web server.

When **testInclude.php** is run, the text placed in **textInclude.txt** will be sent to the browser that invoked it. In the same manner html **or** php files can be included.

Output: (Refer to diagram 18.8)

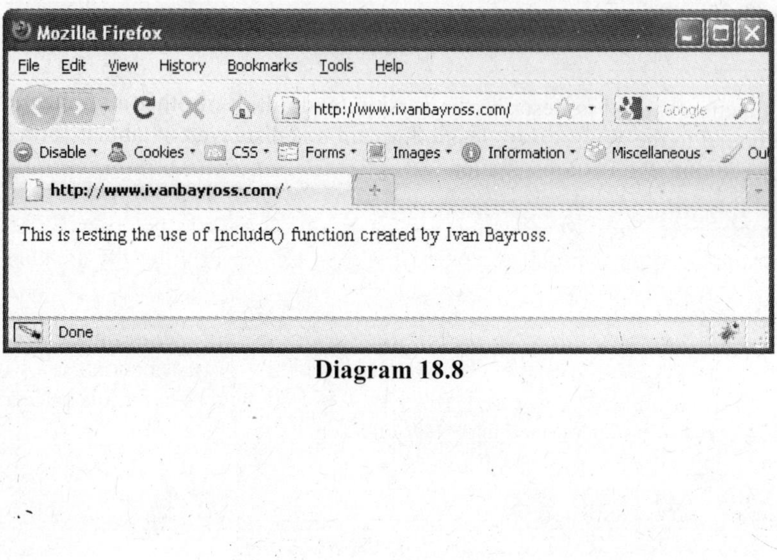

Diagram 18.8

header()

This function allows sending a raw HTTP header to the client browser. Most of its applications are technical, but one of its most common usages is relatively simple, redirecting a user elsewhere i.e. to another URL. This has the same effect as the META redirection tag in HTML.

This will re-direct the browser to load a different page.

Consider the following example:

```
<?php
    header("Location:http://www.ivansmusings.com/");
    exit;
?>
```

NOTE

If the **header()** function is used, it must be called **before** sending any information to the browser, either from PHP or HTML. If not, then an error such as "headers already sent" will be displayed.

This function also takes a second parameter, which is optional and can hold either TRUE or FALSE to determine if the current header should replace the previous header. By default, it is **TRUE**. However, if **FALSE** is passed as the second argument, multiple headers of the same type can be FORCED.

Consider the following example:

```
<HTML>
    <BODY>
        <?php
            header("WWW-Authenticate: Negotiate");
            header("WWW-Authenticate: NTLM", FALSE);
        ?>
    </BODY>
</HTML>
```

The above example sends header information multiple times. The first header function does not use second argument while the second header function uses FALSE as the second argument to send or force the header information the second time.

phpinfo()

The **phpinfo()** function is used to describe the version (and a host of other attributes) of the PHP runtime installed at and bound to the Web server. This information is displayed in tabular form in a Browser and is useful for troubleshooting the PHP installation.

The **phpinfo()** function options:

Name	Description
INFO_GENERAL	The configuration line, php.ini location, build date, Web Server, System and more
INFO_CREDITS	PHP credits
INFO_CONFIGURATION	Local and master values for php directives
INFO_MODULES	Loaded modules
INFO_ENVIRONMENT	Environment variable information
INFO_VARIABLES	All predefined variables from EGPCS (Environment, GET, POST, Cookie, Server)
INFO_LICENSE	PHP license information
INFO_ALL	Shows all of the above. This is the default value

Example:

```
<HTML>
    <BODY>
    <?php
    /* Displaying all PHP information available */
        phpinfo();
    /* Displaying only the general information about PHP */
        phpinfo(INFO_GENERAL);
    ?>
    </BODY>
</HTML>
```

Output: (Refer to diagram 18.9)

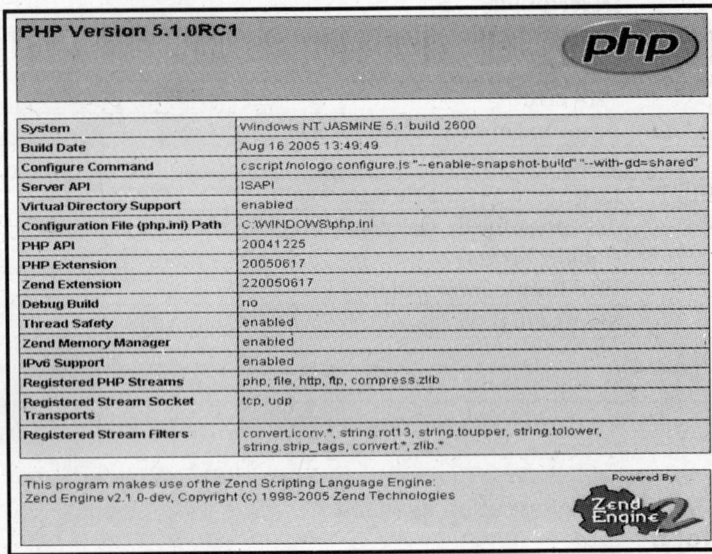

PHP Version 5.1.0RC1

System	Windows NT JASMINE 5.1 build 2600
Build Date	Aug 16 2005 13:49:49
Configure Command	cscript /nologo configure.js "--enable-snapshot-build" "--with-gd=shared"
Server API	ISAPI
Virtual Directory Support	enabled
Configuration File (php.ini) Path	C:\WINDOWS\php.ini
PHP API	20041225
PHP Extension	20050617
Zend Extension	220050617
Debug Build	no
Thread Safety	enabled
Zend Memory Manager	enabled
IPv6 Support	enabled
Registered PHP Streams	php, file, http, ftp, compress.zlib
Registered Stream Socket Transports	tcp, udp
Registered Stream Filters	convert.iconv.*, string.rot13, string.toupper, string.tolower, string.strip_tags, convert.*, zlib.*

This program makes use of the Zend Scripting Language Engine:
Zend Engine v2.1.0-dev, Copyright (c) 1998-2005 Zend Technologies

Diagram 18.9: Page generated after executing the function **phpinfo**(INFO_GENERAL)

PHP SERVER VARIABLES

All Web servers capture and hold information such as the URL from which the user request came from, which browser is being used and so on. This information is stored in several **server variables**.

In PHP, **$_SERVER** is a reserved variable that contains all such Web server information. $_SERVER is a **global** variable, which means that it is available for access by the code spec of any/all PHP scripts.

The following example will dispatch to the user's Browser the URL the server request came from, the user's browser name and the user's IP address:

```
<HTML>
    <BODY>
        <?php
            echo "Referer: " . $_SERVER["HTTP_HOST"] . "<BR />";
            echo "Browser: " . $_SERVER["HTTP_USER_AGENT"] . "<BR />";
            echo "User's IP address: " . $_SERVER["REMOTE_ADDR"];
        ?>
    </BODY>
</HTML>
```

Save the above code snippet and run the file by invoking it via the Web Browser to get an output as shown in diagram 18.10.

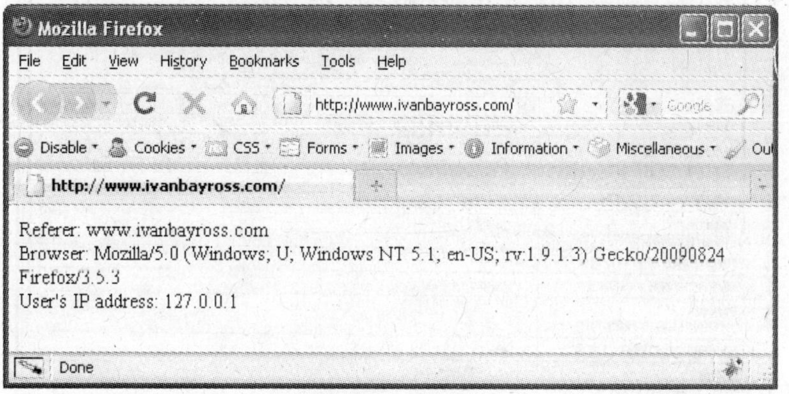

Diagram 18.10

To check the type of browser a client is using, scan the Web server variable HTTP_USER_AGENT for the **user agent string** each browser sends as part of its HTTP request. The variable of interest right now is:

```
$_SERVER['HTTP_USER_AGENT']
```

NOTE

The **$_SERVER** is a special reserved PHP variable that contains all Web server information. It is known as autoglobal (**or** superglobal). These special variables were introduced in PHP 4.1.0. Prior this older $HTTP_*_VARS arrays were used instead, such as $HTTP_SERVER_VARS. Although deprecated, the older variables still exist.

To display the contents of this variable, use:

```
<?php
    echo $_SERVER['HTTP_USER_AGENT'];
?>
```

A sample output of this script may be:

```
Mozilla/5.0 (Windows; U; Windows NT 5.1; en-US; rv:1.9.1.3)
Gecko/20090824 Firefox/3.5.3
```

There are many types of variables available in PHP. In the above example an **array element is printed**.

The variable **$_SERVER** is just one variable that PHP automatically makes available to programmers.

A list can be seen in the Reserved Variables section of the PHP manual **or** a complete list can be obtained by running a PHP script like this: (Refer to diagram 18.11)

```
<?php
    phpinfo();
?>
```

When this PHP code spec executes on the Web server a well-formatted HTML page, full of information about PHP, will be displayed along with a list of all the Web server variables available.

PHP Variables

Variable	Value
_SERVER["ALL_HTTP"]	HTTP_ACCEPT:image/gif, image/x-xbitmap, image/jpeg, image/pjpeg, application/x-shockwave-flash, application/vnd.ms-powerpoint, application/vnd.ms-excel, application/msword, */* HTTP_ACCEPT_LANGUAGE:en-us HTTP_CONNECTION:Keep-Alive HTTP_HOST:localhost HTTP_USER_AGENT:Mozilla/4.0 (compatible; MSIE 6.0; Windows NT 5.1; SV1) HTTP_ACCEPT_ENCODING:gzip, deflate
_SERVER["HTTPS"]	off
_SERVER["SCRIPT_NAME"]	/phpinfo.php
_SERVER["HTTP_COOKIE"]	*no value*
_SERVER ["AUTH_PASSWORD"]	*no value*
_SERVER["AUTH_TYPE"]	*no value*
_SERVER["AUTH_USER"]	*no value*
_SERVER ["CONTENT_LENGTH"]	0
_SERVER["CONTENT_TYPE"]	*no value*
_SERVER ["PATH_TRANSLATED"]	c:\inetpub\wwwroot
_SERVER["QUERY_STRING"]	*no value*
_SERVER["REMOTE_ADDR"]	127.0.0.1
_SERVER["REMOTE_HOST"]	127.0.0.1
_SERVER["REMOTE_USER"]	*no value*
_SERVER ["REQUEST_METHOD"]	GET

Diagram 18.11: The PHP variable section in the output for the function **phpinfo()**

Multiple PHP statements can be put inside PHP tags creating little blocks of code that do more than just echo text. For example, **to check for Internet Explorer** and print a line of text based on a condition do this:

```
<?php
    if (strpos($_SERVER['HTTP_USER_AGENT'], 'MSIE') !== false)
    {
        echo 'The Web Browser is Internet Explorer';
    }
?>
```

If I.E. was the Client Browser, a sample output of this script may be as shown in Diagram 18.12:

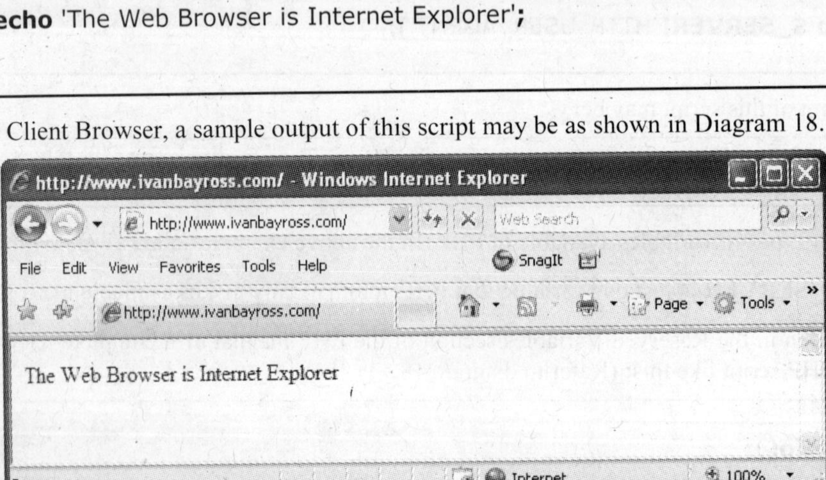

Diagram 18.12: Internet Explorer

The above code spec uses the **strpos()** function, which searches a character, word or string from within another string.

In this case **Internet Explorer** is being searched for inside $_SERVER['HTTP_USER_AGENT']. If found, the function returns the position of **Internet Explorer** relative to the start of the string. Otherwise, it returns FALSE.

If it **does not** return FALSE, (i.e. if expression evaluates to TRUE) the code within {braces} is executed. Otherwise, the code does not run.

To take this a step further, jump in and out of PHP mode in the middle of a PHP block. Store the following script in **testBrowser.php:**

```
<HTML>
   <HEAD>
      <TITLE>Identifying The Web Browser</TITLE>
   </HEAD>
   <BODY>
      <?php
         if (strpos($_SERVER['HTTP_USER_AGENT'], 'Opera') !== false)
         {
      ?>
      <H3>The Web Browser is <B> Opera </B></H3>
      <CENTER>The function <B>strpos()</B> has returned <U>TRUE<U> for
         <B>Opera</B></CENTER>
      <?php
         }
         elseif (strpos($_SERVER['HTTP_USER_AGENT'], 'MSIE') !== false)
         {
      ?>
      <H3>The Web Browser is <U>Internet Explorer</U></H3>
      <CENTER>The function <B>strpos()</B> has returned <U>TRUE</U> for
         <B>MSIE</B></CENTER>
      <?php
         }
     else
     {
      ?>
      <H3>The Web Browser is neither Opera nor Internet Explorer</H3>
      <CENTER>The function <B>strpos()</B> has returned <U>FALSE</U> for
         BOTH conditions</CENTER><BR>
      <B>Browser Type Is - </B>
      <?php
            echo $_SERVER['HTTP_USER_AGENT'];
         }
      ?>
    </BODY>
  </HTML>
```

Output: (Refer to diagrams 18.12.1, 18.12.2 and 18.12.3)

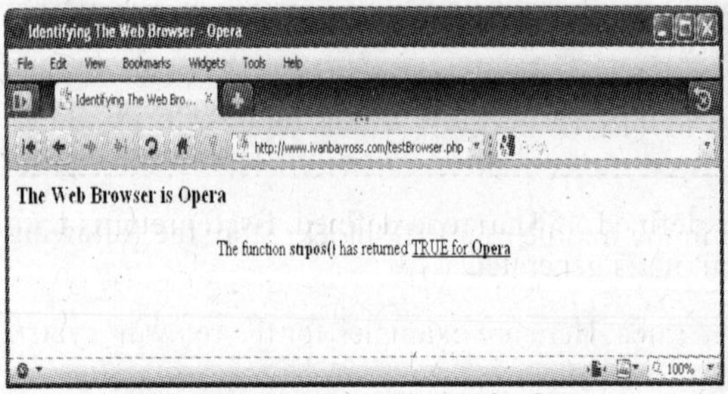

Diagram 18.12.1: Output in Opera

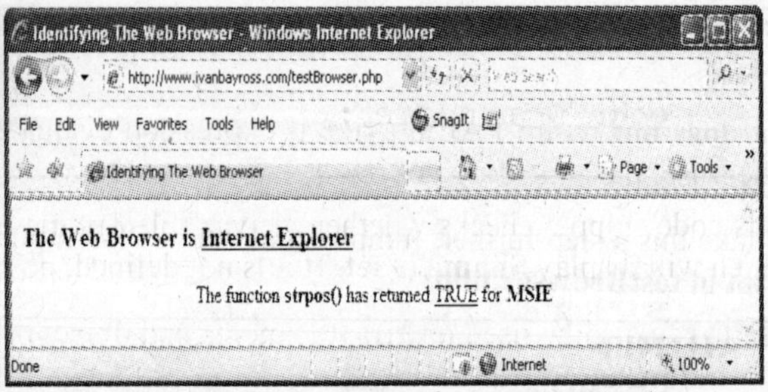

Diagram 18.12.2: Output in Internet Explorer

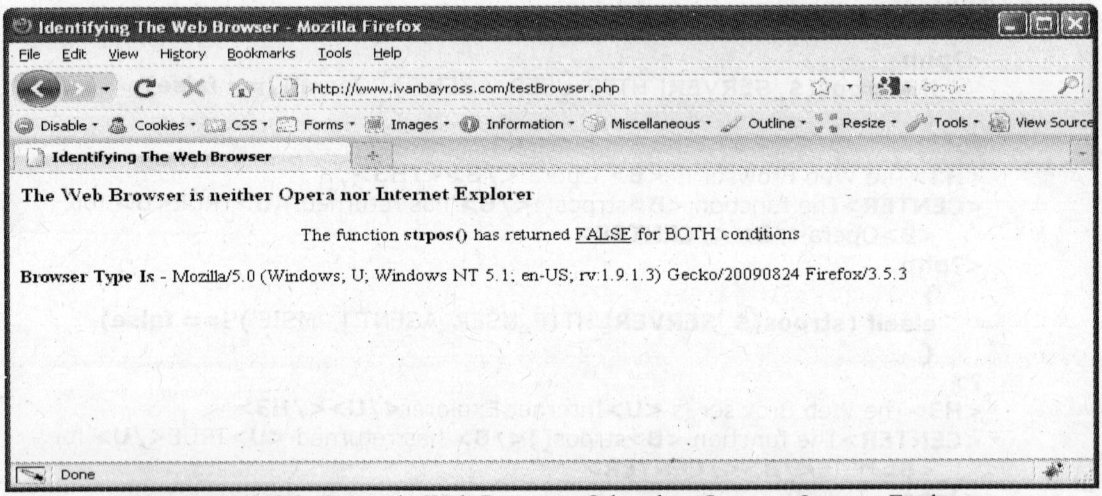

Diagram 18.12.3: Output in Web Browsers Other than Opera or Internet Explorer

Instead of using the PHP **echo** statement to output something, the PHP code block exits and straight HTML is sent to the browser. The important and powerful point to note here is that the logical flow of the PHP script continues to remain intact.

Functions For Variables

There are three basic functions that are useful while using variables. These are:

- **isset()** - It determines whether a variable has been **declared** and **loaded** with a value by a programmer. Returns TRUE if such a variable is passed to it. If not it returns FALSE. Can take multiple arguments
  - If a variable has been unset with **unset()**, it will no longer be set in such a case **isset()** will return FALSE if testing a variable that has been set to NULL
  - A NULL byte ("\0") is **not equivalent** to the PHP NULL constant
  - **isset()** only works with variables, passing anything else will result in a parse error

Syntax:

```
bool isset (mixed <String> [, mixed <String> [, mixed ...]])
```

Example:

```
if (isset($name))
{
    echo '$name is set';
}
```

This code snippet checks whether the variable **$name** is defined. If **$name** is defined, **isset()** returns **true**, which will display **$name is set**. If it is not defined, no output is generated.

isset() can also be used on array elements and object properties. Here are examples for the relevant syntax, which can be referred to later:

Example: (For checking array element)

```
if (isset($array["offset"]))
{
    ...
}
```

Example: (For checking object property)

```
if (isset($object->property))
{
    ...
}
```

NOTE

Isset() is the only one of the three language constructs that accepts an arbitrary amount of parameters. Its accurate prototype is as follows:

isset($var1, $var2, $var3, **...);**

It only returns true if all the variables have been defined otherwise, it returns false. This is useful when the required input variables has to be checked for the script have really been sent by the client, saving a series of single **isset()** checks.

- **empty()** - It may be used to check if a variable has not been declared or its value is FALSE. This language construct is usually used to check if a form variable has not been sent or does not contain data. When checking a variable's truth value, its value is first converted to a Boolean according to rules and then it is checked for TRUE/FALSE. Returns true if the variable, passed as its *only* parameter, holds FALSE or empty values
    - The following are considered **empty values:**
        - "" (an empty string)
        - 0 (0 as an integer)
        - "0" (0 as a string)
        - NULL
        - FALSE
        - array() (an empty array)
        - var $var; (a variable declared, but without a value)

Syntax:

```
bool empty (mixed <String>)
```

Example:

```
if (empty($name))
{
    echo 'Error: Forgot to specify a value for $name';
}
```

This code prints an error message if **$name** doesn't contain a value that evaluates to TRUE

- **unset()** - It **undeclares** a previously set variable and frees any memory that is used by it if no other variable references its value. A call to **isset()** on a variable that has been unset() returns FALSE. It is used when a variable needs to be deleted
    - The behavior of **unset()** inside of a function can vary depending on what type of variable that unset() is attempting to destroy
    - If a global variable is **unset()** inside of a function, only the local variable is destroyed. The variable in the calling environment will retain the same value as before unset() was called. If it is desired to unset() a global variable inside of a function, use the $GLOBALS statement while referring the variable
    - If a variable that is PASSED BY REFERENCE is unset() inside of a function, only the local variable is destroyed. The variable in the calling environment will retain the same value as before unset() was called
    - If a static variable is unset() inside of a function, unset() destroys the variable and all its references

Syntax:

```
void unset (mixed <String> [, mixed <String> [, mixed ...]])
```

Example:

```
$firstname = "Ivan Bayross";
unset($firstname);
if (isset($firstname))
{
    echo '$firstname is set';
}
```

This example will not generate any output because **isset()** returns false.

<u>**unset()** can also be used on array elements and object properties similar to **isset()**</u>.

Example:

```
<?php
    if(isset($name))
    {
        echo 'The Variable Holds Value.' . "<BR />";
    }
    else
    {
        echo 'The Variable Does Not Hold A Value.' . "<BR />";
        $name = "Ivan Bayross";
        if(isset($name))
        {
            echo 'The Variable Now Holds A Value: ' . $name . "<BR />";
            if(empty($name))
            {
                echo 'The Variable Now Holds FALSE.' . "<BR />";
            }
            unset($name);
            if(!isset($name))
            {
                echo 'The Variable Is Being Deleted.' . "<BR />";
            }
        }
    }
?>
```

Output: (Refer to diagram 18.13)

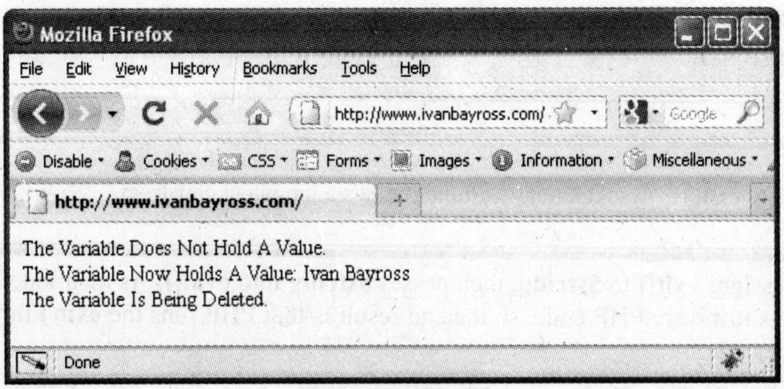

Diagram 18.13

Controlling Script Execution

There are basically three functions, which can control the execution of a script:

- **exit()** - Used for immediately terminating the script execution. **exit()** takes just one optional parameter and terminates execution of the script immediately. If a parameter is passed, this is used as the script exit code and if it is a string, it is printed out

Syntax:

```
void exit ([mixed <Status>])
```

exit() is a very common function and is used wherever needed to end a script with no further work.

Example:

```
if ($str1 != $str2)
{
    print "Access denied.";
    exit;
}
```

NOTE

Since the **exit()** function takes only one parameter, (either a program return value or a string) it is preferred to return a number and link this number with subsequent processing of the PHP script. In this case, **0** (zero) would usually mean, **Everything went OK** and everything else means, **Something went wrong**.

- **eval()** - Takes one string parameter, but it executes that string as if it were PHP code

Syntax:

```
mixed eval ([string <String>])
```

eval() might seem a little pointless, but it is actually very helpful as it allows passing in any text string as PHP code and have it executed. This allows storing the PHP code in a database or to calculate it on the fly, which gives a lot more flexibility. Admittedly, **eval()** is nowhere near as helpful as **exit()**, but it is still good to know.

Here is an example of both **exit()** and **eval()** in action:

```
<?php
    $string = "exit()";
    eval($string);
?>
```

TIP

For many **exit()** is not technically a function, it's a language construct.

The above code assigns **exit()** to **$string**, then passes **$string** into **eval()**. As mentioned, **eval()** will execute the string it gets as if it were PHP code, so the end result is that PHP runs the **exit()** function through **eval()** and terminates the code.

- **die()** - Used for immediately terminating the execution of the script. The function **die()** is an alias of the **exit()** function and works the same way

Syntax:

```
void die ([mixed <Status>])
```

Using **exit()** with a string causes PHP to output the string then terminate the script. This is commonly used by programmers with an exit() alias, such as:

```
perform_action() OR die("Action failed!");
```

In that situation, **perform_action()** will be called and if it returns **false, die()** will be called to terminate the script. This is a fast and easy way to make sure that certain functions have run successfully before getting into the core of the PHP script.

NOTE

The reason that code works is because the **OR** operator is used which means that PHP will only execute the second function if the first function returned false. This is a common use of the **OR** operator.

CAUTION

Remember that the || operator is higher than the **OR** operator in terms of precedence and more importantly, || also higher than =. Consider the processing of the following code:

```
$processfile = fopen("filename", "r") || die("Could not open file!");
```

As || has a higher precedence than =, it is calculated first and PHP attempts to load *filename*. If it succeeds, **fopen()** will return a resource that evaluates to **true**. Naturally all calls to **die()** succeed, so **die()** will also always be evaluated as true.

However, because PHP will short-circuit the || operator, when **fopen()** succeeds **die()** will not be called and the || operator will return **1** (true) because the operand on its left side (the call to **fopen()**) returned true. Thus, PHP reads the line of code like this:

```
processfile = (fopen("somefile", "r") || die("Could not open file!"));
```

Finally, the value **1** will be assigned to **$processfile**. As this is not intended, the **OR** operator comes in handy. As **OR** has a lower priority than =, PHP reads the line of code like this:

```
$processfile = fopen("somefile", "r") or die("Could not open file!");
```

That is, **fopen()** is called and its value is assigned to **$processfile**, which is then put through the comparison operator.

Array Functions

PHP offers a large collection of built-in functions that facilitates working with arrays. A handful of useful array functions are described below:

- **count()** - Takes an array as an argument and returns the number of array elements. It returns zero if the array is not set or if it is set but contains zero elements

Syntax:

```
int count(mixed var)
```

- **in_array()** - This function will search the array **str2** for the value **str1** and returns **TRUE** if **found** in the array or otherwise **false**

Syntax:

```
boolean in_array(mixed $str1, array $str2 [, bool strict])
```

- **reset()** - Every PHP array has an internal pointer that keeps track of the current position in the array. When using constructs such as **foreach**, the function diligently resets the array pointer to the beginning of the array. However, many array functions, such as **prev()** and **next()** move the pointer to a new position in the array. This can then affect future calls to functions, such as **array_walk()**, which begins its processing wherever the pointer happens to be thus calling **reset()** prior using **array_walk()** is a good idea

Syntax:

```
mixed reset(array array)
```

The **reset()** function is used to ensure that an array's pointer is placed at the array's first element. It returns the value of the first element:

Example:

```
reset($book);
/* Setting the pointer at the array's first element */
array_walk($book, "MyFunction");
/* Applying MyFunction() to every element of the array */
```

- **sort()** - It is used to sort values in an array. The optional second parameter **SortFlags** can be used to specify how the data should be sorted. The possible values are **SORT_REGULAR**, **SORT_NUMERIC**, which forces the values to be compared numerically or **SORT_STRING**, which forces the values to be compared as strings

Syntax:

```
void sort(array array [, int <SortFlags>])
```

PHP has several built-in sorting functions whose syntax is very similar to **sort()**. These functions differ in behavior providing various options to the sorting process, such as changes in the direction of the sort, treatment of keys, the comparison algorithms used and so on.

- **explode()** and **implode()** - These two functions are officially considered **string** functions, but they do concern arrays

explode() takes a string and splits it into separate elements of an array, using the argument provided as a **delimiter.**

implode() does the opposite i.e. it traverses the elements of an array and re-creates a single string using a **glue** argument.

Example:

```
<?php
    $fruits= "Banana; Mango; Orange; Apple";
    /* Turning the string $fruits separated by semicolons into array elements */
    $fruitsname = explode("; ", $fruits);
    echo "Using Explode: " . "<BR />";
    echo $fruitsname[0] . "<BR />";
    echo $fruitsname[1] . "<BR />";
    echo $fruitsname[2] . "<BR />";
    echo $fruitsname[3] . "<BR />";
    echo "<HR>";
    /* Turning the array $fruitsname into a sentence separated by a space */
```

```
        echo "Using Implode: " . "<BR />";

        $fruitsarray = implode(" ", $fruitsname);
        echo $fruitsarray;
    ?>
```

Output: (Refer to diagram 18.14)

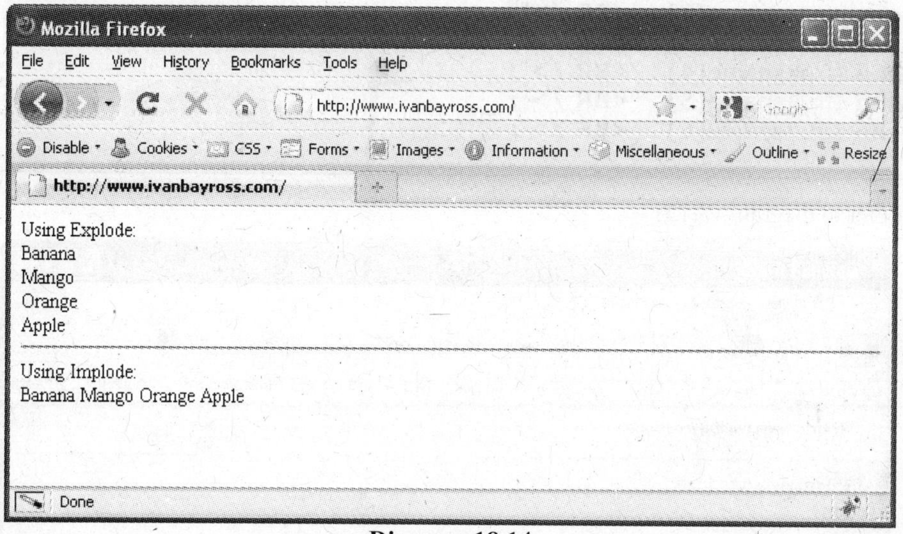

Diagram 18.14

- **array_push** - This function appends an element or a set of elements to the end of an array variable

Syntax:

```
array_push $ArrayToAppendTo, $element [,$element...]
```

Example:

```
<?php
        $fruits= "Banana; Mango; Orange; Apple";
/* Turning the string $fruits separated by semicolons into array elements */
        $fruitsname = explode("; ", $fruits);
        echo "<HR />";
        $newfruits = "Cherry";
        array_push ($fruitsname, $newfruits);
        echo "After Pushing a new fruits" . "<BR />";
        echo $fruitsname[0] . "<BR />";
        echo $fruitsname[1] . "<BR />";
```

```
    echo $fruitsname[2] . "<BR />";
    echo $fruitsname[3] . "<BR />";
    echo "<HR />";
    array_push ($fruitsname, "Avocado", "Blackberry", "Grapefruit");
    echo "After Pushing a set of new fruits" . "<BR />";
    echo $fruitsname[0] . "<BR />";
    echo $fruitsname[1] . "<BR />";
    echo $fruitsname[2] . "<BR />";
    echo $fruitsname[3] . "<BR />";
    echo $fruitsname[4] . "<BR />";
    echo $fruitsname[5] . "<BR />";
    echo $fruitsname[6] . "<BR />";
?>
```

Output: (Refer to diagram 18.15)

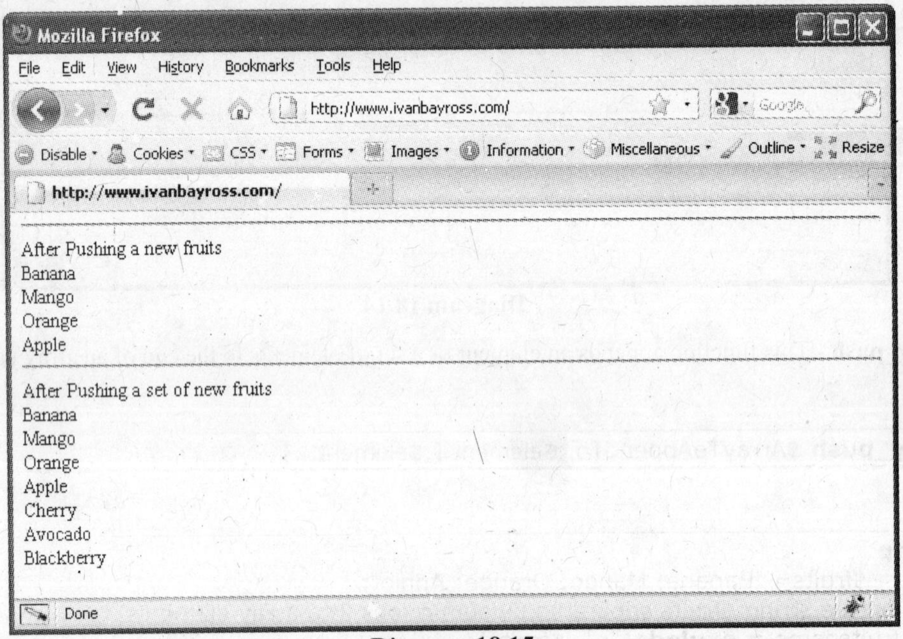

Diagram 18.15

- **array_pop** - It pops out and returns the last value of the array, thus shortening the array by one element. If array is empty (or is not an array), **NULL** will be returned

Example:

```
<?php
    $fruits= " Banana; Mango; Orange; Apple";
/* Turning the string $fruits separated by semicolons into array
 elements */
    $fruitsname= explode("; ", $fruits);
    echo "<HR />";
    while ($element = array_pop ($fruitsname))
    {
        echo $element;
```

```
        echo "<BR />";
        echo "<HR />";
        echo "After Popping $element the array named fruitsname is left with :";
        print_r($fruitsname);
        echo "<HR />";
    }
?>
```

Output: (Refer to diagram 18.16)

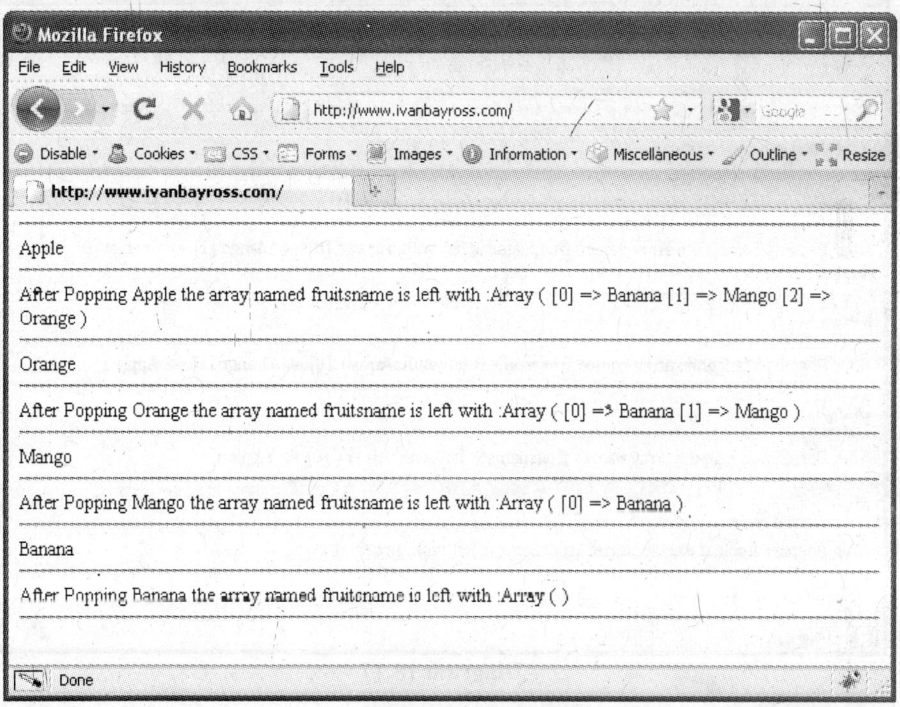

Diagram 18.16

- **array_shift** - It shifts off (removes) the first value of the array and returns it, shortening the array by one element and moving everything up. All numerical array keys will be modified to start counting from zero while literal keys won't be touched. If array is empty (or is not an array), NULL will be returned

Example:

```
<?php
    $fruits = "Banana; Mango; Orange; Apple";
/* Turning the string $fruits separated by semicolons into array elements */
    $fruitsname = explode("; ", $fruits);
    echo "<HR />";
    while ($element = array_shift ($fruitsname))
    {
        echo $element;
        echo "<BR />";
        echo "<HR />";
```

```
        echo "After Popping $element the array named fruitsname is left with :";
        print_r($fruitsname);
        echo "<HR />";
    }
?>
```

Output: (Refer to diagram 18.17)

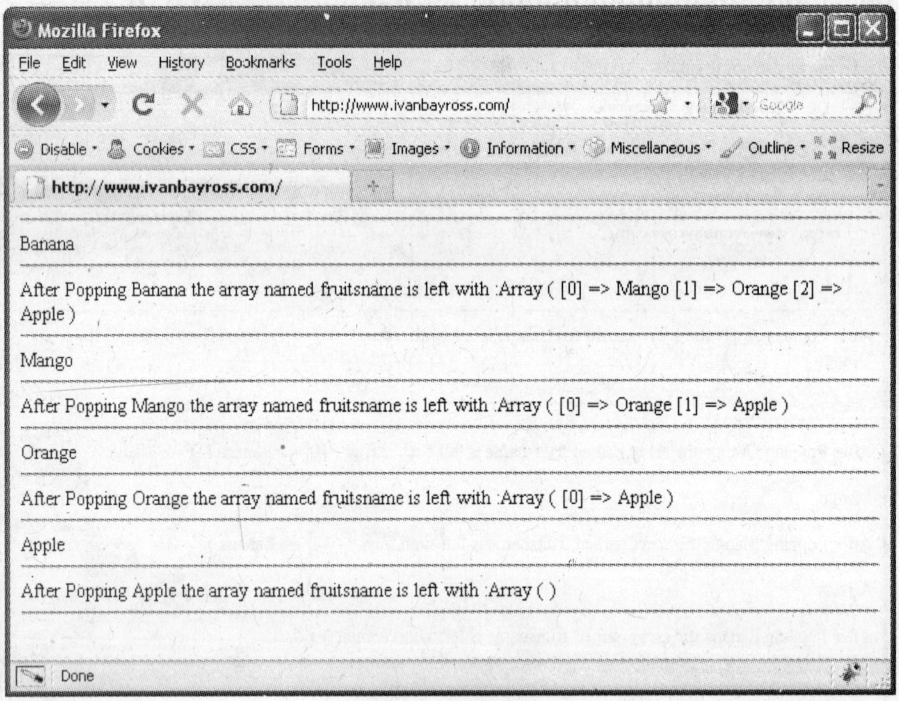

Diagram 18.17

- **array_reverse** - It takes its input from an array and returns a new array with the order of the elements reversed, preserving the array keys if the second parameter is TRUE

Example:

```
<?php
    $fruits = "Banana; Mango; Orange; Apple, Grapes";
    /* Turning the string $fruits separated by semicolons into array
elements */
    $fruitsname= explode("; ", $fruits);
    echo "Before Reversing";
    echo "<HR />";
    print_r($fruitsname);
    $reversefruitsname = array_reverse ($fruitsname);
    echo "<BR />";
    echo "<BR />After Reversing";
    echo "<HR />";
    print_r($reversefruitsname);
    $preversefruitsname = array_reverse ($fruitsname, TRUE);
```

```
    echo "<BR />";
    echo "<BR />After Reversing (Preserving Keys)";
    echo "<HR />";
    print_r($preversefruitsname);
?>
```

Output: (Refer to diagram 18.18)

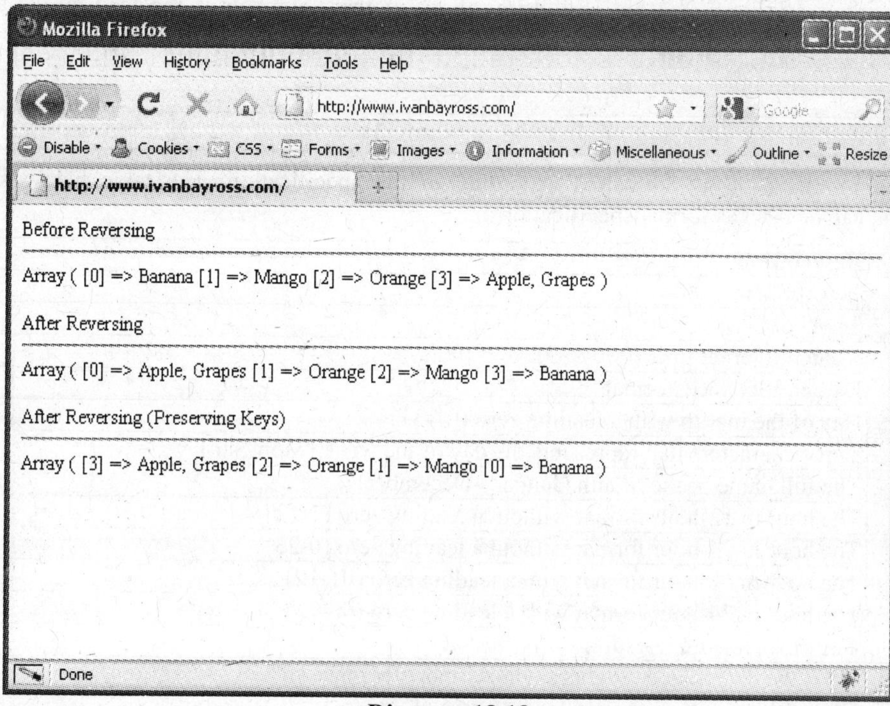

Diagram 18.18

WORKING WITH DATE AND TIME

Most of the date and time functions in PHP are used for printing out the current date and time but apart from that, PHP date and time functions offer many other possibilities.

Being able to work easily with date and time information is a basic skill every PHP programmer should acquire as soon as possible.

NOTE

PHP represents time as the number of seconds that have passed since January 1st 1970 00:00:00 GMT, a date known as the start of the Unix epoch, hence this date format is known as "epoch time" or a "Unix timestamp". This might seem like a peculiar way to store dates, but it is actually remarkably good as internally any date since 1970 can be stored as an integer and converted to a human-readable string wherever necessary. The advantage of working with Unix time is that it is not tied down to any specific formatting.

The Date() Function

The function **date()** is used to **format** either **time** or a **date**.

This function can take the current date and extract specific information from it. For example: the specific day (i.e. Sunday, Monday and so on), whether it is **a.m.** or **p.m.** what time it is.

To do so, call **date()** and provide a string as the first parameter. This string may now contain a list of formatting symbols as shown in table 18.1 below. Each of these symbols is replaced by the associated date/time value.

Syntax:

```
string date(string <Format> [, int <TimeStamp>])
```

This function returns a string formatted according to the specification. The table below shows the characters that can be used as format specifications:

Character	Description
a	"am" or "pm"
A	"AM" or "PM"
B	Swatch Internet time (000-999)
c	Date in ISO 8601 format
d	Day of the month with a leading zero (01-31)
D	Three characters that represents the day of the week (Mon-Sun)
F	The full name of the month (January-December)
g	The hour in 12-hour format without a leading zero (1-12)
G	The hour in 24-hour format without a leading zero (0-23)
h	The hour in 12-hour format with a leading zero (01-12)
H	The hour in 24-hour format with a leading zero (00-23)
i	The minutes with a leading zero (00-59)
I	"1" if the date is in daylights savings time, otherwise "0"
j	Day of the month without a leading zero (1-31)
l	The full name of the day (Monday-Sunday)
L	"1" if the year is a leap year, otherwise "0"
m	The month as a number with a leading zero (01-12)
M	Three letters that represents the name of the month (Jan-Dec)
n	The month as a number without a leading zero (1-12)
0	The difference to Greenwich time (GMT) in hours
r	An RFC 822 formatted date (example: "Tue, 10 Apr 2005 18:34:07 +0300")
s	The seconds with a leading zero (00-59)
S	The English ordinal suffix for the day of the month (st, nd, rd or th)
t	The number of days in the given month (28-31)
T	The local time zone (example: "GMT")
U	The number of seconds since the Unix Epoch (January 1 1970 00:00:00 GMT)
w	The day of the week as a number (0-6, 0=Sunday)
W	ISO-8601 week number of year, weeks starting on Monday
y	The year as a 2-digit number (example: 03)
Y	The year as a 4-digit number (example: 2003)
z	The day of the year as a number (0-366)
Z	Time zone difference to UTC (in seconds)

Table 18.1

NOTE

Almost all of the formatting symbols shown in the above table are available since PHP 3.

There are only two exceptions: Using **W** for determining the week number of a date **was added in PHP 4.1.0** and using **c** for retrieving the ISO 8601 representation for a date (for example: 2006-06-30T12:34:56+01:00) **came in PHP 5**.

The function **date()** is very powerful and offers a broad range of ways to use it. However, especially if the content is localized, then formatting good phrases are needed.

Example:

```
<?php
    /* Printing something like: Monday */
    echo date("l")."<BR />";
    /* Printing something like: Monday 5th October 2009 12:38:11 PM */
    echo date("l dS F Y h:i:s A")."<BR />";
    /* Printing something like: Monday the 5th */
    echo date("l \\t\h\e jS")."<BR />";
?>
```

Output: (Refer to diagram 18.20)

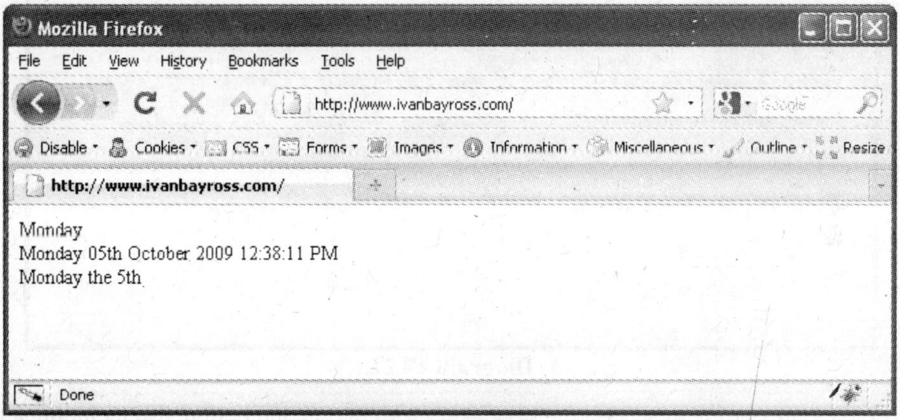

Diagram 18.20

The time() Function

PHP has a basic function **time()** to get the current time in epoch format . **time()** takes no parameters and returns the current timestamp representing the current time.

Example:

```
<?php
    print time();
    $time = time();
    print $time;
?>
```

time() value can be either directly printed or it can be stored in a variable and then the contents of the variable printed. But in either case the result is identical.

Converting From A String

PHP has a built in function to help convert strings to a timestamp. The function **strtotime()** takes two parameters i.e. the string time to convert and a second **optional** parameter that can be a relative timestamp.

Syntax:

```
int strtotime(string <time> [int now])
```

This function returns a timestamp on success, **FALSE** otherwise. Prior to PHP 5.1.0, this function would return **-1** on failure.

In this function the first parameter is important. Consider the following script:

```
<?php
    print strtotime("28 October 2005") ."<BR />";
    print strtotime("28 October 2005 17:30") ."<BR />";
    print strtotime("2005/10/28") ."<BR />";
?>
```

Output: (Refer to diagram 18.21)

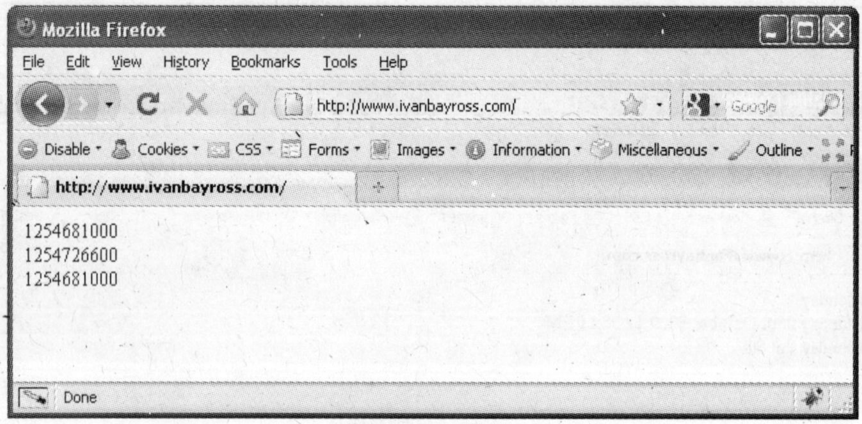

Diagram 18.21

Here there are three ways of representing the same date, with the second option also including a time. If the script is executed, PHP outputs an integer representation for each one. Refer to diagram 18.18.

In the output, the first and third integers are the same, while the second one is slightly higher. These numbers are the Unix timestamps for the dates passed into **strtotime()**, which it has successfully managed to convert.

CAUTION

The function **strtotime()** uses **American-style dates**, which means that if it finds a date like 10/11/2003, it will consider it to be October the 11th as opposed to November the 10th.

Example:

```
<?php
    $UnixDate1 = "Year End 2009";
    $UnixDate2 = "31st Dec. 2009";
    $UnixDate3 = "25 August 2005 05:30";
    $UnixDate4 = "+2 Day";
    $UnixDate5 = "Every Wednesday";
    if (strtotime($UnixDate1) == FALSE)
    {
        print "Date conversion failed for $UnixDate1 !<BR />";
    }
    else
    {
        print "Date conversion succeeded for $UnixDate1 !<BR />";
    }
    if (strtotime($UnixDate2) == FALSE)
    {
        print "Date conversion failed for $UnixDate2 !<BR />";
    }
    else
    {
        print "Date conversion succeeded for $UnixDate2 !<BR />";
    }
    if (strtotime($UnixDate3) == FALSE)
    {
        print "Date conversion failed for $UnixDate3 !<BR />";
    }
    else
    {
        print "Date conversion succeeded for $UnixDate3 !<BR />";
    }
    if (strtotime($UnixDate4) == FALSE)
    {
        print "Date conversion failed for $UnixDate4 !<BR />";
    }
    else
    {
        print "Date conversion succeeded for $UnixDate4 !<BR />";
    }
    if (strtotime($UnixDate5) == FALSE)
    {
        print "Date conversion failed for $UnixDate5 !<BR />";
    }
    else
    {
        print "Date conversion succeeded for $UnixDate5 !<BR />";
    }
?>
```

Output: (Refer to diagram 18.22)

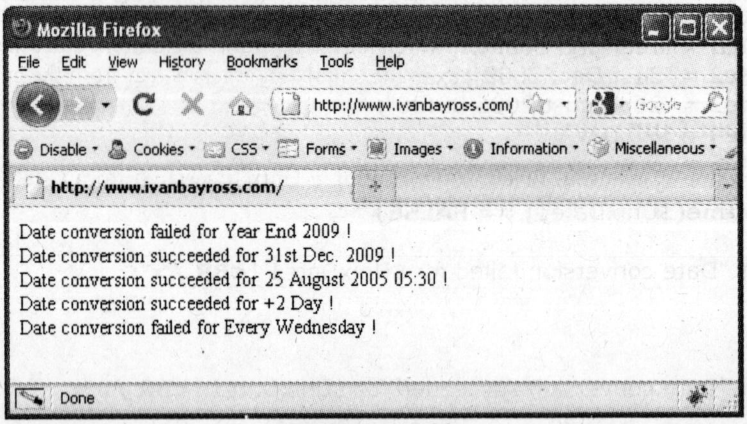

Diagram 18.22

In the above example, the **strtotime()** function is unable to resolve the string "Year End" in the first case and "Every" in the last case.

strtotime() takes two parameters, with the second one being optional. Parameter one is a special string containing formatting codes, which indicate how the timestamp must be converted. Parameter two is the timestamp, which needs conversion. If this information is not supplied, PHP assumes that the current timestamp must be converted.

Example:

```
<?php
    print "Next Sunday is: " . date("l dS F Y h:i:s A", strtotime("Next Sunday")) .
            "<BR />";
    print "Today is: " . date("l dS F Y h:i:s A", strtotime("Today")) . "<BR />";
    print "Two days after the Day Before Yesterday is: " . date("l dS F Y h:i:s A",
            strtotime("2 days", time() - (86400 * 2))) . "<BR />";
    print "A year ago is: " . date("l dS F Y h:i:s A", strtotime("1 year ago",
            time())) . "<BR />";
?>
```

Output: (Refer to diagram 18.23)

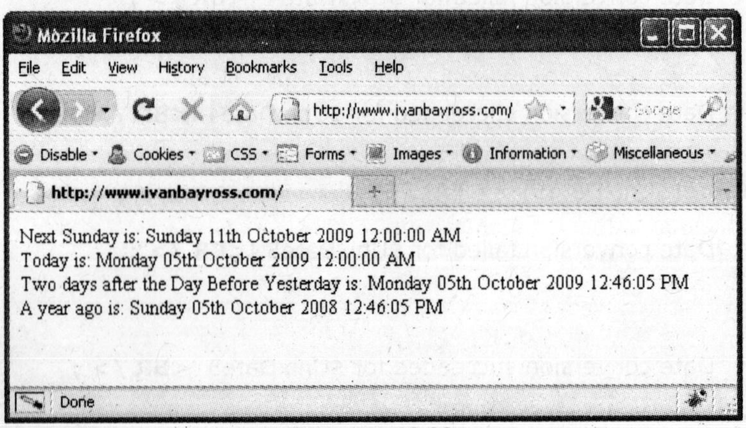

Diagram 18.23

The first line will print the datetime for the next Sunday (not the upcoming Sunday, but the one after). The second line will print the current datetime. The third line actually uses time() minus two days as its second parameter and "2 days" for its first parameter, which means it returns the current datetime (two days time from now minus two days is now). The final example simply subtracts a year from the current datetime.

Converting From Components

The **mktime()** function is a special function for creating a Unix timestamp from a date component. It can be used to store year, month and day in separate variables.

Syntax:

```
int mktime ([int <hour> [, int <minute> [, int <second> [, int <month> [, int <day>
        [, int <year> [, int <is_dst>]]]]]]])
```

The order of the parameters in this function is as: hour (24Hr), minute, second, month, day, year, Is_Daylight_Savings_Time.

Example:
To use the **mktime()** function for passing 2:30 pm on the 31st of October 2005, the command is used like this:

```
$newTime = mktime(14, 30, 0, 10, 31, 2005, -1);
```

The last parameter (i.e. **-1**) tells PHP whether **D**aylight **S**avings **T**ime (DST) should be in effect. The options are:

- **1** to have DST switched ON
- **0** to have DST switched OFF
- **-1** to let PHP decide

Using the **mktime()** function helps in date arithmetic, as it will correct crazy dates quite well.

If 13 months are to be added to the function call above without having to figure out the new settings, just add 13 to the month parameter (currently 10), as shown below:

```
$newTime = mktime(14, 30, 0, 23, 31, 2005, -1);
```

As a year consists of 12 months, PHP will add one to the year value, subtract 12 from the month's value and calculate the date from there.

Example:

```
<?php
    $newTime1 = date("l dS F Y h:i:s A", mktime(14, 30, 0, 10, 31, 2005, -1));
    $newTime2 = date("l dS F Y h:i:s A", mktime(14, 30, 0, 23, 31, 2005, -1));

    print "Original Value: " . $newTime1 . "<BR />";
    print "Modified Value: " . $newTime2 . "<BR />";
?>
```

Output: (Refer to diagram 18.24)

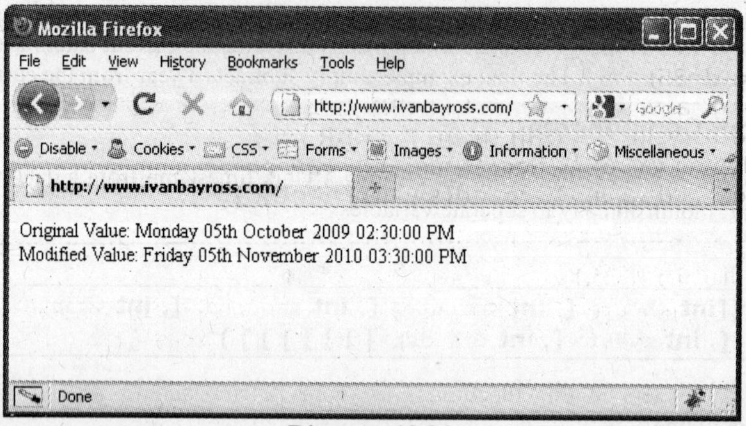

Diagram 18.24

PERFORMING MATHEMATICAL OPERATIONS

PHP has a great number of built-in mathematical functions ready for use, as well as several constants for popular numbers to avoid re-calculations. In PHP, nearly all mathematical functions can be grouped into three areas: rounding, randomization and conversion.

Rounding Up A Number

There are three basic functions, used for rounding up numbers in PHP. These are:

- **ceil()** - It accepts one parameter, a number and returns the round to the nearest integer greater than the number

Syntax:

```
float ceil (float <value>)
```

- **floor()** - It accepts one parameter, a number and returns the round to the nearest integer smaller than the number

Syntax:

```
float floor (float <value>)
```

TIP

The **floor()** function converts a floating-point number to an integer in the same way as typecasting, except typecasting is faster.

- **round()** - It accepts two parameters, a number and returns the round to the nearest integer smaller than the number

Syntax:

```
float round (float <value> [, int <precision>])
```

Example:

```
<?php
    $num1 = 15.85;
    print "Original value: " . $num1 . "<BR />";
    print "Ceiled value: " . ceil($num1) . "<BR />";
    print "Floored value: " . floor($num1) . "<BR />";
    print "Rounded value: " . round($num1) . "<BR />";
?>
```

Output: (Refer to diagram 18.25.1)

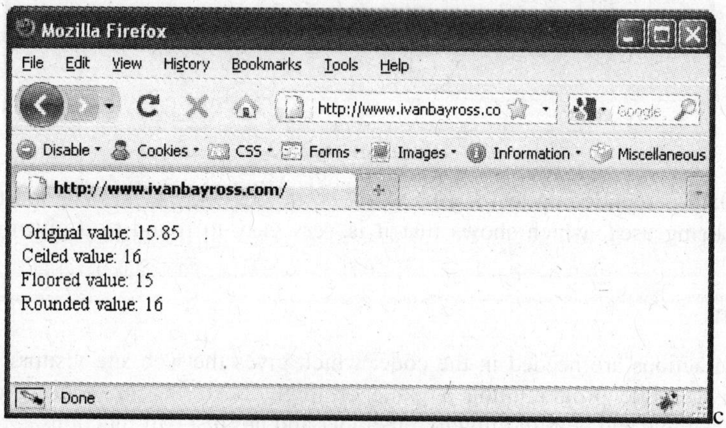

Diagram 18.25.1

Example:

```
<?php
    $num1 = 15.38;
    $num2 = 15.5;
    $num3 = 15.95356;
    print "Round of $num1: " . round($num1) . "<BR />";
    print "Round of $num2: " . round($num2) . "<BR />";
    print "Round of $num3: " . round($num3) . "<BR />";
    print "Round of $num3 with precision as 3: " . round($num3, 3) . "<BR />";
    print "Round of $num3 with precision as 4: " . round($num3, 4) . "<BR />";
?>
```

Output: (Refer to diagram 18.25.2)

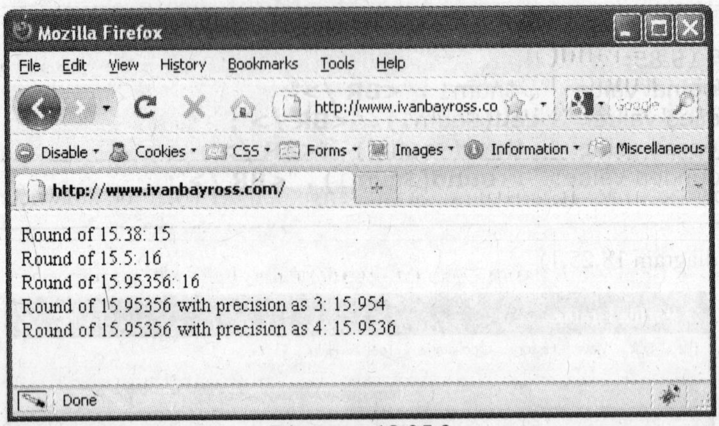

Diagram 18.25.2

As can be seen, 10.45 is rounded up to 10, 10.5 to 11, while 10.95457 to 11. The fourth operation has the second parameter being used, which shows that it is very easy to round to a given number of decimal places.

Randomization

Sometimes random actions are needed in the code, which gives the web site visitors a different greeting each time they visit, while programming a game or might be trying to securing data by hashing it. Randomization is a simple and helpful thing to remember and has just two functions.

They are **rand()** and **mt_rand()**.

- **rand()** - It is a basic randomization function that is very quick but not very random as the numbers it generates are slightly more predictable

Syntax:

```
int rand ( [int min, int max])
```

- **mt_rand()** - It is more complicated. The **mt** parts means **M**ersenne **T**wister as that is the name of the randomization algorithm it uses. **mt_rand()** returns much more random numbers, but does so at the cost of some speed

Syntax:

```
int mt_rand ( [int min, int max])
```

Both functions do the same thing and both take the same parameters i.e. two optional numbers, for the minimum number to return and the maximum number to return. Either supply no parameters, which will result in PHP returning a random number between one and a very high number or supply the two parameters.

Example:

```
<?php
    $randomrange = rand();
    $randrange = rand(1,10);
    $mtrandrange = mt_rand(1,100);
?>
```

The two numbers passed in are **inclusive** i.e. **$randrange** number could be anywhere between 1 and 10 including 1 and 10.

If any parameters are not passed to **rand()** and **mt_rand()** calls, PHP will generate a random number from 1 to a high number. If to find out the maximum number PHP can return from a **rand()** call, use **getrandmax()**. There is a similar function, **mt_getrandmax()** for **mt_rand()**.

Example:
The following example shows how randomization can be used to greet web site visitors in various ways

```
<?php
    switch(rand(1,6))
    {
        case 1:
            $fruits = 'Apple!';
            break;
        case 2:
            $fruits = 'Mango!';
            break;
        case 3:
            $fruits = 'Grapes!';
            break;
        case 4:
            $fruits = 'Blackcurrant!';
            break;
        case 5:
            $fruits = 'Orange!';
            break;
        case 6:
            $fruits = 'Apricot !';
            break;
    }
    print $fruits;
?>
```

Output: (Refer to diagram 18.26)

Diagram 18.26

Diagram 18.26 (Continued)

One important thing to note is that the speed of randomization does not depend on the sizes passed i.e. rand() is just as fast in rand(1,3) as it is in rand(1, 10000000). mt_rand() works just short of 50% slower than rand(), which means use it if extra randomization is needed.

Other Mathematical Conversion Functions

PHP provides several key functions that manipulate numbers in non-trigonometrical ways of which the most important are:

- **abs()** - It is the most basic function and returns the absolute value of the parameter passed to it i.e. the function leaves positive values untouched, while it converts negative values into positive values

Syntax:

```
number abs (number <value>)
```

- **sqrt()** - It is short for square root and takes just one parameter i.e. the value whose square root needs to be calculated

Syntax:

```
float sqrt (float <value>)
```

- **pow()** - It takes two parameters i.e. a base and a power to raise it by. The value in the first parameter is multiplied with itself, one time less than the value entered as the second parameter. The **pow()** function is capable of handling negative powers for the second parameter, in which case it first multiplies the value in the first parameter with itself as many times as one less the absolute value of the second parameter and then use the result to divide the value in the first parameter

Syntax:

```
float pow (number <base value> , number <exponent>])
```

- **hypot()** - It is designed to calculate the length of a vector or the hypotenuse of a triangle. It takes two parameter: X and Y and returns the value **sqrt((X*X)+(Y*Y))**

Syntax:

```
float hypot (float <first side> , float <second side>])
```

Example:

```
<?php
    print "Absolute of 48.5: " . abs(48.5) . "<BR />";
    print "Absolute of -3.1: " . abs(-3.1) . "<BR />";

    print "Square Root of 40: " . sqrt(40) . "<BR />";
    print "Square Root of 60: " . sqrt(60) . "<BR />";

    print "10 to power of 1: " . pow(10, 1) . "<BR />";
    print "10 to power of 6: " . pow(10, 6) . "<BR />";
    print "10 to power of -3: " . pow(10, -3) . "<BR />";
    print "10 to power of  4: " . pow(10, -4) . "<BR />";
    print "1000 to power of 0.8: " . pow(1000, 0.8) . "<BR />";

    print "Vector of 5 & 6: " . hypot(5, 6) . "<BR />";
    print "Vector of 9 & 11: " . hypot(9, 11) . "<BR />";
?>
```

CAUTION

It is important to note that supplying 0.5 as the second parameter to **pow()** is the equivalent of calculating the square root of the first parameter, which means that using any negative number as parameter one and 0.5 as the second parameter will generate an error, because negative numbers hav no square root.

Output: (Refer to diagram 18.27)

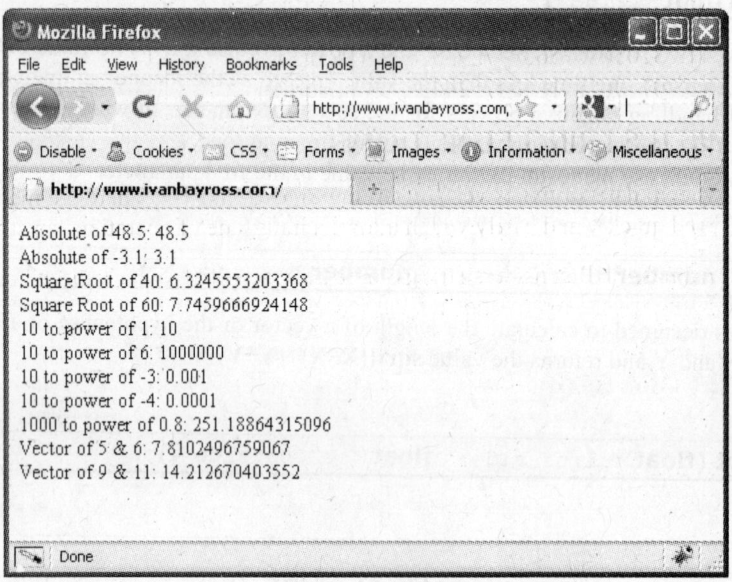

Diagram 18.27

Mathematical Constants

There are several constant values in mathematics, used in maths related scripts, but take some time to calculate. So to save time PHP defines them as constants and these are available to programmers. For example, if the value of **PI** has to be used, just use the PHP built-in constant value **M_PI**.

Example:
To calculate the area **A** of a circle based upon its radius **r**, the formula is **A=pi*r²**. Using PHP it can be written as follows:

```
<?php
    $A = M_PI * ($r * $r);
?>
```

OR

```
<?php
    $A = M_PI * pow($r, 2);
?>
```

Using PHP's built-in mathematical constants saves a lot of lengthy and pointless calculation.

A list of popular PHP constants is as follows:

Constant	Value	Meaning
M_PI	3.14159265358979323846	Pi
M_PI_2	1.57079632679489661923	Pi/2
M_PI_4	0.78539816339744830962	Pi/4
M_1_PI	0.31830988618379067154	1/Pi
M_2_PI	0.63661977236758134308	2/Pi
M_SQRTPI	1.77245385090551602729	sqrt(M_PI)

M_2_SQRTPI	1.12837916709551257390	2/sqrt(M_PI)
M_SQRT2	1.41421356237309504880	sqrt(2)
M_SQRT3	1.73205080756887729352	sqrt(3)
M_SQRT1_2	0.70710678118654752440	1/sqrt(2)

WORKING WITH STRING FUNCTIONS

Learning how to manipulate strings is very rewarding to learn in PHP. There are many helpful functions in PHP that can be used quickly and easily which allows a multitude of operations on strings.

As with variable names, PHP considers strings to be **case sensitive**, which means matching and replacing strings would be quite tricky, were it not for the fact that PHP provides case-insensitive versions of each function, where required.

Extracting Part Of A String

The **substr()** function allows reading just part of a string and takes a minimum of two parameters that is the string to work with and where to start reading from. There is an optional third parameter to allow specifying how many characters are to be read.

Syntax:

```
string substr ( string <source>, int <start position> [, int <length>])
```

NOTE

In PHP, strings and arrays start at index **0** rather than **1**.

If the start position is larger than the actual length of the string, PHP will not return an error. It will just return an empty string.

A negative number can be specified as the third parameter. PHP will consider that number as the amount of characters that have to be **omitted from the end** of the string.

Similarly, a negative number can be specified as the second parameter. PHP will start reading from the string end. A negative length can be used with a negative start index.

Example:

```
<?php
    $str = "String Extraction";
    print "Start at 2: " . substr($str, 2) . "<BR />";
    print "Start at 8: " . substr($str, 8) . "<BR />";
    print "Start at 18: " . substr($str, 18) . "<BR />";
    print "From 7 get 5: " . substr($str, 7, 5) . "<BR />";
    print "From 2 get -11: " . substr($str, 2, -11) . "<BR />";
    print "Start at -8: " . substr($str, -8) . "<BR />";
?>
```

Output: (Refer to diagram 18.28)

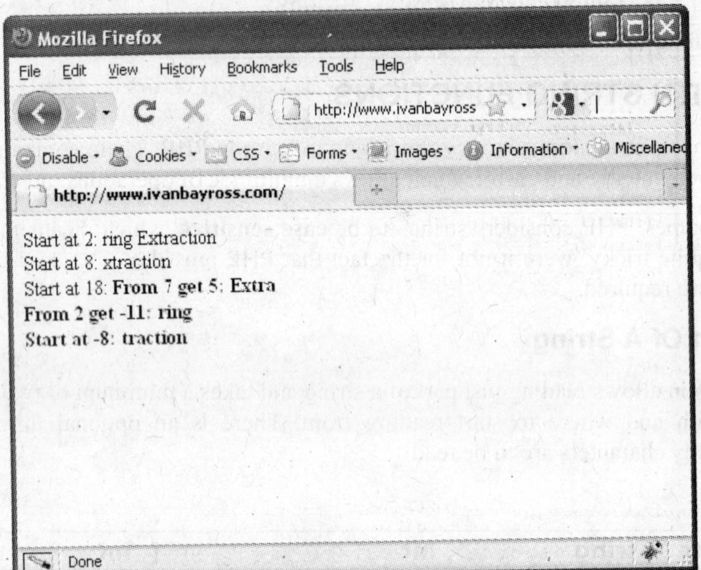

Diagram 18.28

Finding A String Within A String

PHP provides two functions to perform string search. The **strpos()** function and its case-insensitive sibling the **stripos()** functions, returns the index of the first occurrence of a substring within a string.

Syntax:

```
int strpos (string <source>, string <search text> [, int <start position>])
int stripos (string <source>, string <search text> [, int <start position>])
```

If a whole word is specified as the second parameter, the **strpos()** function returns the first position of that word within the string. If the substring specified in the second parameter is not found in first parameter **strpos()** will return **false**.

Example:

```
<?php
    $str = "String Extraction";
    print "Position of c: " . strpos($str, "c") . "<BR />";
    print "Position of ion: " . strpos($str, "ion") . "<BR />";
    print "Position of S: " . strpos($str, "S") . "<BR />";
    print "Position of g: " . stripos($str, "g") . "<BR />";
?>
```

Output: (Refer to diagram 18.28.1)

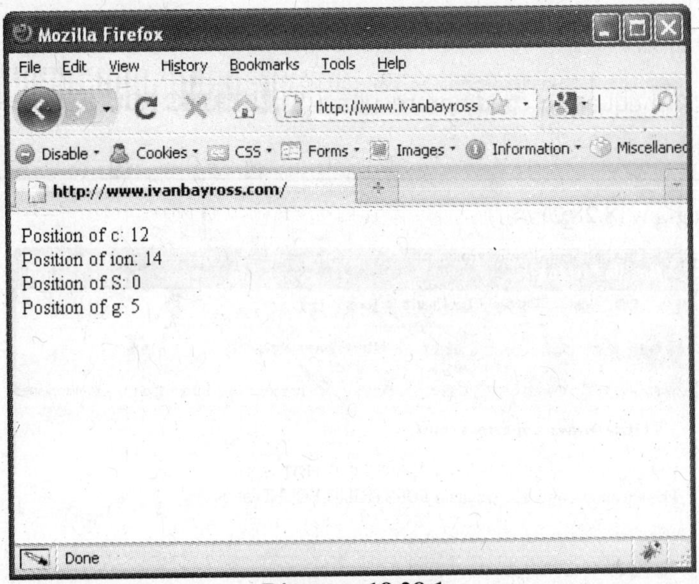

Diagram 18.28.1

CAUTION

While using **strpos()** in a conditional statement, to determine whether the substring exists or not, it is possible that the result fails even though the substring is found at **0** index. This is because, PHP considers **0** to be the same value as **false**, which means that the conditional statement **cannot tell the difference** between Substring not found and Substring found at index 0.

The problem encountered while using a conditional statement can be resolved by using the === (is identical to) operator. In such a situation the comparison will be made between **0** of the type **false** (Boolean) *for substring not found* rather than between **0** of the type integer *for substring found at index 0*.

Example:

```
<?php
   $str = "Using the function strpos() For String Extraction";
   $idx = strpos($str, " Using the function");
   /* Using the 'comparison' (==) operator. */
   if ($idx == false)
   {
      print "The equation condition results a SUBSTRING NOT FOUND<BR />";
   }
   else
   {
      print "The equation condition results a SUBSTRING FOUND at $idx<BR />";
   }
   /* Using the 'is identical to' (===) operator. */
   if ($idx === false)
   {
      print "The equation condition results a SUBSTRING NOT FOUND<BR />";
```

```
    }
    else
    {
        print "The equation condition results a SUBSTRING FOUND at $idx<BR />";
    }
?>
```

Output: (Refer to diagram 18.28.2)

Diagram 18.28.2

Finally, the third parameter to the **strpos()** function allows to specify where to start the search from. Consider the next script, which tries to match the "ing" in "String":

```
<?php
    $str = "Using strpos() For String Extraction";
    $idx1 = strpos($str, "ing");
    $idx2 = strpos($str, "ing", 15);
    /* Using the strpos() without the three parameter. */
    if ($idx1 === false)
    {
        print "First identical condition results a SUBSTRING NOT FOUND<BR />";
    }
    else
    {
        print "First identical condition results a SUBSTRING FOUND at $idx1<BR />";
    }
    /* Using the strops() with the three parameter. */
    if ($idx2 === false)
    {
        print "Second identical condition results a SUBSTRING NOT FOUND<BR />";
    }
    else
    {
        print "Second identical condition results a SUBSTRING FOUND at $idx2
        <BR />";
    }
?>
```

Output: (Refer to diagram 18.28.3)

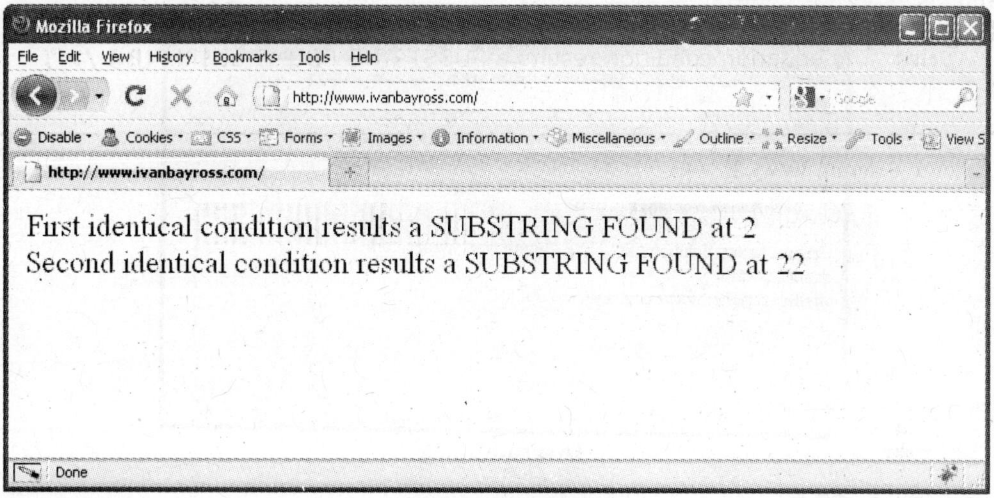

Diagram 18.28.3

In the above example, the **strpos()** function matches the first **ing** it comes across which will be in **Using**. When the third parameter is specified **strpos()** will ignore substring found before the specified starting point.

Returning The First Occurrence Of A String

strstr() extracts a substring or returns the first occurrence of a string within a string.

Syntax:

```
string strstr (string <source>, string <search text>)
string stristr (string <source>, string <search text>)
```

The **strstr()** function is case-insensitive subset of **stristr()** and finds the first occurrence of a substring (specified as the second parameter) inside another string (specified as the first parameter) and returns all characters from the first occurrence to the end of the string.

Example:
The following code snippet uses both **strstr()** and **stristr()** to scan a string for the word **WWW**. When found, it returns the text from the **WWW** until the end of the string:

```
<?php
    $str = "Solutions at -> http://www.ivanbayross.com";
    $strURL1 = strstr($str, "WWW");
    $strURL2 = stristr($str, "WWW");
    echo "Original string: $str<BR />";
    echo "strstr() returns: $strURL1 <BR />";
    echo "stristr() returns: $strURL2 <BR />";
?>
```

Output: (Refer to diagram 18.29)

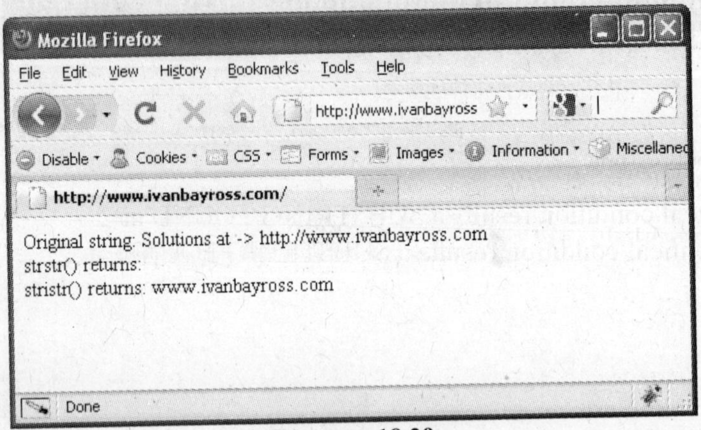

Diagram 18.29

Replacing Parts Of A String

The **str_replace()** and the **str_ireplace()** functions replace one part of a string with new parts. The **str_ireplace()** function is **case-insensitive**.

Syntax:

```
mixed str_replace (mixed <search text>, mixed <replace text>, mixed
                   <source> [, int &<counter>] )
mixed str_ireplace (mixed <search text>, mixed <replace text>, mixed
                   <source> [, int &<counter>])
```

The function accepts a minimum of three parameters i.e. what to look for, what to replace it with and the string to work with. It also has an optional fourth parameter which if passed will hold the number of replacements made.

Example:

```
<?php
    $str = "Java is an open source language. <BR />";
    $newstr = str_replace("Java", "PHP", $str , $count);
    $newStr = str_ireplace("java", "php", $str, $count);
    print "Original: " . $str;
    print "Modified and Case Sensitive: " . $newstr;
    print "Modified and Case Insensitive: " . $newStr;
    print "$count changes were made.<BR />";
?>
```

Output: (Refer to diagram 18.30)

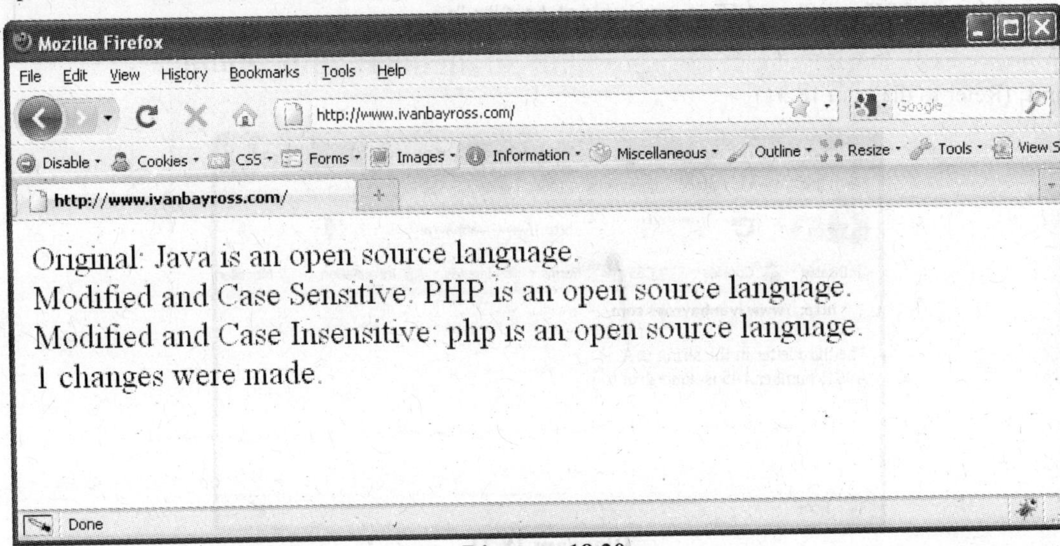

Diagram 18.30

In the above example, both the flavors of the function i.e. case sensitive and case-insensitive are demonstrated.

Converting To And From ASCII

The American Standard Code for Information Interchange is a special set of 255 numbers that evaluate to letters, symbols and actions used in most computers. For example: 74 is J, 106 is j, 123 is { and 32 is a space and so on.

Syntax:

```
string chr (int <ASCII value>)
int ord (string <text>)
```

The **chr()** function is used to convert ASCII to textual characters. This function accepts an ASCII value as its single parameter and returns the text equivalent.

The **ord()** function is the reverse of **chr()** function which converts textual characters to ASCII. This function accepts a string and returns the equivalent ASCII value.

Example:

```
<?php
    $str = "Ivan Bayross is a Professor.";
    if (ord($str{2}) == 97)
    {
        print "The third letter in the string is A<BR />";
    }1
    else
    {
        print "The third letter in the string is not A<BR />";
    }
```

```
    $ltr = chr(105);
    print "ASCII number 105 is equivalent to $ltr ";
?>
```

Output: (Refer to diagram 18.31)

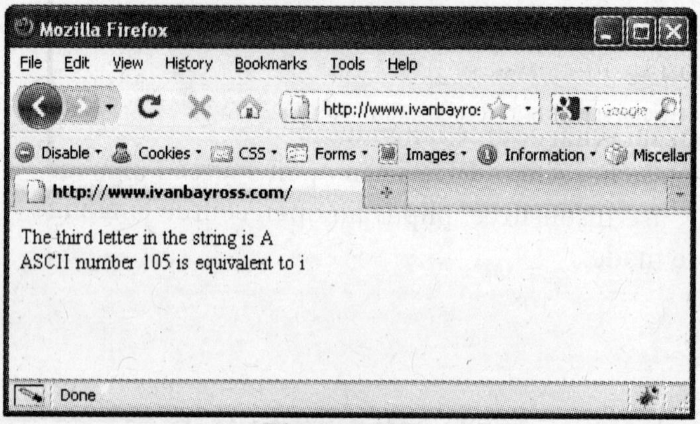

Diagram 18.31

Measuring Strings

Measuring a string and its contents can be done in three separate ways:

- **strlen()** - Is the easiest way to measure a string. **strlen()** counts the number of characters in the string. It takes just one parameter (i.e. the string) and returns the number of characters in it

Syntax:

```
int strlen (string <source>)
```

Example:

```
<?php
    $len = strlen("Linux");
    print "The length of string 1 is: " . $len . "<BR />";

    $len = strlen("Four in One HTML");
    print "The length of string 2 is: " . $len;
?>
```

Output: (Refer to diagram 18.32)

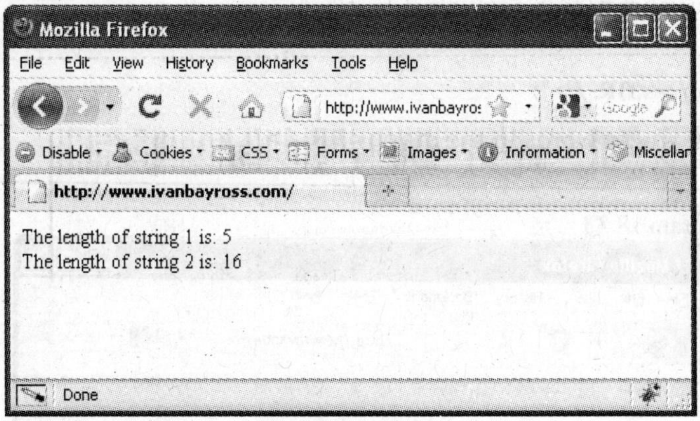

Diagram 18.32

- **count_chars()** - It returns **an array** containing the letters used in that string and how many times each letter was repeated in the string

Syntax:

```
mixed count_chars (string <string> [, int <mode>])
```

Using **count_chars()** is complicated somewhat by the fact that it actually returns an array of exactly 255 elements by default, with each number evaluating to an ASCII code. This can be worked around by filtering through the array to remove items that have a value (frequency) of 0 or, alternatively, pass a second parameter to the function. If 1 is passed, only letters with a frequency greater than 0 are listed, if 2 is passed only letters with a frequency equal to 0 are listed.

- **str_word_count()** - It returns the number of words used if called without any parameters

Syntax:

```
mixed str_word_count (string <string> [, int <format>])
```

Similarly, a second parameter can be passed to **str_word_count()**. By default, it just returns the number of unique words that were found in the string. However, if 1 is passed as the second parameter it will return an array of the words found and passing 2 does the same, except the key of each word will be set to the position that word was found inside the string.

Example:

```
<?php
    $str = "Four in One HTML Book for Beginners.";
    print '$str = "Four in One HTML Book for Beginners."<BR /><BR />';

    $a = count_chars($str, 1);
    $b = str_word_count($str, 1);
    $c = str_word_count($str, 2);
    $d = str_word_count($str);

    print_r($a);
    print "<BR /><BR />";
```

```
        print_r($b);
        print "<BR /><BR />";

        print_r($c);
        print "<BR /><BR />";

        echo "There are $d words in the string<BR />";
?>
```

Output: (Refer to diagram 18.33

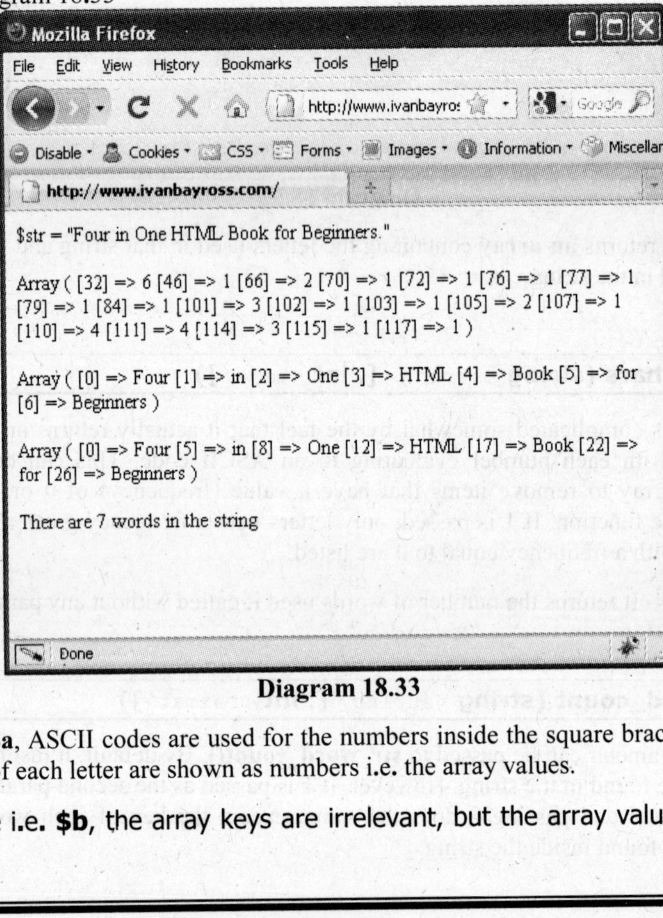

Diagram 18.33

In the first case i.e. **$a**, ASCII codes are used for the numbers inside the square brackets i.e. the array keys and the frequencies of each letter are shown as numbers i.e. the array values.

In the second case i.e. **$b**, the array keys are irrelevant, but the array values are the list of the words found.

NOTE

The punctuation marks such as comma, full stop and numbers are not considered as words in the functions **count_chars()** and **str_word_count()**.

In the third case i.e. **$c**, the array keys mark where the first letter of the word in the value was found, thus **0** means **this** was found at the beginning of the string.

The last case i.e. **$d** shows the default word counting behavior of **str_word_count()**.

Trimming Whitespace

Trimming functions are used to strip whitespaces from left, right or either side of a string variable. Whitespaces include spaces, new lines and tabs.

There are three trimming functions:

- **trim()** - It removes whitespaces from **either sides of the string** passed as the first parameter

Syntax:

```
string trim (string <source> [, string <charlist>])
```

- **ltrim()** - It removes whitespaces **beginning from the left** of the string passed as the first parameter

Syntax:

```
string ltrim (string <source> [, string <charlist>])
```

- **rtrim()** - It removes whitespaces **beginning from the right** of the string passed as the first parameter

Syntax:

```
string rtrim (string <source> [, string <charlist>])
```

The second optional parameter specifies other character(s), which need to be removed from the string.

Example:

```
<?php
    $a = "  Trimming Example ";
    echo "Original text: " . $a . "<BR />";

    $b =ltrim($a);
    echo "LTrim returns: " . $b . "<BR />";

    $c =rtrim($a);
    echo "RTrim returns: " . $c . "<BR />";

    $d =trim($a);
    echo "Trim returns: " . $d . "<BR />";

    $e =trim($a, " ample");
    echo "Trim with 2 params returns: " . $e . "<BR />";
?>
```

Output: (Refer to diagram 18.34)

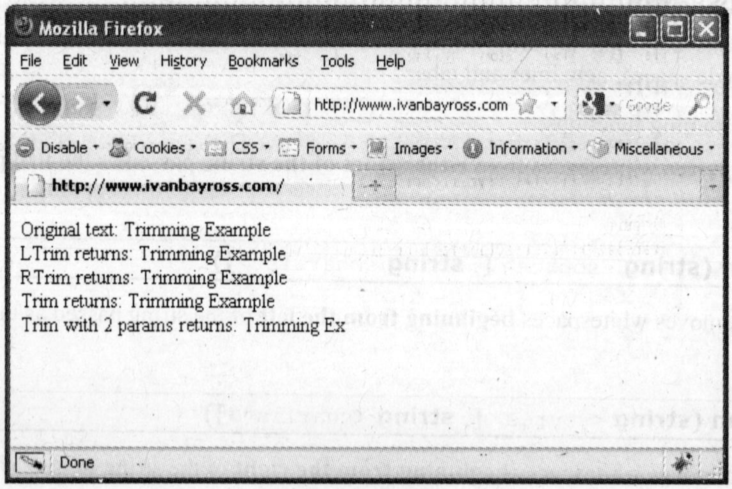

Diagram 18.34

Wrapping Lines In Text Messages

Although web pages wrap text automatically, there are two situations when wrapping the text is required:

- When printing to a console as opposed to a web page, text does not wrap automatically
- When printing to a web page that has been designed to exactly accommodate a certain width of text

Syntax:

```
string wordwrap (string <source> [, int <width> [, string <new line marker> [,
                 boolean <cut>]]])
```

When a sentence of text is passed to **wordwrap()** with no additional parameters, it will return that same string wrapped at the **75-character** mark using **\n** for new lines. To override the defaults, specify the line size and new line marker as parameters two and three respectively.

Example:

```
<?php
    $author = "Ivan Bayross is the author for Four in One HTML Book.";
    print "Original:<BR />" . $author . "<BR /><BR />";
    $author = wordwrap($author, 5, "<BR/>");
    print "Modified:<BR />" . $author;
?>
```

Output: (Refer to diagram 18.35)

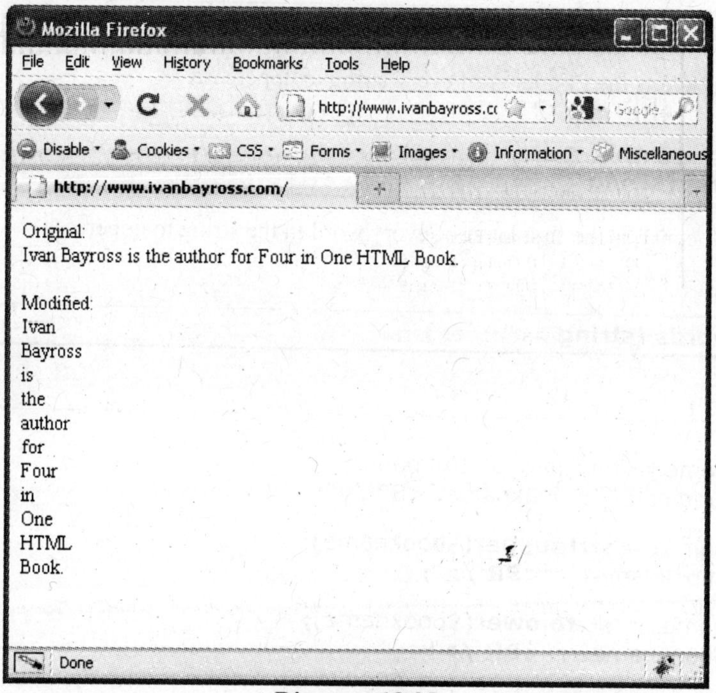

Diagram 18.35

When the script runs within a Web Browser, a page as shown in diagram 18.35 is displayed. While generating the output, **wordwrap()** uses **
**, an HTML new line marker, splits up the words at the 20-character mark, as specified.

NOTE

By default, the **wordwrap()** function wraps words pessimistically. If the second parameter is set to 20, **wordwrap()** will always wrap when it hits 20 characters or under. The only exception to this is if words are individually longer than 20 characters. In such a situation the width of the line increases.

To enforce a specific line width, the value 1 is passed as the fourth parameter, which enables **cut** mode, (i.e. words over the limit will be broken up if this is enabled).

Changing String Case

The following functions affect the case of characters in strings:

- **strtoupper()** - It takes a string parameter as an argument and returns that string entirely in uppercase

Syntax:

```
string strtoupper (string <source>)
```

- **strtolower()** - It takes a string parameter as an argument and returns that string entirely in lowercase

Syntax:

```
string strtolower (string <source>)
```

- **ucfirst()** - It converts the first letter of every string to uppercase

Syntax:

```
string ucfirst (string <source>)
```

- **ucwords()** - It converts the first letter of every word in the string to uppercase

Syntax:

```
string ucwords (string <source>)
```

Example:

```
<?php
    $bookname = "four in one html book";
    echo "Original: " . $bookname."<BR />";

    $bookname1 = strtoupper($bookname);
    echo $bookname1 . "<BR />";

    $bookname2 = strtolower($bookname);
    echo $bookname2 . "<BR />";

    $bookname3 = ucfirst($bookname);
    echo $bookname3 . "<BR />";

    $bookname4 = ucwords($bookname);
    echo $bookname4 . "<BR />";
?>
```

Output: (Refer to diagram 18.36)

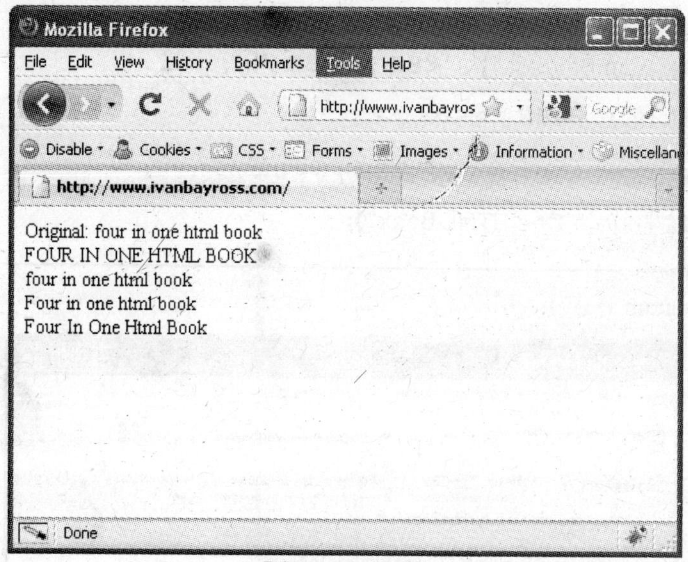

Diagram 18.36

Secure Data Hash

- **sha1()** - sha stands for the **Secure Hash Algorithm**. It is a way of converting a string of any size into a 40-bit hexadecimal number that can be used for verification. Hashes are like unidirectional i.e. one-way encryption designed to check the accuracy of input

Syntax:

```
string sha1(string <source> [, bool <rawoutput>])
```

Well, imagine users enter a password and to check whether the password is correct the following code is written:

```
<?php
	if ($_POST['password'] == "SomePassword")
	{
		// Some Code
	}
?>
```

While that solution certainly works, it means that whoever reads the source code gets the password. Similarly if all the user's passwords are stored in the database and someone cracks it, then all the passwords are hacked. However, if the passwords are stored in a database or in files, after being processed by the **Secure Hash Algorithm** then malicious users will not be able to retrieve the original password.

Hashing is also commonly used to check whether files have downloaded properly i.e. if the hash is equal to the correct hash value, then the file has been downloaded without any problem.

The process of data hashing involves taking a value and converting it into a semi-meaningless string of letters and numbers of a fixed length. **There is no way whatsoever to decrypt a hash to obtain the original value**.

Example:

```
<?php
    print sha1("Ivan Bayross") . "<BR /><BR />";

    print sha1("Hi") . "<BR /><BR />";

    print sha1("Good Afternoon") . "<BR /><BR />";

    print sha1("Four in One HTML Book");
?>
```

Output: (Refer to diagram 18.37)

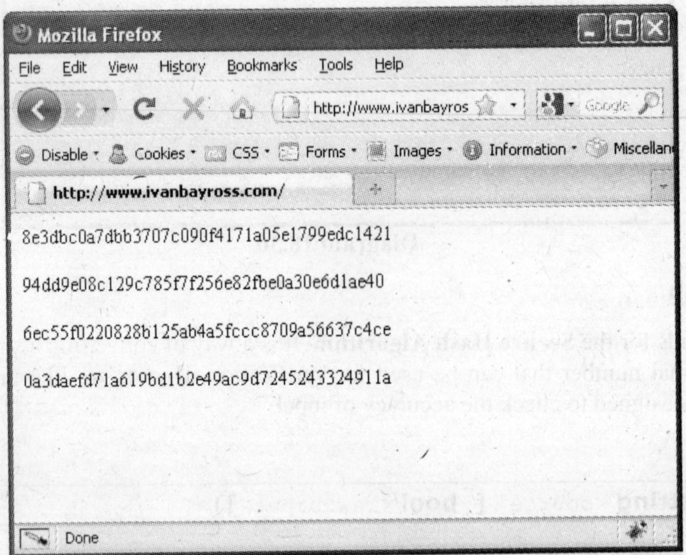

Diagram 18.37

There are three key things to notice:

- All the output is exactly 40 characters in length and always will be
- The difference between the hash of "hello" and the hash of "Hello" is gigantic despite the only difference being a small caps change
- There is no way to distinguish between long strings and short strings because the hash is not reversible (that is, the original input from the hash cannot be extracted)

One thing that is imperative to remember is that **sha1()** will always give the same output for a given input.

NOTE

If an optional second parameter is set to true, the **sha1** hash is returned in raw binary format and will have a length of 20.

The **sha1()** can now be applied to check password as:

```
<?php
    if (sha1($_POST['password'])== "SomeHashedPasswordStoredInDB")
    {
                    // Some Code
    }
?>
```

- **md5()** - md stands for **M**essage **D**igest. The **md5()** function produces a data hash in exactly the same way as **sha1()**, with the difference that it is only 32-bytes long. Having fewer bits in md5 makes it less secure.

  An md5 hash is 32 bytes long, which is equal to 128 bits i.e. an md5 hash can be made up of 3.4028236692093846346337460743177e+38 different possibilities, more commonly referred to as 2 to the power of 128. These are an enormous number of varieties and so is quite secure for most purposes

Syntax:

```
string md5(string <source> [, bool <rawoutput>])
```

Example:

```
<?php
    print md5("Ivan Bayross") . "<BR /><BR />";
    print md5("Hi") . "<BR /><BR />";
    print md5("Good Afternoon") . "<BR /><BR />";
    print md5("Four in One HTML Book");
?>
```

Output: (Refer to diagram 18.38)

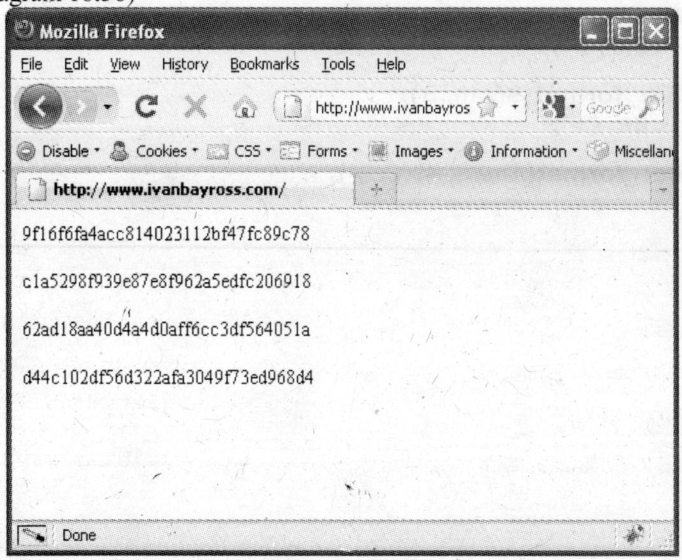

Diagram 18.38

NOTE

sha1() function is recommended for hashing data securely as compared to **md5()** function.

sha1() is longer and is less likely to have a **collision** that is a situation where two different strings share the same hash. However, **md5()** has a slight speed advantage.

Printing Number Formats

number_format() is a remarkably helpful function that takes a minimum of one parameter, the number to format and returns that same number grouped into thousands.

There are two function prototypes for **number_format()**. This means that this function can be passed either one, two or four parameters. Passing it **one or two fits** the **first prototype** and passing **four fits** the **second**.

So, if **number_format()** is passed a parameter of **1234567**, it will return **1,234,567**.

By default, **number_format()** rounds fractions **1234567.89** to **1,234,568**. However, the default can be changed by specifying the second parameter, which is the number of decimal places to include.

Parameter three allows choosing the character to use as decimal point and parameter four allows choosing the character to use as thousands separator.

Syntax:

```
string number_format(float <number>, int <decimalplaces>,
                     string <decimalpoint>, string <thousandsseperator>)
```

Example:

```
<?php
    $num = 9819.012895;
    echo 'Original Number is: ' . $num . "<BR />";

    $a = number_format($num);
    echo $a . "<BR />";

    $b = number_format($num, 3);
    echo $b . "<BR />";

    $c = number_format($num, 4, '.', ',');
    echo $c;
?>
```

Output: (Refer to diagram 18.39)

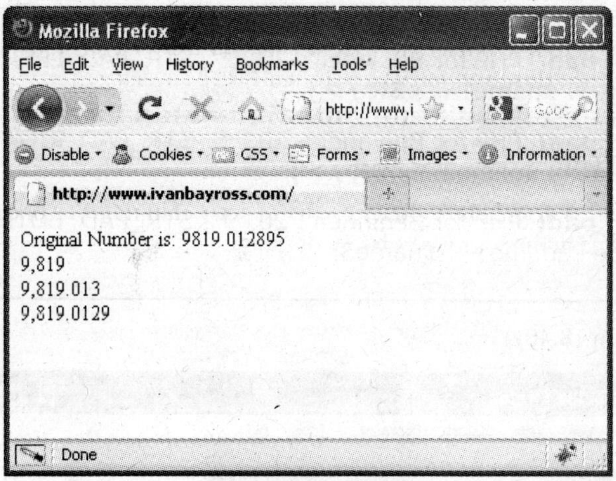

Diagram 18.39

number_format() is incredibly useful when it comes to formatting money for checkout pages in shopping baskets, although it is useful anywhere needed to represent large numbers, adding a thousand separator invariably makes things easier to read.

String Padding

str_pad() makes a given string (parameter one) larger by **N** number of characters (parameter two) by padding on spaces to parameter one.

Syntax:

```
string str_pad(string <input>, int <padlength> [, string <padstring>
                    [, int <padtype>]])
```

Example:

```
<?php
    $string = "PHP";
    $newstring = str_pad($string, 10);
?>
```

The above code would leave "PHP   " in **$newstring**, which is the same string from **$string** except with seven spaces are appended, equaling the total length of that string to 10 (passed in as parameter two).

str_pad() has an optional third parameter that sets the padding character to be applied:

```
<?php
    $string = "PHP ";
    $newstring = str_pad($string, 15, 'a');
?>
```

The above code would put **PHPaaaaaaa** into **$newstring**.

The function can be extended by using an optional fourth parameter, which allows specifying **the side** which needs to be padded. The fourth parameter is specified as a constant and either use STR_PAD_LEFT, STR_PAD_RIGHT or STR_PAD_BOTH.

Example:

```
<?php
    $name1 = str_pad("PHP for Beginner", 20, '*', STR_PAD_LEFT);
    echo 'Left Pad: ' . $name1 . '<BR />';

    $name2 = str_pad("PHP for Beginner", 20, '*', STR_PAD_RIGHT);
    echo 'Right Pad: ' . $name2 . '<BR />';

    $name3 = str_pad("PHP for Beginner", 20, '*', STR_PAD_BOTH);
    echo 'Both side Padding: ' . $name3;
?>
```

Output: (Refer to diagram 18.40)

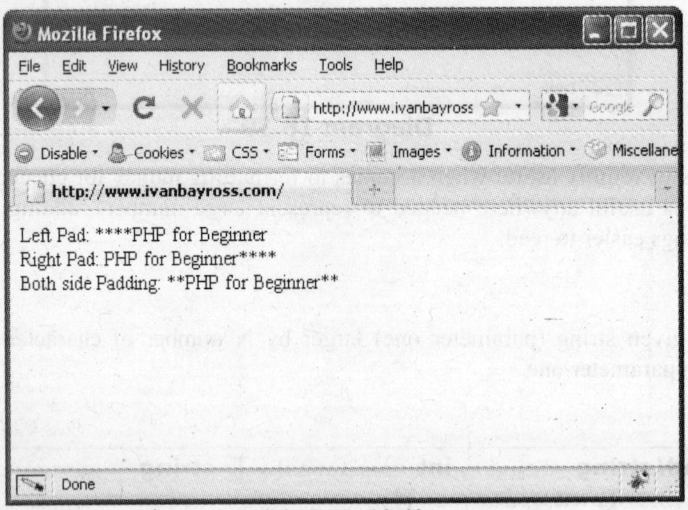

Diagram 18.40

The above code will set **$name1** to be ******PHP for Beginner**, **$name2** to be **PHP for Beginner ****** and **$name3** to be ****PHP for Beginner**** as expected.

NOTE

HTML by itself only allows a maximum of one space at any time. If more padding is needed, use ** ** the HTML code for non-breaking space.

Complex String Printing

The **printf()** function is the **C and C++** way to format text and is also available in PHP. It is not easy to use, but is useful for producing shorter code during code formatting.

Syntax:

```
void printf(string <format> [, mixed <args> [, mixed ...])
```

The function takes a variable number of parameters. A format string is always the first parameter, followed by other optional parameters of various types.

Example:

```
<?php
    $fruitName1="Mango";
    $fruitName2="Apple";
    $fruitName3="Apricot";
    $fruitName4="Orange";
    printf("%s, %s, %s and %s are name of fruits.", $fruitName1, $fruitName2,
$fruitName3, $fruitName4);
?>
```

Output: (Refer to diagram 18.41)

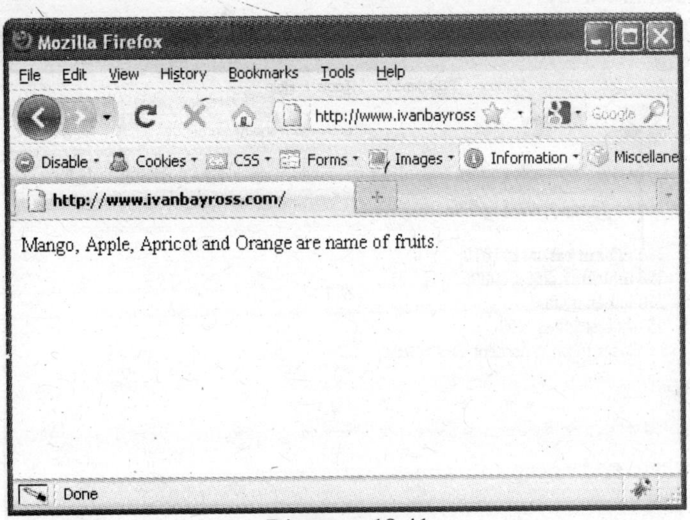

Diagram 18.41

The **%s** is a special format string that means **string parameter to follow**, which means that **$fruitName1**, **$fruitName2**, **$fruitName3**, **$fruitName4** will be treated as text inside the string that **printf()** creates.

The **printf()** function takes a variety of other format strings other than **%s**. The complete list is as mentioned below:

Format	Meaning
%%	A literal percent character; no matching parameter is required
%b	Parameter is an integer; present it as binary
%c	Parameter is an integer; present it as a character with that ASCII value
%d	Parameter is an integer; present it as a signed number
%f	Parameter is a float; present it as a float
%o	Parameter is an integer; present it as octal
%s	Parameter is a string; present it as a string
%x	Parameter is an integer; present it as hexadecimal with lowercase letters
%X	Parameter is an integer; present it is hexadecimal with uppercase letters

Example:

```
<?php
    $number = 250;
    printf("250 in binary is: %b.<BR />", $number);
    printf("250 in float is: %f.<BR />", $number);
    printf("250 in hex is: %x.<BR />", $number);
    printf("250 as a string is: %s.<BR />", $number);
    printf("%% allows to print percent characters.");
?>
```

Output: (Refer to diagram 18.42)

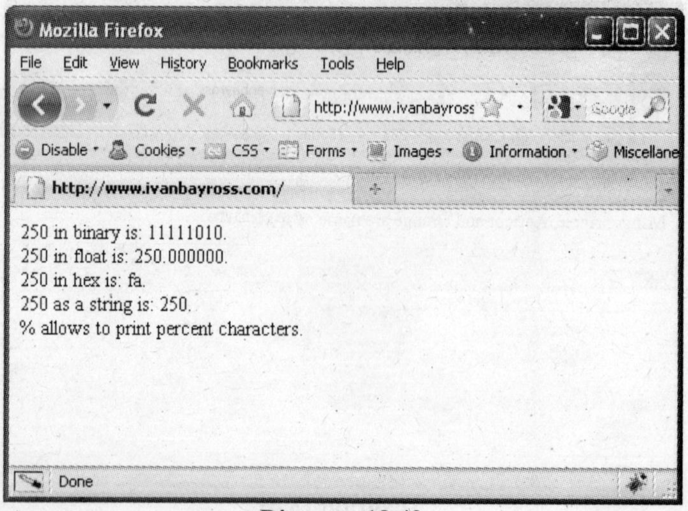

Diagram 18.42

Pausing Script Execution

[

There are two ways to pause execution in a script.

Syntax:

```
void sleep(int <seconds>)
void usleep(int <micro_seconds>)
```

The older way of doing this:

Example:

```
<?php
    $now = time();
    print date("h:i:s A") . "<BR />";
    echo "Pause<BR />";
    while ($now + 4 > time())
    {
    /* Performing no action */
    }
```

```
    echo "Resume<BR />";
    print date("h:i:s A");
?>
```

Output: (Refer to diagram 18.43)

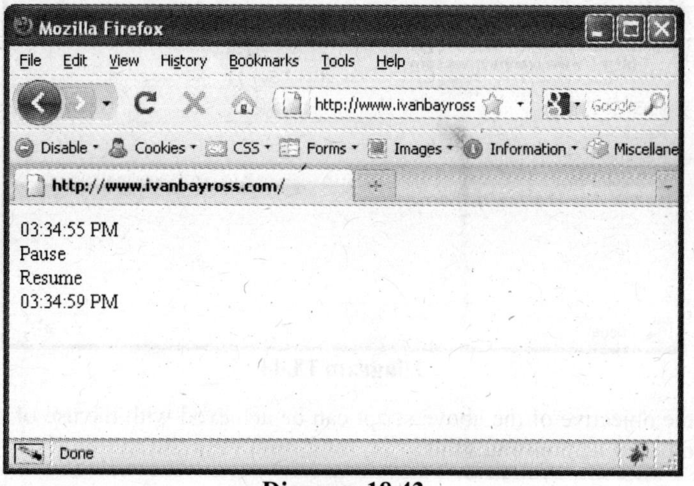

Diagram 18.43

While it does work, there are two problems with it:

- **time()** has a very low precision, only returning the number of whole seconds that have passed, which makes the whole thing quite vague
- PHP has to sit there looping thousands of times while it waits, essentially doing nothing

A much better solution is to use one of the two script sleep functions, **sleep()** and **usleep()**, which take the amount of time to pause execution as their only parameter.

The difference between **sleep()**and **usleep()** is that **sleep()** takes a number of seconds as its parameter, whereas **usleep()** takes a number of microseconds i.e. millionths of a second as its parameter.

Using either of them is far more accurate than the previous **time()** loop and they both have their advantages. The **sleep()** function is better if accuracy is not desired and **usleep()** is better if accuracy is desired.

The above script could be rewritten like this:

```
<?php
    $now = time();
    print date("h:i:s A") . "<BR />";
    echo "Pause<BR />";
    sleep(4);
    echo "Resume<BR />";
    print date("h:i:s A");
?>
```

Output: (Refer to diagram 18.44)

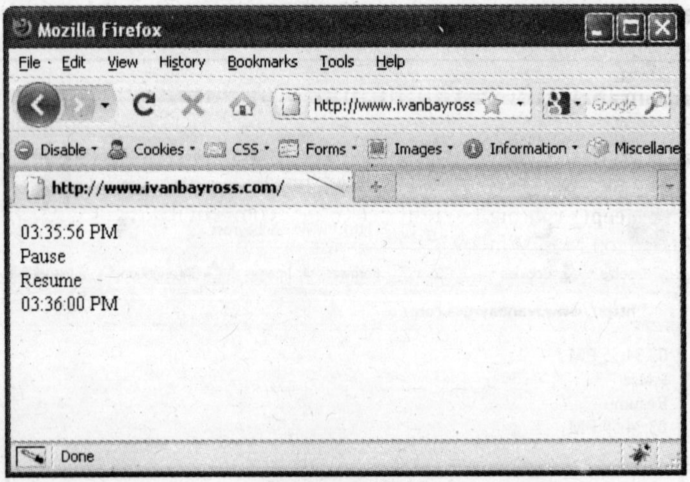

Diagram 18.44

On similar ground, the objective of the above script can be achieved with the use of the **usleep()** function. The script mentioned below demonstrates this:

```
<?php
    $now = time();
    print date("h:i:s A") . "<BR />";
    echo "Pause<BR />";
    usleep(4000000);
    echo "Resume<BR />";
    print date("h:i:s A");
?>
```

Output: (Refer to diagram 18.45)

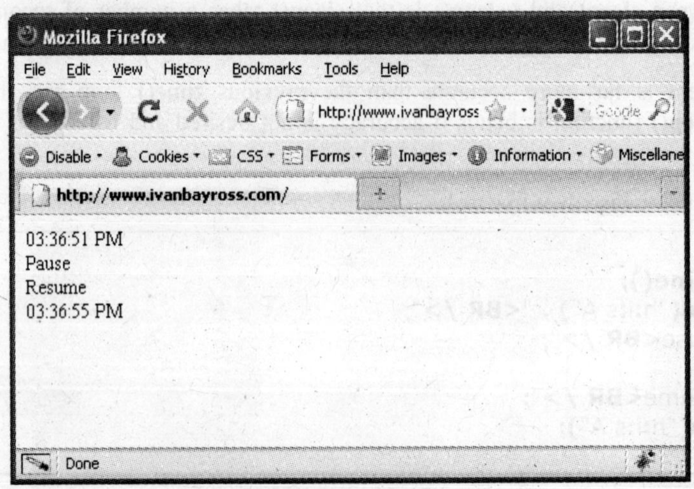

Diagram 18.45

NOTE

The default maximum script execution time is 30 seconds, but **sleep()** and **usleep()** can be used to make the scripts go on for longer than that because technically PHP does not have control during the sleep operation.

CAUTION

The use of **usleep()** is a big no-no if backwards compatibility is desired, because it wasn't available prior to PHP 5, on M.S. Windows.

HANDS ON EXERCISE

1. Create a function to calculate 33% tax on the given salary i.e. Rs. 65,500. The output should look like as shown below:

```
Tax for Rs. 65500 is: Rs. 21615
```

2. Generate Fibonacci series for the numbers 1 to 17. The output should look like as shown below:

```
1, 1, 2, 3, 5, 8, 13, 21, 34, 55, 89, 144, 233, 377, 610, 987, 1597
```

19. WORKING WITH FORMS

A very popular way to make a web site interactive is using HTML based forms by the site. Using HTML forms, a website can interact with a visitor and:

- Obtain registration information prior access to different site offerings
- Permit a visitor to submit information to the website
- Allow a visitor to upload files to the website

and much more.

HTML provides several graphic elements and the means to customize their behavior, thus empowering programmers to create any type of form for use by a web site.

A Form is displayed in a pre-defined area of an HTML document. This area would contain text, which acts as a prompt adjacent to text boxes to fill in with information. Once done the form would return this information back to the web server for further processing by another program. This fulfills the means of permitting a user to interact with the website.

Technically there are HTML tags that spawn, define and label text-entry boxes, check boxes, radio buttons, drop-down menus and so on to create on-screen forms, for collecting information from a user.

The data captured by the HTML form is returned to a server side script by the Browser in which the form runs. The web server side script then processes the information received.

Forms are an excellent way of collecting and processing information from people visiting a web site, thus allowing them to interact with the site. The output of form processing can be sent as an e-mail, stored online, printed and/or returned as an HTML page.

Forms are generally used for:

User Registration	Logging in users
Receiving feedback	Online shopping
Online catalogs	Surveys
Request for information	Conferencing

And so on.

Introducing HTML Form Tags And Elements

A brief overview of commonly used HTML form tags and their attributes, prior creating a form would go a long way in being able to create an HTML form that works exactly as required.

The Main <FORM> Tag

The **<FORM> </FORM>** tags indicate the boundaries of a form on the HTML page. **<FORM>** indicates where the form starts and **</FORM>** indicates where the form ends. All other form elements must be enclosed between **<FORM></FORM>** tags.

Syntax:

```
<FORM NAME="<formname>" ACTION="<server side (PHP) program name>"
  METHOD="<GET or POST>" >
```

The attributes passed within the **<FORM>** tag are:

- **NAME:** The value passed to the NAME attribute uniquely identifies the form so that it may be referenced by style sheets or client side JavaScript
- **ACTION:** The **value** passed to the ACTION attribute is the name of the web server side program which will process the data captured by the form when the data captured is returned to the web server by the Browser. The value passed to the ACTION attribute can either be just the program name or can specify a URL which points to where the program is located on the web server

  Alternatively, if the data is not supposed to be sent from the form to a server-side program, then **action="mailto:<Complete Email Address>"** can also be specified. In this case, the data captured by the form is simply mailed to the Email ID by the browser, rather than being sent to a program on a web server for further processing
- **METHOD:** The value passed to the METHOD attribute defines exactly how the data captured by the form must be sent back from the Browser to the Web server

  There are two possible values accepted by the METHOD attribute:

  - **GET:** With the HTTP GET method, the Browser's processing agent encodes the data captured by the form into a **URL**. The data encoded URL is then returned to the Web Server. The total data that can be dispatched to a Web server, using an encoded URL is limited to **about 1 Kilobyte**
  - **POST:** With the HTTP POST method, the Browser's processing agent returns the data captured by the form to a web server using a **data stream**. There is no limit to the amount of data that can be sent by the Browser to a Web server using a data stream

  POST **is preferred** over GET for returning form data from a Browser to a web server, safely and privately.

  In contrast, the GET method may result in form data being truncated or cached. Additionally, a URL is encoded using plain text hence anyone can read the URL and understand exactly what is being sent back to the Web server.

  All the information that a Browser requires to successfully dispatch data captured in a form to the Web server is **contained as attributes** within the <FORM> tag itself. This is placed there by the programmer creating the form.

TIP

The GET method restricts form data set values to **ASCII characters**. However, when the POST method **with** ENCTYPE="multipart/form-data" is specified the entire **[ISO10646] character set** is covered.

Make absolutely sure that the form ends with a **</FORM>** end tag.

FORM ELEMENTS

There are various HTML form elements that can be used to build a form such as text boxes, text areas, radio buttons, check boxes, command buttons and so on. These elements are always **contained within** the <FORM></FORM> tags.

Text Box

When placed on an HTML form the text box permits the capture of one line of text. A user will be able to key in any textual information into a Text box.

Syntax:

```
<INPUT TYPE="Text" NAME="<textboxname>" SIZE="" MAXLENGTH=""
TABINDEX="" />
```

Where,

- **INPUT** is an HTML keyword that indicates the start of an HTML object being described
- **TYPE** accepts the type of a form element, in this case a text box
- **NAME** accepts any name which is then bound to the text box example: **txtName**
- **SIZE** accepts a size for the text box i.e. how long the text box will appear on a form
- **MAXLENGTH** controls the maximum number of characters the text box will accept
- **TABINDEX** accepts a numeric value that indicates a position of that form object within other objects on a form. The form cursor uses the tab index of form elements when navigating through multiple objects on a form

Text Area

This is a larger text box that allows a user to key in multiple lines of text. The entered text can span across multiple lines. The **size** of a Text Area is specified in **ROWS** and **COLUMNS**. The COLUMNS of the text area determines the number of characters it can capture and the ROWS determines the number of lines of text it can capture.

Syntax:

```
<TEXTAREA NAME="<textareaname>" ROWS="<noofrows>"
  COLS="<noofcolumns>"></TEXTAREA>
```

Where,

- **NAME** is the name of the Text Area
- **ROWS** indicate how many rows of text will be accepted
- **COLS** indicate how many characters will fit in each row of text captured

Example:

```
<TEXTAREA NAME="comment" ROWS=6 COLS=40>
</TEXTAREA>
```

In the above example, the text area will accept 6 rows of text, each row 40 characters long.

TIP

A text area is specified using opening and closing tags i.e. **<TEXTAREA> </TEXTAREA>**.

Password

The password field looks identical to a text box. However, when text is typed in it, the letters are hidden. This provides a level of security when keying in passwords into a form.

Caution

Even though the passwords are displayed as an asterisk (*) in the password text box they **are not** dispatched to the web server **encrypted** in any way.

Syntax:

```
<INPUT TYPE="PASSWORD" NAME="<passwordname>" SIZE="30"
    MAXLENGTH="15" />
```

Where,

- **INPUT** is an HTML keyword that indicates the start of an HTML object being described
- **TYPE** accepts the type of a form element, in this case a password type text box
- **NAME** accepts any name which is then bound to the password box example: **pwdPassword**
- **SIZE** accepts a size for the password type text box i.e. how long the password type text box will appear on the form
- **MAXLENGTH** controls the maximum number of characters accepted by the password type text box

Radio Button

Radio buttons indicate a fixed set of choices. A radio button is an empty circle with a textual prompt displayed beside it. When selected, the circle is partially filled in. Only **one** radio button from a set of radio buttons can be selected at any time. Radio buttons are grouped together by simply naming all the radio buttons used on the form with the same name.

Radio Buttons are sometimes called **Option Buttons** as they allow the selection of any one option out of the list of options. When a second radio button is selected from a group of radio buttons, the first one loses its selection.

Syntax:

```
<INPUT TYPE="radio" NAME="<radiobuttonname>" VALUE="<caption>"
    CHECKED="<True/False>" TABINDEX="" />
```

Where,

- **INPUT** is an HTML keyword that indicates the start of an HTML object being described
- **TYPE** accepts the type of a form element, in this case a radio button
- **NAME** accepts any name, which is then bound to the radio button example: **rdGender**
- **VALUE** accepts a caption for a radio button. It is text placed adjacent to the radio button
- **CHECKED** accepts either **true** or **false**. Is used to select a default radio button

- **TABINDEX** accepts a numeric value that indicates a position of that form object within other objects on a form. The form cursor uses the tab index of form elements when navigating through multiple objects on a form

Checkbox

A checkbox also looks similar to a radio button but can be used for selecting multiple choices from a set. The HTML object placed on the page is a square. The square holds a tick mark in it when selected. The major difference between radio button and check box is that with check boxes multiple choices can be made from a list of choices.

Syntax:

```
<INPUT TYPE="Checkbox" NAME="<checkboxname>" VALUE="<caption>"
    CHECKED="<True/False>" TABINDEX="" />
```

Where,

- **INPUT** is an HTML keyword that indicates the start of an HTML object being described
- **TYPE** accepts the type of a form element, in this case a check box
- **NAME** accepts any name, which is then bound to the check box example: **chkStatus**
- **VALUE** accepts a caption for the check box. It is text, placed adjacent to the check box. Caption text can be placed on the top, bottom or to the left or right of the check button
- **TABINDEX** accepts a numeric value that indicates a position of that form object within other objects on a form. The form cursor uses the tab index of form elements when navigating through multiple objects on a form

The Combo Box Or Drop Down List Box

The Combo Box or Drop Down List box displays multiple options available. The Combo Box or Drop Down List box initially displays one item. When clicked on, it drops down to display a list of items to select from.

Syntax:

```
<SELECT NAME="<selectboxname>" SIZE="1" TABINDEX="">
    <OPTION SELECTED>Opt1 </OPTION>
    <OPTION> Opt1 </OPTION>
    <OPTION> Opt2 </OPTION>
    <OPTION> Opt3 </OPTION>
    <OPTION> Opt4 </OPTION>
    <OPTION> Opt5 </OPTION>
</SELECT>
```

Where,

- **SELECT** indicates the start of the Combo box or DDLB (Drop Down List Box)
- **NAME** accepts any name which is then bound to the combo box
- **SIZE** accepts the size of the box. Here, **1** means one line (or item) is shown by default
- **OPTION SELECTED** accepts which option will appear selected in the box by default
- **OPTION** accepts a string that will be displayed when the Combo box is clicked and drops down
- **/SELECT** indicates the end of the Combo box or DDLB

Hidden Field

Sometimes it is required to have some data returned to the Web server, which is isolated from other form data being captured, generally to satisfy some programming logic need.

For example: Returning a **flag** from the Browser to the Web server that indicates a specific operation must be performed on the form data by the Web server side PHP script. This is usually done when a **single**, Web server side PHP script is coded in such a way that it can perform multiple operations on a database table using the data returned by the form.

This means once form data is submitted to the Web server, the Web server script will need to identify what specific database **write** operation must be performed with the form data returned. i.e. **I**nsert, **D**elete or **U**pdate (i.e. I / D / U) data in a database table with the form data returned.

This is generally done by a hidden variable on the form returning a value either **I** (Insert), **U** (Update), **D** (Delete) which is captured and stored in it depending upon a command button being clicked by the user.

This kind of information is never displayed to the user of the form but is automatically and directly sent to the Web server for super controlling further processing. This is achieved using a hidden form field.

The command to place hidden form field on a form is as follows:

```
<INPUT TYPE="hidden" NAME="<hiddenfldname>" VALUE="<hiddendata>"/>
```

Where,

- **INPUT** is an HTML keyword that indicates the start of an HTML object being described
- **TYPE** accepts the type of a form element, in this case a hidden element
- **NAME** accepts any name which is then bound to the hidden form element example: **frmName**
- **VALUE** accepts a value to be bound to the hidden form element. It is this attribute that will have its value programmatically set (i.e. I, U, D) by JavaScript, depending upon which command button the user clicks on the form

Example:

```
<INPUT TYPE="hidden" NAME="frmName" VALUE="frmClientMaster"/>
```

This will return a name:value pair to the web server:

hidMode:I that helps identify which particulardb operator is intended.

Example:

```
<INPUT TYPE="hidden" NAME="OprMode" VALUE="I"/>
```

This will return the name:value pair to the web server:

OprMode:I that will help identify what table operation must be carried out on form data.

Image

An Image can be used as a clickable element on a form. A form can also be made informative and attractive by adding images as clickable command buttons on the form.

Syntax:

```
<INPUT TYPE="Image" NAME="<imgname>" SRC="<image source path>"
   WIDTH="" HEIGHT="" BORDER="" />
```

Where,

- **INPUT** is an HTML keyword that indicates the start of an HTML object being described
- **TYPE** accepts the type of a form element, in this case an Image
- **NAME** accepts any name which is then bound to the Image element example: **ImgPub**
- **WIDTH** accepts the width of the Image
- **HEIGHT** accepts the height of the Image
- **BORDER** accepts a border size (in pixels) for the Image element

SUBMIT And RESET Buttons

After placing all the form elements required on an HTML page within the <FORM></FORM> tags, there should be some way to have the contents of these elements returned to a particular destination (i.e. The Web server). No form is complete unless the user has a way to submit the data it captures back to the Web server from where it originated. This functionality is brought to a form by a **SUBMIT** button

Syntax:

```
<INPUT TYPE="Submit" NAME="<submitbuttonname>" VALUE="<caption>"/>
```

Where,

- **INPUT** is an HTML keyword that indicates the start of an HTML object being described
- **TYPE** accepts the type of a form element, in this case a button of the type **Submit**
- **NAME** accepts any name which is then bound to the Submit button example: **btnSubmit**
- **VALUE** accepts a string that is displayed on the body of the button as its caption

Some forms also allow erasing all the entries made in form elements prior filling in the form all over again. This functionality is brought to the form by a **RESET** button. The reset button resets all form elements to their default value. **With most forms, this is an empty form.** If form fields have a starting value, the reset button will return the form field to that starting value. **Form field resetting is done at the browser.**

Syntax:

```
<INPUT TYPE="Reset" NAME="<resetbuttonname>" VALUE="<caption>"/>
```

Where,

- **INPUT** is an HTML keyword that indicates the start of an HTML object being described
- **TYPE** accepts the type of a form element, in this case a button of the type **Reset**
- **NAME** accepts any name, which is then bound to the Reset button example: **btnReset**
- **VALUE** accepts a string that is displayed on the body of the button as a caption

ADDING ELEMENTS TO A FORM

To spawn form elements on a form the **<INPUT>** tag is used. The INPUT tag has several attributes. Table 19.1 displays the general attributes used with the INPUT tag:

Attributes	Description	Values
TYPE	Determines the type of form element	Text, Password, Radio, Checkbox, Hidden, Submit, Reset, Image
NAME	Determines the name of an element	Any Suitable Name
SIZE	Determines the size of the element	Any Suitable Number
VALUE	Determines the caption of the element	Any Suitable Caption
READONLY	Permits only reading of the contents of the element	True or False
TABINDEX	Provides an index to form elements	Any Sequential Numeric Value

Table 19.1

An excellent way of learning how HTML forms and their elements behave is by actually creating a form and using it to capture data and return this data to the Web server that served (i.e. delivered) the form to the Browser.

The form as shown in diagram 19.1 will be the end result of this exercise.

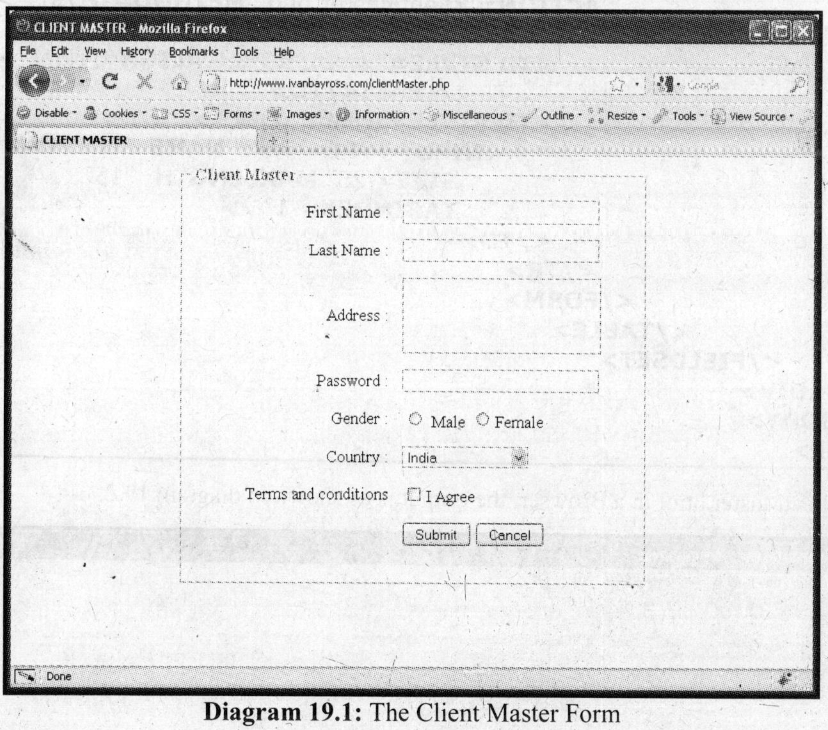

Diagram 19.1: The Client Master Form

The material that follows does just this. A form named **frmClientMaster** will be coded and saved into the **clientMaster.html** file. To begin, a text box is added to this file.

Adding A TextBox

Add a text box between the <FORM></FORM> tags in clientMaster.html with the following specifications:

OBJECT	LABEL	NAME	SIZE	MAX LENGTH	TAB INDEX
Text Box	First Name	txtFirstName	20	15	1

```
<HTML>
    <HEAD>
        <TITLE>CLIENT MASTER</TITLE>
    </HEAD>
    <BODY>
        <DIV STYLE="width: 50%;" >
            <FIELDSET>
                <LEGEND STYLE="color: brown; font-weight: bold;">
                    Client Master</LEGEND>
                    <TABLE  WIDTH="100%"  ALIGN="center"  CELLPADDING="1"
                        CELLSPACING="1"      STYLE="background-background-
                        color: white;">
                    <FORM      NAME="frmClientMaster"      ID="frmClientMaster"
                        ACTION="clientMaster.php" METHOD="POST" >
                        <TR>
                            <TD STYLE="width: 40%;" ALIGN="right">
                                First Name :</TD>
                            <TD STYLE="width: 40%;">
                                <INPUT TYPE="Text" NAME="txtFirstName"
                                    SIZE="25" MAXLENGTH="15"
                                    TABINDEX="1" />
                            </TD>
                        </TR>
                    </FORM>
                </TABLE>
            </FIELDSET>
        <DIV>
    </BODY>
</HTML>
```

On running clientMaster.html in a Browser, the output is as shown in diagram 19.2.

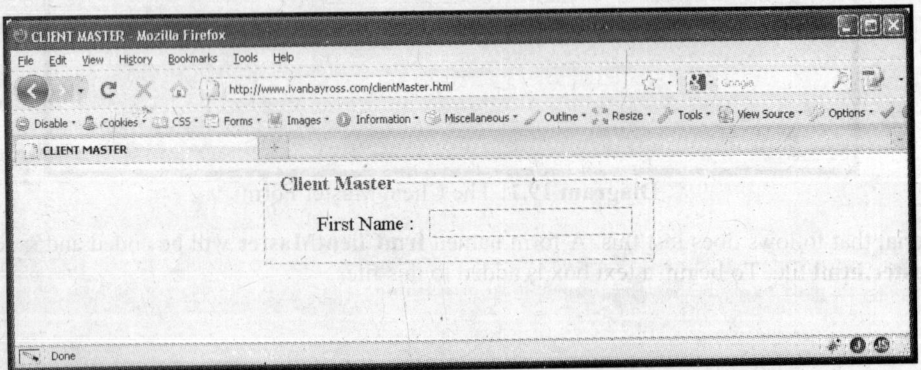

Diagram 19.2: Inserting a Text Box

To carry on building the clientMaster form (Refer to diagram 19.3), add another text box named **txtLastName** to the form with the following specifications.

OBJECT	LABEL	NAME	SIZE	MAX LENGTH	TAB INDEX
Text Box	Last Name	txtLastName	25	15	2

On running clientMaster.html in a Browser, the output as shown in diagram 19.3 is seen.

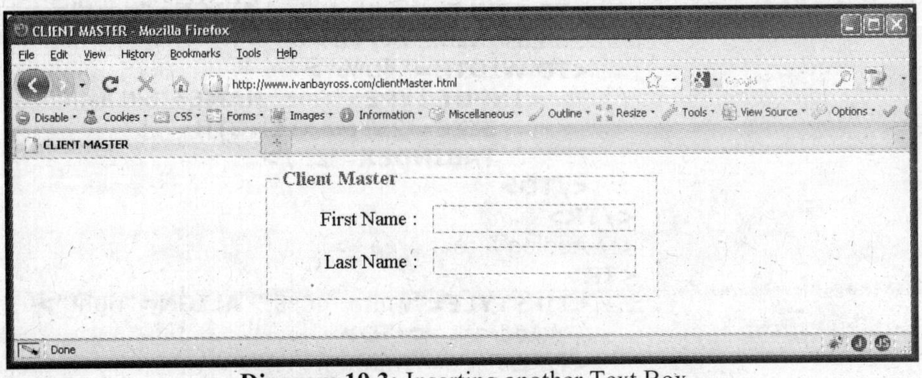

Diagram 19.3: Inserting another Text Box

NOTE

A Read Only text box can be created by setting the **READONLY** property of the INPUT tag as **TRUE**. This text box is **un-editable** that means a user can simply read data displayed in the text box but will not able to edit this data.

Adding A Text Area

Finally add a Text Area to the form with the following specifications:

OBJECT	LABEL	NAME	ROWS	COLS	TAB INDEX
Text Area	Address	taAddress	9	18	3

```
<HTML>
    <HEAD>
        <TITLE>CLIENT MASTER</TITLE>
    </HEAD>
    <BODY>
        <DIV STYLE="width: 50%;" >
            <FIELDSET>
                <LEGEND STYLE="color: brown; font-weight: bold;">
                    Client Master</LEGEND>
                    <TABLE  WIDTH="100%"  ALIGN="center"  CELLPADDING="1"
                            CELLSPACING="1" STYLE="background-color:white">
                        <FORM      NAME="frmClientMaster"      ID="frmClientMaster"
                            ACTION="clientMaster.php" METHOD="POST" >
                        <!--Adding a text box-->
                            <TR>
                                <TD STYLE="width: 40%;" ALIGN="right">
                                    First Name :</TD>
                                    <TD STYLE="width: 40%;" ALIGN="right">
                                        <INPUT TYPE="TEXT" NAME="txtFirstName"
```

```
                         SIZE="25" MAXLENGHT="15"
                         TABINDEX="1" />
                   </TD>
               </TR>
                   <!--Adding another text box-->
               <TR>
                   <TD STYLE="width:40%;" ALIGN="right">
                       Last Name :</TD>
                   <TD WIDTH="40%">
                       <INPUT TYPE="Text" NAME="txtLastName"
                         SIZE="25" MAXLENGTH="15"
                         TABINDEX="2" />
                   </TD>
               </TR>
               <!--Adding a text area-->
               <TR>
                   <TD STYLE="width: 40%;" ALIGN="right">
                       Address :</TD>
                   <TD STYLE="width: 40%;">
                       <TEXTAREA NAME="taAddress" ROWS="3"
                         COLS="18" TABINDEX="3">
                       </TEXTAREA>
                   </TD>
               </TR
           </FORM>
         </TABLE>
     </FIELDSET>
   <DIV>
 </BODY>
</HTML>
```

On running clientMaster.html in a Browser, the output is as shown in diagram 19.4.

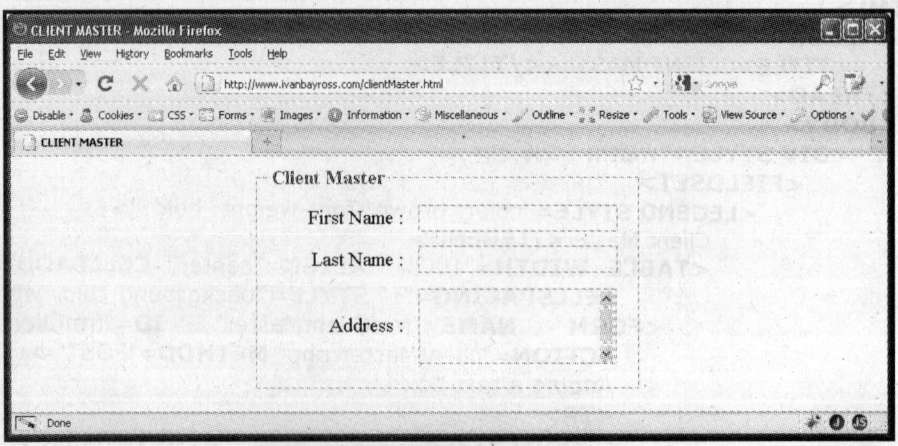

Diagram 19.4: Inserting a text area

Adding A Password Field

Next add a password field to the form with the following specifications:

OBJECT	LABEL	NAME	SIZE	MAX LENGTH	TAB INDEX
Password	Password	pwdPassword	25	15	4

```
<HTML>
    <HEAD>
        <TITLE>CLIENT MASTER</TITLE>
    </HEAD>
    <BODY>
        <DIV STYLE="WIDTH: 50%;" >
            <FIELDSET>
                <LEGEND STYLE="COLOR: BROWN; FONT-WEIGHT: BOLD;">
                    Client Master</LEGEND>
                    <TABLE  WIDTH="100%" ALIGN="center" CELLPADDING="1"
                        CELLSPACING="1"     STYLE="background-background-
                        color: white;">
                        <FORM     NAME="frmClientMaster"     ID="frmClientMaster"
                        ACTION="clientMaster.php" METHOD="POST" >
                        <!--Adding a text box-->
                        <TR>
                            <TD STYLE="width: 40%;" ALIGN="right">
                                First Name :</TD>
                            <TD STYLE="width: 40%;" ALIGN="right">
                                <INPUT TYPE="Text" NAME="txtFirstName"
                                    SIZE="25" MAXLENGTH="15"
                                    TABINDEX="1" />
                            </TD>
                        </TR>
                        <!--Adding another text box-->
                        <TR>
                            <TD STYLE="width: 40%;" ALIGN="right">
                                Last Name :</TD>
                            <TD STYLE="width: 40%;">
                                <INPUT TYPE="Text" NAME="txtLastName"
                                    SIZE="25" MAXLENGTH="15"
                                    TABINDEX="2" />
                            </TD>
                        </TR>
                        <!--Adding a text area-->
                        <TR>
                            <TD STYLE="width: 40%;" ALIGN="right">
                                Address :</TD>
                            <TD STYLE="width: 40%;" >
                                <TEXTAREA NAME="taAddress" ROW="3"
                                    COLS="18" TABINDEX="3">
                                </TEXTAREA>
                            </TD>
                        </TR>
                        <!--Adding a password field-->
                        <TR>
```

```
                        <TD STYLE="width: 40%;" ALIGN="right">
                            Password :</TD>
                        <TD STYLE="width: 40%;">
                            <INPUT TYPE="PASSWORD"
                                NAME="pwdPassword" SIZE="25"
                                MAXLENGTH="15" TABINDEX="4"/>
                        </TD>
                    </TR>
                    </FORM>
                </TABLE>
            </FIELDSET>
        <DIV>
    </BODY>
</HTML>
```

On running clientMaster.html in a Browser, the output is as shown in diagram 19.5.

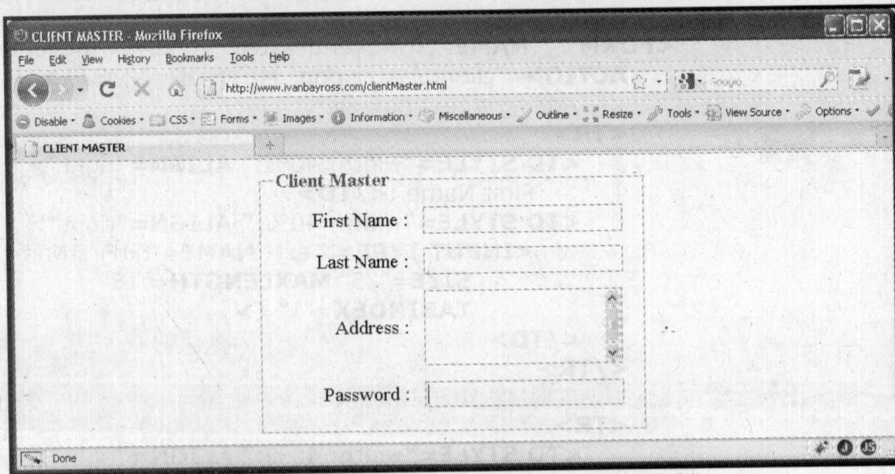

Diagram 19.5: Inserting a Password text field

Adding Radio Buttons

The radio buttons present a range of choices, from which a user can select only one. Each **group** of radio buttons therefore **share the same name**.

Now use the following specifications and place multiple radio buttons on the form:

OBJECT	LABEL	NAME	VALUE	CHECKED	TAB INDEX
Radio Button	Gender	rdGender	male	TRUE	5
Radio Button	Gender	rdGender	Female	--	6

```
<HTML>
<HEAD>
    <TITLE>CLIENT MASTER</TITLE>
</HEAD>
<BODY>
    <DIV STYLE="width: 50%;" >
        <FIELDSET>
            <LEGEND STYLE="color: brown; font-weight: bold;">
```

```
            Client Master</LEGEND>
            <TABLE  WIDTH="100%"  ALIGN="center"  CELLPADDING="1"
                CELLSPACING="1" style="background-background-color:
                white;" >
              <FORM      NAME="frmClientMaster"      ID="frmClientMaster"
                ACTION="clientMaster.php" METHOD="POST"
                <!--Adding a text box-->
                <TR>
                    <TD STYLE="width: 40%;" ALIGN="right">
                        First Name :</TD>
                    <TD STYLE="width: 40%;" ALIGN="right">
                        <INPUT TYPE="Text" NAME="txtFirstName"
                            SIZE="25" MAXLENGTH="15"
                            TABINDEX="1" />
                    </TD>
                </TR>
                <!--Adding another text box-->
                <TR>
                    <TD STYLE="width: 40%;" ALIGN="right">
                        Last Name :</TD>
                    <TD STYLE="width: 40%;">
                        <INPUT TYPE="Text" NAME="txtLastName"
                            SIZE="25" MAXLENGTH="15"
                            TABINDEX="2" />
                    </TD>
                </TR>
                <!--Adding a text area-->
                <TR>
                    <TD STYLE="width: 40%;" ALIGN="right">
                        Address :</TD>
                    <TD STYLE="width: 40%;">
                        <TEXTAREA NAME="taAddress" ROW="3"
                            COLS="18" TABINDEX="3">
                        </TEXTAREA>
                    </TD>
                </TR>
                <!--Adding a password field-->
                <TR>
                    <TD STYLE="width: 40%;" ALIGN="right">
                        Password :</TD>
                    <TD STYLE="width: 40%;">
                        <INPUT TYPE="PASSWORD"
                            NAME="pwdPassword" SIZE="25"
                            MAXLENGTH="15" TABINDEX="4" />
                    </TD>
                </TR>
                <!--Adding a radio button-->
                <TR>
                    <TD STYLE="width: 40%;" ALIGN="right">
                        Gender :</TD>
                        <TD STYLE="width: 40%;">
                            <INPUT TYPE="RADIO" NAME="rdGender"
                                VALUE="male" CHECKED="true"
```

```
                                    TABINDEX="5" />Male
                                      <INPUT TYPE="radio" NAME="rdGender"
                                       VALUE="female" TABINDEX="6" />Female
                              </TD>
                           </TR>
                        </FORM>
                     </TABLE>
                </FIELDSET>
            <DIV>
        </BODY>
    </HTML>
```

On running clientMaster.html in a Browser, the output is as shown in diagram 19.6.

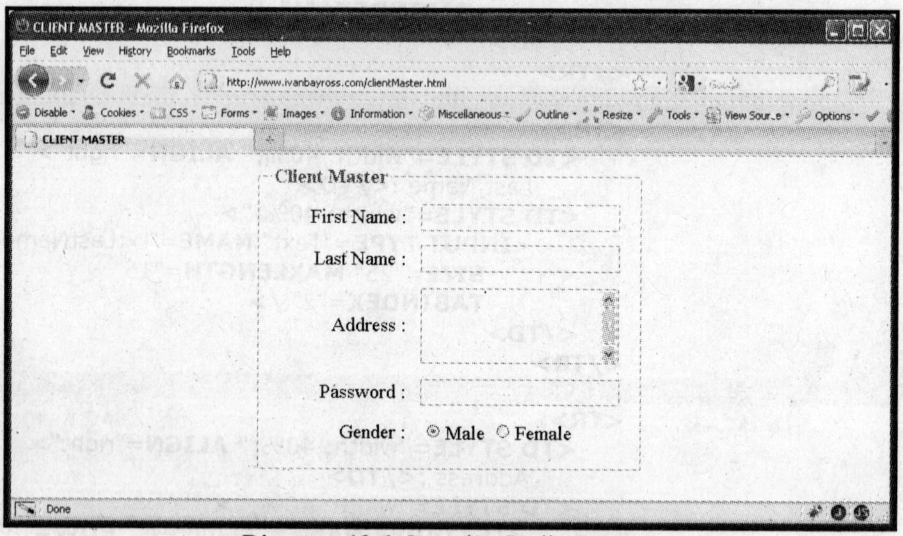

Diagram 19.6: Inserting Radio Buttons

Adding A Select Box

Now add a Drop Down List Box (DDLB) to the form with the following specifications:

OBJECT	LABEL	NAME	SIZE	TAB INDEX
Select Box	Country	selectCountry	1	9

```
    <HTML>
    <HEAD>
        <TITLE>CLIENT MASTER</TITLE>
    </HEAD>
    <BODY>
        <DIV STYLE="width: 50%;" >
            <FIELDSET>
                <LEGEND STYLE="color: brown; font-weight: bold;">
                    Client Master</LEGEND>
                    <TABLE  WIDTH="100%"  ALIGN="center"  CELLPADDING="1"
                            CELLSPACING="1" STYLE="background-color: white;">
```

```
        <FORM     NAME="frmClientMaster"     ID="frmClientMaster"
            ACTION="clientMaster.php" METHOD="POST" >
            <!--Adding a text box-->
            <TR>
                <TD STYLE="width: 40%;" ALIGN="right">
                    First Name :</TD>
                <TD STYLE="width: 40%;" ALIGN="right">
                    <INPUT TYPE="Text" NAME="txtFirstName"
                        SIZE="25" MAXLENGTH="15"
                        TABINDEX="1" />
                </TD>
            </TR>
            <!--Adding another text box-->
            <TR>
                <TD STYLE="width: 40%;" ALIGN="right">
                    Last Name :</TD>
                <TD STYLE="width: 40%;">
                    <INPUT TYPE="Text" NAME="txtLastName"
                        SIZE="25" MAXLENGTH="15"
                        TABINDEX="2" />
                </TD>
            </TR>
            <!--Adding a text area-->
            <TR>
                <TD STYLE="width: 40%;" ALIGN="right">
                    Address :</TD>
                <TD STYLE="width: 40%;">
                    <TEXTAREA NAME="taAddress" ROW="3"
                        COLS="18" TABINDEX="3">
                    </TEXTAREA>
                </TD>
            </TR>
            <!--Adding a password field-->
            <TR>
                <TD STYLE="width: 40%;" ALIGN="right">
                    Password :</TD>
                <TD STYLE="width: 40%;">
                    <INPUT TYPE="PASSWORD"
                        NAME="pwdPassword" SIZE="25"
                        MAXLENGTH="15" TABINDEX="4" />
                </TD>
            </TR>
            <!--Adding a radio button-->
            <TR>
                <TD STYLE="width: 40%;" ALIGN="right">
                    Gender :</TD>
                <TD STYLE="width: 40%;">
                    <INPUT TYPE="radio" NAME="rdGender"
                        VALUE="male" CHECKED="checked"
                        TABINDEX="5" /> Male
                    <INPUT TYPE="radio" NAME="rdGender"
                        VALUE="female" TABINDEX="6" /> Female
                </TD>
```

```
                    </TR>
                    <!--Adding a select box-->
                    <TR>
                        <TD STYLE="width: 40%;" ALIGN="right">
                            Country :</TD>
                        <TD>
                            <SELECT NAME="selectCountry" SIZE="1"
                                    TABINDEX="7">
                                <OPTION SELECTED="selected">
                                    India</OPTION>
                                <OPTION>United Kingdom</OPTION>
                                <OPTION>USA</OPTION>
                                <OPTION>Australia</OPTION>
                            </SELECT>
                        </TD>
                    </TR>
                </FORM>
            </TABLE>
        </FIELDSET>
    <DIV>
  </BODY>
</HTML>
```

On running clientMaster.html in a Browser, the output is as shown in diagram 19.7.

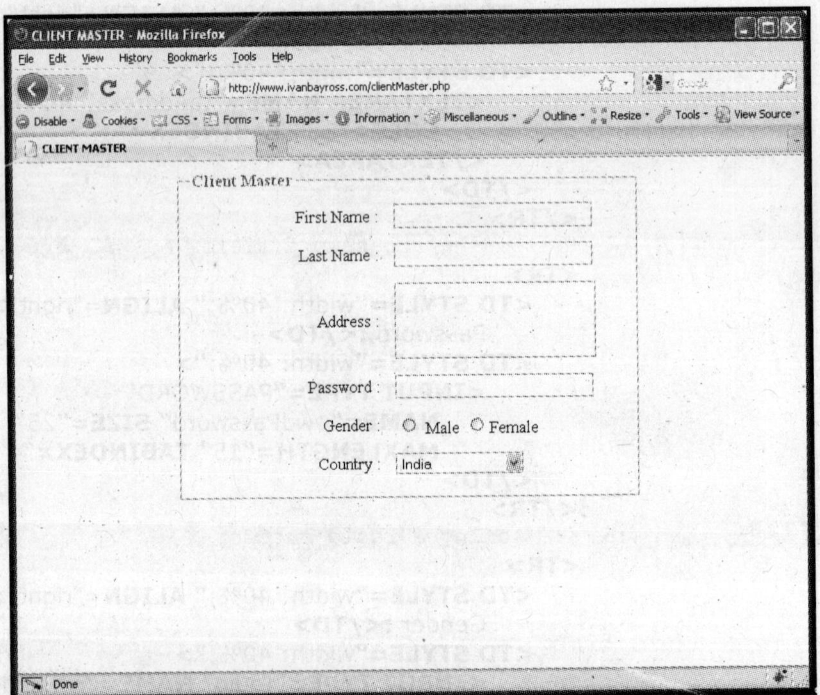

Diagram 19.7: Inserting a Select Box

Adding Check Boxes

Now use the following specifications and place multiple check boxes on the form:

OBJECT	LABEL	NAME	VALUE	CHECKED	TAB INDEX
Check Box	Status	chkStatus	Single	TRUE	7
Check Box	Status	chkStatus	Married	--	8

```
<HTML>
<HEAD>
    <TITLE>CLIENT MASTER</TITLE>
</HEAD>
<BODY>
    <DIV STYLE="width: 50%;" >
        <FIELDSET>
            <LEGEND STYLE="COLOR: BROWN; FONT-WEIGHT: BOLD;">
                Client Master</LEGEND>
                <TABLE WIDTH="100%" ALIGN="center" CELLPADDING="1"
                    CELLSPACING="1" STYLE="background-color: white;">
                    <FORM NAME="frmClientMaster" ID="frmClientMaster"
                    ACTION="clientMaster.php" METHOD="POST" >
                    <!--Adding a text box-->
                    <TR>
                        <TD STYLE="width: 40%;" ALIGN="right">
                            First Name :</TD>
                        <TD STYLE="width: 40%;" ALIGN="right">
                            <INPUT TYPE="Text" NAME="txtFirstName"
                                SIZE="25" MAXLENGTH="15"
                                TABINDEX="1" />
                        </TD>
                    </TR>
                    <!--Adding another text box-->
                    <TR>
                        <TD STYLE="width: 40%;" ALIGN="right">
                            Last Name :</TD>
                        <TD STYLE="width: 40%;">
                            <INPUT TYPE="Text" NAME="txtLastName"
                                SIZE="25" MAXLENGTH="15"
                                TABINDEX="2" />
                        </TD>
                    </TR>
                    <!--Adding a text area-->
                    <TR>
                        <TD STYLE="width: 40%;" ALIGN="right">
                            Address :</TD>
                        <TD STYLE="width: 40%;">
                            <TEXTAREA NAME="taAddress" ROW="3"
                                COLS="18" TABINDEX="3">
                            </TEXTAREA>
                        </TD>
                    </TR>
                    <!--Adding a password field-->
                    <TR>
```

```
                <TD STYLE="width: 40%;" ALIGN="right">
                    Password :</TD>
                <TD STYLE="width: 40%;">
                    <INPUT TYPE="PASSWORD"
                        NAME="pwdPassword" SIZE="25"
                        MAXLENGTH="15" TABINDEX="4" />
                </TD>
            </TR>
            <!--Adding a radio button-->
            <TR>
                <TD STYLE="width: 40%;" ALIGN="right">
                    Gender :</TD>
                <TD STYLE="width: 40%;">
                    <INPUT TYPE="RADIO" NAME="rdGender"
                        VALUE="male" CHECKED="checked"
                        TABINDEX="5" /> Male
                    <INPUT TYPE="RADIO" NAME="rdGender"
                        VALUE="female" TABINDEX="6" /> Female
                </TD>
            </TR>
            <!--Adding a Drop Down List-->
            <TR>
                <TD STYLE="width: 40%;" ALIGN="right">
                    Country :</TD>TD WIDTH="40%">
                    <SELECT NAME="selectCountry" SIZE="1"
                     TABINDEX="7">
                        <OPTION SELECTED="selected">
                            India</OPTION>
                        <OPTION>United Kingdom</OPTION>
                        <OPTION>USA</OPTION>
                        <OPTION>Australia</OPTION>
                    </SELECT>
                </TD>
        </TR>
            <!--Adding check boxes-->
            <TR>
                <TD STYLE="width: 40%;" ALIGN="right">
                    Terms and conditions:</TD>
                <TD STYLE="width: 40%;">
                    <INPUT TYPE="CHECKBOX" NAME="chkAgree"
                        VALUE="Agree" TABINDEX="8" />I Agree
                </TD>
            </TR>
        </FORM>
      </TABLE>
    </FIELDSET>
  <DIV>
 </BODY>
</HTML>
```

On running clientMaster.html in a Browser, the output is as shown in diagram 19.8.

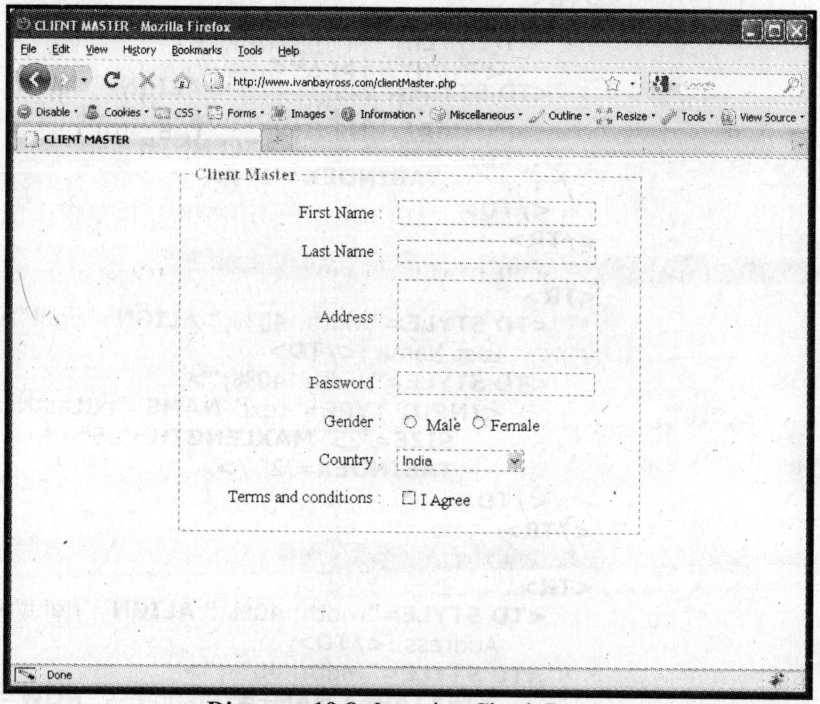

Diagram 19.8: Inserting Check Boxes

Adding A SUBMIT And CANCEL BUTTON

Since the form is completely constructed it is time to add both Submit and Reset buttons to the form. The Submit button will submit the data captured by the form back to the web server from where the form is delivered. The Reset button will reset all the form fields to their datum position for the form to be filled in again when required.

Add Submit and Reset Buttons to the form with the following specifications:

OBJECT	LABEL	NAME	ACTION
Submit	SUBMIT	btnSubmit	Submits form data to a web server
Reset	CANCEL	btnCancel	Resets the form fields

```
<HTML>
    <HEAD>
        <TITLE>CLIENT MASTER</TITLE>
    </HEAD>
    <BODY>
        <DIV STYLE="width: 50%;" >
            <FIELDSET>
                <LEGEND STYLE="color: brown; font-weight: bold;">
                    Client Master</LEGEND>
                    <TABLE WIDTH="100%" ALIGN="center" CELLPADDING="1"
                        CELLSPACING="1" STYLE="background-color: white;">
                        <FORM    NAME="frmClientMaster"    ID="frmClientMaster"
                        ACTION="clientMaster.php" METHOD="POST" >
```

```
<!--Adding a text box-->
<TR>
    <TD STYLE="width: 40%;" ALIGN="right">
        First Name :</TD>
    <TD STYLE="width: 40%;" ALIGN="right">
        <INPUT TYPE="Text" NAME="txtFirstName"
            SIZE="25" MAXLENGTH="15"
            TABINDEX="1" />
    </TD>
</TR>
<!--Adding another text box-->
<TR>
    <TD STYLE="width: 40%;" ALIGN="right">
        Last Name :</TD>
    <TD STYLE="width: 40%;">
        <INPUT TYPE="Text" NAME="txtLastName"
            SIZE="25" MAXLENGTH="15"
            TABINDEX="2" />
    </TD>
</TR>
<!--Adding a text area-->
<TR>
    <TD STYLE="width: 40%;" ALIGN="right">
        Address :</TD>
    <TD STYLE="width: 40%;">
        <TEXTAREA NAME="taAddress" ROW="3"
            COLS="18" TABINDEX="3">
        </TEXTAREA>
    </TD>
</TR>
<!--Adding a password field-->
<TR>
    <TD STYLE="width: 40%;" ALIGN="right">
        Password :</TD>
    <TD STYLE="width: 40%;">
        <INPUT TYPE="password"
            NAME="pwdPassword" SIZE="25"
            MAXLENGTH="15" TABINDEX="4" />
    </TD>
</TR>
<!--Adding a radio button-->
<TR>
    <TD STYLE="width: 40%;" ALIGN="right">
        Gender :</TD>
    <TD STYLE="width: 40%;">
        <INPUT TYPE="RADIO" NAME="rdGender"
            VALUE="male" CHECKED="checked"
            TABINDEX="5" /> Male
        <INPUT TYPE="RADIO" NAME="rdGender"
            VALUE="female" TABINDEX="6" /> Female
    </TD>
</TR>
```

```
            <!--Adding a Drop Down List-->
            <TR>
                <TD STYLE="width: 40%;" ALIGN="right">
                    Country :</TD>TD WIDTH="40%">
                    <SELECT NAME="selectCountry" SIZE="1"
                      TABINDEX="7">
                        <OPTION SELECTED="selected">
                            India</OPTION>
                        <OPTION>United Kingdom</OPTION>
                        <OPTION>USA</OPTION>
                        <OPTION>Australia</OPTION>
                    </SELECT>
                </TD>
          </TR>
          <!--Adding a Checkbox-->
          <TR>
              <TD STYLE="width: 40%;" ALIGN="right">
                  Terms and conditions :</TD>
              <TD STYLE="width: 40%;">
                  <INPUT TYPE="CHECKBOX" NAME="chkAgree"
                      VALUE="Agree" TABINDEX="8" />I Agree
                  </TD>
          </TR>
          <!--Adding a Submit and Reset buttons-->
              <TR>
                  <TD STYLE="width: 40%;" ALIGN="right">
                      <INPUT TYPE="SUBMIT" NAME="btnSubmit"
                        VALUE="Submit" TABINDEX="9" />
                  </TD>
                  <TD STYLE="width: 40%;" >
                       <INPUT TYPE="RESET" NAME="btnCancel"
                        VALUE="Cancel" TABINDEX="10" />
                  </TD>
              </TR>
        </FORM>
      </TABLE>
    </FIELDSET>
  <DIV>
 </BODY>
</HTML>
```

On running clientMaster.html in a Browser, the output is as shown in diagram 19.9.

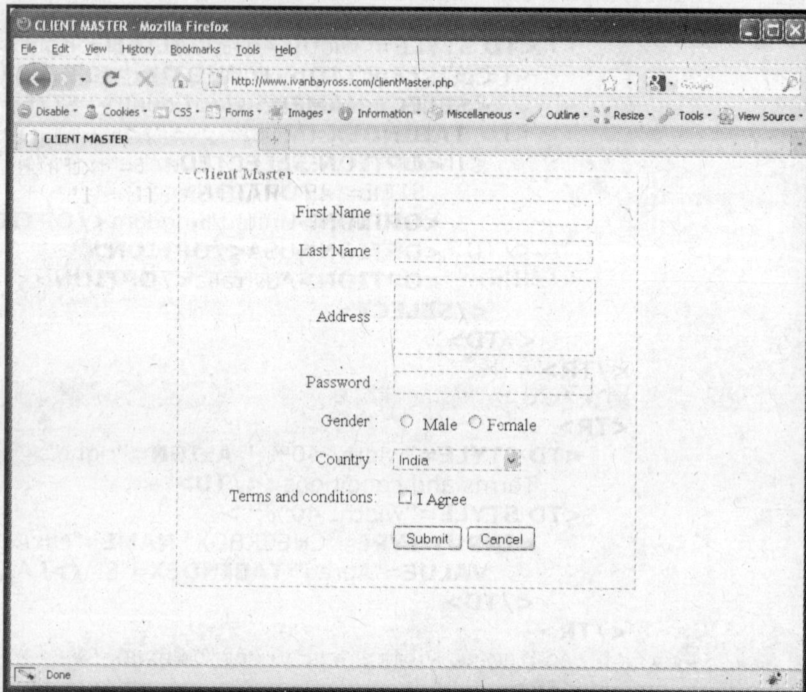

Diagram 19.9: Inserting a SUBMIT and RESET buttons

Adding A Hidden Field

Once the form is ready for operation it is time to add a hidden field to the form. The content of the hidden field ensures that appropriate information for form data processing is returned to the Web server from where the form originated.

Add a hidden field to the form with the following specifications:

TYPE	NAME	VALUE
Hidden	frmClientInfo	Client Master Details

The following code places a hidden field on the form:

```
<HTML>
    <HEAD>
        <TITLE>CLIENT MASTER</TITLE>
    </HEAD>
    <BODY>
        <DIV STYLE="width: 50%;" >
            <FIELDSET>
                <LEGEND STYLE="color: brown; font-weight: bold;">
                    Client Master</LEGEND>
                    <TABLE  WIDTH="100%"  ALIGN="center"  CELLPADDING="1"
                            CELLSPACING="1" STYLE="background-color: white;">
                        <FORM     NAME="frmClientMaster"     ID="frmClientMaster"
                            ACTION="clientMaster.php" METHOD="POST" >
```

```
<!--Adding a text box-->
<TR>
    <TD STYLE="width: 40%;" ALIGN="right">
        First Name :</TD>
    <TD STYLE="width: 40%;" ALIGN="right">
        <INPUT TYPE="Text" NAME="txtFirstName"
            SIZE="25" MAXLENGTH="15"
            TABINDEX="1" />
    </TD>
</TR>
<!--Adding another text box-->
<TR>
    <TD STYLE="width: 40%;" ALIGN="right">
        Last Name :</TD>
    <TD WIDTH="40%">
        <INPUT TYPE="Text" NAME="txtLastName"
            SIZE="25" MAXLENGTH="15"
            TABINDEX="2" />
    </TD>
</TR>
<!--Adding a text area-->
<TR>
    <TD STYLE="width: 40%;" ALIGN="right">
        Address :</TD>
    <TD STYLE="width: 40%;">
        <TEXTAREA NAME="taAddress" ROW="3"
            COLS="18" TABINDEX="3">
        </TEXTAREA>
    </TD>
</TR>
<!--Adding a password field-->
<TR>
    <TD STYLE="width: 40%;" ALIGN="right">
        Password :</TD>
    <TD STYLE="width: 40%;">
        <INPUT TYPE="PASSWORD"
            NAME="pwdPassword" SIZE="25"
            MAXLENGTH="15" TABINDEX="4" />
    </TD>
</TR>
<!--Adding a radio button-->
<TR>
    <TD STYLE="width: 40%;" ALIGN="right">
        Gender :</TD>
    <TD STYLE="width: 40%;">
        <INPUT TYPE="radio" NAME="rdGender"
            VALUE="male" CHECKED="checked"
            TABINDEX="5" /> Male
        <INPUT TYPE="radio" NAME="rdGender"
            VALUE="female" TABINDEX="6" /> Female
    </TD>
</TR>
<!--Adding a Drop Down List-->
```

```
                <TR>
                    <TD STYLE="width: 40%;" ALIGN="RIGHT">
                        Country :</TD>
                        <TD STYLE="width: 40%;">
                            <SELECT NAME="selectCountry" SIZE="1"
                        TABINDEX="7">
                            <OPTION SELECTED="selected">
                                India</OPTION>
                            <OPTION>United Kingdom</OPTION>
                            <OPTION>USA</OPTION>
                            <OPTION>Australia</OPTION>
                        </SELECT>
                    </TD>
                </TR>
                <!--Adding a Checkbox-->
                <TR>
                    <TD STYLE="width: 40%;" ALIGN="right">
                        Terms and conditions :</TD>
                    <TD STYLE="width: 40%;">
                        <INPUT TYPE="CHECKBOX" NAME="chkAgree"
                            VALUE="Agree" TABINDEX="8" />I Agree
                        </TD>
                </TR>
                <!-- Adding a Submit and Cancel buttons -->
                    <TR>
                        <TD STYLE="width: 40%;" ALIGN="right">
                            <INPUT TYPE="SUBMIT" NAME="btnSubmit"
                              VALUE="Submit" TABINDEX="10" />
                        </TD>
                        <TD STYLE="width: 40%;">
                            <INPUT TYPE="RESET" NAME="btnCancel"
                                VALUE="Cancel" TABINDEX="11" />
                        </TD>
                    </TR>
                    <!-- Adding hidden input tag -->
                    <TR>
                        <TD STYLE="width: 100%;" ALIGN="right"
                            COLSPAN="2">
                            <INPUT TYPE="Hidden" NAME="frmClientInfo"
                                    VALUE="Client Master Details" />
                        </TD>
                    </TR>
                </FORM>
            </TABLE>
        </FIELDSET>
    <DIV>
  </BODY>
</HTML>
```

NOTE

Although hidden form items may be invisible when the form is displayed on-screen, it is still perfectly possible for a user to read them by viewing the page's underlying HTML source code. **They are not at all a sensible place to store sensitive information such as passwords.**

Converting clientMaster.html To clientMaster.php

Once the entire form is coded and tested and runs successfully in a Browser the same form must be converted to PHP code spec. This is because it's the PHP code spec that converts a static HTML form to a dynamic one. It is the PHP program that runs at the Web server and delivers the HTML form, loaded with appropriate information where necessary and appropriate to the Browser that requested it.

To achieve this, simply save clientMaster.html as clientMaster.php. Then open clientMaster.php in an ASCII editor and make a few minor changes in the code spec as shown in the following code snippet below.

For example:

```
<TD STYLE="width: 40%;" ALIGN="RIGHT"> First Name : </TD>
   <TD>
      <INPUT TYPE="Text" NAME="txtFirstName" SIZE="25" MAXLENGTH="15"
         TABINDEX="1"/>
   </TD>
```

Will now look like:

```
<TD STYLE="width: 40%;" ALIGN="RIGHT"> First Name : </TD>
   <TD>
   <INPUT TYPE="Text" NAME="txtFirstName" SIZE="25" MAXLENGTH="15"
         TABINDEX="1"
               VALUE="<?php echo $_POST['txtFirstName']?>" />
   </TD>
```

This is done so that the form elements **retain their old values** whenever control is passed back to the form after performing any server side validations (usually by a server side PHP script).

The code spec of clientMaster.php will now be as follows:

```
<HTML>
   <HEAD>
      <TITLE>CLIENT MASTER</TITLE>
   </HEAD>
   <BODY>
      <DIV STYLE="width: 50%;" >
         <FIELDSET>
            <LEGEND STYLE="color: brown; font-weight: bold;">
               Client Master</LEGEND>
               <TABLE  WIDTH="100%"  ALIGN="center"  CELLPADDING="1"
                     CELLSPACING="1" STYLE="background-color: white;">
                  <FORM     NAME="frmClientMaster"      ID="frmClientMaster"
                     ACTION="clientMaster.php" METHOD="POST" >
                  <FORM NAME="frmClientMaster" ID="frmClientMaster"
                     ACTION="clientMaster.php" METHOD="POST"  >
```

```
<!--Adding a text box-->
<TR>
    <TD STYLE="width: 40%;" ALIGN="right">
      First Name : </TD>
    <TD STYLE="width: 40%;" >
    <INPUT TYPE="Text" NAME="txtFirstName"
     SIZE="25" MAXLENGTH="15" TABINDEX="1"
    VALUE="<?php echo $_POST['txtFirstName']?>"
    />
    </TD>
</TR>
<!--Adding another text box-->
<TR>
    <TD STYLE="width: 40%;" ALIGN="right">
       Last Name : </TD>
    <TD STYLE="width: 40%;" >
     <INPUT TYPE="Text" NAME="txtLastName"
      SIZE="25" MAXLENGTH="15" TABINDEX="2"
      VALUE="<?php echo $_POST['txtLastName']?>"
     />
    </TD>
</TR>
<!--Adding a text area-->
<TR>
    <TD STYLE="width: 40%;" ALIGN="right">
      Address :</TD>
    <TD STYLE="width: 40%;">
      <TEXTAREA NAME="taAddress" ROW="3"
          COLS="18" TABINDEX="3"
      VALUE="<?php echo $_POST['taAddress']?>" >
          <?php echo $_POST['taAddress']?>
      </TEXTAREA>
    </TD>
</TR>
<!--Adding a password field-->
<TR>
    <TD STYLE="width: 40%;" ALIGN="right">
      Password :</TD>
    <TD STYLE="width: 40%;">
     <INPUT TYPE="PASSWORD"
      NAME="pwdPassword" SIZE="25"
      MAXLENGTH="15" TABINDEX="4"
     VALUE="<?php echo $_POST['pwdPassword']?>"
     />
    </TD>
</TR>
<!--Adding a radio button-->
<TR>
    <TD STYLE="width: 40%;" ALIGN="right">
      Gender :</TD>
    <TD STYLE="width: 40%;">
     <INPUT TYPE="radio" NAME="rdGender"
```

```
                VALUE="male" CHECKED="checked"
                TABINDEX="5"
                  <?php echo (isset($_POST['rdGender']) &&
                      $_POST['rdGender']=="male" ?
                      'checked="true"': '')?> /> Male
              <INPUT TYPE="radio" NAME="rdGender"
                VALUE="female" TABINDEX="5"
              <?php echo (isset($_POST['rdGender']) &&
                      $_POST['rdGender']=="female" ?
                      'checked="true"': '')?> /> Female
              </TD>
          </TR>
          <!-- Adding a select Box -->
          <TR>
              <TD STYLE="width: 40%;" ALIGN="right">
                  Country :</TD>
              <TD STYLE="width: 40%;">
                  <SELECT NAME="selectCountry" SIZE="1"
                      TABINDEX="7">
                  <OPTION
                      <?php if ($_POST['selectCountry']==
                      'India') echo 'SELECTED';?>>India
                  </OPTION>
                  <OPTION
                      <?php if ($_POST['selectCountry']==
                        'United Kingdom') echo 'SELECTED';?>>
                          United Kingdom
                  </OPTION>
                  <OPTION
                      <?php if ($_POST['selectCountry']=='USA')
                      echo 'SELECTED';?>>USA
                  </OPTION>
                  <OPTION
                      <?php if ($_POST['selectCountry']==
                      'Australia') echo 'SELECTED';?>>
                      Australia
                  </OPTION>
                  <!-- Adding check boxes -->
          <TR>
              <TD STYLE="width: 40%;" ALIGN="right">
                  Terms and Conditions :</TD>
              <TD STYLE="width: 40%;">
                  <INPUT TYPE="CHECKBOX" NAME="chkAgree"
                    VALUE="Agree" TABINDEX="8"
                 <?php echo (isset($_POST['chkAgree']) &&
                  $_POST['chkAgree']=="Agree" ?
                  'checked="true"': '')?> />I Agree
              </TD>
          </TR>
          <!-- Adding a Submit and Cancel buttons -->
          <TR>
              <TD STYLE="width: 40%;" ALIGN="right">
```

```
                    <INPUT TYPE="SUBMIT" NAME="btnSubmit"
                        VALUE="Submit" TABINDEX="9" />
                </TD>
                <TD STYLE="width: 40%;">
                    <INPUT TYPE="RESET" NAME="btnCancel"
                        VALUE="Cancel" TABINDEX="10" />
                </TD>
            </TR>
            <!-- Adding hidden input tag -->
            <TR>
                <TD STYLE="width: 40%;" ALIGN="right"
                    COLSPAN="2">
                    INPUT TYPE="Hidden" NAME="frmClientInfo"
                    VALUE="Client Master Details" />
                </TD>
            </TR>
        </FORM>
    </TABLE>
  </FIELDSET>
 <DIV>
</BODY>
</HTML>
```

Once all these changes have been made the PHP code spec inserted within HTML code spec guarantees a degree of dynamism that did not exist in the static HTML form.

Once this is done code spec for **error handling** can be done. During this process, if an error is detected in the form data filled in by the user, then the old values are shown on the form along with an appropriate error message when the form is dispatched back to the user.

Error handling, i.e. error detection and the error message sent back to the Browser, is done by another PHP program on the Web server. The name of this program is **clientMast.php**. This is the value that is bound to the form's **ACTION** attribute. Refer to the code snippet explained earlier.

The following validations are run on form data that is returned to the Web server by the Browser:

1) That none of the form fields have been left empty
2) That some type of book was selected from the drop down list box
3) That an appropriate check box was checked
4) That the publisher's code was not left empty and that a numeric value was entered

If an error is detected, the form carrying all the data previously entered in the form is returned to the Browser, together with an appropriate error message, printed in red, at the top of the form.

The code of the **clientMast.php** is shown in the code snippet below.

```
<?php
    if ($_POST['txtFirstName']=="")
    {
        echo "<center><SPAN style="color: red;">
                Please Enter Client's First Name.</SPAN></center>";
        echo "<HR>";
```

```
    include("clientMaster.php");
  }

  else if ($_POST['txtLastName']=="")
  {
    echo "<center><SPAN style="color: red;">
          Please Enter Client's Last Name.</SPAN></center>";
    echo "<HR>";
    include("clientMaster.php");
  }

  else if ($_POST['taAddress']=="")
  {
    echo "<center><SPAN style="color: red;">
          Please Enter Client's Address.</SPAN></center>";
    echo "<HR>";
    include("clientMaster.php");
  }

  else if (($_POST['pwdPassword'] ==""))
  {
    echo "<center><SPAN style="color: red;">
          Please Enter Password.</SPAN></center>";
    echo "<HR>";
    include("clientMaster.php");
  }
  else if(!isset($_POST['rdGender']))
  {
    echo "<center><SPAN style="color: red;">
          Please Select Gender.</SPAN></center>";
    echo "<HR>";
    include("clientMaster.php");
  }
  else if(!isset($_POST['chkAgree']))
  {
    echo "<center><SPAN style="color: red;">
          Please accept the terms and conditions.</SPAN></center>";
    echo "<HR>";
    include("clientMaster.php");
 }
  else
  {
    echo "<center><SPAN style="color: blue;">The Form Name is " .
       $_POST['frmClientInfo'] . " -- This is a hidden Variable </FONT>
       <BR /> </center>";
    echo "<center><SPAN style="color: brown;">
          Data Entered Successfully</SPAN></center>";
    echo "<HR>";
    $_POST="";
```

```
        include("clientMaster.php");
    }
?>
```

Running clientMaster.php At The Web Server

Create clientMaster.php and clientMast.php using any text editor such as Notepad. Place these files under a virtual host **or** Apache's htdocs directory as the case may be. Run PublisherMaster.php file using a web Browser such as I.E. or Mozilla by entering the file URL in the Browser's address bar and clicking **GO** as shown in diagram 19.10.

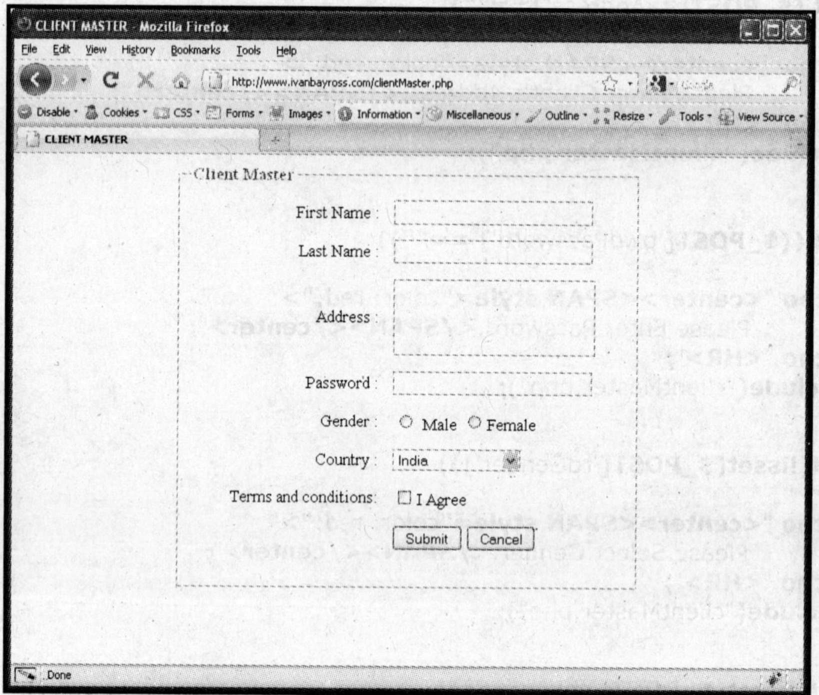

Diagram 19.10: The Client Master form

Ensure that the validation of form data occurs by deliberately introducing errors when loading the form with data and click **Submit** button to return this data back to the Web Server from where the form originated. First leave entire form blank and click **Submit** button.

A form as shown in diagram 19.11 is returned to the Browser. Note the error message, **Please Enter Clients' First Name**, displayed in red, at the top of the form. Next, use the same form enter a Client's name **Ivan Bayross**, leave the rest of the form empty and click **Submit** button.

The form as shown in diagram 19.12 is returned by the web server. Note the appropriate error message, **Please Enter Clients Last Name**, displayed in red at the top of the form.

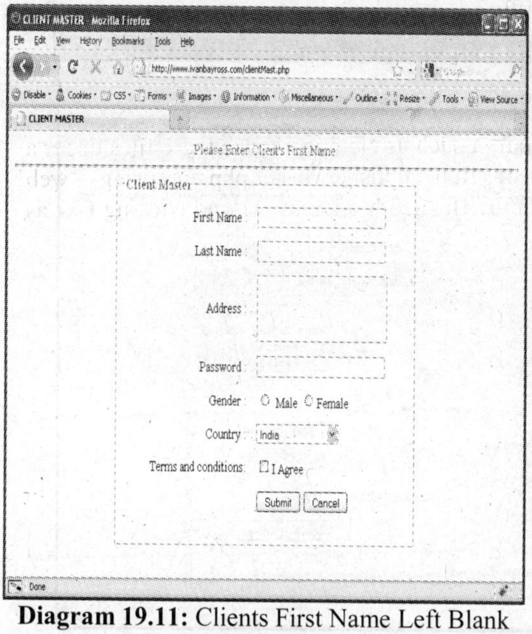

Diagram 19.11: Clients First Name Left Blank

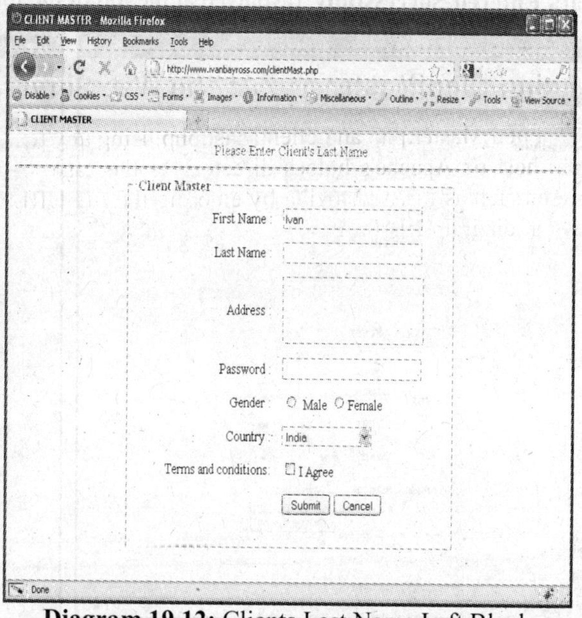

Diagram 19.12: Clients Last Name Left Blank

Use the same form. Now enter the Client's Last Name **Bayross** as shown in diagram 19.13 leave the rest of the form empty. Click **Submit**.

clientMast.php does error handling once again. The form is returned back to the Browser with an appropriate error message, **Please Enter Client's Address**, displayed in red at the top of the Browser as shown in diagram 19.13.

Now enter the client's address as shown in diagram 19.14. Do not select or fill in anything else in the form. Click **Submit**.

The form is returned back to the Browser with an appropriate error message, **Please Enter Password**, displayed in red at the top of the Browser as shown in diagram 19.14.

Now enter the client's password as shown in diagram 19.15. Do not select or fill in anything else in the form. Click **Submit**.

The form is returned back to the Browser with an appropriate error message, **Please Select Gender**, displayed in red at the top of the Browser as shown in diagram 19.15.

Now select the appropriate gender as shown in diagram 19.16. Do not select or fill in anything else in the form. Click **Submit**.

The form is returned back to the Browser with an appropriate error message, **Please accept the terms and conditions**, displayed in red at the top of the Browser as shown in diagram 19.16.

Finally check on **Terms and Condition**. Click **Submit**. Since the form is fully and correctly filled in, it is accepted by the Web Server as shown in diagram 19.17. Notice the appropriate message of success, **Clients Data Entered Successfully**, displayed at the top of the form.

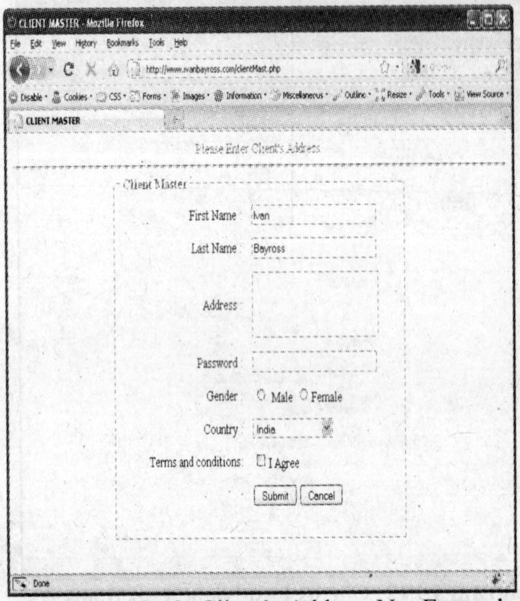

Diagram 19.13: Client's Address Not Entered

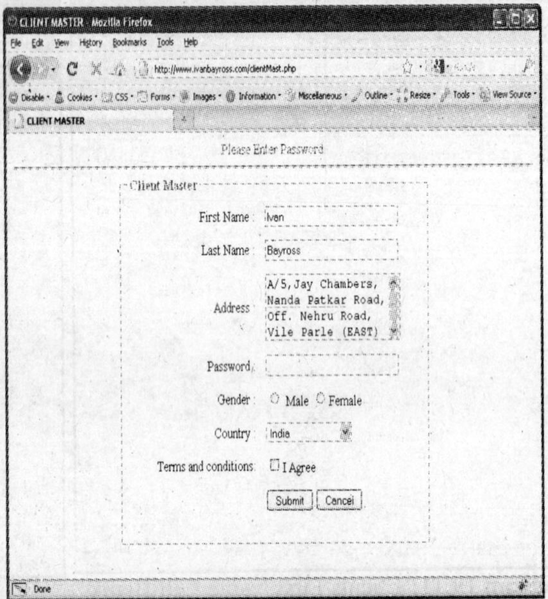

Diagram 19.14: Clients' Password Not Entered

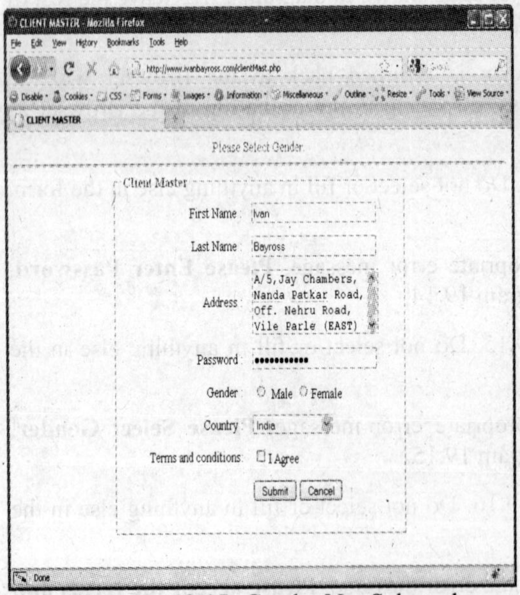

Diagram 19.15: Gender Not Selected

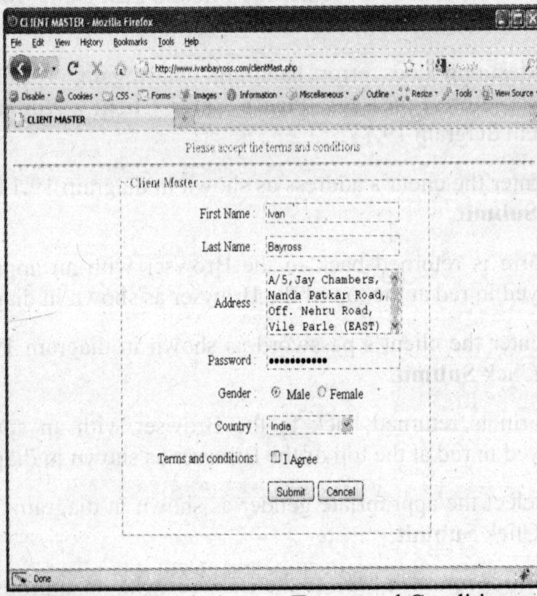

Diagram 19.16: Accept Terms and Conditions

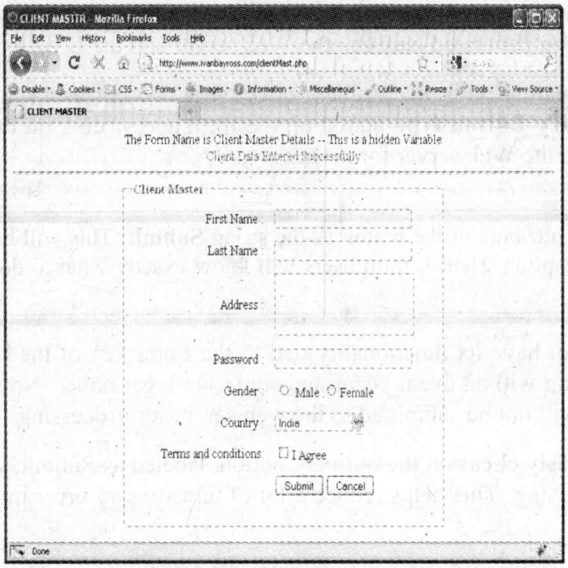

Diagram 19.17: Client Data Entered Successfully

Notice that on each error, the previous data captured in a form element is returned to the Browser. This is possible as the form had appropriate PHP syntax embedded in it, which ensures that the original data captured is returned when an error occurs. All validation checks can be tested as described above.

Diagram 19.16 **returns the first line** as:

```
The Form Name is Client Master Details. -- This is a hidden Variable
```

This is just to demonstrate the use and retrieval of hidden form elements.

The following code spec written in the clientMast.php is responsible to print this line.

```
echo "<SPAN style="color: blue;">The Form Name is " . $_POST['frmClientInfo'] .
    " -- This is a hidden Variable.</SPAN><BR/>";
```

The **next line says:**

```
Client Data Entered Successfully
```

This line is of prime importance as it indicates that the data captured by the clientMaster.php has passed all the validations that were written in the clientMast.php file.

Preventing Forms Being Automatically Submitted To A Web Server

Users often hit the **Enter** key on their keyboards out of a force of habit especially when the user's form cursor is in a text box during data entry. If a form has a **Submit** (type) command button placed on the form, (whose functionality is to return the data captured by the form to the Web server), this creates a bit of a problem.

This is because the Submit button's functionality is tied to the **Enter** key, i.e. if the Enter key is pressed the form's data is immediately submitted to the Web Server by the Browser. Hence without the user clicking **Submit** button, form data is dispatched to the Web server for processing.

This often results in incomplete form data being sent back to the Web server, resulting in a lot of unnecessary error traffic being generated between the Web server and the Browser.

There is a simple way of dealing with this problem effectively. Do not use a **Submit type** button on the form. Instead use an **ordinary Button type** button on the form and write a bit of JavaScript into its Click event to Submit data back to the Web server for processing.

NOTE

Pass the **VALUE** attribute of the button as the string **Submit**. This will be displayed on the body of the button as its caption. Hence, form users will know exactly what to do to pass form data back to the Web server.

The ordinary button does not have its functionality tied to the Enter key of the keyboard. Only when the user clicks this type of button will an event occur and some work get done. Now even if the user hits the Enter key often, form data will not be submitted to the web server for processing.

Only when the user consciously clicks on the ordinary button, labeled as Submit, will form data be returned to the Web server for processing. This helps reduce a lot of unnecessary error traffic between the Browser and the Web server.

Use the following technique to return form data back to the Web server:

```
<INPUT TYPE="Button" VALUE="Submit" onClick="submit()"/>
```

NOTE

Make a call to the forms built-in method **submit()** in the **onClick** attribute of the ordinary button. This is the method that automatically returns form data to the Web server from where the form originated.

Automatically Selecting The Contents Of Text Boxes

Another simple convenience that can be built into forms is the automatic selection of the content in a text box if the user uses a mouse to navigate to a text box.

TIP

Automatic selection of the contents of any text box occurs even if the user uses the **tab** key on the keyboard to navigate to a text box.

The following code snippet, when added to a text box ensures that text box content will be automatically selected if the user uses a mouse and navigates to a text box.

```
<INPUT TYPE="Text" NAME="txtEmail" onFocus="this.select()"
    VALUE="enter your email"/>
```

Where,

- **INPUT** is an HTML keyword that indicates the start of an HTML object being described
- **TYPE** indicates the type of form element in this case a text box
- **NAME** is any suitable name which will be assigned to the element example: **txtEmail**

- **VALUE** - When the attribute VALUE is passed, a string as shown, is displayed in the text box as a prompt when the text box is visible on the form. This really is a default value that must be overwritten by the user at form data entry time. Hence, as soon as the form cursor navigates to the text box this default text must be selected to be overwritten

  This ensures that only what the user types in is sent back to the Web Server for processing.

- **onFocus="this.select()"** - This is a form element event that fires when the form cursor navigates into a form element. When the event fires the code snippet **this.select()** ensures that the text already in the text box is selected ready to be over written by the user. **select()** is a built in function. The keyword **this** binds the function to the current element on which the form cursor rests

UPLOADING FILES TO THE WEB SERVER USING PHP

Often Web sites offer users the functionality of uploading their files, such as photographs and textual captions for these photographs to the web site to get users and their friends to visit/re-visit the web site often. PHP has several built in functions that assist in managing file uploads to a Web server.

To empower users to upload files to the Web server, a user interface must be created first that will allow users to have a standard way for communicating with the web site. Most web site user interfaces are basically forms written in HTML, which use PHP code spec to add dynamism to the form.

The user interface (i.e. HTML form) delivered by the Web server to the Browser must have a form element that permits the user to navigate through their hard disk directories and sub-directories to select the appropriate file(s) for upload to the Web server.

Once the file(s) were selected on the local hard disk at the Client, a clickable **Upload File** button on the form completes its functionality.

The following HTML code spec does just this (i.e. **upload.html**)

```
<HTML>
  <HEAD>
    <TITLE>File Upload</TITLE>
  </HEAD>
  <BODY>
    <FORM ENCTYPE="multipart/form-data" ACTION="upload.php"
          METHOD="POST">Please Choose a file to upload:<BR />
      <INPUT TYPE="File" NAME="file4Upload"></INPUT>
      <BR />
      <INPUT TYPE="Submit" VALUE="Upload File"></INPUT>
    </FORM>
  </BODY>
</HTML>
```

Focus on the following form attributes:

- **ENCTYPE="multipart/form-data"** - Necessary for the form element of the type **file** to function properly
- **ACTION="upload.php"** - The name of the PHP page that holds the code spec that actually uploads the file to the web server

Save this file as **upload.html**. To view this file, request it from a Web server using a Browser. A form will be displayed in the Browser as shown in diagram 19.18.

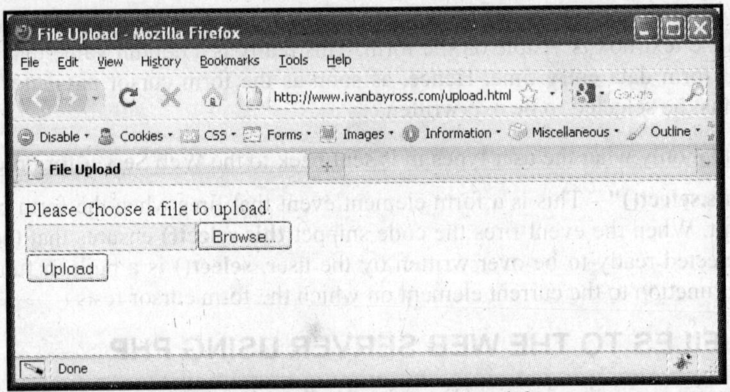

Diagram 19.18: The upload.html form

When Browse... button is clicked a directory tree is displayed. The directory tree is the structure of the hard disk, on the client computer, on which the Browser is running.

Simply navigate to the file to be uploaded and select it. This will automatically get assigned to the text box adjacent to the Browse... button.

Once the file to be uploaded is selected, click Upload the file data will be streamed to the web server and processed by **upload.php** located on the web server.

Since the **upload.html** form is ready, it is time to code the PHP script **uploader.php** that is going to handle the file upload and its storage to the Web server.

upload.php, uploads the file to **temporary storage** on the Web server. If the file is not moved to a different (safe) location it will be destroyed when the Web server purges its temporary storage area to make place for other file uploads.

Hence its necessary to move the uploaded file to a secure area on the hard disk of the Web server from where it will be available to users on demand.

To move this file to a secure area of the Web server's hard disk a programmer has to make use of the **$_FILES** associative array, created and maintained by the Web server.

The **$_FILES** associative array is where a Web server automatically stores all information about files uploaded to it.

The **$_FILES** associative array will have an **array index** and a **value** bound to each array index. **file4upload** will be the array index and **the name of the file** captured in it will be the value bound to this array index.

TIP

file4upload is the name of the textbox and Browse... button combination used as the HTML form element to capture the name of the file for upload on the Client machine.

This name is passed back by the Browser to the web server and is stored in the **$_FILES** array at the web server as the array index. The actual filename uploaded being stored as the value bound to this array index.

Now all that the server side PHP program **upload.php** needs to do is extract the uploaded file name from the **$_FILES** associative array (to identify the file uploaded) and process it appropriately.

Additionally, the **$_FILES** associative array contains the following:

- The **name** index of the **$_FILES** array contains the original path from where the user uploaded file
- The **tmp_name** index of the **$_FILES** array contains the path to where this file temporarily stored on the Web server's hard disk. The uploaded file must exist on the Web server in a temporary directory with a temporary name

The following code spec demonstrates how to get the temporary file name, choose a permanent name and choose a safe place to store the file so that it is available to users on demand:

```
// The path of the file i.e. where the file is going to be placed
$target_path = "uploadFile/";
// Adding the original filename to our target path
$target_path = $target_path . basename( $_FILES['file4Upload']['name']);
// Getting the temporary file
$_FILES['file4Upload']['tmp_name'];
```

NOTE

To save the files uploaded create a new directory called **uploads** in the same subdirectory where uploader.php resides.
(In this material's case it was c:/sct/phpproj/**uploads**)

The move_uploaded_file( ) Function

The next step is to call a built-in **move_uploaded_file()** function. The **move_uploaded_file()** requires the following parameters:

1) The path to where the temporary file is located on the Web server
2) The path where it should be moved to on the Web server

```
<?php
    $target_path = "uploadFile/";
    $target_path = $target_path . basename( $_FILES['uploadedFile']['name']);
    if(move_uploaded_file($_FILES['uploadedFile']['tmp_name'], $target_path))
    {
        echo "The file ". basename($_FILES['uploadedFile']['name'])." has been
            uploaded Successfully.";
    }
    else
    {
            echo "Sorry there was an error uploading the file, please try again!";
    }
?>
```

Save all this code in a file named **upload.php**.

Now run upload.html in a browser. A form as shown in the diagram 19.18 will be displayed that will allow browsing for a file to be uploaded to the Web server on the Client's hard disk. Click [Upload] after selecting a file for upload.

$move_uploaded_file returns **true** if the file is moved and **false** if a problem occurrs. Therefore, if the upload is successful, then a text **The file <filename> has been uploaded** will be displayed in an HTML page that is returned to the Browser as shown in diagram 19.19.

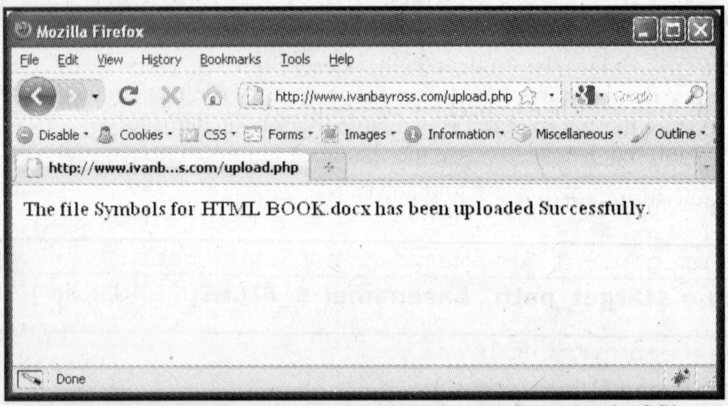

Diagram 19.19: Message indicating successful upload of file

TIP

If the file is uploaded successfully, it will be saved in the **uploads** directory that is created in the same subdirectory where uploader.php resides.

If the upload is not successful then an error message **Sorry there was an error uploading the file, please try again!** will be displayed as shown in diagram 19.20.

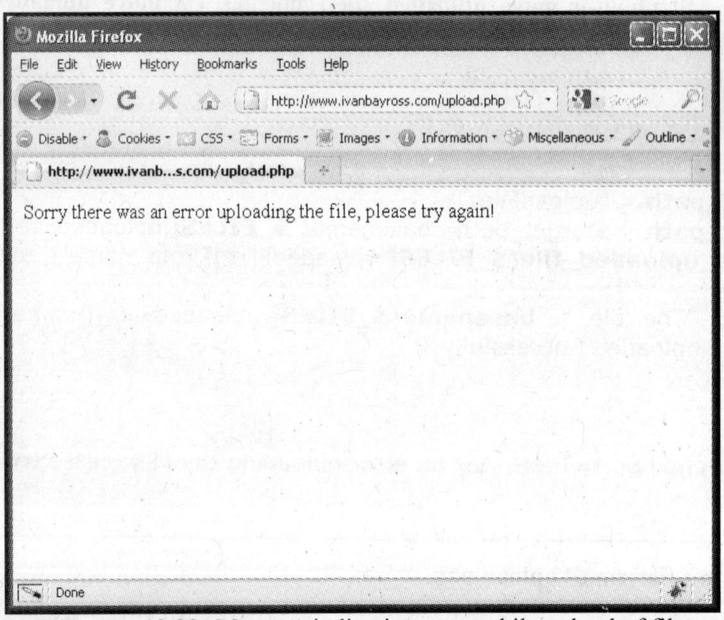

Diagram 19.20: Message indicating error while upload of file

NOTE

Any file including an image file (*<filename>*.**jpg**) can be uploaded to the Web server using upload.php.

HANDS ON EXERCISES

1. Create a form to capture Product Master and PHP code which will retrieve the data captured by the HTML form display the name of the form and message **"Product Data Entered Successful"** as shown in diagram 19.21 and diagram 19.22 The HTML form should perform the following:
   - ❑ Capture the data such as the Product Name, Description, Quantity, Price, and Product Image.
   - ❑ Clears the form fields when Cancel button is clicked
   - ❑ Submit the captured data and upload the file when Submit button is clicked
   - ❑ Product Name form field is not left blank
   - ❑ Product Description field is not left blank
   - ❑ Product Quantity field is not left blank and only number
   - ❑ Product Price field is not left blank and only number
   - ❑ Product Image upload a the image of the product

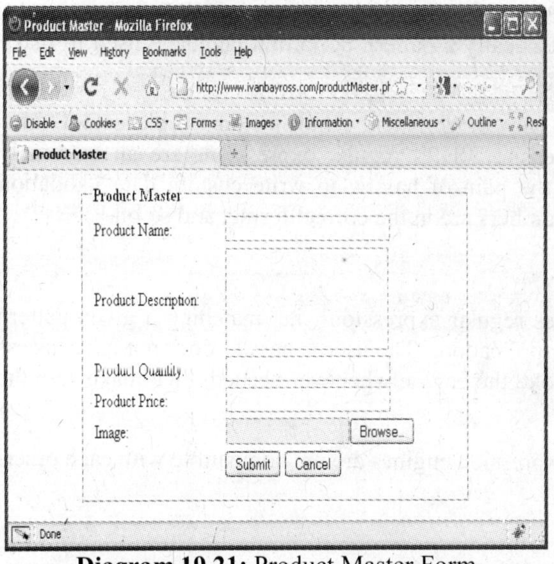

Diagram 19.21: Product Master Form

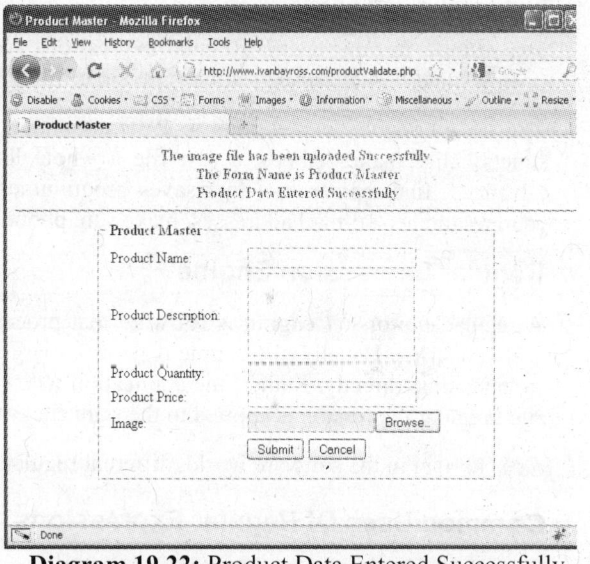

Diagram 19.22: Product Data Entered Successfully message

20. REGULAR EXPRESSIONS

The use of regular expressions in PHP helps create neatly coded PHP programs. Having said that, regular expressions are something that programmers seem to avoid. PHP based regular expressions are quite simple to implement once their concept is understood.

Regular expressions started out as a feature of the Unix shell. They were designed to make it easy to find, replace and work with strings. Regular expressions haves been used widely in many different areas of Unix based Operating Systems.

A regular expression is a specially formatted pattern that can be used to find instances of one string within another.

Several programming languages including Visual Basic, PERL, JavaScript and PHP support regular expressions. In other words Regular expressions are basically a pattern definition language used to make complex and flexible string searches possible.

The use of regular expressions in PHP is similar to any modern text editor's find / replace tool. This functionality makes editing a text file a whole lot easier. PHP's regular expressions are an extremely advanced, find-replace tool that saves programmers the pain of having to write custom data validation routines to check e-mail addresses, make sure phone numbers are in the correct format and so on.

Regular Expression Engine

A regular expression **engine** is software that processes regular expressions, i.e. matching a given pattern within a string. Usually, the engine is part of a larger application. The user generally does not have access to the engine directly. Rather, the application will invoke the engine whenever needed, then make sure the right regular expression is applied to the right file.

As is normal in the software world, different regular expression engines are not compatible with each other.

Common Uses Of Regular Expressions

A common use of regular expressions is in form data validation. For example, regular expressions can be used to check that an email address entered into a form contains the @ symbol and a period (**.**) which are definitely part of the email address, without which the Email address is not an Email address at all.

They can also be used to complete complex search and replace operations within a body of text that would not be possible with PHP's standard **str_replace** function.

In a web application, regular expressions would work well for:

- Data entry form input validation
- Verifying input format, example, the format of an Email address
- Parsing data from pre-defined variables
- Searching for and replacing data (when required) in a file or database
- If PHP code spec is being used to create user-defined functions to validate or manipulate portions of a string, then these user-defined functions could be scrapped and regular expressions used instead

- If custom written functions are being used:
  - To make sure form data contains valid information such as an @ and a **dot** in an Email address

  OR

  - To loop through each character in a string and replace it, if it matches a certain criteria, such as if it's upper case or if it's a space

Regular expressions are really simple to implement. Once a few regular expressions, which are specially formatted strings, used to tell the PHP regular expression engine, which portion of a string to match, are understood, using regular expressions becomes essentially commonplace.

Types Of Regular Expressions

While the basics of regular expressions are pretty much the same across the board, there are different flavors. PHP supports two flavors of regular expressions. **P**erl **C**ompatible **R**egular **E**xpressions (PCRE) and POSIX Extended Regular Expressions have both been available since PHP 3.

PCRE is generally considered a bit faster, performance wise, than POSIX, but the syntax of POSIX is easier to grasp. The basic concepts of regular expressions **are the same** for both types.

The following is code spec commonly used to validate e-mail addresses. The first function performs exactly the same as the second. The second function uses a regular expression.

Function One:

```
<?php
    function emailValidate($email)
    {
        $emailSymbol = strpos($email, "@");
        $dotSymbol = strpos($email, ".");

        if($emailSymbol && $dotSymbol)
            return true;

        else
            return false;
    }

    echo emailValidate("ivanbayross@ivanbayross.com");
?>
```

Function Two:

```
<?php
    function emailValidate($email)
    {
        return ereg("^[a-zA-Z]+@[a-zA-Z]+\.[a-zA-Z]+$", $email);
    }
    echo emailValidate("ivanbayross.com");
?>
```

The first function looks easy and well structured, but it would be easier to validate an e-mail address using the **one-line** version **emailValidate()** shown in **Function Two**.

Function Two above uses regular expressions only and contains one call to the **ereg** function. The **ereg** function always returns **true** or **false**, indicating whether its string argument matched what is specified in the regular expression or not.

Regular Expression Functions

Before a string can be matched to a regular expression, the regular expression has to be created. The syntax of regular expressions is a little quirky at first. Each phrase in the expression represents some sort of search criteria. A list of some of the most common regular expressions as well as an example of how to use each one is provided.

PHP has six functions that work with regular expressions. They all take a regular expression as their first argument and are shown below:

ereg()	The most common regular expression function, ereg() allows searching a string for a match with a regular expression(s).
eregi()	Performs exactly the same as ereg(), but is case **insensitive**.
ereg_replace()	Allows searching a string for a regular expression and then replace any occurrence of that string with a new string.
eregi_replace()	Has exactly the same search-replace functionality as ereg_replace(), but is case **insensitive**.
split()	Allows searching a string for a regular expression and returns the matches as an array of strings.
spliti()	Performs exactly the same as spilt(), but is case **insensitive**.

The simplest form of regular expressions is to match a single character or word. This does not require any knowledge of regular expressions or how to create patterns. In fact, it is as simple as the **Find** option used in word processing software. All that needs to be done is to specify the character or word that must be matched.

Symbols Used In Regular Expressions

Using ^ and $

Let's take a look at two special symbols '^' and '$'. These symbols indicate the start and the end of a string, respectively, as follows:

- "**^Ivan**" : Matches any string that starts with **Ivan**
- "**Bayross$**" : Matches a string that ends with **Bayross**
- "**^xyz$**" : Matches a string that starts and ends with **xyz.** (This can be the string **xyz** itself)
- "**Professor**" : Matches a string that has the text **Professor** in it

The last example shows that if either of the two symbols are not used this indicates that the pattern may occur anywhere inside the string i.e. the string is not bound to any of the edges start or end.

Using *, + and ?

Symbols like '*', '+', and '?', denote the number of times a character or a sequence of characters may occur. The '*' means **zero or more**, '+' means **one or more** and '?' means **zero or one**.

They can be used as:

- "**iv***": Matches a string that has a character **s** followed by zero or more **v**. The possibilities are "**i**", "**iv**", "**ivvv**" and so on
- "**iv+**": Matches a string that has a character **s** followed by at least one or more a. The possibilities are "**iv**", "**ivv**" and so on
- "**iv?**": Matches a string that has a character **s** but may or may not be followed by a single character **v**. The possibilities are "**i**", "**iv**"
- "**i?v+$**": Matches a string that may have a character **s** but compulsorily ends with at least one or more **v**. The possibilities are "**v**", "**iv**", "**ivvv**", "**ivan**" and so on

Using Bounds {}

Bounds can also be used, which come inside braces and indicate ranges in the terms of occurrences. They are used as:

- "**iv{2}**": Matches a string that has a character **s** followed by exactly two **h**. The possibility is "**ivv**"
- "**iv{2,}**": Matches a string that has a character **s** followed by at least two **h**. The possibilities are "**ivv**", "**ivvvv**" and so on
- "**iv{3,5}**": Matches a string that has a character **s** followed by at least three but not more than five **v**. The possibilities are "**ivvv**", "**ivvvv**", "**ivvvvv**"

NOTE

The first number/parameter in a range should always be specified. This means **{0,2}** or **{2,}** are valid and not **{,2}**. Also, notice that the symbols used earlier such as '*', '+' and '?' have the same effect as using the bounds **{0,}**, **{1,}** and **{0,1}** respectively.

Using Quantifiers

To quantify a sequence of characters, put them inside round brackets as:

- **"i(va)*"**: Matches a string that has a character **s** followed by zero or more copies of the sequence **"va"**
- **"i(va){1,5}"**: Matches a string that has a character **s** followed by at least one but not more than five copies of **"va"**

Using | The OR Operator

The '|' symbol works similar to the OR operator and can be used as:

- **"Ivan|Mr.Ivan"**: Matches a string that holds either **"Ivan"** or **"Mr.Ivan"**
- **"(Cynthia|Ivan)Bayross"**: Matches a string that holds either " **CynthiaBayross**" or **"IvanBayross"**
- **"(i|v)*a"**: Matches a string that has a sequence of alternating characters i.e. **i** and **v** but ending with a character **a**. The possibilities are **"ia"**, **"iia"**, **"iiia"** and so on or **"va"**, **"vva"**, **"vvva"** and so on

Using . The Period

A period '.' stands for any single character and can be used as:

- **"s.[0-9]"**: Matches a string that has a character **s** followed by any one character further followed by a digit. The possibilities are **"iv2"**, **"iv1"** and so on
- **"^.{8}$"**: Matches a string with exactly **8** characters. The possibilities are **"Ivan"**, **"Cynthia"** and so on

Using [ ] Bracket Expressions

Bracket expressions specify which characters are allowed in a single position of a string and can be used as:

- **"[iv]"**: Matches a string that has either the character **s** or **h**. This is same as **"i|v"**
- **"[a-d]"**: Matches a string that holds lowercase characters **'a'** through **'d'**. This is equal to **"a|b|c|d"** or **"[abcd]"**
- **"^[a-zA-Z]"**: Matches a string that begins with a letter
- **"[0-9]%"**: Matches a string that has a single digit before a percent sign
- **",[a-zA-Z0-9]$"**: Matches a string that ends in a **comma** followed by an alphanumeric character
- **"%[^a-zA-Z]%"**: Matches a string with a character that is not an alphabet between two percent signs

Using Regular Expression Functions

NOTE

With **ereg()**, matching is **case sensitive**. For **case insensitive** matching, use **eregi()**.

Example:

```
ereg("professor", "Ivan Bayross is a Professor.");
```

In the above example the signature (i.e. code spec) of the function **ereg()**, will look for the word **professor** in the supplied string. If it locates the word, **true** is returned. Otherwise, **false** is returned. Obviously, in this example the result would be false as **ereg()** is case sensitive.

Now consider the following:

```
eregi("professor", "Ivan Bayross is a Professor.");
```

In this example the signature (i.e. code spec) of the function **eregi()**, will look for the word **professor** in the supplied string. In this example the result would be **true**, as the match performed here is case insensitive.

Now, a simple pattern using the (.) meta-character is being introduced. A meta-character is a character that PHP expands to mean something else. The (.) meta-character, expands to represent any character **except** a new line. Here the original example is slightly modified, to show the use of this special character.

```
ereg("Mu...i", "Ivan Bayross stays in Mumbai");
```

The regular expression of **Mu...i** will match any occurrence of the letter **Mu** that is followed by **any three** other characters and then by the letter **i**. This will match the word Mumbai in the string, so the expression will return **true**.

The ^ and **$** symbols can be specified in the **ereg** function. ^ denotes that a match should be found at the **beginning** of a string, while the **$** modifier denotes that the match should be found at the end of a string.

```
ereg("^Mumbai", "Ivan Bayross stays in Mumbai");
```

The preceding line of code returns **false** because Mumbai is **not** at the **beginning** of the string in which pattern matching is attempted.

```
ereg("Mumbai$", "Ivan Bayross stays in Mumbai");
```

The preceding line of code returns **true** because Mumbai is at the **end** of the string in which pattern matching is attempted.

There are also meta-characters that specify the number of times a particular pattern can occur in a match. One is the **?** character. When this meta-character is used, the preceding pattern or character will be matched **zero** or **one** times.

```
ereg("MumbaiX?", "Ivan Bayross stays in Mumbai");
```

This expression will evaluate to **true** because the letter X **can occur once**, **or not at all**.

NOTE

Since the characters preceding the meta-character (**X**) are not placed in brackets, the **meta-character applies only to the letter X**.

The next meta-character is the (*) character. It will match the preceding pattern or character, zero or more times. This character is used as a **wildcard** character in many different applications. The difference in regular expressions is that **it must follow the pattern** to be matched, rather than just replace it.

```
ereg("M*bai", "Ivan Bayross stays in Mumbai");
```

This expression matches the letters **M**, followed by zero or more letters, followed by the letters **bai**.

The + meta-character can also be used and provides **almost the same functionality** as the * character, except that the pattern **must occur at least once**.

```
ereg("Mu+bai", "Ivan Bayross stays in Mumbai");
```

That would match the letters **Mu**, followed by one or more letters, then followed by the letters **bai**.

The previous modifiers are useful when matching varying occurrences of a pattern, what if an exact amount of occurrences must be matched? Regular expressions provide a simple means of doing so using **bounds**.

```
ereg("Mum{1}bai", "Ivan Bayross stays in Mumbai");
```

This would match the word **Mumbai**. The **{1}** signifies that the preceding character or pattern (in this case **m**) should be matched exactly once. This would match the letters **Mu**, followed by exactly one occurrence of the letter **m**, then followed by the letters **bai**.

Now, let's take a look at specifying a range for the number of matches.

```
ereg("Mum{1,3}bai", "Ivan Bayross stays in Mumbai");
```

This would match the word Mu**m**bai, Mu**mm**bai or Mu**mmm**bai. The bound **{1,3}** allows matches of at least one but not more than three **m**.

Up to this point single characters have been dealt with. Take a look at grouping with parentheses, in order to use the different meta-characters on more than one character at a time.

```
ereg("Mu(mm)+bai", "Ivan Bayross stays in Mummmmbai");
```

In this example, the regular expression will match the letters **Mu**, followed by one or more occurrences of **mm**, then followed by the letters **bai**. In this case, the expression would return **true**. It would have also returned true if the string being matched against had the word **Mummbai** in it or the word **Mummmmmmbai**.

The (|) character permits an **either or** situation.

```
ereg("(Ivan Bayross|Mr. I Bayross)", "Mr. I Bayross stays in Mumbai");
```

This example will match either **Ivan Bayross** or **Mr. I Bayross**. Because the string being matched contains the word **Mr. I Bayross**, this expression will return **true**.

Using **[ ]** (square brackets), a range of characters to be matched can be expressed. This can be especially useful when matching numbers (i.e. digits) or a specific range of letters.

Multiple ranges can be placed within the square brackets as follows:

```
ereg("Mumba[0-9g-j]", "Ivan Bayross stays in Mumbai");
```

The preceding example will match the word **Mumba**, followed by a **digit** or a **letter** in the range of **g** through **j**. In this example, the expression would evaluate as **true**, because the letter **i** falls within this range.

To match the space character in a search string, use the predefined POSIX class **[[:space:]]**. The **square** brackets indicate a related set of sequential characters and **:space:** is the actual class to match (which, in this case, is any white space character).

White spaces include the tab character, the new line character and the space character. Alternatively, use **one space** character (" ") if the search string must contain **just** one space and **not** a tab or new line character.

In most circumstances use **:space:** because it signifies a programmers intention a bit better than a single space character, which can easily be overlooked. There are several POSIX standard predefined classes that can be used as part of a regular expression, including **[:alnum:]**, **[:digit:]**, **[:lower:]** and so on.

Match a single space character like this:

```
<?php
    echo ereg("Ivan[[:space:]]Bayorss", "Ivan Bayross");
?>
```

Match either **no** spaces or **one** space by using the **?** character after the expression, as follows:

```
<?php
    echo ereg("Ivan[[:space:]]?Bayross", "IvanBayross");
?>
```

The following expression uses escape characters and involves placing a backslash **before any special symbols**. To include the **or** symbol (|) in the search:

```
<?php
    echo ereg("^[a-zA-z]+\|[a-zA-z]+$", "Ivan|Mr.Bayross");
?>
```

There are only a handful of symbols that require escape characters placed before them, they are:

- ^
- $
- (,)
- .
- [
- |
- *
- ?
- +
- \
- {

The following regular expression validates a standard URL (with **no** port number).

```
ereg("^(http|ftp)://(www\.)?.+\.(com|net|org)$", "www.ivanbayross.com");
```

^(http|ftp) indicates matching the protocol part of the URL. This makes sure that only **http** or **ftp** can be used. The ^ character specifies the beginning of the string and by enclosing http and ftp in brackets and separating them with the **or** character (i.e. the | symbol), the PHP regular expression engine is told that either the characters **http** or **ftp** must be at the beginning of the string.

(www\.)?.+\.(com|net|org)$ indicates that a domain name usually consists of www.somewebsite.com, but can optionally be specified without the **www** part. This example only allows **.com**, **.net** and **.org** domain names to be considered valid.

Example:
The above illustration can be built as shown below:

```
<?php
    function validDomain($nameOfDomain)
    {
        return ereg("^(http|ftp)://(www\.)?.+\.(com|net|org)$",
                    $nameOfDomain);
    }
    echo validDomain("http://www.ivanbayross.net");
    echo validDomain("ftp://downloads.com");
    echo validDomain("ftp://www.gmail.co.in");
    echo validDomain ("www.ivanbayross.com");
?>
```

In the above example, the first two calls to **validDomain()** will return **true**, while the last two calls will return **false**.

Similarly, the **eregi()** can be used to perform **case insensitive** matching as required while performing email address validation:

```
<?php
    function validCheckEmail($cEmail)
    {
        if(!eregi("^[a-z0-9\._-]+" . "@" . "([a-z0-9][a-z0-9-]*[a-z0-9]\.)+"
            . "([a-z]+\.)?". "([a-z]+)$", $cEmail))
        {
            return TRUE;
        }
        return FALSE;
    }
?>
```

Examining the regular expression portion line by line:

^[a-z0-9\._-]+	This portion of the expression will match any letter, any digit, a period, an underscore or a hyphen. The match must occur at the beginning of the string and it will match one or more of those characters.
@	This next piece of the regular expression will match a single occurrence of an @ symbol. Because this is appended to the previous portion of the regular expression, it would occur after the first portion was matched.
([a-z0-9][a-z0-9-]*[a-z0-9]\.)+	This portion will match a single letter or digit. Then zero or more letters or digits are matched, followed by a single letter or digit again. At the end of this piece, a single period must be matched.
([a-z]+\.)?	This part of the regular expression will match one or more occurrences of any letter, followed by a period. This entire part of the expression can occur once or not at all as defined by the ? character.
([a-z]+)$	This final piece of the regular expression will match any letter and that letter must occur at least once.

NOTE

With **ereg_replace()**, matching is **case sensitive**. For **case insensitive** matching, use **eregi_replace()**.

Example:

```
ereg_replace("Professor", "Project Leader", "Ivan Bayross is an Professor.");
```

In this example the signature (i.e. code spec) of the function **ereg_replace()**, will look for the word **Professor** in the supplied string and replace it with **Project Leader**. If it locates the word, **the modified string** is returned. Otherwise, **original string** is returned. Obviously, in this example the result would be the original string as **ereg_replace()** is case sensitive.

Now consider the following:

```
eregi_replace("Professor", "Project Leader",  "Ivan Bayross is a Professor.");
```

In this example the signature (i.e. code spec) of the function **eregi_replace()**, will look for the word **Professor** in the supplied string and replace it with **Project Leader**. In this example the result would be the modified string, as the match performed here is case insensitive.

```
ereg_replace("Mumbai$", "Goa", "Ivan Bayross stays in Mumbai");
```

The preceding line of code returns **the modified string** because **Mumbai** is at the **end** of the string in which pattern matching was attempted.

The (|) character permits an **either or** situation.

```
ereg_replace("(Mumbai|Goa)$","Chennai", "Ivan Bayross stays in Mumbai");
```

This example will match either **Mumbai** or **Goa** at the end of the string. Because the string being matched ends with the word **Mumbai**, the string returned will be "**Ivan Bayross stays in Chennai**".

The **ereg_replace()** function can be used to replace URLs with HTML links. Consider the following code:

```
<?php
    $url = "http://www.ivanbayross.com";
    $link = ereg_replace("[[:alpha:]]+://[^<>[:space:]]+[[:alnum:]/]", "<a
                         href=\"\\0\">\\0</a>", $url);
?>
<HTML>
    <HEAD>
        <TITLE>Link to a URL</TITLE>
    <BODY>
        The converted URL is :<BR />
        <?php
            echo $link;
        ?>
    </BODY>
</HTML>
```

Output: (Refer to diagram 20.1)

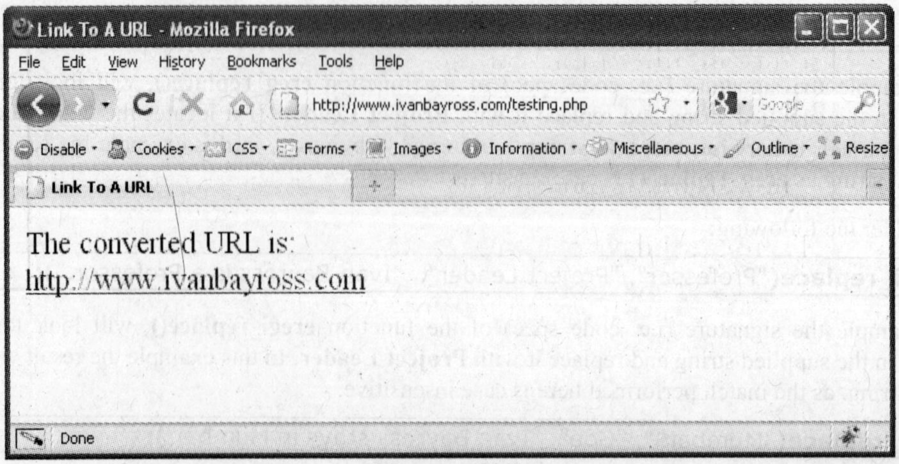

Diagram 20.1

NOTE

If an integer value is used as the replacement parameter, the expected result may not be achieved. This is because **ereg_replace()** will interpret the number as the ordinal value of a character and apply that.

Example:

```
<?php
    $aNumber = 5;
    $bString = "There are five days in a week.";
    $bString = ereg_replace("five", $aNumber, $bString);
    echo $bString . "<BR />";

    $aNumber = '5';
    $bString = "There are five days in a week.";
    $bString = ereg_replace("five", $aNumber, $bString);
    echo $bString;
?>
```

Output: (Refer to diagram 20.2)

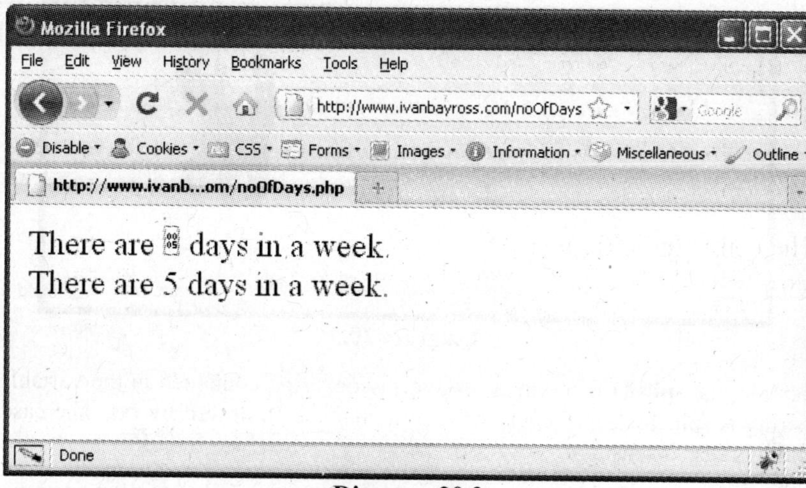

Diagram 20.2

In the above example, the first block of code fails in the replace operation because the variable **$num** holds a numeric value. The second block of code is able to perform the replacement as the variable **$num** holds a string.

The **split()** can be used to parse a date which may be delimited with slashes, dots or hyphens:

```
list($month, $day, $year) = split('[/.-]', $date);
```

The variable **$date** may hold the date in the formats such as **mm/dd/yyyy**, **mm.dd.yyyy** or **mm-dd-yyyy**.

The above code spec, after splitting the value held by the variable **$date** in three parts, will transfer them into variables **$month**, **$day** and **$year**.

NOTE

With **split()**, matching is **case sensitive**. For **case insensitive** matching, use **spliti()**.

Example:

Now consider the following example, which demonstrates the technique that can be used in **spliti()**:

```
<?php
    $str = "http://www.ivanbayross.com?txtName=Ivan
                    &txtSurname=Bayross&txtDOB=23/06/1952";
    $columns = spliti(".txt", $str, 4);
    echo "The parameters and their corresponding values passed are: <BR />";
    print_r($columns);
?>
```

Output: (Refer to diagram 20.3)

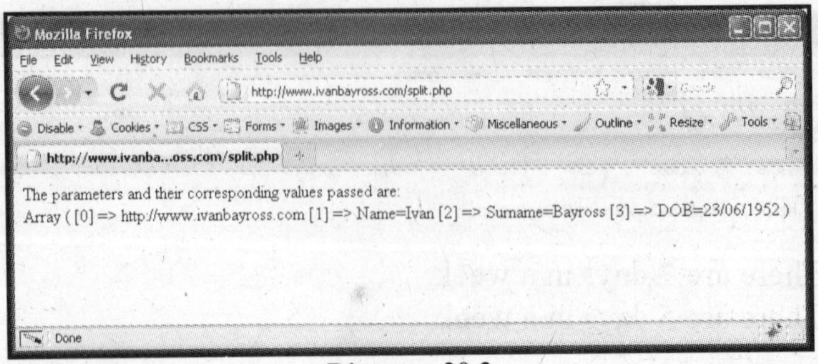

Diagram 20.3

In the above example, the **spliti()** function is used to divide string contained in the variable **$str**, into four segments. The string is split for every occurrence of a character followed by **txt**. The case used for **txt** is irrelevant as **spliti()** is case insensitive.

In the above example, if the third parameter for **spliti()** was not specified, the value contained in **$str** would have been segmented into four parts (as the combination of a character followed by **txt** appears three times).

Example:
Consider the following example. It is a data entry form, generated by a PHP program. The form captures data such as name, date of birth, qualifications and specialty in four individual form elements. The captured values are submitted to a PHP program, which uses regular expressions to **validate** and **format** the data before sending it back to the client's browser.

Create a file with the following contents:

```
<?
     /*
          Date      :- 04/10/05
          Author    :- Ivan Bayross
          Filename:- clientMaster2.php
          Purpose  :- Validates and displays Client's name, email id and
                        telephone number using regular expressions.
     */
     /* A variable holding the developers name. */
   $author = 'Ivan Bayross';
?>
<HTML>
   <HEAD>
   <TITLE>Client's Details</TITLE>
   </HEAD>
   <BODY STYLE="FONT-FAMILY: georgia;">
   <CENTER>
   <FIELDSET STYLE="WIDTH:50%">
        <LEGEND STYLE="FONT-WEIGHT: bold; FONT-FAMILY: georgia;
             FONT-SIZE: 12px;">CLIENT'S DETAILS:</LEGEND>
             <FORM ACTION="clientForm2.php" METHOD="post"
                  NAME="frmClientInfo">
```

```
<TABLE ID="tableForm" BORDER="0" BGCOLOR="#FFFFFF"
    CELLPADDING="4" CELLSPACING="6" WIDTH="100%" >
    <TR>
        <TD COLSPAN="2" STYLE="COLOR: #ff0000;">
            <?php echo $alertmessage ?>
        </TD>
        <TR>
            <TD COLSPAN="2"><CENTER>
                Please enter the information to get access to our resources.
                </CENTER>
            </TD>
        </TR>
        <TR>
            <TD ALIGN="right" WIDTH="30%">
                Client Name:
            </TD>
            <TD>
                <INPUT NAME="txtname" TYPE="text"
                    VALUE="<?php echo $_post['txtname'];?>"
                    SIZE="50" />
            </TD>
        </TR>
        <TR>
            <TD> </TD>
            <TD> (Format: <Strong>Surname</Strong>[:Space:]
                    <Strong>Name</Strong>[:Space:]
                    <Strong>Second/Middle Name</Strong>)
            </TD>
        </TR>
        <TR>
            <TD ALIGN="right" WIDTH="30%"> Email Id: </TD>
            <TD>
                <INPUT NAME="txtemail" TYPE="text"
                    VALUE="<?php echo $_post['txtemail'];?>"
                    SIZE="50" />
            </TD>
        </TR>
        <TR>
            <TD> </TD>
            <TD> (Format: <Strong>Email Id</Strong>[@]
                  <Strong>Domain Name</Strong>)
            </TD>
        </TR>
        <TR>
            <TD ALIGN="right" WIDTH="30%"> Telephone: </TD>
            <TD>
                <INPUT NAME="txtphone" TYPE="text"
                    VALUE="<?php echo $_post['txtphone'];?>"
                    SIZE="50" />
            </TD>
        </TR>
```

```
            <TR>
                <TD> </TD>
                <TD> (Format: <Strong>Only Numeric Values Are Allowed</Strong>)
                </TD>
            </TR>
            <TR>
                <TD ALIGN="right" WIDTH="30%">  </TD>
                <TD>
                  <INPUT NAME="cmdsubmit" TYPE="submit" VALUE="Submit"/>
                  <INPUT NAME="cmdreset" TYPE="reset" VALUE="Cancel" />
                </TD>
            </TR>
          </TABLE>
        </FORM>
      </FIELDSET>
    </CENTER>
  </BODY>
</HTML>
```

Save the file as **clientMaster2.php** and run it via a web browser. The HTML page as shown in diagram 20.4 will be displayed.

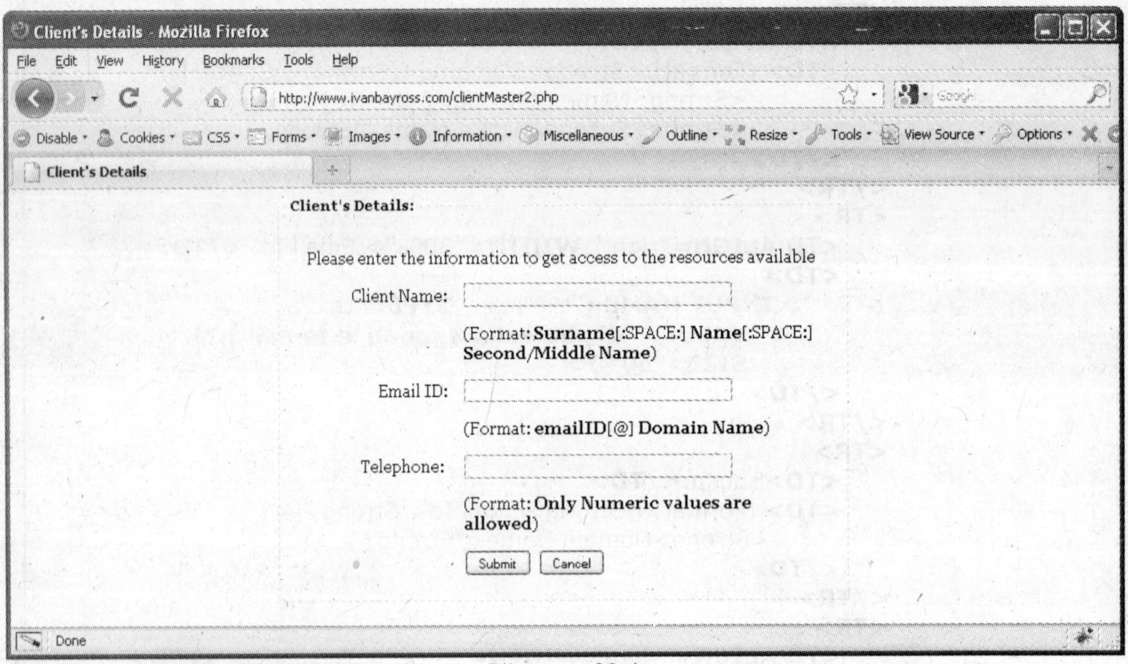

Diagram 20.4

Enter the information as asked for into the form fields and click [Submit] to pass the data captured to be processed by clientForm2.php.

On receiving the data, the other file processes the code snippet mentioned below:

```
<?php
	/*
		Date       :- 04/10/09
		Client     :- Ivan Bayross
		Filename   :- clientForm2.php
		Purpose    :- Validates and Displays Client's name, email id and telephone number using
		              Regular Expressions
	*/
	/* A Variable Holding the Developers Name. */
		$author = 'Ivan Bayross';

	/* Storing the System Date In the Format 1st Jan, 2009. */
		$sysdt = date("js m, y");

	/* Storing The System Time In the Format 00:00. */
		$systm = date("h:i");

		/* Checking If the Variable For Client's Name Is Empty, (I.E. A Blank Client's Name
		   Field Was Submitted). */
		if(empty($_post['txtname']))
		{
			/* Returning To The Data Entry Form If the Clients Name Is Empty. */
			$alertmessage = '<center>Field For Client\'S Name Is Empty!</center>';
			include ("clientMaster2.php");
			exit;
		}
		/* When The Client's Name Is Submitted. */
		else
		{
			/* Using Regular Expressions With the ereg() Function, To Identify An
			Occurrence of Double Spaces In the Client's Name. */
			if(ereg("([[:space:]]){2}", $_post['txtname']))
			{
				/* Returning To the Data Entry Form, If the Client's Name Contains
				   Double Spaces. */
				$alertmessage = '<center>Double Spaces Found in Client\'s
						Name</center>';
				include ("clientMaster2.php");
				exit;
			}
		}
		/* Checking If the Variable for Client's Email Id Is Empty,
		   (i.e. A Blank Date Of Email Field Was Submitted). */
		if(empty($_post['txtemail']))
		{
		    /* Returning To The Data Entry Form, If The Client's Email Id Is Empty. */
			$alertmessage = '<center>Field for Email Id is Empty! </center>';
			include ("clientMaster2.php");
			exit;
		}
	/* When The Client's Email Id is Submitted. */
```

```
        else
        {
                /* Returning To the Data Entry Form, If the Format for the Client's Email Id
                   is Not As Specified In The Data Entry Form. */
            $regex = '/^([a-zA-Z0-9\.\-\_])+\@ (([a-zA-Z0-9\.\-])+\.)+([a-zA-Z0-9]{2,4})+$/';
            if(!preg_match($regex,$_post['txtemail']))
            {
                $alertmessage = '<center>Invalid Client\'s email id! </center>';
                include ("clientMaster2.php");
                exit;
            }
        }
                /* Checking If The Variable For Client's Telephone No Is Empty, (I.E. A Blank
                   Telephone Number Field Was Submitted). */
        if(empty($_post['txtphone']))
        {
            /* Returning To The Data Entry Form, If The Client's Telephone No Is Empty. */
            $alertmessage = '<center>Field for Client\'s Telephone Is Empty! </center>';
            include ("clientMaster2.php");
            exit;
        }
        else
        {
                /* Checking If The Variable For Client's Telephone is a numeric value
                   (i.e a blank character value was submitted). */
                $regex = '/[0123456789]/' ;
                if(!preg_match($regex,$_post['txtphone']))
                {
                    $alertmessage = '<center>Invalid Client\'s telephone number! </center>';
                    include ("clientMaster2.php");
                    exit;
                }
        }
?>
/* The following output will be generated when valid set of client's data is submitted */
<HTML>
        <HEAD>
                <TITLE>Result after using Regular Expression</TITLE>
        </HEAD>
        <BODY STYLE="Font-Family: georgia;">
                <H4>Details Submitted As On: </H4>
                <TABLE BORDER="1" CELLSPACING="1" WIDTH="250">
                        <TR>
                            <TD ALIGN="right" WIDTH="100">Server Date : </TD>
                            <TD ALIGN="left" WIDTH="100">
                                <?php echo $sysdt; ?>
                            </TD>
                        </TR>

                        <TR>
```

```
                <TD ALIGN="right" WIDTH="100">Server Time : </TD>
                <TD ALIGN="left" WIDTH="100">
                    <?php echo $systm; ?>
                </TD>
            </TR>
    </TABLE>
    <HR>
<?php
    /* Using the split() Function To Extract Client's Last Name, First Name And
       Second Name into Variables $lname, $fname and $mname respectively. */
    list($lname, $fname, $mname) = split(" ", $_post['txtname'], 3);
?>
    <H4>Client's Name: </H4>
    <TABLE BORDER="1" CELLSPACING="1" WIDTH="500">
            <TR>
              <TD ALIGN="center" WIDTH="150">
                <?php echo $lname; ?>
              </TD>
              <TD ALIGN="center" WIDTH="150">
                <?php echo $fname; ?>
              </TD>
            <TD ALIGN="center" WIDTH="200">
                <?php echo $mname; ?>
            </TD>
          </TR>

          <TR>
            <TD ALIGN="center" WIDTH="150">Surname</TD>
            <TD ALIGN="center" WIDTH="150">First name</TD>
            <TD ALIGN="center" WIDTH="150">Second/Middle Name</TD>
          </TR>
    </TABLE>
    <HR>

    <H4>Email Id: </H4>
    <TABLE BORDER="0" CELLSPACING="1" WIDTH="300">
        <TR>
          <TD ALIGN="left" WIDTH="150">
              <?php echo $_post['txtemail']; ?>
          </TD>
        </TR>
    </TABLE>
    <HR>

    <H4>Telephone: </H4>
    <TABLE BORDER="0" CELLSPACING="1" WIDTH="400">
     <TR>
       <TD ALIGN="left" WIDTH="150">
         <?php echo  $_post['txtphone']?>
       </TD>
     </TR>
```

```
                </TABLE>
            </BODY>
    </HTML>
```

Save the changes made to the file **clientForm2.php** and execute the file by passing a call through the file **clientForm2.php**.

Following validations are performed by the **clientForm2.php** file.

- The Client Name textbox is not empty
- No double spacing in the client name captured
- Email textbox is not empty
- Email textbox should be in correct format
- Telephone textbox field is not empty
- Telephone textbox field should be only numeric value

Verify the validations as:

- Client Name cannot be left empty

Submit the form deliberately keeping the Client Name field empty and press Submit. The PHP code checks the contents of the Client Name field returned by the Browser. As it is empty, an error message is generated and stored in the variable **$alertmessage**. This error message is included in the form at the top of the HTML code spec and the combination of the error message and the HTML form is returned to the Browser. Refer to diagram 20.5.1.

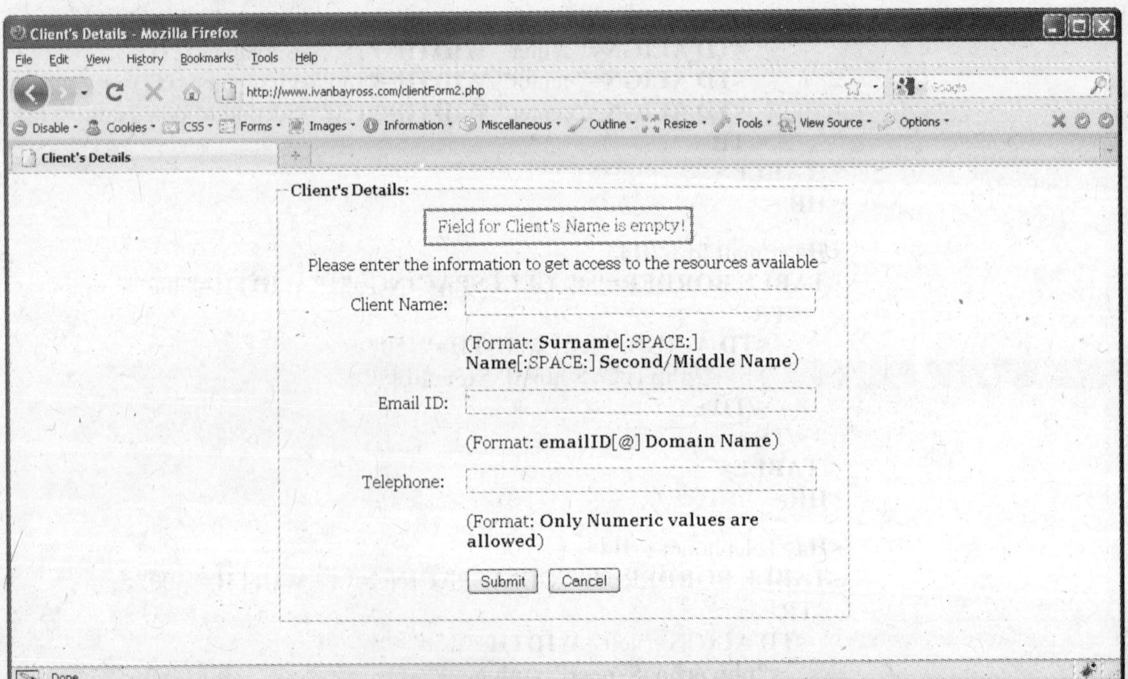

Diagram 20.5.1: An error message indicating an empty client's name field

As seen in diagram 20.5.1, the error message is displayed after the form title.

The above validation is done using the following code spec:

```
/* Checking if the variable for Client's name is empty, (i.e. a blank Client's name field was submitted). */
  if(empty($_POST['txtName']))
  {
    /* Returning to the data entry form if the Client's name is empty. */
      $alertmessage = '<center>Field for Client\'s Name is empty! </center>';
      include("clientMaster2.php");
      exit;
  }
```

- No double spacing in the Client's name captured

To test double spacing validation, insert double spaces in between the Client Name and click Submit. The PHP code checks the contents of Client Name field returned by the Browser. As it has double spacing, an error message is generated and stored in the variable **$alertmessage**.

To validate the name for double spaces, the **ereg()** function is used which will scan the contents of client's name for the occurrence of double spaces:

```
ereg("([[:space:]]){2}", $_POST['txtName'])
```

This error message is included in the form at the top of the HTML code spec and combination of error message and HTML form is returned to the Browser. Refer to diagram 20.5.2

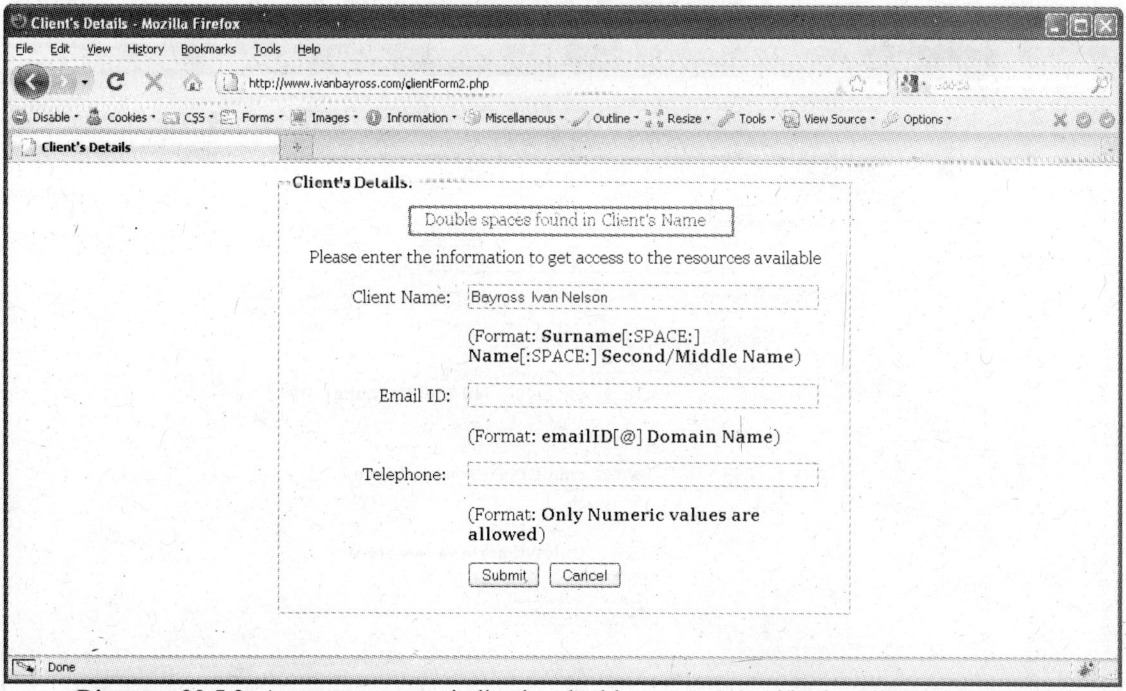

Diagram 20.5.2: An error message indicating double spaces passed in the Client's name field

The above validation is done using the following code spec:

```
/* Using regular expressions with the ereg() function, to identify an occurrence of double
spaces in the client's name.*/
   else
   {
      if(ereg("([[:space:]]){2}", $_POST['txtName']))
      {
         /* Returning to the data entry form, if the client's name contains double
            spaces. */
         $alertmessage = '<center>Double spaces found in Client\'s Name</center>';
         include ("clientMaster2.php");
         exit;
      }
   }
```

The above regular expression uses the **[[:space:]]** to identify space. Since double spacing is to be identified bound **{2}** is used to search two continuous spaces.

- Email cannot be left empty

Submit the form by passing a valid Client Name and deliberately keeping Email Id field empty and press Submit. The PHP code checks the contents of the Client Name and Email Id field returned by the Browser. As the email id field is empty, an error message is generated and stored in the variable **$alertmessage**. This error message is included in the form at the top of the HTML code spec and the combination of the error message and the HTML form is returned to the Browser. Refer to diagram 20.5.3.

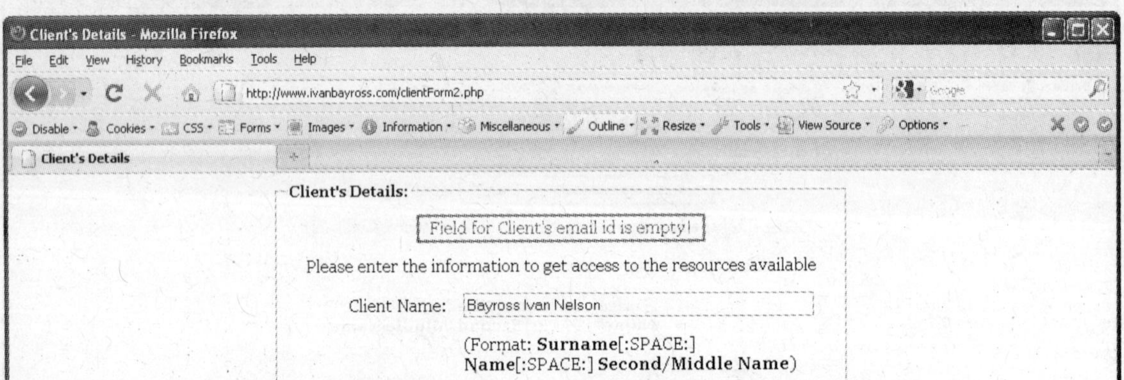

Diagram 20.5.3: An error message indicating an empty Email id field

As seen in diagram 20.5.3, the error message is displayed after the form title.

The above validation is done using the following code spec:

```
/* Checking if the variable for Client's Email Id is empty, (i.e. a blank Email id field was submitted) */
        if(empty($_POST['txtEmail']))
        {
                /* Returning to the data entry form, if the client's email id is empty. */
                $alertmessage = '<center>Field for Client\'s email id is empty!</center>';
                include ("clientMaster2.php");
                exit;
        }
```

- Invalid Client's email id!

Submit the form by passing a valid Client Name and deliberately passing a wrong Email Id format i.e. ivan.com and press Submit. The PHP code checks the contents of the Client Name and Email Id fields returned by the Browser. As the Email Id value is in wrong format, an error message is generated and stored in the variable **$alertmessage**. This error message is included in the form at the top of the HTML code spec and the combination of the error message and the HTML form is returned to the Browser. Refer to diagram 20.5.4.

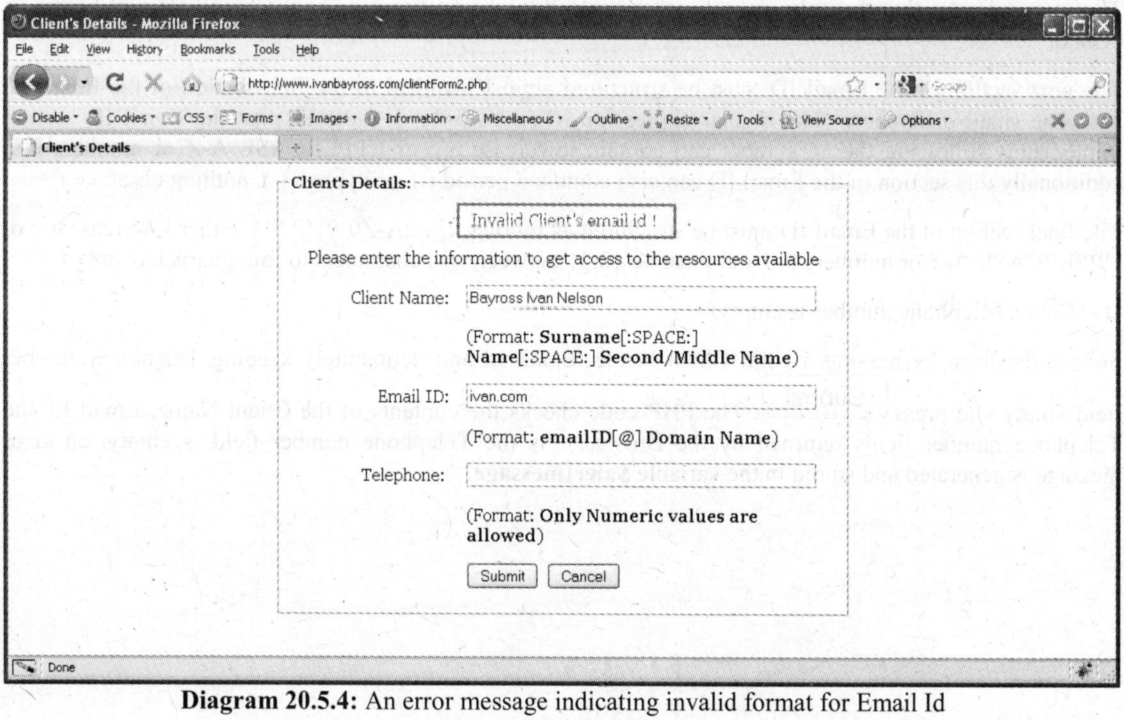

Diagram 20.5.4: An error message indicating invalid format for Email Id

As seen in diagram 20.5.4, the error message is displayed after the form title.

The above validation is done using the following code spec:

```
/* When the Client's Email Id is submitted. */
else
{
  /* Returning to the data entry form, if the format for the Client's Email Id is not as specified in
     the data entry form. */
  $regex = '/^([a-zA-Z0-9\.\-\_])+\@ (([a-zA-Z0-9\.\-])+\.)+([a-zA-Z0-9]{2,4})+$/';
  if(!preg_match($regex,$_POST['txtEmail']))
  {
      $alertmessage = '<center>Invalid Client\'s Email Id !</center>';
      include ("clientMaster2.php");
      exit;
  }
}
```

In the above regular expression /^([a-zA-Z0-9\.\-_]) indicates that the start of the Email ID can contain either lowercase a-z or UPPERCASE A-Z or numbers 0-9, additionally this section of the Email ID can also contain a period (.), or hyphen (-), or underscore (_), nothing else.

The +\@ indicates that the only character that can follow the first section of the Email ID will be the @ symbol.

The next section of the Email ID must be structured almost identical to the first section of the Email ID with one small difference. The regular expression (([a-zA-Z0-9\.\-]) indicates that the Email ID section immediately following the @ symbol can contain lowercase a-z or UPPERCASE A-Z or numbers 0-9, additionally this section of the Email ID can also contain a period (.), or hyphen (-), nothing else.

The final section of the Email ID must be structured as follows, ([a-zA-Z0-9]{2,4}) either lowercase a-z or UPPERCASE A-Z or numbers 0-9 and must be {2,4} between two characters to four characters only.

- Client Telephone number is empty!

Submit the form by passing a valid Client Name, Email Id and deliberately keeping Telephone number field empty and press Submit. The PHP code checks the contents of the Client Name, Email Id and Telephone number fields returned by the Browser. As the Telephone number field is empty, an error message is generated and stored in the variable **$alertmessage**.

This error message is included in the form at the top of the HTML code spec and the combination of the error message and the HTML form is returned to the Browser. Refer to diagram 20.5.5.

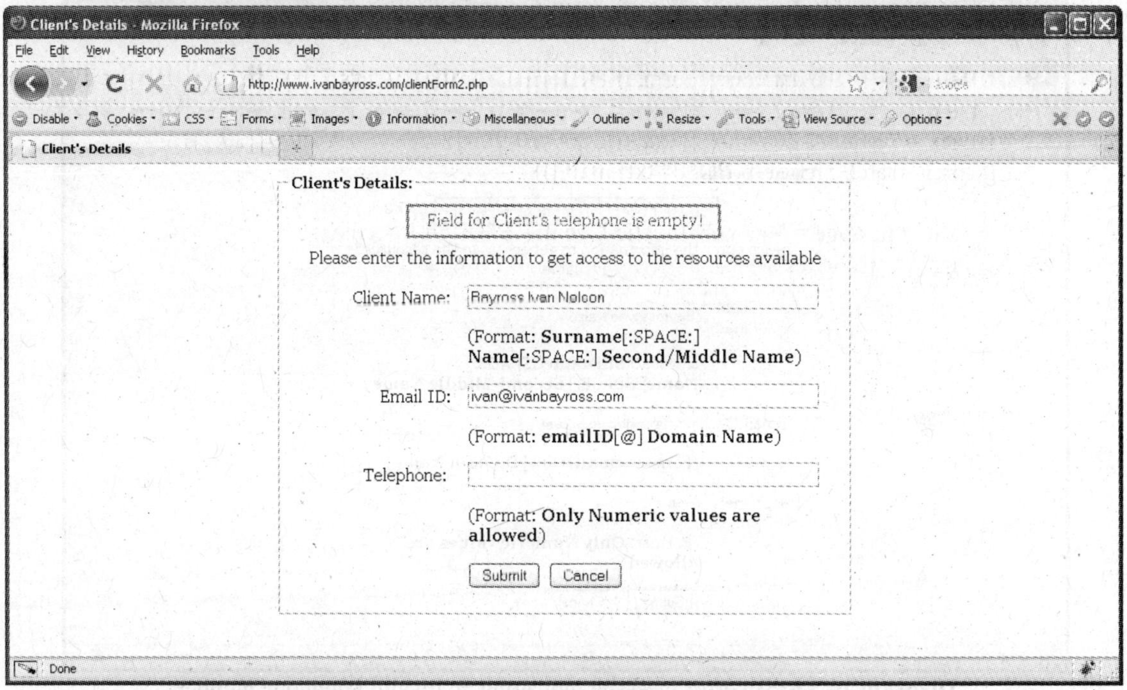

Diagram 20.5.5: An error message indicating an empty telephone field

As seen in diagram 20.5.5, the error message is displayed after the form title.

The above validation is done using the following code spec:

```
/* Checking if the variable for Client's Telephone number is empty, (i.e. a blank telephone
field was submitted). */
   if(empty($_POST['txtPhone']))
   {
      /* Returning to the data entry form, if the Client's Telephone number is
      empty. */
      $alertmessage = '<center>Field for Client\'s telephone is empty! </center>';
       include ("clientMaster2.php");
       exit;
   }
```

- Invalid client's telephone number!

Submit the form by passing a valid Client Name, Email Id and deliberately passing a character value in Telephone number field and press  . The PHP code checks the contents of the Client Name, Email Id and Telephone number fields returned by the Browser. As the Telephone number holds a character value, an error message is generated and stored in the variable **$alertmessage**.

This error message is included in the form at the top of the HTML code spec and the combination of the error message and the HTML form is returned to the Browser. Refer to diagram 20.5.6.

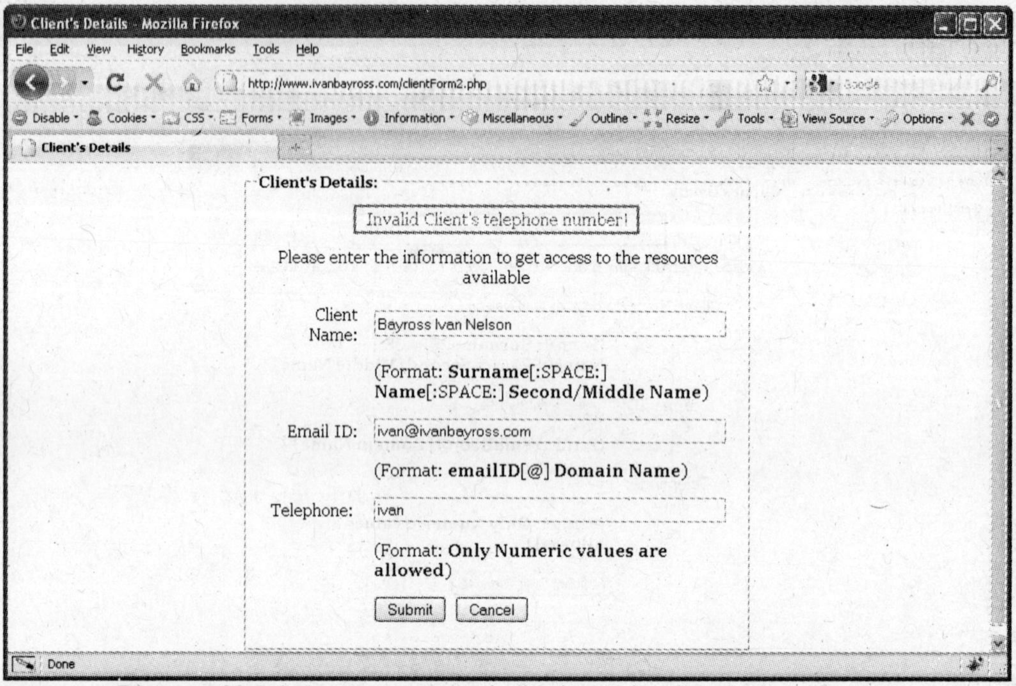

Diagram 20.5.6: An error message indicating an invalid telephone number

As seen in diagram 20.5.6, the error message is displayed after the form title.

The above validation is done using the following code spec:

```
/* Checking if the variable for Client's Telephone is valid. */
    else
    {
       $regex = '/[0123456789]/' ;
/* Returning to the data entry form, if the format for the Client's telephone is not as specified in the data entry form. */
       if(!preg_match($regex,$_POST['txtPhone']))
       {
         $alertmessage = '<center>Invalid Client\'s telephone number!
                            </center>';
         include("clientMaster2.php");
         exit;
       }
    }
```

Submit the form by passing a valid Client Name, Email Id and Telephone number and press Submit. Refer to diagram 20.5.7.

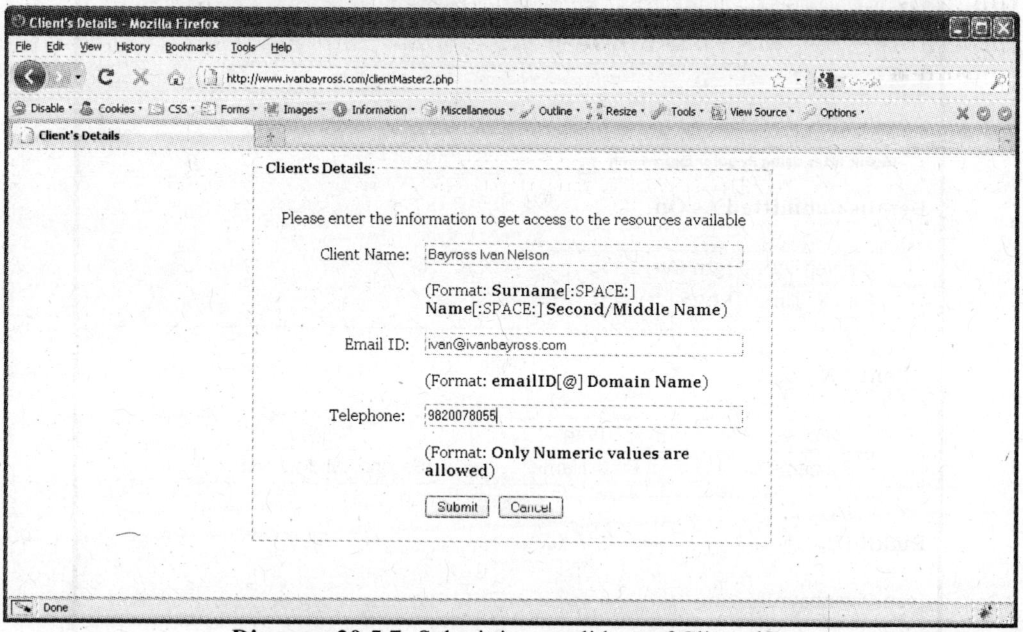

Diagram 20.5.7: Submitting a valid set of Client data

When valid data is received by **clientForm2.php**, Regular expression functions are used to decide the layout for display, which includes:

- Separating elements for the name on the bases of spaces. This is done using the **split()** function:

```
/* Using the split() function to extract Client's last name, first name and second name
into variables $lname, $fname and $mname respectively. */

    list($lname, $fname, $mname) = split(" ", $txtName, 3);
```

The above code spec extracts the last name, first name and the middle name from the form field **txtName** and stores it in the variables **$lname**, **$fname** and **$mname** respectively.

Submit the form by passing a valid Client Name, Email Id and Telephone number and press Submit. The PHP code checks the contents of the Client Name, Email Id and Telephone number fields returned by the Browser.

Since all the values in all the fields are correctly passed, clientForm2.php will generate output as shown in diagram 20.5.7.

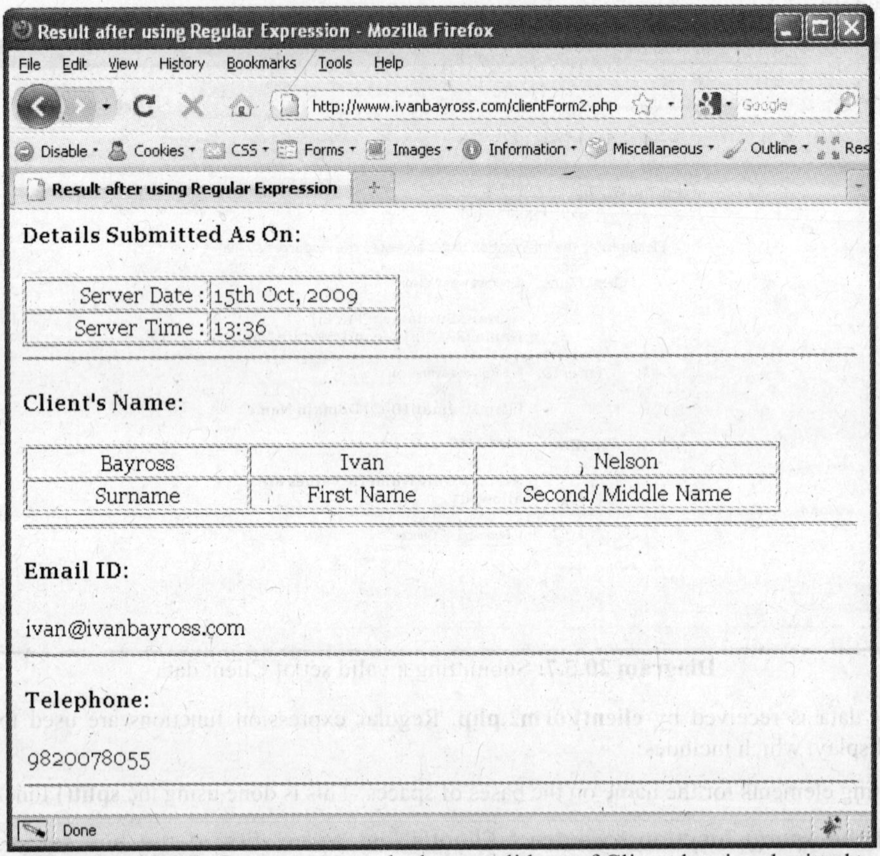

Diagram 20.5.7: Output generated when a valid set of Client data is submitted

HANDS ON EXERCISES

1. Develop a form to capture Product Details as shown in diagram 20.6.1. The HTML based form should perform the following:
   - ❑ Captures data i.e. Product Id, Product Name, and Product Price.
   - ❑ Clear the form fields when the Cancel button is clicked
   - ❑ Product Id should be numeric values only. Alert the user if Product Id is not a numeric value.
   - ❑ Product Price should be numeric values only. Alert the user if Product Price is not a numeric value.
   - ❑ Submit captured information as shown in diagram, 20.6.2, when Save button is clicked

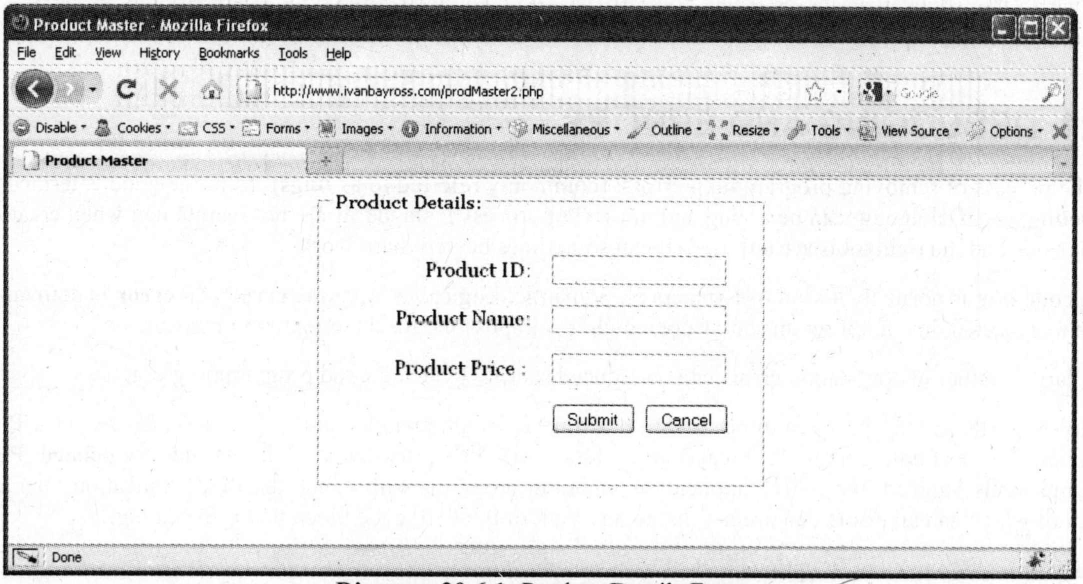

Diagram 20.6.1: Product Details Form

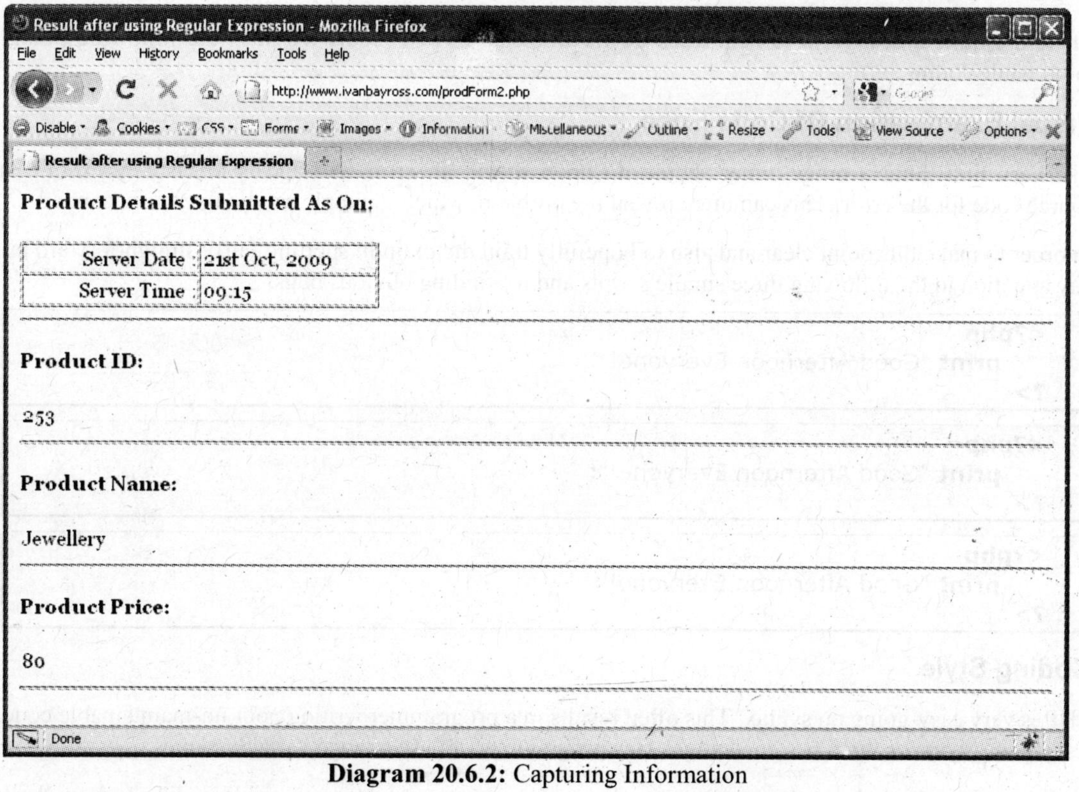

Diagram 20.6.2: Capturing Information

21. DEBUGGING AND ERRORS

The process of removing programming errors, (commonly referred to as **bugs**), from the code is termed as **Debugging**. Debugging can be a long and drawn out process if standards are not maintained when creating the code and the right tools are not used. It can sometimes be very hard work.

A code **bug** is normally a kind of Syntactical, Semantic, Logical or Runtime **error**. An **error** is defined as an unexpected, invalid program state from which it is impossible for the program to recover.

A large number of application errors can be reduced sharply by using good programming practices.

However, there may be many other factors, beyond a programmer's control that cause errors, in a PHP script. For example, Network breakdowns, full hard disks, hardware failure, bugs associated PHP components plugged into a PHP application, errors in programs with which the PHP application interacts All of which can all errors that are not due to any fault of the PHP code block that is executing.

PHP provides a number of options to deal with errors.

GOOD PROGRAMMING PRACTICES

There are quite a few ways to help track down problems in PHP code. Do keep the following points in mind while coding:

Visual Examination Of Code Spec

The very first thing a programmer should do upon seeing an error message is to visually examine the source code for the error. This can often reveal the problem, which if simple can be fixed in seconds

In order to make this point clear and also to hopefully train the brain in spotting fairly straightforward bugs, pay attention to the following three simple scripts and try finding obvious bugs.

```
<?php
    print "Good Afternoon Everyone!
?>
```

```
<?php
    print "Good Afternoon Everyone!":
?>
```

```
<?php
    print "Good Afternoon Everyone!';
?>
```

Coding Style

PHP is very easy-going on syntax. This often results in a programmer writing poor un-maintainable code. Easy-going syntax sometimes encourages lazy programmers to use strange variable names.

Coding style should always be consistent and not vary across modules. A sensible coding style will allow reading PHP code quickly and logically and thus help understand what that particular code spec intended to do. Coding style should be such that different parts of code spec are easily distinguishable.

Adopt a smart logical coding style. Ensure that fellow programmers on the team use the same style of:

- o Documenting code spec with appropriate REM statements
- o Standardized Variable and Function naming
- o Approved spacing between code segments in one module
- o Well indented Bracing

and so on. Rigidly following a specified pattern allows scripts to look almost identical in structure and easy to maintain.

When using the same coding style (i.e. following a set of coding standards), two independent programmers should be able to create code that is indistinguishable from each other.

To Improve Code Spec Readability

Use spaces, tabs and new lines wherever possible to help improve readability.

- o Operators should have a space on either side
- o Function parameters should have a space after the comma
- o Use braces even when they are optional. Without braces readability is lost and logic errors are more than possible

Example:
Use the second option rather than the first one

```
/* Option 1 */
$number=function($a,$b,$c);
/* Option 2 */
$number = function($a, $b, $c);
```

Example:
Use the second option rather than the first one

```
/* Option 1 */
if($number1 == $number2) print "number1 equals number2!";
/* Option 2 */
if ($number1 == $number2)
{
    print "number1 equals number2!";
}
```

NOTE

Note that there is a space after the **if** statement in second option, which makes it clear that if is not a function.

TIP

Using lots of whitespace will not slow the script, so use whitespace liberally.

Commenting Code Spec

Avoid using # comments.

/* */ or // are much more common and can do all that is required.

Use extensive comment statements throughout any code block.

This will help:

- Refresh a programmer's memory when editing the script months or years from creation
- Other programmers who take over a code maintenance task understand what the code is supposed to do

Meaningful Variable Names

Use meaningful variable names where appropriate. This means choose variable names based on the data they hold or the process they belong to or both.

For Example: **$FirstName** is likely to hold the first name of a person, whereas **$fnm** could hold anything.

Consider using the underscore to separate words in a variable name because **$FirstName** is harder to read than **$First_Name**.

TIP

Variables should be named such that they are really easy to type. This will help avoid the chance of being spelt incorrectly.

Good variable names: $Date_Of_Birth, $First_Name
Average variable names: $dob, $f_name, $first_name_of_current_member
Bad variable names: $d, $fn, $fnc1

Using variables names as $i, $j, $k and so on are fine when used as temporary variables inside loops, but elsewhere are just meaningless and will cause confusion at code maintenance time. Example: It's quite sensible to use **$ctr** to represent variable which works as a counter inside a loop.

Functions

Consider using **include_once()** and **require_once()** to avoid possible errors caused by one file being included several times. This is particularly important when a class is defined in one file and many other programmers require to use it.

NOTE

It is generally good practice to put commonly used functions into a standard include file. Then use **include_once()** in PHP scripts that require to access those functions.

After adopting this method it is always the case that some functions are local to each script. In such a scenario, appropriately name those local functions as to make it clear that they are local. This will help ensure that a programmer not to look for them in the standard include file.

PHP Code Block Indicators

Although **<?** and **<%** are available for use to enter PHP mode, their use is not encouraged for several reasons:

- They are not enabled by default
- They may not be recognized by the PHP runtime on all computers
- <? is not XML compliant

Hence, always use **<?php**

ERROR HANDLING IN PHP

PHP provides different ways to handle errors:

- Display errors
- Log Errors
- Ignore Errors
- Act on Errors / Exceptions

Each of these options has an important place in a robust error-handling system. Consequently none of these options supersede another in importance or functionality.

Displaying errors is usually beneficial in a development environment and **logging** them is usually more appropriate in a production environment.

Some errors can be safely **ignored** and others **demand reaction**. The exact mix of error handling techniques a programmer employs depends on individual needs.

Displaying Errors

When a need arises to display errors, the error is sent to the standard output stream, which in the case of a web page means that it is sent to the Browser.

Displaying errors is very helpful for development because it enables a programmer to get instant feedback on what went wrong with a script without having to look through a long log file. Nothing needs to be done except read the 'Error' web page returned.

The only thing required is to toggle the **error level** setting **on** and **off**. This can be easily done via the php.ini file.

TIP

To display the error messages, the **display_errors** directive needs to be set **ON** in the **php.ini** file.

To edit the **php.ini** file do the following:

1. Open the **php.ini** file in any ASCII editor (Example: Notepad on Windows or KATE on Linux). Refer to diagram 21.1.1

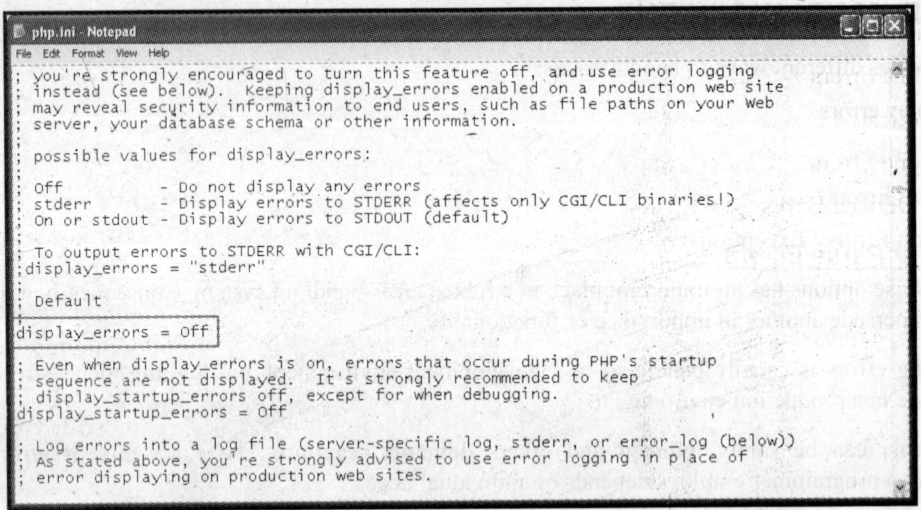
php.ini - Notepad

File Edit Format View Help

```
; you're strongly encouraged to turn this feature off, and use error logging
; instead (see below).  Keeping display_errors enabled on a production web site
; may reveal security information to end users, such as file paths on your Web
; server, your database schema or other information.
;
; possible values for display_errors:
;
; Off          - Do not display any errors
; stderr       - Display errors to STDERR (affects only CGI/CLI binaries!)
; On or stdout - Display errors to STDOUT (default)
;
; To output errors to STDERR with CGI/CLI:
;display_errors = "stderr"
;
; Default
display_errors = Off

; Even when display_errors is on, errors that occur during PHP's startup
; sequence are not displayed.  It's strongly recommended to keep
; display_startup_errors off, except for when debugging.
display_startup_errors = Off

; Log errors into a log file (server-specific log, stderr, or error_log (below))
; As stated above, you're strongly advised to use error logging in place of
; error displaying on production web sites.
```

Diagram 21.1.1: display_errors directive is set to off

2. Search for the following line: (Refer to diagram 21.1.1)

```
display_errors = off
```

3. Uncomment the line if it is commented and set the value from **OFF** to **ON** as shown in the diagram 21.1.2

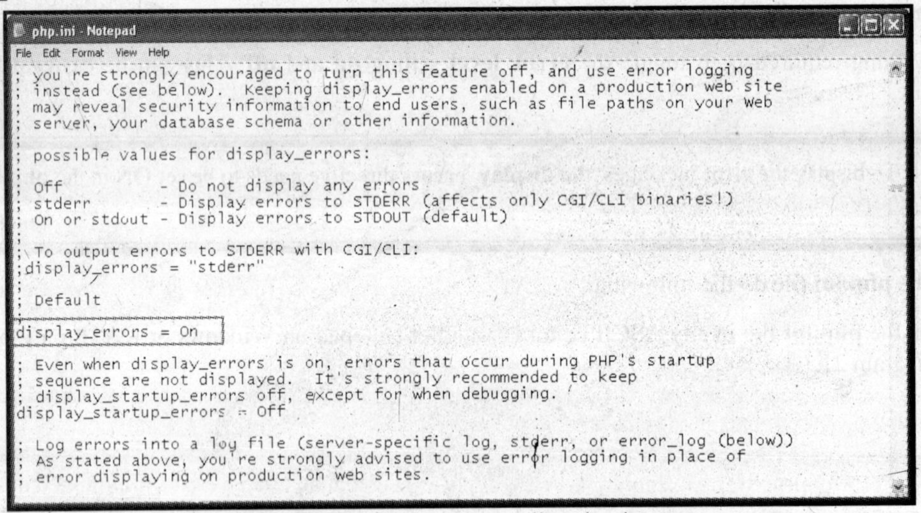
php.ini - Notepad

File Edit Format View Help

```
; you're strongly encouraged to turn this feature off, and use error logging
; instead (see below).  Keeping display_errors enabled on a production web site
; may reveal security information to end users, such as file paths on your Web
; server, your database schema or other information.
;
; possible values for display_errors:
;
; Off          - Do not display any errors
; stderr       - Display errors to STDERR (affects only CGI/CLI binaries!)
; On or stdout - Display errors to STDOUT (default)
;
; To output errors to STDERR with CGI/CLI:
;display_errors = "stderr"
;
; Default
display_errors = On

; Even when display_errors is on, errors that occur during PHP's startup
; sequence are not displayed.  It's strongly recommended to keep
; display_startup_errors off, except for when debugging.
display_startup_errors = Off

; Log errors into a log file (server-specific log, stderr, or error_log (below))
; As stated above, you're strongly advised to use error logging in place of
; error displaying on production web sites.
```

Diagram 21.1.2: display_errors directive is set to on

4. Save the **php.ini** file and restart the Web Server (i.e. the Apache Service)

Type Of Errors

An error message that the PHP interpreter generates falls into one of the following categories:

- Syntax or Parse Errors
- Fatal Errors
- Warnings
- Notices

- Logical Errors
- Environmental Errors
- Runtime Errors
- Core Errors
- Compile Errors
- User Defined Errors

Syntax or Parse Errors

Syntax and Parse errors are identified when a PHP file is processed, before the PHP interpreter starts executing it. Syntax errors are the most common and easily detected category of errors.

Common syntax errors involve:

- Missing (;) semi-colons (Every instruction of PHP code must end with a semi colon)
- Missing () parenthesis
- Misspelled keywords
- Missing ($) dollar sign before variables
- Missing {} curly brackets
- Strings not closed properly and so on

Strings usually cause the most common errors because a lot of PHP code spec actually echoes HTML back to the Browser and HTML needs to use quotes around certain elements.

The following is code spec with a string left un-terminated.

```
<?php
    print "Ivan Bayross Says Hi: ;
    print "<BR />";
    print "Hope Every one is Understanding Handling of PHP Errors.";
?>
```

In the above code spec the part marked in gray color indicates a syntax error in the **print** statement. The **print** statement is used to print the data to the Browser. Data to be printed being the string enclosed between " ".

NOTE

In the above code, the syntax error is produced intentionally to display the error message.

Before the PHP runtime starts executing a PHP file, syntax errors and parse errors are trapped at the time of file compilation. As the code contains a **print** statement where the ending double quote " is missing, an error message is displayed as shown in diagram 21.2.

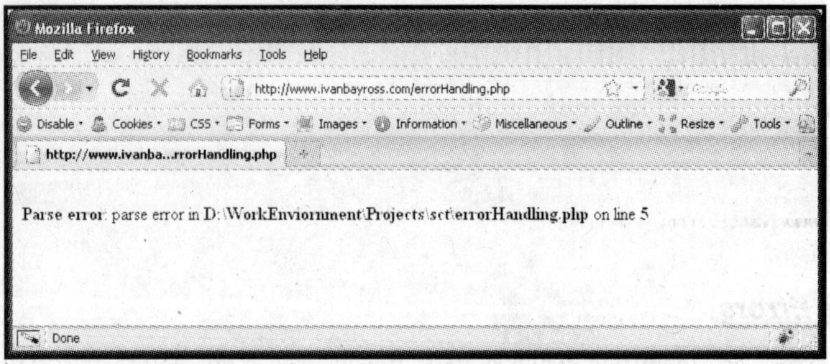

Diagram 21.2: Error message displayed

When PHP includes another file in the current file and if the other file has a syntax or parse error, compilation will stop. The code spec and declarations preceding the parse error are compiled and those following the error are discarded. The output will be a partially compiled file.

To demonstrate this, use following two files:

- errorHandling.php
- testing.php

The following is the code spec of **testing.php**.

```
<?php
    // Using require to include another file
    require "errorHandling.php";
    print "This file includes the contents of testing.php";
?>
```

In the above code spec, the portion marked in gray indicates the inclusion of another file using the **require** keyword. Using **require** the contents of the file **errorHandling.php** are included in the file **testing.php**.

The following is the code spec of **errorHandling.php**.

```
<?php
    print "Ivan Bayross Says Hi:;
    print "<BR />";
    print "Hope everyone is understanding the handling of PHP Errors.";
?>
```

When **testing.php** file is compiled, PHP will locate the file **errorHandling.php** using **require** keyword. As **errorHandling.php** contains a syntax error in it, the PHP runtime will identify the error and display an error message as shown in diagram 21.3.

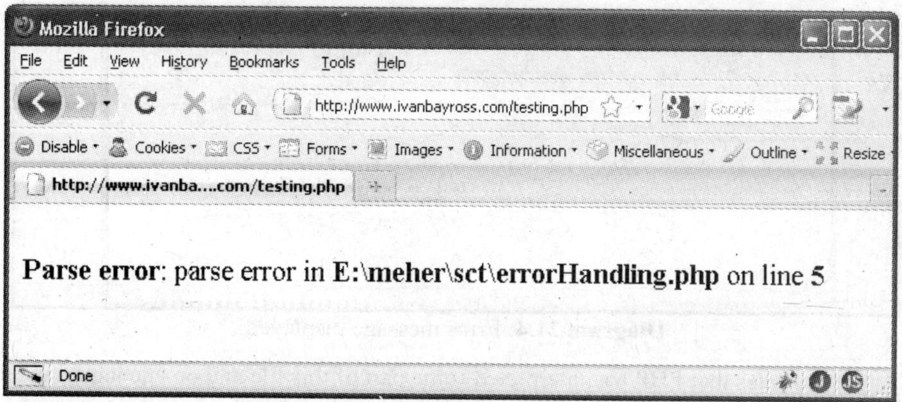

Diagram 21.3: Error message displayed

PHP file compilation also aborts with an error message whenever it encounters an undefined function or class.

One thing that helps reduce syntax errors is writing PHP code in an editor that is PHP-aware, such as BBEdit, Emacs, XEmacs, Komodo, Dreamweaver, PHPEd, PHPEdit, Zend Studio and so on.

All these editors automatically handle syntax highlighting. This feature changes the color of different parts of the code spec based on what those parts are.

For example, strings are displayed in pink, keywords in blue, comments in grey and variables in black.

Syntax highlighting makes it easier to detect errors such as a string that has a missing closing quote. This is possible as the pink text (which is supposed to be a color for string) continues past the line that the string is on, all the way to the end of the file or to the next quote that appears later in the program.

These editors also permit quote and bracket matching. This helps to make sure that all the quotes and brackets used in the codespec are balanced.

Further these editors also show line numbers alongside the code spec. This is very helpful when an error message is rendered by the PHP interpreter which complains about a parse error in line 72.

Fatal Errors

A **fatal error** occurs when there is a severe problem with the code spec, such as calling a function that has not been defined. The interpreter simply stops executing the code spec when a fatal error is encountered.

The following PHP code tries to call a function, which is not defined or declared.

```
<?php
    print "Calling an Undefined function and error occurs!";
    // Calling a function named UnknownFunction which is not defined
    UnknownFunction();
?>
```

A user defined function named **UnknownFunction()** is included in the above code spec. As the PHP run time can not find the **UnknownFunction()**, an error message is displayed in the browser as shown in diagram 21.4.

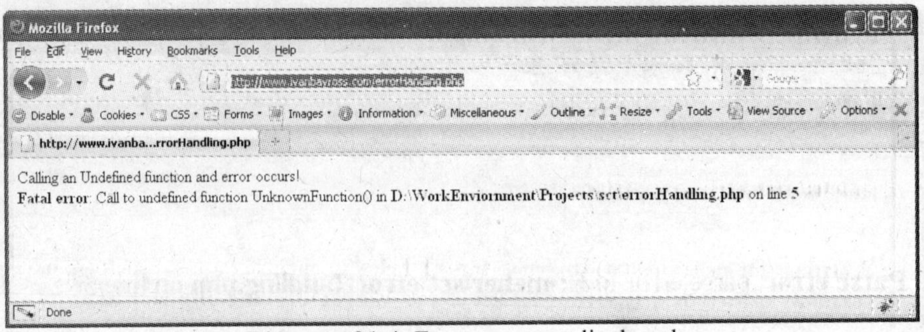

Diagram 21.4: Error message displayed

The above output indicates that PHP has interpreted some part of this file and on encountering an error, has halted. This is proved by the fact that the PHP code block has dispatched the contents passed to the print statement to the Browser prior the **Fatal error**.

Warnings

Warning errors are fairly common and will not interrupt PHP script execution. Warnings are usually errors, which are serious enough to **prevent the correct execution** of the program but not cause it to halt. Usually invalid regular expressions or missing files will generate warnings.

Many environmental errors also result in warnings. If there is no error handling in place to react to these environmental errors, the original failure will often produce more errors as the script continues to execute. When warnings are encountered, PHP will try to continue executing the code after giving the warning message.

For example: When **include()** cannot locate the specified file, this would cause a warning if the condition were not gracefully handled by the program's logic.

Example: (errorWarning.php)

```
<?php
    // Opening a file named testing.txt in Read Only Mode.
    fopen("testing.txt","r");
    echo "<BR /><HR>";
    echo "After warning error still continue processing further code!";
?>
```

The above code spec tries opening a non existent file named **testing.txt** using **fopen()** function. A warning is displayed as shown in diagram 21.5, however the PHP run time still continues executing the next line.

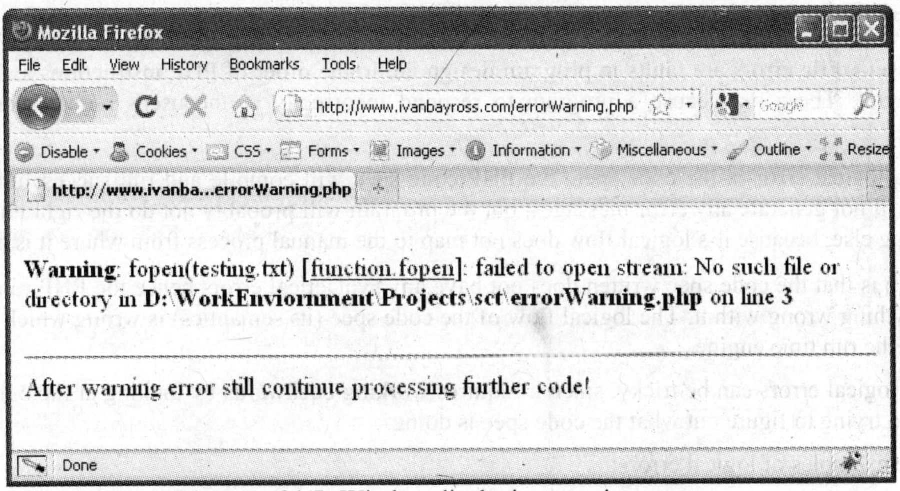

Diagram 21.5: Window displaying warning message

Notices

Notices will never terminate the script and can be quite helpful. These will be displayed when PHP encounters something, which could be an error, but could also be correct, when the script is running normally.

Notices are PHP's way to tell the programmer that the code it runs may be doing something unintentional, such as reading a variable, which is undefined.

Since PHP assigns a default value when operations are performed on such variables, these do not result in fatal conditions requiring termination of the script.

Example:

```
<?php
   echo($no * 9000);
?>
```

The above code spec attempts, using the variable **$no** before any value has been assigned to it. The output is a PHP **Notice** displayed, followed by 0 as shown in diagram 21.6.

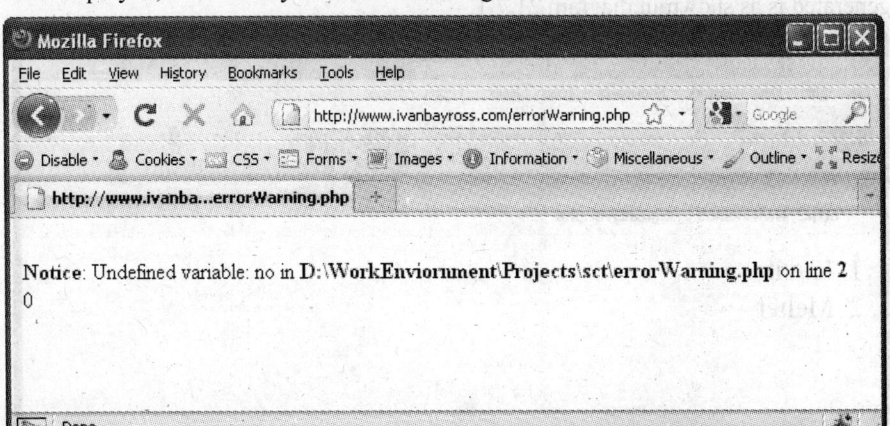

Diagram 21.6: Window displaying Notice Error

Logical Errors

Logical or **semantic** errors are faults in program design **i.e.** in the order of PHP instructions as laid out in the PHP script. These may cause a program to respond incorrectly to the user's requests or to crash completely.

If there is a logical error in the code spec, the PHP code spec will compile and run successfully, i.e. the computer will not generate any error messages, but the program will probably not do the right thing. It will do something else, because it's logical flow does not map to the manual process from where it is derived.

The problem is that the code spec written does not have any syntactical errors hence the PHP run time will not find anything wrong with it. The logical flow of the code spec (its semantics) is wrong which cannot be checked by the run time engine.

Identifying logical errors can be tricky, since it requires working backwards by looking at the output of the program and trying to figure out what the code spec is doing.

Some of the examples of logical errors:

- PHP code spec that does **not print out the last message**. One reason may be that the **print counter started from 0 and not 1**
- An infinite loop was entered into. Here the reason may be that the value of the loop's control variable is neither being increased nor decreased

Example:
In the following example, the code spec iterates through an array containing clients names and displays each client.

```
<?php
    $clients= array("Ivan", "Kavita", "Meher");
    for ($b = 1; $b < count($clients); $b++)
    {
        echo "$b: $clients [$b]<BR />";
    }
?>
```

Here, the counter variable **$b** started from 1 **and not** from 0, hence the first client's name will not be displayed. This is not what the code spec is expected to do.

The output generated is as shown in diagram 21.7.1.

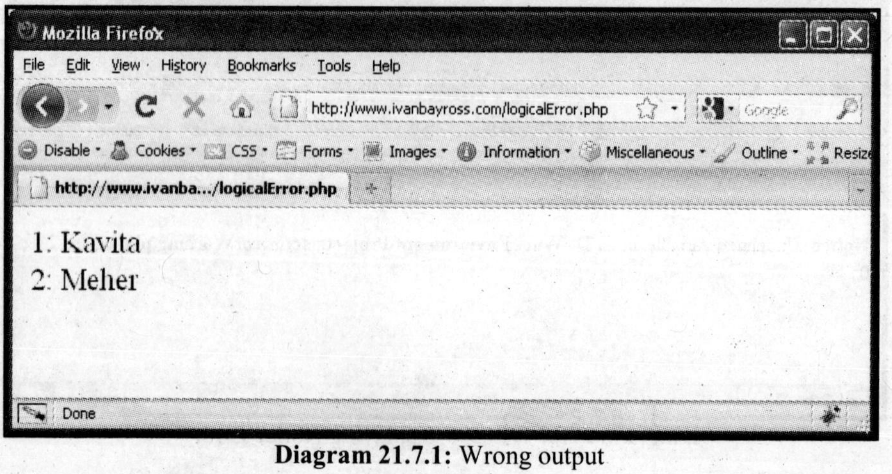

Diagram 21.7.1: Wrong output

This problem can be solved by setting the counter variable in the **for loop** to 0 instead of 1.

```
<?php
    $clients= array("Ivan", "Kavita", "Meher");
    for ($b = 0; $b < count($clients); $b++)
    {
        echo "$b: $clients[$b]<BR />";
    }
?>
```

Here, the counter variable **$b** started from 0 **and not** from 1, hence the first client's name is displayed.

Now the output generated is as shown in diagram 21.7.2.

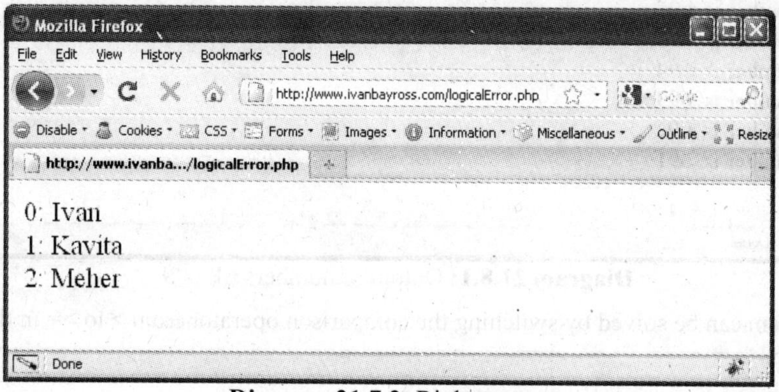

Diagram 21.7.2: Right output

Example:
In the following code spec, the programmer intends the script to print the numbers in descending order from 700 to 690.

```
<?php
    print ("Printing Numbers " . "<BR />");
    for($a = 700; $a > 690; $a--)
    print("Number is :" . $a . "<BR />");
?>
```

Since the comparison operator > was used as opposed to >= the last comparison 690 > 690 did not succeed and only the numbers 700 to 691 were printed as shown in diagram 21.8.1.

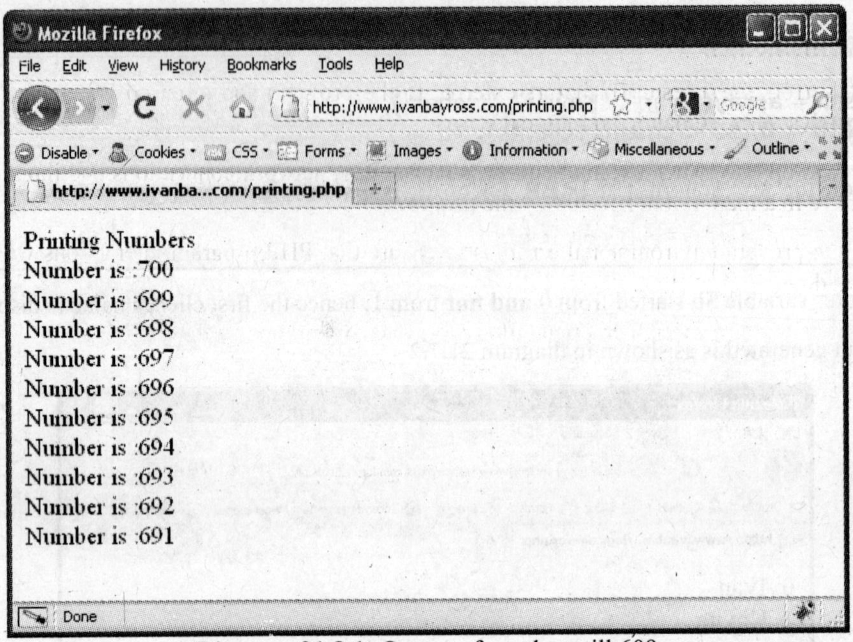

Diagram 21.8.1: Output of numbers till 609

This logical problem can be solved by switching the comparison operator from > to >= in the **for loop**.

```
<?php
    print ("Printing Numbers " . "<BR />");
    for($a = 700; $a >= 690; $a--)
    print("Number is :" . $a . "<BR />");
?>
```

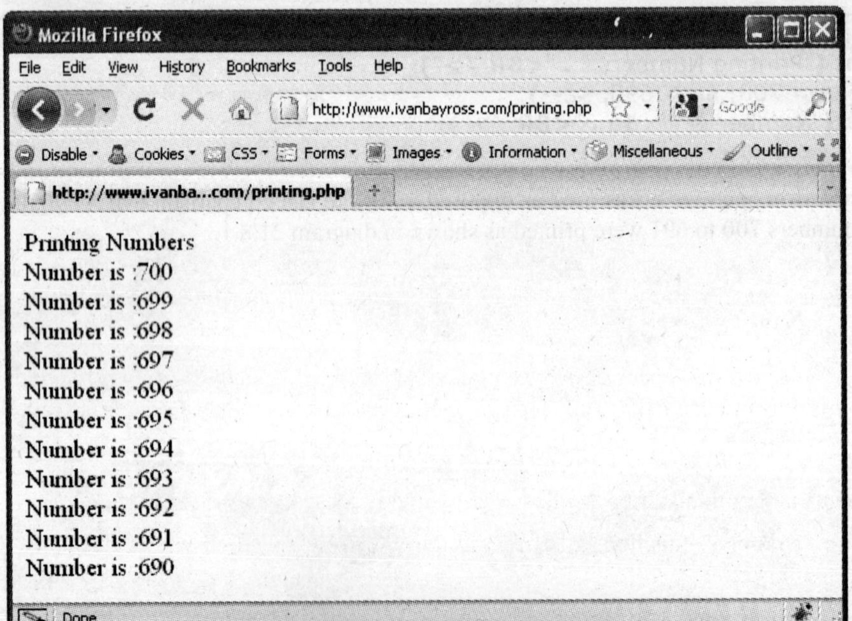

Diagram 21.8.2: Output of numbers till 690

Environmental Errors

Environmental errors are a result of factors external to the program and often go undetected by test cases designed to catch syntax, semantic and logical errors.

These errors crop up only when external entities such as files, network connections and input data assumes a form or behave in a manner unexpected by the program.

The only way to prevent environmental errors is to ensure that PHP program interactions with all external entities are valid.

For example consider a script, which opens files and writes operations on the server's local disk. This script might work fine in a development environment, but will fail in a production environment where **disk access privileges are much more restrictive** than on the development workstation.

Example:
The following is code spec, which

- Establishes a connection between **PHP** and **MySQL engine**.
- User tries to connect to a database named **test**
- If an error occurs, an appropriate message is sent by the **die()** function to the requestor of the program, generally a Browser

This script might work fine in a development environment, but will fail in a production environment if proper configuration between PHP and MySQL was not done.

```
<?php
  $user="root";
  $pwd="sct2306";
  $db="learn";
  $host="localhost";

  @mysql_connect($host, $user, $pwd) or die("Sorry MySql connection Failed");

  $db_link=mysql_select_db($db) or die("Sorry could not select the database!");
  echo "MySQL Database Connection Established!";

  mysql_close();
?>
```

Runtime Errors

Once the code is up and running (and perhaps tested), **non-fatal**, **runtime errors**, are the most common type of errors in PHP.

Runtime refers to errors that occur during execution of the code, which are not usually programming errors but caused by factors outside PHP itself, such as disk or network operations or database calls.

For example:

- The **fopen()** function fails because the file passed to it does not exist
- The **mysql_connect()** function fails because the username specified was accidentally deleted by the MySQL administrator
- If a user tries inserting a row into a table without providing an appropriate value for a mandatory (i.e. NOT NULL) column

Example:

```
<?php
    // Opening a file named Information.txt in Read Only Mode.
    fopen("learn.txt", "r");
?>
```

The above code spec tries opening a non existent file, named **learn.txt** using **fopen()** function. An error message is displayed as shown in diagram 21.9.

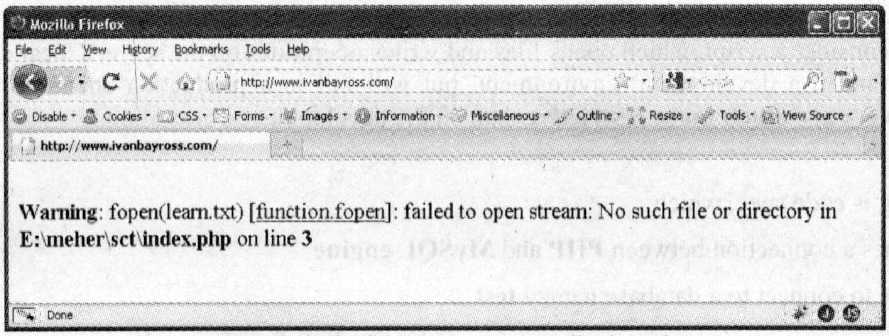

Diagram 21.9: Error message displayed

Core Errors

Core errors are those that are generated by the PHP run time core i.e. caused by an extension that failed to start up and caused PHP to abort.

E_CORE_ERROR is a fatal error detected in PHP's internals indicating a serious problem with the PHP installation.

E_CORE_WARNING is a compile time warning generally indicating a problem with the PHP installation.

Compile Errors

The underlying ZEND scripting engine identifies and generates error levels. Even in the case badly written user-defined functions or any other PHP code spec, it is the ZEND scripting engine, which will identify and generate appropriate errors.

E_COMPILE_ERROR is a fatal compile time error generally occurring during compilation, indicating a syntax error in the PHP script that can not be recovered from causing PHP to abort.

E_COMPILE_WARNING is a compile time error warning users about deprecated syntax and indicating a non-fatal syntax error in the PHP script.

User Defined Errors

Often when programmers require raising user defined errors in their applications, (i.e. other than any of the ones reported above), the User-defined (E_USER_*) error level fulfills this requirement. This is never raised by the underlying ZEND scripting engine automatically, but specifically by the PHP programmer writing the code spec.

E_USER_ERROR is a user generated error message, which causes PHP to abort execution. This is generated from inside PHP scripts to halt execution with an appropriate message.

E_USER_WARNING is a user generated warning message, which will not cause PHP to exit. Scripts may use it to signal a failure corresponding to one that PHP would signal with E_WARNING. This is generated from inside PHP scripts to flag a serious warning message without halting execution.

E_USER_NOTICE is a user generated notice message, which may be used in scripts to signal possible errors (analogous to E_NOTICE). This is generated from inside PHP scripts to print a minor notice to the screen, usually regarding potential problems with scripts.

The error mechanism in PHP is used by all built-in PHP functions. By default, this simple mechanism prints an error message with file and line number and exits.

Error Levels In PHP

PHP errors are categorized by an error level ranging from **notices** to **fatal** errors. The error level tells the programmer how serious the error is.

The **error_reporting** configuration directive in the php.ini file controls which kinds of errors the PHP runtime reports.

The default value for **error_reporting** is **E_ALL** as in **PHP 5.1.0RC1**, which tells the PHP runtime to report all errors.

PHP defines some constants that can be used and applied to set the value of **error_reporting** so that only errors of certain types get reported.

These constants are:

- **E_ALL** - For all errors **except strict notices**
- **E_PARSE** - For parse errors
- **E_ERROR** - For fatal errors
- **E_WARNING** - For warning messages
- **E_NOTICE** - For notices
- **E_STRICT** - For strict notices. This error level is the only one not included in the **E_ALL** constant. **E_STRICT** error level displays Run time notices. This enables the PHP runtime to suggest changes to code, which will ensure the best interoperability and forward compatibility of user code

STRICT messages ensure that a programmer is definitely informed about using deprecated functions and so on in PHP code spec.

Hence, to instruct the PHP runtime to pass on all information that could possibly be an error, set **error_reporting** to **E_ALL | E_STRICT**.

Setting Error Reporting Levels Via PHP.INI

1. Open the **php.ini** file in any ASCII editor (Example: Notepad on Windows or Kate on Linux)
2. Search for the following line: Refer to diagram 21.10.1

```
error_reporting = E_ALL
```

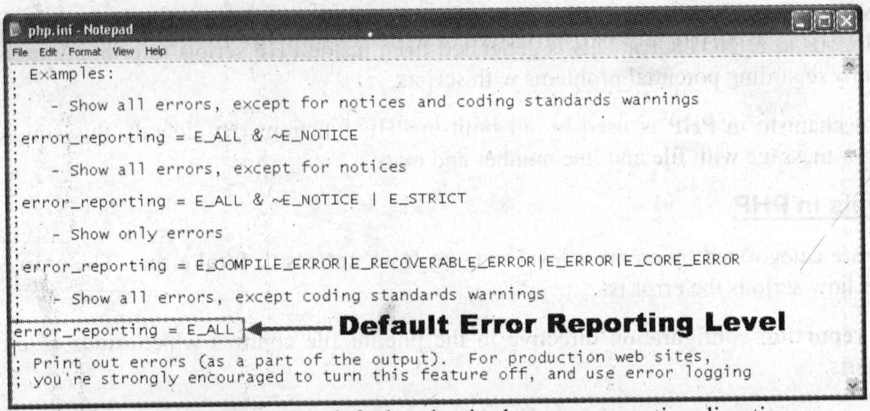
php.ini - Notepad
File Edit Format View Help

```
; Examples:
;
;   - Show all errors, except for notices and coding standards warnings
;
;error_reporting = E_ALL & ~E_NOTICE
;
;   - Show all errors, except for notices
;
;error_reporting = E_ALL & ~E_NOTICE | E_STRICT
;
;   - Show only errors
;
;error_reporting = E_COMPILE_ERROR|E_RECOVERABLE_ERROR|E_ERROR|E_CORE_ERROR
;
;   - Show all errors, except coding standards warnings
;
error_reporting = E_ALL

; Print out errors (as a part of the output).  For production web sites,
; you're strongly encouraged to turn this feature off, and use error logging
```


Diagram 21.10.1: The default value in the error_reporting directive

3. Modify the line of **error_reporting** as shown in the diagram 21.10.2

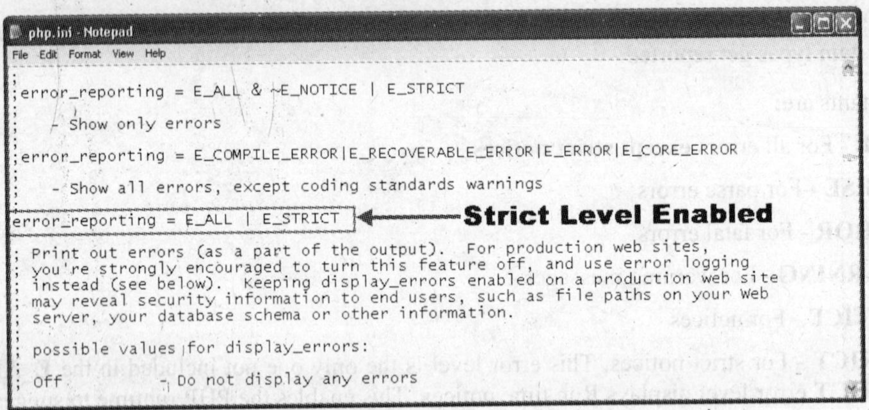
php.ini - Notepad
File Edit Format View Help

```
;error_reporting = E_ALL & ~E_NOTICE | E_STRICT
;
;   - Show only errors
;
;error_reporting = E_COMPILE_ERROR|E_RECOVERABLE_ERROR|E_ERROR|E_CORE_ERROR
;
;   - Show all errors, except coding standards warnings
;
error_reporting = E_ALL | E_STRICT

; Print out errors (as a part of the output).  For production web sites,
; you're strongly encouraged to turn this feature off, and use error logging
; instead (see below).  Keeping display_errors enabled on a production web site
; may reveal security information to end users, such as file paths on your Web
; server, your database schema or other information.
;
; possible values for display_errors:
;
; Off          - Do not display any errors
```


Diagram 21.10.2: Enabling strict levels of error reporting

4. Save the file **php.ini** and restart the Apache Service

When a user sets an error level via editing **php.ini** file, the change is reflected to all **.php** files executed. For example: If a user sets **error_reporting = E_ALL** every single **.php** file run in the same environment will display **Notices**, if encountered.

To have such strict error reporting done for only a single **.php** file set the error reporting level at its runtime using **error_reporting()** embedded within it.

Setting Error Reporting Levels Via error_reporting()

error_reporting() sets the value of the **error_reporting** directive at runtime. PHP has many levels of error reporting. Using this function, different levels of error reporting can be set for the duration (runtime) of a script.

The function accepts either a bitmask or named constants. Using named constants is strongly encouraged to ensure compatibility for future versions.

Syntax:

```
int error_reporting([ int level ]);
string ini_set(string <VariableName>, string <NewValue>);
```

The available error level constants are listed below. The actual meanings of these error levels are described in the predefined constants.

Value	Constant
1	E_ERROR
2	E_WARNING
4	E_PARSE
8	E_NOTICE
16	E_CORE_ERROR
32	E_CORE_WARNING
64	E_COMPILE_ERROR
128	E_COMPILE_WARNING
256	E_USER_ERROR
512	E_USER_WARNING
1024	E_USER_NOTICE
2047	E_ALL
2048	E_STRICT

Table 21.1

TIP

To understand the functionality of **error_reporting()**, undo all the changes made in **php.ini** file.

Undoing Changes in php.ini file

Follow the steps to undo the changes in **php.ini** file:

1. Open the **php.ini** file in any ASCII editor (**Example:** Notepad on Windows or Kate on Linux). Refer to diagram 21.11.1
2. Search the following line: (Refer to diagram 21.11.1)

```
display_errors = on
```

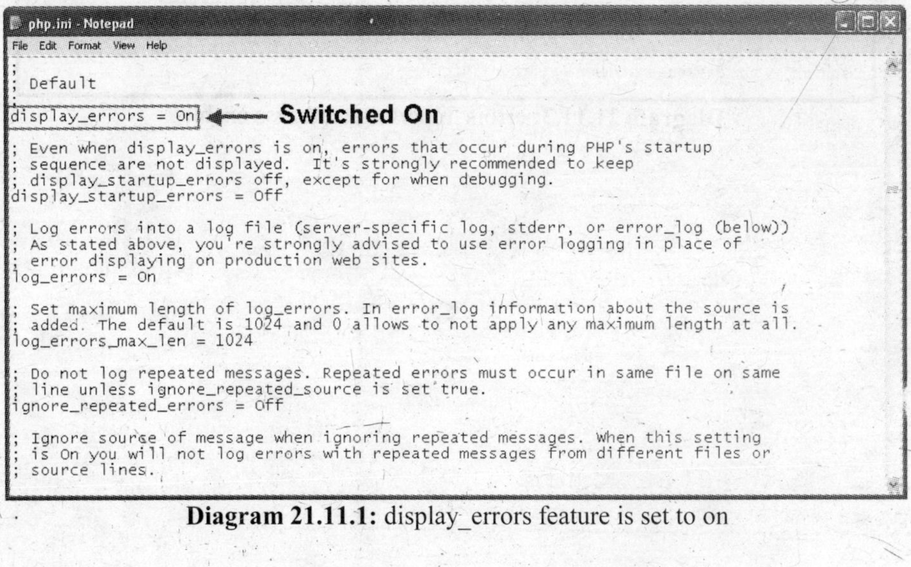

```
php.ini - Notepad
File Edit Format View Help
;
; Default
;
display_errors = On
; Even when display_errors is on, errors that occur during PHP's startup
; sequence are not displayed.  It's strongly recommended to keep
; display_startup_errors off, except for when debugging.
display_startup_errors = Off

; Log errors into a log file (server-specific log, stderr, or error_log (below))
; As stated above, you're strongly advised to use error logging in place of
; error displaying on production web sites.
log_errors = On

; Set maximum length of log_errors. In error_log information about the source is
; added. The default is 1024 and 0 allows to not apply any maximum length at all.
log_errors_max_len = 1024

; Do not log repeated messages. Repeated errors must occur in same file on same
; line unless ignore_repeated_source is set true.
ignore_repeated_errors = Off

; Ignore source of message when ignoring repeated messages. When this setting
; is On you will not log errors with repeated messages from different files or
; source lines.
```


Diagram 21.11.1: display_errors feature is set to on

Set the value **OFF** instead of **ON** as shown in the diagram 21.11.2

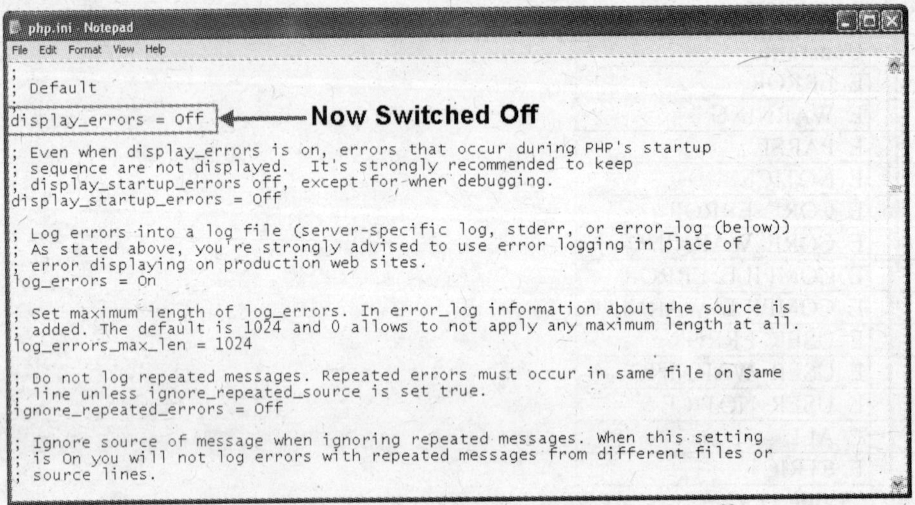

Diagram 21.11.2: display_errors feature is set to off

3. Search for the following line: (Refer to diagram 21.11.3)

error_reporting= E_ALL | E_STRICT

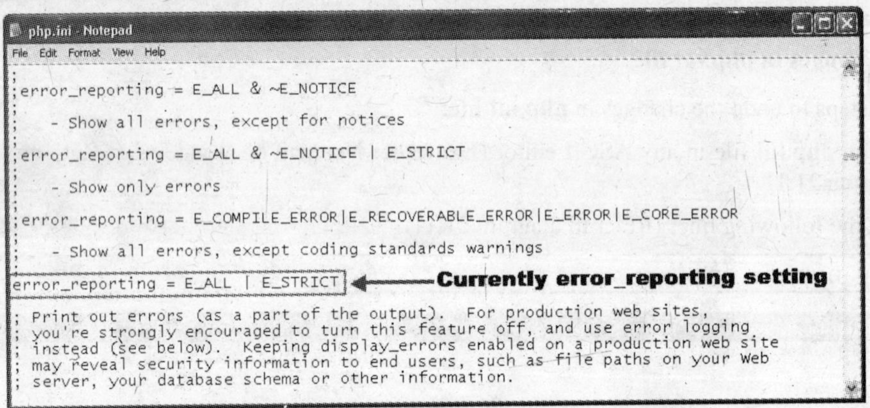

Diagram 21.11.3: errors_reporting feature is enabled

4. Comment the line of **error_reporting** as shown in the diagram 21.11.4.

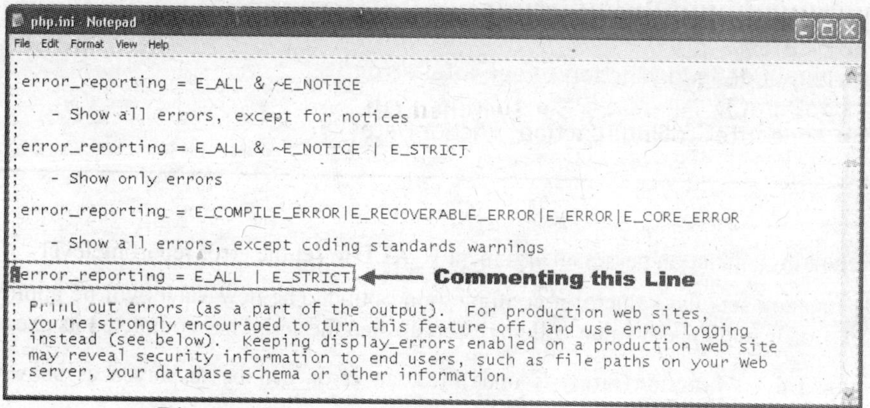

Diagram 21.11.4: error_reporting feature is disabled

5. Save the file **php.ini** and restart the Apache Service

To understand the changes made in **php.ini** file, execute the following code spec in a browser:

```
<?php
    echo "Line Before calling function functionData()";
    echo "<BR />";
    // Calling undefined function to see fatal error
    functionData();
    echo "Line After calling function functionData()";
?>
```

As no error level is set within the **php.ini** file, first **echo** statement will execute successfully and no error message will be displayed as shown in diagram 21.12.1.

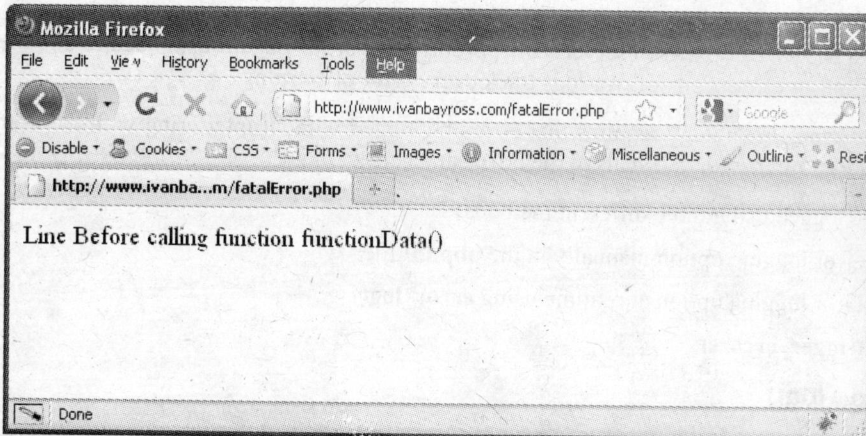

Diagram 21.12.1: No error message is displayed

Now edit the above code spec (fatalError.php) and insert the following two lines marked as gray:

```
<?php
    // Calling undefined function to see fatal error
    error_reporting(E_ALL);
    ini_set("display_errors", "on");
```

```
    echo "Line Before calling function functionData()";
    echo "<BR />";
    // Calling undefined function to see fatal error
    functionData();
    echo "Line After calling function functionData()";
?>
```

Where,

- **error_reporting()** function passes an argument **E_ALL** to set the error reporting level
- **ini_set()** function sets the value of a configuration option. The new value will be applied during the script's execution and the old value will be restored when the script has completed its execution

As the function named **functionData()** is undefined, an error will be displayed as shown in diagram 21.12.2 and the execution will terminate.

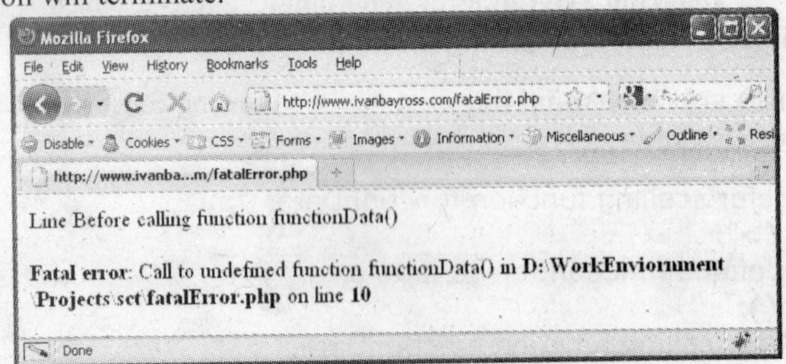

Diagram 21.12.2: **Fatal Error message displayed**

Logging Errors

What Is A Log?

A log is a text file saved on a Web server. An appropriate error message is appended to this file by the Web sever every time an error occurs. Error logs track every error or warning.

A good error handling strategy requires that errors be logged without interfering with the user interface so that a web site administrator can analyze the errors and correct them.

Errors can be logged using three different methods:

- Set the error logging option manually in the **php.ini** file
- Set the error logging option at runtime using **error_log()**
- Use of **trigger_error()**

Using error_log()

PHP provides the built in **error_log()** for logging any errors when they occur. Using **error_log()** error messages will be logged directly into log files at the Web server rather than being dispatched to a Web browser.

error_log() function appends a user defined error message into log file which resides specified in directory on the Web Server. These log files can then be viewed later, on demand.

Syntax:

```
int error_log(string <Message>, int <MessageType> [, string <Destination>]
              [,string <ExtraHeaders>])
```

Where,

- **Message** is the error message that must be appended into the log file
- **Message type** is the type of error message being logged (Refer to table 21.2)

Type	Explanation
0	Depending on what the **error_log** configuration directive is set to in php.ini the error message will either be routed to the Operating System's system logging mechanism **or** a file. This is the **default** option
1	The error message is sent by email to the email address in the destination parameter. This is the only message type where a fourth parameter, **ExtraHeaders** is used
2	The error message is sent through the PHP debugging connection. This option is only available if remote debugging has been enabled. In this case, the destination parameter specifies the host name or IP address and optionally, port number, of the socket receiving the debug information
3	The error message is appended to a destination file. A newline is **not automatically** added to the end of the message string

Table 21.2

Example:

```
<?php
    $filename = "learn.php";
    if (is_file($filename))
    {
        print("file $filename does exist!");
    }
    else
    {
        error_log("File does not exist!", 3, "D:/sct/error/errorlog.txt");
    }
?>
```

In the above code spec, if **is_file()** returns the Boolean value TRUE, (i.e. the file exists) **print()** is used to return a statement to the caller.

If **is_file()** returns the Boolean value FALSE which indicates that file does not exists then **error_log()** will log the error message in the file **errorlog.txt**.

NOTE

To understand the functionality of **error_log()**, **learn.php** intentionally **does not exist**.

As **learn.php** does not exist, an appropriate error message is appended to **errorlog.txt** which exists (or will be created) in **D:/WorkEnviornment/Projects/sct/errors/errorlog.txt** as shown in diagram 21.13.1.

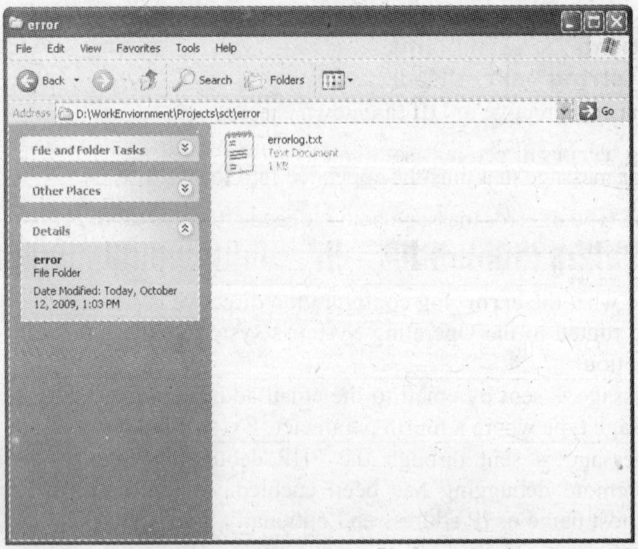

Diagram 21.13.1: Log file is created

To view the **error details**, open the file **D:/WorkEnviornment/Projects/sct/errors/errorlog.txt** using an ASCII editor such as Notepad, as shown in diagram 21.13.2.

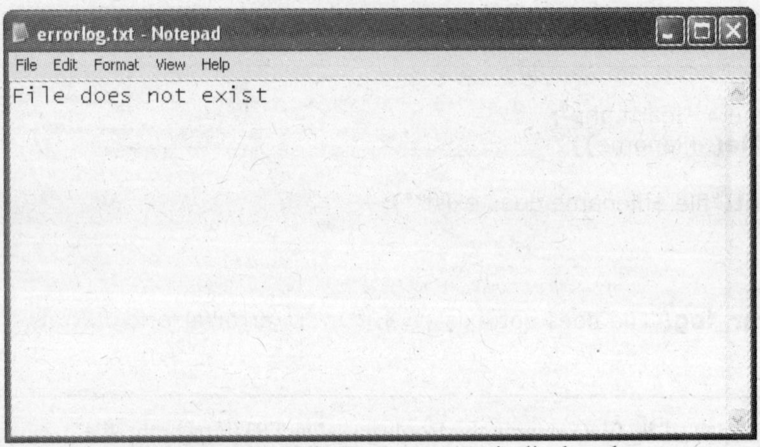

Diagram 21.13.2: Error message is displayed

Using php.ini File To Set Error Log File Path

Instead of using **error_log()** every time in a code spec, PHP allows the programmer to create such an environment via manually editing the **php.ini** file where,

- Only one *<filename>*.log file is bound to the system path
- Which will hold all system generated error messages

To understand this functionality, the php.ini file must be modified to set different log options.

PHP internally supports **both** logging to a **file** and logging via **syslog** through two settings in the **php.ini** file.

Logging errors to a file

Open **php.ini** in an ASCII editor like Notepad:

1. Set the **display_errors** directive to **Off** (as shown earlier)
2. Ensure that the **log_errors** directive is set to **on** as shown in diagram 21.14.1

```
log_errors = On
```

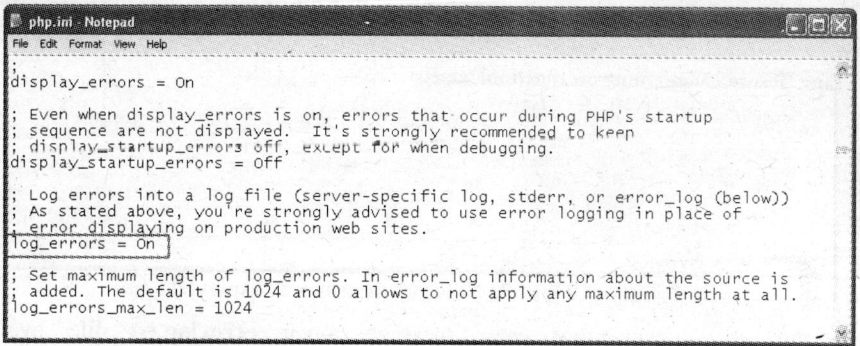

Diagram 21.14.1: log_errors directive is set to on

3. Search for the following line:

```
error_log = filename
```

4. **Uncomment** the line and provide a valid path to where the error log file can be placed in which all errors can be appended / captured as shown in diagram 21.14.2

```
error_log = "D:\WorkEnviornment\Projects\sct\error\errorlog.txt"
```

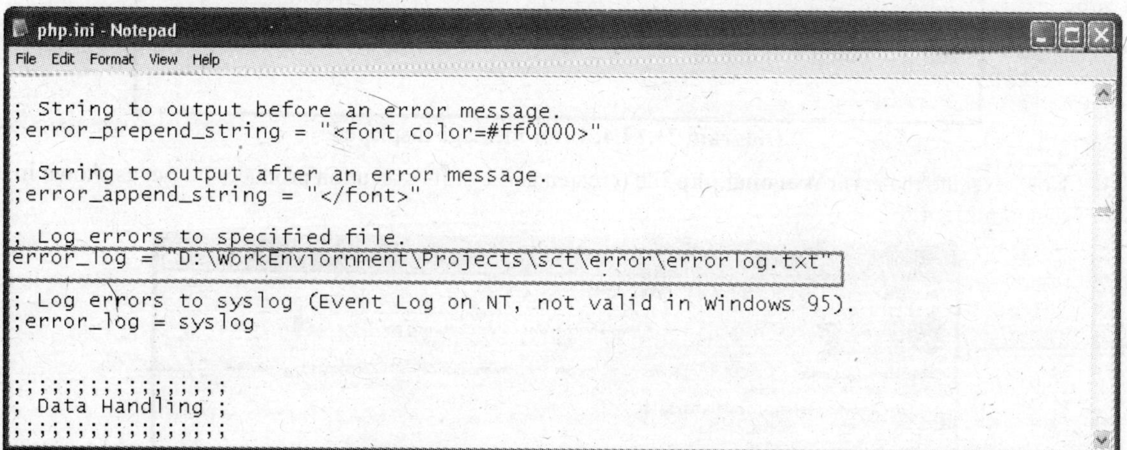

Diagram 21.14.2: path is set to error_log

5. Save changes made in **php.ini** file and restart the Apache Service

To view all the errors in **errorlog.txt**,

1. Execute the **fatalError.php** file (created earlier). Its execution produces output as shown in diagram 21.14.3

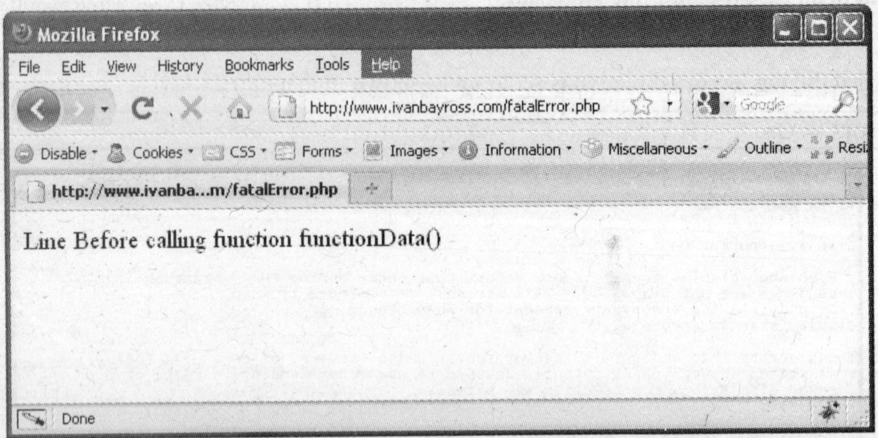

Diagram 21.14.3: No error message is displayed

2. To view the system generated error message, open **errorlog.txt** file available under **D:\WorkEnviornment\Projects\sct\error\errorlog.txt** as shown in diagram 21.14.4

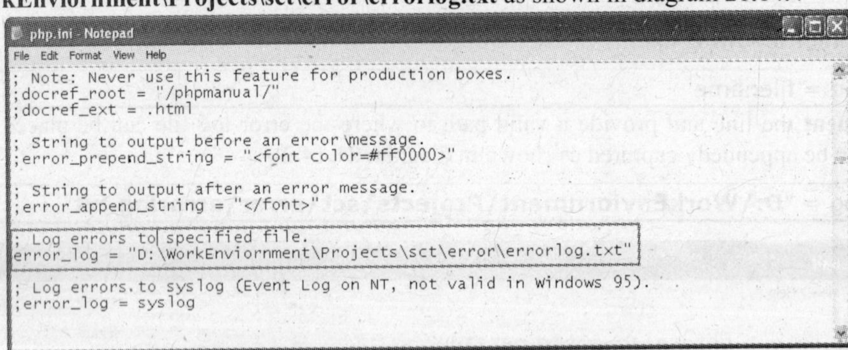

Diagram 21.14.4: Error message displayed

3. Now, execute the **errorWarning.php** file (created earlier). Its execution produces output as shown in diagram 21.14.5

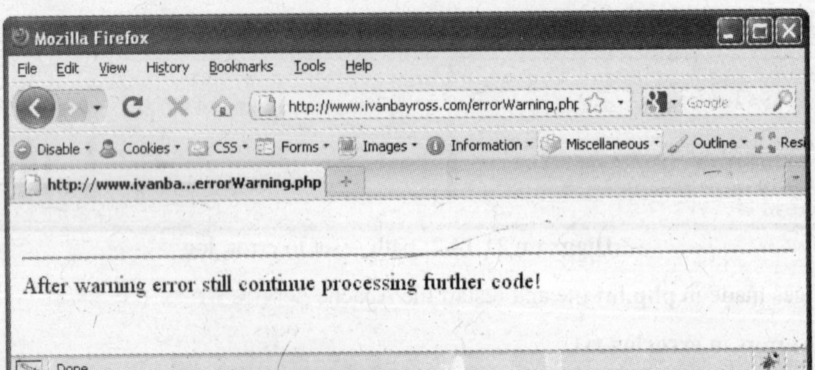

Diagram 21.14.5: No error message displayed

4. To view the system generated error message, open the **errorlog.txt** file using the path **D:\WorkEnviornment\Projects\sct\error\errorlog.txt** as shown in diagram 21.14.6

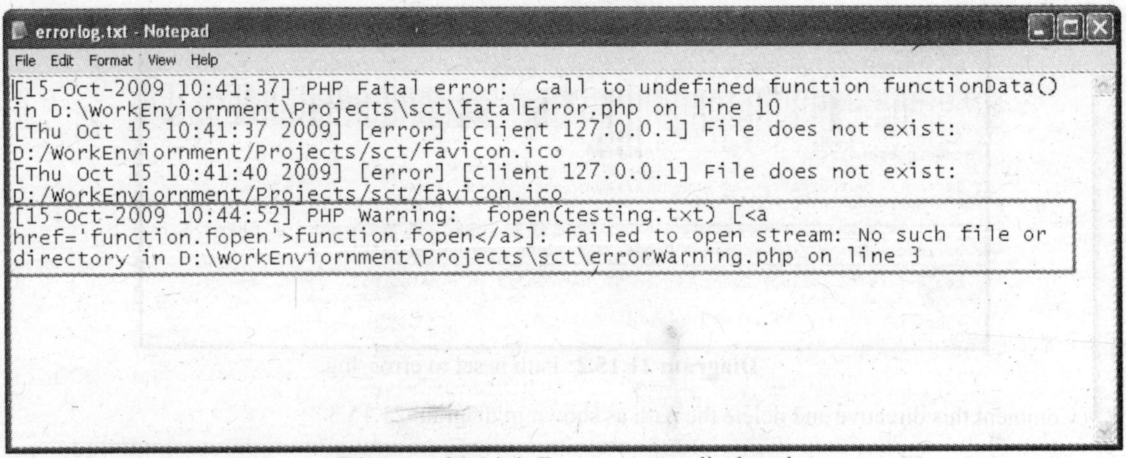

errorlog.txt - Notepad

File Edit Format View Help

```
[15-Oct-2009 10:41:37] PHP Fatal error:  Call to undefined function functionData()
in D:\WorkEnviornment\Projects\sct\fatalError.php on line 10
[Thu Oct 15 10:41:37 2009] [error] [client 127.0.0.1] File does not exist:
D:/WorkEnviornment/Projects/sct/favicon.ico
[Thu Oct 15 10:41:40 2009] [error] [client 127.0.0.1] File does not exist:
D:/WorkEnviornment/Projects/sct/favicon.ico
[15-Oct-2009 10:44:52] PHP Warning:  fopen(testing.txt) [<a
href='function.fopen'>function.fopen</a>]: failed to open stream: No such file or
directory in D:\WorkEnviornment\Projects\sct\errorWarning.php on line 3
```

Diagram 21.14.6: Error message displayed

Hereafter, all error messages generated by any **.php** file will get stored in: **D:\WorkEnviornment\Projects\sct\error\errorlog.txt**.

Logging Errors Via Syslog

To log errors via syslog (through the php.ini file):

1. Set the **display_errors** directive to **Off** (as shown earlier)
2. Set the **log_errors** directive to **On** as shown in to diagram 21.15.1

```
log_errors = On
```

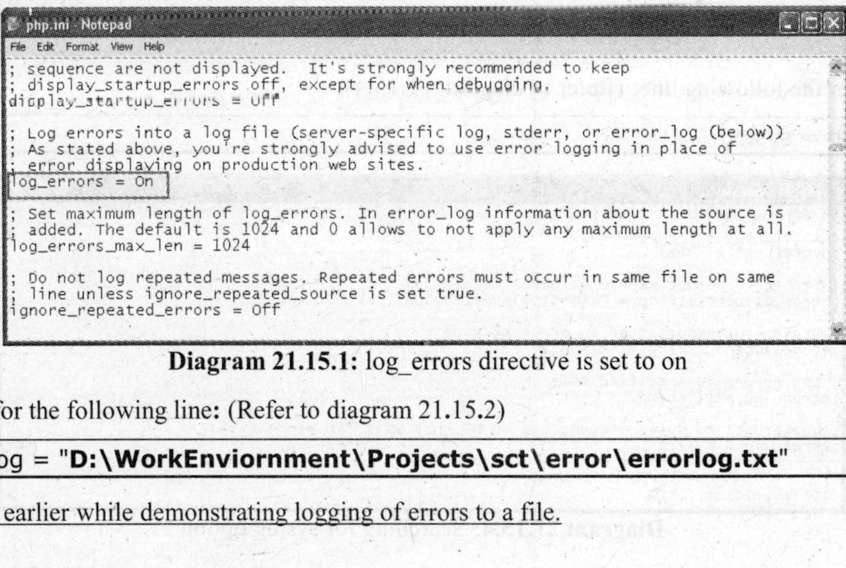

php.ini - Notepad

File Edit Format View Help

```
; sequence are not displayed.  It's strongly recommended to keep
; display_startup_errors off, except for when debugging.
display_startup_errors = Off

; Log errors into a log file (server-specific log, stderr, or error_log (below))
; As stated above, you're strongly advised to use error logging in place of
; error displaying on production web sites.
log_errors = On

; Set maximum length of log_errors. In error_log information about the source is
; added. The default is 1024 and 0 allows to not apply any maximum length at all.
log_errors_max_len = 1024

; Do not log repeated messages. Repeated errors must occur in same file on same
; line unless ignore_repeated_source is set true.
ignore_repeated_errors = Off
```

Diagram 21.15.1: log_errors directive is set to on

3. Search for the following line: (Refer to diagram 21.15.2)

```
error_log = "D:\WorkEnviornment\Projects\sct\error\errorlog.txt"
```

This was set earlier while demonstrating logging of errors to a file.

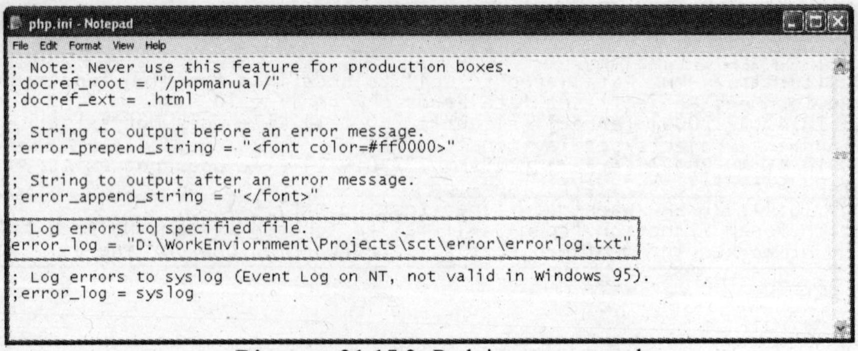

Diagram 21.15.2: Path is set to error_log

4. Comment this directive and delete the path as shown in diagram 21.15.3

```
;error_log = filename
```

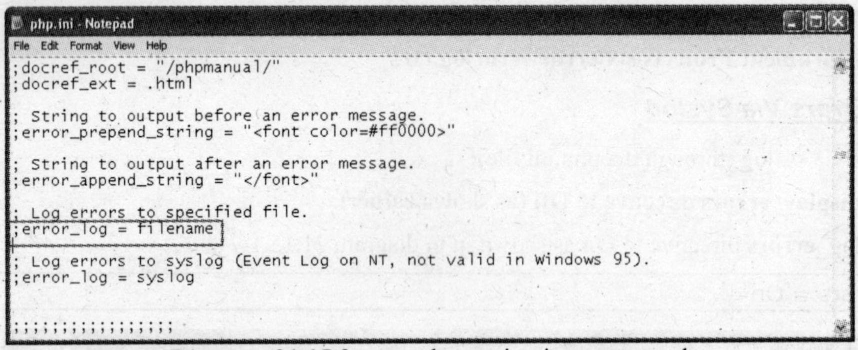

Diagram 21.15.3: error_log option is commented

5. Search for the following line: (Refer to diagram 21.15.4)

```
error_log = syslog
```

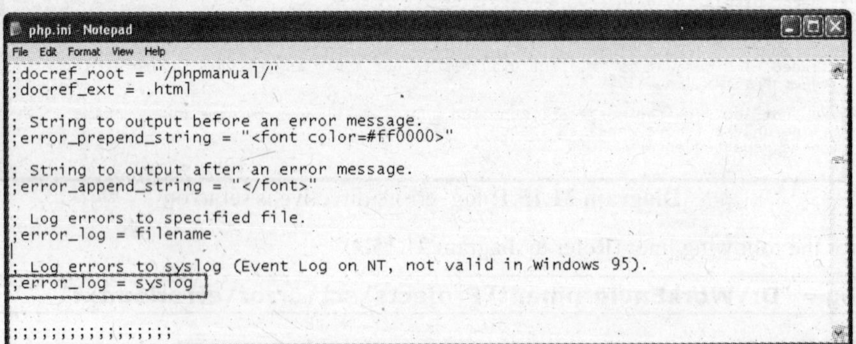

Diagram 21.15.4: Searching for syslog option

6. Uncomment the directive of **error_log** having the value **syslog**. Refer to diagram 21.15.5

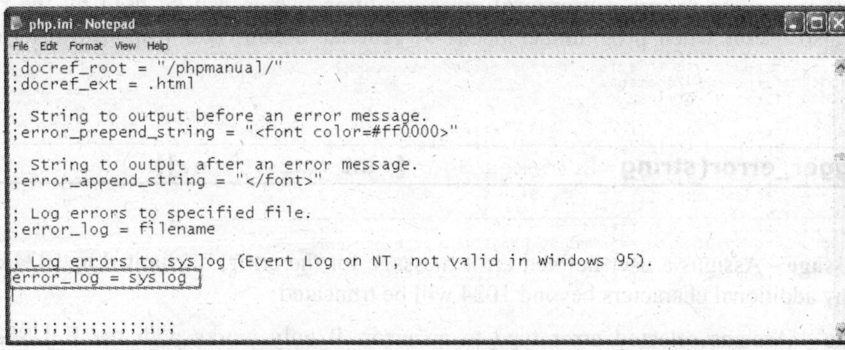

Diagram 21.15.5: Uncommented the option for syslog

7. The errors logged via syslog technique can be viewed using an **Event Viewer** available as a System Software in any O/s. For example to view these errors in Windows XP open the Event Viewer available under **Start → Control Panel →Administrative Tools → Event Viewer**. Refer to diagram 21.15.6

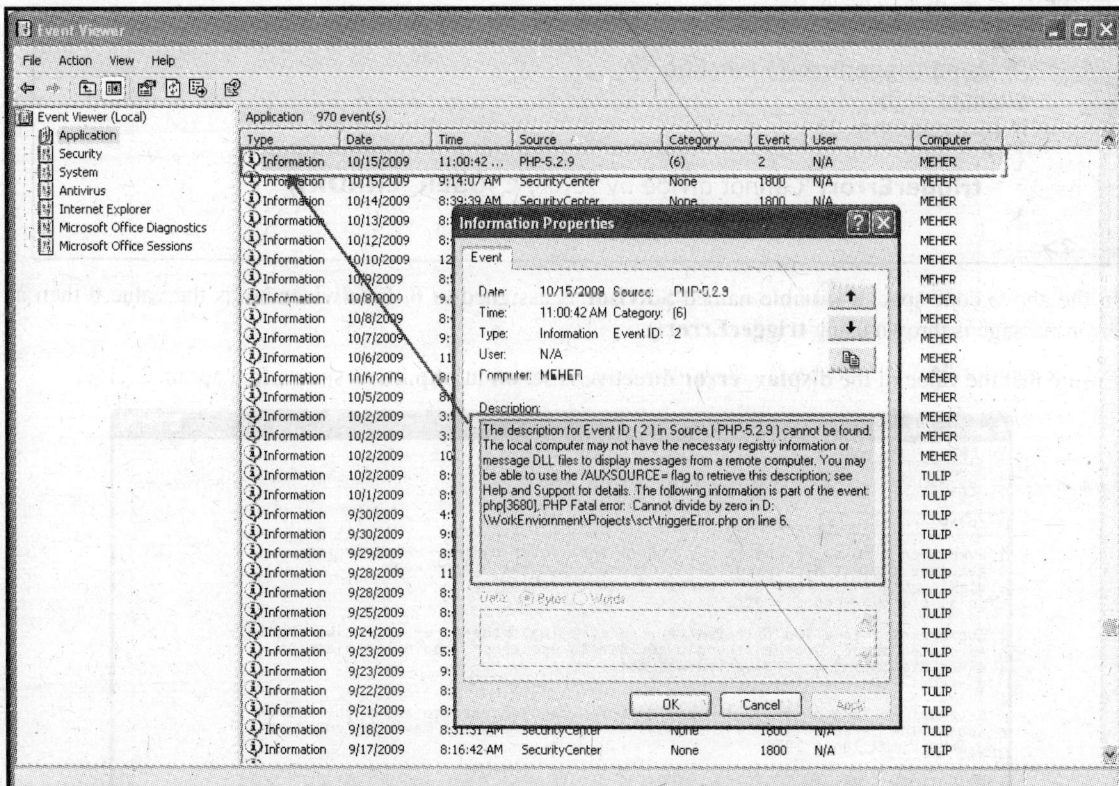

Diagram 21.15.6: Event Viewer in Windows XP

Using trigger_error()

trigger_error() generates a user-level error, warning or notice message.

trigger_error() is used to trigger a user-level error condition, which can be used by the built-in error handler. It is also useful when programmer needs to generate a particular response to an exception at runtime.

Syntax:

```
bool trigger_error(string <ErrorMessage> [, int <ErrorType>])
```

Where,

- **ErrorMessage** - Assigns a user defined error message for the error. It's limited to 1024 characters in length. Any additional characters beyond 1024 will be truncated
- **ErrorType** - Assigns selected error type to an error. It only works with the E_USER family of constants and will default to E_USER_NOTICE

Return Values

trigger_error() returns FALSE if a wrong ErrorType is specified and TRUE otherwise.

Example:

```
<?php
    /* Using triggerError() function */
    $divisor = 0;
    if ($divisor == 0)
    {
        triggerError("Cannot divide by zero", E_USER_ERROR);
    }
?>
```

In the above code spec, a variable named **$divisor** is assigned to **0**. If **$divisor** holds the value **0** then an error message is thrown using **triggerError()**.

Ensure that the value of the **display_error** directive is set **on** in **php.ini** as shown in diagram 21.16.1

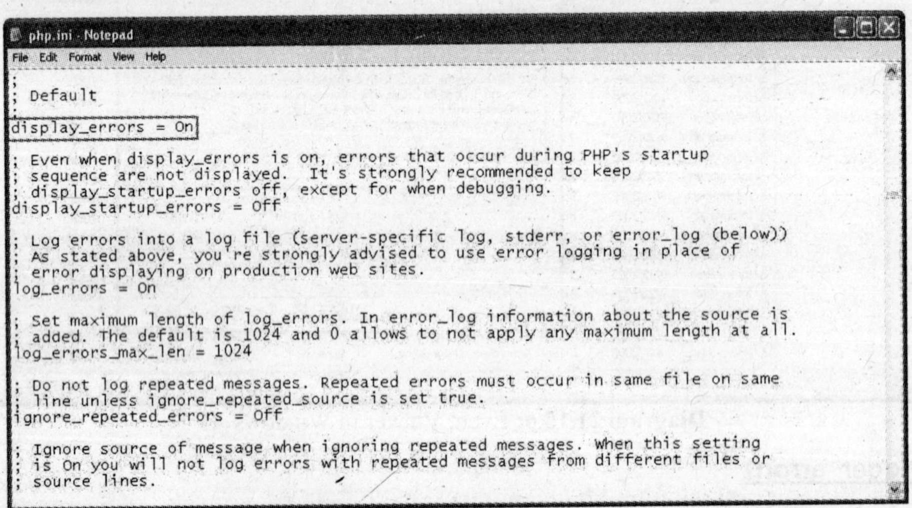

Diagram 21.16.1: display_errors feature is set to on

Execute the code spec shown in the example. Since the error is trapped using **triggerError()**, the user generated error message will be displayed as shown in diagram 21.16.2.

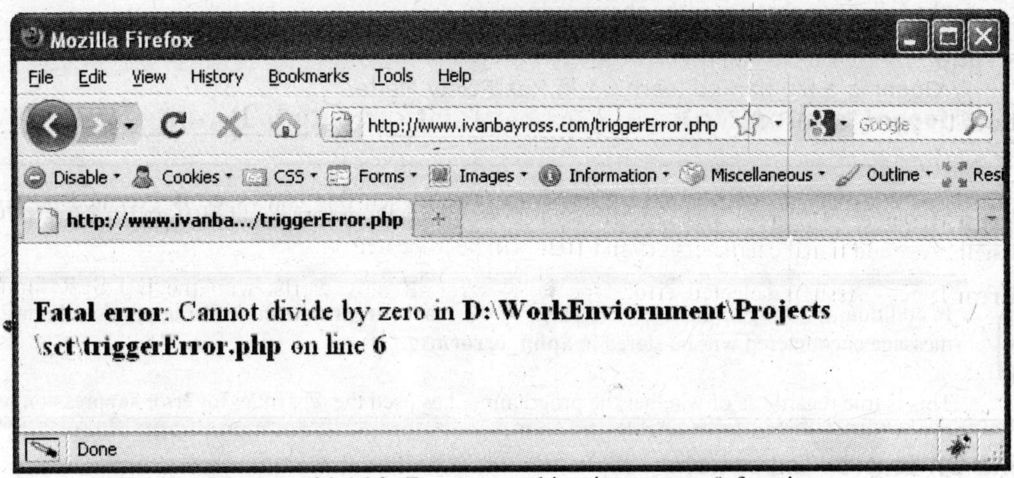

Diagram 21.16.2: Error trapped in trigger_error() function

Ignoring Errors

PHP allows the selective suppression of error reporting when errors occur with the @ syntax. If a programmer wants to open a file that may not exist **and** suppress any errors that arise, this can be done using the syntax given on the next page.

Syntax:

```
$fp = @fopen($file, $mode);
```

<u>PHP's error facilities do not provide any flow control capabilities.</u>

Consider the following code spec having a function **fopen()**, that attempts to get the contents of a file that does not exist:

```
<?php
    // Opening a file named learn.txt in Read Only Mode.
    fopen("learn.txt", "r");
?>
```

An error message is displayed as shown in diagram 21.17.

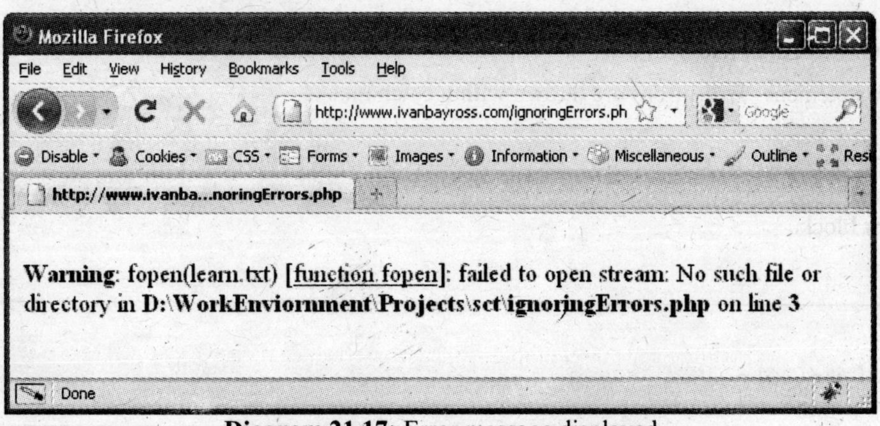

Diagram 21.17: Error message displayed

Now make the following changes in the above code spec:

```
<?php
    // Opening a file named learn.txt in Read Only Mode.
    @fopen("learn.txt", "r");
?>
```

Since an error is expected, it is suppressed using @. Now when this code spec is executed no error is displayed.

TIP

In addition, if a programmer sets the value of the **track_errors** directive **On** in php.ini, the last error message encountered will be stored in **$php_errormsg**.

This is true regardless of whether the programmer has used the @ syntax for error suppression or not.

Acting On Errors / Exceptions

An exception is an event that occurs during the execution of a program that disrupts the normal flow of its instructions. They provide a way to react to exceptional circumstances such as runtime errors in a program by transferring control to special functions called **handlers**.

Exceptions are a high-level, built-in error mechanism. **PHP 5** introduced exceptions, a new mechanism for handling errors in an object context. Exceptions provide significant advantages over more traditional error management techniques.

When an error occurs within a method, the method spawns an object and delivers this to the runtime system. The object, called an **exception** object, contains information about the error, including its type and the state of the program when the error occurred. Programmatically creating an exception object and handing it to the runtime system is called **throwing an exception**.

PHP 5 has an exception model similar to that of other programming languages. An exception can be thrown, tried and caught within a PHP code block. An exception is thrown by using the **throw** keyword from inside a **try** block. Exception handlers are declared with the keyword **catch**, which must be placed immediately after the **try** block.

Exceptions are handled using:

- Try block - A block of PHP code spec for execution, which must include at least one catch block
- Catch block - Multiple catch blocks can be used to catch different exception class types, program execution will continue until after that last catch block defined in the code block sequence
- Throw statement - Exceptions are thrown within catch blocks

Try Block

The first step in constructing an exception handler is to enclose the code that might throw an exception within a **try** block.

Syntax:

```
try
{
        //Some Code
}
```

If an exception occurs within the try block, an exception handler associated with it handles that exception. To associate an exception handler with a try block, the programmer must add a catch block after the try block.

Catch Block

Each catch block is an exception handler and handles the type of exception indicated by its argument. The catch block contains code that is executed if and when the exception handler is invoked.

When an exception is thrown, PHP code following the statement at which the exception was thrown **will not** be executed **and** the PHP runtime will attempt to find the first matching catch block.

Syntax:

```
try
{
    ...
}
catch (ExceptionType Name)
{
    ...
}
```

Throw Statement

All methods use the **throw** statement to throw an exception. The throw statement requires a single argument i.e. a throwable object.

Syntax:

```
throw <SomeThrowableObject>;
```

Example:

```
<?php
    /* Using Exceptions */
    try
    {
        $number = 40;
        if ($number < 50)
        {
            throw new Exception("Value is lesser than 50");
        }
        $message1 = "Value is Correct";
        print $message1;
    }
    catch(Exception $exception)
    {
        print "Value must be greater than 50";
    }
?>
```

In this example, PHP enters the **try** block and starts executing code. When it hits the line **throw new Exception**, it will stop executing the **try** block and jump to the **catch** block.

Once PHP has left the **try** block, it will not return to it. Here it checks each exception option against the list in **catch** and executes the appropriate code. In this example there is only one catch option.

Execution of the above code spec will display output as shown in diagram 21.18.1.

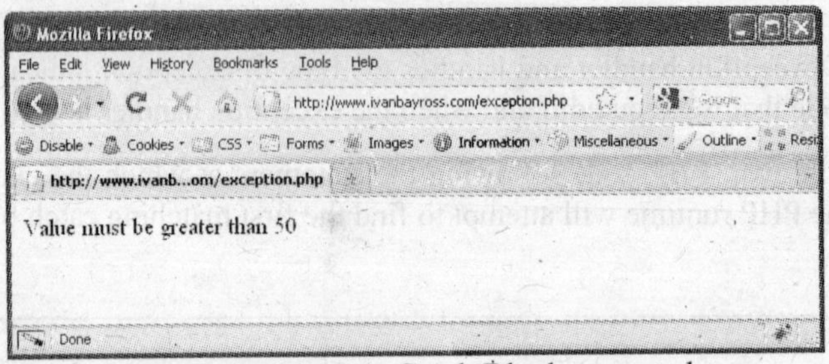

Diagram 21.18.1: Catch Block executed

Change the value of the variable **$number** as follows in the above code spec:

```
$number = 70;
```

Now **$number** holds value which is greater than **50**.

Re-execute the code spec. Refer to diagram 21.18.2.

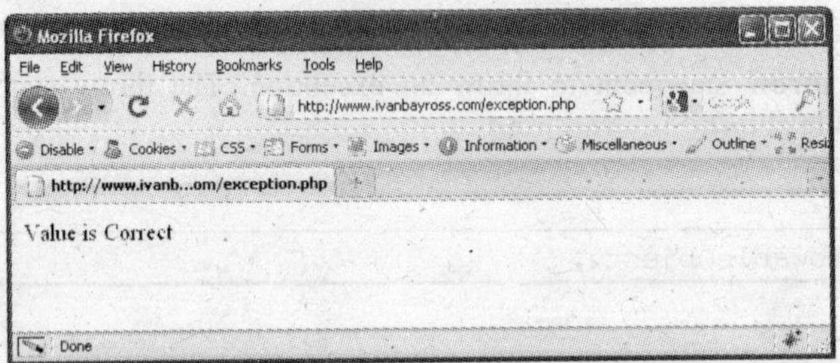

Diagram 21.18.2: Try Block executed

Example:

```
<?php
    $user="root";
    $pwd="sct2306";
    $db="learn";
    $host="localhost";
    $link= @mysql_connect($host, $user, $pwd);
    try
    {
        if (!$link)
        {
            throw new exception("MyException");
        }
        echo "MySQL Connection Established!";
    }
    catch(Exception $connection)
    {
        print "Connection Failed!";
    }
```

```
    echo "<BR />";
    $db_link=@mysql_select_db($db);
    try
    {
        If (!$db_link)
        {
            throw new exception("Sorry database does not exists!");
        }
        echo "Database ". $db . " Exists!";
        mysql_close();
    }
    catch(Exception $database)
    {
        print "Sorry could not select the database!";
    }
?>
```

The above code spec when executed will display an output as shown in diagram 21.19

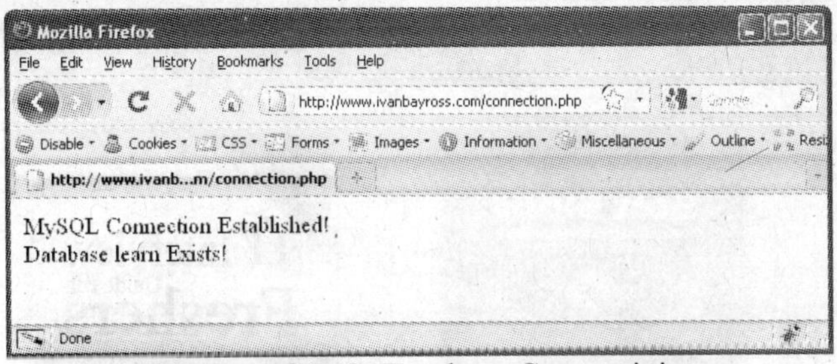

Diagram 21.19: Database Connectivity

In the above code spec

- An attempt to establish a connection is made using **@mysql_connect()** with the following parameters
  - **$host** is the host of MySQL **or** the **localhost** of MySQL
  - **$user** is the user (in this case the **root** user) to login into MySQL
  - **$pwd** is the password bound to root

```
$link = @mysql_connect($host, $user, $pwd);
```

- The following **if** statement checks if a connection was established or not. If no connection was established then the **if** condition continues execution and throws an exception

```
if (!$link)
{
    throw new exception("Myexception");
}
```

  - Since the connection is not valid **and** an exception is thrown a valid catch block takes appropriate action

```
catch(Exception $connection)
{
    print "Connection Failed!";
}
```

- After connecting successfully to a valid database, using **@mysql_select_db()** a database named **learn** is selected

```
$db_link=@mysql_select_db($db);
```

- In case, the database named **learn** is not selected the **if (!$db_link)** takes over and throws an exception

```
If (!$db_link)
{
    throw new exception("Sorry database does not exists!");
}
```

- Since an exception is thrown a valid **catch** block takes appropriate action

```
catch(Exception $database)
{
    print "Sorry could not select the database!";
}
```

22. A STANDARD CHALLENGE AND RESPONSE SYSTEM

All interactive websites which are PHP and database (MySQL) driven will deliver a challenge and response system to a site visitor at some time or the other. The challenge and response system is basically a Login system which validates whether website resources should be delivered to the visitor or not.

When a visitor wishes to access specific website resources, not normally available to unregistered visitors, a login ID and password form is displayed to the user. Please refer to diagram 22.1. The combination values of an Email ID and Password captured via the form. These values are then checked against registered Email ID's and Passwords stored in a database table on the Web server.

If the combination login ID and password captured exists in the registered users database table, website resources will be released to the visitor or the visitor will be required to register first then log in, else the visitor will simply be displayed an appropriate message and denied access to the website resources.

This in essence is what an Internet based Challenge and Response system is all about.

The Login Sub system:

THE LOGIN FORM:

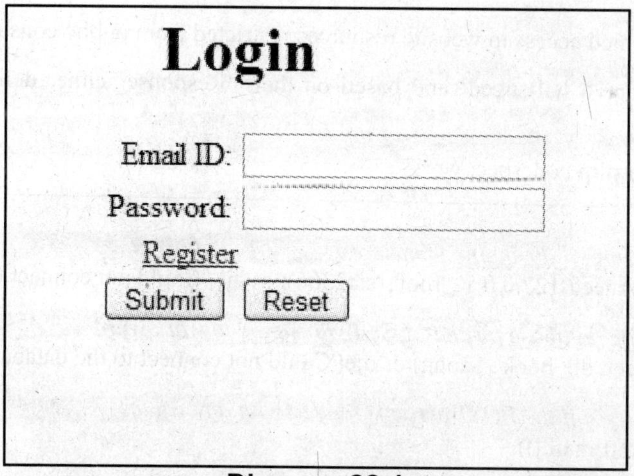

Diagram 22.1

When the Login sub system runs the form as shown in diagram 22.1 is displayed in the visitor's Browser. This form permits any visitor to access website resources not available to unregistered visitors.

All the visitor has to do is enter the Email ID and Password that they originally registered with and the restricted website's resources will be immediately accessible to them.

Form Functionality:

When a visitor loads an Email ID and Password into the Login form and clicks the Login button the data captured in the form is immediately delivered to the Web server by the Browser.

Assuming that the form's Method attribute was loaded with the value POST then the form data is delivered to Web server using a bit stream. This data is then stored within the POST array at the Web server.

The form's Action attribute will be loaded with the name of the PHP file that must handle the data returned by the Browser. The PHP file name is another block of data delivered by the Browser to the Web server when the rest of the form data is delivered.

Hence, the Web server knows exactly which PHP program on the Web server is supposed to handle the data being returned from the Browser. The Web server will invoke the PHP program and its code spec will begin to deal with the form data returned by the Browser and held in the POST array at the Web server.

This PHP program will:

- Access the POST array at the Web server
- Locate the Email ID and Password values
- Extract these values and load them into memory variables
- Then create a SQL Select sentence with these values in its WHERE clause and fire this against the 'Registered Users' table at the Web server
- If the SQL Select runs successfully the login ID / password combination have been located in the 'Registered Users' table. Hence, the visitor is considered as registered.
- The Website resources are then immediately available for access by the logged in visitor
- If the SQL Select fails then the login ID / password combination is not available in the 'Registered Users' table. The visitor is considered as unregistered. An error message is displayed in the visitor Browser from where the attempt to login took place
- The visitor can then either 'Register' with the website by clicking on the Register link at the bottom of the login form, complete the website's registration process and then login in.

OR

- Will simply be denied access to website resources restricted from public consumption

This is how visitors are 'Challenged' and based on their 'Response' either delivered or denied website resources.

Here is how the **Login.php** codespec, works.

```
<?php
    //connecting to the mysql db engine in memory
    $conn = mysql_connect('127.0.0.1', 'root', 'sct2306') or die('Could not connect to MySQL');

    //selecting a specific database for the MySQL db engine to work with
    $db  = mysql_select_db('book', $conn) or die('Could not connect to the database');

    //A simple check to see if the POST array is loaded with any values
    if(isset($_POST['txtEmail']))
    {
    //Creating a query against the regvisitor table to seek if the visitor is registered
    $qryLogin = " SELECT emailid, password FROM regvisitor WHERE emailid = '". $_POST['txtEmail']
    ."' AND password = '". $_POST['txtPassword'] ."' ";

    //Firing the query against the regvisitor table to perform the seek
    $rsLogin =mysql_query($qryLogin);

    //Checking the number of rows returned by the query
    //If there are no rows returned the visitors LoginID and Password do not exist in the regvisitors table
    // i.e. The visitor is not registered
    //If a single row is returned the visitors LogiID and Password exists in the regvisitors table
    // i.e. The visitor is registered
    $numRowsLogin=mysql_num_rows($rsLogin);
```

```
    if($numRowsLogin)
    {
        //If the visitor is registered a call is made to the login success HTML page
        header('location:loginSuccess.php');
    }
    else
    {
        //If the visitor is not registered a call is made to the login invalid HTML page
        header('location:loginInvalid.php');
    }
  }
?>
```

When the PHP codespec begins execution at the Webserver a connection is setup with the MySQL database engine running in memory. To establish a connection three blocks of information are required, the ip of the computer on which the MySQL Db engine is running on, a legitimate user ID and finally a Password. All three of these values are passed to a built in MySQL method:
mysql_connect('127.0.0.1', 'root', 'sct2306') or die('Could not connect to MySQL');

The **die()** method permits a user defined error message to be displayed to the visitor in case a connection to the MySQL Db engine failed.

Once a connection to the MySQL DB engine running in memory is established, the next step is to connect to a specific database. The MySQL method:
mysql_select_db('book', $conn) or die('Could not connect to the database');
The **die()** method permits a user defined error message to be displayed to the visitor in case a connection to the database failed.

Once a connection to the database has been established its time to craft a Query string to be fired against the database selected. The table name will be within the query string.

```
$qryLogin = " SELECT emailid, password FROM regvisitor WHERE emailid = '". $_POST['txtEmail']
        ."' AND password = '". $_POST['txtPassword'] ."' ";
```

The Query string is created by accessing the POST array and retrieving values returned by the Browser that are stored there. The $_POST['txtEmail'] and $_POST['txtPassword'] retrieve the Email ID and Password returned by the Browser and stored in the POST array at the Web server.

NOTE

Be very careful when crafting concatenated values within the query WHERE clause.

This must be structured as follows:
A single quote ('), followed by a double quote (") followed by a period (**.**) followed by the $_POST['*textbox name value*'] followed by a period (**.**), followed by a double quote ("), finally terminated by a single quote ('). It is most often in this structure that programmers make mistakes.

Then fire the Query. The PHP **mysql_query(**$qryLogin**);** method does exactly this.

If the query returns a single row, (*remember that the Email ID is the primary key of the table and hence the combination of Email ID and password will always return a single row* **or** *no row at all*) display the Login successful PHP page to the visitor. If the query runs and returns nothing then display the Login Invalid PHP page to the visitor.

The following block of PHP code does exactly this.

```
if($numRowsLogin)
{
  //If the visitor is registered a call is made to the login success HTML page
  header('location:loginSuccess.php');
}
else
{
  //If the visitor is not registered a call is made to the login invalid HTML page
  header('location:loginInvalid.php');
}
}
```

ERROR HANDLING IN THE CHALLENGE AND RESPONSE SUB SYSTEM:

All interactive modules that belong to an application should have some sort of error handling built in to them. The challenge and response system being explained has. This is because interactive modules should be able to trap user errors and prevent these from destroying the integrity of the business data being captured. In addition to being able to trap user errors, appropriate simple to understand, descriptive error messages should be displayed to the user when an error does occur.

Error handling can be done at two different locations. At the visitor's Browser when data is being entered into the Login form or at the Web server after the submission of form data.

For simplicity purposes this material chooses to use Browser based error trapping. To achieve this Javascript code is included within the <head></head> tags. To separate the Javascript code from all other HTML code, the Javascript codespec is enclosed within the <script></script> tags.

The Javascript codespec used for error trapping in this Challenge and Response sub system:

```
//client side javascript validation codespec starts
  <script type="text/javascript" language="javascript">
        function validateLogin()
        {
          //A check to ensure that the text box Email ID is not blank
          if(document.getElementById('txtEmail').value == "" )
          {
                alert('Please enter an email id');
                return false;
          }
          //A check to ensure that the text box Password is not blank
          else if(document.getElementById('txtPassword').value == "" )
          {
                alert('Please enter a password');
                return false;
          }
          else
          {
                return true;
          }
        }
```

```
    </script>
//client side javascript validation codespec ends
```

When the Login form's Submit button is clicked this code block in invoked via the Login form's onSubmit attribute which calls the Javascript method validateLogin (). Using the form's onSubmit attribute to invoke data validation codespec is taken so that if any data validation If condition fails, the form data submit process is automatically aborted.

Here checks are being performed to ensure that neither the Login text box nor the Password text box is left empty. If they are, the form data submit process is aborted and an appropriate error message is displayed to the visitor within a Javascript Alert as shown in diagrams 22.2.1 and 22.2.2.

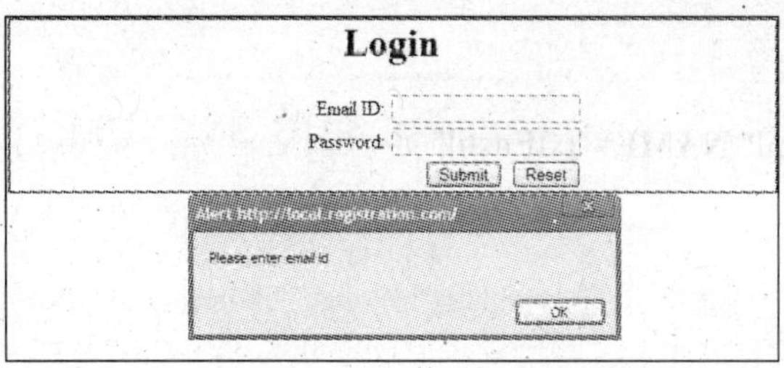

Diagram 22.2.1.

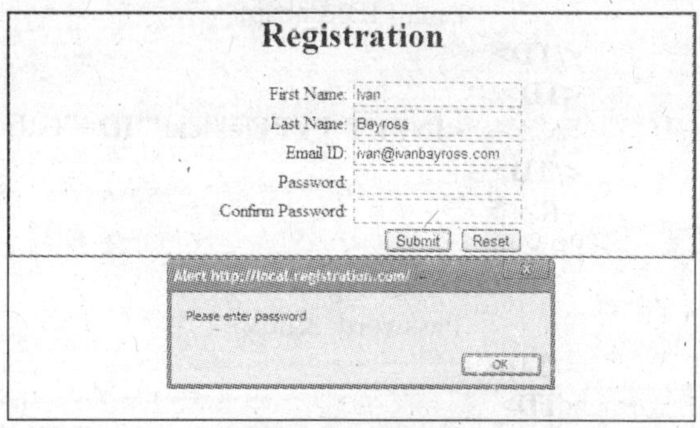

Diagram 22.2.2.

This approach is perfect for data being entered into a form in the visitors Browser, but there is also another level of data validation that needs to take place at the Web server level.

If a visitor types in a wrong Email ID and Password combination and dispatches this to the Web server, these values can only be validated at the Web server when they are compared to values previously stored in the regvisitor table when a visitor registered with the website.

Hence, this Challenge and Response sub system contains PHP based data validation codespec which runs at the Web server and returns a simple to understand, descriptive error message to the user if the Email ID / Password combination fails the validation check at the Web server.

To understand this please do a quick review of the PHP codespec on page 514 and 515. Here a Select query is fired against the regvisitor table. The WHERE clause uses the Email ID and Password entered by the user in the Login form and thus searches for these values within the regvisitor table.

If the Select query succeeds a PHP file named loginSuccess.php is invoked which returns an HTML page to the user as shown in diagram 22.2.3.

If the Select query fails a PHP file named loginInvalid.php is invoked which returns an HTML page to the user as shown in diagram 22.2.4.

You are successfully login to ivanbayross.com	**Email ID or Password you provided might be wrong please check**
Diagram 22.2.3.	**Diagram 22.2.4.**

Now for a quick look at the HTML code spec that displays the Login form in the visitors Browser and how this functions. Diagram 22.2.1 displays the login form.

```
<HTML>
<BODY>
<CENTER>
  <FORM ID="frmlogin" NAME="frmlogin" METHOD="POST" ACTION="login.php"
        ONSUBMIT="return validatelogin(document.frmlogin);">

   <TABLE BORDER="0" CELLSPACING="0" CELLPADDING="0" WIDTH="40%">
     <TH COLSPAN="2"><H1>Login</H1></TH>
     <TR>
       <TD ALIGN="right" WIDTH="50%">
             Email ID: 
       </TD>
       <TD>
             <INPUT TYPE="text" ID="txtEmail" NAME="txtEmail" />
       </TD>
     </TR>
     <TR>
       <TD ALIGN="right">
             Password:  
       </TD>
       <TD>
             <INPUT TYPE="password" ID="txtPassword" NAME="txtPassword" />
       </TD>
     </TR>
     <TR>
       <TD COLSPAN="2"> </TD>
     </TR>
     <TR>
       <TD ALIGN="right">
             <INPUT TYPE="SUBMIT" ID="cmdSubmit" NAME="cmdSubmit"
             VALUE="Submit" /> 
       </TD>
       <TD>
             <INPUT TYPE="reset" ID="cmdReset" NAME="cmdReset" />
       </TD>
     </TR>
   </TABLE>
  </FORM>
</CENTER>
</BODY>
</HTML>
```

In the HTML codespec, the value of the **method** attribute indicates that the Browser should return the form's content to the Web server using a bit stream. The value of the **action** attribute indicates that the Web server must invoke **login.php** to process the contents returned to it by the visitors Browser.

The **onSubmit** attribute of the form invokes the user defined method named **validateLogin()**, which then executes and validates that neither of the text boxes in the form are left empty.

If any text box is left empty then an error message is displayed to the visitor in their Browser and the form's data submission to the Web server is aborted.

THE REGISTRATION SUB-SYSTEM:

When a visitor clicks on the Register link in the login form, a form as shown in diagram 6 is displayed in the visitors Browser.

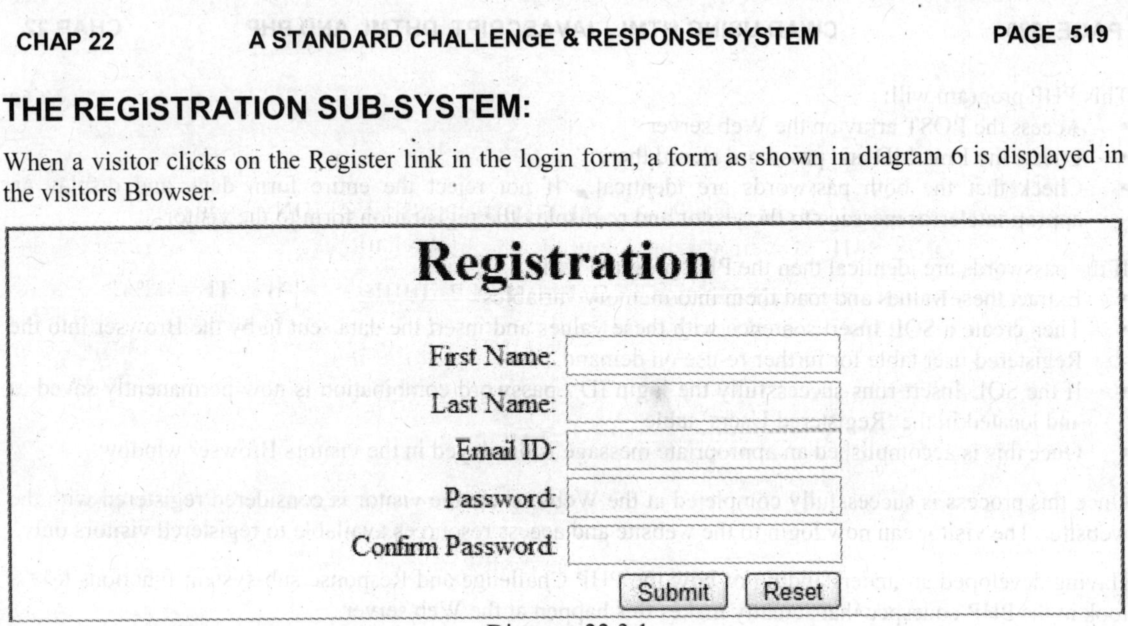

Diagram 22.3.1

This registration form captures the following information from the visitor:

1) Their first name
2) Their last name
3) Their Email ID
4) Password chosen
5) The confirm password value

An Email ID is unique across the Internet. While a first / last name combination need not be. Hence, the Challenge and Response sub-system uses the visitor's unique Email ID as the value to identify the visitor whenever the visitor wishes to login and access restricted website resources.

The visitor is required to key in a password value of their choice and confirm the password value by keying in exactly the same password value a second time. The sub-system checks to see that both the password value and the confirm password value are identical before being accepted and stored permanently.

If during this check, if these values are not identical an error message is displayed to the Visitor and the forms content is rejected from any further processing.

When the Submit button is clicked, the Browser checks the form's Method and Action attributes for their values. The value held in form's Method attribute determines how the Browser will return form data to the Web server. Assume the value is POST. The Browser will then use a bit stream to return form data to the Web server.

The value held in the form's Action attribute will have the name of the PHP file which will process this data at the Web server. The Browser will send this PHP file name back to the Web server along with all the other information being sent back.

Hence, the Web server knows exactly which PHP program, located at the Web server is supposed to handle the data being returned from the Browser. The Web server will then invoke this PHP program which in turn will handle the form data now resident in the POST array of the Web server.

This PHP program will:

- Access the POST array on the Web server
- Locate the Email ID and password stored there
- Check that the both passwords are identical. If not reject the entire form data, and display an appropriate error message to the visitor and re-display the registration form to the visitor

If the passwords are identical then the PHP program will:

- Extract these values and load them into memory variables
- Then create a SQL Insert sentence with these values and insert the data sent in by the Browser into the Registered user table for further re-use on demand.
- If the SQL Insert runs successfully the login ID / password combination is now permanently saved to and located in the 'Registered Users' table
- Once this is accomplished an appropriate message is displayed in the visitors Browser window.

Once this process is successfully completed at the Webs server the visitor is considered registered with the website. The visitor can now login to the website and access resources available to registered visitors only.

Having developed an understanding of how the PHP Challenge and Response sub-system functions take a look at the PHP codespec that actually makes this happen at the Web server.

Here is how the **Login.php** codespec, works.

```
<?php
//connecting to the mysql db engine in memory
$conn = mysql_connect('127.0.0.1', 'root', 'sct2306') or die('Could not connect to MySQL');
//selecting a specific database for the MySQL db engine to work with
$db  = mysql_select_db('book', $conn) or die('Could not connect to the database');
//A simple check to see if the POST array is loaded with any values
if(isset($_POST['txtFname']))
{
//Retrieving values from the POST array and creating a SELECT query
//to be fired against the regvisitor table to check for a duplicate registration
$qryLogin = " SELECT emailid, password FROM regvisitor WHERE emailid = '". $_POST['txtEmail'] ."'
AND password = '". $_POST['txtPassword'] ."' ";
```

NOTE

Be very careful when crafting concatenated values within the query WHERE clause.

This must be structured as follows:
A single quote ('), followed by a double quote ("), followed by a period (.), followed by the $_POST['*textbox name value*'] followed by a period (.), followed by a double quote ("), finally terminated by a single quote ('). It is most often in this structure that programmers make mistakes.

```
//Firing the SELECT query
$rsLogin =mysql_query($qryLogin);
```

```
//Checking the number of rows that have been returned by the SELECT statement
$numRowsLogin=mysql_num_rows($rsLogin);
//If any rows are returned by the SELECT query a duplicate registration is being attempted hence invoke duplicateEmail.php to handle this situation
if($numRowsLogin)
{
header('location:duplicateEmail.php');
}
//Since the SELECT query failed to return any rows
//Create an INSERT statement using values stored in the POST array at the Web server
else
{
$qryAddUser = " INSERT INTO regvisitor (emailid, fname, lname, password)
VALUES ( '". $_POST['txtEmail']."', '". $_POST['txtFname'] ."', '". $_POST['txtLname']."', '".
$_POST['txtPassword'] ."') ";
//Fire the INSERT statement against the register table
mysql_query($qryAddUser);
//Invoke thankYou.php to inform the visitor of a successful registration
header('location:thankYou.php');
}
}
?>
```

Here is how the visitor Registration.php, javascript code works, which validates the Registration form data before it is dispatched to the Web server for further processing.

```
<!doctype html public "-//w3c//dtd html 4.0 transitional//en">
<html>
<head>
<title>User Registration System</title>
//client side javascript validation codespec starts
<script type="text/javascript" language="javascript">
    function validateRegistration()
    {
        if(document.getElementById('txtFname').value == "" )
        {
            alert('Please enter first name');
            return false;
        }
        else if(document.getElementById('txtLname').value == "" )
        {
            alert('Please enter last name');
            return false;
        }
        else if(document.getElementById('txtEmail').value == "" )
        {
            alert('Please enter email id');
            return false;
        }
```

```
    else if(document.getElementById('txtPassword').value == "" )
    {
      alert('Please enter password');
      return false;
    }
    else if(document.getElementById('txtConfPassword').value == "" )
    {
      alert('Please enter confirm password');
      return false;
    }
    else if(document.getElementById('txtPassword').
            value!= document.getElementById('txtConfPassword').value)
    {
      alert('Password and confirm password values must be the same');
      return false;
    }
    else
    {
      return true;
    }
}
</script>
//client side javascript validation codespec ends
</head>
```

CLIENT SIDE JAVASCRIPT BASED ERROR HANDING

The Registration form uses client side javascript to validate the content of the Registration form prior it being submitted to the Web server for processing.

When the form's Submit button is clicked, the javascript function validateRegistration() is invoked by the form. When this method is invoked, multiple If conditions check to see if any of the text boxes, have been left blank in the form.

If any of the text boxes on the form have been left blank and the Submit button is clicked a simple to understand error message is displayed to the visitor in the form of a Javascript Alert and the form's data submit process to the Web server is automatically aborted by the code spec **return false;**. Please refer to diagrams 22.4.1, 22.4.2, 22.4.3, and 22.4.4.

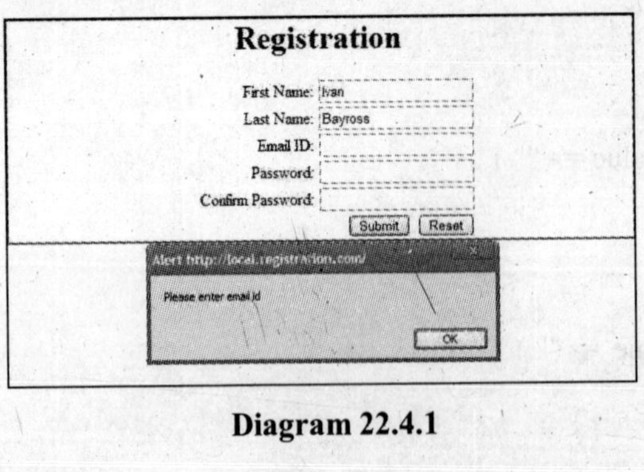

Diagram 22.4.1

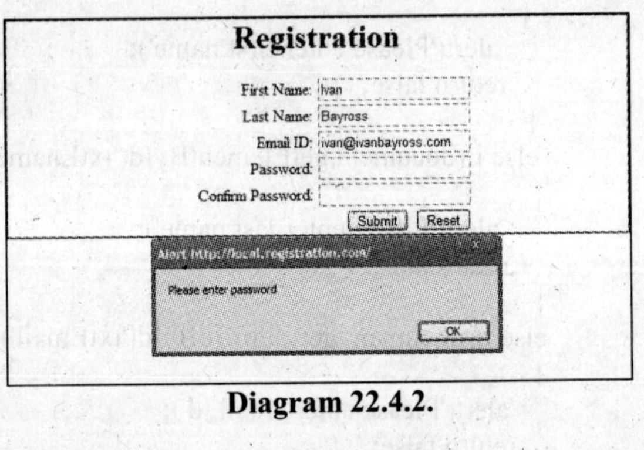

Diagram 22.4.2.

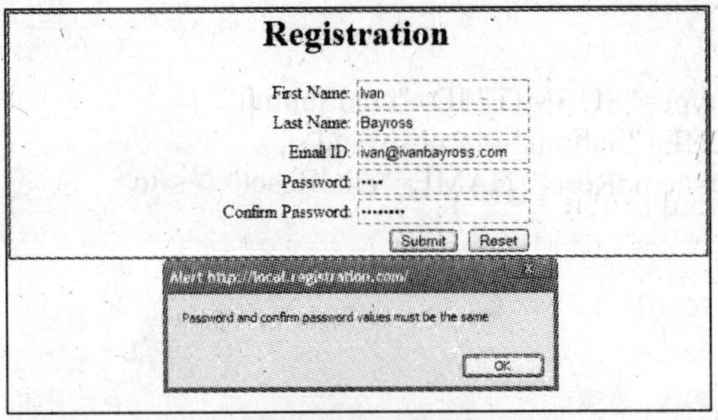

Diagram 22.4.3

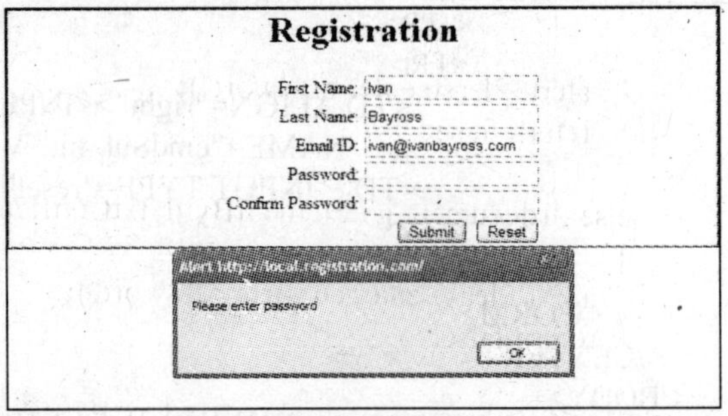

Diagram 22.4.4

Identical JavaScript Alerts are displayed in case the user has left the First Name or Last Name text boxes empty.

Once all the form's textboxes are loaded with appropriate values these are immediately submitted by the Browser to the Web server for processing at the Web server.

Now for a look at the HTML code spec that displays the Registration form in the visitors Browser and how this functions.

```
<HTML>
<BODY>
<CENTER>
  <FORM ID="frmRegistration" NAME="frmRegistration" METHOD="post"
   ACTION=" registration.php" onSubmit="return validateRegistration(document.frmRegistration);">
        <TABLE BORDER="0" CELLSPACING="0" CELLPADDING="0" WIDTH="40%">
              <TH COLSPAN="2"><H1>Registration</H1></TH>
              <TR>
                    <TD ALIGN="right" WIDTH="50%">First Name: </TD>
                    <TD><INPUT TYPE="text" ID="txtFname" NAME="txtFname"  /></TD>
              </TR>
              <TR>
                 <TD ALIGN="right">Last Name: </TD>
                 <TD><INPUT TYPE="text" id="txtLname" NAME="txtLname"  /></TD>
              </TR>
              <TR>
                 <TD ALIGN="right">Email ID: </td>
                 <TD><INPUT TYPE="text" id="txtEmail" NAME="txtEmail"  /></TD>
              </TR>
              <TR>
                 <TD ALIGN="right">Password: </td>
                 <TD><INPUT TYPE="password" ID="txtPassword" NAME="txtPassword"  /></TD>
              </TR>
              <TR>
                 <TD ALIGN="right">Confirm Password: </td>
                 <TD>
                      <INPUT TYPE="password" ID="txtConfPassword" NAME="txtConfPassword"  />
                 </TD>
              </TR>
              <TR>
                 <TD COLSPAN="2"> </TD>
```

```
            </TR>
            <TR>
                <TD ALIGN="right"><INPUT type="SUBMIT" ID="cmdSubmit"
                    NAME="cmdSubmit" VALUE="Submit" /> </td>
                <TD><INPUT TYPE="reset" ID="cmdReset" NAME="cmdReset" /></td>
            </TR>
        </TABLE>
    </FORM>
  </CENTER>
 </BODY>
</HTML>
```

In the HTML codespec, the value of the **method** attribute indicates that the Browser should return the form's content to the Web server using a bit stream. The value of the **action** attribute indicates that the Web server must invoke **registration.php** to process the contents returned to it by the visitors Browser.

WEB SERVER SIDE PHP BASED ERROR HANDLING

The form data submitted to the Web server is handled by registration.php at the Web server. registration.php does a simple duplicate check for the Email ID / Password combination submitted to see if this has been registered before at the website. If the Email ID has been registered with the Web site, then:

- An error page is displayed to the user
- The data returned by the Browser is not stored at the Web server in the regvisitor table

Please refer to Diagrams 22.4.5 and 22.4.6

Email Id you have entered is already registered please choose different Email Id	**Thank you for registering with ivanbayross.com**

Diagram 22.4.5 **Diagram 22.4.6**

Should a visitor wishing to register with the website enter an Email ID and Password combination that already exists at the Web server an error message HTML page is displayed in the visitor's Browser as shown in diagram 11.

If the Email ID and Password combination is unique and not saved within the regvisitors table before a Thank You HTML page is displayed in the visitor's Browser as shown in diagram 12.

NOTE

A MySQL database system must be running at the Web server. This will contain a **regvisitor** table having the following structure.

Tablename	regvisitor
Primary Key	Email ID

Column Name	Datatype	Width	Explanation
emailid	Varchar	50	Primary Key (Holds the Email Id of a registering visitor)
fname	Varchar	100	Holds the first name of the registering visitor
lname	Varchar	100	Holds the last name of the registering visitor
password	Varchar	50	Holds the password value entered by the registering visitor

The PHP program which Selects and validates a visitor's Email ID and Password on login or Inserts a visitor's Registration data accesses the **regvisitor** table.

SOLUTIONS TO HANDS ON EXERCISES

17. THE BASICS OF PHP

1. Create and display Names of Fruit (using an array).

```
<?php
	$fruits = array(0=>"Apple", 1=>"Appircot", 2=>"Grapes", 3=>"Banana",
	4=>"Mango", 5=>"Grapefruit" );

	echo ("List of Fruit Name (using array) <BR />");
	echo $fruits[0] . "<BR />";
	echo $fruits[1] . "<BR />";
	echo $fruits[2] . "<BR />";
	echo $fruits[3] . "<BR />";
	echo $fruits[4] . "<BR />";
	echo $fruits[5] . "<BR />";

?>
```

2. Display current date, month, year and day of the week of the machine serving PHP pages

```
<?php
	echo $dt=date("d") . " ";
	echo $mnth=date("M") . " ";
	echo $yr=date('Y') . "<BR />";
	echo $dayofweek=date("D");
?>
```

3. Display current day of week(using ifelse() condition)

```
<?php
	$dayofweek=date("D");
	echo "Hello Everyone ";

	if ($dayofweek=="Monday")
	{
		print "Today is Monday, starting of a new week.";
	}
	elseif ($dayofweek=="Tues")
	{
		print "Today is Tuesday.";
	}
	elseif ($dayofweek=="Wed")
	{
		print "Today is Wednesday.";
	}
```

```
elseif ($dayofweek=="Thur")
{
        print "Today is Thurday.";
}
elseif ($dayofweek=="Fri")
{
        print "Today is Friday, starting of a weekend.";
}
elseif ($dayofweek=="Sat")
{
        print "Today is Saturday.";
}
else
{
        print "Today is Sunday.";
}
?>
```

4. Display Fruits Name and their prices in a Tabular Layout (using key and value pairs)

```
<HTML>
    <HEAD>
        <TITLE>Tabular Layout</TITLE>
    </HEAD>
    <BODY>
        <?php
            $arryFruitName = array('Apple' => 'Rs. 35/-', 'Appricot' => 'Rs. 45/-',
            'Mango' => 'Rs. 150/-', 'Watermelon' => 'Rs. 75/-', 'Banana' => 'Rs. 20/-' ,
            'Grapes' => 'Rs. 30/-' , 'Grapefruit' => 'Rs. 40/-');
            echo "<TABLE Width='50%' Border='1', cellpadding='1', cellspacing='5'>";
            echo "<TR>";
            echo "<TH>Fruit's Name</TH>";
            echo "<TH>Price</TH>";
            echo "</TR>";
            reset($arryFruitName);
            while (list($key, $value) = each($arryFruitName))
            {
                echo "<TR>";
                echo "<TD>$key</TD>";
                echo "<TD>$value</TD>";
                echo "</TR>";
            }
            echo "</TABLE>";
        ?>
    </BODY>
</HTML>
```

18. FUNCTIONS

1. **Create a function to calculate 33% tax on the given salary i.e. Rs. 65,500**

```
<?php
    function Tax($sal)
    {
        $tax = ($sal *33)/100;
        return($tax);
    }
    $ sal = 65500;
    $taxamount = Tax($sal);
    echo "Tax for Rs. ".$ sal." is: Rs. ".$taxamount;
?>
```

2. **Generate Fibonacci series for the numbers 1 to 17**

```
<?php
    function fibonacci($number, $showseries="no")
    {
        $retval = "";
        if ($number == 1)
        {
            return 1;
        }
        $number1 = 1;
        $number2 = 0;
        $retval = "1";

        for ($i = 1; $i < $number; $i++)
        {
            $fib = $number2 + $number1;
            $number2 = $number1;
            $number1 = $fib;
            if ($showseries == 'yes')
            {
                $retval .= ", ".$fib;
            }
        }
        if ($showseries == 'yes')
        {
            return $retval;
        }
        else
        {
            return $fib;
        }
    }
    echo (fibonacci(17, "yes"));
?>
```

19. WORKING WITH FORMS

1. Create a form to capture Product Details for submitting it and for clearing the data

```
<HTML>
  <HEAD>
       <TITLE>Product Master</TITLE>
  </HEAD>
  <BODY>
       <center>
            <FIELDSET STYLE="width:50%;">
                 <LEGEND STYLE="color:Blue"><b>Product Master</b></LEGEND>
                      <TABLE WIDTH="396" ALIGN="center" CELLPADDING="1"
                           CELLSPACING="1" BORDERCOLOR="#000000"
                           BGCOLOR="#FFFFFF">
                           <FORM ACTION="productValidate.php" METHOD="POST"
                                NAME="frmProductMaster" enctype="multipart/form-data">
                                <TR>
                                     <TD COLSPAN="2">Product Name:</TD>
                                     <TD><INPUT TYPE="Text" NAME="txtProdName"
                                          SIZE="28" MAXLENGTH="15" TABINDEX="1"
                                          VALUE="<?php echo $_POST['txtProdName']?>">
                                     </TD>
                                </TR>
                                <TR>
                                     <TD COLSPAN="2">Product Description:</TD>
                                     <TD><TEXTAREA NAME="taProdDesc" ROWS="4"
                                          COLS="21" TABINDEX="2">
                                               <?php echo $_POST['taProdDesc'];?>
                                          </TEXTAREA>
                                     </TD>
                                </TR>
                                <TR>
                                     <TD COLSPAN="2">Product Quantity:</TD>
                                     <TD><INPUT TYPE="text" NAME="txtProdQuantity"
                                          SIZE="28" MAXLENGTH="15" TABINDEX="3"
                                     VALUE="<?php echo $_POST['txtProdQuantity']?>" />
                                     </TD>
                                </TR>
                                <TR>
                                     <TD COLSPAN="2">Product Price:</TD>
                                     <TD><INPUT TYPE="Text" NAME="txtProdPrice"
                                          SIZE="28" MAXLENGTH="15" TABINDEX="4"
                                          VALUE="<?php echo $_POST['txtProdPrice']?>">
                                     </TD>
                                </TR>
```

```
                <TR>
                  <TD COLSPAN="2">Image:</TD>
                  <TD><INPUT TYPE="file" NAME="file4upload"
                              TABINDEX="5"/> </TD>
                </TR>
                <TR>
                  <TD> </TD>
                <TD colspan="2"><INPUT TYPE="Submit" NAME="btnSubmit"
                                    VALUE="Submit" tabindex="6" />
                                   <INPUT TYPE="Reset" NAME="btnCancel"
                                      VALUE="Cancel" tabindex="7" />
                  </TD>
                </TR>
                <TR>
                    <TD><INPUT TYPE="Hidden" NAME="hiddProdName"
                              VALUE="Product Master" />
                    </TD>
                </TR>
            </FORM>
          </TABLE>
      </FIELDSET>
    </center>
  </BODY>
</HTML>
```

2. Create a PHP code, which will retrieve the data captured by the HTML form, display the name of the form and also display the message Data Entered Successfully on the HTML form page after performing the validations

```
<?php
        if ($_POST['txtProdName']=="")
        {
                echo "<center><span style='color: Red;'>Please Enter Product's Name.</span></span>";
                echo "<HR>";
                include("productMaster.php");
        }
        else if ($_POST['taProdDesc']=="")
        {
                echo "<center><span style='color: Red;'>Please Enter Product's
                        Description.</span></center>";
                echo "<HR>";
                include("productMaster.php");
        }
        else if ($_POST['txtProdQuantity']=="")
        {
                echo "<center><span style='color: Red;'>Please Enter Product's
                        Quantity.</span></center>";
                echo "<HR>";
                include("productMaster.php");
        }
```

```
else if (!is_numeric($_POST['txtProdQuantity']))
{
        echo "<center><span style='color: Red;'>Please Enter Numeric Value for Product
                        Quantity.</span></center>";
                echo "<HR>";
                include("productMaster.php");
}
else if ($_POST['txtProdPrice']=="")
{
        echo "<center><span style='color: Red;'>Please Enter Price of the
                        Product.</span></center>";
        echo "<HR>";
        include("productMaster.php");
}
else if (!is_numeric($_POST['txtProdPrice']))
{
        echo "<center><span style='color: Red;'>Please Enter numeric value for Product
                        Price.</span></center>";
        echo "<HR>";
        include("productMaster.php");
}
else if ($_FILES['file4Upload']['name']=="")
{
        echo "<center><span style='color: Red;'>Please Choose a Image to be
                uploaded.</span></center>";
        echo "<HR>";
        include("productMaster.php");
}
else
{
        $target_path = "uploadFile/";
        $target_path = $target_path.$_FILES['file4Upload']['name'];
        if(move_uploaded_file($_FILES['file4Upload']['tmp_name'], $target_path))
        {
                echo "<center><span style='color: Red;'><b>The image file has been uploaded
                                Successfully.</b></span></center>";
        }
        else
        {
                echo "Sorry there was an error uploading the file, please try again!";
        }
        echo "<center><span style='color: Red;'><b>The Form Name is
                        " . $_POST['hiddProdName'] . "</b></span><BR></center>";
        echo "<center><span style='color: Red;'><b>Product Data Entered
                        Successfully</b></span></center>";
        echo "<HR>";
        $_POST="";
        include("productMaster.php");
}
?>
```

20. REGULAR EXPRESSIONS

Develop a PHP code, which will generate a Personnel Information form

```
<!--
            Date            :- 04/10/09
            Client          :- Ivan Bayross
            Filename        :- prodMaster2.php
            Purpose         :- Displays of product details form
-->

<html>
  <head>
    <title>Product Master</title>
  </head>
  <body style="font-family: georgia;">
    <center>
        <fieldset style="width:40%">
          <legend style="font-weight: bold; font-family: georgia; font-size:12px; color: blue;">
            Product Details:</legend>
          <form action="prodForm2.php" method="post" name="frmProdInfor">
            <table id="tableForm" border="0" bgcolor="#ffffff" cellpadding="4" cellspacing="6"
              width="100%" align="center">
              <tr>
                <td colspan="2" style="color:#FF0000;"><?php echo $alertmessage?></td>
              </tr>
              <tr>
                <td align="right" width="50%"> Product ID:</td>
                <td><input name="txtProdID" type="text"
                    value="<?php echo $_POST['txtProdID'];?>" size="20" />
                </td>
              </tr>
              <tr>
                <td align="right" width="50%"> Product Name: </td>
                <td><input name="txtProdName" type="text"
                    value="<?php echo $_POST['txtProdName'];?>" size="20" />
                </td>
              </tr>
              <tr>
                <td align="right" width="50%"> Product Price : </td>
                <td><input name="txtProdPrice" type="text"
                    value="<?php echo $_POST['txtProdPrice'];?>" size="20" />
                </td>
              </tr>
              <tr>
                <td align="right" width="50%">  </td>
                <td>
                  <input name="cmdSubmit" type="submit" value="Submit">  
                  <input name="cmdReset" type="reset" value="Cancel">
                </td>
              </tr>
```

```
            </table>
        </form>
      </fieldset>
    </center>
  </body>
</html>
```

Create a PHP file that will validate data captured by the form. This program uses regular expressions to validate and format data.

```
<?php
        /*
            Date            :-  04/10/09
            Client          :-  Ivan Bayross
            Filename        :-  prodForm2.php
            Purpose         :-  Validates and displays product details using regular expressions.
        */
        /* A variable holding the developers name. */
            $author = 'Ivan Bayross';
        /* Storing the system date in the format 1st Jan, 2009. */
            $sysdt = date("jS M, Y");
        /* Storing the system time in the format 00:00. */
            $systm = date("H:i");
        /* Checking if the variable for Product ID is empty*/
            if(empty($_POST['txtProdID']))
            {
                    /* Returning to the data entry form, if the Product ID is empty. */
                    $alertmessage = '<center>Product ID is empty! </center>';
                    include ("prodMaster2.php");
                    exit;
            }
            else
            {
                    $regex = '/[0123456789]/' ;
                    if(!preg_match($regex,$_POST['txtProdID']))
                    {
                            $alertmessage = '<center>Invalid Product ID!</center>';
                            include ("productMaster2.php");
                    exit;
                    }
            }
    /* Checking if the variable for Product's name is empty, (i.e. a blank name field was submitted). */
            if(empty($_POST['txtProdName']))
            {
            /* Returning to the data entry form if the product name is empty. */
                    $alertmessage = '<center>Product Name is empty!</center>';
                    include ("prodMaster2.php");
                    exit;
            }
```

```
/* When the Product's name is submitted. */
		else
		{
/* Using regular expressions with the ereg() function, to identify an occurrence of double spaces in the product name. */
	if(ereg("([[:space:]]){2}", $_POST['txtProdName']))
	{
		/* Returning to the data entry form, if the product name contains double spaces. */
		$alertmessage = '<center>Double spaces found in Product Name</center>';
		include ("prodMaster2.php");
		exit;
	}
	}
/* Checking if the variable for Product Price is empty, (i.e. a blank field was submitted). */
		if(empty($_POST['txtProdPrice']))
		{
			/* Returning to the data entry form, if the Product Price is empty. */
				$alertmessage = '<center>Product Price is empty! </center>';
				include ("prodMaster2.php");
				exit;
		}
		else
		{
				$regex = '/[0123456789]/' ;
				if(!preg_match($regex,$_POST['txtProdPrice']))
				{
					$alertmessage = '<center>Invalid Product Price!</center>';
					include ("prodMaster2.php");
					exit;
				}
		}
	?>
	<html>
		<head>
			<title>Result after using Regular Expression</title>
			<style>
				#tableForm{font-size:12px;}
				input{font-family:georgia;}
			</style>
		</head>
		<body style="font-family:georgia;">
			<H4>Product Details Submitted As On:</H4>
			<table border="1" cellspacing="1" width="250">
			  <tr>
				<td align="right" width="100">Server Date :</td>
				<td align="left" width="100"><?php echo $sysdt; ?> </td>
			  </tr>
```

```
                <tr>
                        <td align="right" width="100">Server Time :< /td>
                        <td align="left" width="100"><?php echo $systm; ?></td>
                </tr>
                </table><hr>

                <h4> Product ID: </h4>
                <table border="0" cellspacing="1" width="300">
                <tr>
                    <td align="left" width="150">
                        <?php echo $_post['txtProdID']; ?>
                    </td>
                </tr>
                </table>
                <hr>

                <h4> Product Name: </h4>
                <table border="0" cellspacing="1" width="400">
                <tr>
                    <td align="left" width="150">
                        <?php echo  $_post['txtProdName']; ?>
                    </td>
                </tr>
                </table>
                <hr>

                <h4> Product Price: </h4>
                <table border="0" cellspacing="1" width="400">
                <tr>
                    <td align="left" width="150">
                        <?php echo  $_post['txtProdPrice']; ?>
                    </td>
                </tr>
                </table>
                <hr>
        </body>
    </html>
```

SECTION - VI: Appendix

APPENDIX - A

HTML Color Codes

Color	RRGGBB	Color	RRGGBB	Color	RRGGBB
White	FFFFFF	Red	FF0000	Green	00FF00
Blue	0000FF	Magenta	FF00FF	Cyan	00FFFF
Yellow	FFFF00	Black	000000	Aliceblue	F0F8FF
Aquamarine	70DB93	Baker's chocolate	5C3317	Blue violet	9F5F9F
Brass	B5A642	Bright gold	D9D919	Brown	A62AA2
Bronze	8C7853	Bronze II	A67D3D	Cadet blue	5F9F9F
Cool bopper	D98719	Copper	B87333	Coral	FF7F00
Cornflower blue	42426F	Dark brown	5C4033	Dark green	2F4F2F
Dark green copper	4A766E	Dark olive green	4F4F2F	Dark orchid	9932CD
Dark purple	871F78	Dark slate blue	6B238E	Dark slate grey	2F4F4F
Dark tan	97694F	Dark turquoise	7093DB	Dark wood	855E42
Dim grey	545454	Dusty rose	856363	Feldspar	D19275
Firebrick	8E2323	Forest green	238E23	Gold	CD7F32
Goldenrod	DBDB70	Gray	C0C0C0	Green copper	527F76
Green yellow	93DB70	Hunter green	215E21	Indian red	4E2F2F
Khaki	9F9F5F	Light blue	C0D9D9	Light gray	A8A8A8
Light steel blue	8F8FBD	Light wood	E9C2A6	Light green	32CD32
Mandarin orange	E47833	Maroon	8E236B	Medium aquamarine	32CD99
Medium blue	3232CD	Medium forest green	6B8E23	Medium goldenrod	EAEAAE
Medium orchid	9370DB	Medium sea green	426F42	Medium slate blue	7F00FF
Medium turquoise	70DBDB	Medium violet red	DB7093	Medium wood	A68064
Midnight blue	2F2F4F	Navy blue	23238E	Neon blue	4D4DFF
Neon pink	FF6EC7	New midnight blue	00009C	New tan	EBC79E
Old gold	CFB53B	Orange	FF7F00	Orange red	FF2400
Orchid	DB70DB	Pale green	8FBC8F	Pink	BC8F8F
Plum	EAADEA	Quartz	D9D9F3	Rich blue	5959AB
Salmon	6F4242	Scarlet	8C1717	Sea green	238E68
Semi sweet chocolate	6B42226	Sienna	8E6B23	Silver	E6E8FA
Sky blue	3299CC	Slate blue	007FFF	Spicy pink	FF1CAE
Spring green	00FF7F	Steel blue	236B8E	Summer sky	38B0DE
Tan	DB9370	Thistle	D8BFD8	Turquoise	ADEAEA
Very dark brown	5C4033	Very light gray	CDCDCD	Violet	4F2F4F
Violet red	CC3299	Wheat	D8D8BF	Yellow green	99CC32

Resource On World Wide Web

The world wide web (w3) constorium	http://www.w3.org/
Home to general information on the World Wide Web and links to all areas of WWW and HTML.	

The WWW Section of Yahoo!	http://www.yahoo.com/Computers/World_Wide_Web
Links to hundreds of pages regarding WWW and HTML.	

OpenText	http://www.opentext.com/
An extensive database of Web sites.	

Resources On HTML Editors

FrontPage	http://www.microsoft.com/msoffice/frontpage/default.html
Microsoft's Web page and site development application.	

GNNPress	http://www.tools.gnn.com/press/index.html
A multiplatform Web page design tool.	

HomeSite	http://www.dexnet.com/homesite.html
A full-featured shareware Web page designer.	

HTML Assistant Pro	http://www.brooknorht.com/istar.html
A commercial HTML editor based on popular shareware editor.	

HTML Writer	http://www.lal.cs.byu.edu/people/nosack/index.html
An HTML editor that allows to edit more than one document at a time.	

InContext Spider	http://www.incontext.ca/products/spider1.html
A commercial Web page tool that supports advanced HTML features.	

Symposia	http://www.grif.fr/prod/sympro.html
A web design application for UNIX and Windows.	

Webber	http://www.csdcorp.com/webber.htm
An HTML editor that includes a validator program to look for invalid HTML markup.	

WebMedia Publisher	http://www.wbmedia.com/publisher/
A web page tool that supports the latest Microsoft and Netscape HTML extensions.	

Web Wizard	http://www.halcyon.com/webwizard/index.html
An HTML editor available in 16-bit and 32-bit versions	

Resources On HTML Document Development

HTML 2.0 Specification	http://www.w3.org/hypertext/www/MarkUp/html-spec/index.html
A full description of the final draft of HTML 2.	

HTML 3.2 Draft Specification	http://www.w3.org/pub/www/MarkUp/
A full description of the current draft of HTML 3.2.	

HTML Style Guide	http://www.w3.org/hypertext/www/Provider/Style/Overview.html
Tim Berners-Lee's excellent guide to designing WWW documents.	

NetSpace Guide for HTML Developers	http://netspace.org/netspace/wwwdoc.html
Lots of links to documents on creating effective HTML documents.	

URL Descriptions	http: //www.w3.org/hypertext/www/Addressing/Addressing.html
Definations of the various types of URLs, as well as discussion of URNs and URIs.	

WWW Development Page (Virtual Library)	http://www.charm.net/web/Vlib/
Links to a wide range of HTML development documents.	

Net Tips for Writers and Designers	http://www.dsiegel.com/tips/
Design tips for effective Web pages from a leading designer.	

Frames Tutorial	http://www.newbie.net/frames/
A step by step tutorial for creating pages using frames.	

APPENDIX - B

Resources For JavaScript

Gamelan JavaScript Scripts	http://www.gamelan.com/
A repository of many JavaScript scripts.	

JavaScript Scripts	http://www.geocities.com/SiliconValley/9000/
A set of useful JavaScript scripts by the same set of authors.	

JavaScript Tip of the Week	http://www.webreference.com/javascript
Numerous tips and tricks on using JavaScript.	

Babyak's JavaScript Resources	http://www.epix.com/~mbabyak/
Links to JavaScript resources across the Web	

JavaScript Overview	http://home.netscape.com/comprod/products/navigator/version2.0/script/index.html

JavaScript Documentation	http://home.netscape.com/eng/mozilla/Gold/handbook/javascript/index.html

JavaScript Index	http://www.c2.org/~andreww/javascript/

JavaScript Library	http://www.c2.org/~andreww/javascript/lib/

Learning JavaScript with Windows Help	http://www.webconn.com/javahelp/javahelp.htm

APPENDIX C

HTTP

HTTP replies and requests both consist of a header and a body. Scripts that want to return HTTP directly to a client must create their own header. This header starts on a line distinguishing it as HTTP and expresses the status of the HTTP request. This line has the form:

HTTP/version status_code message

The message is often OK or an error message. This error message can be used by the client to tell the user what happened. The status code is an integer between 200 and 599. It should be one of the status code listed in the HTTP specification. The valid codes are listed in the table below.

Code	Meaning
200	The request was successful
201	The POST request was successful

Code	Meaning
202	The request was received but the result was unknown
203	The GET request was accepted, but only partially fulfilled
204	The request was successful, there is no body information to update the client
300	The request can be provided from multiple locations at the client's choice, the location fields should be used to make this choice
301	The requested resource has moved and can be found at the URL in the location: field of the header. The browser should retrive the new URL automatically
302	The requested resource is not at the specified location and can be found at the URL in the location: field of the header. The browser should retrieve the new URL automatically
304	The resource requested with a GET request and an If-Modified-Since field is not modified and will not be returned
400	The request has a wrong syntax
401	The requested resource requires authentication. The header should contain WWW-authenticated fields to allow the user to negotiate with the server for authentication
402	The requested resource has a cost and the client did not send a valid Chargeto:field in the request header
403	The requested resource is forbidden
404	The requested resource could not be found
405	The requested resource does not support the type of request made
406	The requested resource is not one of the client's accepted types or encoding
410	The requested resource was available, but is not any longer
500	There was a server error
501	The sever does not support the type of request that was made
502	The request required that the server retrieve information from another server and this retrieval
503	The requested service is not available at this time
504	Same as 502, but the retrieval timed out instead of failed

After the first line, the header can contain a number of lines, including the content type of the HTTP body. Following the header is a blank line and the body, HTML for a reply with the content type text/HTML. A list of the standard HTTP response header fields is provided in the table below.

Field	Meaning
Allow:method_list	A comma-delimited list of the HTTP request methods supported by the requested resource. These methods can be any of GET, HEAD, POST, PUT, DELETE, LINK and UNLINK. As one would expect, CGI scripts usually allow GET and/or POST
Content-Encoding:encoding	The encoding used on the message body. Currently this can be either compress or gzip. Only one of these fields is allowed. If supported by the browser, this allows data to be compressed during transfer and automatically decompressed by the browser without the user knowing
Content-length:length	The length in bytes of the message
Conient-Transfer-Encoding:type	The encoding method used by the method, this is uncommon in HTTP requests, but is used in MIME
Content-type:general/specific	The MIME type for the message, often text/HTML
Date:date	The date and time that the message is sent. The format for this field is week day, day month year hours:minutes:seconds time zone. The time zone should be Greenwich Mean Time(GMT) for compatibility. For example, this field could be WED, 01 Apr 1995 13:13:13: GMT
Derived-From:version	The version of the information from which the resource came
Expires:date	The date and time that this reply should become invalid. Clients should use this information to refresh a page if necessary

Field	Meaning
Forwarded:by url for domain	Used by proxy Web servers to tell the client that a proxy was used. If multiple proxies are used, this field will be present multiple times
Last-modified:date	The date and time when this resource was last modified. This value should be in GMT
Link:thelink	Similar to the HTML link tag
Location:url	The URL for a resource that the Web server should return instead of this one.
MIME-version:version	The version of the MIME protocol that is supported
Public:methods	A list of non standard methods supported by this resource
Retry-after:date	If a resource is unavailable, the status code 503 should be returned and this field should have the date and time or number of seconds that the client should wait before retrying
Server:app/version	The Web server application name and version
Title:title	The title of the resource
URL:url	The Uniform Resource Identifier for a resource that should be returned instead of the requested one. This field is replacing Location:
Version:version	The version of the resource itself
WWW-Athentication:scheme message	This field is used to support user authentication

APPENDIX - D

Resources For PHP

PHP Source	http://php.net/index.php
Download the latest versions of PHP from here. New builds occur almost daily	

PHP Helpful Information	http://www.w3schools.com/PHP/
A repository which provides a great deal of useful information.	

The PHP Manual	http://php.net/manual/en/index.php
The latest updated PHP manual	

INDEX

<

<DIV>...</DIV> 222
<LINK> 221
<SPAN>...</SPAN> 220
<STYLE>...</STYLE> 213
  Type=text/css 213

A

Action 165
Action attribute 165
ALIGN 25, 47
ALT 38
ALT attribute 41
anchors 59
Anonymous Functions 352
Apache 239
Apache 2 Installation 240
Arithmetic Operators 133
ARPAnet 1
array methods 132
Arrays 131, 307
Assignment Operators 135

B

Bold 25
Boolean .... See
BORDER 38, 47
BORDER attribute 38
button 166
button element 169

C

Caption 48
Cascading Style Sheets (CSSs) 213
CELLPADDING 47
CELLPADDING attribute 49
CELLSPACING 47
CELLSPACING attribute 50
Centering 27
checkbox 173
checkBox 166

Client / Server 12
Client IP Address 6
COLSPAN 47
COLSPAN and ROWSPAN attributes 52
communicating on the Internet 2
Comparison Operators 134
Compile Errors 492
Conditional Statement
  if (...else) 309
  switch 315
Conditional Statements 309
Configuration file php.ini 259
Constants 289
Constants Declaration Function define() 289
cookies 191
Core Errors 492

D

Data Rows 47
Data Types
  Array 278
  Boolean 278
  Float 278
  Integer 278
  Object 278
  Resource 278
  String 278
Date object 182
DD 34
Debugging 478
Declaring functions 140
Definition description 34
Definition Lists 34
Definition term 34
dense array 131
DL34
Document Body 19
Document Head 19
Document Object Model(DOM) 150
Domain Name Extension 5
Drawing Lines 24
Dynamic website 268

E

Environmental Errors 491
Error handling function
  error_log() 498
  error_reporting() 49
  trigger_error() 50

Escape characters 457
- " 457
- $ 457
- (........ 457
-) 457
- * 457
- 457
- ? 457
- [........ 457
- ^ 457
- | 457
- + ... 457

Establishing connectivity on the internet 5
eval( ) function 139
Event handlers 157
Exceptions 508
- Catch Block 509
- Throw Statement 509
- Try Block 508

Expressions 133
Extended Regular Expressions 451
Extracting String Function
- substr() 385

F

Fatal Errors 485
Font Attributes 214
Footer 21
FOR loop 138
Form Attributes
- ACTION 411
- METHOD 411
- Method Attributes
  - GET 411
  - POST 411
- NAME 411

Form Elements
- Checkbox 414
- Combo Box 414
- Hidden Field 415
- Image 415
- Password 413
- Radio Button 413
- RESET 416
- SUBMIT 416
- Text Area 412
- Text Box 412

Form Methods
- ENCTYPE 445

Forms 160, 410
Frames 74

FRAMESET 74
FTP 10
Function For Array
  array_pop 368
  array_reverse 370
  array_shift 369
  each() 324
  explode() 366
  implode() 366
  in_array() 365
  list() 324
  reset() 324
  sort() 366
Function For Changing String Case
  strtolower() 397
  strtoupper() 397
  ucfirst() 398
  ucwords() 398
Function For Controlling Script Execution
  die() 364
  eval() 364
  exit() 363
Function For Converting String
  strtotime() 374
Function For Coverting Components
  mktime() 377
Function For Finding A String
  stripos() 386
  strops() 386
Function For Measuring String
  count_chars() 393
  str_word_count() 393
  strlen() 392
Function For Pausing Script Execution
  sleep() 406
  usleep() 406
Function For Printing Number
  number_format() 402
Function For Randomization
  mt_rand() 380
  rand() 380
Function For Replacing String
  str_ireplace() 390
  str_replace() 390
Function For Returning String
  stristr() 389
  strstr() 389
Function For Rounding Numbers
  ceil() 378
  floor() 378
  round() 378

Function For Securing Data
md5() 401
sha1() 399
Function For String Padding
str_pad() 403
Function For Trimming Whitespace
ltrim() 395
rtrim() 395
trim() 395
Function for Variables
empty() 361
isset() 360
unset() 362
Function For Wrapping Word
wordwrap() 396
Function To Convert From ASCII
chr() 391
Function To Convert To ASCII
ord() 391
Functions 139, 339
Date() 372
header() 354
include() 348
phpinfo() 354
INFO_ALL 355
INFO_CONFIGURATION 355
INFO_CREDITS 355
INFO_ENVIRONMENT 355
INFO_GENERAL 355
INFO_LICENSE 355
INFO_MODULES 355
INFO_VARIABLES 355
print() function 339
printf() 404
Time() 373
Functoin For Array
array_push 367
count() 365
reset() 365

G

Get 165

H

Header Rows 47
HEIGHT 38
HERE Documents 291
hidden object 166
Hierarchy 151
HREF 58
HTML 15, 36, 268

HTTP.................... 14
Hyperlinks 58

I

If - then - else 137
IIS
  Installation.................... 231
Image maps.................... 63
IMG 38
Immediate if (Conditional expression).................... 137
Infinite loops 330
Instance 150, 185
Instance Hierarchy 150
Instantiation 185
Interactive event handlers 157
Internet.................... 1
Internet Address 8
Internet Domains 4
Internet Information Server.................... 230
INTERNET PROTOCOL 9
InterNIC.................... 2
Interpreted language 126
IP Addressing 7
ISP 1, 6
Italics.................... 25
Iterations 319
  Looping.................... 319
    do...while loop 326
    for loop 319
    foreach loop.................... 327
    while loop 322

J

Joining Strings 283
JSSS DOM 151

L

Length property 133
LI 33
Line Breaks.................... 21
Live Wire.................... 125
log 498
Logical Errors 488
Logical Operators.................... 134
Loops Within Loops 332

M

math object 181
Mathematical Constants 384
Mathematical Functoins
abs() 382
hypot() 383
pow() 383
sqrt() 382
meta-character 455
Method 165
Methods 153
Multiple Virtual Domains 3

N

NAME 75
NAME=value 191
Network Class 9
Newline Character 282
Non Interactive event handlers 157
Notices 487
Null 130

O

OL34
OnChange( ) 167
onSelect( ) 167
Opearotrs
Binary Operators 296
Operator Precedence 303
operators 133
Operators 292
Binary Opeartors
Assignment Operators 298
Bitwise Operators 301
Comparison Operators 299
Concatenation Operator 299
Logical Operators 300
Numeric Operators 296
Ternary Operator 303
Unary Opeartors
Cast Operators 295
Increment / Decrement Operators 293
Negation Operators 293
Unary Operators 292
Ordered Lists 33

P

paired 15
Paragraph breaks 21
parseFloat( ) function 139
parseInt( ) function 139
Passing parameters 140
password 166
password element 168
Perl **C**ompatible **R**egular **E**xpressions 451
PHP
  Comments 275
  Logical Operators 301
PHP Command
  date() 312, 314, 315, 317
  echo 280, 324
  oci_connet() 312
PHP Iteration
  do ... while 319
  for 319
  foreach 319
  while 319, 324
PHP Language
  parsed 228
PHP Statement
  if (...else) 312
PHP Superglobals
  $_COOKIE 288
  $_ENV 289
  $_FILES 288
  $_GET 288
  $_GLOBALS 28
  $_POST 28
  $_REQUEST 28
  $_SERVER 28
  $_SESSION 28
POSIX 45
POSIX standard predefined classes
  alnum 45
  digit 45
  lower 45
Post 16
Programming Statements 13
Properties 15

R

radio 16
radio button 17
Recursion Functions 34

Recursive Functions 142
References 304
Registering A Virtual Domain 4
Regular Expression
 $ 453
 * 453
 . The Period 454
 ? 453
 [ ] 454
 ^ 453
 {} 453
 + ... 453
 OR operator 454
 Quantifiers 454
Regular Expression Engine 450
Regular Expression Function
 ereg() 452
 ereg_replace() 452
 eregi() 452
 eregi_replace() 452
 split() 452
Regular Expression Functions 452
Regular Expression Functoin
 spliti() 452
Regular Expressions 450
reset 166
reset button 171
Resolving Domain Names 7
Return keyword 343
Return values 142
ROWSPAN 47
Runtime Errors 491

S

select 166
select object 178
Servers 13
Servers and Clients 1
set-cookie 191
singular 15
SIZE 25, 28
Spacing 28
Special Loop Keywords 331
 break 331
 continue 331
Special Operators 135
Static website 268
String 129
string object 181
String Operators 135

Styles 24
submit 166
submit button 170
Super Controlled - endless loops 138
Symbols Used In Regular Expressions 453
Syntax or Parse Errors 483

T

TABLE 47
TARGET 76
TCP/IP 2, 8
TD 47
TELNET 11
text 166
TEXT 20
Text fields 168
textarea 176
textArea 166
The World Wide Web 10
Title 20
TR 47
TRASMISSION CONTROL PROTOCOL 10
TYPE 28
Types Of Regular Expressions 451

U

UL33
Underline 25
Unordered List 33
USEMAP 64
User Defined Errors 492

V

VALIGN 47
Variable 128
Variable Scope 142, 283
Variable Variables 286
Variables 278
Virtual Domain 3
VSNL 6

W

Warnings 486
Web Server 1
Web servers 229
WHILE loop 138
WIDTH 25, 38, 47
wildcard 455